Brief Lives:
Sitters and Artists
in the Garrick Club Collection

Brief Lives:
Sitters and Artists
in the Garrick Club Collection

KALMAN A. BURNIM and JOHN BASKETT

With Contributions by
Edward A. Langhans

GARRICK CLUB

Text by Kalman A. Burnim and John Baskett with contributions by Edward A. Langhans

First published 2003 by Garrick Club,
Garrick Street, London WC2E 9AY
in association with Unicorn Press,
76 Great Suffolk Street, London SE1 0BL

ISBN 0 906290 73 2

Typesetting by Ferdinand Pageworks, Surrey
Printed and bound in Great Britain

Cover: *The Exterior of the Garrick Club* (Cat. 925)
by Frederick Marrable

Contents

Foreword

by Sir Donald Sinden C.B.E.

At school the only names of the 'Ancients' that impinged themselves on my brain were those connected with mathematics: Pythagoras, Euclid and Archimedes. Of Sophocles, Euripides and Aristophanes I knew nothing. When I first discovered Hamlet I thought that 'Seneca cannot be too heavy, nor Plautus too light' probably referred to the handicapping of two horses in the Wittenberg Stakes. I was a late developer.

When I started as an actor in Brighton in 1942 I was extremely lucky to meet many luminaries who then appeared at the Theatre Royal: Marie Tempest, Henry Baynton, Lillian Braithwaite, John Martin Harvey, Irene Vanbrugh, Henry Ainley, Ruth Draper, the Lunts, Sybil Thorndike, Franklin Dyall, Zena Dare and many more. Desperate to learn, I sat at their feet and heard them tell of the theatre they had known in their youth. Strange names cropped up: Benson, Terry, Beerbohm Tree, Irving. Who were they? I acquired biographies and read avidly. More names cropped up: Phelps, Macready, Compton. More biogs to read. More names: Kean, Cooke, Kemble, Mathews, Siddons. I was learning my theatrical history backwards! But I was hooked.

In 1949 I appeared in London for the first time. Gerald Lawrence, who played Henry II with Irving as Beckett on the night the great man died in Bradford on the 13th of October 1905, proposed me for the Green Room Club – 'and in due time I would like to propose you for the Garrick.' Garrick – I had just been reading about him, so what was THE Garrick? Around Covent Garden were roads named after actors: Kemble Street, Kean Street and sure enough a Garrick Street! On the south side was a very dirty building with no number or name. It was six o'clock on an autumn evening and the building appeared blacker in contrast to the lights blazing inside. Looking up I could see paintings – dozens of them – in gilt frames hanging on blood red walls. Someone was coming out of the door: 'Is this the Garrick Club,' I asked. 'It most certainly is!' replied a man in a Fedora who I assumed to be an actor. I could see up the stairs to a lighted hall and there was a large bronze bust on a plinth. I knew it! 'That is HENRY IRVING!' I cried. 'Is it?' said the man in the Fedora.

From that moment I used any excuse to stand outside feeling like Howard Carter peering at the treasures of Tutankhamen. He could not have been more excited than I was. I could see only the ceilings of two rooms and the top row of paintings. An extremely large painting of Corinthian columns against a sky took up an entire wall. Why? I wondered, it didn't look theatrical … but this was the Garrick: Irving, Tree, Seymour Hicks, *etc*, had talked and written about it.

I never set foot in the place until I was elected a member in 1960. Dear Gerald Lawrence had died and Charles La Trobe of the Haymarket Theatre had proposed me. Tentatively I approached the uniformed porter at the door. 'I am a new member,' I said nervously, and I proffered the letter I had received from the Secretary. 'Oh yes. I will inform Commander Satterthwaite. You will find the bar at the top of the stairs.'

Sinews stiffened and blood summoned, I made my way up into the hall. There was Henry Irving in bronze, which I hope nobody saw me touch. 'Here's to our enterprise' he had said when he first appeared on the stage in Sunderland. Slowly I made my way up the great staircase, pausing before each picture. Vast portraits of Sarah Siddons and Charles Kean glowered down at me. 'Upstart!' they seemed to say. Straight ahead into the bar. A full-length portrait of Quin as Falstaff hung between the windows. I knew about Quin. There was the Commander, gin in hand, who introduced me to several other members. 'You seem interested in the pictures,' said one. 'Oh indeed yes! Is there someone who can tell me about them?' 'Well, there is the Picture Committee,' he replied as he tried to read the label on a large portrait of a man in white tie and tails – 'this seems to be someone called Seymour Hicks.' Surely I thought, this member cannot be an actor. (He was a judge.)

I discovered later that a catalogue had been produced in 1936 but with very few illustrations. Not until 1997 was a complete and illustrated catalogue printed. This awakened a great interest in the Collection and it became clear that a companion volume of biographies of the sitters and artists would be welcomed. Not all the members could be expected to have touched hands with generations of actors back to Richard Burbage. Present and new members and scholars across the world will be grateful for this volume, which could not have been produced but for the expertise of Kalman Burnim and John Baskett. New members can sit at their feet and read of a magical Theatre of Long Ago – and not so long ago.

Donald Sinden
Rats Castle, Isle of Oxney, 2003

Preface

We have compiled this collection of 'Brief Lives' of the sitters and artists represented in the great collection of pictures and sculpture in the Garrick Club in response to comments by members that such information would be useful to have at hand when viewing items in the collection. The biographies are by no means intended to be complete or even comprehensive, or to replace the notices to be found in various compendiums such as *The Dictionary of National Biography, Who's Who in the Theatre, The Oxford Companion to the Theatre,* and the *Biographical Dictionary of Actors, Actresses, Musicians, Dancers, Managers, and Other Stage Personnel in London 1660-1800*, Thieme-Becker's *Künstler-Lexikon* and Emmanuel Bénézit's *Dictionnaire des Peintres, Sculpteurs, Dessinateurs et Graveurs*. We have tried to avoid repeating in too much detail the information contained in the individual notices in Geoffrey Ashton's *Pictures in the Garrick Club*, edited by Kalman A. Burnim and Andrew Wilton. *Brief Lives* may stand on its own but it is intended to be used in conjunction with that catalogue.

Our main purpose in compiling these *Brief Lives* – a title borrowed from John Aubrey, of course – is to offer the reader and viewer some sense of who the sitters and artists were (and are) and what they did (and do). We hope that in so doing, the lives of these hundreds of persons, many of whom were or are members of the Garrick Club, will take on richer meaning and that appreciation of the pictures and sculpture in which they are represented in the Club's magnificent collection will be enhanced.

K. A. B.
J. B.

Acknowledgments

The authors wish to express their gratitude to the following persons for their assistance and support: Brian Allen, Julian Barrow, John Hayes, Henry Magee, Michael Clint Phillips, Penny Treadwell, Andrew Wilton and Christopher Wood. Special thanks are extended to Martin Harvey, the Garrick Club Secretary; the Works of Art Sub-Committee and the Secretary to that Committee, Betty Beesley; Enid Foster, Club Librarian; Marcus Risdell, archive researcher and compiler of the Garrick Club Art Database; and Hugh Tempest-Radford, our publisher. Sir Donald Sinden has kindly obliged us with an engaging foreword. Especially, we acknowledge our debt to the sixteen-volume *Biographical Dictionary of Actors, Actresses, Musicians, Dancers, Managers, and Other Stage Personnel in London, 1660-1800* (herein called the *BDA*), written by Philip H. Highfill, Jr, Kalman A. Burnim and Edward A. Langhans and published by the Southern Illinois University Press, from which much of the information about the eighteenth-century people has been culled, and we recommend that the reader who wishes to have additional information should consult those volumes.

Our special gratitude is extended to Edward A. Langhans, Professor of Drama and Theatre, *Emeritus*, at the University of Hawaii, who contributed a number of the notices published here (and noted with 'EAL'). His assistance has hastened the completion of the work and enriched its interest.

Abbreviations

BDA: Philip H. Highfill, Jr, Kalman A. Burnim and Edward A. Langhans. *A Biographical Dictionary of Actors, Actresses, Musicians, Dancers, Managers, and Other Stage Personnel in London, 1660-1800.* 16 vols, 1973-1993.

BEBB: Kalman A. Burnim and Andrew Wilton. *The Richard Bebb Collection in the Garrick Club. 2001.*

DNB: *Dictionary of National Biography*, edited by Leslie Stephen and Sidney Lee. 1927-1968.

EB: *Encyclopaedia Britannica Online*

OCT: *Oxford Companion to the Theatre*, edited by Phyllis Hartnoll, various editions.

PGC: Geoffrey Ashton. *Pictures in the Garrick Club. A Catalogue*, edited by Kalman A. Burnim and Andrew Wilton. 1997.

WW: *Who's Who*, cd-rom.

WWW: *Who Was Who*, cd-rom.

WWT: *Who's Who in the Theatre*, various editions.

WWWT: *Who Was Who in the Theatre*, various editions.

Numbers of pictures prefixed with the letter 'G' – as in G1002, for example – indicate acquisitions acquired and catalogued after the publication of *Pictures in the Garrick Club*. Numbers prefixed with 'B' are in the Bebb Collection. Those prefixed with 'S' are sculpture. If there is no prefix the picture is catalogued in *PGC*.

Notices marked EAL are written by Edward A. Langhans. The other notices of the sitters are written by Kalman A. Burnim, and the notices of the artists are written by John Baskett. Professor Burnim has served as general editor.

Bibliography

(in addition to the references cited in the abbreviations above)

Bénézit, E. *Dictionnaire critique et documentaire des peintures, sculpteurs, dessinateurs et graveurs* … 1999.

Bryan, Michael. *Biographical and Crticial Dictionary of Painters and Engravers.* 1813-1816.

Burnim, Kalman A. and Philip H. Highfill Jr. *John Bell. Patron of Theatrical Portraiture.* 1998.

Crookshank, Anne and the Knight of Glin. *The Painters of Ireland, c. 1600-1920.* 1927.

Graves, Algernon. *Art Sales from Early in the Eighteenth Century to Early in the Twentieth Century.* 3 vols. 1918-1921.

—— *The Royal Academy of Arts, a Complete Dictionary of Contributors and their Work from its Foundation in 1769-1904.* 8 vols. 1970 ed.

Gunnis, Rupert. *Dictionary of British Sculptors, 1660-1851.* 1951.

Hall, Lillian. *Catalogue of Dramatic Portraits in the Theatre Collection of the Harvard College Library.* 4 vols. 1930.

Lugt, Frits. *Les Margues de Collections des dessins & d'estampes.* 1921.

Millar, Oliver. 'Zoffany and his Tribuna,' *PMFBA* (1967).

Read, Benedict. *Victorian Sculpture.* 1982.

Redgrave, Richard. *Dictionary of Artists of the English School.* 1878.

Spalding, Frances. *Twentieth Century Painters.* 1990.

Strickland, Walter G. *A Dictionary of Irish Artists.* 2 vols. 1913.

Thieme, Ulrich and Felix Becker. *Allgemeines Lexikon der bildenden Künstler von der Antike bis sur Gegenwart.* 1926.

Walpole, Horace. *Anecdotes of Painting in England.* 4 vols. 1762-1771.

Waterhouse, E. K. *The Dictionary of British Eighteenth-Century Painters.* 1981.

Waters, Grant M. *Dictionary of British Artists Working 1900-1950.* 1975.

Welcome, John. *The Sporting World of R. S. Surtees.* 1982.

Whitley, William T. *Artists and their Friends in England 1700-1799.* 2 vols. 1928.

—— *Art in England 1800-1820.* 1928.

Wood, Christopher. *Victorian Painters.* 1995.

Brief Lives of the Sitters

A

ABINGTON, Frances **1-3, G1036**

1737-1815

She was born Frances Barton in 1737, the daughter of a cobbler in Vinegar Yard, Windmill Street, an address not far from Drury Lane Theatre. Colourful tales abound about her early childhood and youth in poverty to her rise to luxury and high social circles. Though many are false there is much truth in the mythology. Certainly she sold flowers at about the age of fourteen in the Covent Garden Piazza, and she became an assistant to a French milliner in Cockspur Street and a cookmaid in the kitchen of Robert Baddeley, who also became a famous actor. By the summer of 1755 she was a member of Theophilus Cibber's company – Bayes's New-rais'd Company of Comedians – at the Haymarket Theatre, where she made her first recorded appearance, announced as a young gentlewoman, in the role of Miranda in *The Busy Body*. Among her other roles there, when she was now billed as Miss Barton, was Kitty Pry in *The Provok'd Husband*, Desdemona, and her first time in boy's clothes (soon to be one of her specialities), Sylvia in *The Recruiting Officer*. Stints at Bath and Richmond were followed by an engagement with Garrick at Drury Lane Theatre in the autumn of 1756, where she made her first appearance as Lady Pliant in *The Double Dealer*. But she was used sparingly. After her marriage in 1759 to James Abington, a King's Trumpeter, she and her husband left for Dublin, where she appeared at the Smock Alley Theatre on 11 December 1759 as Mrs Sullen in *The Beaux' Stratagem*. In 1760 she transferred to the Crow Street Theater.

Her professional and social success in Dublin caused the breakup of her marriage. She became the mistress of a wealthy Irish M. P. named Needham and returned with him to England, where he died, at Bath, in 1763. Solicited by Garrick, Mrs Abington went back to Drury Lane Theatre. Though she and Garrick frequently quarreled, mostly over petty matters, she remained at Drury Lane throughout his management and into Sheridan's until 1782. Dissatisfied with her salary under Sheridan, she finally transferred to Covent Garden Theatre, making her first appearance there on 29 November 1782 as Lady Flutter in *The Discovery*. She continued her career at Covent Garden until 1790, when she suddenly retired. But in 1797, leaving a quiet and settled existence at her house in Hammersmith near the Thames, she re-engaged at Covent Garden, coming back on 6 October to act Beatrice in *Much Ado about Nothing*, a role which had been one of her most successful and flattering. Time had taken somewhat of a toll but had not diminished her charm. James Boaden wrote: 'Her person had become full, and her elegance somewhat unfashionable; but she still gave to Shakespeare's Beatrice what no other actress in my time has ever conceived; and her old admirers were still willing to fancy her as unimpaired as the character itself.' After acting a few more times that season, she wisely retired, making her final appearance on 12 April 1799 as Lady Racket in *Three Weeks after Marriage*. Frances Abington died at her Pall Mall apartment on 4 March 1815 and was buried in St James's, Piccadilly.

In the fullness of her talent, Abington was an excellent comedienne, exhibiting gaiety, ease, elegance and grace. She had a fresh spirit and a sparkling eye. Those attributes served her as well in her social life and made her especially attractive to a number of male suitors. Her clothes often set the fashion for duchesses to dairy maids. In addition to Beatrice, among her best roles were Mrs Oakly in *The Jealous Wife*, Charlotte Rusport in *The West Indian* and Lady Teazle in *The School for Scandal*. She had created the last-named role at the premiere at Drury Lane on 8 May 1777, and Lady Teazle was as much Mrs Abington as Mrs Abington was Lady Teazle (*BDA*). She was, however, not served well in James Roberts's canvas of the screen scene (**2**). General Burgoyne had expressly written for her the part of Lady Bab Lardoon in *The Maid of the Oaks*, in which she was pictured by Hickey (**1**). Numerous other portraits of Mrs Abington exist, including her as the Comic Muse by Reynolds at Waddesden Manor. A portrait of her as Beatrice by James Roberts was anonymously engraved and published in *Bell's Shakespeare*, and another by J. H. Ramberg, engraved by C. Sherwin, appeared in the same publication (see K. A. Burnim and P. H. Highfill, Jr, *John Bell, Patron of Theatrical Portraiture*, 1998). (*BDA*)

ABRAMS, Harriet **4**
1760-1825?
Harriet Abrams was one of the ten children of the Drury Lane house servant John Abrahams (fl. 1775-1779) who performed in the London theatres during the last half of the eighteenth century. The most famous of her siblings was John Braham (**90**, **652**), the great tenor. A prize voice pupil of the composer Thomas A. Arne, she made her debut at the age of 15 as the Little Gipsy in Garrick's afterpiece *May Day, or, the Little Gipsy* at Drury Lane in October 1775. Her next role was Leonora in *The Padlock* that December, and she made occasional appearances at Drury Lane until the spring of 1780, including in 1778 Sylvia in *Cymon*, the role in which she is pictured in the Garrick Club drawing (**4**). She also had concert engagements, often with her sisters, at the Concerts of Ancient Music, the Oxford Music Room, Astley's Amphitheatre, and other venues. She composed 16 sentimental and popular songs. (*BDA*)

ACHURCH, Sarah
See Sarah WARD

AICKIN, James **5, 5, 613**
c. 1735-1803
The actor James Aickin was born in Dublin about 1735, the son of a weaver and the younger brother of the actor Francis Aickin (d. 1805). He spent the early part of his career as a strolling player in Ireland, and then acted in Edinburgh until he went down to London to make his debut as Young Belmont in *The Foundling* at Drury Lane on 6 November 1767. He remained an active player at that theatre 32 seasons until, after suffering several strokes, he died in London in March 1803, at the age of 69. He played a large number of supporting roles, mainly blunt, honest and elderly men, such as Brabantio in *Othello*, Buckingham in *Richard III*, Capulet in *Romeo and Juliet*, Gloster in *King Lear*, Colonel Blunt in *The Committee* (**613**), Major O'Flaherty in *The West Indian* and Lord Randolph in *Douglas*. In those pictures of him at the Garrick Club his corpulence, which earned him the nickname Belly, can be seen. Other portraits of Aickin show him as King Henry VI (engraved by Walker after Dighton), and as Horatio in *The Fair Penitent* and Phocion in *The Grecian Daughter* (both engraved by W. Walker after D. Dodd). (*BDA*)

ALEXANDER, Sir George **7, 8**
1858-1918
Born George Alexander Gibb Samson in 1858, he first acted in London in 1881 and by the end of that year was associated with Irving's company at the Lyceum, playing Caleb Deecie in a revival of *Two Roses*. After eight years with Irving, Alexander took up management on his own, producing over 80 plays at the St James's Theatre, especially encouraging English dramatists at a time when adaptation of French farces was the predominant fare in the West End. In 1906 he presented Pinero's *His House in Order*, described as the most typical of the St James's plays. But he also produced plays by Shakespeare, Wilde and the verse dramatist Stephen Phillips.

Handsome and charming, Alexander was the epitome of the stage leading man. Perhaps his greatest success was in the dual roles of Rudolph and the King in Edward Rose's *The Prisoner of Zenda* (adapted from Anthony Hope's novel), first produced at the St James's on 7 January 1896. Brough painted him in that role in 1902 (**7**). Other important roles included Vilon in *If I Were King*, Karl Heinrich in *Old Heidelberg* and John Worthing in *The Importance of Being Earnest*. He became a member of the Garrick Club in 1886 and was knighted in 1911. He died in 1918, of diabetes. A. E. W. Mason's biography, *Sir George Alexander and the St. James's Theatre*, was published in 1935.

ALLAN, Maude **9**
1879-1956
The classical dancer Maude Allan (misspelled Allen in the *Catalogue of Pictures*) was born in Toronto in 1883, the daughter of the physicians William and Isabel Allan. She studied piano in San Francisco (where she was raised), Berlin and Vienna. She taught herself dance, and made her

dancing debut in Vienna in 1903, when she performed and choreographed dances to the music of Bach, Mendelssohn and Schubert. She appeared in many European cities before she made her London debut at the Palace Theatre in March 1908, creating a sensation with her *Vision of Salomé*, an exotic piece in which she had first appeared in Vienna in 1903. That dance, for which she wore a translucent skirt and a halter of beads, became her most famous offering over many years, and brought her international acclaim.

After dancing in St Petersburg and Moscow in 1909, she appeared at Carnegie Hall in New York on 20 January 1910 and subsequently toured much of the world, including India, Burma, China, the Philippines, Australia, New Zealand and the United States. She returned to London in October 1917, appearing at the Court Theatre on 12 April 1918 as Salomé in Oscar Wilde's play. That May she performed at the London Pavilion and then resumed far-flung tours to the Near East, the United States and Argentina, Chili and Brazil. Allan danced in Paris in December 1924, the Metropolitan Opera House in New York and the Hollywood Bowl in 1925. She returned again to England in 1928, appearing at the Lyceum Theatre in April 1932 and in a revival of *The Miracle* at the Manchester Repertory Theatre in September 1934. She contributed articles on the art of dance to several journals and published *My Life in Dancing*, 1908. Allan died in Los Angeles on 7 October 1956. (*See* Felix Cherniavsky, *The Salomé Dancer: the Life and Times of Maud Allan*, 1991.)

ALLEN, Mary
See Mary JERROLD

ALMAR, George **10**
1802-c. 1854
Almar was the author of some 45 melodramas and spectacles, most of them performed at Sadler's Wells between 1830 and 1854. He also acted in some of them, including *The Cedar Chest* on 14 July 1834, in which he played Carnaby Cutpurse, the role in which Buss pictured him. He was also shown in penny-plains as Coral Crown in *The Cedar Chests* and Sir Brian Debois Guilbert in *Ivanhoe*. Almar managed Sadler's Wells between 1833 and 1835.

AMIS, Sir Kingsley **965**
1922-1995
Born in London in 1922, he was educated at the City of London School and St John's College, Oxford. During the Second World War he served as a Lieutenant in the Royal Corps of Signals. He taught English literature at University College, Swansea, from 1949 to 1961, and at universities in England and the United States.

His first novel, *Lucky Jim* (1954), perhaps remains his best known (filmed in 1957) and associated him with the movement of social discontent called the Angry Young Men. As with *Lucky Jim*, much of his writing concerned young antiheroes who rise by stint of hard work and scholarship, only to discover that the highest places remain occupied by the well-born. He wrote some 40 books, including about 20 novels, volumes of poetry and collections of essays. His novels include *That Uncertain Feeling* (1955), *I Like it Here* (1958, prompted by his visit to Portugal), *One Fat Englishman* (1963, based on his experiences teaching in America), *The Green Man* (1969) and *The Old Devils* (1986, Booker Prize). He was knighted in 1990 and published his *Memoirs* in 1991. Sir Kingsley has been characterised as an angry young lefty who matured into a conservative curmudgeon. He had strong dislikes of snobbery and arrogance, both of the left and right, and political correctness, and although his tastes may have got stuck in the mud (*National Review*, 14 September 1998), he was foremost a masterly professional writer. In 1973 he became a member of the Garrick Club, where he could often be seen until his death in 1998. For a biography, see Eric Jacobs, *Kingsley Amis* (1998).

ANDERSON, E. Abbot
See Allan AYNESWORTH

ANDERSON, Harry **966**
d. 1918
Harry Anderson was a popular performer in South London music halls in the late nineteenth and early twentieth centuries. Some information about him is in the *Catalogue of Pictures*.

ANDERSON, James Robertson **793**
1811-1895
Born in Glasgow on 8 May 1811, Anderson spent the early years of his acting career in provincial theatres and then appeared at Covent Garden on 30 September 1837 as Florizel in *The Winter's Tale*. He then was active as a London actor and Drury Lane manager for some 47 years and also toured America and Australia. He had a fine voice and figure. Among his last roles was Tybalt in *Romeo and Juliet* at the Lyceum on 1 November 1884. In 1843 Anderson became a member of the Garrick Club, where he was frequently to be seen. After leaving the Club late one night on his way to his lodgings in the Bedford Hotel he was garroted and robbed. He never fully recovered from his injuries and died at the Bedford Hotel on 3 March 1895; he was buried at Kensal Green. In addition to his placement in O'Neil's Billiard Room group, engraved portraits of him as Macbeth and other characters are listed in the *Harvard Catalogue of Dramatic Portraits*. (*DNB*)

ANDREWS, John **750**
fl. 1817
Nothing more is known by us about the John Andrews who is pictured as No. 8 in Harlow's painting of the Trial Scene in *Henry VIII*.

ANDREWS, Julie **11**
b. 1935
This leading musical star, whose original name was Julia Elizabeth Wells, was born in Walton-on-Thames, Surrey, on 1 October 1935. By the age of ten she was appearing in a music hall act with her pianist mother and singer stepfather. Having legally adopted his surname of Andrews, she made her solo debut in 1947 in the revue *Starlight Roof* at the London Hippodrome. Her Broadway debut was in *The Boy Friend* in 1954. In New York in 1956 she triumphed as Eliza Doolittle in *My Fair Lady* (also in London in 1958), and in 1960 appeared as Guinevere in *Camelot*, another hit by Lerner and Loewe. Though she did not reprise either role in the film versions of those productions, she became one of the most popular film-stars of the 1960s by her performances of the title role in Disney's *Mary Poppins* (1963) – for which she received an Academy Award 1964) – and as Maria in *The Sound of Music* (1965), for which she received a nomination for an Academy Award. Both films became enormous money-makers throughout the world and remain perennial favourites. Other films include *The Americanization of Emily* (1964), *Torn Curtain* (1966), *Hawaii* (1966), *Thoroughly Modern Millie* (1966) and the less successful *Star!* (1968), *Darling Lili* (1970) and *S.O.B.* (1981). She received another Academy Award nomination for her tour-de-force performance of a woman impersonating a male female-impersonator in *Victor/Victoria* (1982), a film by her husband Blake Edwards. She brought that role to Broadway in 1995, when she refused to accept a Tony because the rest of the cast and her husband had been overlooked. Though a fine and versatile actress – as evidenced by her performances in her husband's films and in occasional television specials – she is admired primarily and adored by the public for her charm and her crystalline, four-octave voice and perfect pitch. *See* Robert Windeler, *Julie Andrews: A Life on Stage and Screen* (1997), and James Arntz and Thomas S. Wilson, *Julie Andrews* (1995).

ANGELO, Henry **12**
1755-1835
He was the son of the riding and fencing master Domenico Angelo (1717?-1802), whose *L'école des armes* was published by Dodsley in London, 1763. The elder Angelo was a friend of Garrick, and Henry Angelo in his *Reminiscences* (London, 2 vols 1828) offers a considerable amount of information (not always reliable) about the London theatres and his family's relationships with Garrick and his contemporaries. De Wilde's painting (**12**) pictures Angelo in his only performance on the London stage, at the King's Theatre on 29 March 1792, although he appeared as an amateur actor in various private theatres. In addition to his *Reminiscences*, Angelo also published *Instructions for the Sword Excercise* (1835) and *Angelo's Pic Nic; or, Table Talk* (1834). For more about him see J. D. Aylward, *The House of Angelo; a Dynasty of Swordsmen* (1953).

ANGLESEY, 3rd Marquis of, William George Paget **973**
d. 1869
William George Paget who is pictured as No. 17 in O'Neil's scene of members in the Billiards

Room, was the son of Henry William George Paget (1768-1854), 1st Marquis of Anglesey, noticed in the *DNB*. He became a member of the Garrick Club in March 1845; he died on 7 February 1869.

ARDEN, Joseph FSA **793**
d. 1879
Joseph Arden, pictured as No. 23 in O'Neil's large canvas of a game in the Billiards Room, was a Fellow of the Royal Society of Antiquarians. He was elected to the Garrick Club on 18 January 1834 and died in January 1879. He was the author of *The Orations of Hyperides for Lycophron and for Euyxenippus* (1853).

ARMSTRONG, Charles? or John? **13**
fl. 1780 or John 1709-1779
Ashton speculates that the sitter in **13** is Charles Armstrong, but there is also the possibility that he is, as the bequest states, Dr John Armstrong (1709-1779), the writer and physician who is noticed in the *DNB*. A post in the army took John Armstrong to Germany. He returned to London in 1770 and wrote a number of verses, prose and travel essays, including two volumes of *Miscellanies* (1770), *A Short Ramble Through France and Italy* (1771) and *Medical Essays* (1773).

ARNE, Susanna Maria
See Susanna Maria CIBBER

ARNOLD, Elizabeth
See Elizabeth CLENDINING

ARNOLD, Samuel James **14**
1774-1852
The prolific dramatist and well-known London manager Samuel James Arnold was born in London in 1774, the son of the eminent eighteenth-century composer Dr Samuel Arnold (1740-1803) and his wife Mary Ann (née Napier). Trained as an artist, between the ages of 26 and 34 he exhibited portraits regularly at the Royal Academy; he painted a portrait of Erasmus Darwin at that time. His portrait of the showman Charles Dibdin is in the Garrick Club (**154**). But Arnold adopted his father's profession and was engaged for the major part of his career writing and producing a large number of plays, mostly with music. His first musical play, *Auld Robin Gray* was produced at the Haymarket in 1794. A series of his plays followed, among them *Who Pays the Reckoning?* (Haymarket 1794), *The Shipwreck* (Drury Lane 1796), *The Irish Legacy* (Haymarket 1797), *The Veteran Tar* (Drury Lane 1801) and *Man and Wife* (Drury Lane 1809). In 1809 he became the licensee of the new English Opera House (the Lyceum in the Strand) where the Drury Lane company was playing while its burned-down theatre was being replaced. He later opened the Lyceum under his own management, producing there a number of his own operas, which were characterised by Hazlitt as threadbare in plot and sickly in sentiment. – 'Mr Arnold writes with the fewest ideas possible.' Arnold managed Drury Lane Theatre from 1812 to 1815 and then reopened his enlarged English Opera where he presented for the first time in England a version of Weber's *Freischutz*. Arnold was a fellow of the Royal Society and a magistrate. He was an original member of the Garrick Club in 1831 and served as one of its first Committee members but resigned on 6 November 1835. Soon after, having taken to heavy drinking and deep in debt, he went to live in Boulogne. He died in 1852. Arnold also had been a leading member of the Beefsteak Club, where he was called 'the Bishop' and often performed a mock grace in a large white mitre. He was generally known by the sobriquet 'Sambo.'

(*DNB*, R. H. Barham, *The Garrick Club: Notices of One Hundred and Thirty-Five of its Former Members* (1896).

ASTLEY, Hannah Waldo née Smith **15**
fl. 1791-1834
Hannah Waldo Smith was riding in Philip Astley's Royal Amphitheatre in Dublin by 1791 and in 1801 married the manager's son John Astley (**16**). She performed with her husband for a number of years, and he wrote several spectacle-melodramas for her. At her husband's death in 1821 she attempted to keep the Astley enterprises going; she remained involved in equestrian performances there in collaboration with James West and Andrew Ducrow until at least 1834. In addition to the formal Garrick Club

portrait by Saxon, she was pictured as Joanna in *Ferdinand of Spain* in a penny-plain engraving published in 1828 by W. West.

ASTLEY, John Philip Conway 16
1767-1821
This equestrian, actor, manager and playwright was the son of Philip Astley (1742-1814), the equestrian manager who in the late 1760s established exhibitions of horsemanship in St George's Fields, Lambeth, between Blackfriars and Westminster bridges, and erected his Royal Amphitheatre in Peter Street, Dublin, in 1789. Young Astley was appearing in his father's equestrian ring in London by the age of six and was a precocious sensation – somewhat hyperbolically described 'as the greatest performer that ever appeared … and as a horseman, stands unparalleled by all nations.' As a horseman, acrobat and general all-around performer, he remained one of the chief attractions of the Astley enterprise and in 1784 took over the Amphitheatre in Lambeth. He devised a number of spectacles and equestrian dramas, including *The Pirates* (1800), *The Iron Tower* (1801), *The Man in the Moon* (1808) and *The Brave Cossack* (1812). In the last-mentioned he was pictured as Count Staffo in an engraving by W. Heath. In 1814 he inherited all his father's enterprises in London, Dublin and Paris, but he proved not to be the energetic and devoted showman that his father had been. He was more interested in society, where he was found to be a handsome, witty and amiable (though coarse and somewhat indolent) fellow. When he died in 1821, of a liver disease, his diminished enterprises were carried on by his widow, the equestrian Hannah Astley (**15**), whom he had married in 1801.

ATTENBOROUGH,
Lord Richard CBE, KC G1003
b. 1923
Richard Attenborough was born at Cambridge on 29 August 1923, the son of a teacher, Frederick Levi Attenborough and his wife, the writer Mary Attenborough. His brother Sir David Attenborough (b. 1927) is the well-known writer, television executive, and maker and presenter of television documentaries on wildlife and evolution. Richard attended Wyggeston Grammar School for Boys in Leicester and the Royal Academy of Dramatic Art (1941), then moved to film acting and film making. His fine film performances include a Seaman in *In Which We Serve* (1942), Pinkie in *Brighton Rock* (1947), the Leader of *The Great Escape* (1963), the Murderer in *10 Rillington Place* (1971) and the Ringmaster in *Jurassic Park* (1993). He received the Best Actor Award at the San Sebastian Film Festival in 1964 for his performance in *Seance on a Wet Afternoon* and Golden Globe Awards as best supporting actor in *The Sand Pebbles* (1966) and *Dr Doolittle* (1967). Attenborough made his film directing debut with *Oh! What a Lovely War* (1969), followed by such films as *A Bridge Too Far* (1977), *Young Winston* (1972) and the multi-award winning *Ghandi* (1982). Other excellent films include *Magic* (1978), *A Chorus Line* (1985), *Cry Freedom* (1987), *Chaplin* (1992) and *Shadowlands* (1993).

Attenborough was honoured with a CBE in 1967 and was knighted in 1976. He became a member of the Garrick Club in 1950. Lord Attenborough serves as president or board member on numerous arts and charitable organizations in Britain. In January 1945 he married Sheila Sim (b. 1922), former actress and magistrate. They had been at RADA together and appeared in the original West End production of *The Mousetrap* in 1952. They have two daughters, Jane and Charlotte, and a son Michael, who is an executive of the Royal Shakespeare Company and a member of the Garrick Club.

AUGUSTUS, Frederick.
See SUSSEX, Duke of

AYLMER, Sir Felix Edward Jones OBE 17
1889-1978
He was born on 21 February 1889 at Corsham, Wiltshire, the son of Lt Col Thomas Edward Aylmer-Jones and his wife Lilian. After being educated at Magdalen College School and Exeter College, Oxford, Aylmer studied for the stage under Rosina Filippi. In March 1911 he made his stage debut at the Coliseum, London, as the Italian in *Cook's Man*, embarking on a stage career that would last some 58 years, during which he would play numerous roles on stage

and film and television. Early on he played minor roles with Fred Terry's company and then with Sir Herbert Beerbohm Tree and in the Birmingham Repertory Company, appearing in such characters as Subtle in *The Alchemist*, Orsino and Malvolio in *Twelfth Night*, Morell in *Candida* and Sergius in *Arms and the Man*. He became one of the most familiar faces on the twentieth-century stage, in later life mainly in the line of noblemen, judges, professors and elder gentlemen. Among his dozens of parts in London and New York were Sir Colenso Ridgeon in *The Doctor's Dilemma* (Kingsway November 1926), the Earl of Warwick in *Saint Joan* (Old Vic November 1934), Professor Sigelius in *Power and Glory* (Savoy April 1938), the Reverend Josiah Crawley in *Scandal at Barchester* (Lyric October 1944), Henry Fanshaw Beringer in *First Person Singular* (Duke of York's February 1952) and the Judge in *The Chalk Garden* (Haymarket March 1956). His many roles in films included the Bishop in Olivier's *Henry V* and Polonius in Olivier's *Hamlet*. Aylmer was President of British Actors Equity Association for 20 years, 1949-1969, and was vice-president of the Royal Academy of Dramatic Art, 1953-1955. In 1950 he was awarded the OBE, and he was knighted in 1965. He became a member of the Garrick Club in 1937 and was also a member of the Green Room and Beefsteak clubs. (*WWWT*)

AYNESWORTH, Allan **18**

1865-1959

Born E. Abbot-Anderson on 14 April 1865 at the Royal Military College, Sandhurst, he was the son of General E. Abbot-Anderson. He was educated at Chatham House and in France and Germany. His first stage appearance was at the Comedy Theatre, London, on 28 April 1887, when he walked on in *The Red Lamp*. Having adopted the stage name Allan Aynesworth, at the St James's Theatre from 1887 to 1892 he played minor roles and then appeared at the Criterion and Daly's Theatre. At the Garrick Theatre in May 1894 he played Sir Frederick Blount in *Money*, and back at the St James's in February 1895 he appeared as the original Algernon in *The Importance of Being Earnest*. Between 1903 and 1907 Aynesworth filled leading characters in productions with Marie Tempest. During his next three decades on the stage he was seen in numerous roles at many London theatres, notably Jackson Ives in *Ready Money* on 12 August 1912 at the New Theatre – where he also engaged in management. That play ran for over 200 performances. He also shared management at the Garrick Theatre in 1913 and with Irving Albery at the Criterion and Prince of Wales in 1914. Later roles included Lord Porteus in *The Circle* (Haymarket January 1921), Dominic in *The Dover Road* (Haymarket June 1922), Colonel Sapt in *The Prisoner of Zenda* (Haymarket August 1923), Wilfred Everitt in *All the King's Horses* (Globe January 1926) and Dawkins in *Bees and Honey* (New Theatre July 1929). In 1895 Aynesworth became a member of the Garrick Club, where he was held in high esteem. Codner's portrait of him (**10**) was presented by some of his fellow members in 1937. He died on 22 August 1959 at the age of 95.

B

BACON, Elizabeth
See Elizabeth POOLE

BADDELEY, Robert **19-23**
1733-1794
Robert Baddeley was born on 20 April 1733, probably in London, and it said that as a youth he was a cook to the theatrical manager, actor and playwright Samuel Foote. He made his first appearance as Sir William Wealthy in Foote's comedy *The Minor* on 28 June 1760 at the Haymarket Theatre. In his first season at Drury Lane in 1760-61, under Garrick's management, he acted Frankly in *The Register Office*, Gomez in *The Spanish Fryar* and a role in Foote's new comedy *Taste*. After touring Irish towns for two seasons. Baddeley returned to Drury Lane, where in 1763-64 he took on some 20 roles, establishing a line of parts of older men in low comedy, such as Sir Harry Grubbin in *The Tender Husband*, the role in which he is depicted by De Wilde (**20**). He remained an established member of the Drury Lane company for another 31 years. And after Garrick's death in 1779 Baddeley became one of the original group of actors that formed a club called 'The School of Garrick' – and was pictured as a member of that society by Hardy (**21**) and Spicer (**22**). Zoffany's scene in the Garrick Club of *The Clandestine Marriage*, showing Mrs Baddeley as Fanny Sterling and Tom King as Lord Ogleby (**23**), is one of loveliest of eighteenth-century pictures; but the figure of Baddeley as Canton is in the far background. Cosway drew a portrait of Baddeley in the same role (**19**). Among Baddeley's best roles was Moses in Sheridan's *The School for Scandal*, which he created on 8 May 1777, and in which he is shown by Zoffany in a fine painting now in the Lady Lever Collection (*BDA* I: 199). Though never an actor of high talent, he did excel at playing national types, like Moses, the Frenchman in *The Recruiting Officer* and Fluellen in *Henry V*; his Swiss, Germans, and Frenchmen 'were admirably characteristic' (*BDA* I: 200).

Baddeley's marriage to eighteen-year-old Sophia Snow in 1763 was to prove unhappy and tumultuous. She was very beautiful, vain and reckless, and she engaged in a series of amours; moreover when she took to the stage she became a more popular and favourite performer than her husband. Eventually they separated, and Baddeley lived his later years with the actress Katherine Sherry (1745-1782) and finally with Mrs Catherine Strickland, who became known as Mrs Baddeley. Robert Baddeley died in London at his house in New Store Street on 20 November 1794, having suffered several strokes over the years since 1780. Baddeley is best remembered today for the bequest in his will, proved at London on 18 December 1794, in which he left the interest of £100 to provide the actors at Drury Lane with cakes and ale on Twelfth Night, a ritual observed to this day at that theatre. He also left money to the Drury Lane Theatrical Fund – he was a founding member for the establishment of an asylum for needy or indigent actors in a dwelling in West Molesey, Surrey. That house was lived in by Catherine Strickland until her death; but the opening of 'Baddeley Asylum' never occurred.

BADDELEY, Mrs Robert,
Sophia née Snow **23**
1745?-1786
This remarkably beautiful woman, who became one of the most controversial personalities of her time, was born about 1745 in the parish of St Margaret, Westminster, the daughter of Valentine Snow, serjeant-trumpeter to George II, and his wife Mary Snow. The details of her early life are shrouded in mythology, perpetuated by a highly novelized account of her life published in six volumes in 1787, bearing the name of Elizabeth Steele, but probably actually written by one Alexander Becknell. Born into a musical family of some modest affluence, at the age of about 18 in 1763 she eloped with the actor Robert Baddeley. They proved incompatible and unfaithful, and later separated. But through his influence she made her first recorded appearance, announced as a young gentlewoman, at Drury Lane Theatre on 27 September 1764, as Ophelia to Holland's Hamlet. When she played the role for the third time, on 27 April 1765, she was named in the bills as Mrs Baddeley. As a

regular member of the Drury Lane company from 1766 to 1780 she became exceedingly popular in a line of singing ingenues and young pretty heroines, including Celia in *As You Like It*, Patty in *The Maid of the Mill*, Uganda in *Cymon*, Fedelia in *The Foundling*, Violante in *The Wonder* and Olivia in *Twelfth Night*. She was not the original Fanny Sterling in the première of *The Clandestine Marriage* on 20 February 1766 (that was Mrs Palmer), but it is said that during a command performance of the play the King was so taken with Mrs Baddeley in the role that he ordered Zoffany to paint the picture now in the Garrick Club (**23**). Mrs Baddeley also sang at the various London pleasure gardens in summers and occasionally acted at the Haymarket and in the English provinces and Ireland.

Obliged to leave London to escape her creditors in 1782, she went to Dublin, where she became the mistress of Richard Daly, the Smock Alley Theatre manager. He was but one of her numerous lovers, who included a string of actors and several titled men. Mrs Baddeley was as reckless as she was beautiful and went through suitors almost as quickly as she went through money. After Daly it was Lord Melbourne, then the Duke of York and Sir Cecil Bishop. Her excesses and escapades eventually took their toll. After several years in the Edinburgh company, until the 1784-85 season, she 'fell into consumption' and died on 1 July 1786 in her lodgings in Shakespeare Square, Edinburgh, and was buried in the Calton cemetery, at about the age of 41. (*BDA*)

BAILEY, William stage name of William O'Reilly **24, 25**
d. 1791
William O'Reilly, who later adopted the stage name of Bailey, was a merchant in London by 1772 but by 1774 was the manager of the theatrical circuit in the Norwich area. The major portion of his theatrical career was spent in the provinces or (occasionally) on the fringes of London, where he seems first to have appeared at Richmond in August 1776. During his brief management of the China Hall Theatre in Rotherhithe in May and June 1778, he portrayed a great variety of roles, 17 in all, before fire destroyed the building soon after the performance of 26 June. Among his roles at China Hall were Jollup in *The Mayor of Garratt*, Catesby in *Jane Shore*, Hardcastle in *She Stoops to Conquer* and Peter in *Romeo and Juliet*. Subsequently he acted at Dublin and other cities in Ireland, at Edinburgh and under Wilkinson's management on the York circuit. At the Smock Alley Theatre in Dublin in November 1782 he appeared under his real name, O'Reilly. He died on 23 May 1791 and was buried at St James's Church, Dublin. (*BDA*)

BANCROFT, Lady Marie née Wilton **S1**
1839-1921
See Sir Squire BANCROFT

BANCROFT, Sir Squire **26-29, S2**
1841-1926
The actor-manager Squire Bancroft was born on 14 May 1841 and was educated privately in England and France. He made his first appearance on the stage at the Theatre Royal, Birmingham, in January 1861 as Lt Manley in *St Mary's Eve*. After playing numerous roles in provincial theatres he appeared in London for the first time on 15 April 1865 at the Prince of Wales's Theatre as Jack Crawley in *A Winning Hazard*. There he met Marie Effie Wilton, the daughter of provincial players and already a well-established actress in London and co-manager of the theatre. They married in 1867 and embarked on distinguished co-managerial careers that made the Prince of Wales's Theatre one of the most successful of its time and brought them into eminence as innovative producers. They made significant increases in the performers' compensation and used more realistic and practical scenery, a practice started by Mme Vestris. They also played numerous leading roles. Among his finest were Sidney Daryk in *Society* (1865), Captain Hawtree in *Caste* (1867), Triplet in *Masks and Faces* (1875) and Orloff in *Diplomacy* (1878). She excelled in a number of the productions. They made their last appearances on 20 July 1885 in a mixed bill of their showpieces. They made occasional appearances thereafter under other managements.

Bancroft was knighted in 1897. He served as President of the Royal Academy of Dramatic Art and received an honorary doctorate at St Andrew's University (1922). Bancroft, who cut a tall elegant figure, became a member of the Garrick Club in 1869; he was also a member of the Athenaeum and Green Room clubs (and was president of the latter). The Bancrofts published their memoirs *On and Off Stage* in 1888. He died on 19 April 1926 at the age of 84. Lady Bancroft, who also wrote several plays and a novel, died on 22 May 1921 at the age of 82. Their son George Pleydell Bancroft (1868-1956) also acted on the London stage and wrote novels; he was also a member of the Garrick Club. (*OCT, WWWT*)

BANKS, Leslie James CBE S3
1890-1952
Born in West Derby, near Liverpool, on 9 June 1890, Leslie Banks was educated at Trinity College, Glenalmond, Perthshire, and Keble College, Oxford. He made his first stage appearance with Frank Benson's company on 27 October 1911 at the Town Hall, Brechin, as Old Gobbo in *The Merchant of Venice.* After a stint with Benson's company in the provinces in 1911 and a tour of America, Banks made his first appearance in London at the Vaudeville Theatre on 5 May 1914 as Lord Murdon in *The Dangerous Age.* He served in the Army during the First World War and returned to play with the Birmingham Repertory. He re-appeared in the West End in 1921 to take up a long and estimable career as an actor and producer. Among his most successful roles were Petruchio in *The Taming of the Shrew* (1937 with Edith Evans), the schoolmaster title role in *Goodbye, Mr. Chips* (1938), Lord Porteus in *The Circle,* Tattle in *Love for Love* and Claudius in *Hamlet* (1944-45) – all at the Haymarket. In New York he played Hook in *Peter Pan* (1924) and Henry in *Springtime for Henry* (1931). He became a producer in 1926, presenting such plays as *Crime and Punishment* (1927), *The Lady with the Lamp* and *Emma Hamilton* (1929), *The Way to the Stars* (1932) and *Good-Night Children* (1942). Banks also appeared in numerous films. He became President of British Actors' Equity in 1948 and was honoured with a CBE in 1950. The *OCT* describes him a 'distinguished presence, with a fine speaking voice,' and an actor whose performances were touched with 'imagination and subtle humour.' He became a member of the Garrick Club in 1928 and was also a member of the Green Room, Savage, Beefsteak and Stage Golfing Society. (*OCT, WWWT*)

BANNISTER, Charles 30-33, 652
1741-1804
Born at Newland, Gloucestershire, in 1741, the son of John and Rebecca Powell Bannister, he was employed in the government victualing office at Deptford by 1760. Having engaged in amateur theatricals as a youth, Bannister, it is said, brashly applied to Garrick for a position at Drury Lane Theatre. Rebuffed, he spent some time in provincial companies until he was taken on by Samuel Foote at the Haymarket Theatre and appeared on 28 April 1762 in one of Foote's satirical entertainments called *The Orators,* in which Bannister played Will Tirehack, an Oxford student who did imitations of well-known players. He developed a talent and reputation for taking off performers, especially foreign singers, but received no immediate engagement at a London patent theatre. He bounced about, singing at taverns and pleasure gardens, and soon went to act at the Crow Street Theatre, Dublin, and for several summers seasons at Richmond. Finally, in 1767-68 he was taken on at Drury Lane, where he made his first appearance on 22 September 1767 as Merlin in *Cymon.* Bannister remained underemployed at Drury Lane, but enjoyed some success again at Foote's Haymarket in the summer of 1768. In 1768-69 his fortunes improved and he became a well-regarded standby through much of the remainder of his long career. He continued to appear regularly at the Haymarket in summers. He was especially good in dialect characters such as Cadwallader in *The Author,* Don Diego in *The Padlock* and O'Flannagan in *The Cozeners.* Among his many other characters were Hawthorn in *Love in a Village,* Major Sturgeon in *The Mayor of Garratt,* Steady in *The Quaker* (**31**), Caliban in *The Tempest,* Antonio in *The Merchant of Venice,* Casca in *Julius Caesar* and Claudius in *Hamlet.* Bannister's main attribute was his strong bass voice, complemented by a pleasant personality and a large figure.

Attributed to Zoffany is the portrait of him in the Garrick Club as Launce (with his dog) in *The*

Two Gentlemen of Verona (**33**), a role he seems not to have played in London. He was one of the founders of the society of actors called 'The School of Garrick' (**32**). Bannister died in London on 19 October 1804 and was interred in the family vault under the communion table in St Martin-in-the-Fields. His son John Bannister (*q.v.*) also became a much-loved comic actor.

BANNISTER, John **34-42**
1760-1836
John Bannister was born on 12 May 1760 at Deptford, where his father Charles Bannister (*q.v.*) was employed in the government victualing office. Shortly after John's birth, his father took up acting and eventually became a leading comic actor whose career in London extended some 42 years. Young John had a talent for drawing and in 1777 was placed in the Royal Academy Schools, where he became a close friend of Thomas Rowlandson; but insufficient funds required his withdrawal, and he, too, turned to acting. He played Dick in Murphy's *The Apprentice* at Drury Lane on 27 August 1778, and then appeared as Palmira in *Mahomet* on 11 November 1778. It is said that Garrick (who was in retirement) coached him line by line. In 1779-80 Bannister began a regular engagement at Drury Lane, where his father was a leading actor. In the 1790s he gradually assumed many of his father's parts and soon commanded a higher salary – £16 per week to his father's £6. His popularity extended through 1814-15. He also played summers at the Haymarket for 17 consecutive years, until 1797, acting at that theatre some 150 different characters. Thereafter he spent his summers touring the provinces in the three kingdoms. His repertoire at Drury Lane was remarkable in that it consisted of over 425 characters, although many were in short comic afterpieces or skits.

He is seen in some of his favourite and best characters in paintings now in the Garrick Club, where there are nine depictions of him. (*See Pictures in the Garrick Club* for details on those characterizations.) Among other roles in which he demonstrated his comic abilities were Bob Acres in *The Rivals*, Bobadil in *Every Man in his Humour*, Colonel Oldboy in *Lionel and Clarissa*, Lovewell in *The Clandestine Marriage*, Scrub in *The Beaux' Stratagem*, Touchstone in *As You Like It* and Tony Lumpkin in *She Stoops to Conquer*.

He was as popular offstage as on. Among his many influential friends were the Duke and Duchess of Bedford, Lord and Lady Holland, Sir Joshua Reynolds, Sir Thomas Lawrence, the musician William Linley, the banker Thomas Coutts, Richard Brinsley Sheridan, Leigh Hunt and William Hazlitt. He was a member of the club called 'The School of Garrick' (**37**).

Bannister died at his house at No 65, Gower Street, Bedford Square, on 7 November 1836, and was buried in the family vault at St Martin-in-the-Fields. In addition to the pictures of him in the Garrick Club, there are numerous other portraits of him in private and theatrical character. (*BDA*)

BARKER, Frederick **43, 892**
fl. 1940s-1970s
Frederick Barker, who was on the Garrick Club staff by the late 1940s, was a wine waiter, who, according to Richard Hough, *The Ace of Clubs* (1976), was a great character and 'gave his whole life to the Garrick.'

BARKER
See GRANVILLE-BARKER

BARNETT
See BERNARD

BARRIE, Sir James Matthew **44**
1860-1937
Born at Kirriemuir, Scotland, the son of a poor weaver, Barrie studied for several years at Edinburgh University and served as a journalist for the *Nottingham Daily Journal* before he settled in London as a free-lance writer in 1885. He became a successful playwright with *The Professor's Love Story* in 1894; his novel *The Little Minister*, a best-seller in 1891, made him wealthy and was adapted into a highly-successful play in 1897. In the early decades of the twentieth century he wrote a series of magical and sentimental plays that became stage triumphs, including *Quality Street* (1901), *The Admirable Crichton* (1902), *What Every Woman Knows* (1908), *The Twelve-Pound Look* (1910), *The Old Lady*

Shows her Medals (1917), *A Kiss for Cinderella* (1916) and *Dear Brutus* (1917). In the last-mentioned, Barrie abandoned his whimsicalities and fancifulness for a melancholy look at the disenchanting failure of a second chance in life. But the most enduring of his plays, which grew out of his short stories published in *The Little White Bird* in 1902, was *Peter Pan, the Boy Who Wouldn't Grow Up*, first acted in December 1904 with Nina Boucicault in the title-role. His last play, *The Boy David*, was written for and performed by Elizabeth Bergner in 1936. Barrie died in June the following year. In 1913 Barrie had been created a baronet and in 1922 was awarded the Order of Merit. He became president of the Society of Authors in 1928 and chancellor of Edinburgh University in 1930. He had been elected to membership in the Garrick Club in January 1890.

BARRINGTON, John **45, 46**
1715-1773
Born in 1715 in County Cork, Ireland, Barrington was intended for the law, but he turned to acting by 1735, when he was engaged at the Rainsford Street Theatre in Dublin. During his long career his peregrinations took him throughout Ireland, during which time he established himself, as one critic put it, as 'an excellent comic Actor of Infinite Humour, a much desir'd pleasing Companion.' The first record of his playing Teague in *The Committee* – the character in which he is depicted in Garrick Club portraits **45** and **46** – was at Waterford in the summer of 1737. In this character he made his London debut on 5 April 1739 at Covent Garden. Tate Wilkinson, manager of the York circuit, called Barrington's Teague the best stage Irishman he ever saw. Barrington was in and out of London for several years and in 1749-50 joined the company at Covent Garden, where he remained through 1762-63. During that period his wife also acted there. She was the former Mrs Sacheverel Hale, born Anne Hallam, the sister of the Hallams who acted earlier in London and were instrumental in founding the theatre in America. As the premiere stage Irishman of his time, Barrington played numerous such roles, including Foigard in *The Stratagem*, O'Cutter in *The Jealous Wife* and Macmorrice in *Henry V*. He died on 15 January 1773 and was buried in the ground of St George the Martyr, near the Foundling Hospital. (*BDA*)

BARRY, Elizabeth **47**
c. 1658-1713
Elizabeth Barry, who became the first great actress on the English stage, was born about 1658, the daughter of the barrister Robert Barry, who was ruined by his raising a regiment for Charles I at his own expense. There are many stories about Elizabeth's early life, including one that the Earl of Rochester had trained her in the role of Isabella in *Mustapha*, which she performed before Charles II. But her first performance of record was in the small part of Draxilla in Otway's *Alcibiades* at the Dorset Garden Theatre in late September 1675. Over the next several years she appeared in such roles as Leonora in *Abdelazer*, Elvira in *The Wrangling Lovers*, Lucia in *The Cheats of Scapin* and Emilla in *The Fond Husband*. She also gave birth to a daughter by Rochester in December 1677. In the 1679-80 season she took on several major roles, including Lavinia in Otway's *Caius Marius*, and the following season she was the leading lady of the Duke's company, playing Cordelia in the Tate version of *King Lear*, Leonora in *The Spanish Fryar*, and Belvidera in Otway's *Venice Preserv'd*, in the premiere, probably on 9 February 1682. Otway, with whom she had an affair, had written the role expressly for her. There were other lovers, including the dramatist Sir George Etherege and the Earl of Dorset. She became notorious for her amours, prompting several satires, including one called 'Three Late Marriages,' in which she is referred to as 'slattern Betty Barry.'

She displayed in her acting a high pitch of emotion coupled with a great degree of control that suited her for the great roles of Lady Macbeth, Calista in *The Fair Penitent*, Roxana in *The Rival Queens*, Evadne in *The Maid's Tragedy* and Cleopatra in *All for Love*. She retired from the stage in 1709 and died on 7 November 1713, at about the age of 55. As an actress she had been of the highest order. The portrait of her after Kneller in the Garrick Club (**47**) is a copy of the original at Strawberry Hill. She is pictured kneeling by William III, with the actress Ann Bracegirdle by her side, in another canvas by

Kneller at Hampton Court Palace. There is an extensive notice of her in the *BDA*.

BARRY, Spranger **48, 49**
1717?-1777
He was born about 1717 in Dublin, the son of William Barry, a silversmith of Skinner Row, and his wife Catherine. He tried several occupations, but having inherited a comfortable sum from his father and possessed of a handsome figure and fine voice, eventually he turned actor. He made his first appearance on 15 February 1744 at the Aungier Street Theatre, Dublin, as Othello. According to the prompter that night, Barry 'seem'd a finish'd Actor dropt from the Clouds.' He had a 'perfect' figure and a voice 'the harmony and melody of whose silver tones were resistless.' He next played the major roles of Pierre in *Venice Presev'd* and Varanes in *Theodosius*. After acting a series of heroic roles in Dublin (some with the young actors David Garrick and George Anne Bellamy), Barry made his Drury Lane debut on 4 October 1746 as Othello, a role it seems he had been born to play; after seeing him in the part Garrick gave up playing it himself. Barry continued at Drury Lane in 1747-48, where Garrick was now manager, performing a repertoire of leading parts.

At the close of the 1749-50 season he left Drury Lane for Covent Garden, a move that prompted the famous 'Romeo rivalry.' On 28 September 1750 Barry and Mrs Cibber appeared as Romeo and Juliet, and on the same night at Drury Lane Garrick and Bellamy appeared in the same roles. After 12 nights at both houses the play was withdrawn from Covent Garden when Mrs Cibber tired, and a triumphant 13th performance went on at Drury Lane. In the controversy over the better Romeo, though Garrick was admired for his great passion, the palm went to Barry, whose natural physical beauty and grace more suited him to the role. As one practical female audience member put it, had she been Juliet to Garrick's Romeo she certainly would have expected him to scale up to the balcony, but as Juliet to Barry's Romeo, she would 'certainly have *gone down* to him!'

Now at the blossoming of his talents, at Covent Garden Barry came on in a series of capital roles that established him as a major player and a continuing rival to Garrick: Lothario in *The Fair Penitent*, Phocyas in *The Siege of Damascus*, Pierre and Jaffeir in *Venice Preserv'd* and Osmyn in *Zara*. In 1754-55 he went back to Ireland to act at Smock Alley, but he returned to Covent Garden the next season and stayed through 1757-58, adding Lear and Douglas to his impressive repertoire.

Barry left Covent Garden to venture into management in Dublin, building a new theatre on the site of the old Music Hall in Crow Street, which he opened in October 1758. Dublin could not support two theatres, and after taking on several mortgages Barry was obliged to give up his theatre to Mossop, the manager of the rival Smock Alley. He also had to sell his other properties in Ireland, including a farm in Dublin and a theatrical venture he had started in Cork. Once more back in London in the summer of 1766 he and his wife Ann Barry (née Dancer) acted for Foote at the Haymarket, and in 1767-68 they engaged at Drury Lane, where their performances as Rhadamistus and Zenobia in the premiere of Murphy's *Zenobia* on 27 February 1768 were acclaimed. The Barrys gave Garrick problems by being difficult and temperamental. Moreover, Barry was often ill and could not play. The couple continued to travel back and forth between Drury Lane and Dublin, and in 1776 they engaged at Covent Garden, where Barry made his last stage appearance on 28 November 1776 as the elderly Evander in Murphy's *The Grecian Daughter*.

Barry died on 10 January 1777, at about the age of 60, and was buried in the North Cloister of Westminster Abbey. Clearly he had been one of the finest actors of his time. Many paintings and engravings of Barry were made, among them the oil by an unknown artist (**48**) and Hayman's scene from *Hamlet* (**49**). Barry's first wife Anne seems to have been dead by 1753, when he took up with the young Covent Garden actress Maria Isabella Nossiter. Early in 1768 he married Ann Dancer, an estimable actress, who had first performed as Miss Street, then as Mrs Dancer (she married the actor William Dancer in 1754), and after Barry died she became Mrs Crawford, having married the Irish barrister

Thomas Crawford in July 1778. In her best performances, as Lady Randolph in *Douglas*, in the title role in *Euphrasia*, and Monimia in *The Orphan*, for example, she was favourably compared to Mrs Siddons. (*BDA*)

BARRYMORE, William **50**
1759-1830
William Barrymore, whose real name was Blewit, was born at Taunton in 1759, the son of a hair dresser. Various memoirs of his early life differ, but in July 1780 he was with a company of strollers at Plymouth. He made his way to London in 1782, appearing for the first time at Drury Lane on 3 October as Young Meadows in *Love in a Village*. He remained at that theatre for most of his career, at least through 1808-9, playing a considerable number of roles in musical pieces and comedies. He was also a leading actor at the Haymarket Theatre for many summer seasons. Critical reports describe him as an awkward performer, who acted with stiff knees, and had trouble retaining his lines; but at least one friendly source praised his judgment, noted his improvement over the years and suggested that he was industrious and steady as a second-rate actor. The last several years of his career he spent in the provinces, making his final appearance as Charles Beverley opposite Mrs Siddons as Mrs Beverley in *The Gamester* at Brighton in the summer of 1809. He died at Edinburgh in July 1830. Among his more effective roles had been Laertes in *Hamlet*, Dumont in *Jane Shore* and Osmond in *The Castle Spectre*.

His son William Henry Barrymore acted in pantomimes and spectacles in London in the mid-nineteenth century and went to America, where he died in 1845. Our subject seems not to have been related to the famous family of Barrymores who played in America in the twentieth century. (*BDA*)

BARTLEY, George **51, 447**
1782?-1858
Born in Bath about 1782, Bartley, the son of a boxkeeper at the Bath theatre, appeared in children's roles, and then, according to conflicting memoirs, was apprenticed as a waiter and cook at the York House Hotel in Bath or was placed in a counting house. In the summer of 1800, however, he appeared as Orlando in *As You Like It* at Cheltenham. While in a touring company he met his first wife, a Miss Stanton, who may have been one of the daughters of the provincial manager John Stanton. Bartley made his first appearance in London at Drury Lane on 18 December 1802, as Orlando. Dissatisfied with his roles and salary, Bartley left London and from 1809 to 1811 was the unsuccessful manager at Glasgow. He also began to build a reputation as an actor in Manchester, Liverpool and elsewhere. In 1814 he married Sarah Smith (1783-1850), a tragic actress of considerable reputation, and returned with her to Drury Lane, where, on 12 April 1815, he appeared as Falstaff, a character that would prove to remain his favourite. (Ashton speculates that the portrait in the Garrick Club catalogued as William Lovegrove in the role of Realize in *The Will* (**447**) may actually be of Bartley as Falstaff.) After a successful tour with his wife in America in 1818, he was engaged at Covent Garden winters and at the Lyceum summers. In 1829 he became stage manager of Covent Garden Theatre, a post he retained for some 14 years. He retired in 1852, taking his farewell benefit on 18 December. He died, probably from a stroke, in Woburn Square on 22 July 1858 and is said to have been buried in the churchyard of St Mary's, Oxford. Though not a first-line actor, Bartley served his profession well. For many years he was treasurer of the Covent Garden Theatre Theatrical Fund. He was an original member of the Garrick Club in 1831, but later resigned.

The picture reproduced as **51** in *Pictures in the Garrick Club* and intended to be Bartley as Hamlet is in error. That picture is of Edward Shuter as Scapin and was also reproduced, correctly, as **740**. (A similar mixup occurs in the *BDA*, where Bartley's portrait as Hamlet is reproduced, incorrectly, in 13: 377 as Shuter as Scapin). Bartley seems never to have acted Hamlet in London, nor was Pocock's picture ever engraved.

BARTLEY, Sarah
See Sarah SMITH

BARTOLOZZI, Lucia Elizabeth
See Lucia Elizabeth VESTRIS

BARTON, Elizabeth
See Mrs William HOPKINS

BARTON, Frances
See Frances ABINGTON

BATESON, Lieutenant-General Richard CVO 793
d. 1905
Lieutenant-General Bateson, who is pictured as No. 7 in O'Neil's large canvas of members in the Billiards Room (**793**), was elected to the Garrick Club on 5 May 1852. He died on 11 September 1905.

BECHER, Eliza
See Eliza O'NEILL

BEECHAM, Sir Thomas, 2nd Baronet 52
1879-1961
The English conductor and impresario Thomas Beecham was born on 29 April 1879 at St Helens, Lancashire, the son of the wealthy businessman Joseph Beecham and the grandson of the founder of the Beecham's pill business. Educated at Wadham College, Oxford, he studied composition but had no formal musical training. He first conducted in London in 1905 and in 1906 formed his own New Symphony Orchestra. In 1909, supported by a private fortune that would enable him to embark on a number of musical ventures, Beecham created the Beecham Symphony Orchestra that gave concerts at Wigmore Hall. He began presenting operas at Covent Garden and other theatres, introducing London audiences to the music of Strauss, Delius and Berlioz. During his long career he developed a repertoire encompassing every style and school and produced and conducted about 120 operas, about half of which were new to Britain. After World War I financial constraints forced the closing of his opera company, but it was later revived as the British National Opera Company.

Beecham became widely known as a guest conductor in Britain, Germany, Canada and America. In 1932 he formed the London Philharmonic Orchestra and became conductor at Covent Garden; he became artistic director of the latter the following year. Magnificent sound recordings and tours throughout the English provinces and Europe enhanced his fame. In the United States he conducted the Seattle Symphony (1941-1944) and the Metropolitan Opera (1942-1944). In 1947 he founded the Royal Philharmonic Orchestra in London, and remained principal conductor until 1960. He died in London on 8 March 1961.

Beecham had inherited his father's baronetcy in 1916. He had been knighted in 1915. He became a member of the Garrick Club in 1938 but resigned in December 1945. His autobiography *A Mingled Chime* was published in 1943, and he also wrote a biography of Frederick Delius (1959). His biographical notice in *Grove's Dictionary* praises him highly for his musicality: 'he lends a unique perfection and subtlety of phrasing, a blending of grace and vitality that defy analysis.'

BEITH, Major-General John Hay CBE 53
1876-1954
Beith, who wrote under the pen name of Ian Hay, was born on 17 April 1876 in Manchester, the sixth child of John Alexander Beith, a cotton merchant, and his wife Janet (née Fleming). He was the grandson of Alexander Beith, one of the founders of the Free Church of Scotland in 1843. After attending St John's College, Cambridge, John Beith served as a teacher and junior master at Fettes until in 1912 he left there to take up writing. His first novel, *Pip* (1907), became a best-seller and was followed by a number of other novels. He gave distinguished service in World War I, during which he rose to the rank of major. For his work in America from 1916 to 1918 with the information bureau of the British War Mission he was awarded the CBE.

Beith took up the theatre in 1919, and he successfully adapted his own novels into plays on the London stage, including *A Safety Match* (1921) and *Housemaster* (1936). In collaboration with others he wrote a number of plays: *Orders are Orders*, with Anthony Armstrong (1932); *A Song of Sixpence*, with Guy Bolton (1930); *Good Luck*, with Seymour Hicks (1823); and with P. G. Wodehouse *A Damsel in Distress* (1928) and *Leave it to Psmith* (1930).

In the Second World War, Beith became a Major-General as Director of public relations for the War Office. He is pictured by Dugdale in the uniform of that rank (**53**). Subsequently he wrote a tribute to Malta entitled *The Unconquered Isle* (1948) and *Hattie Stowe,* a play about Harriet Beecher Stowe that was a failure.

Beith was esteemed for his striking personality, charm and after-dinner speeches. He was chairman of the Society of Authors twice (1921-1924, 1935-1939), a member of the council of the League of British Dramatists and President of the Dramatists Club from 1937. For his long service as a Governor of Guy's Hospital he was awarded the Order of St John of Jerusalem.

He became a member of the Garrick Club in 1919. He had married in 1915 Helen Margaret Spiers, the only daughter of Peter Alexander Spiers of Polmont Park, Stirlingshire; they had no children. Beith died in Petersfield on 22 September 1952. (*DNB*)

BELLAMY, George Anne 54, 967
1731-1788
The troublesome and spirited actress George Anne Bellamy stated that she was born in Fingal, Ireland, on 23 April 1733, though there is some considerable doubt about the accuracy of that assertion. Much of the information about her earlier years derives from her 'autobiographical' *Apology for the Life of George Anne Bellamy* (1785), a not entirely reliable source and actually attributed to Alexander Bicknell. She was the daughter of the actress Mrs Bellamy (née Seal, later Mrs Walter, d. 1771) and resulted from her mother's liaison with James O'Hara, second Baron of Tyrawley. After supposedly having been placed in an Ursuline convent for five years, she was brought under the care of a Mr Du Vall, a London peruke maker. Lord Tyrawley took her to live for a while at Bushey Park but he soon went off to be ambassador to Russia.

By her own account George Anne made her first appearance on the stage in the capital role of Monimia in *The Orphan* at Covent Garden on 22 November 1744, at the age of 14. But she actually made her London debut at that theatre, at the tender age of 10, on 20 April 1741, as a servant to Colombine in the pantomine *Harlequin Barber*. Again announced as her first appearance on any stage she played Miss Prue in Congreve's *Love for Love* on 27 March 1742, a role that suggests she must have been more than 11 years of age at the time.

Subsequent to her November 1744 appearance as Monimia she took on a number of leading parts at Covent Garden and at the Smock Alley Theatre, Dublin, in 1745-46. After three years in Dublin, she returned to Covent Garden and triumphed as Belvidera in *Venice Preserv'd* on 20 October 1748. Quickly she became a great rage both on and off the stage, playing such roles as Imoinda in *Oroonoko*, Volumnia in *Coriolanus*, Statira in *The Rival Queens* and Anne Bullen in *Henry VIII*. She also entered into a relationship with George Montgomery Methan that would last some five years before she moved on to John Calcraft of Grantham, who would not marry her, but by whom she had a daughter and was supported in great style in a grand house in Parliament Square. In the autumn of 1750 Garrick was successful in his campaign to bring Bellamy to Drury Lane, where she appeared on 28 September as Juliet to his Romeo (**967**). He was 33 and she was about 19. The production was rivaled by Barry and Mrs Cibber in the same roles at Covent Garden, provoking the famous 'Romeo and Juliet War' that lasted 12 nights until the Covent Garden production faltered and Garrick and Bellamy added a triumphant 13th night. Though Mrs Cibber had greater beauty and tragic expression, Mrs Bellamy showed a natural loveliness and amourous rapture. As one observer put it, 'For my own part I shed more tears in seeing Mrs *Cibber*, but I am more delighted in seeing Mrs *Bellamy*.' She spent another three seasons at Drury Lane and then returned to Covent Garden, where off and on she was engaged for the remainder of her career. During that time she had a succession of paramours, including the actors West Digges and Henry Woodward.

George Anne retired in 1770 to a residence in Strand-on-the-Green, near Kew, where despite having been recipient of several legacies she lived in some privation. She died on 16 February 1788 in Eliot's Row, St George's Fields, having lived under the rules of the King's Bench and having suffered from a broken ankle that never healed and required her to need help to walk, George Anne Bellamy was always a great public favourite, but she ranked just below the great actresses of her day, Mrs Cibber and Mrs Pritchard. Her beauty well suited her for roles like Juliet and Cordelia, and with tears at her command she excelled as Monimia. In addition to Lindo's portrait (**54**) and the scene from *Romeo and Juliet*, she was pictured in a number of paintings and engravings (see *BDA* 2: 19-20).

BENDA, Kenneth **892**
d.1978
The actor Kenneth Benda, shown as No. 38 in Gilroy's painting of the Garrick Club Outing in 1967, was elected to the Garrick Club in March 1965. He died on 27 July 1978.

BENNETT, Harriet Pye
See ESTEN

BENNETT, Jill **941**
1931-1990
Born in Penang, Malaya, on 4 December 1931, the daughter of the rubber plantation owner James Randle Bennett and his wife, her full name was Nora Noel Jill Bennett. After education at Priors Field, Godlaming, she attended the Royal Academy of Dramatic Art (1944-1946) and became a member of the company at the Royal Shakespeare Theatre in Stratford-upon-Avon in 1949. While at Stratford she began a love affair with the actor Sir Godfrey Tearle, who was about 42 years her senior. Her first appearance on the London stage was as Anni in *Captain Carvallo* at the St James's in August 1950. In May 1951 at the St James's she played Iras in Olivier's productions of *Antony and Cleopatra* and *Caesar and Cleopatra*. She established her reputation with her performance as Masha in *The Seagull* at the Saville in August 1956 and appeared on the London stage in a variety of roles in the 1960s and 1970s. At the Royal Court in June 1972 she was highly praised for her portrayal of Hedda in an adaptation of *Hedda Gabler* by John Osborne, to whom she was married from 1968 to 1977. (A first marriage, to Willis Hall, was dissolved.) In Osborne's play *Time Present* in 1968, based on her passionate relationship with Tearle, her performance as Pamela won her the Variety Club and Evening Standard awards for best actress. Later (1983) in her book *Godfrey: A Special Time Remembered* she called her relationship with him the four happiest years of her life. At the Royal Court in August 1971 she appeared as Frederica in Osborne's *West of Suez*. Other roles included Fay in *Loot* at the Royal Court and then for the National Theatre (at the Old Vic in February 1975 and subsequently at the Lyttelton in March 1976) Sally Prosser in *Watch It Come Down*.

On television she played in productions of *The Heiress*, *The Three Sisters* and *Design for Living*, among others. Jill Bennett also made a major career in films, appearing in *The Charge of the Light Brigade, Moulin Rouge, Equus, Giant, The Purple Rain, Shampoo, The Big Heat, The Manchurian Candidate, Inadmissable Evidence* and *The Sheltering Sky*. She died in London on 4 October 1990. She has been described as an actress 'noted for projecting emotional vulnerability and, alternately, elegant comedy'. *(EB)*

BENSLEY, Robert **55-59**
1742-1817
Robert Bensley, sometimes mistakenly called Richard in the records, was a principal actor on the London stage for some 31 years. Details of his early life are confusing, but after military service, perhaps in the Marines in North America, he was introduced as a 'Gentleman' making his first appearance at Drury Lane Theatre on 2 October 1765, as Pierre in *Venice Preserv'd* (**58**). In that and the following season under Garrick's management at Drury Lane he enjoyed moderate success in such roles as Hamet in *The Orphan of China*, Standard in *The Constant Couple*, Polydore in *The Orphan*, Constant in *The Provok'd Wife* and Horatio in *The Fair Penitent*. The next season, 1767-68, he went over to Covent Garden, where he remained engaged for eight consecutive seasons. He returned to Drury Lane in 1775-76, and was a loyal and busy actor there until his retirement in 1796. He also played at the Haymarket during summers and purchased a portion of the Bristol playhouse in 1772.

During his many years in London his repertoire included some 76 roles. About 23 portraits of him (including those at the Garrick Club) in his various roles were done by a number of artists. He first acted Hubert in *King John* (**59**) on 23 September 1767 at Covent Garden. At Drury Lane he played Prospero in *The Tempest* (**57**) on 1 January 1777, Harold in *The Battle of Hastings* (**55**) on 24 January 1778 and Oakly in *The Jealous Wife* (**56**) on 25 September 1788. Bensley was regarded as a serviceable but undistinguished actor whose experience carried him through his cast of characters with 'a tolerable good grace.' He had, according to one harsh critic, 'neither face, voice, manner, or scarce any theatrical requisite.' Garrick had nicknamed him 'Roaring Bob' – because of his old-style acting in the manner of James Quin. Nevertheless, Benson had a steadying influence upon the company, and his large repertoire and substantial knowledge of the drama entitled him to a place as a principal performer. Bensley died at Stanmore on 12 November 1817. The portrait in the Garrick Club (**58**) attributed to Roberts in *PGC* is now attributed to Ryley and shows Bensley as Pierre in *Venice Preserv'd*. (*BDA*)

BENSON, Sir Frank Robert **60**

1858-1959

Born at Alresford, Hampshire, on 4 November 1858, the son of a wealthy barrister, this actor-manager was educated at Winchester and Oxford. While at New College, Oxford, and a member of OUDS, he produced *Agamemnon* in the original Greek and acted Clytemnestra. In 1882 he made his professional debut as Paris in *Romeo and Juliet* under Irving at the Lyceum. In 1883 he formed a touring company and over the years in the provinces produced all of Shakespeare's plays except *Troilus and Cressida* and *Titus Andronicus*. He brought his company to London for the first time in 1889-90, playing at the Globe, and returned to London numerous times. He regularly acted such Shakespearean roles as Hamlet, Lear, Coriolanus and Richard II and also performed in Canada and South Africa.

Benson devoted himself mainly to the producing of Shakespeare's plays, organizing 26 of the annual festivals from 1886 at Stratford-upon-Avon, where he served as a Governor of the Shakespeare Memorial Theatre and Trustee of the Birthplace. As a manager and teacher at the acting school he founded in 1901, he trained a number of young actors who became known as 'Bensonians.' He became the only actor ever to be knighted in a theatre, when in 1916 George V knighted him at Drury Lane on the occasion of the Shakespeare Tercentenary celebration. In 1930 he published his *Memoirs*, and also wrote *I Want to Go on the Stage*. He had married in 1886 the actress Gertrude Constance Featherstonhaugh (1860-1946), who played leading roles in his company. Benson, who became a member of the Garrick Club in March 1893 (and also was a member of the Green Room Club), died in London on 31 December 1939 at age 81. (*OCT*, *WWWT*)

BERKELEY, Thomas Mortimer Roland **61-63**

d. 1924

The barrister Thomas Berkeley was elected to the Garrick Club in 1904. He served as Chairman of the Picture Committee, in which capacity he is pictured by Munnings in **62**. Berkeley died in 1924.

BERNARD, John **64**

1756-1828

Born in 1756 at the Portsmouth Naval Station, the son of a navy lieutenant John Bernard and his wife Ann (the daughter of a naval captain), young John was sent to a Latin grammar school near Chichester. After leaving school and determined to become an actor, he had an aborted engagement at Farnham and then was taken on by the eccentric country manager Henry Thornton, who sometime in 1773 presented him as Jaffeir in *Venice Preserv'd* at the village of Chew Magna. Bernard had assumed the name of Mr Budd for his debut, and then took on the name of Mr Barnett for his subsequent country campaigns. He bounced about several provincial companies playing in Taunton, Weymouth, Braintree, Needham, Dedham and Norwich. At the last place in 1774 he married his first wife, an actress named Mrs Cooper, and they acted as the Barnetts. Eventually they assumed the name of Bernard, and continued on their peregrinations at Norwich, York (under Tate Wilkinson), Bath,

Exeter and elsewhere until they joined Daly's company in Ireland in 1782, playing at Cork and then at the Capel Street Theatre, Dublin, in 1782-83. Back in England Bernard became a 'ruling favourite' of the Bath Theatre in 1785-86. He then signed articles with Harris at Covent Garden and made his debut there on 19 October 1787 as Archer in *The Beaux' Stratagem.* At that theatre through November 1795, he acted such roles as Flutter in *The Belle's Stratagem,* Jack Meggot in *The Suspicious Husband* (**64**) and Gratiano in *The Merchant of Venice.* The *Candid and Impartial Strictures* in 1795 called him 'A performer of merit in many parts ... but not so good as a London audience ought to expect.'

After failing as manager at Hull and Dover and elsewhere, he set sail for America in 1797 (now accompanied by his second wife, a Miss Fisher of the Guernsey company) and made his debut at the Greenwich Street Theatre in New York as Goldfinch in *The Road to Ruin.* His subsequent career in America was successful and he was popular with audiences. He had a useful stint as manager (with Snelling Powell and James Dickson) of the Federal Street Theatre in Boston between 1806 and 1811, and his touring took him throughout the United States and Canada. His second wife died in 1806 and he soon had a third, the former Miss Wright, also an actress.

Bernard's main contribution to the American Theatre was his two-volume *Retrospections of the Stage* (1830), brought out after John's death by his son Bayle Bernard. (The parts about America were edited by Laurence Hutton and Brander Matthews and were published in 1887 as *Retrospections of America 1797-1811.*) Soon after 1819, Bernard returned to England where he died destitute on 29 November 1828.

While he was acting in London, Bernard was a clubable fellow, having been made an honorary member of the Anacreontic Society; he also founded a comedians' club called 'The Strangers at Home.' His social acceptance is testified to by his having been made secretary of the Beefsteak Club. His portrait for his appointment in that club was painted by P. Marshall; it was presented to the Garrick Club in 1900 by his daughter-in-law Mrs Bayle Bernard, but the picture is missing. *See* also K. A. Burnim and P. H. Highfill, Jr, *John Bell, Patron of British Theatrical Portraiture,* No. 110.

BERNHARDT, Sarah Henriette Rosine S4, B132, B156

1844-1923

Regarded by many as the greatest actress of the second half of the nineteenth century, she was born in Paris about 22 October 1844, the illegitimate daughter of a Dutch courtesan, Julie Bernard. Her real name was Henriette Rosine Bernard, but she was destined to be called 'The Divine Sarah.' After training at the Paris Conservatoire she was accepted at the Comédie-Française in 1862, but soon she was discharged. She acted at the Odéon between 1866 and 1872, having a great success as Anna Damby in *Kean* (1868) and a triumph as Zanetto in *Le Passant* (1869). Bernhardt returned to the Comédie-Française in 1872 and proceeded to a number of great portrayals: the Queen in *Ruy Blas,* the title roles in Voltaire's *Zaire* and Racine's *Phèdre,* Doña Sol in Hugo's *Hernani,* Desdemona in Shakespeare's *Othello* and Marguerite in Dumas' *La dame aux camélias.* Tours in England, throughout continental Europe, the United States, Australia and South America in the 1880s and 1890s established her international reputation. She also became famous for her series of affairs and for her independent and sometimes unconventional behaviour. In the 1880s Victorien Sardou wrote four plays for her: *Fèdora* (1882), *Thèdora* (1884), *La Tosca* (1887) and *Cléopâtre* (1890). In 1893 she became manager of the Théâtre de la Renaissance, then in 1899 of the Théâtre des Nations, which she renamed the Théâtre Sarah Bernhardt and managed until her death. (That theatre is now known as the Théâtre de la Ville.) She acted Hamlet in 1899, at the age of 55, and created the role of the Duke of Reichstadt in Rostand's *L'Aiglon* in March 1900. In 1915 her right leg had to be amputated as a result of an accident when jumping off the parapet in the last scene of *La Tosca* some years before, but she continued to act, appearing in roles that allowed her to remain seated. She died in Paris on 26 March 1923. (*See* Burnim and Wilton, *The Richard Bebb Collection in the Garrick Club,* B132 and B156.)

BETTERTON, Juliana
See Juliana GLOVER

BETTERTON, Thomas **65**
1635-1710
Born about August 1735 in Tothill (or Tuttle) Street, Westminster, Thomas Betterton was the son of Matthew Betterton and his second wife, Frances. Matthew styled himself a gentleman of Westminster and was apparently an under-cook to Charles I. Christened at St Margaret's, Thomas was given what was then called a polite schooling, though his earliest biographer, Charles Gildon, said in 1710 that the lad did not receive 'an Education in the learned Languages,' – though he studied French and made use of it later. He was apprenticed to the bookseller John Holden, and it was presumably through his master that he made his early theatrical and literary contacts. By 1659-60, when, after 18 years of suppression, professional acting was again allowed, young Betterton was a member of a troupe led by John Rhodes, another bookseller. The prompter John Downes said Tom's 'Voice [was] then as Audibly strong, full and Articulate, as in the Prime of his Acting.' That emphasis on his voice is significant, for Betterton lived in an age when people, as Hamlet says, go to 'hear' a play. Further, our hero, according to the actor Anthony Aston, 'labour'd under an ill Figure, being clumsily made, having a great Head, a short thick Neck, stoop'd Shoulders, and had fat short Arms ...' His voice and his control of it must have more than made up for these deficiencies, however, for early on he was given important roles: the Bondman, Pericles, Deflores in *The Changeling* and Archas in *The Mad Lover*.

On 24 August 1661 Betterton, just 26, appeared at the Duke's Company's Lincoln's Inn Fields theatre as Hamlet, which he acted to the end of his career to great applause. Downes said that the troupe's manager, Sir William Davenant, '(having seen *Mr. Taylor* of the *Blackfryars* Company Act [Hamlet], who being Instructed by the Author *Mr. Shakespear*) taught Mr. *Betterton* in every Particle of it; which by his exact Performance of it, gain'd him Esteem and Reputation, Superlative to all other Plays.' The diarist and playgoing addict Samuel Pepys found in Betterton his favourite actor, and Betterton's Hamlet on 31 August 1668 was 'the best part, I believe, that ever man acted.'

Many of Betterton's 120 or more roles between 1662 and 1704 were in plays now forgotten, but we recognize some of them: Mercutio in *Romeo and Juliet*, Bosola in *The Duchess of Malfi*, Sir Toby Belch in *Twelfth Night*, the title role in *Henry VIII*, Macbeth, Dorimant in *The Man of Mode*, King Lear (in Tate's adaptation), Brutus in *Julius Caesar*, Othello, Manly in *The Plain Dealer*, Valentine in *Love for Love*, Sir John Brute in *The Provok'd Wife*, Fainall in *The Way of the World* and Falstaff in *The Merry Wives of Windsor*. He was remarkably versatile and had, according to his contemporaries, a highly disciplined and commanding stage presence.

Early in his career he became involved in theatre management and staging. He went on an official trip to Paris in 1662 to examine French and Italian staging practices. That was the first of at least three Paris trips Betterton made, and the growth of stage spectacle and operatic productions in the late Restoration period in England was largely stimulated by his efforts. After Davenant's death in April 1668 Betterton and Henry Harris, the two leading actors in the Duke's Company, served the widow Davenant as acting managers, and Betterton took over Sir William's training of young performers, particularly new actresses (for which service he paid himself an extra twenty shillings a week). He was involved in the absorption of the King's Company by the Duke's in 1682, and in 1694 he led a player's revolt from the United Company. During the joint troupe's life from 1682 to 1694, Betterton was squeezed out of management by the crafty lawyer-manager Christopher Rich, but when London once again had two rival companies in 1695, Betterton renovated the old Lincoln's Inn Field Theatre and with his leading ladies Elizabeth Barry and Anne Bracegirdle ran his own troupe for ten years.

The aspect of theatre management that seemed to appeal most to Betterton and which had a profound effect on the English theatre was staging. The Dorset Garden Theatre, which Betterton had helped open in 1671, was equipped with elaborate scenes and machines and became over the years the home of most of London's spectacle productions. Betterton's familiarity with the Parisian stage and the scenes and machines of Italian designer-machinists, led to English productions like Dryden's *King Arthur* and *Albion and Albanius* that dazzled audiences. Musical theatre, with the help of Betterton's staging and Henry Purcell's music, became a London staple.

Having evidently prospered financially from the 1660s to the early 1690s, Betterton lost all he had in an East Indies venture and had to continue acting to the end. Three days after playing Melantius in *The Maid's Tragedy* on 13 April 1710 he died from complications of the gout. His wife-actress Mary, distressed at Thomas' financial loss in 1692 and at his physical deterioration in his later years, had lost her reason some time before his death. She died in 1712.

The greatest actor between Burbage in Shakespeare's day and Garrick in the heart of the eighteenth century, Thomas Betterton had a remarkable talent for capturing spectators through his carefully controlled creation of a tension so palpable that, as *The Laureate* declared in 1740 in describing his Hamlet, 'The whole audience hath remain'd in a dead Silence for near a Minute, and then – as if recovering all at once from their Astonishment, have joined as one Man, in a Thunder of universal Applause.' (*BDA*) [EAL]

BETTY, William Henry West **66, 67, B2, B157**

1791-1874

Called 'The Young Roscius,' or Master Betty, William Henry West Betty was born in Shrewsbury, Shropshire, in 1791, and before the age of 12, on 16 August 1803, he appeared on the stage in Belfast as Osman in *Zara.* His success as a child performer in Dublin, Glasgow and Edinburgh brought the prodigal to London in 1804, when he appeared on 1 December at Covent Garden, at the age of 14, as Achmet in *Barbarossa* (**66**). Thus began the Master Betty craze, and it is said that his salary was immediately raised to £100. He played alternately at Covent Garden and Drury Lane that season as Norval in *Douglas* (**67**), Hamlet, Romeo, Rolla, Tancred and Richard III and other roles. He was so much the rage that William Pitt once adjourned the Commons so that members could see Betty play Hamlet, a role he supposedly mastered in four days. But he was a short-lived phenomenon and was gone from the London stage by 1808 and forgotten. He then attended Christ's College, Cambridge. After a failed attempt to return to the stage Betty lived in obscurity off what was left of his squandered fortune until he died in London in 1874, at the age of 83. In his *Life of Mrs Siddons*, Thomas Campbell dismissed Betty as 'An hallucination in the public mind, and a disgrace to our theatrical history.' (*See* Burnim and Wilton, *The Richard Bebb Collection in the Garrick Club*, B2 and B157.)

BILLINGTON, Elizabeth née Weichsel **68, 69**

1765 or 1768-1818

Born in 1765 or 1768, Elizabeth Weichsel was the daughter of Carl Weichsel, a Freiberg native who was principal oboist at the King's Theatre, and his wife Fredericka (née Weirman), who was a singer at Vauxhall Gardens. Elizabeth was a prodigy on the harpsichord by 1774, when she and her father performed in a concert at the Haymarket on 10 March. Other concerts followed, and in October 1783 she married James Billington, a double-bass player and one of her singing teachers. While she was performing in Dublin for several years her marriage was threatened by a series of liaisons she had, including one with the Irish manager and celebrated debaucher Richard Daly. She also suffered the death of a daughter. But the marriage held together and the Billingtons returned to London, where at Covent Garden on 13 February 1786 she made her first appearance in a theatrical role, playing Rosetta in *Love in a Village.* Over the next decade she acted little but sang in numerous concerts and oratorios, at Vauxhall Gardens, in the Concerts of Ancient Music and in the successive Handelian Commemorations at Westminster Abbey. While on tour with her in Italy her husband died, in May 1794; she was remarried in 1799, to a young Frenchman named Felissent, who proved to be a blackguard and from whom she remained separated much of the time. She continued performing in operas and concerts throughout Italy, and in 1801 she returned to London to sing alternately at Drury Lane and Covent Garden, appearing as Mandane in *Artaxerxes*. She also sang at the King's Theatre in the 1802-03 season, becoming the recognized *prima donna* in the Italian operas and charming audiences with her beauty and brilliant soprano voice. Mrs Billington retired in May 1811 and rejoined Felissent on her property near Venice, where she died on 25 August 1818, some say as the result of a beating by her husband.

Reynolds painted her as Saint Cecilia, on a life-size canvas that is now at the Beaverbrook Art Galley in Frederickton, New Brunswick. A portrait of her by Romney as Saint Cecelia is at the Boston Museum of Fine Arts. Her portrait was also painted by other artists, including Lawrence and Masquerier (**68**). In the latter she appears somewhat heavier than in the more idealized images of her, and Gillray caricatured her as a rotund Mandane. For a list of other portraits see the *BDA* 2. 128-29.

BIRCH, Christiana Ann, later Mrs William Macready 70
1765-1803
Born in Lincolnshire in 1765, Christiana Ann Birch was the daughter of a surgeon and the grand-daughter of William Frye, president of the Council of Montserrat. She was a newcomer to the Liverpool-Manchester company in 1786, where she met the actor William Macready (1755-1829). She became his first wife at the Collegiate Church in Manchester in June 1786. Among her roles was Julia in *The Rivals*. The Macreadys moved to London in September 1786, he to take up an engagement at Covent Garden, she to settle down as a housewife and mother. Among her three surviving children was William Charles Macready (1793-1873), who became an eminent tragedian (**450**, **451**). She died at Sheffield on 3 December 1803.

BLANCHARD, Thomas 71, 72
1760-1797
The comic actor and tenor singer Thomas Blanchard was born in 1760, the son of the actor Thomas Blanchard. For some years he toured with his father in the provinces and made his London debut at Drury Lane on 13 October 1773, as Cupid in *A Trip to Scotland*. After filling similar boy's roles there that season, he returned to play in the provinces, mainly at Bath and Bristol, for some 11 years, until 3 October 1787, when he appeared at Covent Garden as the rustic Hodge in *Love in a Village*. He stayed at Covent Garden until he was dismissed in June 1794 because of his heavy drinking. He was in and out of London during the remainder of his career – he had a great success at Jones's Royal Circus, St George's Fields, in March-April 1796. In October he was engaged at the Fishamble Street Theatre in Dublin, where he died on 30 December 1797 and was buried in St Mark's churchyard. He was survived by his widow Charlotte Blanchard (b. 1761), an actress, and several children. His son Thomas John Blanchard (b. 1789) – 'Blanchard the Pantaloon' – acted in London into the 1830s. Two of Blanchard's sisters also performed in London. Blanchard, who had an 'excellently resonant tenor voice' – was especially successful in rural rustics when he was sober. Among his numerous roles was Ralph in *The Maid of the Mill*, in which he is pictured by De Wilde (**71**, **72**).

BLANCHARD, William 73, 477, 750
1769-1835
Born at York on 2 January 1769, he was orphaned at a young age and was cared for by his uncle William Blanchard, publisher of the *York Chronicle*. He joined a company of strollers, playing under the name of Bentley for four years as he acted in various provincial theatres. His first London appearance was on 1 October 1800 at Covent Garden Theatre, playing Bob Acres in *The Rivals*. Blanchard's talent secured him a long engagement and higher salary, and a position of recognised eminence in the Covent Garden company. Except for a brief visit to America in 1832, he remained for many years at Covent Garden until his death. The critics wrote warmly of many of his characterizations and especially praised his portrayals of Polonius, Fluellen, Pistol and Sir Andrew Aguecheck. Among the best pictures of him are De Wilde's portrait as the Marquis de Grand Château (**73**) and Clint's scene for *Love, Law, and Physic* (**477**). De Wilde also pictured him as Andrew Aguecheek and Ralph in *The Maid of the Mill* (see Burnim and Highfill,

John Bell). Blanchard's last character was Counsellor Crowsfoot in Jerrold's comedy *Nell Gwynne* at Covent Garden on 9 January 1833. He died on 8 May 1835, at age 66, and was buried in the graveyard of St Luke's, Chelsea.

BLAND, Dorothea
See Dorothy JORDAN

BLAND, Maria Theresa Catherine Romanzini née Terzi **74-76**
1770-1838
Considerable confusion and contradiction surround Maria Bland's origins. The most reliable documentation is a manuscript at the Folger Library in the hand of James Winston, that states she was baptised Maria Theresa Catherine Terzi in the Catholic Church of Notre Dame in Caen, Normandy, on 10 September 1770, and she was the daughter of an itinerant musician from Rome named Alexander Tersi and his wife Catherine Zeli, a Florentine Jewess. When the family came to England in 1773 they changed their professional name to Romanzini, and on 10 April four-year-old Maria appeared with her father on stage at Bristol. She soon was performing in London at Hughes' Riding School, Blackfriars Bridge, and at Sadler's Wells, and by the age of 11 she was singing at the King's Theatre and at Drury Lane. Maria spent most of her professional career at Drury Lane, though she often played summers at the Haymarket and in the provinces. Among her numerous roles at Drury Lane were Fanny in *The Maid of the Mill*, Rose in *The Double Surprise*, Jenny in *The Deserter*, Annette in *Lord of the Manor* and Ariel in *The Tempest*.

Maria Romanzini married the actor George Bland on 21 October 1791 at St Paul, Covent Garden. It proved to be an unfortunate marriage, and by 1795 Mrs Bland was living openly with the actor Thomas Caulfield. Finding himself in an untenable situation, George Bland took himself off to America, where he acted in New York and Boston and died in the latter city in 1807. Eventually Thomas Caulfield left Mrs Bland and also went to America; he died in a drunken fit while acting on a stage in Kentucky in 1815. Mrs Bland, however, thrived professionally in London, and, according to Oxberry, was recognized 'as perfect as an English ballad-singer.'

Though she was unattractively short and stumpy, looked like a most unharmonious person, and was the brunt of unkind remarks concerning her Jewish background, she remained a stage favourite for more than 30 years. She sang admirably in Italian and French, but the English ballad style was her forte. In her later years she taught singing. By 1824 she was suffering from a nervous disorder that edged on madness. She benefited by some £800 from a public subscription on her behalf that brought her an annuity of £80. Mrs Bland lived her final years with a family named Western, at the Broadway, Westminster, where she died of a stroke on 15 January 1838; she was buried at St Margaret, Westminster. Information about her children is in the *BDA*, where also are lists of her many roles and portraits. (*BDA*)

BLEDISLOE, Benjamin Ludlow Bathurst, the 2nd Viscount **77**
1889-1979
Born on 2 October 1899, the elder son of the 1st Viscount Bledisloe and Bertha Susan (youngest daughter of the 1st Baron Ludlow), Ben Bathurst was educated at Eton and Magdalen College, Oxford. He served in the RAF in World War I and was a squadron leader and then wing commander in the Second World War. In 1927 he was called to the Inner Temple, became a bencher at Lincoln's Inn in 1956 and QC in 1952. In 1958 he succeeded to 2nd Viscount Bledisloe. His interest in flying and gardening, among other pursuits, continued throughout his life. Viscount Bledisloe became a member of the Garrick Club in 1936, served as a Trustee, and was often seen in the card room, where Gilroy has pictured him. His heir, Christopher H. L. Bathhurst (b. 1934), 3rd Viscount Bledisloe, became a member of the Garrick Club in 1959.

BLESSINGTON, Marguerite Power, Countess of **78**
1789-1849
Born Marguerite Power on 1 September 1789 near Clonmel, County Tipperary, at the age of 15 she was sold into marriage by her father to

Captain Maurice St Leger Farmer. He proved a sadist from whom she fled in three months. In 1817 he was killed in a drunken brawl and she was free to marry Charles Gardiner, the Earl of Blessington. With her husband she went abroad in 1822, accompanied by the young Alfred Count D'Orsay (1801-1852), who was the husband of Blessington's daughter by his first wife. After two months in Genoa with Lord Byron, they travelled in Italy and France until the earl died in May 1829. Lady Blessington, with a fortune much diminished by extravagance, returned to England with D'Orsay, who was now in a broken marriage. They lived together for the rest of her life, and she turned to writing in order to support herself. She wrote a successful first novel, *Grace Cassidy, or The Repealers* in 1833, and then *The Idler in Italy* in 1839 and *The Idler in France* in 1841. Her associations with Byron yielded her *Conversations of Lord Byron* in 1834. In constant debt, she found it necessary to flee with D'Orsay to Paris in April 1849, where she died several months later, on 4 June 1849. D'Orsay (who painted **78**) died there in 1852. Reputedly a woman of beauty and wit, Lady Blessington conducted a brilliant salon. Her portrait was also painted by Sir Thomas Lawrence. (*EB*)

BLOOM, Claire G0978

b. 1931

Born Claire Blume in North Finchley, London, the daughter of an advertising executive, she was a war evacuee in the United States from 1940 to 1943 and returned to London in 1944 to train at the Guildhall School of Music and Drama and Central School. She was at the Oxford Playhouse in 1946 and made her London debut in 1947 in *The Wind Devil.* In 1948 she became a member of the Royal Shakespeare Company, with which she acted Ophelia, Blanche in *King John* and Perdita in *A Winter's Tale.* International fame came when Charlie Chaplin cast her in his film *Limelight* (1951). In 1952 she toured the United States as Juliet. Subsequently she received superb notices for her appearances in *Rashomon* (1964), *A Doll's House* (1970, in New York), *A Streetcar Named Desire* (1974) and *The Cherry Orchard* (1981, at the American Repertory Theatre in Cambridge, Massachusetts). Procktor's (**G0978**) portrait shows her as Mme Ranevskaya in the last mentioned play. Her film roles include Lady Anne in Olivier's *Richard III* and Helena in *Look Back in Anger* (1959), *The Clash of the Titans* and *Yesterday's Children.* Her television credits include *Brideshead Revisited* (1981) and *Shadowlands* (1985, for which she received a BAFTA award as Best Actress. She was married to the film actor Rod Steiger for ten years 1959-1969); to Hilliard Elkins (1969-1976); and to the novelist Philip Roth for some five years (1990-1995). In 1987 she published her autobiography, *Limelight and After,* and in 1996 her *Memoirs.*

BLUNT, Arthur Cecil

See Arthur CECIL

BOAS, Guy 79

1896-1966

Guy Boas was born 9 December 1896, the son of Frederick S. Boas, OBE, and was educated at Christ Church, Oxford. He served as a Lieutenant in the Oxford Hussars, 1916-1918. He was a Senior English Master at St Paul's School, a lecturer in English Literature at Oxford, Vice-President of the English Association and Headmaster of Sloane School, Chelsea, where he produced 15 Shakespearean plays. Boas wrote as 'G. B.' for *Punch,* and was General Editor of *The Scholar's Library.* His *Shakespeare and the Young Actor* appeared in 1955. Boas also published several collections of light verse and *The Garrick Club 1831-1964.* He had become a member of the Garrick in November 1943 and was Hon. Librarian from 1943 until he died on 26 March 1966.

BOLTON, Mary Catherine, later Lady Thurlow 80

1790-1830

Born Mary Catherine Bolton in 1790, she made her London debut as Polly in *The Beggar's Opera* on 8 October 1801. She acted as Miss Bolton until 1813, when she married Edward, 2nd Baron of Thurlow (1781-1829), who is noticed in the *DNB.* Lady Thurlow died on 28 September 1830. In addition to **80** by De Wilde, there are portraits of her as Ophelia, Eliza and Princess Badroulboudour in *Aladdin.* (*Era Almanac* 1879)

BOOTH, Barton **81, 82**

1679?-1733

The actor Barton Booth was born about 1679 in Lancashire, the third son of John Booth. The family estate may have been impaired, and they moved to London, where Barton was placed with Dr Busby at Westminster School about 1688 and received a classical education that marked his acting style in later years. Young Booth's first professional acting seems to have been the title role in *Oroonoko* at the Smock Alley Theatre, Dublin, in the summer of 1698. He began performing in Thomas Betterton's troupe at the Lincoln's Inn Fields Theatre in London about the autumn of 1700, playing mostly secondary roles but making useful theatrical and social contacts and drawing notice as a hard-drinking but hard-working actor. By 1707 he was making his mark in such volatile parts as Shakespeare's Hotspur and Laertes but also in roles requiring the majesty of the Ghost in *Hamlet*. The prompter John Downes in 1708 wrote that Booth was 'A Gentleman of liberal Education, of form Venust; of Mellifluent Pronuntiation, having proper Gesticulations, which are Graceful Attendants of true Elocution; of his time a most Compleat Tragedian.'

That description is rather typical of the many comments on Barton Booth's acting throughout his career at Drury Lane, where he became from 1708 a solid, stolid fixture for twenty years. By 1710 he was established in such important roles as Othello, Castalio in *The Orphan*, Valentine in *Love for Love*, Brutus in *Julius Caesar* and Horatio in *Hamlet*, and by the time he became a sharer in the Drury Lane management in 1713-14 he had added King Lear, Jaffeir in *Venice Preserv'd*, Pinchwife in *The Country Wife*, and, most importantly, the title role in Addison's immensely popular *Cato*. His 'line' was firmly established, and he did little to expand his talent during the rest of his career. But he was evidently very good at what he did. His fellow actor and manager, Colley Cibber, claimed that 'The tones of his voice were all musical, and he had so excellent an ear, no one ever heard a dissonant note come from him … And his articulation was so excellent, he was heard to the farthest part of the theatre when he almost whispered.' Aaron Hill admired Booth's control over his voice and body: 'one would almost be tempted to borrow the aid of a very bold figure, and to express this excellence the more significantly … that the *blind* might have seen him, in his *voice*, and the *deaf* have heard him, in his *visage*.' Booth was a very good actor who lacked that extra quality – charisma, we would probably call it – that we look for in the very best players.

Rough-hewn and wild in his early years, Booth settled down and sobered up about 1701, when his father died. Details are missing, but within a few years he was married, to the daughter of Sir William Barkham, and he took on the responsibility of helping to support his brother and sister. His wife died in 1710, and Booth, having established some useful social connections, began to manoeuvre for a portion of the Drury Lane patent.

The trio of actors who managed Drury Lane so successfully from 1713 to the early 1730s, Booth, Cibber, and Robert Wilks, made it the premier playhouse in England, partly because they were all hard-working and talented performers who complimented one another in their acting lines and won the admiration of their fellow players as well as their audiences. They also succeeded because they had the necessary business acumen to keep their theatre operating smoothly and profitably. Before and after them were periods of great difficulty, and not until David Garrick bought into the Drury Lane patent in 1747 did the company regain the dominance the triumvirate gave it. Exactly what part of the management Barton Booth took care of is not always apparent, for he was not the company's leading man, like Wilks, nor one of the favourite playwrights, like Cibber. But Aaron Hill praised Booth for his learning and judgment, qualities that informed his acting and must have been especially valuable in management.

In 1719 Booth had married the dancer-actress Hester Santlow, to whom he willed the bulk of his estate. He died after a long and excruciating illness on 8 or 10 May 1733; his will is a candid, caring document that hints at a lifetime of difficult relations with his unappreciative siblings and a tender affection for his wife. (*BDA*) [EAL]

BOOTH, Cockran Joseph **83, 84**

d. 1789

After spending over 10 years acting in provincial companies, mainly at Bristol and Richmond, Cockran Joseph Booth made his London debut at Covent Garden on 4 October 1774 as Polyperchon in *Alexander the Great.* That season he acted a number of substantial roles, including Stockwell in *The West Indian*, Don John in *Much Ado about Nothing* and Cloten in *Cymbeline.* Booth remained at Covent Garden through 1788-89 and acted summers at the Haymarket. His line was mainly old men in comedy (**83** and **84**). He died in London on 7 July 1789. Though his obituary claimed he was a 'respectable figure' in many roles, most accounts indicated he was not a very good actor. (*BDA*)

BOOTH, Junius Brutus **85**

1796-1852

Born in London on I May 1796, the son of Richard Booth, a lawyer in Bloomsbury, the eccentric Booth was intended for the law, but turned actor instead. After appearances in struggling provincial companies in England and Belgium, he made his debut at Covent Garden as Sylvius in *As You Like* It on 18 October 1815. On 12 February 1817 he appeared with success as Richard III. Kean brought him to Drury Lane and on 20 February 1817 he acted Iago to Kean's Othello. He appeared as Lucius Junius Brutus in Payne's *Brutus* – the role in which the Garrick Club picture depicts him (**85**) – at the Royal Coburg early in 1820. He soon became a leading actor and for a while was considered a rival to Kean. He deserted his wife, whom he seems to have married while in Brussels, for Mary Ann Holmes, a Bow Street flower girl, and in 1821 went to America, making his debut in Richmond, Virginia, as Richard III. He also played that role for his New York debut at the Park Theatre on 5 October 1821.

In 1825 Booth returned to London for an engagement at Drury Lane, where he acted Brutus on 8 October, Richard III on 13 October and Othello on 17 October. He returned to America and achieved great popularity in such roles as Hamlet, Iago and Sir Giles Overreach and was hailed as second only to the famous American tragedian Edwin Forrest. His regular tours took him to California, New Orleans and up the Mississippi. He died in 1852 on a Mississippi steamboat.

His sons by Mary Ann Holmes, all born out of wedlock, became actors. The eldest, Junius Brutus Booth Jr (1821-1883) had a modest career as an actor-manager, mainly in California. Edwin Thomas Booth (1833-1893) became a renowned American actor, especially famous for his portrayal of Hamlet. The youngest son, John Wilkes Booth (1839-1865) was also an outstanding actor but became infamous for his assassination of President Abraham Lincoln at Ford's Theatre, Washington, on 14 April 1865.

BOURCHIER, Arthur **86**

1863-1927

The actor-manager Arthur Bourchier was born at Speen, Berks, on 22 June 1863, the son of Capt Charles Bourchier; he was educated at Eton and Christ Church, Oxford, and he was one of the founders of the OUDS, playing with that organisation Feste, Shylock, Hotspur and Brutus, among others. His first professional appearance was at Wolverhampton in 1889, as Jaques in *As You Like It*, with Mrs Langtry's company. He played the same role for his London debut at the St James's Theatre on 24 February 1890, thus beginning a long career during which he acted at and managed a number of theatres, including the Garrick, the Criterion and the Strand. Some of his notable roles included Long John Silver in *Treasure Island* (**86**), the title roles in *The Admirable Crichton* and *Henry VIII* and Joseph Surface in *The School for Scandal.* With Tree's company at Her Majesty's (1910-11) he acted Henry VIII, Bottom, Brutus, Sir Toby Belch and Macduff. He was at his best in 'truculent, fiery, or broad hearty parts ...' (*OCT*).

Bourchier married the fine actress Violet Vanbrugh (1867-1942) in 1894, and they often appeared together on stage. His second wife, Violet Marion Kyrle Bellew, whom he married in 1918, was also an actress. Bourchier died while on tour in South Africa on 14 September 1927, at age 63. He had become a member of the Garrick Club in 1885.

BOWDEN, Wright **87**

1752-1823

Born in 1752, the son of a publican in Manchester, Bowden made his first appearance on any stage at Covent Garden Theatre on 18 October 1787 in the title role of *Robin Hood* (**87**) and was greatly applauded for his 'deep tenor' voice. After playing the role 29 times that season, Bowden went to act in Ireland and Scotland, and did not return to London until 2 May 1794, when he again performed Robin Hood at Covent Garden. He remained at that theatre for three seasons, appearing in such singing roles as Ferdinand in *The Duenna*, Sileno in *Midas* and Fairlop in *The Woodman* and singing patriotic speciality songs. In 1797 he resigned from Covent Garden and went to play that summer at Richmond, his last theatrical engagement. He then became a stockbroker. Bowden died on 16 April 1823 at the age of 71 and was buried in St Mary's churchyard, Manchester. He was respected for his singing but not for his acting. In addition to the portrait of him as Robin Hood at the Garrick Club, a small watercolour by W. Loftis of Bowden in that character is at the Folger Library. (*BDA*)

BRACEGIRDLE, Anne **88**

c. 1663 or 1673-1748

She was born in Northamptonshire, the daughter of Justinian and Martha Bracegirdle, and Anne's birth year has been argued as about 1663 or 1673. Her parents fell on hard times and placed young Anne with the actors Thomas and Mary Betterton in London, where she received her early stage training and may have spoken prologues and epilogues as a girl. She was not listed as a player in the United Company in the Lord Chamberlain's accounts until 12 January 1688, and the following month at Drury Lane Theatre she is known to have acted Atelina in *The Injured Lovers*, a new play by the actor Mountfort. She was cited as Mrs Bracegirdle, not because she was married, which she was not, but because she had reached or was near her majority. Her first recorded breeches part was Semernia in *The Widow Ranter* on 20 November 1689, and by early 1690 she may have acted Statira in *The Rival Queens*, a part that became one of her favourites with audiences. Most of her acting at this time was at Drury Lane, though the United Company also performed at the Dorset Garden playhouse.

Few other performers of her day attracted so much attention, and most of the scribbling had less to do with her acting than with her bewitching beauty and apparent virtue. The actor Colley Cibber remembered that Anne in 1690 was 'blooming to her Maturity; her Reputation as an actress gradually rising with that of her Person; never any Woman was in such general Favour of her Spectators, which, to the last Scene of her Dramatick Life, she maintain'd by not being unguarded in her private Character.' In 1692 she and her mother were at the centre of a fumbled abduction attempt by an unwanted suitor that ended with the murder of her friend and fellow actor William Mountfort. The trial was the talk of the town, and long after the event the pundits and satirists gave Anne little peace.

The notoriety did not harm her theatrical career, of course, and by 1695, when Betterton broke away from Drury Lane and the tyrannical management of Christopher Rich, he made Anne and the actress Elizabeth Barry his co-leaders of the Lincoln's Inn Fields Theatre. His new troupe opened their venture with Congreve's *Love for Love* on 30 April 1695 with Anne acting Angelica, a part the love-struck author wrote especially for her, and the work was a great success. Congreve went on creating other parts for her, the most famous and indicative of her brilliant talent in comedy being Millamant in *The Way of The World.* Then Nicholas Rowe, another dazzled playwright, began writing tragic roles for her. Anne's salary by 1707 was a minimum of £120 annually, equal to Betterton's. Then, with a fine sense of timing, the '*Celebrated Virgin*' as Gildon called her in 1702, quit the stage at the height of her career and lived out her singular life quietly and untheatrically.

Anthony Aston, who in 1748 provided us with candid sketches of the players of his day, said Anne was 'of a lovely Height, with dark-brown Hair and Eye-brows, black sparkling Eyes, and a fresh blushy Complexion; and, whenever she exerted herself, had an involuntary Flushing in her Breast, Neck and Face, having continually a chearful Aspect, and a fine Set of even white

Teeth.' He thought her best at genteel comedy and in breeches parts, in which she could display her shapely legs. She lived to see David Garrick take the stage, recognizing and welcoming his genius. Anne Bracegirdle died on 12 September 1748 at the age of 85 and was buried, at her request, at Westminster Abbey. If there is an error in the Abbey registers, evidence of Anne's probable appearances as a child would suggest that she was born in 1673 instead of 1663. (The Index of Sitters in *Pictures in the Garrick Club* contains a typographical error and on p. 536 gives her death date as 1718.) (*BDA*; Lucyle Hook, 'Anne Bracegirdle's First Appearance,' in *Theatre Notebook*, 1959.) [EAL]

BRADSHAW, Anna Maria.
See Anna Maria TREE

BRADSHAW, Mrs William, Mary 89
d. 1780
Mary Bradshaw was probably the wife of the Drury Lane boxkeeper William Bradshaw. She first appeared on the stage at Lincoln's Inn Fields Theatre on 7 January 1743 as Nell in *The Devil to Pay* and a few weeks later acted Lucy in *The Beggar's Opera*. In the season 1743-44 she joined the company at Drury Lane, where she was to remain, for the most part, for 37 years, playing first a line of young ladies and then older woman. Her first role at Drury Lane was Kitty Pry in *The Lying Valet* on 17 September 1743. Among other roles were Phillis in *The Concious Lovers*, Miss Prue in *Love for Love* and Emilia in *Othello*. She acted Dorcas in Garrick's romance *Cymon* at the premiere on 2 January 1767 (**89**). She appears with Garrick in a painting by Zoffany of a scene from *The Farmer's Return from London*, an interlude which was first acted at Drury Lane on 10 March 1762; that painting was once owned by the Garrick Club but is now in the collection of Viscount Lambton. Toward the end of her career, she had great difficulty making ends meet. In the summer of 1780 Mrs Bradshaw, now poverty-stricken, was acting at Plymouth, where her daughter Elizabeth appeared and was hissed off the stage. Mrs Bradshaw apparently fell into a raging fit, turned mad and died in early August. (*BDA*)

BRAHAM, John 90, 652
1777-1856
John Braham, one of the greatest singers of the English musical stage, was born in Goodman's Fields, London, on 20 March 1777, the son of a German Jew, John Abraham, and his wife Esther (née) Lyon. John was the youngest of John Abraham's ten children who had musical careers in London (see their notices in the *BDA*). John Braham grew to love music in the Great Synagogue in Duke's Place, where he was educated and came under the tutelage of his uncle Michael Leoni (Meyer Lyon, d. 1797), a chorister at the synagogue and a professional singer on the London stage. John Braham made his singing debut at Covent Garden, at the age of 10, on 21 April 1787, for his uncle's benefit. His first speaking part was Joe in *Poor Vulcan!* at the same theatre on 2 June 1788. Under the patronage of the philanthropist Abraham Goldsmid (1756?-1810), he soon established a reputation by his appearances at leading concert venues in London, Gloucester and Birmingham. In 1797, accompanied by the singer Nancy Storace, with whom he lived for some time, he went to study in Italy and France. He enjoyed great success in Venice and Vienna, and after singing throughout Germany, he returned to Covent Garden for the season of 1801-2. He soon became much adulated by the public, and was described somewhat hyperbolically by one admirer, Jane Porter, in her diary, 'without any exception, the most glorious singer that ever appeared in the world.' Over the next 52 years on the popular London stage he achieved great wealth, earning an average of £14,000 per annum. During his exceptional career he appeared in numerous roles in operas and other musical pieces (though he was not an accomplished actor). He owned and managed for some time the Colosseum and St James's, ventures that were not financially successful. The vast number of songs he introduced achieved great popularity. He electrified audiences when he toured America, 1840-1842. His voice was especially suited to Handelian oratorios, but he was small of stature. Yet, according to Leigh Hunt, when he stood on the concert stage and opened his mouth, his voice 'became a veritable

trumpet of grandeur and exaltation.' After 65 years on the stage, Braham retired in March 1852 and resided at the Grange, Brompton, until his death on 17 February 1856. He was buried at Kensal Green Cemetery. Some years earlier, evidently, he had converted to the Anglican Church. In addition to the pictures of him in the Garrick Club, the *BDA* notes some 40 different portraits of him. Braham was one of the original members of the Garrick Club in 1831. (*BDA*)

BRAITHWAITE, Dame Lilian **91**
1873-1948
Born in Ramsgate in 1873, the daughter of the Reverend J. M. Braithwaite and his wife Elizabeth Jane (née Powell), Lilian Braithwaite engaged in amateur theatricals before making her first professional appearance in 1897 in a series of Shakespearean productions in Durban, Natal. Her first appearance on the London stage occurred on 4 June 1900 at the Crouch End Opera House, when she acted Celia in *As You Like It.* She then appeared at the Haymarket on 30 August 1900 as Lady Olivia Vernon in *Sweet Nell of Old Drury.* At the Comedy Theatre in 1901 as a member of Frank Benson's company she played a number of Shakespearean roles. During her career of over four decades on the London stage, until 1945, she played dozens of parts, her last being Abby Brewster in *Arsenic and Old Lace* at the Strand in December 1942, a production that ran three years. She also acted in America, Canada and Ireland, and made several films. In 1943 she was honoured with a DBE. Dame Lilian died on 17 September 1948, at the age of 75. She had been the first wife of the actor Gerald Lawrence.

BRANSCOMBE, Maud **92**
fl. 1876-1892
The singer Maud Branscombe first appeared on the New York stage in 1876 as Cupid in *Ixion* at the Eagle Theatre. At the Lyceum in New York on 10 March 1879 she appeared as Hebe in pirated productions of *H. M. S. Pinafore* and in 1880 in Philadelpia and Baltimore with the D'Oyly Carte organisation in *Pirates of Penzance* and *H. M. S. Pinafore.* She was performing at the Adelphi, London, in 1882 and 1883. In February 1889 she played Cinderella at the New Theatre Royal, Liverpool. In 1892 her name was mentioned in the *Era Almanac* mail box. Maud Branscombe was reported 'the most constantly photographed beauty of her day.'

BRASSEUR, Isidore **793**
fl. 1853-1869
Isidore Brasseur, a professor at King's College, London, was elected to the Garrick Club in February 1853. The Roll of Members indicates that he resigned in 1859, but he is shown as No. 38 in O'Neil's scene of members in the Billiards Room in 1869.

BREEDON, E. A. **793**
d. 1877
Breedon, who is pictured as No. 19 in O'Neil's scene of members in the Billiards Room, was described as late of the Royal Horse Guards and living at the Carlton Club when he was elected to the Garrick Club in January 1868.

BRIERS, Richard OBE **G1003**
b. 1934
The character actor Richard Briers was born on 14 January 1934 at Merton, Surrey, the son of Joseph Briers and his wife Morna (née Richardson). After training at the Royal Academy of Dramatic Arts, he made his London debut in *Gilt and Gingerbread* in 1959. Though over the years he appeared in such plays as *Present Laughter* (1965), *The Real Inspector Hound* (1968), *Butley* (1972) and *Run for Your Wife* (1983), his main reputation has been achieved in films and television, particularly in *The Good Life* (1975-1978). Other series included *The Other One* (1977-79), *Ever Decreasing Circles* (1984-1987, 1989) and *All in Good Faith* (1985-1988). As a member of the Renaissance Theatre Company, Briers played classical roles, including King Lear and Uncle Vanya. There he began his association with Kenneth Branagh, who later cast him in a series of films: Bardolph in *Henry V* (1989), Fry's Father in *Peter's Friends* (1992), Don Leonato in *Much Ado about Nothing* (1993) and Polonius in *Hamlet* (1996), being among them. Briers received the OBE in 1989 and became a member of the Garrick Club in 1990. He married Ann Davies in 1957 and has two daughters. Among his books are *A Little Light*

Weeding (1993) and *A Taste of the Good Life* (1995).

BROOK, Clive **93**
1887-1974
Clive Brook was born in London on 1 June 1887, the son of George Alfred Brook. After serving in the army in World War I, he made some stage appearances in the provinces and then appeared in London as Hugh Cranford in *Just Like Judy* on 11 February 1920 at the St Martin's Theatre. Later that month he acted Foxcroft Grey in *Over Sunday* and then toured the provinces and began to appear in silent films. After a long hiatus he reappeared on the London stage at Wyndham's in January 1945 as Michael Wentworth in *The Years Between*. He was seen in several other West End productions and, in 1950-51, acted in New Haven and New York. Though pictured by Codner as Gaskany in *The Judge's Story* (**93**), he did not appear in the role; however, he was co-author of the stage version of Charles Morgan's novel. Most of his acting was done in films, and in England and Hollywood he appeared in 102 pictures over 25 years, beginning in 1920. These included *Interference* (his first 'talkie'), *Cavalcade*, *On Approval* and *The List of Adrian Messenger*. Brook became a member of the Garrick Club in 1946. He died in 1974. (*WWWT*)

BROOKE, Gustavus Vaughan **94**
1818-1866
Gustavus Vaughan Brooke was born on 25 April 1818 at Hardwick Place, Dublin. Legend has it that at the age of 14 he appeared in Edmund Kean's place – during one of Kean's benders – at the Theatre Royal, Dublin, as Virginius, Douglas, Young Norval and William Tell. After touring the Irish and Scottish theatres, described as the Irish Roscius he appeared in London at the Victoria as Virginius. On 3 January 1848 at the Olympic he acted Othello and caused some stir, and was hailed as the successor to Kean. That year he also played Shylock, the role in which he is pictured in the Garrick Club (**94**). He acted in America in 1851-52; his attempt at management of the Astor Place Opera House in 1852 was a disaster and he quickly abandoned the venture. He returned to play again in London and then went to Australia, where another attempt at management in Melbourne left him penniless. By then he was a hopeless drunkard, all his great promise dissipated. In 1866 he set out again for Australia, but his ship 'The London' went down in the Bay of Biscay, with the loss of almost all passengers, including Brooke.

Brooke had a noble presence, a fine voice, and 'a careless, happy-go-lucky spirit.' His promise ended in an acting style that had turned to rant. But there are some 20 engravings of Brooke in various roles, signifying his one-time popularity and talent. W. J. Lawrence wrote *The Life of Gustavus Vaughan Brooke* (1897). (*DNB, OCT*)

BROOKS, Mrs née Watson **95**
fl. 1786-1794
She was the daughter of a London merchant named Watson. According to her notice in *Thespian Magazine*, Miss Watson received a genteel education at a boarding school and in France. At 18 she married a wallpaper manufacturer, whose bankruptcy forced her upon the stage. Announced as a gentlewoman making her first appearance on any stage, she acted Lady Townley in *The Provok'd Husband* at the Haymarket Theatre on 19 July 1786. She was regularly engaged at that theatre in the summers through 1794 and also played at Dublin and Edinburgh. Among her characters were Elvira in *The Spanish Fryar* and Elvira in *A Key to the Lock*, Yarico in *Inkle and Yarico* and Primrose in *The Young Quaker*. She never acted Leonora in *The Revenge* in London, though De Wilde pictured her in that role (**95**) in the painting he provided to be engraved for publication in *Bell's British Theatre*. She was tall and elegant and modelled her acting upon Elizabeth Farren's style. Nothing is known of her life after 1794. (*BDA*)

BROOKS, Charles William Shirley **793**
1816-1874
Brooks was born in London on 29 April 1816, the son of the architect William Brooks (d. 1867). Though he passed the Incorporated Law Society's examination in 1838, he seems not to have become a solicitor but turned to writing. He wrote numerous articles for leading periodicals and was a regular contributor to *Punch* from 1851 to his death, often under the name 'Epicurus Rotundus.' He was editor of that magazine from

1870. His best-known series of articles was 'The Essence of Parliament.' Several of his plays were produced in London, including *The Creole* at the Lyceum in 1847 and *Daughter of the Stars* at the New Strand in 1850.

He became a member of the Garrick Club in January 1850. Brooks died at No. 6, Kent Terrace, Regent's Park, on 23 February 1874 and was buried at Norwood Green. (*DNB*)

BROOME, Captain J. E. DSC, RN ret 892
fl. 1947-1980
Captain J. E. Broome, who is listed in Ashton's Index of Sitters as being in Gilroy's scene of members at the Garrick Club Outing but is not found in the key to the picture, was elected to the Garrick Club in March 1947 and resigned in 1980. He was described in the Candidate's Paper as retired from the Royal Navy and an editor.

BRUNTON, Anne, later Mrs Robert Merry, Mrs Thomas Wignell, and Mrs William Warren the second 96
1769-1808
Anne Brunton was born on 30 May 1769, probably in London. She was one of the fourteen children of the actor-manager John Brunton (1741-1822) and his wife (née Friend). Five of Anne's siblings had stage careers (see the *BDA*). After receiving some experience at Bristol and Bath, Anne Brunton made her London debut at Covent Garden on 17 October 1785, as Horatia in *The Roman Father*. She enjoyed great success in that portrayal, which was followed by even more acclaim as Euphrasia in *The Grecian Daughter* on the twenty-eighth. That season she subsequently acted an impressive array of capital roles, especially for someone about seventeen years of age: Juliet, Monimia in *The Orphan*, Hermione in *The Distrest Mother*, Zara in *The Mourning Bride* and Cordelia. The following season she added Alicia in *Jane Shore*, Calista in *The Fair Penitent*, Perdita in *The Winter's Tale* and Beatrice – her first comic role – in *Much Ado about Nothing*. She remained at Covent Garden through 1791-92, expanding her repertoire and earning a reputation as a truly affecting actress with elegant taste.

Elizabeth Brunton's career was to be closely tied with her series of husbands. On 22 August 1791 she married the Della Cruscan writer and bon vivant Robert Merry and returned to Covent Garden in September as Mrs Merry. At the end of the 1791-92 season she left Covent Garden and went into temporary retirement. In September 1796 the Merrys sailed to America, where Mrs Merry was engaged by Thomas Wignell for his Chestnut Street Theatre in Philadelphia. She made her debut there on 5 December 1796 as Juliet and was a great success; the press claimed she would not fail 'at once to establish her own fame, and to reflect honour on the American drama.' In her first season at Philadelphia she acted fifteen major roles, including some she had never played in London: Belvidera in *Venice Preserv'd*, Portia in *The Merchant of Venice* and Gertrude in *Hamlet*. On 23 August 1797 she made her New York debut at the Greenwich Street Theatre as Belvidera. In Baltimore on 24 December 1798 Merry died from a stroke.

Mrs Merry continued to act in major east coast cities, but mainly at Philadelphia, where on 1 January 1803 she married her manager Thomas Wignell. But seven weeks later he died from an infected arm. Three years later, on 28 August 1806, she married William Warren, an actor and at the time lessee of the Chestnut Street Theatre. She appeared as Mrs Warren for the first time in Baltimore in October 1806. She gave her last performance, as Belvidera, at Baltimore on 23 May 1808 and died on 28 June 1808 from complications of giving birth to a stillborn son at Alexandria, Virginia, where she was buried in the churchyard of Christ Church. One obituary writer mourned that the American stage had been 'deprived of its brightest ornament.'

Anne Brunton is the subject of an excellent study by Gresdna Doty, *The Career of Mrs. Anne Brunton Merry in the American Theatre* (1971). In addition to her portrait in the Garrick Club by De Wilde of her as Alzira (**96**), numerous other portraits of her were done. (*BDA*)

BUCKSTONE, John Baldwin 97, B159
1802-1897
Born at Hoxton on 14 September 1802, he was, at the age of 11 (according to an early memoir), placed on board a man-of-war, but at the

intercession of a relative he was brought home and articled to a solicitor. Soon he left the law for the stage, making his first appearance at Peckham as Captain Aubri in *The Dog of Montargis*. After gaining experience and a good reputation in the provinces, and with the encouragement of Edmund Kean, he appeared in London at the Surrey Theatre on 30 January 1823 as Ramsay in *The Fortunes of Nigel*. He acted at the Coburg for three seasons and then became a member of Daniel Terry's company at the Adelphi, where on 1 October 1827 he appeared as Bobby Trot in his own play *Luke the Labourer*. Back at the Surrey he was the original Gnatbrain in Jerrold's *Black-Eyed Susan* on 8 June 1829. In 1833 he engaged at the Haymarket Theatre, where he acted summers until 1839, and where many of his farces were produced, including *Ellen Wareham* (1833), *Uncle John* (1833), *Married Life* (1834) and *Single Life* (1839). Except for short stints at the Lyceum and Drury Lane and a visit to America, Buckstone spent most of his career at the Haymarket, where he became manager in 1853 and produced some 200 of his own plays. He also wrote some novels and pantomimes. It was said that he acted Buckstone in every part, but he displayed an 'abundant geniality' which he also possessed in private life until he became somewhat misanthropic in his later years. He was best in such broad comic roles as Tony Lumpkin, Launcelot Gobbo, Scrub and Bob Acres.

Buckstone became a member of the Garrick Club in 1854. He died on 31 October 1879. His ghost is said to haunt the Haymarket Theatre. A version of Knight's portrait of him (**97**) was done by Maclise and was engraved by R. Page. A number of engravings of him in various characters were also published. (*See* Burnim and Wilton, *The Richard Bebb Collection in the Garrick Club*, B159.)

BULLOCK, Christopher 98

c. 1690-1722

Born about 1690, Christopher Bullock was the first son of William Bullock the elder, a popular player and fair booth operator (*q.v.*). The younger Bullock made his first stage appearance, probably, on 31 December 1707 at the Queen's Theatre in the Haymarket, playing the small comic role of Appletree in *The Recruiting Officer*. Similar parts came to him at the Queen's and at Drury Lane, and in 1714 he settled at the new Lincoln's Inn Fields Theatre under the management of John Rich for a successful career as a player of fops (like Sir Novelty Fashion in *Love's Last Shift*), comic servants (Scrub in *The Stratagem*) and lovers (Constant in *The Provok'd* Wife), and as the author of light, popular plays like *Woman's a Riddle*. Bullock also shared in the theatre's management. He was described by the *London Chronicle* in 1758, long after his death, as tall and agreeable in person, with 'a comic kind of voice, which vented itself in a shrillness of tone, but never sunk into meanness.' As a 'smart sprightly actor' he was the closest thing Rich's company had to the successful Drury Lane comedian Colley Cibber.

Young Bullock's popular and promising career was cut short in 1720-21, when he was frequently too sick to perform. He died of consumption and a fistula on 5 April 1722, leaving a shrewish wife and three children. She was the former Jane Rogers the younger, a minor actress in Rich's troupe. (*BDA*) [EAL]

BULLOCK, William 99

c. 1667-1742

The patriarch of the Bullock clan of London actors in the late Restoration and early eighteenth century was William Bullock, who was probably born about 1667, perhaps at York. He was acting in London under the manager Christopher Rich at Drury Lane by September 1695, playing a skirts part in *The Mock Marriage*. The first names of some of his characters in the late 1690s tell us his speciality: Sly, Shuffle, Sir Tunbelly Clumsey (in *The Relapse*), Frowzy, Mockmode, Sir Fickle, Sauny the Scot and the like. William (and his sons, too) seem to have made their careers in fops, bumpkins, silly Irish and Scots men, old ladies – the farcical types that critics often scorn but audiences love. But, remarkably, Bullock was praised for his tomfoolery by such formidable critics as Addison and Steele. Tom Davies the biographer called Bullock 'an actor of great glee and much comic vivacity,' and Charles Macklin called him 'a true genius of the stage.' Many of Bullock's roles he kept for years, and a few of them were in plays we still know: the Gravedigger in *Hamlet*, Falstaff in *1 Henry IV*, the Host in *The Merry Wives of Windsor*.

At the new Covent Garden Theatre, which opened in 1732, the old trooper made few appearances. He was kept on salary, however, and appears to have ended his career as a pensioner, being given about £57 a season. He augmented his salary over the years by operating a summer fair booth. William Bullock outlived almost all of his family, dying in January 1742. (*BDA*) [EAL]

BURNETT, Jenny
See Jenny LEE

BURT, Clive Stuart Saxon **892**
1900-1981
Clive Burt was born on 11 June 1900. Educated at Eton and Oxford, he was called to the Bar, Gray's Inn, in 1925, and became QC in 1954. He served in the Second World War and received the Croix de Guerre. He was chairman of the Performing Rights Tribunal, 1957-58. In March 1951 he became a member of the Garrick Club. Burt died on 30 September 1981.

BURTON, John **100**
c. 1749-1797?
Born in London about 1749, the son of the Drury Lane actor Edmund Burton (d. 1772), he first appeared at Drury Lane playing a page in *Love Makes a Man* on 28 October 1762. He filled children's roles as Master Burton until 1767-68, when he began to be billed as J. Burton and assumed roles that denoted his maturity. He remained with Drury Lane for many years, through the end of Garrick's management and beyond, until 1795-96. At the end of his career he suffered from debt and ended up in Newgate, where he died in great distress in 1797. Burton was a useful if innocuous player in minor roles, yet he was accounted one of the actors who formed the School of Garrick, many of whom were painted by Spicer (**100**). Other portraits of him are listed in the *BDA* 2: 242. He was also a landscape painter. (*BDA*)

BUTLER, Mrs Pierce
See Frances Anne KEMBLE

C

CAMPBELL, Mrs Patrick
née Stella Tanner **101**
1865-1940
A leading actress of her time, whom Bernard Shaw described as 'perilously bewitching,' Beatrice Stella Tanner was born on 9 February 1865 in Kensington, London. She was educated in Hampstead and Paris and received a scholarship for music at the Guildhall School. She married Patrick Campbell in 1884 and subsequently used that name for the stage even after her husband died in 1900 and she married Major George Cornwallis-West, in 1914. Her first professional appearance was with Ben Greet's company as Sophia Moody in *The Bachelors* on 22 October 1888 at the Alexandra Theatre, Liverpool. After Liverpool she toured with Greet's company throughout the provinces, acting such Shakespearean roles as Rosalind in *As You Like It* and Helena in *A Midsummer Night's Dream*. She appeared in London at the Adelphi in 1890 in *The Hunchback*, *The School for Scandal* and *As You Like It*. Her outstanding performance as Paula Tanqueray in Pinero's *The Second Mrs Tanqueray* at the St James's Theatre in 1893 established her as a leading actress. She returned to that role frequently during her subsequent forty-year career. In 1895 she acted Juliet to Sir Johnston Forbes-Robertson's Romeo, and also acted Ophelia to his Hamlet. Other notable performances by her included Hedda in *Hedda Gabler* (1907), Mélisande (in English and French, the latter to Sarah Bernhardt's Pelléas), Mrs Alving in *Ghosts* and Lady Macbeth. Though she received high praise for her performances in London and New York of the title role in Sudermann's *Magda*, Bernard Shaw disapproved, and he also criticised her Rita in *Little Eyolf* (the role in which she is pictured in **101**). Nevertheless, Shaw wrote for her the role of Eliza Doolittle in his *Pygmalion*, which she created on 11 April 1914 at Her Majesty's Theatre; on her return to New York that year she acted that role at the Park Theatre on 12 October and toured America during the 1914-15 season. In London during the

1920s she acted a number of her favourite roles, returned to New York in 1927, and back at the Lyric, Hammersmith, in July 1927 began a series of speeches on 'Diction in Dramatic Art.' In 1929 at the Royalty Theatre she was excellent as Anastasia in *The Matriarch,* a play based on a novel by G. B. Stern. She made her film debut in 1933 in *Riptide* and was in several other films.

Mrs Campbell's correspondence with Shaw, edited by Alan Dent, was published in 1952, twelve years after her death. An arrangement of those letters by Jerome Kilty, *Dear Liar,* had a successful stage run in America and London in 1959-60, with Kilty as Shaw and Cavenda Humphrey as Mrs Campbell, and was published in 1960. Biographies of Mrs Campbell by Alan Dent and Margot Peters were published in 1961 and 1984, respectively. (*EB, OCT, WWWT*)

CAMPION
See Maria Ann POPE (Mrs Alexander the second)

CANDELON, Catherine
See Kate VAUGHAN

CANE, Dr Cuthbert S. VRD, MREC, LREP **892**
fl. 1957-1979
Dr Cuthbert Cane, shown as No. 28 in Gilroy's scene of the Garrick Club Outing in 1967, was a Harley Street physician. He was elected to the Club in December 1957 and resigned in December 1979.

CAREY, Master
See Edmund KEAN

CARR, Mr **355**
fl. 1813-1820
We know little more about Mr Carr other than he was included as Wildo by Clint in his large painting of a scene from *A New Way to Pay Old Debts,* 1820. He was acting at Drury Lane in 1813, appearing as Gratiano in *Othello* and the Lord Mayor in *Richard III.*

CARR, Joseph William Comyns **102**
1849-1916
This art critic and sometime dramatist was born on 1 March 1849; he attended London University and the Inner Temple. He became a barrister in 1869, and served as art critic for the *Pall Mall Gazette* and English editor of *L'Art.* He also was director and one of the founders of the New Gallery. In addition to essays and books on art, Carr wrote or adapted several plays: *King Arthur* (1895), *Faust* (freely adapted from Goethe, 1908) and (with Arthur Wing Pinero) the libretto for a sound recording of Sir Arthur Sullivan's *The Beauty Stone* (1884). He became a member of the Garrick Club in February 1886. Carr died on 12 December 1916.

CASSON, Sir Lewis Thomas **103**
1875-1969
One of the important actors of the first half of the twentieth century, Lewis Casson was born at Birkenhead on 26 October 1875, the son of Thomas and Laura Casson. He made his first professional appearance at the Royalty Theatre, London, on 7 November 1903 as Polixenes in *The Winter's Tale.* After some touring he joined the Barker-Vedrenne company at the Court Theatre from 1904 to 1907, appearing in a number of Bernard Shaw's plays and in Shakespearean roles. He also appeared at Frohman's Duke of York and in New York in 1910. In 1911 he became director of the Gaiety Theatre in Manchester, where he also acted many roles, including Brutus in *Julius Caesar.* There he met Sybil Thorndike, whom he married. He assumed the directorship of the Royalty Theatre in Glasgow in 1914, directing and acting in many productions. Casson spent much of his career directing plays and touring throughout the world, often in productions with his wife. He was President of Actors' Equity 1940-1945. In 1945 Casson was knighted for his services to the theatre. He received honorary degrees from Glasgow and Wales. In 1954 he became a member of the Garrick Club. Casson first appeared in films in 1933 and on television in 1946. He continued an active professional life into the 1960s, playing Telyegin in *Uncle Vanya* at the Chichester Festival in July 1963 and Harding in *Queen B* at Windsor in September 1963. He died on 16 May 1969 at 93. (*WWWT*)

CAULFIELD, Thomas **104**

1766-1815

Thomas Caulfield was born in 1766, the son of a Clerkenwell music engraver. His brother James Caulfield (1764-1826) became a printseller and publisher and his brother Joseph a music engraver. Two brothers, John and Samuel, were singers. After acting in the provinces from 1787 to 1791, Thomas made his London debut with the Drury Lane company (playing at the King's Theatre while a new Drury Lane was under construction) as Trophonius in *The Cave of Trophonius* on 15 October 1791. Caulfield played numerous supporting roles that season and continued to be engaged at Drury Lane in winters and the Haymarket in summers through 1805, when he went to America. He acted in Boston, Providence, Charleston and New York. He died on stage in Kentucky in May 1815, as a result of 'fit' probably brought on by 'taking too much refreshment.' (*BDA*)

CECIL, Arthur **105-107, G0989**

1843-1896

Arthur Cecil, whose real name was Arthur Cecil Blunt, was born near London in 1843. After making some appearances in amateur theatricals he appeared under the name of Arthur Cecil in the professional productions of *No Cards* and the musical version of *Box and Cox.* In 1874 he joined the company at the Globe Theatre, appearing on 24 January as Jonathan Wagstaff in Gilbert's *Committed for Trial.* Then followed numerous roles at the Globe, the Comedy Theatre and eventually the Court Theatre, where he created many roles, including Baron Verduret in *Honour,* Connor Hennessy in *The Rector*, Posket in *The Magistrate* (**106**) and the Hon Vere Queckett in *The Schoolmistress* (**105**). Among his last characters were Charles Deakin in *The Widow* on 21 April 1892 (at the Comedy) and Sir James Bramston in *The Guardsman* on 20 October 1892 (at the Court). He died at the Orleans Club, Brighton, on 16 April 1896 and was buried at Mortlake. His friend Joseph Knight described him as a 'thorough artist and a clever actor, more remarkable for neatness than robustness or strength' – qualities that seem to have been captured in Ward's drawing (**107**). A caricature drawing of Cecil by an unknown artist is also in the Garrick Club (**G0989**). Cecil was a long-time member of the Club, having joined in 1867.

CHAPMAN, Charlotte Jane **108**

1762-1805

Born in America in 1762, Charlotte Jane Chapman went to live in Yorkshire with relatives. She was on the stage at York by 1780 and married a strolling actor named Morton, who treated her badly. She left him, resumed her maiden name and played in the provinces until she was taken on by Covent Garden Theatre, where she first appeared as Yarico in *Inkle and Yarico* on 22 October 1788. Miss Chapman continued at that theatre through the 1805-06 season, playing many significant roles, including Ann Lovely in *A Bold Stroke for a Wife,* Araminta in *The Old Bachelor,* Lavinia in *The Fair Penitent,* Gertrude in *Hamlet* and Mrs Fainall in *The Way of the World.* She made a comely figure in breeches: the *Authentic Memoirs of the Green Room* (1799) reported that her 'figure is prepossessing, her expression good, but her musical powers indifferent; she performs those characters where *person*, more than power, is required.' She died in February 1805 and was buried on the 14th at St Paul, Covent Garden. In addition to her picture as Augusta Aubrey (**108**), De Wilde also painted her as Celia in *The School for Lovers*, for *Bell's British Theatre.* Bell published the same engraving on 26 January 1793, but captioned it 'Miss Heard as Celia.' (*BDA*)

CHAPMAN, William? **109**

fl. 1770-1820?

It is not certain that the actor depicted in an unknown character by De Wilde (**109**) was actually named William Chapman, and little is known of his early career until he appeared at Drury Lane on 3 October 1782 as Hawthorn in *Love in a Village.* He was in and out of engagements there and at the Haymarket and Covent Garden until 1804, and he may have been the Chapman acting at Covent Garden in 1819-20. Though not a strong singer, he filled the roles of old men in sentimental comedies respectably. (*BDA*)

CHARKE, Charlotte née Cibber, later Mrs Richard Charke, then Mrs John Sacheverell 110
1713-1760
Charlotte Cibber was the seventh child of the actor-manager Colley Cibber and his wife Katherine. Charlotte was born on 13 January 1713 and died on 6 April 1760. In between she was a transvestite, scholar, hunter, quack, wife to Richard Charke, actress, singer, satirist, manager, versifier, puppeteer, suitor to an heiress, wife to John Sacheverell, debtors' prison inmate, conjurer's assistant, pastry cook, farmer, touring player, autobiographer, novelist and other eccentricities. It is no surprise that her portrait at the Garrick Club (**110**) is lost, stolen or strayed. (*BDA*) [EAL]

CHARLES I, King 39, 40, 42
1600-1649
The second son of King James VI of Scotland, later James I of England, and Anne of Denmark, he did not become heir apparent until the premature death of his elder brother Henry, Prince of Wales, in 1612. Following the death of his father, Charles was crowned King, at the age of 25, on 27 March 1625. Soon after he married Henrietta Maria, sister of Louis XIII of France. During his reign, England's colonial possessions expanded, with the establishment of the royal colony of Virgina and the granting of charters for Massachusetts, Maryland and the Carolinas.

His domestic policies were less successful and led to his downfall. Given bad advice by his ministers and queen, Charles stubbornly opposed Parliament over financial affairs and between 1625 and 1629 summoned and dismissed Parliament three times. For another 11 years he reigned without Parliament. His imposition of a new prayer book upon Scotland resulted in rebellion. He further alienated the emerging middle class and tradesmen of the Puritan movement by his hospitality to a flood of his wife's Catholic friends at the royal court. The long feud with Parliament resulted in civil war between his supporters (Cavaliers) and opponents (Roundheads) and the defeat of the King's forces by Cromwell's army at Naseby in 1645. A year later, having been taken by Scottish forces, Charles was surrendered to Parliament and put on trial. Found guilty of treason by one vote (68 to 67), he was beheaded on 30 January 1649.

CHARLOTTE SOPHIA, Queen 257
1744-1818
Charlotte Sophia was born in 1744, the youngest daughter of Charles Lewis, who was the brother of Frederic, the third duke of Mecklenburg-Strelitz. She was betrothed in 1761 to George III, who had become King upon the death of his father George II on 25 October 1760. She landed in England on 7 September 1761 and the next day met George; they were married that evening. Their coronation occurred several weeks later, on 22 September. During their long reign she confined herself mainly to domestic matters, and her union with George was devoted and decorous. They had 15 children, three of whom died young. When George became ill and intermittently insane, his care was mainly in her hands. She died at Kew on 17 November 1818 and was buried in St George's Chapel, Windsor. George III died on 29 January 1820 and was succeeded by the eldest surviving son, George IV, who since 5 February 1811 had been the Prince Regent because of his father's insanity.

CHATTERLEY, Mrs William, Louisa née Simeon 111, 112
1797-1866
Born Louisa Simeon in 1797, probably at Bath, she married the actor William S. Chatterley (1787-1822) in 1814 and made her debut at the Lyceum Theatre in July 1816 as Harriet in *Is He Jealous?*. She appeared at the Olympic in 1820 and in 1821 acted Julia in *The Rivals* at the Haymarket. She made her debut at Covent Garden on 6 November 1821 as Kate Hardcastle in *She Stoops to Conquer*. Her husband died in 1822, and in 1830 she married a Mr Place and retired from the stage. But she eventually returned, joining Wigan's company at the Olympic. At the Adelphi she acted in *Born with Good Luck* in 1856 and in *The French Lady's Maid* in 1858. She died in 1866. She had no extraordinary talents, it is said, but she did play well her line of characters in genteel comedy. In addition to **111** and **112**, she was pictured as Marguerite in *Raymond and*

Agnes in an anonymous plate to *The British Stage* in 1820.

CHERRY, Andrew **113, 114**
1762-1812
Born in Limerick on 11 January 1762, the son of the printer and bookseller John Cherry, Andrew Cherry left grammar school at eleven and was employed by a bookseller in Dublin. He appeared in amateur theatricals at fourteen and three years latter joined a strolling company. After some years as a starving actor, he was engaged at Smock Alley Theatre, Dublin, where over some five years he earned a reputation as a comic actor. After engagements in the English provinces, mainly with Tate Wilkinson's company on the York circuit, Cherry made his first appearance at Drury Lane Theatre on 25 September 1802 as Sir Benjamin Dove in Cumberland's *The Brothers*. He remained at Drury Lane until 1807 and subsequently managed a troupe in Wales. He died at Monmouth on 12 February 1812. According to some accounts, Cherry possessed merit and 'peculiar excellence' as a comedian. He wrote about ten plays, several of which were produced in London; they are well constructed but display little literary merit. The most successful was *The Soldier's Daughter* (see **124**), acted at Drury Lane on 7 February 1804 and printed in 12 editions. (*DNB*)

CHILD, Ludia
See Mrs Richard WEBB

CHRISTIE, James Stirling **793**
d. 1897
James Christie was the son of James Christie the younger (1773-1831) and the grandson of James Christie the elder (1730-1803), who established the famous auction house in London in 1756. This James Christie and his brother George Henry took in William Manson as a partner, and then when Thomas J. Woods came into the firm in 1859, the name was changed to Christie, Manson and Woods. The third James Christie has two notations in the roll of admissions to the Garrick Club, one on 20 December 1851 and the other on 18 November 1854. Both entries indicate that Christie died in July 1897.

CHUDLEIGH-LILLIES, Arthur **115**
1858-1932
He was born at Chudleigh, Devonshire, on 8 December 1858, the son of George William Lillies, M. D., and his wife Charlotte Welch (née Collyns). Though he attended the Royal Medical College, Epsom, Arthur became an actor, making his first London appearance at the Globe on 30 June 1883 as Gilbert in *The Flowers of the Forest*. He was seen as Hurt in *A Sailor and His Lass* at Drury Lane on 15 October 1883 and soon turned to management, becoming joint proprietor with Mrs John Wood of the Court Theatre. From September 1888 he co-produced a number of plays, including *Aunt Jack*, *The Cabinet Minister*, *The Amazons*, *A Royal Family* and *His Excellency the Governor*. He then became lessee and manager of the Comedy Theatre, where he offered, among other productions, *Raffles*, *The Truth*, *Alias Jimmy Valentine* and *A Woman's Way*. He still had the Comedy Theatre when he died on 5 February 1932 at the age of 73. He became a member of the Garrick Club in 1891. Buchel's portrait of him (**115**) was apparently painted after Chudleigh-Lillies's death.

CIBBER, Charlotte
See Charlotte CHARKE

CIBBER, Colley **116**
1671-1757
One of the most important theatre people between Betterton and Garrick, Colley Cibber was born on 6 November 1671, the son of the sculptor Caius Gabriel Cibber. Colley showed an interest in theatre and, against his parents' wishes, he joined the United Company of players at Drury Lane Theatre, playing bit parts and learning his trade under London's leading actor, Thomas Betterton. Cibber's first recorded part was a servant in *Sir Anthony Love* in September 1690, but his real break came in January 1694, when he substituted for Edward Kynaston as Lord Touchwood in *The Double Dealer*. The author Congreve was so delighted that he helped get Cibber a five-shilling raise (to £1 weekly). Then Betterton and many of the older players rebelled against Drury Lane's lawyer-manager Christopher Rich; Cibber chose to stay with

Rich, where he probably felt his opportunities were more promising. Indeed, they were: in May 1695 he took Thomas Doggett's old part of Fondlewife in *The Old Bachelor* and did an imitation of Doggett that even pleased the actor himself. The next year Cibber tried his hand at playwriting and turned out *Love's Last Shift*, creating for himself the role of Sir Novelty Fashion. Though he went on to try a variety of other types, comic fops became his specialty, and Cibber, almost from the beginning of his stage career, was London's most successful comedian-playwright.

Then, as both actor and playwright, he attempted tragedy. In December 1699 his adaptation of Shakespeare's *Richard III* came out at Drury Lane, with Colley casting himslf in the title role. The adaptation was successful enough – indeed, it held the stage into the twentieth century, but Cibber as Richard, a role he insisted on playing for years, was damned by almost all of the critics. In 1734 Aaron Hill in *The Prompter* said Cibber played Richard with 'the distorted heavings of an unjointed caterpillar,' and the *Grub Street Journal* reported that 'he foams, struts, and bellows with the voice and cadence of a watchman rather than a hero and a prince.' Near-obliviousness to harsh criticism was one of Cibber's most remarkable qualities. It saw him through repeated attacks by rival authors, players and critics; he simply did not let the barbs bother him. Perhaps he was just indifferent, for that is how he seems to have treated his wife for years, but it may be closer to the mark to see Cibber as one who enjoyed attention, even when it was ridicule at his own expense.

In addition to establishing one career as an actor and another as a playwright, Cibber began, as early as November 1704, to share in the management of the Drury Lane troupe. He signed a contract with Rich for five years at a weekly wage of £3 10s and accepted a verbal agreement to receive an additional 10s weekly for casting parts, reading plays and 'other services.' He was paid 20s for assisting in the management of the theatre. Still young, Colley was the highest-paid and most influential actor at Drury Lane, and he remained a successful sharer in the management, with Barton Booth and Robert Wilks, into the 1730s. A master at conciliation and keeping cool under fire, Cibber was the ideal middle man.

He continued churning out plays over these years, too, the most successful after *Love's Last Shift* and *Richard III* being *Love Makes the Man, She Wou'd and She Wou'd Not, The Careless Husband, The Double Gallant, The Non-Juror* (an adaptation of Molière's *Tartuffe*) and *The Provok'd Husband.* In 1730 Cibber was appointed poet laureate, much to the chagrin or delight of pundits, and in the years that followed he dutifully composed undistinguished verses for the crown. Then, in 1740, he published *An Apology for the Life of Mr Colley Cibber*, a rambling, windy, self-deprecating, self-indulgent but priceless history of the London theatre of his time. With all its faults it is a delightful and informative work, and, remarkably, it became a very successful publication, reprinted regularly over the centuries.

Colley retired from the stage several times, but his last real season was 1732-33, when at Drury Lane he acted, among other popular roles, Bayes in *The Rehearsal*, Foppington in *The Relapse* and *The Careless Husband*, Fondlewife in *The Old Bachelor*, Richard III, Ben in *Love for Love*, Subtle in *The Alchemist*, Sir Fopling in *The Man of Mode*, Sir John Brute in *The Provok'd Wife* and Witwoud in *The Way of the World* – most of which had been in his repertoire for years. He retired comfortably, made a few return engagements and entertained the public with squabbles in print with Dennis, Fielding and Pope. He seems, especially after his retirement in 1733, to have relaxed and enjoyed his carefree twilight years. He died on 11 December 1757, quietly, in his bed, at the age of 86. James Ralph in 1758 said that 'Cibber was a Player, Writer, and Manager too, and, over and above, a Bottle of as pert small Beer, as ever whizz'd in any Man's Face.' Grisoni's famous portrait of him as Lord Foppington (**116**) sums up the man. (*BDA*)[EAL]

CIBBER, Mrs Theophilus the second, Susanna Maria née Arne 117, 118, 252
1714-1766

Susanna Maria Arne, the daughter of the upholsterer Thomas Arne and his wife Anne, was christened at St Paul, Covent Garden, on 28 February 1714. Her brother Thomas Augustine was to become an important composer and she one of the better singers and best tragic actresses of her time. She may have acted as a child, but her first professional appearance was on 13 March 1732, when at the Haymarket Theatre she sang the title role in *Amelia*; a repeat performance was given for her benefit on 24 March. At the Lincoln's Inn Fields Theatre, the King's, the Haymarket, Drury Lane and Hickford's Music Room from 1732 to 1734 she appeared in title parts and had solo benefits that gave her a remarkable amount of exposure for one just embarking on a stage career. Then, in April 1734 at a Catholic embassy chapel, she married Theophilus Cibber. Cibber was the scapegrace son of Colley Cibber and, like his father an actor-manager. Theophilus was also one of the most outrageous personalities in the London theatre world and within a few years led his bride through a very public, farcical marital caper.

But first Susanna Maria began to construct her stage career, establishing herself as a singer and actress. She developed a repertoire that included some of the best characters in English drama, starting with the title role in Aaron Hill's *Zara* on 12 January 1736. By the end of the 1736-37 she had added Indiana in *The Conscious Lovers*, Amanda in *Love's Last Shift*, Andromache in *The Distrest Mother*, Desdemona in *Othello*, Statita in *The Rival Queens*, Isabella in *Measure for Measure* and Monimia in *The Orphan*. Her musical training stood her in good stead; though not the best of singers, she was blessed with a fine soprano that developed into a rich contralto, and Handel composed for her some of his most affecting oratorio arias. Music had given her discipline, too, and though some critics thought her strong control over her voice was sometimes too rigid, she was capable of projecting both a tenderness that brought tears to her auditors and a passion that made her scenes exciting. She had a sense of humor, especially in some of her cheerful letters to David Garrick, but she seldom showed it in public; what she did reveal was a toughness that drove her managers to distraction and a physical frailty (quite real) that frequently made her unable to perform. But how did she let herself get into the notorious court case involving her husband and her lover?

Theophilus actually introduced her to and encouraged her to have an affair with a moneyed fellow, William Sloper. It was Cibber's plan to push his wife into a relationship with Sloper and then sue him for adultery, asking for £5000. After a trial that had all London talking Cibber was awarded only £10. (For all the absurdly lurid details see the *BDA*.) The notoriety Susanna received during the trial and after – for she clearly found Sloper much to her liking and remained with him the rest of her life – should have destroyed her stage career. But since in the eighteenth century the public rather expected theatre folk to misbehave, Mrs Cibber not only survived the trial but continued her remarkably successful career as a singer and actress, helping to pack theatres in Dublin and London and bring herself an annual income almost equal to that of Garrick. Though she arranged with the managers of Drury Lane and Covent Garden (for she appeared at both in the 1740s) to keep Cibber from performing at the same theatre, she kept calling herself Mrs Cibber in the bills.

In 1755-56, when Garrick at Drury Lane was paying her £700 for the season, she acted only thirteen times. With many performers that was taken as almost standard prima donna behaviour, but Mrs Cibber had real health problems, and she sometimes refused to accept a salary when she could not perform. She was, when she was well, a hard worker, and she acted many very strenuous roles. Two of her most popular and demanding characters were Alicia in *Jane Shore* and Juliet in *Romeo and Juliet*. She also, in addition to characters already mentioned, was seen as Margery Pinchwife in *The Country Wife*, Calista in *The Fair Penitent*, Polly in *The Beggar's Opera*, Belvidera in *Venice Preserv'd*, Ophelia in *Hamlet* and Cordelia in *King Lear*. The actor Samuel Foote in 1747 said 'Her Expressions of the Passion of Grief, surpass every thing of the sort I have seen. There is a melancholly Plaintiveness in her voice, and such a Dejection of Countenance (without Distortion,) that I defy any Man, who has the least Drop of the Milk of Human Nature about him, to sit out the distresses of *Monimia* and *Belvedira*, when represented by this Lady, without giving the most tender and affecting Testimonies of his Humanity.' In her final full season, 1764-

65, she carried a heavy schedule and even when plagued with illness managed to act many of her favourite roles. She was clearly so good at what she did that managers and audiences were willing to suffer her vagaries. Her last appearance, at Drury Lane on 13 December 1765, was as Lady Brute in *The Provok'd Wife*. She died on 30 January 1766. When Garrick heard the news he is reported to have said, 'Then tragedy expired with her.' (*BDA*) [EAL]

CLARKE, Nobby 892

'Nobby' Clarke, identified as No. 50 in the key to Gilroy's painting of the Garrick Club Outing, served as cellarman and assistant barman at the Club for many years.

CLARKE, Rt Hon Sir Edward George S6

1841-1931

Edward George Clarke was born in London on 15 February 1841, the eldest son of J. G. Clarke, a jeweller in King William Street. After serving as a writer in the India Office from 1859 to 1860, he was called to the Bar at Lincoln's Inn in 1864 and practised law and wrote treatises on the law and religion. He was a Member of Parliament for many years, and served as Solicitor General from 1885 to 1892. He retired from law in 1914. Among the books he wrote are *Treatise on the Law of Extradition* (1866 and three subsequent editions), *The National Church* (1916), *The Story of My Life* (1918) and *Benjamin Disraeli; the Romance of a Great Career* (1926). He became a member of the Garrick Club in February 1864. He was knighted in 1886. Sir Edward died on 26 April 1931. A portrait of him by S. J. Solomon hangs in the Royal Courts of Justice. (*DNB*)

CLAY, Frederick 793

1839-1889

The musician Frederick Clay was born in Paris on 3 August 1839, the son of the writer and Garrick Club member James Clay (see below). After some positions in political life, Frederick turned to music, collaborating with Sir Arthur Sullivan and W. S. Gilbert on several theatrical pieces: *Years Ago* (1869), *The Gentleman in Black* (1870) and *Happy Arcadia* (1872). He wrote music for a number of other operas, among them *Court and Cottage* (1862) and *The Merry Duchess* (1883). A few hours after conducting the first performance of his *The Golden Ring* at the Alhambra on 3 December 1883, he suffered a stroke from which he never fully recovered. He died on 24 November 1889 at Oxford House, Great Marlow. Among Clay's most successful pieces is 'I'll sing thee songs of Araby,' a richly harmonised song that has always pleased. Clay became a member of the Garrick Club in April 1862. (*DNB*)

CLAY, James 793

1805-1873

Born in London in 1805, he was the son of a merchant. His uncle was Sir William Clay, MP for Tower Hamlets. James Clay was educated at Winchester, and in 1830 he travelled the East with Benjamin Disraeli, with whom he maintained a friendship throughout his life. In 1847 Clay was elected to Parliament for Hull, a position he held until he died in 1873 at Regency Square, Brighton. He had become a member of the Garrick Club in 1866 and is pictured in O'Neil's group in the billiards room (**793**) with his son Frederick Clay (also a member, *q.v.*). His son Cecil Clay was well known in literary circles, and his son Ernest Clay was a distinguished diplomat. James Clay's authoritative *Treatise on the Game of Whist* appeared in many editions. (*DNB*)

CLEMENTS, Sir John Selby CBE 119

1910-1988

The actor, manager, and director, John Clements was born in London on 25 April 1910, the son of Herbert William Clements and his wife Mary Elizabeth (née Stevens). After attending St Paul's School and St John's College, Cambridge, he made his debut on the stage at the Lyric Theatre, Hammersmith, on 1 April 1930 as Lucas Carey in *Out of the Blue*. He acted in and about London for several years and then toured with Ben Greet's company, acting young leading roles in Shakespeare. In his 47 years on the London stage and in films Clements played a wide spectrum of capital characters: Petruchio, Coriolanus, Arnold Holt in *Edward My Son*, John Tanner in *Man and Superman*, Archer in *The Beaux'*

Stratagem, Macbeth and Antony in *Antony and Cleopatra*. He also directed numerous successful productions in London and at the Chichester Festivals. He received the CBE in 1956 and a knighthood in 1968. He became a member of the Garrick Club in 1943 and a life member in 1978. Sir John also served as Vice-President of British Actors Equity, 1950-1959. He died on 6 April 1988.

CLENDINING, Mrs William, Elizabeth née Arnold **120**

1768-1799

Elizabeth Clendining was born at Stourhead, Wiltshire, in 1768, the daughter of Mr Arnold, a prominent choir singer at Salisbury, Wells and Dublin. She sang at the Dublin Rotunda in 1785, and soon married William Clendining, a surgeon. She retired from singing, but after six years her husband's debts drove her back on to the concert stage. She sang at Bath in 1792 and came under the tutelage of the eminent teacher Rauzzini. She came to London in June 1792 and made her first appearance at Covent Garden as Clara in *Hartford Bridge* on 3 November, when the press hailed her as having 'musical talents of the very first rank.' Mrs Clendining continued at Covent Garden for five more seasons, playing a series of singing ingenues: Clara in *The Duenna*, Rosetta in *Love in a Village*, Lucy in *Love and War*, Mary in *Sprigs of Laurel*, Lorenza in *The Castle of Andalusia* and Yarico in *Inkle and Yarico*. Her husband died at Portsmouth in April 1793. Mrs Clendining was discharged from Covent Garden at the end of the season 1797-98 and went to act at Edinburgh. But she was already quite ill, and she died in Edinburgh on 16 July 1799.

CLIFTON

See Mary Anne STIRLING

CLINT, George

See Index of Artists

CLIVE, Mrs George, Catherine née Raftor **121, 122**

1711-1785

Kitty Clive was born Catherine Raftor on 15 November 1711, the daughter of William Raftor, a lawyer of Kilkenny. It seems likely that the actor manager Theophilus Cibber and his father Colley had a hand in her teenage career. Her initial stage appearance may have been as early as April 1728, though her first role of record is Bianca in *Othello* at Drury Lane on 12 October, and during the rest of the 1728-29 season she was also seen as Minerva in *Perseus and Andromeda*, Dorinda in the altered *Tempest*, Honoria in *Love Makes a Man* and the title part in *Phebe*, among other characters – a large number of appearances for a beginner and a display of her talent as both a singer and an actress. She excelled in comedy and song and consequently appeared in dozens of light comic afterpieces, now long forgotten, that on the printed page give little inkling of her genius. What she did with what she had made her the most popular comedienne of her time. Contemporary commentary suggests that she was born with exquisite timing, a malleable face and body and a perfect sense of how to handle her material.

Our heroine's personal life was as interesting and colourful as her stage career. She was famous for her chastity, like Anne Bracegirdle before her, and when she married in 1733, it was not within her profession but to George Clive, a nonpracticing barrister (not to be confused with the famous Clive of India, George's relative). She took his name and appeared as Mrs Clive for the rest of her life; though the marriage virtually ended by 1735, they were never divorced. Then, as her career continued successfully at Drury Lane, she developed a friendship with Horace Walpole, the eminent man of letters and son of Sir Robert Walpole. He lived in his quaint Gothic castle, Strawberry Hill, near Twickenham, and she, rent free, in a pleasant cottage on his property which was variously called Clive-den and Little Strawberry Hill. The couple evidently had a sexless but very affectionate relationship, and Kitty moved comfortably in Walpole's elegant social circle whenever she was not busy earning a livelihood as the town's premiere farceur, songstress and would-be tragedienne.

Mrs Clive was not the first comic performer to attempt serious drama – the most absurd example of the period was Colley Cibber, who never gave up trying to establish himself in

Richard III, to the howls of critics, who thought he should have known better. Kitty's most constant attempts were Ophelia in *Hamlet* and Portia in *The Merchant of Venice*, neither of which found favour with either playgoers or critics. But through the ages performers have felt that only success in serious characters can give them lasting fame.

Her stage career came to an appropriate close on 24 April 1769, when she acted Flora in *The Wonder*, with David Garrick playing Don Felix and, to conclude the evening, Garrick's popular *Lethe*, featuring Mrs Clive as the Fine Lady (**121**). Her career consisted of many such slight comic pieces, but she was also seen over the years in some famous characters, among them Polly and Lucy in *The Beggar's Opera,* Prue and Mrs Frail in *Love for Love*, Margery Pinchwife in *The Country Wife*, Lady Wou'dbe in *Volpone*, Hoyden in *The Relapse*, Dol Common in *The Alchemist*, Laetitia in *The Old Bachelor*, Millamant, Mrs Marwood and Lady Wishfort (a perfect part for her to play with) in *The Way of the World*, Caelia in *As You Like it*, Widow Blackacre in *The Plain Dealer* and Mrs Heidelberg in *The Clandestine Marriage*. But these important roles in memorable plays were not her bread and butter; more typical was Nell in *The Devil to Pay*, which she acted as early as 1730-31 to great applause and continued playing for the rest of her career – a vehicle for her comic talent and her singing ability and just what the critics and audiences liked.

Kitty also had a modest writing career, her first attempt being *The Rehearsal; or, Bayes in Petticoats*, a burlesque she created in 1749-50, with herself as Bayes in breeches. She wrote three farces in the 1760s with little success. Garrick at Drury Lane staged all her trifles to little avail. Yet she was an entertaining writer – her letters to the actress Jane Pope and to Garrick are full of fun – and she delighted in conversation. Dr Johnson said, 'Clive, sir, is a good thing to sit by; she always understands what you say …' and, 'in the sprightliness of humour, I have never seen [her] equalled … she was a better romp than any I ever saw in nature.' That quality of playfulness in Mrs Clive must have been something she brought to her stage performances that made her so universally enjoyed. She died on 6 December 1785, years after leaving the stage. She had been feisty in the management of her career, but she enjoyed her retirement; in a 1777 letter to Garrick, with whom she had battled over the years and who was now thinking of his own retirement, she wrote 'we will talk and dance and sing and send our hearers laughing to their beds.' (*BDA*)[EAL]

COATES, Robert **123**
1772-1848
This colourful and eccentric personality was born on Antigua in 1772, the son of Alexander Coates, a wealthy sugar-planter. All eight of Robert's siblings died in infancy, so upon the death of his father, he inherited a substantial fortune, including a large collection of diamonds. He took himself to England, where he settled in Bath and began to live in grand style. His carriage, drawn by white horses, was shaped like a kettledrum and bore the motto 'Whilst I live I'll crow.' On 9 February 1810 he made his debut upon the Bath stage as Romeo, and thus earned the nickname 'Romeo Coates.' Among other names, he became known as 'Cock-a-doodle-doo Coates' and 'the Amateur of Fashion.' He appeared in London in 1811 as Lothario in *The Fair Penitent*, and later as Romeo, prompting Charles Mathews to ridicule him in his 'At Home' performances as Romeo Rantall. Coates made appearances in other English towns, but was seen mainly at Bath until audiences grew tired of his antics. His acting, according to most accounts, was very bad. Eventually he squandered his fortune and was forced to flee to Boulogne, where he married. Coming to terms with his creditors, he returned to London, and while leaving a concert at Drury Lane on 15 February 1848 he was crushed between two carriages and died on 21 February at his residence in Montague Square. (*DNB*)

COCHRAN, John
See John MOODY

COLLINS, Thomas **124**
1775-1806
Born in Chichester in 1775, the son of a country manager, Thomas Collins was placed at an early age under the tutelage of a violinist named

Brooks. After his apprenticeship he took to the stage, first appearing in Chichester as Young Philpot in *The Citizen* in 1793, and he soon became a favourite on his father's circuit in the west of England. In 1802 he was engaged at Drury Lane, where he made his first appearance on 2 October as Jabal in *The Jew* and Robin Roughhead in *Fortune's Frolic*. According to the *Thespian Dictionary* there was a peculiarity in his voice and manner that made his humour 'irresistible.' In addition to the scene in *The Soldier's Daughter* (**124**), Collins was pictured by De Wilde as Slender in *The Merry Wives of Windsor* (engraved by W. Ripley, 1804) and as Sharp in *The Lying Valet* (engraved by W. Leney, 1805).

COLMAN, George the elder 125, 126

1732-1794

The playwright and manager George Colman was born at Florence about 15 April 1732, the son of the aristocratic Francis Colman and his wife Mary Gumley. His father was at the time British ambassador to the court of the Grand Duke of Tuscany. George was given his Christian name because his baptismal sponsor was King George I. After attending Westminster School and Christ Church, Oxford, he entered Lincoln's Inn in 1755 and was called to the bar in January 1757. Though he practised some law he mainly turned his efforts to writing odes and pamphlets, including *Critical Reflections on the Old English Dramatists* (1761), in which he made flattering remarks about David Garrick, with whom he was to become associated in writing and managing. His first play was the short afterpiece, *Polly Honeycombe*, which Garrick brought out at Drury Lane on 5 December 1760. Colman's full-length *The Jealous Wife* was successfully produced by Garrick on 12 February 1761 and became a mainstay of the eighteenth-century repertory. Subsequently he wrote numerous theatre pieces: full-length, one acters, musical interludes and adaptations; among the best were *The Clandestine Marriage* (written with Garrick, first played at Drury Lane on 20 February 1766, with Tom King as Lord Ogleby), *The Deuce is in Him* (1763) and *The Spleen* (1776).

While Garrick was on his grand tour on the Continent from 1763 to 1765, Colman directed the production of plays at Drury Lane. In 1767 he became a partner with Harris and Rutherford in the management of Covent Garden Theatre. He enjoyed a successful seven-year reign there, despite his constant bickerings with Harris and some actors and his dispute with the nasty critic William Kenrick over his *The Duellist*. It was as manager of the Haymarket Theatre, however, that Colman demonstrated his greatest managerial skills. In 1776 he bought that theatre from Samuel Foote and operated it under the summer patent until 1789, when its affairs were taken over by his son George Colman the younger (1762-1836). Stricken by a paralytic stroke, the elder Colman spent his last days in an asylum in Paddington, often suffering delusions, until his death on 14 August 1794.

Colman occupied much of his life pursuing his literary interests and cultivating his circle of high-society friends and associates. He also was involved in the publication of some newspapers and periodicals. In addition to the portraits of him in the Garrick Club after Reynolds and Zoffany, Colman was painted by Gainsborough (NPG). For more details of the life of this important figure of the eighteenth century, see the *BDA* (3: 404-420) and K. A. Burnim, *The Plays of George Colman, the Elder*, 6 vols (1983).

CONWAY, William Augustus 127, 750

1789-1828

Born in London in 1789, Conway spent his youth in Barbados, where he had been sent because of poor health. Upon his return to England he became an actor, and at the age of eighteen he made his first appearance, it is said, at Chester as Zanga in *The Revenge*. After strolling the provinces, in 1812 he joined the company at the Crow Street Theatre, Dublin, and then was recommended by Charles Mathews for an engagement at Covent Garden, where he came out as Alexander the Great on 4 October 1813. After leaving Covent Garden in 1816 he acted at Bath until 1820 and then returned to London for a season at the Haymarket, first appearing on 5 July 1821 as Lord Townley in *The Provok'd Husband*. Conway then left for America, appearing in New York on 12 January 1824 as Coriolanus, followed by a number of major roles.

While sailing to Charleston early in 1828, despondent by debt, he threw himself overboard and drowned. On stage Conway had 'a noble person, a strain of brilliant declamation, and no small power of depicting agony and sorrow.' In private, however, he was self-conscious and ill at ease. Conway seems to have had an intimate relationship with Hester Lynch Thrale Piozzi (1741-1821). *See* John Tearle, *Mrs Piozzi's Young Beau. William Augustus Conway* (1991). (*DNB*)

COOKE, George Frederick 128-136, 957
1756?-1812
One of the greatest acting talents of the late eighteenth and early nineteenth century, George Frederick Cooke told his biographer Dunlap that he was born on 17 April 1756, but his birth may have been three years earlier. Though he was probably from Westminster, some sources say Berwick or Dublin. In any case, as a youngster he was drawn to the stage, and by the early 1770s he was acting in Berwick. His first appearance as a professional there was as Dumont in *Jane Shore* in the spring of 1776. He was a strolling player in 1777 and made his London debut, as Castalio in *The Orphan*, at the Haymarket Theatre on 9 April 1778. Following that he was seen, but hardly noticed, as Modely in *The Country Lasses* and Lovewell in *The Clandestine Marriage*. In May and June he acted with the company at the China Hall Theatre in Rotherhithe, playing a variety of small and large roles in comedies and tragedies. Cooke returned to the Haymarket in 1779 and toured with several companies during the 1780s, finding Manchester a useful home base but appearing also at Newcastle, York (with Tate Wilkinson's company), Sheffield, Chester and Liverpool – all northern towns where he established a reputation for exciting acting and heavy drinking. By 1794 he had built a repertoire of major characters, chiefly in serious works, among them Shylock in *The Merchant of Venice* (**133**), Hamlet, Petruchio in *The Taming of the Shrew*, Joseph Surface in *The School for Scandal*, Macbeth, and Richard III (**128**, **130**, **132**, **957**) Apparently reluctant to test himself in a major London theatre, he went instead to Dublin, appearing first as Othello on 19 November 1794 at the Crow Street Theatre under the poor management of Richard Daly. The weakness of Daly's troupe was an excuse for Cooke's leaving Crow Street in March 1795, but his own bouts of drunkeness were really to blame, and he disappeared from all stages for a year.

In the late 1790s Cooke resumed his career – at Manchester, Chester, Dublin (at the new Fishamble Street Theatre) – and, finally, in the autumn of 1800 at Covent Garden Theatre in London at £6 weekly, beginning with Richard III on 31 October. Thomas Harris, the manager, mounted a new production for the occasion, and Cooke, aware of the importance of this opportunity, gave a performance that demonstrated his talent at its best and drew exceptionally detailed reviews. especially in *The Monthly Mirror*: Cooke 'seems to possess an active and capacious intellect, with a profound knowledge of the *science* of ACTING. He has read and thought for himself. He appears to have borrowed neither from contemporary nor deceased excellence. He sometimes passes over what have been usually conceived to be *great points* in the character and he exalts other passages into importance ...' On 10 November he brought the same kind of fresh approach to Shylock, and on the thirteenth he showed off his talent at comedy as Sir Archy Macsarcasm in *Love à la Mode* (**129**), in both of which roles he invited comparison with Charles Macklin, who years before had dared to bring to the London stage new approaches to standard characters. Cooke's first season at a major London theatre must have helped him control his drinking, and in the summer of 1801 he toured to Edinburgh, Glasgow, Liverpool and Manchester, where he was welcomed as a returning hero.

By 1802-3 his salary at Covent Garden was over £14, and he remained there through 1809-10, spending his summers touring, as he had previously. But after his great success in 1800-1 he gradually deteriorated, missing performances and having to apologize to his audiences for his inebriation. Cooke was able to get an engagement in America, making his debut in New York as Richard III on 21 November 1810 and playing also in Boston, Philadelphia, Baltimore and Providence. He was the first really great English actor to appear in America, and the excitement surrounding his season was great, even when his drinking threatened to ruin his welcome. It certainly ruined his health: Cooke died in New York on 26 September 1812. With him at the end was his third wife, who had become Mrs Cooke on 20 June 1811. Of his two previous relationships with women little is known, though his second wife, Alicia Daniels was an actress and is noticed in the *BDA*.

The theatre historian Genest said that 'Cooke did not play many parts well, but ... he played those which he did play well better than anybody else.' Dunlap thought that Cooke's great appeal was his ability to seize 'the perfect image of the person he would represent, and identifying it with his own feelings, so as to express every emotion designed by the author, as if that emotion were his own.' Yet this romanticism in Cooke's approach was accomplished with an almost academic preparation, as the careful details in his promptbooks show (especially the *Hamlet* copy now at Newcastle). He was a remarkable blend of technique and emotion, tragically damaged by an uncontrollable thirst. (*BDA*) [EAL]

COOKE, Thomas Potter 137, B4

1786-1864

Cooke was born in Marylebone on 23 April 1786, the son of a surgeon. As a lad he was with the Royal Navy on board HMS Raven at the siege of Toulon in 1796, and in the battle off Cape St Vincent in 1797. After several other engagements, at the end of the hostilities in 1802 he returned to London to make his debut in a small part at the Royalty Theatre in Wellclose Square in January 1804. He performed at Astley's Amphitheatre (where he appropriately appeared as Nelson) at the Lyceum and in Dublin and in 1809 he was engaged as stage manager at the Surrey Theatre. Over the years, at Drury Lane, the Lyceum, the Adelphi, and Covent Garden he appeared in a number of characters in melodramas, including Ruthven in *The Vampire*, Hans Ketzler in *Castle Spectre*, and Frankenstein in *The Fate of Frankenstein*. At Covent Garden on 19 October 1822 he played Zenocles in *Ali Pasha,* the role in which he was pictured by Clint (**137**). Among his most successful roles was William in *Black-Eyed Susan* on 6 June 1829 at the Surrey, where he played it for 100 nights and then transferred with the production to Covent Garden and subsequently to Drury Lane. Cooke's last appearance on the stage was in that role at Covent Garden on 20 October 1860, for the benefit of the Dramatic College. He died on 10 April 1864 at No 37, Thurloe Street and was buried in Brompton cemetery. He was one of the original members of the Garrick Club in 1831.

Cooke was shown in numerous penny-plain and tuppence-coloured prints. A Staffordshire pottery figure of him as William is in the Garrick Club (**B4**).

COOPER, Dame Gladys, Mrs Philip Merrivale DBE 138

1888-1971

The actress Gladys Cooper was born at Lewisham on 18 December 1888, the daughter of William Frederick Cooper and his wife Mabel (née Barnett). Her career, which would extend for 66 years, began at the Theatre Royal, Colchester, where on 18 December 1905 she played Bluebell in a touring production of *Bluebell in Fairy Land*. Her first appearance in London was as Lady Swan in *The Belle of Mayfair* at the Vaudeville Theatre on 23 June 1906. After some years in the chorus of musical productions she enjoyed success as Cecily in *The Importance of Being Earnest* at the St James's Theatre in June 1911. She played leading roles through the 1910s and entertained troops in France in 1914. She gave a virtuoso performance (**138**) in seven roles in Knoblach's *My Lady's Dress* at the Royalty Theatre beginning 21 April 1914. In 1917 she became joint manager with Frank Curzon of the Playhouse Theatre, of which she was also sole lessee for six years beginning in 1926. Some of her roles during that period were Paula in *The Second Mrs Tanqueray* in June 1922 (a role that established her as a star), the title role in *Magda* (March 1923), the title role in Pinero's *Iris* (March 1925) and Stella Tabret in *The Sacred Flame* (February 1929). Her first appearance on the New York stage was as Mariella Linden in *The Shining Hour* at the Booth Theatre on 13 February 1934. Notable performances later in her career included Felicity in Coward's *Relative Values* in London (1951), Mrs St Maugham in the premiere of Bagnold's *The Chalk Garden* in New York (October 1955) and Mrs Moore in *A Passage to India* in New York (January 1962)

Numerous films include *Now Voyager* (1942), *The Song of Bernadette* (1943), *Green Dolphin Street* (1947) – she received Academy Awards nominations in supporting roles in the first two – and *Separate Tables* (1958), and she also appeared on television in the 1960s. In 1967 she was honoured with a DBE. Her writings include two volumes of memoirs, *Gladys Cooper* (1931) and *Without Veils* (1953). She was married three times: to H. J. Buckmaster, Sir Neville Arthur Pearson, and Philip Merrivale. Dame Gladys died in London on 17 November 1971. *See* Sheridan Morley, *Gladys Cooper* (1941, 1979). (*WWWT*)

COPELAND
See Fanny Elizabeth FITZWILLIAM

COURTENAY, Sir Tom **G1003**
b. 1937
Tom Courtenay, who is one of the group of actors caricatured on the programme for 'A Garrick Celebration' of A. A. Milne, on 10 June 2001, was born in Hull on 25 February 1937, the son of Thomas Henry Courtenay and his wife Anna Eliza (née Quest). He was educated at University College, London, and trained at RADA, 1960-1961. His stage career, which has spanned some 40 years, includes such roles as Hamlet, Malcolm in *Macbeth*, Feste in *Twelfth Night*, Trofimov in *The Cherry Orchard*, Lord Fancourt Baberly in *Charley's Aunt* and Raskolnikov in *Crime and Punishment*. He was outstanding as Norman in *The Norman Conquests* (1974-1975) as Norman in *The Dresser* and most recently in *Art* (1996). Over the past 30 years he has appeared in many influential films that established him as the master of the fatalistic, working class hero, including *Billy Liar*, *Dr Zhivago* and *The Loneliness of the Long Distance Runner*. Courtenay was knighted in 2001. He has received many awards for his stage work, including Academy Award nominations for *The Dresser* and *Dr Zhivago*. Sir Tom became a member of the Garrick Club in 1968.

COUTTS, Harriot
See Harriot MELLON

COWARD, Sir Noel Pierce
1899-1973 **139, G0973, G1002**
The multi-talented Noel Coward was born at Teddington on 16 December 1899, the son of Arthur Coward and his wife Violet (née Veitch). He made his first appearance on the stage when a child as Prince Mussel in *The Goldfish* at the Little Theatre on 27 January 1911 and continued to act for many years, often in his own plays and films. His first success as a playwright came with *The Vortex*, in which he played Nicky Lancaster, at the Everyman and then the Royalty in 1924. Even greater success came with *Hay Fever* in 1925, followed by *Private Lives* (Phoenix Theatre, 1930, and Times Square Theatre in New York, 1931) and *Design for Living* (1932). His reputation as a composer of highly polished and witty comedies of manners was firmly established. In 1935 he introduced 'Tonight at 7.30' (later called 'Tonight at 8.30'), three programmes of nine one-act plays of his own writing, which he also directed and in which he played, among these being *Family Album, Red Peppers, Fumed Oak, Hands Across the Sea* and *Shadow Play*. At the St James's in 1942 he acted Charles Condomine in his *Blithe Spirit*, a comedy that ran 1987 performances, breaking records for a non-musical run. Other notable plays included *Present Laughter* (1942), *Peace in Our Time* (1947), *Nude With Violin* (1956), *Quadrille* (1952) and *Waiting in the Wings* (1960). Coward composed the music for a number of his productions, among them, the popular *Bitter* Sweet (1929), *Operette* (1938), *Words and* Music (1938), *After the* Ball (1954) and *The Girl Who Came for Supper* (1963), adapted from Rattigan's *The Sleeping* Prince. He also wrote the screenplay for *In Which We Serve*, which he directed and in which he acted, and for *Blithe Spirit, The Happy Breed* and the memorable *Brief Encounter*. Appearances in films included *Around the World in 80 Days, The Italian Job* and *Our Man in Havana*. Among his other writing, which include short stories, novels, verses, and lyrics, are two autobiographical volumes, *Present Indicative* (1937) and *Future Indefinite* (1954). He entered management several times, including with the Lunts at the Ethel Barrymore Theatre in New York in 1933.

Coward was knighted in 1970. He became a member of the Garrick Club in October 1966. He died at St Mary, Jamaica, on 26 March 1973.

In addition to his portrait by Seago (**139**), also in the Garrick Club is a small oil painting by Coward of a beach scene in Jamaica (**G0973**) which came to the Club in 1996.

CRABBE, Edward **793**
d. 1904
Edward (or Edmund) Crabbe, who is pictured as No. 20 in O'Neil's large picture of a group in the Billiards Room, was from Streatham in Surrey when he was elected to the Garrick Club on 5 February 1853. A Henry Crabbe, also of Streatham and probably related, was elected on the same date. Edward Crabbe died on 24 December 1904.

CRAMER, Johann Baptiste **750**
1771-1858
Johann Baptist Cramer was born in Mannheim on 24 February 1771, the eldest son of the musician Wilhelm Cramer (1749-1788). His brother Franz Cramer (1772-1848) was a violinist and impresario who between 1790 and 1848 played at various venues in London and at the King's Theatre. Johann had come to London with his father in the 1770s. He became a member of the Royal Society of Musicians in 1802. In 1813 he was a founding member of the Philharmonic Society that began a series of concerts in the Argyll Rooms, Regent Street. That organization became the Royal Philharmonic Society in 1912. He was an esteemed music teacher and composed in a variety of musical forms, including 105 sonatas. Cramer also was partner in the music publishing company Cramer and Keys, and in 1812 he became a partner of Samuel Chappell. Johann Cramer died in London on 16 April 1858. In addition to having his portrait put into the Trial Scene in *Henry VIII* by Harlow (**750**), engravings of him were published, among the best being the engraving by J. Thomson, after A. Wivell (1823). (*BDA*)

CRESWICK, Thomas RA **793**
1811-1869
The landscape painter Thomas Creswick was born on 5 February 1881 at Sheffield. At the age of seventeen he had two of his pictures exhibited at the Royal Academy, where for some 30 years he was a regular exhibitor. He was elected to the Academy in 1851. Known as a keen observer of nature in his landscapes, Creswick also designed many book illustrations. At the London International Exhibition of 1873, 109 of his paintings were shown; a catalogue of the exhibition was published by T. O. Barlow. He was elected to the Garrick Club in 1864. Creswick died at his residence in Linden Road, Bayswater, on 28 December 1869 and was buried at Kensal Green. In addition to appearing in O'Neil's Billiard Room group, his portrait was engraved by M. Jackson, after T. Scott. (*DNB*)

CROSS, Ludia
See Mrs Richard WEBB

CROUCH, Anna Maria
née Phillips **140, 141, 142**
1763-1805
This actress and singer was born in Gray's Inn Lane, London, on 20 April, 1763. She was one of six children of Peregrine Phillips, an official of the Wine Licence Office, who may have been connected through his French mother to Charlotte Corday, the assassin of Marat. Ann Maria was apprenticed for three years to Thomas Linley, the music master and joint patentee of Drury Lane Theatre, and made her first professional appearance on 11 November 1780 at Drury Lane as Mandane in Arne's *Artaxerxes*. She became a popular performer in London and Ireland. In January 1785 she married a young lieutenant named Rawlings Crouch. She had a series of amours, notably one with the singer Michael Kelly and one with the Prince of Wales. By 1790 her talents were diminishing and her health worsening. She died at Brighton on 20 October 1805, evidently of cancer. Mrs Crouch at her peak, however, had extraordinary beauty, grace and singing talent. In addition to those portraits of her at the Garrick Club, she was painted by a number of artists, including Romney, whose pictures of her are at Kenwood and the Pennsylvania Museum. (*BDA*)

CUBITT, Marie Caroline **630**
1800-1829
Marie Cubitt made her debut at Drury Lane on

14 June 1817 as Margaretta in *No Song No Supper* and was well received. According to a note by O. Smith in his 'Collection of Original Letters' (vol 2) at the Garrick Club, she possessed at an early age a voice of considerable 'sweetness' and played a number of characters in a highly accredited manner. In addition to being shown behind the grill in Clint's scene from *Lock and* Key (**630**), she had her portrait painted by R. E. Drummond (engraved by J. Thomson, 1818) and by Meadows as the Gypsy Girl in *Guy Mannering* (engraved by Page, 1827). She died in 1829.

CUMMINGS, Constance CBE 143
b. 1910
The estimable American actress Constance Cummings was born in Seattle, Washington, on 15 May 1910, the daughter of Vernon Halverstadt and his wife Kate Logan. She first appeared on the stage with the Savoy Company in San Diego in 1926. On 8 November 1928 she made her debut in New York at the Alvin Theatre in the chorus of Treasure Girl. Between 1931 and 1934 she appeared in some films and then went to London, where she made her English debut on 22 July 1934 as Alice Overton in Sour Grapes at the Comedy Theatre. She then remained on the London stage for over 40 years and also acted regularly in America. Among her numerous roles were Linda Brown in Accent on Youth (1934), Katherine in Goodbye Mr Chips (1938), Juliet in Romeo and Juliet (1939), Joan in St Joan (1939), Gabby in The Petrified Forest (1942), Martha in Who's Afraid of Virginia Woolf? (1964) and, memorably, Mary Tyrone in the National Theatre's production of Long Day's Journey into Night (1971). Among her fine performances in English provincial theatres was Claire in The Visit at the Belgrade Theatre in Coventry in October 1970. During the Second World War she appeared in films for HM Forces. She performed on television and in some 20 films, including This England, Blithe Spirit, American Madness and The Criminal Code. In 1933 she married the playwright Benn Levy. In 1974 she was honoured with the CBE. See Michael Gertside, For All Seasons: The Story of Stage and Screen Star Constance Cummings (1999). (WWT)

D

DALLAS, Eneas Sweetland 793
1828-1879
He was born in Jamaica in 1828, the elder son of John Dallas, who was a Jamaican physician of Scottish descent. The family went back to Britain when Dallas was four, and he eventually attended Edinburgh University, where he studied philosophy. He became a journalist, writing numerous articles for a variety of journals and papers, but he was mainly renowned for his articles in *The Times* on biography, politics and literary affairs. He wrote a 'careful, graceful English' with profundity. Dallas died in London on 17 January 1879 and was buried at Kensal Green Cemetery. He had been the second husband of the actress Isabella Glyn, but the marriage was dissolved in 1874 by her petition. Dallas became a member of the Garrick Club in 1862 and resigned in 1870. (*DNB*)

DANE, Clemence, pseudonym of Winifred Ashton G0974
1888-1965
Born Winifred Ashton in Blackheath in 1888, this playwright, artist and actress turned to writing novels in 1917 with *A Regiment of Women*. Her next novel, *Legends* (1919), was made into the play *A Bill of Divorcement* (1921) starring Katherine Cornell. Among her many other plays were *Will Shakespeare* (1921), *Wild December* about the Brontes (1932), *Mariners* (1927) and *The Saviours* (1942). She also wrote radio and television plays. The critic St John Irvine called her 'the most distinguished woman dramatist in the theatre' in the 1920s and 1930s. She died in London on 28 March 1965. Charles Mozley's portrait of Clemence Dane was presented to the Garrick Club by Roy Fullick in 1996. Portraits of her by Howard Coster and Frederic Yates are in the National Portrait Gallery, as are her bust (NPG4950) and her portrait (NPG4951) of Noel Coward. David Waldron Smither's *The Works of Clemence Dane* was published in 1988.

DANSEY, Herbert **G0992**
1870-1917
Born in Rome on 6 March 1870 and educated in Florence, Herbert Dansey made his first appearance in London on 7 January 1902 as Lane in a revival of *The Importance of Being Earnest* at the St James's. He also appeared there as Valentino in *Paolo and Francesca* (March 1902) and the Comte de Villars in *The End of the Story* before he played Leone Cassavetti (**G0992**) in Forbes-Robertson's production of *The Light that Failed* at the Lyric on 7 February 1903. Dansey had engagements at the Royalty, Duke of York's, Criterion, Lyceum and Covent Garden prior to his going to America in September 1912 to act Lt Duvallet in *Fanny's First Play*, a role he also appeared in back in London at the Kingsway in February 1915. He died on 30 May 1917 at the age of 47. Dansey was secretary of the Argonauts Society. He seems not to have been a member of the Garrick Club. (*WWWT*)

DARBY, Mary
See Mrs Thomas ROBINSON

DAVENPORT, Mary Ann née Harvey **144-146**
1759-1843
Born at Launceston in 1759, Mary Ann Harvey made her debut at Bath in December 1784 as Lappet in *The Miser*. While acting at Exeter in 1785 she met the actor George Gosling Davenport and married him the next year. The two were strollers for some years, until they were hired at Covent Garden, where on 19 September 1794 she was favourably received as Mrs Hardcastle in *She Stoops to Conquer*. Mrs Davenport continued to please Covent Garden audiences for another 35 years. She mainly appeared in good secondary roles like Juliet's Nurse, Mrs Peachum in *The Beggar's Opera*, Mrs Heidelberg in *The Clandestine Marriage*, Dame Ashfield in *Speed the Plow* (**145**), Widow Warren in *The Road to Ruin*, Lady Denny in *Henry VIII* (**144**) and Fiametta in *The Tale of Mystery* (**146**). Her line of 'affected social climbers, tedious granddams, and a whole group of elderly odd fish beloved by English audiences kept her securely a favourite' (*BDA*). Her husband died in March 1814, and she survived him until her death in Brompton on 8 May 1843. Her last performance at Covent Garden had been as Juliet's Nurse on 25 May 1830. Mrs Davenport was also the sitter for a painting by Romney, the present location of which is unknown. (*BDA*)

DAVIES, Mary Stephens
See Mary WELLS

DAVISON, Maria Rebecca née Duncan **147**
1783-1858
Born about 1783, probably in Liverpool, the daughter of strolling actors named Duncan, she played children's parts in the provinces and eventually engaged with Tate Wilkinson on the York circuit. In 1804 she came to Drury Lane, where she made her debut on 8 October as Lady Teazle in *The School for Scandal* and followed with roles like Rosalind in *As You Like It*, Sylvia in *The Recruiting Officer*, Miranda in *The Busy Body* and Letitia in *The Belle's Stratagem*. On 31 January 1805 she created the role of Julianna in *The Honeymoon*, a character she remained closely associated with and in which Singleton pictured her (**147**). She married James Davison on 31 October 1812, and her name subsequently appeared in the bills as Mrs Davison. She remained at Drury Lane most of her career, eventually playing more elderly characters like Mrs Subtle in *Paul Pry*. She seems to have left Drury Lane in 1829 and lived many years in retirement until her death in Brompton on 30 May 1858. Tall in stature and 'strongly formed,' she had a fine voice. She was excellent in such roles as Lady Teazle, Beatrice and Lady Townly and is said to have had no rival as Julianna in *The Honeymoon*. Leigh Hunt wrote many pages about her in his *Critical Essays* (1807) and claimed she was the 'best *lady* our comic stage possesses.'

DAWSON, Nancy née Newton **148**
1730-1767
The celebrated hornpipe dancer called Nancy Dawson was born in London about 1730, the daughter of a staymaker, William Newton, of Martlet Court, Covent Garden, and his wife Eleanor Newton. There are a number of romanticised fabrications concerning her young

life and affairs. She may have performed at Sadler's Wells and Drury Lane earlier, but her first noticed appearance was at Covent Garden on 1 February 1758, when she danced in the chorus of *The Prophetess.* She was under the auspices of the comedian Edward Shuter (*q.v.*), with whom she had a domestic alliance for many years. On 22 May 1758 she was billed for dancing a hornpipe. After three years at Covent Garden dancing in choruses and offering her hornpipe, Nancy went over to Drury Lane, where she danced similar fare. She also made her first speaking appearance on 20 March 1760 in the droll *The English Sailors in America* and on 29 April 1760, for her benefit, she played Colombine in *Harlequin Statue.* The tune of the hornpipe by which Nancy danced into fame and on which she traded the rest of her short career was almost certainly written by the eminent theatrical composer Dr Thomas A. Arne. It is still sung, in a less sophisticated form, as 'Here We Go Round the Mulberry Bush.' It became a popular household tune, and it and Nancy were often mentioned in the press of the day. A full eight-stanza version of the lyrics – beginning with 'Of all the girls in our town' – appeared in her *Authentic Memoirs* [1761?] and was published in *The Vocal Magazine, or Compleat British Songster* (1781).

Nancy Dawson's name appeared in the Drury Lane bills for the last time on 27 December 1763. Why she retired so abruptly is not known. She died on 9 June 1767 at Haverstock Hill, and was buried on 12 June in the cemetery of St George the Martyr, Bloomsbury, behind the Foundling Hospital. A large stone pylon marks her grave. In her will she made a number of bequests, to her parents, her brother William Newton and his wife Bridget and to neighbours and friends. To her paramour Ned Shuter she left a mourning ring. Contemporary memoirs accounted her a woman of great beauty and grace, with a shrewish temper, who led a 'notoriously immoral life.' But these accounts are largely colourful legends, no doubt highly inflated, yet possessing some kernel of truth. In addition to the portrait of her at the Garrick Club (**148**), an anonymous picture of her striking a pose in her hornpipe dance is in the Library of Worcester College, Oxford. (*BDA*)

DAY, Sir Robin **892, 965**
1923-2000
Sir Robin Day was born on 24 October 1923, the son of William and Florence Day, and was educated at Bembridge School and St Edmund Hall, Oxford. After military service from 1943 to 1947 (rising to RAF Wing Commander), he was at Oxford from 1947 to 1951. In 1951 Day received an MA at the Middle Temple; he was called to the Bar in 1952. In the 1950s Day became a radio and television broadcaster, parliamentary commentator and moderator. He appeared on numerous programmes on BBC and ITV as moderator or commentator, including 'Panorama', 'Question Time' and '24 Hours.' Among his many awards was the Richard Dimbleby Award for factual television, 1974. He was knighted in 1981. Sir Robin became a member of the Garrick Club in January 1962. In 1965 he married Katherine Ainslie, who is shown with him (Nos. 33 and 34) in Gilroy's scene of the Garrick Club Outing (**892**). He died in London on 6 August 2000.

DEAN, Basil MBE, CBE **149**
1888-1971
The eminent theatrical impresario and stage director Basil Dean was born on 27 September 1888 at Croydon, the son of Harding Hewar Dean and his wife Elizabeth Mary (née Winton). He was educated at Whitgift School and made his first stage appearance at the Opera House, Cheltenham, in September 1906 as Trip in *The School for Scandal.* He acted a number of roles in Miss Horniman's company at the Midland Hotel Theatre, Manchester, from 1907 to 1910, and in the spring of 1911 he became the first controller of the experimental Kelly's Theatre in Liverpool, out of which emerged the Liverpool Playhouse. In 1912-1913 he was in charge of stage construction work at the Birmingham Repertory Theatre. He was associated with Barry Jackson and Sir Herbert Beerbohm Tree and organized entertainments for the troops during World War I. He was awarded the MBE in 1918. In 1919, with Alec Rea, he formed the Readean Company, in a partnership that made many important contributions to the British theatre in the 1920s. In 1922 he was appointed consultant

on stage lighting for the General Electric Company, Ltd. His partnership with Rea was terminated in July 1926 and the next month he formed Basil Dean Productions. He was managing director of L.B.D. Productions from 1939 to 1946 and also served as Director of the National Service Entertainments.

Dean was among the first to make talking pictures in Britain and was the first Chairman and Managing Director of Associated Talking Pictures, Ltd, British Film Distributors, Ltd, and Ealing Studios. Throughout his distinguished and varied career he also directed and produced numerous plays and films, including many of the films of Gracie Fields. He brought *The Inspector Calls* to the stage at the New Theatre (Old Vic) in October 1946. Among his many significant productions after the Second World War was *The Aspern Papers* (Queen's 1959), with Michael Redgrave and Flora Robson.

Dean became a member of the Garrick Club in 1939 and was honoured with the CBE in 1947. He died in 1971. A very important archive of his papers, covering some 60 years of his career, including correspondence with many leading theatrical figures, press cuttings, promptbooks, set and costume designs, reviews and programmes, is in the John Rylands Library, Manchester University. (*OCT, WWWT*)

DEANE, John Connellan DCL **793**
1816-1887
John Connellan Deane, who is pictured as No. 33 in O'Neil's large 1869 canvas of members in the Billiards Room of the Garrick Club (**793**), became a member of the Club in 1854, at which time he was of the Court Temple.

DE CAMP, Maria Theresa
See Mrs Charles KEMBLE

DE CAMP, Vincent **150-152**
1779-1839
The singing actor Vincent De Camp was born in London in January 1779, the only son of the flutist George Louis De Camp (1752-1787) and his wife Jeanne, née Dufour (d. 1816). He had five sisters, three of whom were on the stage: Maria Teresa Decamp (b. 1780, later Mrs Charles Kemble), Adelaide De Camp (1780-1834) and Sophia De Camp (b. 1785, later Mrs Frederick Brown). Vincent made his debut in the traditional child's role of the Prince of Wales in *Richard III* with the Drury Lane company at the King's Theatre on 5 November 1792. No doubt it was a heady experience for the youth, for that night John Philip Kemble acted Richard and Vincent's sister danced in the afterpiece. He made several other appearances until he joined the company at the new Drury Lane Theatre in April 1794. He remained at that theatre throughout the rest of his career. By 1798 he was appearing in adult roles, including Lovel in *High Life below Stairs*, Careless in *The School for Scandal* and Vapour in *My Grandmother*. He seldom rose above modest secondary supporting roles like Roderigo in *Othello* and Frankly in *The Suspicious Husband*, so it is curious that he would be represented with three pictures in the Garrick Club. His most important role, it seems, may have been Figaro in Holcroft's adaptation of *The Marriage of Figaro* (**150**). In addition to the other two portraits of him at the Garrick, six more pictures were done of him in various roles, including a watercolour by De Wilde in the British Museum of De Camp as Coupée in *The Virgin Unmask'd*.

After 1814 De Camp played in provincial theatres. At some point he went to America, but his activities are obscure. He is said to have managed at Montreal in 1833, and later that year played at Philadelphia; he subsequently acted at Mobile, Alabama. His death in Houston, Texas, was announced in the *Columbian Century* on 26 August 1839. (*BDA*)

DELPINI, Carlo Antonio **652**
1740-1828
Little is known about the continental career of Delpini, who was born in Rome in 1740. His first known appearance in London occurred at Covent Garden on 26 December 1776, when he danced Pierrot in the pantomime *Harlequin's Frolicks*; he injured himself halfway through the performance and could not appear again until 9 January of the following year. He danced and acted at Covent Garden for several years, was seen at the fairs, and in 1779-80 joined Drury Lane. He made his debut at the summer Haymarket Theatre in May 1780.

Delpini appeared off and on at various London theatres until 1800. In 1787-88 he was engaged with Palmer's Royalty Theatre (**652**), and during the next several years he performed and sometime managed events at Hughes's Royal Circus, devising such divertissements as *A Dutch Tea-Garden* and *What You Please*. He also danced in the opera at the King's Theatre, staged amateur theatricals and gave masquerades. Delpini's wife also acted and sang in the London theatres. Because he had never subscribed to any of the theatrical funds, Delpini had to rely on the kindness of friends during the sicknesses he endured during the last years of his life. He died on 28 January 1828 at his lodgings in Lancaster Court, St Martin's Churchyard. (*BDA*)

DENMAN, William **153**
1766-1806
Born in 1766 into a naval family, Denman was apprenticed to a bookseller in Rochester. He did not pursue the book trade long before he joined a provincial company in 1790 and acted at Kingston and Canterbury. He remained in country companies for six years before he made his London debut at Drury Lane as Foigard in *The Beaux' Stratagem* on 27 October 1796 and received negative notices. That season he continued in similar small roles but next year was in Edinburgh where the criticism was also severe. But after engagements on the York circuit beginning in 1799, he was noticed by George Colman and was hired by him for the summer seasons at the Haymarket. There he settled into a line of Irishmen, old men and fatherly figures. By 1804, however, he was back as a stroller in the provinces. He seems to have died either in June or October 1806. In addition to the portrait of Denman as the Quaker by Wellings (**153**), a portrait of him by W. Carroll was reported to be at the Garrick Club; however the editors of *Pictures in the Garrick Club* could not find it. (*BDA*)

DERBY, Countess of
See Elizabeth FARREN

DIBDIN, Charles **154**
1745-1814
The son of Thomas Dibdin, a silversmith from Southampton, Charles Dibdin was christened on 4 March 1745 at Holyrood Church. He received no formal education, not even in music, for which he had a natural talent, but before he was sixteen (he said) he was singing and playing the organ. Dibdin was drawn to London, became acquainted with theatre people, began composing, refined his knowledge of music and, by 1760-61, was singing in the choruses of *Thomas and Sally* and *Romeo and Juliet* for John Rich at Covent Garden Theatre. On 22 May 1764 Dibdin's pastoral operetta, *The Shepherd's Artifice*, his first full attempt at theatrical composing, was performed as an afterpiece for the composer's shared benefit. He took the part of Strephon. In addition to singing and acting at Covent Garden, Dibdin performed at such pleasure gardens as Vauxhall in London and similar venues in provincial towns; indeed, much of his performing career in the summers was on tour.

Dibdin's first real success was as Ralph in *The Maid of the Mill*, a mainpiece which was newly staged at Covent Garden on 31 January 1765. The management negotiated a three-year contract with Dibdin that assured him of three, four, and then five pounds a week for appearing in nothing but musical pieces – which was just as well, since few in his day accused him of having much acting talent, though audiences loved him as a singer and composer. But in 1767 the manager John Beard, with whom Dibdin worked comfortably, sold his Covent Garden patent to George Colman, with whom Dibdin did not. Charles decamped to Drury Lane and the managership of David Garrick in 1768.

Though Dibdin and Garrick had an edgy relationship, things began well, with Dibdin walking into the role of Mungo and sharing composer's chores with Thomas Augustine Arne in the remarkably successful *Padlock*, which opened at Drury Lane on 3 October 1768. So Dibdin in his early 20s was a successful composer and singer at London's premier theatre and, one would suppose, prosperous. But, as John Britton said, Dibdin was 'ill-versed in the science of domestic economy, or the art of saving money.' His biographical writings, which run to volumes, are full of complaints and justifications for his sorry financial state; he played the blame game well, always acting the put-upon artist and constantly wanting restitution and fuller control over his artistic talents. But he regularly sought out as his theatrical associates the most talented and powerful people, and he constantly found himself at odds with them. In 1774-75 he was £200 in debt to Drury Lane, and in 1776 Garrick discharged him. Without regular employment, Dibdin fled to France with several of his illegitimate children, and there he remained for two years, writing and composing works and sending them off for production at Drury Lane, Covent Garden and Sadler's Wells.

When he returned in the summer of 1778 he signed on at Covent Garden, not as a performer, but as composer to the theatre, for which he churned out musical pieces each season. This arrangement, however, did not prevent him from becoming quarrelsome with the manager, Thomas Harris. By 1780 he was ready to leave Covent Garden again and stage, on 1 March 1780 at the Haymarket, a revival of *The Comic Mirror*, a puppet show he had created. The audience rioted, misunderstanding that the performers were not to be human beings. Then Dibdin produced *The Surprise* at Sadler's Wells in April and returned in the autumn to Covent Garden to squabble with the manager. His next attempt was equestrian theatre at the Royal Circus in Southwark, where, during the mid-1780s, Dibdin created some spectacle pieces and fought with his cohorts. Too often his efforts came to naught, as when he provided the Dublin manager Daly with some musical pieces and was bilked of £460, through no fault of his own except his gullibility in dealing with that charlatan in the first place. In May 1787 he set off on a fourteen-month tour of a solo musical entertainment. By 1790 his life settled down to a routine of providing entertainments for the Wargrave theatricals, Royal Circus, Covent Garden and Sadler's Wells while offering his own concoctions, such as an evening he called *Oddities* at the Lyceum. He turned out a periodical called *The Bystander* and wrote a three-volume novel. Then he decided to create a theatre of his own.

The first San Souci was just a room in the Strand, which Dibdin opened in 1791. Five years later he had a new Sans Souci, in Leicester Place, where he offered an entertainment called *The General Election* and displayed some of his own paintings. The *Monthly Mirror*, with heavy irony, said 'Mr. Dibdin is as assuredly as good a *poet* as he is a *painter*.' But Dibdin held forth at the second Sans Souci for ten years with a variety of musical entertainments. He also supplied pieces to Drury Lane and Covent Garden, turned out a five-volume history of the English stage and went on a tour of 43 provincial towns. But he was wearing out: critics noted that his voice and articulation were deteriorating, and his solo entertainments were full of 'blunders and flounders.'

Charles Dibdin died on 25 July 1814, leaving his estate, whatever it was, to his wife Ann. He also left a number of children, including the talented Charles Isaac Mungo Pitt (by the dancer Harriet Pitt) who followed in his father's footsteps and is noticed in the *BDA*. Charles Dibdin composed hundreds of songs and was immensely popular with audiences. The playwright John O'Keeffe said, 'Dibdin's manner of coming on the stage was in happy style; he ran on sprightly, and with nearly a laughing face, like a friend who enters hastily to impart to you some good news ... A few lines of speaking happily introduced his admirable songs, full of wit and character, and his peculiar mode of singing them surpassed all I had ever heard.' (*BDA*) [EAL]

DICKENS, Charles **155, 156**

1812-1870

Charles John Huffam Dickens was born at Portsmouth, Hampshire, on 7 February 1812. He became the greatest English novelist of the Victorian era and in his lifetime enjoyed more popularity than any previous novelist. His numerous works are familiar to millions through print, radio, film and television: *A Christmas Carol, David Copperfield, Great Expectations, Bleak House, Oliver Twist* and *A Tale of Two Cities*. He also enjoyed a successful career as a platform reader, mostly from his own works, and toured throughout the provinces and the United States. He became a member of the Garrick Club in 1837, soon after he wrote the *Pickwick Papers*. Dickens died at Gad's Hill, near Chatham, Kent, on 9 June 1870. *See* his biographies: Edgar Johnson, *Charles Dickens: His Tragedy and Triumph*

(2 vols,1952) and Norman and Jeanne Mackenzie, *Dickens* (1979). For Dickens and the Garrick Club, see Richard Hough, *The Ace of Clubs* (1987).

DICKONS, Mrs Peter, Martha Frances Caroline née Poole 157
c. 1774-1833
Martha Poole, who came to be called Maria, was born in London about 1774, the daughter of William Poole. As a child prodigy she performed in Handel's concerts at six and sang at Vauxhall Gardens at thirteen. After being instructed in singing by Rauzzini at Bath she made her London debut in an unspecified role in her master's opera *La Vestale* at the King's Theatre on 1 May 1787. Miss Poole became well known through her appearances in concerts in London and Bristol. She made her acting debut as Ophelia in *Hamlet* at Covent Garden on 9 October 1793. At that theatre she played a series of singing ingenues until she married the businessman Peter Dickons on 7 August 1800 and retired for seven years, reappearing as Mrs Dickons at Covent Garden in April 1807. When her husband went bankrupt in 1810 they separated. At the King's Theatre on 18 June 1812 she played the Countess in Mozart's *The Marriage of Figaro*. Subsequently she appeared with the Drury Lane company through 1815-16. After two years singing at the operas in Paris and Venice, Mrs Dickons returned to Covent Garden to sing Rosina in *The Barber of Seville* (**157**) on 13 October 1818. She retired from the stage soon after and suffered from cancer and paralysis until her death at her residence in Regent Street on 4 May 1833. Other portraits of Mrs Dickons are listed in the *BDA* 12: 54.

DIGNUM, Charles 158
c.1765-1827
Charles Dignum was born in Rotherhithe about 1765, the son of a poor Irish tailor. After several apprenticeships with tradesmen and musicians he became a pupil of Thomas Linley, the singing master and father-in-law of Richard Brinsley Sheridan. Dignum made his singing-acting debut at Drury Lane on 14 October 1784 as Young Meadows in *Love in a Village* and was received with 'unbounded applause.' After a very successful first season at Drury Lane, he remained engaged at that theatre for over 30 years, playing numerous supporting and leading roles in ballad operas, pantomimes and musical romances. Among them were Macheath in *The Beggar's Opera*, Hawthorne in *Love in a Village*, Lubin in *The Quaker* and Selim in *Blue-Beard.* Dignum also appeared as Tugg in *The Waterman* on 8 May 1788, the role in which De Wilde pictures him (**158**). (The statement in his notice in *Pictures in the Garrick Club* that he did not play the role in London is incorrect.) He also acted a number of Shakespearean roles, the most important of them being Marcellus in *Hamlet*, Pembroke in *King John* and Lorenzo in *The Merchant of Venice.* Many songs composed by Dignum were published. Dignum was a compulsive eater and he became quite corpulent in his later years. He died at his house in Gloucester Street on 29 March 1827 and left an estate reported to be worth £30,000. (*BDA*).

DIMOND, William Wyatt 159
c. 1752-1812
Dimond was born in the early 1750s. Nothing is known of his early life except that he was intended to be a silver engraver. He spent some 35 years in the theatre but a relatively short time on the London stage. After his first appearance at Drury Lane on 1 October 1772 as Romeo, he played that season Dorilas in *Meropé* and Moneses in *Tamerlane.* Although he had some merit, for the most part he was 'insufficient in judgment, voice, and expression.' He was again at Drury Lane in 1773-74 filling some supporting roles and played at the Haymarket in the summer of 1775. His last appearances in London came in the summer of 1779 at the Haymarket, when he acted Charles in *The Jealous Wife* and Lord Newbry in the premiere of Colman's *The Separate Maintenance* (31 August). Since 1772 Dimond had been delving into theatrical management at Canterbury. He was connected with the Bath Theatre from at least 1775, and he was to remain associated there until his death in 1812. By 1786 he was involved in the business of the theatre with William Keasberry, and eventually he became manager and joint proprietor. He quit acting in 1801 but

continued to manage at Bath and at Bristol. In 1805 he took over the new Theatre Royal in Beaufort Square, which he had helped plan. Dimond died at Bath on 2 January 1812 and was buried at Bath Abbey. In addition to the picture by De Wilde of Dimond as Don Felix (**159**), that artist did a watercolour of him as Philaster; it is in the Harvard Theatre Collection and was engraved by Audinet for *Bell's British Theatre*, 1791. (*BDA*)

DIXON, Clara Ann later Mrs Smith, then Mrs Sterling 160, 600
fl. 1795-1822
It is said that Clara Ann Dixon was the daughter of an army officer and granddaughter of Major-General Dixon, and that her uncle was an admiral. She performed in the private theatricals given by the Society of Kentish Bowman at its lodge on Dartford Heath in 1795 (**600**). She made her professional singing debut as Beda in *Blue-Beard* at Drury Lane on 15 April 1799. The following season, billed as Sga Clara, she was engaged at the King's Theatre and then subsequently at Covent Garden, where she first appeared as Polly in *The Beggar's Opera* on 24 September 1800. Other roles followed: Louisa in *The Duenna*, Jessica in *The Merchant of Venice*, Harriet in *The Reprisal* and Olivia in *Twelfth Night*. In her third season at Covent Garden, having in the previous summer married a Mr Smith, deputy manager of the Plymouth and Exeter company, her name appeared in the bills as Mrs Smith ('late Miss Dixon'). She gave up the stage, but when she separated from Smith and had to support three children she returned. After playing for some years at Bath, Bristol, York and other places, she was back at Covent Garden in 1812-13, now called Mrs Sterling. She sang at Vauxhall Gardens and was at Covent Garden through 1821-22. (*BDA*)

DODD, James William 161-166
1740?-1796
He was probably born in 1740, the son of a London hairdresser, and given a classical education at a Holborn grammar school. Dodd set his sights on a stage career from an early age and by 1763 was performing at the Norwich theatre. At Bath he was seen by the playwright John Hoadly who, at David Garrick's request, provided the Drury Lane manager with a detailed judgment on the young actor's prospects: '… his *person* is good enough, but his motion is too much under restraint and form; more the stalk and *menage* of a dancing master, than the ease of a gentleman … He has a white *calf-like* stupid face, that disgusted me much till I heard him speak and throw some sensibility into it.' There were at this early stage in Dodd's career the marks of the coxcomb and fop that were to become his speciality – just what Garrick was looking for. In the autumn of 1765 Dodd and his wife Martha, also a performer, became members of the Drury Lane company. James's debut there was as Faddle (with a song) in *The Foundling* on 3 October.

Though Dodd, usually for his benefits, tried tragic roles – Richard III, Mark Antony, even Hamlet – he failed. He was cut out for comedy, and most of his characters over the decades were in that genre: Plausible in *The Plain Dealer*, Slender in *The Merry Wives of Windsor*, Sparkish in *The Country Girl* (**163**), Sir Novelty Fashion in *Love's Last Shift*, Osric in *Hamlet*, Sir Benjamin Backbite in *The School for Scandal*, Abel Drugger in *The Alchemist* (**161**), Lord Foppington in *The Careless Husband* (**165**), Bob Acres in *The Rivals* and Sir Andrew Aguecheek in *Twelfth Night*. He was regularly in harlequinades and other musical works where his fine voice was heard to advantage. Dodd's position in the Drury Lane company was secure, and by the early 1790s he was earning £12 weekly. He augmented his salary with visits in the summers to Bristol, Bath, Dublin and a few other provincial playhouses and also engaged in some theatre management, but he hurt his reputation with some members of his audience, especially those in the provinces, when he had an affair with the actress Mary Bulkley. Dodd died on 17 September 1796 in London. (*BDA*) [EAL]

DOGGART, James 892
fl. 1951-1976
James 'Jimmy' Doggart, an ophthalmologist, is shown as No. 8 in Gilroy's scene of the Garrick Club Outing. He was elected to the Garrick Club in November 1951 and resigned in 1976.

DOWTON, William 124, 167-171, B161
1764-1851
The actor and manager William Dowton was born at Exeter on 25 April 1764, the son of an innkeeper. Though given a good education and apprenticed to an architect, he joined strolling players in Devonshire, and is said to have made his professional debut in a barn. After appearances in some western provincial towns, Dowton joined Sarah Baker's company in Kent and played at Rochester and Canterbury from 1792 to 1796. He made his first appearance in London at Drury Lane on 10 October 1796 as Sheva in *The Jew*, to mixed reviews. In his first season there he acted a number of roles, including Scrub in *The Stratagem*, the First Gravedigger in *Hamlet* and Sir Francis Wronghead in *The Provok'd Husband.* Except for occasional appearances in the provinces and at the Haymarket in summer, Dowton remained engaged at Drury Lane until 1820. He settled into a line of older men like Peachum in *The Beggar's Opera,* Sir Anthony Absolute in *The Rivals*, Old Mirabel in *The Inconstant*, Obadiah Prim in *A Bold Stroke for a Wife*, Dr Cantwell in *The Hypocrite* and Major Sturgeon in *The Mayor of Garratt* (**171**). He was not successful on a tour to America in 1836, or in his provincial attempts in England, or in his management at Maidstone and Canterbury.

Dowton died in Brixton, Surrey, on 19 April 1851. Leigh Hunt wrote warmly of him in his *Critical Essays*, praising his mercurial qualities as an actor and person. He was an original member of the Garrick Club in 1831. In addition to the pictures of him at the Garrick Club, there are a number of portraits of him in private and theatrical character (see the *BDA* 4: 469-70). (*BDA*)

DU MAURIER, Sir Gerald Hubert Edward Busson 172-174, G0991
1873-1934
Gerald Du Maurier was born in Hampstead on 26 March 1873, the son of George Du Maurier, the novelist and prominent cartoonist of *Punch*, and his wife Emma (née Wightwick). Educated at Harrow, Gerald first appeared on the London stage in 1894, and then for almost 40 years continued as a favourite and distinguished actor, playing dozens of leading roles in many London theatres. Notable among them were Hamlet, Henry IV, Ernest Woolley in *The Admirable Crichton* (**172**), Capt Hook and Darling in *Peter Pan*, the title role in *Raffles*, Lee Randall in *Alias Jimmy Valentine*, Dearth in *Dear Brutus*, the Policeman in *A Kiss for Cinderella*, Ferdinand Gadd in *Trelawney of the Wells* and Drummond in *Bull-Dog Drummond.* Du Maurier practiced a style of acting that was described as delicately realistic, suggesting rather than stating the deeper emotions. With Frank Curzon he co-managed Wyndham's Theatre from 1910 to 1925, and later the St James's Theatre. He served as President of the Actors' Orphanage Fund, of the Actors' Benevolent Fund, and of Denville Hall, the home for aged actors and actresses. Du Maurier became a member of the Garrick Club in January 1903. He was knighted in 1922 and died in London on 11 April 1934. His daughter Daphne Du Maurier (b. 1907) was a dramatist and novelist, and wrote a biography of her father, *Gerald: a Portrait* (1934) and a history of the Du Mauriers (1937).

DUNCAN, Maria Rebecca
See DAVISON

DUNN, William 175
1782-1855
William Dunn, born in 1782, was a clerk at Drury Lane Theatre by January 1798. In 1807-8 he was called the chief clerk and by 1812-13 was serving as deputy treasurer. He was still at Drury Lane in 1817. He was an original member of the Garrick Club in 1831. Dunn died at Norwood, Surrey, on 3 March 1885 and in his will left everything to his widow Rosa.

DUSE, Eleonora S7
1859-1924
This famous Italian actress and international star was born on 3 October 1859 near Venice, the daughter of strolling players Alessandro Duse and his wife Angelica. She appeared as a child in the role of Cosetta in *Les Miserables* in 1863 and toured with various Italian companies until her first success at Turin in 1879 in *La Princesse de Baghdad.* She was acclaimed for her Marguerite in *La dame aux camélias* at Rome in 1828. Playing

a number of leading parts, Duse caused a great sensation in Russia, Germany and New York. She made her first appearance in London as Marguerite at the Lyric Theatre on 24 May 1893. She then acted in *Fedora, Cavaleria Rusticana, La Locanderia, A Doll's House* and *Antony and Cleopatra.* She was at the Adelphi in 1903 in *La Gioconda, Hedda Gabler* and *The Second Mrs Tanqueray.* She retired in June 1908 after appearing at Drury Lane for Ellen Terry's Jubilee performance, but she reappeared at Turin in May 1921 in *The Lady from the Sea.* Duse died in Pittsburgh on 21 April 1924, in a hotel now on the campus of the University of Pittsburgh.

DYALL, Franklin **S8**
1874-1950
The actor and producer Franklin Dyall was born in Liverpool on 3 February 1874, the son of Charles Dyall. He first appeared under George Alexander's management at the St James's on 28 April 1894 in *The Masqueraders*; other roles included Merriman in *The Importance of Being Earnest,* Claudius in *Hamlet* and Josef in *The Prisoner of Zenda.* In 1897 he joined Forbes-Robertson's company at the Lyceum. Then for some 48 years he continued to appear on the London stage and in the provinces and abroad, playing dozens of leading and featured roles. In March 1935 he toured with Gielgud, acting Claudius. As late as 1945 he toured as Svengali in *Trilby.* He also directed many plays at various theatres, and appeared in numerous films. After his first marriage to Mary Phyllis Logan was dissolved, he married Mary Merrall, who in 1953 presented the bronze by Epstein (**S8**) to the Garrick Club. Dyall became a member of the Garrick Club on 5 January 1934. He died on 8 May 1950.

DYKES, John Christopher **892**
d. 1981
John Dykes became a member of the Garrick Club on 4 February 1965. He died on 20 December 1981.

E

EARL, Sebastian **43, 176, 892**
d. 1983
Sebastian Earl was a Company Director of Selfridge's. In November 1946 he became a member of the Garrick Club, where he was often seen, and served as Chairman of the Wine Committee. He died on 11 August 1983.

EDDINGTON, Paul Clark CBE
1899-1973 **G0979, G1003**
Paul Edington was born in London on 18 June 1927, the son of Albert Clark Eddington and his wife Frances Mary (née Roberts). He was educated at Oxford and trained at RADA. He joined the Birmingham Repertory in 1945 and made his first appearance in the West End as the Rabbi in *The Tenth Man* at the Comedy Theatre in 1961. Eddington was with the Bristol Old Vic for some eleven years, during which he acted such leading parts as the title role in *Brand,* Henry II in *Becket,* Brutus in *Julius Caesar* and Disraeli in *Portrait of a Queen.* With that company he played Palmer Anderson in *The Severed Head* at the Criterion Theatre in London in June 1963 and made his first appearance in New York in that role at the Royale in October 1964. In the spring of 1973 he acted James Tyrone in *Long Day's Journey into Night* and Osborne in *Journey's End.* But it was in television that he became widely known for his excellent performances in the BBC comedy series *The Good Life* (1975-1979) and notably, with Nigel Hawthorne, in *Yes, Minister* (1980-1985) and *Yes, Prime Minister* (1986-1990).

Among his many services to the profession were Governor of the Bristol Old Vic Theatre Trust, 1975-1978; International Committee for Artists' Freedom, Equity 1985-1995; Hon Professor of Drama, Sheffield University; and Member of the Council of the Howard League for Penal Reform, 1993-1995. In 1987 he received an Honorary MA from Sheffield, and that year he was also awarded a CBE. His autobiography, *So Far So Good,* was published in 1995, the year in which he died, on 4 November. Eddington had been a member of the Garrick Club from 1982. In 1952 he had married Patricia Scott. They had three sons and a daughter.

EDINBURGH, H. R. H. Prince Philip, Duke of, also Philip Mountbatten, originally Philip, Prince of Greece and Denmark 177

b. 1921

Prince Philip, KG, KT, OM, Ranger of Windsor Park, Great Master of the Order of the Bath, was born on 10 June 1921, at Corfu, Greece, the son of Prince Andrew of Greece and Denmark (1882-1944). His mother was Princess Alice (1885-1969), eldest daughter of Louis Alexander Mountbatten and Princess Victoria of Hesse (a granddaughter of Queen Victoria). Educated at Gordonstoun and the Royal Naval College, Dartmouth, Prince Philip served in the Royal Navy in combat in the Pacific and Mediterranean from 1940 to the end of the Second World War. He was naturalised a British subject in February 1947, the year in which he married on 20 November at Westminster Abbey the Princess Elizabeth, now Queen Elizabeth II. He was also created Baron Greenwich, Earl of Merioneth, and Duke of Edinburgh. Prince Philip is the Royal Patron of the Garrick Club and was made a member in May 1980.

EDWARD VI 178

1537-1553

Edward VI, the young king of England and Ireland from 1547 to 1553, was born in London on 12 October 1537; he was the only legitimate son of Henry VIII, by his third wife Jane Seymour, who died 12 days after Edward's birth. At the age of nine Edward succeeded to the throne on the death of his father on 28 January 1547. The country was managed by the regent, Edward's uncle, Edward Seymour, Duke of Somerset, until the latter was deposed in 1549 by John Dudley, Earl of Warwick and then Duke of Northumberland. When Edward began to suffer from tuberculosis early in 1553, he was persuaded by Northumberland to arrange that his two half-sisters, Mary and Elizabeth, would be excluded from succession and that Northumberland's daughter-in-law, Lady Jane Grey, would assume the throne. After Edward's death on 6 July 1553 (when he was not quite 16), Lady Jane ruled for nine days only and then was overthrown by Mary I (bloody Mary), who died in 1558 and was succeeded by Elizabeth I. (*EB*)

EDWIN, John 182-187

1749-1790

John Edwin, one of England's busiest actors during the eighteenth century, was born on 10 August 1749 in Clare Market, St Clement Danes. He was the son of the watchmaker John Edwin. His mother Hannah was the daughter of the sculptor Henry Brogden. One of John's sisters, Elizabeth, acted in London in the late 1780s. As a lad John Edwin gave declamations at local 'spouting clubs' and taverns and captured the attention of several theatrical people, including the great comedian Ned Shuter and the managers Francis Waldron and John Lee. He obtained an engagement at Manchester in the summer of 1765 and then at Smock Alley, Dublin, that autumn. After another 11 years bouncing round in the provinces, Edwin made his first London appearance at the Haymarket on 19 June 1776 in an unspecified role in *The Cozeners*. While playing some years at Bath in winters and at the Haymarket in summers, he added to his repertoire such parts as Launcelot in *The Merchant of Venice*, the title role in *Midas*, Wingrave in Colman's *The Suicide*, Justice Woodcock in *Love in a Village* (**182**) and Jerry Sneak in *The Mayor of Garratt.* For his first appearance at Covent Garden on 24 September 1779 he played Touchstone in *As You Like It.* In the 1780s at Covent Garden and the Haymarket this busy comedian acted at least 130 different parts, until worn down by overwork and overdrinking he died on 30 October 1790 at the age of 41 and was buried at St Paul, Covent Garden, between Dr Arne and Ned Shuter. He was a talented and creative comic actor. He had a face that enabled him to be irresistibly funny. His style of singing produced roars of laughter. Edwin was celebrated for his occasional songs 'in character,' and several collections of anecdotes, including *Edwin's Jests* and *Edwin's Pills to Purge Melancholy*, were published.

Edwin lived for some 20 years with his

common law wife Sarah Walmsley, who acted in London as Mrs Edwin. Their uneasy relationship produced four sons and a daughter, including John Edwin 'the younger' (1769-1805), who was a fine comic actor during the last years of the eighteenth century and was much esteemed by the public. The younger Edwin married Elizabeth Richards, an actress who is noticed below as Elizabeth Rebecca Edwin (1771?-1854).

In addition to the six portraits of the elder John Edwin in the Garrick Club, the *BDA* lists another 25 pictures of him. No. **186** attributed to Roberts in *PGC* is now credited to C. R. Ryley and shows Edwin as Jerry Blackacre in *The Plain Dealer*. Similarly, **187** is also by Ryley and shows Edwin as Croaker in *The Good Natured Man*.

EDWIN, Mrs John, Elizabeth Rebecca née Richards 179-181

1771?-1854

Elizabeth Rebecca Richards was probably born about 1771, the daughter of the provincial actor William Talbot Richards and his first wife, an actress. Probably when she was a child and young woman she made appearances in the provinces with her parents. She was at the Theatre Royal in Richmond, Surrey, in 1790, but by the time she made her debut at the Haymarket Theatre on 20 June 1792 as Lucy in *The Virgin Unmask'd* she was married to the comedian John Edwin the younger (1769-1805). After having modest success in a few more appearances in London, Mrs Edwin went to act in Edinburgh, Dublin and York. Her husband died in 1805, and she was not re-engaged in London until the autumn of 1809, when she appeared on 14 October with the Drury Lane company playing at the Lyceum. She remained in that company for six years and then went back to the Crow Street Theatre, Dublin. Returning to London in 1818 she acted at the Olympic and had short engagements at Drury Lane, Covent Garden, the Adelphi and other places for several years. She lived on, in relative obscurity, for some 35 years, until she died at her lodgings in Chelsea on 3 August 1854. Though she never achieved distinction as an actress, when at Drury Lane between 1809 and 1815 she acted some major roles, such as Beatrice in *Much Ado about Nothing*, Lydia Languish in *The Rivals*, Fanny in *The Clandestine Marriage* and Miss Prue in *Love for Love*. She made an impression sufficient for De Wilde to have painted the three portraits of her in the Garrick Club. Other pictures of her are listed in her notice in the *BDA*.

EGERTON, Mrs Daniel, Sarah née Fisher 188

1782-1847

Sarah Egerton was born in 1782, the daughter of the Reverend Peter Fisher, rector of Little Torrington, Devonshire. She first appeared on the stage on 3 December 1803 at Bath as Emma in *The Marriage Promise*. She married the actor-manager Daniel Egerton in 1811. After other appearances at Bath and Birmingham, she made her debut at Covent Garden on 25 February 1811 as Juliet. She acted in melodramas mainly, and on 12 March 1816 she appeared as Meg Merrilies in *Guy Mannering*, the role in which De Wilde depicts her (**188**). Portraits of her as Madge Wildfire in *The Heart of* Midlothian were painted by Brooks, Cruikshank and Drummond; she first acted that role at the Surrey Theatre on 13 January 1819. Sarah Egerton continued to appear in London, at Covent Garden, Drury Lane and Sadler's Wells; at the last, in 1821, she was a great success in the title role in *Joan of Arc*. After the death of her husband in 1835 she retired from the stage. Mrs Egerton died at Chelsea on 3 August 1847 and was buried in Chelsea churchyard.

ELLICK, Peter 892

b. 1938

Peter Ellick, who is identified as No. 48 in Gilroy's scene of the Garrick Club Outing, was born in St Helena on 24 April 1938. He was at the Travellers for a short spell before he joined the Garrick Club staff on 24 September 1959. He has spent extended periods of instruction in vineyards in Champagne, Burgundy and Bordeaux, and he has served expertly as head wine steward for many years.

ELLIOTT, Frederic Boileau 793

d. 1881

The barrister Frederic Boileau Elliott, who was elected to the Garrick Club in February 1866, is shown as No. 34 in O'Neil's painting of members in the Billiards Room in 1869. He died in January 1881.

ELLISTON, Robert William
1774-1831 **189-192, G0990**
The son of a watchmaker, Robert William Elliston was born on 7 April 1774 in Orange Street, Bloomsbury. The boy's uncle, the master of Sidney College, Oxford, placed young William in St Paul's School at the age of nine, and it was supposed that the boy was destined for the clergy. But Robert showed an early interest in the stage and was acting in school plays at Mme Cotterille's academy in the Strand by 1790. He made his real debut on 21 April 1791 at Bath under Dimond, playing Tressel in *Richard III.* The press was encouraging, and a few more performances in Bristol led to an engagement with Tate Wilkinson, manager of the York circuit. Elliston acted Eumenes in *Merope* at Leeds on 30 May 1792, causing Wilkinson to write that the lad was happily devoid of rant but needed more 'energy and variety.' The actor stayed on the York circuit for three seasons and learned over 40 roles but showed no great progress. He came to London and was introduced to and encouraged by John Philip Kemble, but Elliston evidently saw as his best opportunity a return engagement at Bath, where he remained until 1804.

He became a favourite with Bath audiences, did better than his fellows at benefits, and acted some 40 roles, many of them important, such as Macheath in *The Beggar's Opera*, Horatio in *The Fair Penitent*, Meadows in *The Deaf Lover*, Oroonoko and King Lear. He also acted at Bristol from 1793 to 1796 and found himself a wife: Elizabeth Randell (or Rundall, Rundell), a dancing teacher. During those years Elliston arranged to make appearances at the Haymarket in London: on 25 June 1796 he played Octavian in *The Mountaineers* (**192**) and Vapour in *My Grandmother* to approving reviews that especially praised his talent in comedy. Then he was Sheva in *The* Jew, Sir Edward Mortimer in *The Iron Chest* and Romeo, making himself much sought after by both main London theatres. In the autumn of 1796 he dickered with Sheridan at Drury Lane for £1000 to cover his forfeits if he disentangled himself from his contract at Bath. He also negotiated with Harris at Covent Garden, who was willing to have Elliston act 12 evenings during 1796-97 at Covent Garden while still keeping his full-season contract at Bath with Dimond. Elliston accepted the latter arrangement and became known as 'The Fortnight Actor.' This became a pattern for the rest of his career: he regularly involved himself in multiple engagements in and out of London and, in addition, began to build a complicated career in theatre management. Like Bottom the weaver he liked being up to his neck in everything. The real bottom line, however, may have been money, which Elliston proved very adept at getting and spending.

While still performing all over the country, including London but with Bath and Bristol as his home base, Elliston in the late 1790s and early 1800s became increasingly involved in management. He may have begun about 1797 at Wells and Shepton Mallet. During the early years of the new century he tried fruitlessly to get patents to open new theatres in London and in Oxford. Then, in 1809, Elliston leased the Royal Circus on the south bank of the Thames and, after refurbishing it, produced melodramas and pantomimes. Also in 1809 he bought and renovated the theatre at Croydon and took over the Manchester Theatre. He petitioned the House of Commons for a proper licence and then a patent for the Royal Circus so he could produce regular plays and not just musical pieces, but all his efforts came to naught. He altered the Royal Circus and changed its name to the Surrey Theatre, presenting musical versions of such plays as *The Beaux' Stratagem.*

Next, along with acting engagements here and there, he tried to work out a joint scheme with the management of the new Drury Lane but failed; so he settled for an acting contract which had him open the new house on 10 October 1812 playing Hamlet. While he continued acting there through 1814-15 he busied himself in his off-duty time running the Surrey Theatre, buying the Olimpic Pavilion in Wych Street and almost buying three other properties: Vauxhall Gardens in London, the Crow Street Theatre in Dublin and the Edinburgh Theatre. In 1813 he leased the Birmingham Theatre and later the Leicester Theatre in London. He managed the Northampton playhouse for a short period in 1818. Elliston was accused of being a dabbler in everything and a master of nothing, and the *Theatrical Inquisitor* of 1813 castigated him for bustling through his roles onstage and disgusting audiences by neglecting his talent and real potential.

Elliston had long wanted the lesseeship of Drury Lane, and in August 1819 he secured it. The lease was for 14 years at an annual rent of £10,200, but the terms also prohibited Elliston from engaging professionally in any other London theatre. He had the wit to hire James Winston as his assistant, and chiefly because of Winston's good sense the new Drury Lane management was able to survive as long as it did. But in 1826 the overreacher reported that he had lost £30,000 and returned control of the theatre to a committee of proprietors. On 11 May 1826 he collapsed acting Falstaff in *1 Henry IV*, and on 10 December, physically and financially broken, Elliston declared bankruptcy. He tried to revive his management career, becoming proprietor again at the Surrey, but he suffered a stroke on 6 July 1831 and died two days later. (*BDA*) [EAL]

ELMORE, Alfred RA **793**
1815-1881
The painter Alfred Elmore, shown as No. 31 in O'Neil's painting of a game in the Garrick Club Billiards Room, was born at Clonakilty, Cork, in 1815, and at the age of 19 he exhibited his first picture at the Royal Academy. He became a member of the Royal Academy in 1877, and died in London on 24 January 1881. He was best known for his semi-historical works, including 'Mary Queen of Scots,' 'After the Fall,' and 'Lucretia Borgia.' Elmore became a member of the Garrick Club in February 1863.

ELMY, Mary née Morse **49**
1712-1792
Born Mary Morse in 1712, she may have been performing at the Haymarket Theatre and Drury Lane by 1732. In January 1734 she became Mrs (William?) Elmy; she appeared under her new name on 31 January 1734 as Charlotte in *Oroonoko*. After several more seasons in London she went to Dublin, making her Irish debut at the Aungier Street Theatre as Mrs Sullen in *The Stratagem* in October 1738. In January 1747 she was back at Drury Lane, where she remained for several seasons, establishing her line of leading and secondary ladies, including Indiana in *The Conscious Lovers*, Desdemona in *Othello*, Mrs Strickland in *The Suspicious Husband*, Dorinda in *The Stratagem*, Octavia in *All for Love* and Hero in *Much Ado about Nothing*. In October 1750 she took her repertoire to Covent Garden, where she was engaged for the remainder of her career. Among her new characters was Gertrude in *Hamlet* (**47**), a role she acted for the first time on 11 October 1751; *The Rosciad of C-v-nt G-rd-n* (1762) praised her performance. Other roles included Belinda in *The Old Bachelor*, the Duchess of York in *Richard III*, Portia in *Julius Caesar*, Regan in *King Lear* and Lady Brute in *The Provok'd Wife*. Mrs Elmy retired from the stage in April 1762. She was accounted an actress of the second rank. After her retirement she lived some 30 years, until her death on 1 April 1792 at the age of 80, in Knightsbridge, where according to her will she seems to have lived in some comfort. (*BDA*)

EMERY, John **193-199, 477, B162**
1777-1822
The comedian John Emery was born in Sunderland, near Durham, on 22 December 1777, the son of the actors Mackle Emery (d. 1825) and his wife (d. 1827). As a youngster John played the violin in the orchestra at the Brighton Theatre and led the band at Plymouth. Though he seemed destined to be a musician, he decided for the stage, appearing in 1792 at Brighton as Old Crazy in the farce *Peeping Tom*. After some touring and three years in the York company, he received an engagement at Covent Garden, where he made his debut as Frank Oatland in *A Cure for the Heartache* and acquitted himself well. He became an important acquisition, especially in roles of rustic simplicity, and in his first season he offered a large number of characters. He was described as a 'young but very promising performer.' In his second season at Covent Garden he was especially good as

Gibbet in *The Beaux' Stratagem*. In the summer of 1800 he made his first appearance at the Haymarket Theatre on 13 June as Zekiel Homespun in *The Heir at Law*.

Emery remained at Covent Garden during the winter seasons through 1821-22, creating a number of original roles, Dan in *John Bull* (**193**), Tyke in *School of Reform* (**196**) and Dandy Dinmont in *Guy Mannering* among them. He first acted Farmer Ashfield in *Speed the Plough* (**194**) at the Haymarket in the summer of 1801. After the 1821-22 season at Covent Garden, Emery engaged at the English Opera House for the summer. His last performance was as Giles in *The Miller's Maid* on 3 July 1822. He became ill and died of pneumonia on 25 July at his home in Hyde Street, Bloomsbury, and was buried in St Andrew, Holborn, on 1 August. He left his widow Ann (née Thompson) and seven children. Several benefits for his family were subscribed to by his admirers and former colleagues.

Emery had kept up his interest in field sports – especially boxing – and pubs. In addition to being an accomplished musician, he was a talented artist who exhibited some 19 pictures at the Royal Academy, of which he was an honorary member. Hazlitt acclaimed his acting: 'It is impossible to praise it sufficiently because there is never any opportunity of finding fault with it.' The press called him 'one of the most real, hearty, and fervid of actors.' The *BDA* (5: 89-90) lists 26 pictures of him, including the nine in the Garrick Club. (*BDA*)

EMERY, Winifred 200

1862-1924

Winifred Emery was born at Manchester on 1 August 1862, the daughter of the actor Samuel Anderson Emery. Her grandfather was the excellent comedian John Emery (1777-1822). She made her first appearance as the child Geraldine in *The Green Bushes* at the Amphitheatre, Liverpool, in 1870, and appeared, again as a child, in London at the Princess's Theatre in a pantomime on 23 December 1874. Her first adult role in London was at the Imperial Theatre in *Man Is Not Perfect* in April 1879. For several years she acted in and out of London and in July 1881 began to play Annette in Henry Irving's production of *The Bells* at the Lyceum. She made two tours with Irving to the United States and was at Drury Lane and the Vaudeville in 1889-90; at the latter she acted, among other roles, Lady Teazle in *The School for Scandal* (**200**). During the remainder of her busy career on the London stage – interrupted by illness between 1902 and 1905 – she was seen in numerous roles, among which were Beatrice in *Much Ado about Nothing* at Her Majesty's (January 1905, with Beerbohm Tree), Kate in *She Stoops to Conquer* at the Waldorf (January 1906), Mistress Ford in *The Merry Wives of Windsor* at Her Majesty's (April 1908), Esther in *Caste* at the St James's (July 1909), Lady Franklin in *Money* at Drury Lane (May 1911), Miss Dyott in *The School Mistress* at the Vaudeville (February 1913) and the Fairy Berylune in *The Betrothal* (her last role) at the Gaiety (January 1921). She was married to the actor Cyril Maude (1862-1951, *q.v.*). She died on 15 July 1924. Winifred Emery had been one of the most popular actresses of her day.

ESSEX, Miss

See Mrs Edward Anthony ROCK

ESTEN, Mrs James, Harriet Pye, later Mrs Scott-Waring née Bennett 201

1765?-1865

Harriet Esten was born about 1765, probably in Tooting, Surrey, where at the time her mother was reputedly housekeeper and mistress to Admiral Sir Thomas Pye. Contemporary memoirs contain colourful stories about the early life of her mother, Agnes Maria Bennett (d. 1808), author of several popular novels. But the *DNB* states that 'there is no evidence of her birth, her parentage, or her condition.' Supposedly her mother was the daughter of a Bristol grocer named Evans and early on married Mr Bennett, a tanner from Brednock. They soon separated, and Mrs Bennett became a slop-seller in Wych Street, London. While working at a chandler's shop in Borough High Street she met Admiral Pye. Eventually she had two children by him: Thomas Pye Bennett, a naval officer, and Harriet Pye Bennett, the subject of this notice.

Harriet Bennett was married to James Esten in Lower Tooting on 24 February 1784. He was a lieutenant in the Royal Navy, and soon after the marriage he had to seek refuge in France because of his financial losses in business undertakings. Left with two children, Harriet Esten turned to the stage, and, probably with her mother's assistance, was engaged at the Smock Alley Theatre, Dublin, in 1786 and then in the Bath-Bristol company. She made her debut at Bristol on 19 June 1786 as Alicia in *Jane Shore* and was subsequently seen as Roxalana in *The Sultan*, Beatrice in *Much Ado about Nothing*, Widow Belmour in *The Way to Keep Him* and the title role in *Isabella*. Successful engagements at Edinburgh and York earned her a London debut at Covent Garden on 20 October 1790 as Rosalind in *As You Like It*, followed by Indiana in *The Conscious Lovers* on 23 October. She received excellent notices and in her first season at Covent Garden took on such capital roles as Ophelia, Monimia in *The Orphan* and Belvidera in *Venice Preserv'd*. She remained at Covent Garden through 1793-94, while her mother managed on her behalf the Edinburgh Theatre, the lease of which Harriet had secured the previous year. At Edinburgh in July 1794 she gave birth to a daughter by the Duke of Hamilton, who then settled her in an elegant house in Half-Moon Street, Piccadilly, with £1000 a year. Her mother joined her to share in her 'magnificent elevation.' When Harriet's husband returned from St Domingo in 1797 with a fortune of some £200,000, he was granted a divorce. The Duke of Hamilton died in August 1798, leaving her an annuity of £3000.

Harriett Esten acted one more season at Edinburgh, in 1802-3. On 15 October 1812 she become the third wife of Major John Scott-Waring, who had previously been married to the actress Maria Hughes. Waring died in May 1819, and Harriet lived another 46 years. She died on 29 April 1865, at No 36, Queen's Gate Terrace, Kensington, at about the age of 100. As an actress, she was placed 'next to Miss Farren in elegant walks of comedy' by F. G. Waldon, who also called her a 'little enchanting made-up piece of elegance.' She had been in the flowering of her career 'a beautiful and agreeable actress.' Evidently Harriett was not particularly intelligent. The shrewdness of her mother had managed her professional and personal life. (*BDA*)

EVANS, Dame Edith Mary 202, B9-B12
1888-1976

One of the greatest English actresses of the twentieth century, Edith Evans was born in London on 8 February 1888, the daughter of Edward and Ellen Evans. After attending St Michael's School in London, she made her first appearance on the London stage on 10 December 1912 at the King's Hall, Covent Garden, as Cressida in a revival of *Troilus and Cressida*, given by the English Stage Society and directed by William Poel. In a career that lasted into the 1970s, she excelled in numerous major roles, especially in comedies, at theatres and festivals throughout Britain. Among her finest parts were Lady Utterwood in the first production of Shaw's *Heartbreak House* at the Court Theatre in April 1921; Mistress Page in *The Merry Wives of Windsor* (December 1923) and Millimant in *The Way of the World* (February 1924) at the Lyric, Hammersmith; the Nurse in *Romeo and Juliet* at the Old Vic, 1925-26; Mrs Sullen in *The Beaux' Stratagem* at the Lyric, Hammersmith, January 1927; Florence Nightingale in *The Lady with a Lamp* at the Arts and the Garrick, 1929; Irina Arcadina in *The Sea Gull* at the New Theatre, 1936; Lady Fidget in *The Country Wife* at the Old Vic, October-December 1936; Lady Wishfort in *The Way of the World* (October 1948) and Mme Ranevsky in *The Cherry Orchard* (November 1948) with the Old Vic company at the New Theatre; and Judith Bliss in *Hay Fever* at the National Theatre, 1964. Perhaps her greatest role was Lady Bracknell in *The Importance of Being Earnest*, which she first acted at the Globe in January 1939. She first appeared as Cleopatra at the Old Vic in 1925-26, but the production in which she is pictured by Topolski (**202**) was at the Piccadilly in 1946. Among her memorable films were *The Queen of* Spades (1948), *The Importance of Being Earnest* (1952), *Look Back in Anger* (1959), *Tom Jones* (1963) and *The Whisperers* (1967).

She was made DBE in 1946 and received honorary doctorate degrees from London, Oxford and Cambridge universities. In 1925 she had married George Booth, who died in 1935. Dame Edith died in London on 14 October 1976.

EVANS, John Marten Llewellyn CBE 892
b. 1909
'Jack' Evans was born on 9 June 1909, the son of Marten Llewelyn Evans and Edith Helena (née Lile). He was educated at Rugby School and Trinity College, Oxford. He was the Official Solicitor to the Supreme Court of Judicature from 1950 to 1970, became the Assistant Master in Lunacy in 1950, and was Vice-Chairman of Austin Reed Group Ltd from 1969 to 1977. Evans joined the Garrick Club in March 1964 and resigned in December 1984. He is shown with his wife Winifred Emily Evans in Gilroy's scene of the Garrick Club Outing in 1967 (**892**, Nos. 21 and 22). (*WW2002*)

F

FAIRS, John
See Sir John HARE

FARLEY, Charles 203-205, 216
1771-1859
Born in London in 1771, Charles Farley was a call boy at Covent Garden Theatre before he made his stage debut there as Prince Edward in *Richard III,* at the age of 13, on 11 October 1784. By the 1790s he grew to adult parts and during his 50 years at that theatre his repertoire was greater than that of any actor of his time. Many of his hundreds of roles were short and anonymous, consisting of footmen and shepherds and dancing in choruses, but some were Shakespearean clowns and fools (Cloten, Osric, Roderigo) and, especially, leading roles in melodramas and pantomimes. His portrayal of the dumb Francisco in *The Tale of Mystery* (**203**) was in the words of John Doran 'as eloquent and touching as though he had a hundred tongues all tuned to tell with irresistible force a tale of suffering.' Canton in *The Clandestine Marriage* (shown in Clint's canvas **216**) was one of his best French parts, according to Doran, and in his representation of similar fop roles, like Jessamy in *Bon Ton* (**204**), 'his voice assisted him, for he had a curious bubbling sound, which he could less control as his very remarkable nose grew larger and larger.' His best roles were Grindoff in *The Miller and his Men* and the title role in *Timour and the Tartar.* By 1801-2 he was devising ballets and pantomimes for Covent Garden. Among his popular successes were *Raymond and Agnes* (March 1797) and *The Magic Oak* (January 1799). He made significant contributions to numerous other pantomimes to which others had their names attached. Joseph Knight in the *DNB* claimed that as a theatrical machinist 'in his time he was without equal.'

Farley retired from the stage in 1834 and died at his house, No 42, Ampthill Square, Hampstead Road, on 28 January 1859. Farley was a promoter and staunch supporter of the Covent Garden Theatrical Fund. He was one of the original members of the Garrick Club in 1831. (*BDA*)

FARMER, Jane
See Jane POWELL

FARREN, Elizabeth later Countess of Derby 206-208, B14
1762-1829

Elizabeth Farren was born on 6 July 1762 (we know not where), the daughter of George and Margaret Farren, both performers. Eliza's first stage appearance was apparently as a child, and perhaps it was in Salisbury, perhaps at Bath. Her father died about 1770, leaving his wife with four daughters; by late 1773 they were with James Whitley's company in the Midlands. Whitley tried to convince Mrs Farren not to pursue a career in acting, and he said Eliza (he called her Betsy) 'seems to possess every natural requisite' but would be better off in the service of a respectable family. The Farrens did not follow his advice but joined Joseph Younger's troupe at Liverpool, where, at the age of 13, Eliza appeared as Rosetta in *Love in a Village*. She was recommended by Younger to Colman, the summer manager of the Haymarket Theatre in London, where on 9 June 1777 she acted Miss Hardcastle in *She Stoops to Conquer*. The critics found her somewhat lacking in grace, energy and force and they thought her voice a bit sharp, but she was 'more perfect' than most actresses from the provinces. Her genteel, expressive face was to turn her into one of the most popular impersonators of modish ladies on the London stage.

Miss Farren also acted that summer Maria in *The Citizen*, Rosetta, Miss Tittup in *Bon Ton* and Rosina in *The Spanish Barber*. David Garrick, then retired, came to see her and wrote a note to Colman on 2 September 1777, saying he found her a 'most promising Piece.' He hoped she would stay in London, for he 'could teach her a capital part in Comedy, ay & tragedy too, that should drive half our actresses mad – she is much too fine Stuff to be worn & soil'd at Manchester & Liverpool.' But Eliza spent the winter of 1777-78 in those provincial towns and the summer of 1778 at the Haymarket again; in September she acted at Covent Garden and beginning in October she was at Drury Lane, playing such important roles as Charlotte Rusport in *The West Indian*, Constantia in *The Chances*, Nell in *The Devil to Pay*, Millamant in *The Way of the World*, Clarinda in *The Suspicious Husband* (**206**) and Ann Lovely in *A Bold Stroke for a Wife*. Also acting at Drury Lane at the time were William and Mary Farren, evidently not related to Elizabeth.

Miss Farren found Drury Lane her home base for the following 17 years, until her retirement in 1797, but she kept acting during the summers at the Haymarket through 1788, and occasionally she toured to Dublin, York and other provincial venues. It was during the 1780s that she reached her peak of popularity in her favourite line: fine ladies. Though she was seen in a great variety of plays and musicals, she succeeded Mrs Abington in the kind of elegant, aristocratic, fashionable female characters that Anne Oldfield had made the talk of the town earlier in the century. Eliza's salary by 1789-90 was £17 weekly, near the top of the scale but several pounds less than Mrs Billington. Thomas Lawrence's full-length portrait dating about 1790 captures that charm and beauty that made her the model for ladies of quality. Among her many roles were Juliet, Statira in *Alexander the Great*, Lady Betty Modish in *The Careless Husband*, Indiana in *The Conscious Lovers*, Lady Teazle in *The School for Scandal*, Mrs Ford in *The Merry Wives of Windsor*, Lady Brute in *The Provok'd Wife*, Beatrice in *Much Ado about Nothing* and Julia in *The Rivals*. Notices of Miss Farren often congratulated her liveliness, her polish and her 'exquisite representations,' but critics also found her affected and vain – typical qualities of the characters she so often played. Did life imitate art? She is reported to have been at times temperamental and obstinate, and John Philip Kemble reported his problems with her when he managed Drury Lane. She seems, in short, to have behaved like a stage queen.

But Elizabeth Farren dazzled audiences, especially men, with her beauty and bewitching ways, and no one was more taken with her than Edward, the twelfth Earl of Derby. He and she carried on a thinly-veiled affair, and when his wife died on 14 March 1797 Eliza retired from the stage (at age 35), making her last appearance as Lady Teazle on 8 April to a crammed Drury Lane. She and Derby were married on 1 May and led a relatively placid life; the couple had three children. Elizabeth, Countess of Derby died on 23 April 1829, her husband on 21 October 1834. (*BDA*) [EAL]

FARREN, William the elder 209-211, 682
1754-1795
Born in 1754, the son of a tallow chandler in Clerkenwell, William Farren was apprenticed to a banker, according to one source, or to a tinman, according to another. In any case, he was attracted to the stage, influenced by his friendship with the actor Richard Yates, who took William as an apprentice. It is likely that his stage career began in Yates's company in Birmingham as early as 1774. Again helped by Yates, Farren made his London debut at Drury Lane, on 20 March 1775 as Jason in *Medea*. One critic thought William's appearance was decent but hoped he would gain variety and expressive powers and learn to walk erect. Farren's engagement at Drury Lane lasted until 1784 and consisted chiefly of playing such secondary roles as Salarino in *The Merchant of Venice*, Macduff in *Macbeth*, Tybalt and Paris in *Romeo and Juliet*, the Ghost and Horatio in *Hamlet*, Sebastian in *Twelfth Night* and Buckingham in *Richard III* – to name a few of his Shakespearean characters. His salary in 1779-80 and the following years was a modest £4 per week.

Farren (no relation to the actress Elizabeth Farren) also filled in at Covent Garden on occasion and acted in the provinces, but his Drury Lane career was standing still, and in 1784-85 he joined the Covent Garden company, playing first Othello on 27 September 1784 and then following it with some of his old Drury Lane characters; he did not show much progress by his change in company. Over the years he was given occasional leading roles – Captain Absolute in *The Rivals* in 1792, for example – but most of his career was spent as a useful secondary player. William Farren died of pneumonia on 9 May 1795 at the age of 41. He left a common law wife, Mary, née Orton, and several children, one of whom, William Farren the younger (see below), had a considerable career as an actor and manager. (*BDA*) [EAL]

FARREN, William the Younger 212-216
1786-1861
William Farren, the second actor of that name, was born in London on 15 May 1786, the second son of the actor William Farren (1754-1795) and the actress Mary Mansell Orton. For details of the large Farren family that lived comfortably in Gower Street, see the elder William Farren's notice above. The younger William Farren attended Dr Barrow's school in Soho, and having inherited some £6000, in 1806 he ventured upon the stage at the Theatre Royal, Plymouth, under the management of his brother Percival, as Archy MacSarcasm in *Love à la Mode*. He then went to Dublin, where he acted for some ten years before he returned to make his London debut at Covent Garden on 10 September 1818 as Sir Peter Teazle in *The School for Scandal* (**215**). A week later, on 18 September, he appeared as Lord Ogleby in *The Clandestine Marriage* (**216**). Subsequently he became one of the leading actors of his day, excelling mainly in light comedy roles like Sir Anthony Absolute, Lovegold in *The Miser*, Sir Fretful Plagiary in *The Critic* and Sir Andrew Aguecheek. He also played at the Haymarket. Farren remained at Covent Garden some ten years, until he went over to Drury Lane on 16 October 1828 to act Sir Peter Teazle. There he stayed until 1837, offering a wide range of parts, including some in tragedy, such as Polonius, Kent and Casca. He returned to Covent Garden for several years and in the early 1840s joined Benjamin Webster's company at the Haymarket, where he also served as stage manager. While acting the title role in *Old Parr* on 24 October 1843 he suffered a stroke, which paralysed one side of his body and left his speech indistinct. Nevertheless, he continued to act at the Haymarket for some ten years, until he became manager of the Strand Theatre and then the Olympic Theatre from September 1850 to September 1853. He took leave of the stage on 16 July 1855 at the Haymarket, playing a scene from *The Clandestine Marriage*. He died at his house, No 28, Brompton Square, on 24 September 1861. It is said that Farren was the best representative of his time of old men in comedies.

By an unknown woman (his first wife?) Farren had two sons: Henry Farren (1826-1860), who acted in London and America and is noticed in the *DNB*, and his elder brother William Farren (1825-1908), who is noticed below. Our subject married late in life, in 1856, the actress Harriet

Diddear Faucit (d. June 1857), who by her previous marriage to the actor Saville Faucit (d. 1853) was the mother of the nineteenth-century actress Helen Faucit (1817-1898).

FARREN, William **217**
1825-1908
William Farren, the third actor of that name, was born at No 23, Brompton Square, London, on 28 September 1825. He was the son of William Farren (1786-1861) by an unknown woman, perhaps his first wife; and he was also the elder brother of the actor Henry Farren (1826-1860). Our subject began his career singing in the Antient Concerts in 1848, and after some provincial training and using the name of Forrester, he made his London stage debut at the Strand Theatre (under his father's management) in September 1849. On 5 March he acted Moses in the premiere of a version of *The Vicar of Wakefield.* Moving with his father to the new Olympic later that year, he assumed his real name. In January 1852 he acted Cassio to his brother Henry's Othello. Subsequently, at the Haymarket, the St James's and the Vaudeville he was seen in a number of roles mainly in light comedy until the 1870s when he assumed more mature parts. His portrayal of Sir Peter Teazle in a revival of *The School for Scandal* at the Vaudeville on 4 February 1882 was favourably compared with the acting of that role by his more famous father. Other roles in London in which he excelled were Sir Anthony Absolute, Mr Hardcastle, Lord Ogleby in *The Clandestine Marriage* and Sir Harcourt Courtly in *London Assurance.* After 1896 he acted infrequently, and upon retirement in 1898 he moved to Rome. He died in Siena on 25 September 1906 and was buried in that city. Farren had become a member of the Garrick Club in June 1864 but resigned in March 1874. By his wife Josephine Elizabeth Davies, whom he married in 1846, he had a daughter (who did not become an actress) and a son, William Percival Farren (1853-1937), who also acted in London. (*DNB*)

FAWCETT, John **218-224**
1768-1837
The actor and dramatist John Fawcett (the younger), who is represented in seven pictures in the Garrick Club collection, was born on 29 August 1768, the son of the London actors John Fawcett (d.1793) and his wife Sarah, née Plaw (fl. 1781-1796). Both parents are noticed in the *BDA.* The younger Fawcett was enrolled at St Paul's School and then was apprenticed to a linen draper, but, despite his father's objections, he was lured to the stage. He made some appearances in the provinces before playing at York, where he acted Young Norval in *Douglas* in May 1787. He earned a reputation as a tragedian on the York circuit, and married a fellow performer, Susan Mills (née Moore), the widow of the actor John Mills (d. 1787). Fawcett was signed on for the 1791-92 season at Covent Garden, where he made his debut on 21 September 1791 as Caleb in *He Wou'd Be a Soldier.* At Covent Garden he ably filled the roles left open by the recent death of the comedian John Edwin. He quickly became a favourite at that theatre, where he remained until 1830, performing numerous parts, among his best being Caleb Quotem (**219**), Robin Roughhead in *Fortune's Frolic*, Job Thornberry in *John Bull* (**220**), Dr Pangloss in *The Heir at Law* and Lingo in *The Agreeable Surprise.* He was the original Bartholo in *The Barber of Seville* on 13 October 1818.

For some years Fawcett also was involved in the stage management of Covent Garden, a position he held until 1829. Fawcett served as treasurer and trustee of the Covent Garden Theatrical Fund for many years. He acted successfully for the younger Colman at the Haymarket for many summers, and also appeared at several provincial theatres. For almost 40 years he was a leading actor in low comedy and rustic characters, specializing in those that required singing. He was described as a brusque and bluff fellow, ideally suited for farce and ridicule. He took his leave of his public on 30 May 1830, acting Captain Copp in *Charles II* (**224**), and then retired to 'a very pretty little cottage at Botley, near Southampton.' He died on 13 March 1837 and was the first to be buried in the local church for which he had raised a building subscription. John Fawcett became a member of the Garrick Club in February 1833 but resigned in February 1837. In addition to those pictures of him at the Garrick Club, a number of other portraits of him were painted and engraved.

After the death of his first wife Susan Moore in 1797, Fawcett married the actress Anne Gaudry, daughter of the actor Joseph Gaudry; she retired from acting and became wardrobe mistress at Covent Garden and later worked in that capacity at Drury Lane as late as 1821-22. She died in 1849. None of Fawcett's children seem to have become performers. (*BDA*)

FENWICK, Elizabeth
See James Frederick Trevor FENWICK

FENWICK, James Frederick Trevor
1901-1979 **176, 892**
Trevor Fenwick (fig 1 in Gilroy's painting, **892**) was born in Newcastle-upon-Tyne on 8 March 1901, the eldest son of Fred and Margaret Fenwick, and was educated at Pembroke College, Cambridge. He was Chairman of Fenwick Limited (on Bond Street and elsewhere) from 1961 to 1972. Fenwick became a member of the Garrick Club in 1955. He died on 1 January 1979. He married Elizabeth Neldsum (fig 3 in Gilroy's painting) at London in June 1930. She was born on 22 October 1907 in Pitlochry, Perthshire, the second daughter of Andrew and June Neldsum. Educated at Queen Margaret's School, Scarborough, she served in British intelligence activities during the Second World War. She died in London on 8 July 2000.

FENWICK, Peter Trevor OBE **892**
b. 1935
Peter Trevor Fenwick, called Trevor Fenwick Jr in Gilroy's picture of the Garrick Club Outing (fig 25), is the second son of Trevor Fenwick (above) and was born at Newcastle-upon-Tyne in 1935. He was Chairman of the British Home Society from 1982 to 1992. His elder brother John James Fenwick, who was not present at the Garrick Club Outing, was born in 1932 at Newcastle-upon-Tyne, and was Chairman of Fenwick Limited from 1979 to 1997; he became a member of the Garrick Club in 1975.

FISHER, Clara later
Mrs James G. Maeder **225, 787**
1811-1898
Clara Fisher was born in London in 1811, the daughter of an auctioneer and librarian. As a child prodigy she appeared at Drury Lane at the age of six in such roles as Richard III, Shylock and Young Norval in *Douglas*. Drummond's portrait (**225**) represents her at that time. She acted Little Pickle (**787**) in *The Spoiled Child* at Drury Lane on 3 December 1822, when she was eleven. She was very popular and subsequently was seen as Ophelia, Viola, Lady Teazle, in the title role in G. H. Payne's *Clari*, and in contemporary comedies and musical plays. After her marriage to the conductor James Maeder in 1844 she retired. An attempted return to the stage in 1880s met with little success. When young she was, according to Ireland, 'below middle height, and just reaching but not exceeding a delicate plumpness.' In Drummond's picture she wears 'rolls, or puffs,' a style adopted by the fashionable young ladies. Her brother John and two sisters, Jane (Mrs George Vernon) and Amelia, also acted and appeared in New York in mid-century. *See* the *Autobiography of Clara Fisher Maeder* (1897), published the year before her death in 1898.

FISHER, Mrs John Abraham
See Elizabeth POWELL

FISHER, Sarah
See Mrs Daniel EGERTON

FITZWILLIAM, Fanny Elizabeth
née Copeland **226**
1801-1854
She was born in 1801 in a dwelling attached to the Dover theatre, where her father Robert Copeland was manager. She appeared on stage about the age of three in *The Stranger*, and at 12 she played the piano in a concert at Margate. Then, after appearing for a few years as a leading actress at Dover, in 1817 she made her London debut at the Haymarket Theatre, appearing as Lucy in *The Review* and Cicely in *The Beehive*. Fanny acted at the Olympic and Surrey theatres and on 5 December 1821 made her first appearance at Drury Lane, as Fanny in *Maid or Wife*. After engagements in Dublin and the provinces, she appeared at the Adelphi in plays of John Baldwin Buckstone, and in 1832 she took over management of Sadler's

Wells. In 1837 she went to America, where she enjoyed a great success. Back in England by 1844, she acted again in provincial towns. Fanny then returned to the Haymarket, where she was engaged until her death from cholera on 11 November 1854 and was buried in Kensal Green Cemetery. Her marriage to the actor Edward Fitzwilliam (1788-1852) produced the musical director and composer Edward Francis Fitzwilliam and the actress Kathleen Fitzwilliam. An actress of the Mrs Jordan school, Mrs Fitzwilliam was excellent in country girls and Irish peasants. She also was highly regarded as Lady Teazle and as Starlight Bess in Buckstone's *Flowers of the Forest.* At the time of her death she was betrothed to Buckstone. (*DNB*)

FLADGATE, Francis 227, 793

1799-1892

The barrister Francis Fladgate was elected to the Garrick Club in 1832. In his *Ace of Clubs*, Richard Hough regards him as one of the 'founder' members. He inherited a 'modest fortune' from his father, an attorney in Essex. Fladgate practiced little law and spent a great deal of his time at the Garrick during his some 60 years as a member. Called 'Papa' Fladgate because he guided the Club through its early difficult years, he revelled in telling stories of his associations with Kemble, Siddons, and members of the School of Garrick. When he died in 1892 he had spent most of his money on acts of kindness and generosity. He was described by fellow member the Reverend Richard Barham as 'one of the most polished gentlemen and good-natured persons I ever met.'

FLADGATE, Sir William Francis 228

1853-1937

William Francis Fladgate was born on 23 April 1853, the son of William Mark Fladgate (d. 1889). Sir William was Chairman of the London Power Company and of Charing Cross Electricity Supply Company, and he was a Director of the Phoenix Insurance Company and the Law Debenture Corporation. Fladgate was awarded the Medaille du Roi Albert, King of Belgium, for his service to Belgian lawyers during World War I. He was knighted in 1932. He became a member of the Garrick Club in February 1878. Sir William died in 1937. His father, William Mark Fladgate became a Garrick Club member in June 1865; he died in September 1889.

FOOT, Rt Hon Michael PC G1020

b. 1913

The prominent politician and writer Michael Foot was born on 23 July 1913, the son of the Rt Hon Isaac Foote, PC. He was educated at Wadham College, Oxford (President Oxford Union 1933), and soon after entered politics, serving in Parliament by 1945. He rose in the Labour Party: Lord President of the Council and Leader of the House of Commons, 1976-1979; Leader of the Opposition, 1980-1983; Deputy Leader of the Labour Party 1976-1980 and Leader 1980-1983. Foot also was sometime editor of the *Tribune* and *Evening Standard* and was a political columnist on the *Daily Herald,* 1944-1964. He was an Hon Fellow of Wadham College. Among his 17 books are *Trial of Mussolini* (1943), *Full Speed Ahead* (1950), *Parliament in Danger* (1959), *The Politics of Paradise* (1988) and *H. G.: the History of Mr Wells* (1995). (*WWW)*

FOOTE, Samuel 229

1721-1777

Samuel Foote was christened on 27 January 1721 at St Mary, Truro, the son of Samuel and Eleanor Foote. The child's father was, among other things, a lawyer, his mother the daughter of a baronet. The younger Samuel attended a grammar school and then Worcester College, Oxford, but it was not long before the lad's independent spirit and eccentricity lost him his scholarship. He tried law at the Inner Temple but never registered formally and preferred spending his inheritance and displaying his wit at the Grecian Coffee House. To make money he published an exploitation of a scandal on his mother's side of the family – the murder of Sir John Dinely Goodere by his brother.

Much of his life was a series of ventures or adventures: a partnership with a swindling brewer and seller of small beer, a brief marriage in 1741 to a girl whose dowry and patience he quickly spent, a long series of brief engagements at major and minor theatres in London and Dublin as an actor with mimic skills and a venomous tongue, authorship of a number of satirical comedies that scared the wits out of his subjects, publication of books on acting and drama, illegal stage productions pretending to be musical concerts or parties with free performances of plays, frequent wars of words in the press with opponents, on-again off-again friendships with the leading theatre professionals of his day, fortune telling in Dublin in 1758, procurement of a patent for the Haymarket Theatre in 1766, the refurbishing and managing of that old playhouse, inventive puppet productions, the operation of Edinburgh's Theatre Royal in 1770-71, libel suits brought against him by offended subjects of his satires, a successful suit brought by Foote in 1776 for accusations of homosexualty, and so on.

Foote's career in acting – the least of his several talents – began on 6 February 1744 at the Haymarket Theatre, where Charles Macklin presented a 'Concert of Music' followed by a performance of *Othello*, with Macklin as Iago and his acting student Foote (identified only as a young gentleman making his stage debut) in the title role. The performance was said by one paper to have received 'Universal Applause' and by another to be 'a masterpiece of burlesque,' and it is now impossible to tell just what came to pass. Foote over the years acted some important characters, such as Lord Foppington in *The Relapse*, Bayes in *The Rehearsal*, Sir Harry Wildair in *The Constant Couple*, Pierre in *Venice Preserv'd*, Sir Novelty Fashion in *Love's Last Shift*, Shylock in *The Merchant of Venice* and many comic roles in his own plays – Cadwallader in *The Author*, Mrs Cole in *The Minor*, and Major Sturgeon in *The Mayor of Garratt* being among the favourites.

His career as a writer consisted not only of academic works like *A Treatise on the Passions* (1747) and entertainments of all sorts but also comic puffs in the papers intended to drum up business at this theatre or that. His fertile mind seemed always to be creating some new tomfoolery or barbed satire like *Taste* or *Tea* or *Auction of Pictures* or *Dish of Chocolate*, most of which were regularly doctored by Foote to keep them topical. He attracted audiences partly because he was so unpredictable. Little David Garrick was, of course, one of his favourite targets. In 1769, for example, Garrick's Shakespeare Jubilee at Stratford, which was a disaster even without Foote's intervention, was a prime target for Foote's wit. He added mocking speeches to his performance of *The Devil upon Two Sticks*, and he planned a parody in rags of the lavishly costumed Jubilee procession Garrick mounted at Drury Lane after the Stratford event was rained out. When Foote announced that he planned on using a puppet of Garrick in his mockery of the Jubilee he was asked if the puppet was to be life-size, and he replied 'Oh no – not much above the size of Garrick.'

Foote avoided long associations with theatrical companies and their playhouses and was happier when running a theatre himself, especially when it was one of the smaller houses like the Haymarket. As a theatre manager he was clever, inventive, always trying to poke fun at some one or some thing and creating merriment for his audiences in the process. Edward Gibbon said, 'When I am tired of the Roman empire I can laugh away the Evening at Foote's Theatre.' Sam could ridicule himself, too. He lost a leg after he was thrown from a frisky horse in 1766 but did not let a wooden leg deter his stage career. He even nicknamed himself Captain Timbertoe, and as Zachary Fungus in *The Committee* he rode on stage on a hobby horse. Anyone with that sense of humour couldn't be all bad.

But when he died on 21 October 1777 there were some who heaved a sigh of relief and not many who mourned. Garrick told Lady Spencer, 'He had much wit, no feeling, sacrific'd friends and foes to a joke, & so has dy'd very little regretted even by his nearest acquaintance.' The writer Arthur Murphy came to a similar conclusion at greater length. Samuel Johnson noted that, after all, Foote exposed only those who were fools already. But when Dr Johnson heard that Foote was planning to caricature *him*, he 'threatened to beat the mimic with an oak stick' and cut off his good leg. (*BDA*) [EAL]

FORBES-ROBERTSON, Sir Johnston
1853-1937 **230, S10, G0998**

Johnston Forbes-Robertson was born in London on 16 January 1853, the eldest son of the Aberdeen art critic and journalist John Forbes-Robertson and his wife Frances (née Cott). His three younger brothers, Ian (1858-1936), Norman (1859-1932, *q.v.*) and Eric (1865-1935) were also actors. Educated at Charterhouse School and the Royal Academy of Arts, he received some elocution lessons from Samuel Phelps and turned to the stage. His first appearance was on 5 March 1874 at the Princess's Theatre, where he played Chastelard in *Mary Queen of Scots*. Subsequently he acted numerous roles on tour in England and in various London venues, including the Gaiety, Olympic and Haymarket. He joined the Bancrofts at the Prince of Wales's in 1878 and later at the Haymarket and remained with them until July 1885. In 1889 he worked under John Hare at the Garrick Theatre and then under Irving at the Lyceum. Among his memorable portrayals were Romeo (to the Juliet of Mrs Campbell, 1895), Macbeth and Othello. His portrayal of Hamlet, which he first played in September 1897 at the Lyceum, was thought the greatest of his time. His ascetic appearance rendered him ideal for self-examining roles. Among other notable portrayals were Dunstan Renshaw in Pinero's *The Profligate* (Garrick, April 1889), Aubrey in *The Second Mrs Tanqueray* and Golaud in *Pelléas and Mélisande*.

In 1895 he took over the management of the Lyceum, where with Mrs Campbell he produced a number of successes. Subsequently he managed at the Prince of Wales's and the Comedy. In 1900 he married the actress Gertrude Elliott, who became his leading lady. They appeared together in Shaw's *Caesar and Cleopatra, The Light that Failed* (February 1903), in which he played Dick Heldar (**G0998**), and the highly successful *Passing of the Third Floor Back* (September 1908). During his final year at Drury Lane, in 1913, he offered a retrospective of his finest roles, closing the season with Hamlet on 6 June. That week he was knighted.

Sir Johnston then went back to America, where he had toured several times during his career. He took his repertory company all over the United States, and gave his last professional performance at Harvard University as Hamlet on 26 April 1916. Back in England he appeared in some charity performances and lectured on Shakespeare at the Wigmore Hall. He also was seen in several films, including *Hamlet* (1912), *Masks and Faces* (1916) and *The Passing of the Third Floor Back* (1917). His book of reminiscences, *A Player Under Three Reigns*, was published in 1925. Forbes-Robertson was awarded honorary degrees from Columbia University (MA) and Aberdeen (LLD). He became a member of the Garrick Club in May 1888 and was also a member of the Athenaeum and Beefsteak. He died on 6 November 1937 at St Margaret's Bay, near Dover.

Forbes-Robertson's handsome features may be seen in Harcourt's portrait of him (**230**). His daughter Jean Forbes-Robertson (1905-1962) became a distinguished actress (see K. A. Burnim and Andrew Wilton, *The Richard Bebb Collection in the Garrick Club*, No. B20). Robertson's first ambition had been to be a painter, as evidenced by his early training at the Royal Academy. The Garrick Club has his painting of Samuel Phelps as Cardinal Wolsey (**665**). He had played alongside Phelps as Cromwell in *Henry VIII*. (*OCT, WWWT*)

FORBES-ROBERTSON, Norman
1859-1932 **231, G1009**

Born in 1859, Norman Forbes-Robertson was the third son of the Aberdeen art critic and journalist John Forbes-Robertson and his wife Frances (née Cott). His eldest brother was the distinguished actor-manager Sir Johnston Forbes-Robertson (1853-1937), noticed above. His brothers Ian (1858-1936) and Eric (1865-1935, who took the name John Kelt) were also actors, as was his son Frank. Norman made his debut at the Gaiety Theatre in 1875, using the name Norman Forbes. He managed the Globe for some time and was associated with other London managements. Forbes-Robertson wrote several plays and adapted for the stage *The Scarlet Letter* and *The Man in the Iron Mask*, in which he played Louis XIV and Marchiali, respectively. He became a member of the Garrick Club in January 1907. (*OCT*)

FORREST, Edwin **232**
1806-1872

Edwin Forrest, who was regarded as the first great tragic actor of the American stage, was born on 9 March 1806 in Philadelphia, the son of impoverished immigrants. Supposedly he made his first appearance on the stage in 1817 at the

Southwark Theatre, Philadelphia, when the desperate manager asked him to replace a sick actress in the female role of Rosina in *Rudolph; or, The Robber of Calabria*. His real debut, however, occurred in 1820 at the Walnut Street Theatre in that city as Young Norval in Home's *Douglas*. He toured the Western circuit (which was comprised of western Pennsylvania, Kentucky and Ohio), performing noble heroes like Jaffeir in *Venice Preserv'd* and Tell in *William Tell*. In July 1826 he made his first New York appearance, as Othello at the Park Theatre, and also appeared in the same role in November at the Bowery Theatre. Forrest's handsome face, deep and powerful voice and muscular build contributed to making him very popular with audiences, although more discriminating playgoers regarded his acting as often vulgar and melodramatic. In order to stimulate the writing of native drama and to find suitable roles for himself, beginning in 1828 Forrest offered prizes for new American plays. The first winner was John Augustus Stone's *Metamora*; the noble savage became one of Forrest's most popular roles. Among other prize-winning plays were Robert Conrad's *Jack Cade* and three plays by Robert Montgomery Bird – *The Gladiator, Oraloossa* and *The Broker of Bogata*. Forrest, however, was accused of not paying the promised prize money to some of the playwrights.

A tour to London brought favour in 1836, but when he returned in 1845 he found hostile audiences that evidently had been urged on by his rival actor William Macready. The antipathy between Forrest and Macready reached an unfortunate climax in May 1849 while Macready was performing at the Astor Place Opera House in New York. A mob of Forrest's supporters stormed the theatre, the militia was summoned, and in the ensuing riot 22 people were killed and 36 were wounded. Though he remained the idol of the masses, Forrest's reputation suffered. Soon after, he was involved in a sensational suit of divorce against his wife, the actress Catherine Sinclair. Thereafter he lived a lonely and embittered life in his Philadelphia mansion, acting infrequently. His last performance was at the Globe Theatre in Boston on 2 April 1872, when he acted Richelieu.

Forrest died on 12 December 1872 in Philadelphia. He had been guilty, as William Winter put it, of 'vanity, pride, self-assertion, and avarice of power.' Winter also described him as 'a vast animal, bewildered by a grain of genius.' But his acting, sometimes leaning to ranting, was bold and strong, and he had been an important force in the American theatre. His major roles included King Lear, Hamlet and Macbeth. Thomas Sully's portrait of him (**232**) shows him as a young man, soon after he returned from his visit to London; the artist gave it to the Garrick Club in 1840. *See* Richard Moody, *Edwin Forrest – First Star of the American Stage* (1960) and *The Astor Place Riot* (1958).

FORRESTER
See William FARREN (1825-1908)

FORSTER, Johann Reinhold
1729-1798 **S17, B135, B136**

S17 in *PGC* and **B135** and **B136** in the *Richard Bebb Collection* catalogue are identified incorrectly as of David Garrick. They are now identified as of Johann Reinhold Forster, the explorer and scholar of natural history. Forster and his son George (1754-1794) accompanied James Cook on his second voyage around the world (1772-1775) and collected animals, ethnological objects and a large herbarium. Their descriptions and drawings were published as *Characteres Generum Plantarum* (1775-76). The son George published in 1777 *A Voyage Around the World*, based on Johann's journals. The elder Forster later became a professor at the University of Halle, in Germany. He died in 1798, recognized as the father of geography in Europe. (*EB*)

FRANCIS, Alfred Edwin OBE **233**
1909-1985

Born in Liverpool on 27 March 1909, the elder son of Reginald Thomas Francis and Ellen Sophia Francis, Alfred attended Liverpool College and Liverpool School of Architecture. Francis began his career as a songwriter and stage designer, but he quickly advanced into a series of important administrative positions, including the directorship of the London Old Vic, Managing Director of Wales Television and Chairman of the Welsh National Opera. He served as a board member of the London Festival Ballet, D'Oyly Carte Trust,

National Theatre, Bristol Old Vic and various arts councils, and he also was a consultant to many major theatre companies in London, Cardiff and Bristol. Francis received his OBE in 1952 and was elected to the Garrick Club in December 1959; he became an honorary life member. In 1966 he was the recipient of the Whitbread Anglo-American Theatre Award. He died on 19 June 1985. In the Garrick Club Library is Francis's typed manuscript, 'A Few Life Sentences: the memoirs of Alfred Francis, up to the lunatic fringe of the theatre.'

FRANCIS, Raymond **G1003**
1910-1987
Raymond Francis was born in 1910 in Finchley. When he was quite young his parents moved to Bexhill on Sea, where he attended the local grammar school. His interest in entertainment was aroused when he saw the great conjurors Jasper Maskelyne and Devant, so impressing him that he took up conjuring and at the age of twelve, advertising himself as Uncle Raymond, became a children's entertainer. While a student at Madame Espenozar's Dancing Academy, he made his first appearance on the London stage at the La Scala Theatre, in *The Wedding of the Painted Doll* from *The Broadway Melody*. In 1929 he acted as a comic Footman in *Cinderella* at the Children's Theatre, Covent Garden. He was next seen in *Lord Byron* at the Lyric, went on tour with Mrs Brandon's company in *Charley's Aunt*, and was in repertory companies in the country.

During the Second World War, Francis served as a wireless instructor in the 51st Training Regiment at Catterick. Posted overseas to join Stars in Battledress, during a production of *The Amazing Dr Clitterhouse* he met Margaret Towner and married her in Germany in 1945. Their son Clive Francis, the actor and caricaturist, was born in 1946 (see Brief Lives of Artists)

In 1946 Francis and his wife headed a company that entertained ex-servicemen in Newfoundland. Upon their return after six months, Francis understudied Peter Finch in *Captain Carvallo* at the St James's Theatre and appeared in *The Deep Blue Sea* at the Duchess and in *Mr Kettle and Mrs Moon*. Among his last stage appearances were in *The Black Mikado* at the Cambridge Theatre, *Lady Frederick* at the Duke of York's, *Gentle Hook* at the Piccadilly and *Crete and Sergeant Pepper* at the Royal Court. On television he played Dr Watson in a long running series of *Sherlock Holmes*, Inspector Lockhart in a documentary series called *Murder Bag*, which became *Crime Sheet* and then the popular detective series *No Hiding Place*. In 1961 he was named television actor of the year. After a long illness, Clive Francis died in 1987.

He had become a member of the Garrick Club in 1960.

FRENCH, Harold **G0977**
1900-1997
Born in London in 1900, Harold French had a prolific stage career, acting in films and theatre from 1912 to 1936. He directed many of the plays of Terence Rattigan and Noel Coward. In the 1940s he emerged as a front-rank British filmmaker with such films as *The House of the Arrow*, *Secret Mission* and *The Day Will Dawn*. His films about middle-class family life include *Dear Octopus*, *English Without Tears* and *Quiet Weekend*. His *My Brother Jonathan* was a box-office success. His last film was *The Man Who Loved Redheads*, based on Rattigan's comedy.

French became a member of the Garrick Club in 1951. He was its oldest living member before he died in 1997 at the age of 97. His wife Phyllis was killed in a bombing raid in 1941.

FRITH, William Powell **793**
1819-1909
The artist William Powell Frith was born in Aldfield, Yorkshire, on 9 January 1819. He entered the Royal Academy Schools in 1837, and in 1840 he exhibited his first picture, 'Malvolio Before the Countess Olivia.' He was a member of the academies at Antwerp, Brussels and Stockholm, and he was elected a member of the Royal Academy in 1852. His numerous works included 'Othello and Desdemona,' 'Scene from the Vicar of Wakefield,' 'Coming of Age' (1849), 'Life at the Sea-side' (1854), 'The Railway Station' (1862), 'Marriage of the Prince and Princess of Wales'(1865) and 'The Road to Ruin' (1878). See his *My Autobiography and Reminiscences* (1887).

He was elected to the Garrick Club in May 1864 and resigned in January 1883. Frith died in London on 2 November 1909.

G

GAMBON, Sir Michael John, CBE G1002
b. 1940
Michael Gambon, who is shown with other actors in a caricature for the programme of 'A Garrick Celebration of A A Milne' on 10 June 2001, was born in Dublin on 19 October 1940, the son of Edward Gambon and his wife Mary (née Hoare). Gambon served a seven-year engineering apprenticeship before he turned to the stage. From his modest debut as a walk-on gentleman in a Dublin production of *Othello* in 1962 and carrying a spear in Olivier's productions at the National Theatre in 1963, Gambon eventually became a leading stage actor in Britain. He appeared regularly at the National Theatre under the tutelage of Olivier. His major roles included Galileo, King Lear, Othello, Tom in *The Norman Conquests*, Coriolanus, Buckingham in *Richard III* and Jack McCracken in *A Small Family Business*. He earned awards and rave reviews for his portrayal of Eddie in a revival of Miller's *A View from the Bridge* in 1987 (Best Actor Award from *Evening Standard*, Olivier Award and *Plays and Players*). Gambon became known to American audiences through his television portrayals of Chief Inspector Maigret in 1985 and the Singing Detective in 1986 (for the latter he won a BAFTA for best actor). His film career took off in Peter Greenaways *The Cook, the Thief, His Wife and Her Lover* (1989), followed by the Magistrate opposite Brando in *A Dry White Season* (1989), the crazy militaristic uncle to Robin Williams in *Toys* (1992), and in *A Man of No Importance* (1994), *The Browning Version* (1994), and *Dancing at Lughnasa* (1998). He recently appeared in the film *Gosford Park*. On television, remarkably, he won BAFTA awards three years in a row: for *Wives and Daughters* (BBC 1) in 2000, *Longitude* (Channel 4) in 2001, and *Perfect Strangers* (BBC 2) in 2002. Gambon became a member of the Garrick Club in 1990. He received the CBE in 1990 and was knighted in 1998.

GARRICK, David 234-253, 967,
1717-1779 **B21-B23, S11-S16, S056**
David Garrick, the second son and third child of Peter and Arabella Garrick, was born at the Angel Inn, Hereford, on 19 February 1717. David's grandfather, David de la Garrique, was a Huguenot who fled France in 1685, and David's father Peter was brought to England in 1687. Our David was for a while one of Samuel Johnson's pupils at the little school at Edial, near Lichfield. Later, in 1737, Garrick and Johnson made their way to London together, with little money in their pockets, but each destined for fame. Garrick was to serve as a wine salesman for the family business, but he soon pushed that trade out of his mind and turned playwright and actor. He wrote a version of *Lethe* that was played by Henry Giffard's company at Drury Lane and then joined Giffard at the small theatre in Tankard Street, Ipswich, where his first character may have been Aboan in the tragedy *Oroonoko* in the summer of 1741. At the time Garrick adopted the stage name Lyddall. But when he made his legendary debut as Richard III at the Goodman's Fields Theatre in east London on 19 October 1741, he was advertised as 'a Gentleman (who never appear'd on any Stage.).' He was an overnight sensation. His revolutionary and exciting acting style 'threw new light on elocution and action,' banished ranting and bombast, and 'restored nature, ease, simplicity, and genuine humour.' On 28 November the anonymity was discarded and his real name appeared in the London bills for the first time for the role of Chamont in *The Orphan*. Two months later, William Pitt proclaimed the 22-year-old Garrick the best actor the English stage had ever produced. From that time on, the name Garrick would be the dominant force in the history of the British theatre in the eighteenth century and his reputation would remain immense to this day.

In the autumn of 1747, with his new partner James Lacy, Garrick took over the management of Drury Lane Theatre, and for 29 years he directed the finest repertory theatre in all Europe. As a pivotal figure in the development of the art of the theatre he instituted new rehearsal techniques and discipline. The techniques of the theatre arts – scenery, costumes, lighting and other stage practices – significantly matured. Garrick maintained a strong company and demanded their adherence to his instructions and regulations. As modern scholars have pointed out, during the period of Garrick's triumphs dramatic criticism turned to the analysis of characters, with emphasis on the significance of these characters as he had played them. Though Garrick is credited with restoring much of the original texts of Shakespeare's plays and rescuing them from the alterations they suffered since the Restoration, he did provide a few corruptions of his own, altering scenes and speeches to suit his needs. His adaptations included a *Hamlet* without the funeral of Ophelia and the need for the gravediggers, a *King Lear* without the Fool and a Cordelia who lives on, an interpolated dying speech for Macbeth and a scene between the two lovers in the tomb before they die in *Romeo and Juliet.* Garrick, however, was one of the leading playwrights of his day, and many of his plays, especially *The Clandestine Marriage* (with Colman), *Cymon*, *The Lying Valet* and *The Guardian*, became mainstays of the repertory.

It is a given that Garrick was the greatest actor of his time and one of the greatest of all time. His fame extended throughout Europe. His performances of King Lear, Hamlet, Macbeth, Ranger in *The Suspicious Husband*, Lord Brute in *The Provok'd Wife* and Lusignan in *The Roman Father* became the yardsticks against which all other actors who played these characters were measured. There are over 250 portraits of Garrick, in private and stage character, original and engraved, more than those of any other actor, and exceeded in the *Catalogue of Engraved British Portraits in The British Museum* only by those of Queen Victoria. The Garrick Club holds some 21 of them, along with his death mask, chair, silver and other memorabilia. Important caches of material and documents about him are in the Garrick Club Library, the British Library, the Folger Shakespeare Library and the Victoria and Albert Museum. When the British Museum was established in the latter half of the eighteenth century, Garrick's fine collection of old plays formed the nucleus of its library.

In 1749 Garrick married the Viennese dancer Eva Maria Veigel (see below). She outlived him by 43 years. They had no children. During their marriage they enjoyed the company of crowned heads, nobility, and the leading figures of London literary and social circles. They owned residences at No. 27, Southampton Street in Covent Garden, on the Adelphi and on the river at Hampton. The Shakespeare Temple that Garrick had erected at the Hampton villa has recently been restored and opened to the public.

Garrick gave up Drury Lane and made his farewell from the stage in a round of emotional performances in June 1776. He died at his home on the Adelphi on 20 January 1779 and was buried in Poet's Corner, Westminster Abbey. The splendid funeral procession, one of the greatest ever seen in London, stretched from the Strand to the Abbey. His old schoolmaster Johnson wrote, 'I am disappointed by that stroke of death which has eclipsed the gaiety of nations, and impoverished the public stock of harmless pleasure.'

There are numerous books and articles on David Garrick. Among them are Ian McIntyre, *Garrick* (1999), G. W. Stone and G. M. Kahrl, *David Garrick* (1979), G. M. Kahrl and D. M. Little, *The Letters of David Garrick* (3 vols, 1962), Harry M. Pedicord and Frederick Bergmann, *The Plays of David Garrick* (7 vols, 1981) and Kalman A.Burnim, *David Garrick Director* (1961). The 'Ace of Clubs' at No. 15, Garrick Street proudly bears his name.

N.B. S17, **B135** and **B136**, identified as Garrick PGC are now identified as John Reinhold FORSTER (q.v.). The portrait in chalk by Worlidge of Garrick as Tancred (**248**), that was reported in PGC as 'location unknown,' has since been found in the Garrick Club.

GARRICK, Mrs David, Eva Maria née Veigel, stage name 'Violette' 254-256

1724-1822

The future wife of David Garrick, Eva Maria Veigel, was born in Vienna on 29 February 1724, the daughter of Johann Veigel and his wife Eva Maria Rosina. After early training in ballet, by the age of ten she was dancing with the Imperial Ballet in Vienna and came under the protection of the Court. Having adopted the professional name of 'Violette,' she was engaged for the Italian company at the King's Theatre in London. After an adventurous journey during which for some reason she was disguised as a young man, she made her debut at the King's on 11 March 1746 dancing in the opera *Artamene* and causing a small sensation by showing in a caper 'a neat pair of black velvet breeches.' Soon she became quite popular on and off stage, attracting the attention of the Prince of Wales, Horace Walpole, and eventually the protection of the Earl and Countess of Burlington, who took her into Burlington House. It was rumoured, incorrectly, that Burlington was her father. She danced for the first time at Drury Lane on 3 December 1746. That season young David Garrick was at Covent Garden, but he became manager of Drury Lane in the autumn of 1747 and began to pursue Eva Maria with determination. They were married on 22 June 1749 in the Reverend Thomas Francklin's Chapel near Russell Street, and on the same day were married again, this time according to the rites of the Catholic Church, at the Chapel of the Portuguese Embassy in South Audley Street. Eva Maria gave up her dancing career to be Davy's faithful companion, enjoying his fame and fortune and the amiable social life it brought them. Their affectionate and tranquil relationship was ended by his death in 1779. Mrs Garrick lived on for another 43 years, living at their house on the Adelphi Terrace and their villa on the river in Hampton, until her death on 16 October 1822 at the former. She was buried next to David in Poet's Corner, Westminster Abbey. The Garricks had no children.

Her late years were spent in correspondence and caring for her husband's estate and reputation. Toward the end of her life she was described as 'a little bowed-down old woman, who went about leaning on a gold-headed cane, dressed in deep widow's mourning, and always talking of her dear Davy.' Details of her informative will are given in the *BDA* (6: 111-112), as is a list of 21 portraits, including the three in the Garrick Club.

GEARNS, Isabella
See Isabella GLYN

GEORGE III **257**
1738-1820
George William Frederick was born on 4 June 1738 (24 May old style) in London, the first son of Frederick, Prince of Wales, and Princess Augusta of Saxe-Gothe. When George II died in 1760, George III came to the throne, his father, the Prince of Wales, having died in 1751 without ruling. George III married Charlotte Sophia of Mecklenburg-Strelitz on 8 September 1761, and they produced 15 children. In his reign Britain developed an empire. Victory in the Seven Years' War with France established Britain's naval superiority. Another war with France at the end of the century ended with victories by Wellington at Waterloo and Nelson at Trafalgar. A second Act of Union brought Ireland into the empire (until 1920). But the American colonies were lost, and at great cost to George's sanity. He suffered from inherited genetic porphyria which induced bouts of insanity throughout much of his reign and was sufficiently incapacitated from 1811 for his son, the future George IV, to act as regent. George III died at Windsor Castle on 29 January 1820.

GIBBS, Mrs Alexander
See Miss P. GRADDON

GIBBS, Mary née Logan **258-260**
1770-c. 1844
Mary Logan was born in 1770, one of three daughters of an Irish theatrical couple. She probably appeared on the stage in Ireland before she made her debut in London at the Haymarket Theatre as Sally in *Man and Wife* on 18 June 1783. At that time she was called 'a Very Young Lady.' She was similarly advertised when she played that role at Covent Garden on 7 May 1784, but when she returned to the Haymarket on 28 June to play the title role in *Polly Honeycombe* she was identified as Miss Logan. After some appearances in Palmer's company at the Royalty Theatre, during which time she changed her name to Mrs Gibbs, she appeared once at Drury Lane in 1788 and then disappeared for five years. She surfaced next at the Haymarket on 15 June 1793 as Bridget in *The Chapter of Accidents*, and began her engagement at Drury Lane in September 1794. In 1797 the peripatetic Mrs Gibbs transferred to Covent Garden for several seasons, and in the early part of the nineteenth century was seen at the winter patent houses and at the summer Haymarket. She developed an

extensive repertoire of roles, mainly in musical comedies, and was especially outstanding as Cowslip in *The Agreeable Surprise*, Mary in *John Bull*, Ciceley in *Heir at Law* and Grace Gaylove in *The Review*. She also succeeded as Blanch in *The Iron Chest* (**258**) and Selima in *The Tale of Mystery* (**260**), roles in which she was shown by De Wilde, who also painted her as Miss Hoyden in *The Relapse* and Lady Elizabeth Freelove. (De Wilde also did several portraits of her in private character).

Mrs Gibbs evoked high praise from the press, which reported her beauty and ability to inspire and her 'rustic innocence, simplicity and artless truth; she was called one of the 'most interesting and beautiful women on the stage.' About 1795 she began to live with George Colman the younger, manager of the Haymarket, in whose pieces she often performed. She was received everywhere as Colman's wife – though he already had a wife – and Mary lived with him in 'perfect domestic happiness' until Colman's death in 1836. She then retired to Brighton, where she died sometime after 1844. (*BDA*)

GIELGUD, Sir Arthur John 261. 262. 969, S18, S46, S47, S061, B24,
1904-2000 **B25, B137, B138, G1002**

John Gielgud, one of the very greatest actors of the twentieth century, was born in London on 14 April 1904, the son of Frank Gielgud and Kate Terry Lewis. Dame Ellen Terry was his maternal grand aunt and the famed Lithuanian actor Aniela Aszpergerows was his paternal great-grandmother. His elder brother Val Henry Gielgud (1900-1981), an actor and author, became a director of drama for the BBC and then the distinguished and influential Head of BBC Television Drama.

After attending Westminster School and receiving some training at Lady Benson's Acting School and RADA, John Gielgud made his professional stage debut at the Old Vic in 1921 as a Herald in *Henry V*. From that modest beginning, Gielgud rose to an unequalled position as the foremost interpreter of Shakespeare and assumed his place in the pantheon of English actors of his generation, along with Olivier, Richardson, Guinness, Scofield and Mills. All in that remarkable group received knighthoods (except for Scofield, who, it is said, declined to accept it). Gielgud first acted Romeo at the Regent Theatre in 1924. His triumph as Hamlet (**S46**, **B137**) came at the Old Vic in 1930, a quintessential portrayal considered by many to have been the greatest of the century and which he performed over his long career some 500 times. That season at the Old Vic he also appeared as Richard II (**S47**, **B138**), a role 'he was born to play.' He was without equal as Prospero. Other Shakespearean roles in which he excelled were Antony, Macbeth, Angelo, Cassius, Leontes and King Lear. In 1932 at the New Theatre he directed and played the title role in Daviot's *Richard of Bordeaux* (**B25**), a performance that established him as a star in the West End. Among the dozens of non-Shakespearean classical roles he played were Valentine in *Love for Love* (**261**), Worthing in *The Importance of Being Earnest*, Jason in *The Medea*, Mirabel in *The Way of the World* and Jaffeir in *Venice Preserv'd*. Though for most of his career Gielgud abjured contemporary drama, with which he was ill at ease, nevertheless later he was brilliant in such plays as *Forty Years On* (Apollo 1968), *Home* (Royal Court 1970) and *Veterans* (Royal Court 1972). He also successfully directed a number of productions with great intelligence and appeared in a number of television performances.

Gielgud's film career included some 43 films, beginning in 1924 with the silent *Who is the Man?* Other films include *Hamlet, Saint Joan, Becket, Oh! What a Lovely War, Caligula, The Shooting Party, Chariots of Fire* and *Murder on the Orient Express*. His only Oscar, however, came in 1981 for Best Supporting Actor, in the role of Hobson, the sharp-witted butler in *Arthur*. His awards were many, including a special Olivier Award in 1985 for his services to the theatre. Oxford, London, St Andrews and Brandeis bestowed honorary doctorate degrees. He was knighted in 1953. Sir John was a life member of the Garrick Club, which he joined in 1970. He died on 21 May 2000, at the age of 96, at his country estate, Wotton Underwood, Aylesbury, Buckinghamshire.

Gielgud's silken and superbly modulated voice has been preserved on numerous sound recordings. His writings include his early autobiography, *Early Stages* (1938), *Stage Directions* (1963), *An Actor in his Time* (with John Miller and John Powell,

1980) and *Backward Glances* (1990). Biographies include *Ages of Gielgud* (edited by Ronald Harwood 1984); *John Gielgud: a Celebration*, by G. D. Brandreth (1984); and *Gielgud, a Theatrical Life* by Jonathan Croll (2001).

GILBERT, Sir John 793
1817-1897
See Index of Artists

GILBERT, Sir William Schwenk 263
1836-1911
The dramatist William Gilbert was born in Southampton Street, London, on 18 November 1836. He was educated at London University and in 1864 was a barrister at the Inner Temple; he also served as a clerk in the Privy Council Office 1857-1862. As a journalist he wrote many articles for humorous papers. His first theatrical effort was a Christmas entertainment commissioned by T. W. Robertson. He next wrote *The Palace of Truth* (Haymarket 1870) and *Pygmalion and Galatea* (1871). After a few more attempts at serious plays, Gilbert began the famous association with Sir Arthur Sullivan with *Trial by Jury* in 1875. That success was followed by a series of comic operas that included, among others, *HMS Pinafore* (1878), *The Pirates of Penzance* (1880), *Iolanthe* (1882), *The Mikado* (1885), *Ruddigore* (1887) and *The Yeoman of the Guard* (1888). These Savoy operas, as they came to be known, were long associated with the D'Oyly Carte Company and have been revived constantly by light opera companies around the world.

Though extremely successful, the association with Sullivan was not a happy one, primarily because of Gilbert's irascible personality. Gilbert wrote some libretti for other composers, but they remain undistinguished. He built the Garrick Theatre in 1889 and was knighted in 1907. Sir William became a member of the Garrick Club in February 1906. He died at Harrow Weald, Middlesex, on 29 May 1911, of a heart attack brought on by his rescuing of a woman who was drowning in a lake on his estate. (*EB, OCT*)

GILROY John T. Y. 264, 892
1898-1865
See Index of Artists

GLOVER, Juliana née Betterton 265, 943
1779-1850
Juliana (but known as Julia) Glover was born on 8 February 1779 at Newry, where her parents Thomas William Betterton and his wife (the widow of the actor Wingfield Palmer) often performed. With her parents she acted on the York circuit and in Ireland, then at Hereford, Bath and Bristol. Her London debut was at Covent Garden on 12 October 1797 as Elwina in *Percy*, followed by Charlotte Rusport in *The West Indian*. She was engaged at Covent Garden through 1801-2. Her father, who treated her brutally, sold her for a thousand pounds to Samuel Glover, scion of a large fortune, whom she was obliged to marry on 20 March 1800. On 21 October 1802 she acted Mrs Oakly in *The Jealous Wife* at Drury Lane where she remained for some years. She also appeared through 1850 in numerous other London theatres, including the Haymarket and the Strand. Among her notable roles were Joanna in *The Deserted Daughter*, Mrs Sullen in *The Beaux' Stratagem*, Clarinda in *The Suspicious Husband*, Mrs Walsingham in *The School for Lovers* and Widow Warren in *The Road to Ruin*. On 5 February 1846, her 66th birthday, the Haymarket manager Webster presented her with a silver cup commemorating her 50 years on the stage.

Soon after playing Mrs Malaprop in *The Rivals* – when she could barely speak – she died on 16 July 1850 and was buried on the 19th in the churchyard of St George the Martyr, Bloomsbury. Her administrator and eldest son, Edmund Glover (1813?-1860) acted and managed in London. Her second son, William Howard Glover (1819-1875), noticed in the *DNB*, became a composer and critic in New York. Her three daughters Georgina, Phyllis and Mary, were also actresses. Juliana Glover was considered a good performer, and James Boaden believed her to be the ablest actress in London in 1823. The *BDA* (6: 241) lists 18 portraits of her in private and theatrical character, including the Garrick Club pictures (**265** and the missing 943) (*BDA*)

GLYN, Isabella, later Mrs Edward Willis and then Mrs Eneas Sweetland Dallas née Gearns
1823-1889 **266, B26-B28**
This actress was born Isabella Gearns in Edinburgh on 22 May 1823, the daughter of an architect. After some acting in amateur theatricals she went to Paris with her first husband, Edward Willis, to study acting. Using her mother's maiden name of Glyn, she first performed professionally at Manchester as Constance in *King John* (**266**) and then was seen as Lady Macbeth and Hermione. She made her London debut on 26 January 1848 as Lady Macbeth at the Olympic. That September she appeared as Volumnia at Sadler's Wells. She remained at that theatre until 1851, making a reputation in strong tragic figures, and on 26 December 1851 she appeared at Drury Lane as Bianca in *Fazio.*

Isabella Glyn continued to play at various London theatres until 1869, after which time her appearances became less frequent and she was mainly occupied with Shakespearean recitals. She gave such readings in Boston, Massachusetts, in 1870. Her popularity diminished in the 1880s, and she died of cancer at her home, No 13, Mount Street, Grosvenor Square, on 18 May 1889. She had married her second husband, Eneas Sweetland Dallas at Edinburgh in December 1853. She was one of the last adherents of the Kemble school, with a commanding figure, large gestures and a powerful voice. (*DNB,* see also Burnim and Wilton, *The Richard Bebb Collection in the Garrick Club,* B26-B28).

GOODALL, Mrs Thomas, Charlotte née Stanton **267**
1765-1830
The daughter of Samuel Stanton, a theatrical manager in the Midlands, Charlotte Stanton was born in 1765. She, her two sisters and at least two brothers probably took to the stage as children, and Charlotte was talented enough to gain a chance with the Bath manager John Palmer to play Rosalind in *As You Like It* on 17 April 1784. Palmer was pleased enough to contract with her for four seasons at Bath and Bristol and gave her Lady Teazle in *The School for Scandal,* Mrs Page in *The Merry Wives of Windsor* and Juliet. In 1787 she married Thomas Goodall, and for the rest of her career she acted under her married name. Blessed with a fine figure, she was especially popular in such 'breeches' parts as Sir Harry Wildair in *The Constant Couple* (**267**). John Philip Kemble at Drury Lane brought her out as Rosalind on 2 October 1788. Though her competition there was strong – Dorothy Jordan, Elizabeth Farren and Sarah Siddons – Charlotte was seen in such major characters as Mrs Sullen in *The Stratagem,* Millamant in *The Way of the World,* Viola in *Twelfth Night* and Nerissa in *The Merchant of Venice.* She restricted herself almost exclusively to comedy. Charlotte Goodall died in July 1830. (*BDA*) [EAL]

GOWARD, Mary Ann
See Mary Ann KEELEY

GRADDON, Miss P., later Mrs Alexander Gibbs **268**
1804-1854?
The singer Miss Graddon, born at Taunton, Somersetshire, in 1804, appeared at some provincial concert rooms before making her debut at Vauxhall in 1822. In October 1824 she sang Susanna in *The Marriage of Figaro* at Drury Lane, and 10 November 1824 she was heard as Linda in *Der Freischutz* (**268**). In 1854 a portrait of her in this character was published on the title page of sheet music for a polka, 'La Bal Costumé,' which she composed. Other roles in which she appeared at Drury Lane included Amanda in *The Fall of Algiers* (1825), Zulema in *Abu Hassan* and Maria in *Two Houses of Granada* (1826). She soon married Alexander Gibbs, of the firm of Graddon and Gibbs, makers of pianofortes. Probably she was related to the partner Graddon. As Mrs Gibbs she appeared in theatres and concert halls in London, Dublin and provincial towns until 1854, when she either retired or died.

GRAHAM, Mary Anne
See Mrs Richard YATES

GRANVILLE-BARKER, Harley **269**
1877-1946
The dramatist and director Harley Granville-Barker, who profoundly influenced the twentieth-

century theatre, was born in Kensington, London, on 25 November 1877, the son of Albert James Barker and Mary Elizabeth Bozzi-Granville. After some early training for the stage he made his debut at Harrogate in *Vice Versa*, performed at the Theatre Royal in Margate, and then came to London in 1892. He was with Ben Greet's Shakespeare repertory company in the West End. In 1900 he joined the experimental Stage Society, with which he first appeared in *The Coming of Peace*, a translation of Hauptmann's *Das Freidenfest*. On 1 July 1900 at the Strand Theatre he appeared as Eugene Marchbanks in the premiere of George Bernard Shaw's *Candida*. Over the next few years he acted in productions by Greet and William Poel, the founder of the Elizabethan Stage Society. Poel's productions on an Elizabethan-style open stage strongly influenced Barker. In 1904 Barker became manager of the Court Theatre with J. E. Vedrenne to begin a significant period in English theatre. There he produced and acted in plays by Maeterlinck, Galsworthy, Ibsen and Masefield. At the Court eleven plays by George Bernard Shaw were performed. Shaw, who seems to have been the main financier, also directed his own plays, and Granville-Barker acted in many leading roles in them, including John Tanner in *Man and Superman*, Valentine in *You Never Can Tell* and Adolphus Cusins in *Major Barbara*. His wife Lillah McCarthy also acted in these plays. In 1906-7 Granville-Barker ended his association with the Court Theatre to establish a successful repertory program at the larger Savoy Theatre, where he directed Shakespearean production on an open stage with rapid and lightly stressed speech.

Granville-Barker's decision in 1915 to divorce Lillah McCarthy and marry the American novelist and poet Helen Huntingdon, whom he had met while on tour in America, ended his acting career and his friendship with Shaw. After serving in the Red Cross in the First World War, Granville-Barker became President of the British Drama League and a leading advocate for a national theatre. Settling in Paris, he began to write his series of *Prefaces to Shakespeare* (1927-1947) in which he analyzed the plays from his experience as a practical playwright and director. In 1937 he became Director of the British Institute in Paris, and then he took refuge in Spain in 1940. During the Second World War he went to the United States, lectured at Harvard and Yale and worked for British Information Services. He returned to Paris in 1946, where he died on 31 August.

Among his most successful plays are *The Madras House* and *Waste*. Other plays include *Prunella*, *The Marrying of Ann Leete*, *The Voysey Inheritance* and *Souls on Fifth*. He became a member of the Garrick Club in 1908. Among his biographies are *Granville Barker* by Eric Salmon (1983) and *Granville Barker and the Dream of Theatre* by Dennis Kennedy (1985).

GREGG, Hubert Robert Harry **892**
b. 1914
The prolific author, composer, actor, and broadcaster Hubert Gregg was born in London on 18 July 1914, the son of Robert Joseph Gregg and Alice Maud (née Bessant). He attended St Dunstan's College and the Webber-Douglas School of Singing and Dramatic Art. Gregg made his first appearance in London as Julien in *Martine* at the Ambassadors' on 23 May 1933. He played Shakespearean roles at Regent's Park and the Old Vic 1933-34, appeared in New York in 1936, and then enjoyed an active career – interrupted by military service in the Second World War – directing and acting in London and elsewhere in England into the 1970s. He appeared in numerous films, and on BBC television and radio. In addition to plays and novels, he wrote many scripts that he presented himself on television, including a series called 'Hubert Gregg and the Forties' (1944); he wrote similar scripts for other decades. For radio he produced over 300 programmes, including 'Hubert Gregg Remembers,' a series for both BBC and ITV. Among his more than 100 songs are the well-remembered and loved 'Maybe it's because I'm a Londoner' and 'I'm going to get lit up.' Gregg became a member of the Garrick Club in May 1954. (*WWT*)

GREGORY, Lady Mary Anne
See Mary Anne STIRLING

GRIEVE, William
See Index of Artists

GRIFFIN, Benjamin **271**

1680?-1740

He was probably born in 1680 in Oxned, Norfolk, the son of a clergyman. Dissatisfied with an apprenticeship to a glazier, Benjamin Griffin joined the Duke of Norfolk's troupe of strollers. In 1714 he tried his hand at playwriting, an adaptation of Dekker and Massinger's *The Virgin Martyr* he called *Injured Virtue*. He soon joined John Rich's company at Lincoln's Inn Fields Theatre in London, where he established himself as a low comedian specializing in skirts parts and testy old men. In 1721 he moved to the Drury Lane company at £4 weekly but had to settle for a pound less when his contract expired in 1724. His career was a modest one, though he had some nice small parts: Tribulation in *The Alchemist* (**271**), Silence in *2 Henry IV*, Sir Politick in *Volpone* and Peachum in *The Beggar's Opera*. His most popular character was Lovegold in *The Miser*. Griffin died on 18 February 1740, remembered as 'a facetious companion and one whom everybody lov'd.' (*BDA*) [EAL]

GRIMALDI, Joseph **272-274, 944**

1778-1837

This 'Great King of Clowns' – known as Joe or Joey, was born on 18 December 1778 in Stanhope Street, Clare Market, London. His father was Giuseppe Grimaldi (d. 1788), a dancer and ballet master at Drury Lane Theatre, who had a reputation as a libertine, and his mother was Rebecca Brooker, a utility dancer at Drury Lane and the daughter of Zachariah Brooker, a butcher of Holborn. The family dynasty dated back at least to John Baptist Grimaldi (d. 1760?), a dancer and dentist in London who was the father of another John Baptist Grimaldi (fl. 1740-1741); that latter Grimaldi was also a dancer and acrobat who was called 'Iron Legs.' They were Joey's great grandfather and grandfather, respectively.

Joey spent the first ten years of his life around the streets of Clare Market. Having been schooled by his father in the skills of pantomime, Joey made his first stage appearance at the age of 23 months, in November 1781 at Drury Lane, as the Clown in *Robinson Crusoe*. From that time, until he retired in May 1823, Grimaldi performed regularly in pantomimes in London – at Drury Lane, Covent Garden and Vauxhall Gardens, but mainly at Sadler's Wells. He was hailed as 'the most wonderful creature of his day, and far more unapproachable in his excellence than Kean or Kemble in theirs.' His great portrayals in such pieces as *Harlequin and Mother Goose; or, the Golden Egg* (**272**), *Harlequin in his Element*, *Harlequin and Blue Beard*, *Aladdin*, *The Wild Man* and *Harlequin and Friar Bacon* were unequalled and his rapport with his audiences magical. The critic in the *Monthly Mirror* wrote of his performance in *Mother Goose*: 'of all the whimsical beings that, by their contortions and vulgarities in pantomime, set the young, ay, and old folks too, in a roar, the clown of Grimaldi is the most surprising, diverting and effective. We can in no way describe what he does … He must be seen.'

Grimaldi's body was racked by the physical abuse it had suffered over the years, and by 1828 he could not go on. He made a round of farewell appearances, barely able to walk. On 17 March 1828 he made his final appearance before a packed house at Sadler's Wells. His last years were spent in agony at his house, No 33, Pentonville Road; George Cooke, the publican of the nearby Marquis of Cornwall, carried him back and forth to the pub on his back. The great clown died on 31 May 1837 in Southampton Street and was buried in the graveyard of St James on Pentonville Hill.

His first wife Maria, whom he had married in 1799, was the daughter of the Sadler's Wells manager Richard Hughes. She died in childbirth in October 1800. Joey mourned her passing for many years, even long after his marriage in December 1801 to the actress Mary Bristow, the daughter of provincial actors. Mary suffered a paralytic stroke in 1832; Grimaldi nursed her constantly until her death in 1834. Their son, Joseph Samuel Grimaldi (*q.v.*), had an undistinguished career on the stage.

Grimaldi's reminisences, which he had completed writing in 1836, were published after his death, in February 1838, as *The Memoirs of Joseph Grimaldi*, edited by 'Boz' (Charles Dickens). Richard Findlater's biography, *Grimaldi King of Clowns*, was published in 1955. Many of

Grimaldi's pantomimes are treated by David Mayer in *Harlequin in his Element* (1969).

The *BDA* lists some 95 pictures and caricatures of Grimaldi.. (*BDA*)

GRIMALDI, Joseph Samuel **275**
1802-1832
He was born on 21 November 1802, the son of the great Joe Grimaldi (*q.v.*) and his wife Mary (née Bristow). According to his father's memoirs, he made his stage debut in 1815 at Sadler's Wells as Friday in *Robinson Crusoe*. His first appearance of record occurred with his father at Covent Garden in 1819, when he played Chittaquae in the pantomime *Harlequin and Fortunio*. He proved to be too poorly disciplined for the stage, and although he continued to be engaged at Covent Garden and elsewhere, he betrayed his high promise and died of delirium on 11 December 1832.

GUERBEL, Countess de
See Dame Geneviève WARD

GUERRABELLA, Mme de
See Dame Geneviève WARD

GUINNESS, Sir Alec **276, G1003**
1914-2000
Born Alec Guiness de Cuffe on 2 April 1914 in London, this wonderful actor was a copy editor in an advertising agency for a while before he began to study at the Fay Compton Studio of Dramatic Art. He made his stage debut at the Playhouse on 2 April 1934 as a walk-on in *Libel!*, spent several years in small parts in London venues, and joined Gielgud's company, appearing again in minor roles. He was with the Old Vic in 1937-38, when his roles included Hamlet (in a modern-dress production) and Bob Acres in *The Rivals*. During the Second World War he served in the Royal Navy but was given leave to appear in New York in a Christmas run of *Flare Path* (1942-43). With the Old Vic again he performed at the New Theatre from 1946 to 1948, playing the Fool in *King Lear*, Abel Drugger in *The Alchemist*, Richard II and the Dauphin in *Saint Joan*. He continued to appear on the stage in London and at various festivals, in Stratford, Ontario, and Chicester, and in New York, where he played the Unexpected Guest in *The Cocktail Party* and the title role in *Dylan in 1964*. One of his last stage roles was as the Father in *A Voyage Round My Father* at the Haymarket in 1971.

It was in films that Guinness became an international star with a series of brilliant portrayals. His initial screen role was Herbert Pocket in *Great Expectations* (1946), followed by the notable Ealing comedies, *Kind Hearts and Coronets* (1949), *The Lavender Hill Mob* (1951), *The Man in the White Suit* (1951) and *The Ladykillers* (1955). His greatest triumph came as the disciplined and inflexible Colonel Nicholson in *The Bridge on the River Kwai*, for which he won an Academy Award (1957). Another splendid performance was as the boorish Scottish Lieutenant-Colonel Jock Sinclair – a role Guinness once claimed to be his favourite – in *Tunes of Glory* (1960). Other films included *Lawrence of Arabia, Dr Zhivago* and *A Passage to India*. He won world-wide popularity for his role of the Jedi warrior Obi-Wan Kenobi in *Star Wars, The Empire Strikes Back* and *The Return of the Jedi*. Guinness professed to have hated the part, but it brought him enormous wealth. He also starred as the master spy George Smiley in the television series *Tinker, Tailor, Soldier, Spy* (1980) and *Smiley's People* (1982).

Guinness became a member of the Garrick Club in 1948. He was awarded a CBE in 1955 and was knighted in 1959. In 1938 he married the actress Merula Salaman; they lived in their later years at their home in Petersfield. Sir Alec wrote his memoirs in *Blessings in Disguise* (1985) and *My Name Escapes Me* (1986). This extraordinarily versatile actor died on 5 August 2000, at the age of 86, in King Edward VII Hospital, in Midhurst. West Sussex. (*WW, OCT, EB*)

GUITRY, Lucien-Germain **S19, B39**
1860-1925
The French actor, dramatist and manager Lucien-Germain Guitry was born in Paris on 13 December 1860. After leaving the Conservatoire, Guitry first appeared as Armand in a revival of *La dame aux camélias* at the Gymnase in 1878. In 1891 he acted the romantic title role in Dumas's *Kean*. In 1902 he became manager at the Théâtre de la Renaissance, where he also acted. When

the actor Coquelin died during rehearsals for Rostand's *Chantecler* in 1909, Guitry took on the title role. He also appeared in many plays written by his son Sacha Guitry (1895-1957), who presented the sculpture of his father (**S19**) to the Garrick Club. Guitry gave a notable performance in *Pasteur*. He was considered one of the greatest actors of his time. *See* Burnim and Wilton, *The Richard Bebb Collection in the Garrick Club*, B30, and James Harding, *The Last Boulevardier* (1968).

GWYN, Eleanor nicknamed Nell 277, 278
1650?-1687
Nell Gwyn's horoscope at the Bodleian Library, Oxford, gives her birthdate as 2 February 1650, though she may have been born earlier; her place of birth and parentage are uncertain. She may have begun her stage career in 1664-65, though not until late February 1667, when she appeared in the breeches part of Florimel in Dryden's *Secret Love*, can we be very sure of her stage activity. Samuel Pepys saw her in that role on 2 March and was quite carried away: 'so great performance of a comical part was never, I believe, in the world before as Nell do this, both as a mad girle, then most and best of all when she comes in like a young gallant; and hath the motions and carriage of a spark the most that ever I saw any man have.' Pepys told his *Diary* again and again how smitten he was by Nell's beauty, or how disappointed he was when she attempted serious roles, or how sad that she could not dance better, or how shocking that Lord Buckhurst should 'erept' her from the stage (as the prompter Downes put it), or how happy he was at her return, or how disenchanted he was seeing her up close in her makeup, or what a 'bold merry slut' she was.

Nell Gwyn's stage career was very short; she gave it up about February 1671. As a mistress she advanced from her leading man Charles Hart to Buckhurst to Charles II, with some affairs in between. By King Charles she had two sons and enough money that, had she managed her estate more prudently, she could have been very wealthy indeed. But she was a generous jade, bright (though not very literate), witty and as amiable a companion as the King could ask. The playwright Aphra Behn dedicated her *Feign'd Curtizans* in 1679 to Nell: 'you glad the hearts of all that have the happy fortune to see you, as if you were made on purpose to put the whole world into a good Humour.' There seems to have been much truth in that. Kathleen Winsor's popular novel *Forever Amber*, published in 1944, was based on Nell's life and became a box office hit in the film version.

Nell Gwyn died on 14 November 1687. (*BDA*; David Bond, 'Nell Gwyn's Birthdate' in *Theatre Notebook* (1986), 40: 3-9 and 'Some Notes on Nell Gwyn's Stage Career 1663-1668' in *Theatre Notebook* (1987), 41: 107-114. [EAL]

H

HALLAM, Isabella
See Mrs George MATTOCKS

HAMMERTON, Mr **438**
fl. 1812-1814
Mr Hammerton, who was a native of Dublin, acted on many Irish stages and in Liverpool before coming to London to appear at Covent Garden Theatre on 24 October 1812, when he played Serjeant Crump in *The Lord of the Manor* (**438**). Other roles that he acted over the following several seasons included Virolet in *The Mountaineers*, Paris in *Romeo and Juliet* and the First Actor in *Hamlet.*

HANNEN, Nicholas James OBE **279-280**
1881-1972
Born in London on 1 May 1881, the son of Sir Nicholas John Hannen and Jessie Woodhouse, he spent much of his early life in China and Japan. He was educated at Radley and Heidelberg and then studied for the Foreign Office before becoming an apprentice to the architect Sir Edwin Lutyens. He went on the stage in 1910, played in musical comedies, and joined the Glasgow Repertory Company in 1914. When the war broke out Hannen was at the St James's Theatre in London and then joined Granville-Barker's company. He joined the RASC and served in France. Between the wars he was seen in a number of companies in a wide repertory, including *Accent on Youth, Sour Grapes* and *Waste.* At the Old Vic from 1944 to 1947 he appeared in the plays of Shaw, Shakespeare and Chekhov. His films included *Fear, Henry V, Quo Vadis* and *Richard III.* His first wife, Muriel Melbourne Victoria Morland, whom he married in 1907, died in 1960, and soon after he married the well-known actress Athene Seyler (1889-1990), with whom he toured. Mrs Grey-Edwards's portrait of him (**279**) is a companion to that of Athene Seyler (**736**). Seago's oil portrait of him (**280**) shows him at age 80, some 11 years before he died on 25 June 1972. He was a life member of the Garrick Club, having been elected on 2 February 1922.

HARE, Sir John original name John Fairs
1844-1921 **281-284**
Originally named John Fairs, he was born on 16 May 1844, in London, according to his entry in *Who Was Who,* or in Giggleswick, Yorkshire, according the *Encyclopaedia Britannica.* He was educated at the Giggleswick Grammar School. In September 1864 he made his first appearance on the stage in Liverpool, assuming the name of John Hare, after a family name of his wife Mary Adela Elizabeth, whom he had married that year; she was the daughter of John Hare Holmes. His London debut came on 25 September 1865 in *Naval Engagement* at the Prince of Wales's Theatre, which was being managed by the Bancrofts. There he appeared for a number of years, featured in plays by Robertson. In 1875 he became actor-manager of the Court Theatre; there on 8 January 1876 he originated the role of Lord Kildare in *A Quiet Rubber* (**283**). From 1879 to 1888 he was a leading actor at the St James's. Hare managed the new Garrick Theatre from 1889 to 1894, producing plays by Pinero and especially Sydney Grundy's *A Pair of Spectacles,* in which he acted Benjamin Goldfinch, one of his most popular roles. In 1895 he made his first appearance in New York on 23 December in *The Notorious Mrs Ebbsmith.*

Because he was one of the finest character actors of his time, Hare was knighted in 1907. He retired from the stage in 1911 and died in London on 28 December 1921. Hare had become a member of the Garrick Club on 16 May 1868.

HARLEY, George Davies **2855**
d. 1811
His real surname was Davies, and he was probably born in London, where his father kept a shop in Sidney's Alley, Leicester Square. As a youth Harley served as a bank clerk and then in an insurance firm. It is said that the estimable actor John Henderson taught him acting. Assuming the name Harley, he made his ambitious debut at Norwich on 20 April 1785 as Richard III. During four years at Norwich he became successful enough to be dubbed the 'Norwich Roscius' and to play capital roles like King Lear, Tamerlane and Dumont (to Sarah Siddons's Jane Shore). In 1789 he moved to

London, where he made his debut on 25 September at Covent Garden as Richard III; when the critics noted that he 'possessed some power' and 'may be useful.' Other roles that season included Iago, Shylock, Macbeth, Horatio in *The Fair Penitent* and Ventidius in *All for Love*. He remained at Covent Garden through 1795-96, but by 1792 the management reduced his status to that of supporting actor. Harley also acted summers at Birmingham; he joined the company at Bath and Bristol in 1796, and was seen at Sheffield, Liverpool, Worcester and Manchester. He acted at Dublin in 1799-1800 and 1802. Harley, who remained a bachelor, died at Leicester on 28 October 1811. He had written some volumes of poems and ballad stories, including *A Monody on the Death of Mr. John Henderson,* and a biography of the child-actor phenomenon Master Betty. In addition to De Wilde's portrait of him as Caled (**285**), a portrait by the same artist of him as Lusignan in *Zara* was reported to be in the Garrick Club, but is not there. It was engraved by W. Bromley for *Bell's British Theatre* (1791); see Burnim and Highfill, *John Bell,* No. 173.

HARLEY, John Pritt 286, 287, 355, G1040
1786-1858
The son of John Harley, a draper and silk mercer, and his wife Elizabeth, John Pritt Harley was born in February 1786 and baptised at St Martin-in-the-Fields, London, on 5 March. During his apprenticeship with a linen draper in Ludgate Hill and later during his employment as a clerk to Windus and Holloway, attorneys in Chancery Lane, Harley engaged in amateur theatricals and then acted from 1806 at Cranbrook, Canterbury, Brighton, Rochester and Southend. He remained at Southend for some time, where his singing won him favour. After an engagement in the north of England from 1812 to 1814, he engaged with Samuel J. Arnold at the English Opera House, where he made his London debut on 15 July 1815 as Marcelli in *The Devil's Bridge* and then acted several other roles. Soon after he went over to Drury Lane Theatre, where he first appeared as Lissardo in *The Wonder* on 16 September 1815. Harley remained at Drury Lane, continually appearing before the public in a number of comic heroes, especially in operas, until the 1840s; he made occasional summer excursions and had some engagements at the Lyceum, where for some time he served as stage manager. He also was at the St James's Theatre under Braham's management in the mid 1830s. He was with W. C. Macready at Covent Garden in 1838, and remained at that theatre when Mme Vestris and Charles Mathews took up management in 1840. He also joined Charles Kean at the Princess's Theatre during the 1850s.

Harley was much enjoyed in the roles of Shakespearean clowns and as Bobadil in *Every Man in His Humour*. On 20 August 1858, while acting Lancelot Gobbo he suffered a stroke in the wings and died penniless two days later at his residence at No 14, Upper Gower Street; he was buried at Kensal Green Cemetery on 28 August. Harley was considered an eccentric. An avid collector of walking sticks, he amassed some 300, which were in the sale of his effects. He was an original member of the Garrick Club in 1831, and served as master and treasurer of the Drury Lane Theatrical Fund. He never married.

HARLOW, George Henry
See Index of Artists

HARLOWE, Sarah, stage name of Miss Wilson? and later of 'Mrs' Francis Godolphin Waldron the second 288, 289, 787
1765-1852
Sarah Harlowe was the stage name of an actress who was born in 1765 and whose real name was apparently Wilson. Sarah's first appearance on stage in London was on 19 July 1786 at the Windsor Castle Inn in Hammersmith, as Kitty Sprightly in *All the World's a Stage.* And sprightly she was as an actress, according to critics of the time, who referred to her as spirited, even impudent on stage, where she was seen over the years as a singer, dancer and actress – especially in breeches parts, such as Adeline in *The Battle of Hexham* (**289**) and male characters, like William in *Rosina*. In London Sarah was seen frequently at the Haymarket in both summer and winter and at Drury Lane, Covent Garden, Sadler's Wells and the Royalty, and she was on the road

often, acting at Richmond, Brighton, Margate, Birmingham, Wolverhampton and Weymouth. She seems clearly to have been a capable actress who could play a variety of secondary and tertiary roles in comedy, and she was not unwilling to try more serious parts, such as Gertrude in *Hamlet* and Emilia in *Othello* (both at the Haymarket). Not until fairly late in her career, at the turn of the century, did she settle down: at Drury Lane, for £3 weekly, and there she remained for some 26 years.

Mrs Harlowe, in 1786 at Hammersmith, had acted in a troupe led by Francis Godolphin Waldron, and at some point they became lovers – perhaps in 1788, when Waldron's wife seems to have either left him or died. Sarah's relationship with Waldron continued until his death in 1818. She acted until 1826 and died in 1852. In her later years she depended on an annuity from the Drury Lane Theatrical Fund, and at her death she was identified as Sarah Waldron. [EAL]

HARRIS, Henry **290**
c. 1634-1704
An actor, singer, dancer, manager and possibly scene painter, Henry Harris was born about 1634 and became involved in theatrical activities in London as early as 5 November 1660. On that date he was named in an agreement concerning the Duke's Company of players; he was evidently a sharer but was listed as a painter rather than an actor. He may therefore have joined Sir William Davenant and his troupe as a scene painter. He also received, for much of his life, payments from the crown for positions he held in the revels and the engraved seals offices. But his main career from 1660-61 onward was performing. The diarist Pepys, who became a good friend, frequently commented on Harris's abilities as an actor, singer and dancer. The player's first recorded part was Alphonso in both parts of *The Siege of Rhodes* at the Lincoln's Inn Fields playhouse beginning on 28 June 1661, and in August he appeared as Horatio to Thomas Betterton's Hamlet. Among his other notable roles were Sir Andrew Aguecheek in *Twelfth* Night, Duke Ferdinand in *The Duchess of Malfi*, Cardinal Wolsey in *Henry VIII* (**290**) and Macduff in *Macbeth*. When the Duke's Company opened its new Dorset Garden Theatre in 1671, Harris added numerous new roles in plays now forgotten, but throughout his career he was second to Betterton, even in their shared management, and infrequently gained the choicest roles in the best plays.

Harris thought himself worthy of better treatment. In 1663 he had threatened to bolt the Duke's Company; Pepys heard that Harris had grown proud and wanted £20 for acting in a new play and £10 for 'every revive' – more than Betterton – but the manager refused. Perhaps because of that rebuff, Henry spent part of his time dabbling in property, and the Lord Chamberlain's accounts show him regularly being sued for debts (even his wife took him to court, sueing for maintenance). Yet he led a vigorous and perhaps spendthrift social life, as Pepys frequently noted. Harris seems to have had too many irons in the fire. He retired from the stage in 1681 after a career that began with promise; he died on 3 August 1704. (*BDA*) [EAL]

HARRIS, Henry **750**
d. 1839
The Henry Harris who is identified as figure 13 in the key to Harlow's painting of the Trial of Queen Katherine is not known to us. We speculate that the Covent Garden manager Thomas Harris (d. 1820), who is noticed in the *DNB*, was intended. Thomas Harris was involved in the management of that theatre from 1767 and also sometimes served as stage-manager. He formed an impressive collection of theatrical portraits, many by Gainsborough Dupont. *See* his notice in the *BDA*.

HARRIS, Robert Louis Anstruther **945**
1900-1995
Robert Harris was born on 28 March 1900, the son of Alfred H. Harris and his wife Susanne Amelie (née Anstie). After being educated at Sherborne and at New College, Oxford, he began his stage career in 1922. He appeared with the Old Vic-Sadler's Wells Company at Stratford and in many West End productions. Among his numerous roles were Hamlet, Oberon, Prospero, Henry IV, Shylock, Eugene Marchbanks in *Candida*, Thomas More in *A Man for All Seasons*, Pope Pius XII in *The Deputy* and

Orin Mannon in *Mourning Becomes Electra.* He also appeared in films, television (Old Jolyon in *The Forsythe Saga*) and on radio. Harris was elected to the Garrick Club on 6 March 1952 and resigned in December 1974. He died on 18 May 1995.

HARRIS, Sarah
See Sarah SMITH

HARRIS, Thomas
See Henry HARRIS

HART, Michael **892**
fl. 1967
Michael Hart, identified as No. 45 in Gilroy's scene of the Garrick Club Outing in 1967, was a kitchen porter at the Garrick Club who came to the outing to assist with the hard work.

HARTLEY, Elizabeth née White **291**
1750?-1824
The daughter of James and Eleanor White of Berrow, Somerset, this beautiful actress was born in 1750 or 1751. As a young woman she became the mistress of a Mr Hartley, probably a provincial actor, and though she never married him she took his name. As Mrs Hartley she appeared in Edinburgh on 4 December 1771 in the role of Monimia in *The Orphan.* That season at Edinburgh she acted substantial tragic roles, suggesting some considerable previous experience, Desdemona, Cordelia, Belvidera in *Venice Preserv'd* and Calista in *The Fair Penitent* among them. After enjoying success in similar roles during several seasons at Edinburgh, and then at Bristol, Mrs Hartley made her London debut on 5 October 1772, at Covent Garden, acting Jane Shore. By the end of her first season in London, though she had not very much impressed the critics by her acting, she was universally acclaimed as a very beautiful woman. She continued to be engaged at Covent Garden through 1779-80, acquitting herself in leading roles in the repertory. The large painting in the Garrick Club by Angelica Kauffmann of her as Hermione (**291**) commemorates her single appearance in that role on 12 March 1774. During her last several seasons at Covent Garden she was plagued by illness that often prevented her playing. She retired from the stage in May 1780 and died many years later, at the age of 73, at her house in Woolwich on 26 January 1824. Reynolds and Romney also made portraits of her. The *BDA* (7: 162-64) lists 35 portraits of her. The actor-playwright Thomas Hull accounted her as the only one beautiful enough to personate the fair Rosamond – a nickname that became attached to her – in his *Henry II.* (*BDA*)

HARVEY, Sir John Martin **457, B168**
1863-1944
The actor-manager John Martin-Harvey was born at Wyvenhoe, Essex, on 22 June 1863, the son of the yacht builder John Harvey and his wife Margaret Diana Mary. He studied drawing and painting, and although intended for naval architecture he turned to the stage, making his first appearance at the old Court Theatre in 1881. He was in one of Wyndham's companies of *Betsy*, and then in 1882 joined Irving's company at the Lyceum, where he remained for 14 years. In 1889 he took over management of that theatre, with an adaptation of *A Tale of Two Cities* called *The Only Way*, in which he played Sydney Carton. He remained associated with that melodramatic role the remainder of his career. Subsequently Harvey managed the Prince of Wales, Covent Garden and other theatres. Among his notable productions were *Hamlet, Richard III* (**457**), *Henry V, The Taming of the Shrew* and *Everyman.* In 1912 he gave a splendid performance in *Oedipus Rex* that was memorialized by Macqueen-Pope as 'savage in its stark horror.' In 1930 Harvey published his *Autobiography.* He became a member of the Garrick Club in 1919 and received a knighthood in 1921. He was awarded an Honorary LL D from Glasgow University in 1938. Sir John died at his home, Primrose Cottage, East Sheen, Surrey, on 14 May 1944. His wife Angelina Helena (Nina) de Silva (1869-1949), whom he had married in 1889, was his leading lady in many productions. (*OCT, WW*)

HARVEY, Martin James **G1041**
b. 1945
Martin Harvey was born on 4 February 1945 at

Farnborough, Hampshire, the son of Robert James Harvey and his wife Marjorie Diana (née Morrison). After being educated at Stubbington House Preparatory School in Fareham and King's School, Ely, in Cambridgeshire, he trained for five years from 1962 to 1967 in the management training scheme at the Savoy Hotel in London.

In March 1975 Harvey was appointed Secretary of the Garrick Club; he was one of the first and youngest of the new breed of club secretaries to come trained and experienced in the hotel and catering industry. The Garrick Club has benefited greatly from his talent at management and innovation. He introduced the Grill Room after-theatre suppers and made the Milne Room a venue for ladies' luncheons. Harvey established a link with Angers Catering College in France that allowed students to work a minimum of one year at the Club to learn English, and he purchased a hostel to accommodate female students from Angers and catering colleges in the United Kingdom. Under his direction the basement and kitchen were reorganised and a satellite kitchen on the ground floor was introduced. He also oversaw the conversion of the two top floors of the Club premises from staff bedrooms to bedrooms for members and the installation of the passenger lift. The membership, feeling a collective debt of gratitude for the dedication Martin Harvey has shown towards the Garrick Club's interests, recently made him a member.

In June 1969 Harvey married Diana Stirling, and they have two children. Since 1975 they have lived in Claygate, Surrey.

HARVEY, Mary Ann
See Mary Ann DAVENPORT

HARWOOD, Ronald CBE, FRSL G1032
b. 1934
The writer Ronald Harwood was born on 9 November 1934, the son of Isaac Horwitz and his wife Isabel (née Pepper). He was educated in Cape Town and at RADA. He was an actor from 1953 to 1960, was Chairman of the Writers Guild of Great Britain in 1969, served as Artistic Director of the Cheltenham Festival of Literature in 1975, and has taught and lectured at various colleges and universities. Harwood has written a number of novels and short stories and biographies of Sir Donald Wolfit, John Gielgud and Alec Guinness. His plays have been especially successful on the London stage: among them *Country Matters* (1969), the award-winning *The Dresser* (1980) and *Taking Sides* (1995). Harwood wrote the screen plays for *A High Wind in Jamaica* (1965), *Evita Perón (1981), The Dresser* (1983), *Mandela* (1987), *The Browning Version* (1994), *Cry, the Beloved Country* and *The Pianist* (2003). He became a member of the Garrick Club in 1967.

HAVERS, Sir Robert Michael Oldfield, Baron of St Edmunds 892
1923-1992
Robert Michael Havers, shown as No. 31 in Gilroy's painting of the Garrick Club Outing in 1967, was born on 10 March 1923, the son of Sir Cecil Havers and his wife Enid (née Snelling). He was educated at Westminster School and Corpus Christi College, Cambridge, and was called to the Bar, Inner Temple, in 1948. His distinguished career in the law and public service culminated in his being appointed Lord High Chancellor of Great Britain in 1987. He was knighted in 1972. In October 1954 he had become a member of the Garrick Club. He was co-author of *The Royal Baccarat Scandal* (1977, made into a play by Royce Ryton), *Tragedy in Three Voices* (1980), *The Poisoned Life of Mrs Maybrick* (1977) and *Murder With A Double Tongue* (1978).

HAWKESLEY, Eric Dickons Bouchier 892
d. 1975
Eric Hawkesley became a member of the Garrick Club in November 1951. He was assistant secretary of the British South Africa Company and an associate of the Royal Academy of Music. He died in 1975.

HAWKINS, Anthony Hope
See Anthony HOPE

HAWKINS, Jack CBE S059
1910-1973
The estimable actor Jack Hawkins was born in London on 14 September 1910, the son of Thomas George Hawkins and his wife Phoebe

(née Goodman). He made his first appearance on the stage at the Holborn Empire on 26 December 1923, walking on in *Where the Rainbow Ends*. Subsequently he appeared at many London venues, including the Savoy, Vaudeville, Royalty, Lyceum and Globe, and also in New York. Among his many roles were Claudius in *Hamlet*, Edmund in *King Lear*, Caliban in *The Tempest*, Othello, Morell in *Candida* and Mercutio in *Romeo and Juliet*. Hawkins was best known to international audiences through his films: *The Fallen Idol*, *The Cruel Sea*, *The Intruder*, *The Bridge on the River Kwai*, *Ben Hur* and *Lawrence of Arabia*. During the Second World War Hawkins served in the Royal Welsh Fusiliers and the Second British Division in India; he became colonel in command of the ENSA administration for India and was demobilized in 1946. He became a member of the Garrick Club in November 1948, and he received the CBE in 1958. Hawkins died on 18 July 1973. His first wife was Jessica Tandy.

His second wife, Doreen Lawrence, presented the bust of him by David Rawnsley (**S059**) to the Garrick Club in 1993.

HAWTHORNE, Sir Nigel Barnard CBE G1002

1929-2001

The 'bleakly intelligent actor' (*Guardian* 26 December 2001) Nigel Hawthorne was born in Coventry on 5 April 1929 to Dr Charles Bernard Hawthorne and his wife Agnes Rosemary. The family emigrated to Cape Town, South Africa, in 1931. After some acting in Cape Town, Hawthorne returned to England in 1951, failed to succeed, went back to South Africa, and returned again to England in 1963. He made his London debut as Fancy Dan in *Talking to You* in October 1966. His first big success came as Field Marshal Haig in Joan Littlewood's production of *Oh! What a Lovely War* at Stratford East. Other memorable stage roles included Major Flack in *Privates on Parade*, Prince Albert in *Early Morning* and George III in *The Madness of King George;* he was nominated for an Academy Award for his performance in the film version of *Madness*. He was with the Royal Shakespeare Company in 1983-84, and with that company in 1999 he acted King Lear, a performance not enthusiastically received. Hawthorne's greatest success and lasting fame came with his portrayal of the manipulative civil servant Sir Humphrey Appleby in the TV series *Yes, Minister* with Paul Eddington and Derek Fowlds, followed by *Yes, Prime Minister*, in the 1980s and early 1990s. Hawthorne acted in over 50 films and TV programmes. Among those were *The Winslow Boy*, *Twelfth Night*, *Barchester Chronicles*, *Ghandi* and *Holocaust*. He won five BAFTA awards.

Hawthorne received a CBE in 1987. He was knighted in 1998 and became a member of the Garrick Club in 1999. He lived for many years in Hertfordshire with his partner, the writer Trevor Bentham (b. 1943), whom he had met at the Royal Court Theatre in 1968. After a long struggle with cancer, Sir Nigel died in Hertfordshire on 26 December 2001. His autobiography, *Straight Face*, was published posthumously in 2002.

HAY, Harriet

See Mrs John LITCHFIELD

HELP, Mrs 892

fl. 1967

Mrs Help, who is shown as No. 46, serving behind the tables in Gilroy's scene of the Garrick Club Outing, probably was a server on the Garrick Club staff.

HENDERSON, John 292-297

1747-1785

Considered by the playwright Richard Cumberland as next to Garrick in some respects, John Henderson was born in Cheapside in February 1747. Most of his contemporaries commented on his lack of physical appeal and his inadequate voice, though they praised his feeling, perfect ear, good sense and remarkable memory. So his road to stardom was rocky almost from the beginning. He decided in 1768 on a stage career and was auditioned by David Garrick's brother George, who told him his voice was too weak for the theatre. John then approached the dramatist Hiffernan for help in meeting *the* Garrick, but Hiffernan's excuse for turning him down was that he was afraid Henderson was too short (though so was Garrick). Then Henderson tried to earn the attention of the Drury Lane manager by giving recitations at a hall in Islington, including an imitation of Garrick's Stratford Jubilee Ode. Perhaps Garrick saw Henderson at work, for he gave him a hearing, but the manager criticized the young man's poor articulation. With his retirement not many years away Garrick clearly did not want to encourage a possible successor who was wanting some of the fundamentals in an actor, so he persuaded Henderson to go to Bath and gain experience.

Using the stage name Courtney, Henderson appeared at Bath on 6 October 1772 as Hamlet (**296**). Thomas Davies, Garrick's (and Henderson's) biographer, said that when word got around that Henderson had Garrick as his patron, the posh people of Bath flocked to the theatre and made his debut a great success. The choice of Hamlet for his Bath debut must have had Garrick's approval, if not his blessing, and the rest of Henderson's career consisted largely of the other greatest roles in English drama; from the beginning, Henderson seems to have aimed for the top, despite his deficiencies. At Bath he acted Richard III, Benedick in *Much Ado about Nothing*, Macbeth (**297**), Bobadil in *Every Man in His Humour*, and Bayes in *The Rehearsal* – all before the end of the month. He then added Don Felix in *The Wonder*, the title role in *The Earl of Essex*, Hotspur in *1 Henry IV* (on 26 December, using his own name) and King Lear. His repertoire looked very like Garrick's, and, of course, he was inviting comparison. In the summer of 1773, when Henderson was in London trying to get an engagement for the winter season, Garrick showed little interest. John signed on at Bath again and added to his repertoire Pierre in *Venice Preserv'd*, Don John in *The Chances*, Comus, Othello, Archer in *The Beaux' Stratagem*, Ranger in *The Suspicious Husband*, Sir John Brute in *The Provok'd Wife*, Belville in *The School for Wives* and Beverly in *The Man of Business*. Garrick still wasn't interested, and Henderson stayed at Bath for a third season. The master's reluctance was probably due, in part, to his own situation; with retirement in the offing, he clearly hoped for a new leader for Drury Lane, but Henderson did not qualify. He was good, but not very very good. Further, Henderson was a difficult negotiator, insisting on control over what parts he would act; Garrick was not yet willing to give up that kind of control to young John. What Garrick wanted was another Garrick.

Henderson had powerful friends who supported his cause, and they probably protested too much, making Garrick all the more adamant. Henderson signed on for a second three-year engagement at Bath, and in April 1775 Garrick (finally) went to see him act. He was not impressed, though he saw 'sparks of fire which might be blown to warm even a London Audience.' But he wished Cumberland and Henderson's other supporters would stop corrupting the young man with their advice.

For the summer of 1777 Henderson negotiated an engagement at the Haymarket Theatre in London, using, with reservations, Shylock for his London debut. It occurred on 11 June 1777, and he pulled it off with fair success and was compared favourably with Charles Macklin, who was still London's favourite Shylock after reinventing the character in the 1740s. Then Henderson went on to play Leon in *Rule a Wife and Have a Wife*, Falstaff in *1 Henry IV* (with great success) and other characters from his Bath experience. Garrick finally solved Henderson's problem by retiring, and Richard Brinsley Sheridan engaged John at Drury Lane for the 1777-78 season at £10 weekly. Then Henderson was wanted everywhere. He was the leading actor at Drury Lane, went off to Dublin and then Liverpool in the summer of 1778, acted again at Bath, returned for a second season at Drury Lane with some appearances also at Covent Garden, toured in Ireland in the summer of 1779 and then joined Covent Garden for 1779-80, where he remained in the winters for the rest of his career. By 1785-86 he was earning over £17 weekly and was at the top of his profession. Then, on 25 November 1785, John Henderson died in his sleep, most likely of a heart attack, at age 38. He was buried at Westminster Abbey on 3 December, in Poets' Corner, near Garrick. Jane Henderson (née Figgins), whom he married in 1779, died in 1819 and was buried beside her husband. (*BDA*) [EAL]

HENSON, Leslie **298**

1891-1957

The actor and producer Leslie Henson was born

on 3 August 1891, the son of Joseph Lincoln Henson and his wife Alice Mary (née Squire), and was educated at Cliftonville College and Emanuel School. After early appearances in musical comedies at Bath, he performed in *To-Night's the Night* at the Winter Garden Theatre in New York in 1914 and the Gaiety Theatre in London in 1915. After service in the First World War, he became a familiar face in numerous London comedies and revues, some of which he also produced. He made extensive tours entertaining troops in the Second World War. His most famous performance probably was the title role in *Harvey* at the Prince of Wales and Piccadilly in 1950, and he was a success as Pepys in the musical version of *And So to Bed* at the Strand and on tour in 1954. Henson appeared in several pantomimes and films, and at the time of his death on 2 December 1957 he was rehearsing the role of Widow Twanky for a pantomime at Windsor. His particularly amusing and rubber-like face 'could keep a theatre in gales of laughter without saying a word' (*OCT*).

Henson was thrice married: in 1919 to Madge Saunders (divorced), in 1925 to Gladys Gunn (divorced), and in 1944 to Harriet Martha Day. He served as Vice-President of the Actors' Orphanage and the Actors' Benevolent Fund, as Counsellor to the King George V Pensions Fund for Actors and Actresses, and as President of the Royal General Theatrical Fund for 20 years. He became a member of the Garrick Club in November 1948 and was also a member of the Green Room Club and the Stage Golfing Society. (*WWW*)

HERBERT, Charles T. 793

d. 1908

Charles T. Herbert (not Hebbert), who is shown as No. 13 in O'Neil's large picture of members in the Billiards Room, was elected to the Garrick Club on 5 June 1847. No other information was on his candidate's paper.

HICKS, Sir Seymour Edward 299, S20

1871-1949

Sir Seymour Edward Hicks was born at St Helier, Jersey, the eldest son of Major Hicks and Grace Seymour. Although he was originally intended for the Army, he entered the theatrical profession in November 1887 and was a principal light comedian in the Gaiety company. He toured for a long time with the Kendalls in America and Britain, and with his own company in Africa, Australia and Canada. He appeared with equal success in musical comedy, straight plays and music halls. Hicks was among the first to entertain troops in France during the First World War. He received the Legion of Honour from the French government in 1931; he was knighted in 1935.

Hicks wrote and produced 64 plays, including *The Man in Dress Clothes*, in which he is pictured as Lucien in the painting by Codner (**299**). Other plays included *Under the Clock, Catch of the Season* and *Bluebell in Fairyland*. His performance in his *Sleeping Partners* was especially memorable. He also published several volumes of memoirs, among them *Twenty Four Years of an Actor's Life* (1910) and *Vintage Years* (1943). In 1931 he published *Acting: A Book for Amateurs*. He enjoyed a happy marriage with the actress Ellaline Terriss.

Sir Seymour became a member of the Garrick Club in February 1899. He died on 6 April 1949.

HICKS, Ellaline, Mrs Seymour

See Ellaline TERRISS

HICKS, William Robert S45

1808-1868

The humourist William Robert Hicks was born on 1 April 1808 at Bodmin, Cornwall, the son of the schoolmaster William Hicks and his wife Sarah. The younger Hicks kept a boarding school for boys from 1832 to 1840 in Bodmin and became proficient at mathematics. In 1840 he was appointed domestic superintendent of the Cornwall mental asylum, where he instituted more humane modern treatment. He served as mayor of Bodmin in 1865 and 1866. An especially witty speaker, Hicks was a popular story teller and became known as the 'Yorick of the West.' Many of his narratives were in the Cornish dialect. Among his most famous stories were 'The Coach Wheel,' 'The Blind man, his Wife, and his Dog Lion,' 'Dead March in Saul' and 'The Jury.'

Hicks resigned from the Cornwall asylum in

1860 and retired to his house at Westheath, Bodmin. He died on 5 September 1868 and was buried in the local cemetery.

HIPPISLEY, John **300**
1696-1748
Born on 14 January 1696 at Wookey Hole, near Bristol, John Hippisley learned the acting trade from the eighteenth century's greatest harlequin, the London theatre manager John Rich. Hippisley's first recorded role was at Lincoln's Inn Fields Theatre on 7 November 1722: Fondlewife in *The Old Bachelor*. After that he acted two dozen characters during the 1722-23 season, including Marplot in *The Busy Body*, the title role in *Hob* and Polonius in *Hamlet* – parts important enough to suggest he had been performing for some time before that. He acted for Rich at Lincoln's Inn Fields and (from 1732) Covent Garden Theatre through 1746-47 in important comic roles, the most notable being the Mad Welshman in *The Pilgrim* (his Welsh parts earned him such nicknames as Ap Leek and David Ap-Shinkin), Corbaccio in *Volpone* (he was especially good as old men) and Peachum in *The Beggar's Opera* (he was a singer, too). Skirts parts, dialect characters, fools, bumpkins, rascals and clowns in a variety of plays made him a favourite with audiences, as his receipts at benefits year in and year out show.

In addition to his heavy London schedule during the regular season with Rich's troupe, Hippisley was a theatre manager at Bristol and Bath from 1728 and worked the late summer fairs in London in the 1730s. In his spare time he dabbled in playwriting, ballad operas being his specialty and *Flora* (1727) his most popular work. By 1747 he had worn himself out. Though 'lower'd in spirits' he acted Scrub in *The Stratagem* on 2 April for his Covent Garden benefit, after which he was at Bristol and then Richmond. He played Trincalo in *Albumazar* on 3 November 1747 back at Bristol. There he died, on 12 February 1748. The *Public Advertiser* gave him a nice complimentary close: '*Laughter lamented that her Fav'rite dy'd.*' His main claim to fame and posterity is his inclusion as Peachum in Hogarth's famous picture of the prison scene in *The Beggar's Opera*. (*BDA*) [EAL]

HOARE, Sarah
See Mrs Thomas WARD

HOLLAND, Charles **301**
1733-1769
The actor Charles Holland was born in Chiswick on 12 March 1733, the son of a baker, John Holland, and his wife Sarah. Young Charles tried amateur acting and fancied himself talented enough to apply to David Garrick at Drury Lane, where he made his debut (advertised as 'A Young Gentleman') on 13 October 1755 playing the title role in Oroonoko to great applause, according to the prompter Richard Cross. Garrick then showed off Holland as Dorilas in *Merope*, George Barnwell in *The London Merchant*, Florizel in *The Winter's Tale* and Hamlet (for his benefit on 20 April 1756). That was a heady opening season for young Holland, and it is little wonder that he became Garrick's disciple and remained at Drury Lane for the rest of his career. Holland must have been a talented actor. Critics noted his handsome looks, fine voice, and understanding. His repertoire included some of the best roles in English drama: Jaffeir and Pierre in *Venice Preserv'd*, Romeo, Douglas, Richard III, Macbeth, Iago in *Othello*, Ferdinand and Prospero in *The Tempest*, Hotspur in *1 Henry IV*, Osmyn in *The Mourning Bride*, Hastings in *Jane Shore* and Bajazet in *Tamerlane*.

Holland's curse, however, was that he was regarded as a copy of Garrick – an excellent copy, to be sure, but still a copy, and in London he would always be so, even when Garrick was on the Continent for an extended vacation and gave many of his parts to Holland. There were some critics who could not accept Holland but found him, as Kelly did in his *Thespis* in 1767 'sententious, dull, and heavy.' Descriptions of Holland's personal behaviour may give a clue: he was seen as good, natural, cheerful, generous, sober – a person whose epitaph could truly be flattering; indeed, Garrick was able to say on Holland's monument that the actor's career supported 'the credit of the Stage by just and manly Action.' Contemporaries evidently liked Charles Holland very much but did not find him exciting. His last performance was as Prospero on 20 November 1769. He died on 7 December at 36, of smallpox.

Pictures in the Garrick Club reproduces two pictures showing Charles Holland, but one of them (**355**) is of his nephew, also named Charles Holland (1768-1849), playing in *A New Way to Pay Old Debts* in the nineteenth century with Edmund Kean. (*BDA*)[EAL]

HOLLAND, Charles 355

1768-1849

Charles Holland, the son of Thomas and Sarah Holland and the nephew of Charles Holland the actor (1733-1769), was born in 1768, probably at Chiswick. Under the name of Harford he made his debut as Pierre in *Venice Preserv'd*, at Bath on 4 January 1791. At some point Holland dropped his pseudonym, and it was as Holland that he made his first appearance at Drury Lane, on 31 October 1796 as Marcellus in *Hamlet*. He was then seen in other minor characters during the season, and in the summer of 1797 he acted at Richmond, playing Richard III and Macbeth. Then Holland returned to Drury Lane, where he spent the rest of his career playing supporting roles – 'Walking Gentleman in Farces Dumb Lords and attendants in Tragedies' as he called his typical characters in a letter now at the Folger Library. Winston said Holland was 'of very moderate talent.' The actor left the stage after the 1820-21 season and became a gentleman farmer. He died, probably at Chiswick, in 1849.

Pictures in the Garrick Club reproduces a painting by George Clint showing a scene from *A New Way to Pay Old Debt* (**355**); in it a Mr Holland is shown as Lord Lovell, with Edmund Kean as Sir Giles Overreach. This Holland could not have been (as the Index of Sitters in *PGC* has it) the well-known Charles Holland, who died in 1769, but surely was our subject. Kean first played Overreach at Drury Lane in 1816, when our Charles Holland was in the company. (*BDA*) [EAL]

HOLMAN, Joseph George 302-306

1764-1817

Born in August 1764, Joseph George Holman was the son of Major John Holman, who died when his son was only two. His uncle sent the boy to school and intended him for the clergy, but the lad had been attracted to school theatricals at Soho Academy. He very likely had other stage experience, for at the age of twenty he made his debut at Covent Garden Theatre, playing Romeo to Elizabeth Younge's elderly Juliet on 25 October 1784. Holman then went on to appear as Macbeth, Richard III, Chamont in *The Orphan* (**303**), Hamlet, and Lothario in *The Fair Penitent* – to name a few of his characters. It was a remarkable first season, and the critic writing for the *Public Advertiser*, sounding quite modern, predicted that the 'easy and natural performance of Holman … will prove a fatal blow to the cause of the Attitudinarians and Face-makers; to those who think dramatic excellence consists in … finding out meanings that were never meant … [and] in stretching out their fingers like monkies dying in convulsions … ' Alas, it was not to be. Though Holman had a popular following at Covent Garden, Smock Alley Theatre in Dublin, Drury Lane (briefly), the Haymarket, Liverpool and other provincial theatres, he developed the very bad habits his early critics had praised him for avoiding. Again and again over the years he was cautioned to restrain his energetic, ranting style and posturing.

Yet critics often described him as having a genteel person, an elegance and intelligence that promised much. At Covent Garden he was encouraged by a good salary – £12 weekly by 1791-92 plus good receipts at his benefits, and he was a useful actor with a wide range of roles in his head. He gained experience in management and in theatre life in America, wrote some forgettable plays, had three wives (the first by common law) and died at the age of 53 in August 1817 at Rockaway, Long Island, New York. (*BDA*) [EAL]

HOPE, Anthony Sir Anthony Hope Hawkins 307

1863-1933

Born on 9 February 1863, the son of the Reverend E. C. Hawkins, Vicar of St Bride, Fleet Street, Anthony Hope Hawkins was educated at Balliol College, Oxford, where he was President of the Oxford Union Society; and was called to the Bar at the Middle Temple in 1887. His first success as a novelist came with *The Prisoner of Zenda* (1894); then followed *Rupert of Hentza*

(1898). He soon turned to writing fulltime. Some of his subsequent works were *Mrs Maxon Protests, A Young man's Year, Captain Dieppe* and *Lucinda*. His plays included *The Adventure of Lady Ursula* and *Pilkerton's Peerage*. In 1918 he was knighted for his war service.

He was elected to the Garrick Club on 15 January 1903. Sir Anthony died on 8 July 1933.

HOPKINS, Mrs William, Elizabeth née Barton **769**
1731-1801
Elizabeth Barton, the daughter of a publican in York, was born in 1731. She had done some acting in York by the time she married, at the age of 22, the actor and prompter William Hopkins at York Minster on 22 April 1753. She spent some eight years in the provinces, engaged at Edinburgh and in Ireland, where audiences saw her as Lady Brute in *The Provok'd Wife*, Olivia in *Twelfth Night*, Miranda in *The Tempest*, Lavinia in *The Fair Penitent* and Hermione in *The Distrest Mother*. When her husband became prompter at Drury Lane, she accompanied him to that theatre, making her first appearance on 14 November 1761 as Almeria in *The Mourning Bride*. Mrs Hopkins remained busily employed at Drury Lane for 34 years, playing major roles in comedies and tragedies. Even in her later years, when she had grown to some 19 stone, she was accounted a useful actress and towards the end of her career was 'perfectly suited to old maids and crabbed aunts.' In her prime, however, she often appeared in leading roles in the repertory, such as Jane Shore, Ophelia, Cleopatra in *All for Love*, Lavinia in *The Fair Penitent*, Roxanna in *The Rival Queens,* Mrs Heidelberg in *The Clandestine Marriage* and Gertrude in *Hamlet* (**769**). She retired in 1796, claimed on the Drury Lane Theatrical Fund that year, and died at Bath on 8 October 1801 in her seventieth year. Two daughters were actresses and married well. Elizabeth (b. 1756) married the oboist Michael Sharp and became the mother of the painter Michael William Sharp. Priscilla (1758-1854) was first married to the actor William Brereton and after his death in 1787 to John Philip Kemble. A watercolour drawing by De Faesch of Mrs Hopkins as Gertrude in *Hamlet* is in the Folger Shakespeare Library. (*BDA*)

HORDERN, Sir Michael **946, G1002, G1038**
1911-1995
Born on 3 October 1911 at Berkhamsted, Hertfordshire the son of Capt Edward Joseph Calverly Hordern and Margaret Emily (née Murray), Michael Hordern was educated at Brighton College. After acting in amateur productions at the St Pancras People's Theatre, he made his first professional appearance as Lodovico in *Othello* at the People's Palace in March 1937. He was in repertory at the Little Theatre, Bristol, for several years and then served in the Royal Navy from 1940 to 1946. Subsequently he embarked on a career full of fine performances in plays and films. In the Old Vic season 1953-54 he played Polonius, King John and Prospero and there in 1958-59 he acted Cassius, Pastor Manders in *Ghosts* and Macbeth. Other major roles included Beutler in *The Physicists* at the Aldwych, 1963; King Lear at Nottingham Playhouse, 1969 (also on television); and George Moore in *Jumpers* at the National Theatre, 1972. Hordern excelled in comedies by Pinter, Ayckborn, Shaw and Mortimer. He also appeared in numerous films, including *Passport to Pimlico* and *A Funny Thing Happened on the Way to the Forum*. His honours include Honorary Fellow, Queen Mary's College 1987; Honorary DLitt Exeter 1985 and Warwick 1987; and CBE 1972 and a knighthood in 1983. His autobiography *A World Elsewhere* was published in 1993. Sir Michael became a member of the Garrick Club in 1953. He was an avid fisherman. He died in Oxford on 2 May 1995. His wife Grace Eveline Mortimer, whom he married in 1943, died in 1986.

HORN, Charles Edward **308**
1786-1849
Born in London in 1786, this composer and vocalist was the son of Karl Friedrich Horn (1762-1830), who came from Saxony to London and, about 1789, became music-master to the Princesses Augusta and Elizabeth and was appointed organist at St George's Chapel in 1823. Charles made his debut at the English Opera House (the Lyceum) as Meddle in *Up All Night* on 26 June 1809 (**308**); he was severely criticized but the production was fairly popular. He did not reappear on the London stage until 1814, when

he played Seraskier in *The Siege of Belgrade,* but not until he performed Casper in *Der Freischutz* at Drury Lane in 1824 did he become established as a favourite singer. He also composed a number of operas; some of his songs became national ballads, including 'I know a Bank' and 'Child of Earth.' When he lost his voice in 1835 he left the stage and moved to New York, where he established a music publishing business. Upon his return to London in 1843 Horn was appointed director of music at the Princess's Theatre. In 1848, he went back to America to become conductor of the Haydn and Handel Society in Boston. He died in Boston on 21 October 1849. (*DNB*)

HOWARD, Leslie **309**
1893-1943
Born in London on 3 April 1893 and christened Leslie Howard Steiner, this charming and popular actor was educated at Dulwich College, was employed as a bank clerk, then served in the First World War, and subsequently appeared on the stage in 1917 as Leslie Howard. He made his first London appearances in 1918 at the New Theatre. In 1920 he appeared in *Just Suppose* at the Henry Miller Theatre in New York and acted in that city until 1925. Howard played alternately in London and New York into the mid-thirties, starring in such plays as *Her Cardboard Lover* (1927, with Tallulah Bankhead), *Berkeley Square* (1929), *The Petrified Forest* (which he produced in New York with Gilbert Miller, 1935) and *Hamlet* (1936). His own play, *Murray Hill,* was performed in New York in 1927. Howard made his film debut in *Outward Bound* in 1930 and then appeared in a number of estimable films, including *Of Human Bondage* (1934), *The Scarlet Pimpernel* (1935), *The Petrified Forest* (1936), *Romeo and Juliet* (1936), the first major film version of Shaw's *Pygmalion* (1938) and *Gone With The Wind* (1939). He died when a plane that was carrying him to London from Lisbon was shot down on 1 June 1943. Howard had become a member of the Garrick Club in July 1933.

HOWE of Aberavon, Sir Richard Edward Geoffrey, Baron of Tandridge **965**
b. 1926
Lord Howe was born on 20 December 1926, the elder son of B. E. Howe and Mrs E. F. Howe (née Thomson). He was educated at Winchester College and Trinity Hall, Cambridge, and served as a Lieutenant in the Royal Signals, 1945-1948. He was called to the Bar, Middle Temple, in 1952. As a distinguished statesman, he has held a number of important posts, including M. P., House of Lords, Minister for Trade and Consumer Affairs, Chancellor of the Exchequer and President of the Conservative Political Centre National Advisory Committee. He has also served on many international councils, committees and foundations, has been a fellow at numerous prestigious universities, including Harvard and Stanford, and is the recipient of numerous honours. He was knighted in 1970. Lord Howe became a member of the Garrick Club in 1983.

HUGHES, Mr **355**
b. 1789
The actor Hughes (whose first name eludes us), who is shown by Clint in the group scene from *A New Way to Pay Old Debts* (**355**), was born in 1789 in Hatton Garden and first appeared on the stage at Cheltenham. After performances at Woolwich and Richmond he went to Drury Lane in 1813, playing the Mock Duke in *The Honeymoon.* He was still occasionally filling small parts in low comedy and farce when William Oxberry's *Dramatic Biography* was published in 1825. He sometimes served as Edmund Kean's secretary.

HULL, Thomas **310, 311, 682**
1728-1808
The son of an apothecary in the Strand, Thomas Hull was born in 1728. By 1753-54 he was acting at the Smock Alley Theatre in Dublin; subsequently he joined the Bath company and played there through 1757-58. He acted the Elder Woud'be in *The Twin Rivals* for his London debut on 5 October 1759 at Covent Garden, and there he remained for the following 48 years during the winter seasons, playing mostly solid, secondary roles such as Edgar in *King Lear,* Cassius in *Julius Caesar,* Johnson in *The Rehearsal,* Stanley in *Richard III* and the like. He was a dependable, hard-working, journeyman actor year in and year out, respected and appreciated but never mistaken for a top performer. He was equally diligent as a

theatrical manager or actor in the summers in provincial theatres like Birmingham, Bristol, Margate and Brighton and as an author and adaptor of plays, especially musical pieces. Hull wrote at least two oratorios (unperformed), a number of nondramatic works (including a four-volume novel), some successful stage works and translations. Hull's most lasting accomplishment, however, was his founding of the Covent Garden theatrical fund to assist retired and disabled performers who had fallen on hard times. He married the actress Anna Maria Morrison in the early 1760s, and they apparently had a son. Mrs Hull died in 1805, Thomas Hull on 22 April 1808.

Pictures in the Garrick Club, p. 357, reproduces a scene from Moore's *The Gamester* (**682**) with Hull pictured as Jarvis (he is shown in the same character in **310**); in the commentary with **682** Hull is listed, in error, as Stukely and Inchbald as Jarvis. Jarvis was Hull's role at Covent Garden by 3 January 1782 (*BDA*) [EAL]

HUNT, Martita **312**
1900-1969
Martita Hunt was born in Argentina on 30 January 1900, the daughter of Alfred Hunt and his wife Marta (née Burnett), and was educated at Queenwood, Eastbourne. After preparing for the stage under Geneviève Ward and Lady Benson, she made her debut in 1921 with the Liverpool Repertory Company. Her first appearance in London was with the Stage Society at the Kingsway Theatre on 6 May 1923 as the Third Woman in *The Machine Wreckers*. During her London career, which lasted some 33 years, she acted numerous roles, including the Tsarina in *Rasputin* (Strand, April 1929), the Nurse in *Romeo and Juliet*, Portia in *The Merchant of Venice* and Portia in *Julius Caesar*, Lady Macbeth, and the Queen in *Hamlet* (all at the Old Vic, 1929-30). She also played Masha in *The Seagull* (New, May 1936), Mrs Cheveley in *An Ideal Husband* (Westminster, November 1943) and Cornelia in *The White Devil* (Duchess, March 1947). Perhaps her greatest triumph came with her New York debut at the Belasco Theatre as Countess Aurelia in *The Madwoman of Chaillot* (**312**) on 27 December 1948. She also was seen in numerous films. Martita Hunt died on 12 June 1969. (*WWWT*)

I

INCHBALD, George **682**
d. 1800
George Inchbald, the son of the actor Joseph and (stepson?) of the actress-author Elizabeth Inchbald, had a modest stage career. At Elizabeth's urging George was hired by Tate Wilkinson of the York circuit in July 1779 and proved, said Wilkinson in his *Wandering Patentee*, 'a young man of great service' as an actor and singer. (Wilkinson referred to Elizabeth as George's mother-in-law.) Inchbald stayed on the York circuit until 1786, spending the summers of 1780 and 1781 in Edinburgh acting such parts as Strickland in *The Suspicious Husband* and Merlin in *Tom Thumb*. He tried London in the autumn of 1786, acting Stukely in *The Gamester* (**682**) at Covent Garden, substituting for Francis Aickin. His voice failed him on 16 October when he tried the title part in *Richard Coeur de Lion*, and he resigned. Inchbald returned to the provinces – Norwich, Spalding and probably Dublin and Worthing – and married. He died on 28 October 1800.

Pictures in the Garrick Club, p. 357, reproduces a scene from Moore's *The Gamester* (**682**) with Inchbald pictured as Stukely; in the commentary Hull is listed, in error, as Stukely and Inchbald as Jarvis. (*BDA*)[EAL]

INCHBALD, Mrs Joseph, Elizabeth, née Simpson **313, 314**
1753-1821
Born on 15 October 1753 at Standingfield, Suffolk, Elizabeth Simpson was the daughter of John and Mary Simpson, Roman Catholic farmers. Elizabeth was born with a stutter, which she eventually mastered but never conquered, yet she had a successful career as an actress, playing leading roles in both comedies and tragedies in the provinces and in London. Then, in 1789, having proved to herself that she could succeed as an actress but having accepted the fact that she was not going to reach the top of her profession, she left the stage and became one of the most prolific and successful of English authors.

Elizabeth Simpson was a beautiful, strong-minded woman, but her applications to Thomas King and Samuel Reddish at Drury Lane in 1772 were unsuccessful, and, according to her biographer Boaden, her appeal to James Dodd, also of Drury Lane, got her an indecent proposal and Dodd a basin of hot water in the face. So she set her sights on Joseph Inchbald, a provincial and London actor twice her age, to whom she was wed on 9 June 1772. Two days later the couple headed for Bristol, where Joseph was scheduled to perform. He arranged for Elizabeth to play Cordelia to his Lear – very appropriate casting – on 4 September. The seasons following found the Inchbalds restlessly touring: Glasgow, Edinburgh, Aberdeen, Haddington, Kelso, Liverpool, Manchester, Canterbury, Hull, Halifax. The couple also made friends on the road with the Siddons and Kemble families. Suddenly, on 6 June 1779 at Leeds, Joseph Inchbald died. By that time Elizabeth had managed to control her speech impediment enough to build up a repertoire of important characters, among them Calista in *The Fair Penitent*, Lady Anne in *Richard III*, Miranda in *The Tempest*, the title role in *Lady Jane Grey* (**313**), Violante in *The Wonder*, Monimia in *The Orphan*, Silvia in *The Recruiting Officer*, Desdemona in *Othello*, Cleopatra in *All for Love* and Julia in *The Rivals*.

Soon after Joseph's death Elizabeth, who had always enjoyed writing, finished a draft of her first novel and sent it off to a publisher, who turned it down. She then decided to give up the rough and tumble life of a touring player and try again what she could do in London. On 3 October 1780 she appeared at Covent Garden playing Bellario in *Philaster*. Her salary was a modest £2 weekly. She remained there for nine years, but she also, in the summers, went over to the Haymarket or off to Dublin or Shrewsbury; she could not bring herself to settle down, even in her London abodes, which changed constantly. Then, at the end of her 1788-89 season at Covent Garden, she left the stage and turned to writing full time. In addition to novels, plays, translations and critical articles, she edited several multi-volume anthologies of plays, saved a diary that ran to 52 volumes and burned a four-volume autobiography. Her four-volume novel, *A Simple Story* (1791), was probably her most influencial work. Elizabeth Inchbald died on 1 August 1821. (*BDA*) [EAL]

INCLEDON, Charles Benjamin
1763-1826 **315, 316, 947**

Christened Benjamin Incledon but later naming himself Charles, our subject was baptized on 5 February 1763, the son of the surgeon and apothecary Bartholomew Incledon of St Keverne, Cornwall. At eight he was singing in the Exeter Cathedral choir and receiving musical training; then he served in the Navy from 1779 to 1783 and was called 'Singer to the British Fleet.' After some appearances as a singer at Southampton and tuition under Rauzzini at Bath, he made his London debut at Vauxhall Gardens on 29 May 1786. Incledon established himself as a singer, especially of ballads and most particularly of such songs as 'Rule Brittannia,' 'The Storm' (**315**, **947**) and 'Black-Eyed Susan.' He sang solos regularly at pleasure gardens like Vauxhall in the summers, but his main career was in the winters in musicals, chiefly at Covent Garden Theatre, where he made his debut on 17 September 1790 as Dermot in *The Poor Soldier*. That season he also played the title role in *Cymon*, Sandy in *The Highland Reel*, Carlos in *The Duenna*, Wilfred in *The Woodman*, Young Meadows in *Love in a Village* and other characters in light works. In addition, he participated in the oratorios at Covent Garden in the spring of 1791. Then as now, good singers were forgiven and well paid despite not displaying much ability as actors, and Incledon at Covent Garden rose to £12 weekly by 1793-94, the third highest in the troupe. In 1795 Francis Waldron described Incledon's voice: 'Clear, mellow, and extensive in its tones, it is capable of executing almost any piece of vocal music. His forte is evidently in the plain English ballads; and the sea songs, which have always been peculiarly grateful to a British ear, were never better sung than by this gentleman. The less we say of his acting powers the less cause he will have to blame our freedom of observation.'

Incledon also appeared at provincial theatres, especially at Southampton (where he got his start), Liverpool, Manchester, Edinburgh, York, Dublin, Bristol, Bath and many others, one of his favourite roles with audiences being Macheath in *The Beggar's Opera* (**316**). Further, he developed showcase entertainments, such as in 1802, when he concocted a potpourri of songs and recitations aptly called *Variety*. In 1817 and 1818 he tried America, was called 'The Wandering Melodist,' and brought back £5000. He found time in his peregrinations to have three wives and at least eight children. He continued his career even after his vocal powers waned. Incledon retired first on 19 April 1822 at the English Opera House and again at Southampton in October 1824. He died on 11 February 1826 at Worcester. (*BDA*) [EAL]

IRVING, Sir Henry John Henry Brodribb **317-327, 948, S21-S23, S48, S058 B34-B35, B139-B142, B163 G0983**
1838-1905

Henry Irving, who was the leading force in the English theatre during the second half of the nineteenth century, was born John Henry Brodribb at Keinton, near Glastonbury, on 6 February 1838, the son of Samuel and Mary Brodribb. He received some early schooling at the City Commercial School in Lombard Street, London, where he took elocution lessons to overcome a stutter. His first professional stage appearances were at Sunderland in 1856, and he first performed in London in 1859. After some more years in the provinces he returned to London, where on 6 October 1866 he played Doricourt in *The Belle's Stratagem* and Rawdon Scudamore in *Hunted Down* at the St James's Theatre. Over the next five years he performed at several London venues, until, on 25 November 1871 at the Lyceum, he scored his first great success as Matthias in *The Bells* (**326**), an adaptation by Leopold Lewis of Erckmann-Chatrian's *Le Juif polonais*; that role became one of his signature parts for the rest of his life. Irving was associated with the Lyceum some 30 years, 21 as lessee. Under his management, which began on 30 December 1878 with *Hamlet*, he produced many of Shakespeare's plays with magnificence and archeological accuracy in costumes and scenery. His acting in these productions won him accolades and immense prestige. 'To Irving acting was movement. He drew a character in sharp, sudden, delicate, superb movements, each guided by a craftsmanship on which he had worked with what seemed to his associates almost inhuman concentration' (*OCT*). The notable productions included *The Lady of Lyons, The Merchant of Venice, The Corsican Brothers, Romeo and Juliet, Henry VIII* (**327**), *Faust* (**318**), King *Lear* (**324**), *Beckett* and *Cymbeline*. He first appeared in America in 1883 and often returned there.

His lease at the Lyceum expired in 1901; that year he acted Coriolanus, and in 1902 he made his last appearance there, as Shylock. Thereafter he toured America, Canada and the English provinces. While at Bradford playing Becket he died on 13 October 1905.

Irving was the first British actor to be knighted, in 1895. Many other distinctions came to him, including honorary degrees from Dublin, Cambridge and Glasgow. He served as President of the Actors' Benevolent Fund, the Actors' Association and the Managers' Association of Great Britain. Irving was a member of the Athenaeum, the Marlborough, the Reform and the Beefsteak clubs, but it was at the Garrick Club, of which he became a member in 1874, where he was most often seen, holding court at the head of the long table at after-theatre suppers. His chair still occupies that venerable place in the Coffee Room. In the Garrick Club Library are some 22 volumes of materials on the life and works of Irving, collected by Percy Fitzgerald.

Irving's marriage to Florence O'Callaghan in 1869 was not a happy one, and they separated in 1879. They had two sons, both of whom became actors. Henry Brodribb Irving is noticed below. (*OCT, Garrick Club Library)*

IRVING, Henry Brodribb **238, 329, S24**
1870-1919

The actor-manager and author H. B. Irving was born in London on 5 August 1870, the eldest son of the famous Sir Henry Irving and his wife Florence (the daughter of Surgeon-General Daniel James O'Callaghan). He was the brother of the actor Laurence Irving (1871-1914). He was educated at Marlborough College and at New College, Oxford, and was called to the Bar at the Inner Temple in 1894. But he had already turned to his father's profession, making his first appearance on the London stage at the Garrick Theatre on 19 September 1891 as Lord Beaufoy in *School*. After a hiatus from the stage until 1894, he re-appeared and continued to act until 1914. He also was lessee and manager of several West End theatres, including the Shaftesbury, the Queen's and the Savoy. In 1911-12 he toured Australia and in 1912-13 South Africa. Irving appeared in a number of plays made famous by his father: *The Bells*, *Louis XI*, and *Charles I*. He created the title role in J. M. Barrie's *The Admirable Crichton* on 4 November 1902, the role in which Buchel pictured him (**328**). His writings include *The Life of Judge Jeffreys* (1858), *French Criminals of the 19th Century* (1901) and *The Trial of Mrs Maybrick* (1913). Irving died in London on 17 October 1919. He had become a member of the Garrick Club in 1896 and was also a member of the Athenaeum, Beefsteak and Green Room clubs. (*WWWT*, *WWW*)

IVERS, Mary Anne
See Mary Anne ORGER

J

JAMES, Lord Henry QC, MP **793**
d. 1902
Lord Henry James is shown as No. 37 in Henry O'Neil's large picture of Garrick Club members in the Billiards Room in 1869. He was elected to membership in the Garrick Club on 15 February 1862 and died on 22 March 1902.

JEANS, Isabel **330**
1891-1985
The actress Isabel Jeans was born in London on 16 September 1891, the daughter of Frederick George Jeans and his wife Esther (née Matlock). She made her first appearance on the London stage as Daffodil in *Pinkie and the Fairies* at Her Majesty's Theatre on 16 December 1909, beginning a busy career of some 55 years in numerous plays in the West End. Some of her major roles included Fanny in *Fanny's First Play,* Raina in *Arms and the Man* and Hypatia in *Misalliance*, all at the Everyman in 1922; and Margery Pinchwife in *The Country Wife* (Regent 1924), Lady Underwood in *Heartbreak House* (Cambridge 1943), Mrs Erlynne in *Lady Windermere's Fan* (Haymarket 1945), Lady Elizabeth Mulhammer in *The Confidential Clerk* (Edinburgh Festival 1953, Lyric, London 1953) and Lady Bracknell in *The Importance of Being Earnest* (Haymarket 1968). She was married to the actor Claude Rains and then to Gilbert Edward Wakefield. Isabel Jeans died in 1985.

JEFFERSON, Thomas **613**
1732-1807
The actor and manager Thomas Jefferson was born on 31 January 1732, the son of a farmer in the North Riding of Yorkshire. He was articled to an attorney, but a visit to London, where he was almost killed in an accidental explosion at a coffee house in Tilt Yard, turned him toward the stage. After some country engagements he appeared for the first time at Drury Lane on 24 October 1753 as Vainlove in *The Old Bachelor*. Jefferson remained at Drury Lane through 1757-58, playing a number of modest supporting roles, such as Essex in *King John,* Paris in *Romeo and*

Juliet, Catesby in *Jane Shore* and Pedro in *The Spanish Fryar*. In the autumn of 1758 Jefferson and his actress-wife went to Ireland, where they acted in Dublin and the county towns for several years. He was back at Drury Lane in 1767 and acted there until the mid-1770s, taking on a repertoire somewhat more ambitious, including Colonel Restless in *The Committee* (**613**), Mirabel in *The Way of the World*, Claudius in *Hamlet*, Orsino in *Twlfth Night*, Major O'Flaherty in *The West Indian* and Iachimo in *Cymbeline*. Jefferson also managed the theatres at Plymouth, Richmond and several other towns.

Jefferson died at Plymouth in 1807, probably from complications of gout. Jefferson was a likeable actor who served as an able journeyman under Garrick, to whom he often played the comic foil. He had a large family by his two wives. By his first wife he had a son, Joseph Jefferson (1774-1832), who acted in America with some success and married into the Warren family of actors. Another son, also named Joseph Jefferson (1804-1842), acted in America and was the father of the famous American actor Joseph Jefferson (1829-1905), the third of that name, who made a career playing Rip Van Winkle. A portrait of our subject, Thomas Jefferson, was published as a plate to *Hibernian Magazine* with the erroneous caption: 'Mr. Thomas Jefferson. Late President of the United States of America,' thus inflating his status on the world's stage.

JEFFREY, Peter **1003**

1929-2000

Born in Bristol on 18 April 1929, the son of Arthur Winifred Gilbert Jeffrey and his wife Florence Alice (née Weight), Peter Jeffrey was educated at Harrow and Pembroke College, Cambridge. After appearances with the Chorlton-cum-Hardy Repertory Company in 1951, he toured for two years with the Elizabethan Theatre Company, playing Julius Caesar, Exeter in *Henry V*, Horatio in *Hamlet*, Escalus in *Romeo and Juliet* and Carlisle in *Richard II*. He was with the Bristol Old Vic from 1957 to 1959 and then joined the Royal Shakespeare Company in 1960. With the RSC, at Stratford and at the Aldwych in London, Jeffrey acted, among other roles, Agamemnon in *Troilus and Cressida*, Delio in *The Duchess of Malfi*, Banquo in *Macbeth* and Albany in *King Lear*. With the Prospect Theatre company he toured in 1966 in the title role in *Macbeth*. Back with the RSC in August 1975 he played Percy in *Jingo* at the Aldwych. He also appeared in some films. Jeffrey became a member of the Garrick Club in 1991. He died in January 2000. (*WWT17*)

JERROLD, Mary **331**

1877-1955

The actress Mary Jerrold was born in London on 4 December 1877, the daughter Philip F. Allen; she was the great-granddaughter of the playwright and journalist Douglas William Jerrold (1803-1857). She attended the Gower Street School and began her long stage career at the St James's Theatre, London, on 14 April 1896 as Prudence Dering in *Mary Pennington, Spinster*. That success brought other roles at that theatre, and she engaged with the Kendals for three and a half years, 1902-1905. During her next 45 years on the stage Jerrold acted dozens of roles in popular West End plays, including Rose Sibley in *Milestones*, the role in which she is pictured by Cushla Parker (**331**), Peggy Ingledew in *Under the Greenwood Tree*, Marion Yates in *The Madras House*, Sarah in *Trelawny of the Wells*, Lady Beaconsfield in *Disraeli* and Mrs Frail in *Love for Love*. She toured Australia in 1926-1927 with Dion Boucicault and acted in New York in 1928. At the age of 65, in 1942, she began a three-and-a half-year run as Mrs Brewster in *Arsenic and Old Lace* at the Strand. Some of her last roles were at the Lyric, Hammersmith, in 1950: Lady Wrathie in *Shall We Join the Ladies?*, Cuthman's Mother in *The Boy With a Cart* and Lady Amorest in *The Old Ladies*. She began making films in 1931. She was married to Hubert Harben. Mary Jerrold died in 1955. (*WWT*)

JEYNES, Alban **892**

d. 1980

Alban Jeynes, who is shown as No. 6 in Gilroy's picture of the Garrick Club Outing in 1967, was an Associate of the Royal Academy of Music. He was elected to the Garrick Club in January 1946 and died on 4 May 1980.

JOHN, a Club Servant **793**

fl. 1867

A Garrick Club servant called John is identified as No. 44 in O'Neil's scene of members in the Billiards Room in 1867.

JOHNSON, Benjamin **271**

1665-1742

Born in 1665, Benjamin Johnson seems to have begun his stage career with some strolling players, after which he joined Christopher Rich's troupe at Drury Lane Theatre in London. His first known part was Sir Simon Barter in *The Mock Marriage* in September 1695. He was then seen at Drury Lane or the Dorset Garden Theatre in mostly small comic parts in plays now forgotten. Johnson was also a painter, said the prompter John Downes in 1708, though no examples of his work have been found. He became a popular comedian, his most praised parts being Corbaccio in *Volpone,* Morose in *The Silent Woman* and Numps in *Bartholomew Fair,* all by Shakespeare's contemporary, Ben Jonson (not an ancestor), which suggests that the natural quality praised in Johnson's acting was a stress on character comedy rather than slapstick. It is as Ananias in Jonson's *Alchemist* that he is shown in Van Bleeck's painting (**271**). Johnson also played such parts as the Gravedigger in *Hamlet,* Foresight in *Love for Love* and Caliban in *The Tempest.* He was compared to the comedians Underhill and Doggett, which was high praise, and when Colley Cibber was one of the Drury Lane managers he appropriated some of Johnson's parts for himself, a nice compliment, though left-handed. It is difficult to tell now whether Benjamin Johnson was shabbily treated or just not very ambitious; his acting line was similar in some ways to that of Cibber and the popular John Hippisley, but Johnson's career was not as successful as one would have expected from an actor who appears to have been fairly talented. He acted until 26 May 1742 and died, according to the *Daily Advertiser,* on 31 July, aged 77. (*BDA*) [EAL]

JOHNSTON, Henry Erskine **332, 333**

1777-1845

Legend surrounds the origins of the actor Henry Erskine Johnston, who may or may not have been the son of a hairdresser, his real name may or may not have been Somerville, and he may or may not have been apprenticed to a signet and then to a linen draper. He did, it seems certain, make his stage debut as Hamlet at the Theatre Royal, Shakespeare Square, Edinburgh, on 9 July 1794, under Stephen Kemble's management. When he acted Young Norval in *Douglas,* in full Highland attire on 23 July, he received a warm reception. Johnston acted in Edinburgh and in Irish towns until he made his London debut on 23 October 1797 as Young Norval, at Covent Garden. Among his excellent notices was the *Monthly Mirror*'s praise of his 'finer qualities, figure excepted, for any actor on the stage.' He remained engaged in capital roles at Covent Garden most years from then until 1816. He was then at Drury Lane from 1817-18 through 1820-21, acting such roles as Pierre in *Venice Preserv'd* and the original Rob Roy in an adaptation from Scott.

Johnston also managed various theatres: Astley's Amphitheatre in Dublin, 1811-12, and at Aberdeen, Greencock and Glasgow. In 1823 he opened the Caledonian Theatre in London but gave it up after several months. Though his application for an engagement at the Walnut Street Theatre in Philadelphia was rejected, Johnston went to America. He obtained a position at the National Theatre in New York, where he made his American debut on 7 November 1837 as Sir Archy Macsarcasm in *Love-à-la Mode.* After a few more appearances he returned to London, where he died on 9 February 1845 at his residence in Gillingham Street, Vauxhall Road, and was buried in the Lambeth parish church.

Johnston was a popular and versatile actor, if not an excellent one. The critic Gilliland called him 'highly useful.' In June 1796 he married Nannette Parker (b. 1782), the daughter of the equestrian producer William Parker. But Johnston and his wife were estranged for many years and were divorced in 1820. He then married Magdalen Johnson. As his widow, she presented the portrait by Allan (**332**) of Johnston as Young Norval to the Garrick Club. (*BDA*)

JOHNSTONE, John Henry 334-337
1749?-1828
The *DNB* settles on 1 August 1749 as John Henry Johnstone's probable birth date, though early sources are contradictory. He was apparently born in Kilkenny, the son of a military quartermaster. He was articled to a Dublin attorney but gave that up, came to London, squandered his money, spent some troublesome time in the military and, back in Dublin, was engaged as a singer at the Smock Alley Theatre. His debut was as Lionel in *Lionel and Clarissa* on 9 November 1775 and won him a salary of four guineas weekly in a variety of singing parts at several Dublin playhouses and in the county towns. At the Crow Street theatre was Maria Ann Portier, an actress and singer from a theatrical clan, who he married in 1778. In 1783 the couple came to London and were hired at Covent Garden. John Henry (called Jack) sang Lionel for his debut on 2 October 1783 and demonstrated 'excellence of person, voice and deportment' to the *Theatrical Review* critic. His first seasons were auspicious, bringing him on as Macheath in *The Beggar's Opera*, Lord Aimworth in *The Maid of the Mill* and, most importantly, Dermot in O'Keeffe's new comic opera *The Poor Soldier*, on 4 November 1784, with music by Shield. Thereafter Shield provided Johnstone with more stage Irishmen and insured his popularity. Jack stayed at Covent Garden in the winters and the Haymarket in the summers, specializing in onstage Irishmen and offstage mistresses, through 1802-3. He made occasional trips to the provinces, especially Ireland, where he was a great favourite. He was a fair enough singer, though Haydn found him 'most unmusical.'

His last 17 years in London were spent at Drury Lane (and at the Lyceum with the Drury Lane company), beginning on 20 September 1803; his peak salary was £17 weekly. He died in December 1828. Though described as handsome and convivial, Johnstone was called by Oxberry 'tyrannical at home, inconstant abroad – mean at his table, and an interloper at the table of others.' (*BDA*) [EAL]

JONES, Richard 216, 338-341, 438
1779-1851
The actor and dramatist Richard Jones was born in Birmingham in 1779, the son of a builder and surveyor. Though originally intended for an architect, Jones turned to the stage, playing his earlier years in the northern towns. After a season at Birmingham he went to Manchester, and then to the Crow Street Theatre, Dublin, where he appeared in November 1799. He played most of the principal Irish towns and then came to London, where he made his debut at Covent Garden Theatre on 9 October 1807 as Goldfinch in *The Road to Ruin*. He was not favourably received, but he persisted against bad notices, eventually obtained a London engagement and made his debut at the Haymarket on 5 June 1809 as the Copper Captain in *Rule a Wife and Have a Wife*. Acting there in a number of other comedies in a wide range of roles, he developed into a popular comedian, as evidenced by his portraits by De Wilde. He was admirable as eccentric gentlemen – becoming known as 'Gentleman Jones' – and as heroes in madcap farces. It is said he was the best-dressed actor on the stage. He wrote several plays that were not successful: *The Green Man*, *Carnival* and *Hoaxing* among them. He left the stage in 1833 and gave elocution lessons. Jones died on 30 August 1851. He was one of the original members of the Garrick Club in 1831. (*DNB*)

JORDAN, Dorothy née Bland 342, 343
1761-1816
Dorothy Jordan was baptised at St Martin-in-the-Fields on 22 November 1761, the daughter of Francis and Grace Bland. Her father was reputed to be a captain. Her mother (née Phillips) was one of nine children of a Welsh clergyman. At least two of her sisters became actresses. Dorothy made her debut at the Crow Street Theatre, Dublin, as Lucy in *The Virgin Unmask'd* on 3 November 1779. After acting several more roles there and at the Smock Alley Theatre in July 1782, she joined Tate Wilkinson's company on the York circuit. She was originally advertised in the bills as Miss Bland, but Wilkinson dubbed her Mrs Jordan, saying now that she was a full-fledged actress she had 'crossed over.'

As Mrs Jordan she remained with Wilkinson in the north for three years, until she made her first London appearance, at Drury Lane, on 18

October 1785 as Peggy in *The Country Girl*, a character that became one of her signature roles, and in which she was painted by De Wilde (**342**) and by Romney (now at Waddesdon Manor). When she acted Viola in *Twelfth Night* on 16 November the critic in the *Public Advertiser* wrote, 'The great powers of Mrs Jordan cannot be better displayed than in the wonderful contrast of her *Country Girl* and *Viola*. In one all archness and vivacity; in the other serious, gentle, tender and sentimental.' Soon she appeared as Priscilla Tomboy in *The Romp*, another distinctive role in her repertoire.

Over the next twenty years at Drury Lane Mrs Jordan added dozens of roles, including Juliet, Lady Teazle and Mrs Hardcastle. It was in breeches parts that she excelled and became a celebrated performer. As a 'star' she attracted a number of suitors and lovers, including the Dublin manager and profligate Richard Daly, the young baronet Richard Ford (by whom she had three children) and finally the Duke of Clarence, with whom she lived to the end of her life in an extravagant fashion and by whom she had ten children. She also continued her stage career during her years with Clarence. The relationship with Clarence in the beginning spawned numerous ribald and vulgar commentaries and caricatures. Many viewed her as a royal concubine living off the public purse, while others sympathized with her because she seemed to be kept working on the stage to support the prince's life style.

Mrs Jordan – she never received a title – died on 5 July 1816 in Paris and was buried in the cemetery at St Cloud. She had been an actress with excellent comic talents and also had been affecting in serious roles. Hazlitt called her 'the child of nature,' whose voice was 'a cordial to the heart.' Charles Lamb and Leigh Hunt also lavished praise upon her. The *BDA* lists some 85 portraits of her. Among those are Hoppner's portrait of her as Viola, at Kenwood, and his portrait of her as the Comic Muse, now at Buckingham Palace. (*BDA*)

K

KEAN, Charles John 344, B36

1811-1868

The actor-manager Charles John Kean, the second son of Edmund Kean (*q.v.*), was born on 18 January 1811 in Waterford, Ireland. After three years at Eton he made his first appearance on the stage at Drury Lane on 1 October 1827 as Young Norval in *Douglas*. He played at that theatre for two seasons without creating much excitement. Among his roles in 1828-29 was Frederick in *Lovers' Vows*, a production in which his future wife Ellen Tree (*q.v.*) acted Amelia. That season he failed to succeed as Romeo and retired to the provinces. After some engagements in Dublin and Cork, he made his debut in New York at the Park Theatre as Richard III in September 1830. Upon his return to London he was engaged at Covent Garden, where he made an appearance with his father on 25 March 1833, acting Iago to Edmund's Othello. That night Edmund Kean collapsed on the stage and soon died. Charles again toured the provinces, returned to New York (with his new wife whom he had married in Dublin in 1842), played at the Haymarket and gave performances at Windsor Castle.

Though he was receiving some recognition as an actor, Kean's main contribution to the English theatre was to be in managing and the producing of a series of meticulously mounted plays at the Princess's Theatre. In August 1850 he and Robert Keeley leased that theatre and opened it on 28 September with *Twelfth Night*, followed by *Hamlet* (with Kean in the leading role) on 30 September. At the end of the season Keeley withdrew, and Kean began a series of spectacular revivals, beginning with the lavishly produced *King John* on 9 February 1852 and extending through 1858-59. His notable productions – in which he also acted the leading roles – included *The Corsican Brothers* (February 1852), *Macbeth* (February 1853), Byron's *Sardanapalus* (June 1853), *Louis XI* (January 1855, **344**), *The Winter's Tale* (April 1856), *Pizarro*, in which he acted Rolla (September 1856, **B36**), *The Tempest* (July 1857), *King Lear* (April 1858) and *The Merchant of Venice* (June 1858). His last

Shakespearean revival was *Henry V* (in which he played Henry) on 28 March 1859. These productions, mounted with historically accurate costumes and scenery, greatly influenced the direction of the modern theatre towards realism, and they were inspirations for Duke George II and his Saxe-Meininger company. Kean gave up the Princess's at the end of 1858-59, then at the top of his profession. A dinner was given in his honour at St James's Hall on 20 July 1859.

Kean continued to act in the country and at Drury Lane, but he was never an inspired performer, and he possessed a number of mannerisms. In July 1863 he set off with his wife on a tour around the world, acting in Melbourne, San Francisco, Vancouver Island, Kingston and New York. In 1866 he appeared at Liverpool and the Princess's again in London. He made his final appearance on the stage at Liverpool on 28 May 1867 as Louis XI, his greatest role. After a long illness, Charles Kean died in Queensborough Terrace, Chelsea, on 22 January 1868, and was buried near the small estate of Keydall, in Catherington, Hampshire. His wife Ellen died in 1880. Kean became a member of the Garrick Club in 1833. (*DNB, OCT, BEBB*)

KEAN, Mrs Charles, Ellen née Tree
See Ellen TREE

KEAN, Edmund **345-355, 959, S062**
1787?-1833 **B37-B42, B164**

One of the greatest of English actors, described as a 'turbulent genius' (*EB*), Edmund Kean was born in March 1787 (or 1789) in London, the bastard son of a sometime actress named Ann Carey and Edmund Kean, a disturbed young actor who committed suicide at the age of 22 and is noticed in the *BDA*. His uncle was Moses Kean (d. 1793), also an actor noticed in the *BDA*. Supposedly young Edmund began his theatrical career playing Cupid in a production of *Cymon* at Drury Lane on 31 December 1791, and the Master Kean who is listed in the Drury Lane playbill for Robin in *The Merry Wives of Windsor* on 8 June 1796 was undoubtedly Edmund. After some schooling in London and lessons in elocution from his uncle Moses, he was seen again at Drury Lane as Prince Arthur to the King John of J. P. Kemble and the Constance of Mrs Siddons in May 1801. Kean was regularly running off, sometimes to play at the fairs and in the provinces, advertised as Master Carey. He made his first appearance at the Haymarket on 9 June 1806 as Ganem in *The Mountaineers*. But he continued to play in country towns. In July 1808 in Stroud he married Mary Chambers, an actress nine years his junior. Their son Charles John Kean (*q.v.*) was born in Waterford in 1811.

Finally, his great early triumph came on 26 January 1814, when at Drury Lane he brought forward a gripping portrayal of Shylock (**354**), a performance that indicated his intense and fiery style of acting would outmode the more measured and classical style of Kemble. Specializing in stage villains, notably Richard III (**345, 346, 348, 352, 353**), Iago, Macbeth and later Sir Giles Overreach in *A New Way to Pay Old debts* (**351, 355**), Kean clearly was the premier actor of his day. His performances of Othello (**347**), King Lear and Hamlet were also estimable. Watching Kean act Shakespeare, in the famous words of Coleridge, was having the Bard revealed 'by flashes of lightning.' But his offstage demon – drink – and his passionate and turbulent personality often rendered him ineffective and drew hostile responses from the press and public both in England and America. His reputation was considerably sullied when he was sued for adultery and criminal conversation by Alderman Robert Cox in the mid-1820s because of Kean's relationship with Mrs Cox.

Kean squandered his substantial earnings as an actor (some £10,000 a year) in debauchery as he slowly but surely was committing suicide by drinking. At Covent Garden on 25 March 1833 he acted Othello to his son's Iago and collapsed during the performance. Several months later he died, on 15 May, at his home in Richmond, Surrey. He was buried in Poet's Corner, Westminster Abbey, near Garrick. A number of books have been written on Kean, among them *The Flash of Lightning, a Portrait of Edmund Kean*, by Giles Playfair (1983) and *Edmund Kean*, by Harold Newcomb Hillebrand (1934).

KEAN, Ellen
See Ellen TREE

KEEGAN, Sir John Desmond Patrick OBE, FRSL **G1031**

b. 1934

The military historian John Keegan was born on 15 May 1934, the eldest son of Francis Joseph Keegan and his wife Eileen Mary Keegan (née Bridgman). He was educated at Balliol College, Oxford (BA 1957, MA 1962). He served as a Political Analyst at the US Embassy, London, from 1958 to 1960, and as Senior Lecturer in Military History at Sandhurst, from 1960 to1986. Keegan has held a number of fellowships and has lectured at universities in the United States and Canada. His more than a dozen books on the history of the Second World War include *Six Armies in Normandy* (1982), *The Second World War* (1989), *Churchill's Generals* (1991), *A History of Warfare* (1993, Duff Cooper Prize 1994) and *The Battle for History* (1996). Since 1986 he has been Defence Editor at the *Daily Telegraph*. He has been a member of the Garrick Club since 1977.

KEELEY, Mary Ann, née Goward **356, 357**

1805-1899

Born Mary Ann Goward at Ipswich in 1805, she was trained as a singer and made her debut at the Lyceum on 2 July 1825 in the title role of *Rosina*. She appeared on 28 November, at Covent Garden as Margaretta in *No Song, No Supper*. After marrying the low comedian Robert Keeley (*q.v.*) in 1829, she appeared with him regularly at Covent Garden and the English Opera (the Lyceum), and in June 1833 they were engaged at the Coburg, renamed the Victoria. After a journey to America, they joined Madame Vestris at the Olympic in 1838 and in 1841 were with Macready at Drury Lane. In 1844 they took over the management of the Lyceum with Strutt, playing there in many farces and burlesques until 1847. Subsequently they engaged with Charles Kean at the Princess's Theatre, with Webster at the Haymarket, and then at the Adelphi for five years. After her husband's death in 1869, Mrs Keeley retired from the stage, lived another 30 years, and died in 1899. In addition to the title role in *Jack Sheppard*, she excelled in such characters as Dame Quickly in *Henry IV*, Mrs Page in *The Merry Wives of Windsor*, Nydia in *The Last Days of Pompeii* and Smirke in an adaptation of *Nicholas Nickleby*. (*DNB, OCT*)

KEELEY, Robert **358-360**

1793-1869

Robert Keeley was born into a large family in 1793 at No. 3 Grange Court, Carey Street, Lincoln's Inn Fields. His father was a watchmaker. Although he was apprenticed to a printer, Keeley's appetite for the stage was whetted by participation in amateur theatricals, and he joined a strolling company in Richmond, and then passed four years on the Norwich circuit under Brunton. He was engaged by Elliston for the Olympic, where he appeared in 1818 as the original Leporello in *Don Giovanni in London*, and then he appeared at the Adelphi for two seasons as the original Jemmy Green in *Tom and Jerry*. He joined Charles Kemble at Covent Garden in 1822, where he acted a number of low comic and pathetic roles. With his wife Mary Goward, whom he married in 1829 (*q.v.*), he was engaged at the Coburg (renamed the Victoria) in 1833, and, after a visit to America, with Madame Vestris at the Olympic in 1838 and with Macready at Drury Lane in 1841-42. In 1844 the Keeleys joined Strutt in the management of the Lyceum until 1847, producing burlesques and adaptations of Dickens's novels. Keeley continued engagements at various London theatres until his retirement in 1857. He died at Brompton on 3 February 1869. His widow survived another 30 years. A genuine comedian, with a small stature and many mannerisms, Keeley was a master of pathos. Dickens praised his acting of Dogberry and Verges, and those characters 'into which, by a few words or a little touch, he threw a certain homely tenderness quite his own.' He became a member of the Garrick Club in 1859. One of his daughters, Mary Lucy (1831-1870), made her debut at the Lyceum in 1845 and married the comedian Albert Smith. Another daughter, Louise (1833-1877), appeared at Drury Lane in July 1856 and acted as Toole's leading lady; she married the police magistrate Montagu Williams. (*DNB, OCT*)

KEEN, Frederick Grinham

See KERR

KEHL, Anne

See Mary Anne STERLING

KELLY, Frances Maria **361**

1790-1882

The actress and singer Frances Maria Kelly, born at Brighton on 15 October 1790, was the daughter of the actor Mark Kelly (1767-1833) and his wife Mary Singleton (she was the widow of a Mr Jackson and the mother of the Anne Jackson who became the wife of the elder Charles Mathews). Frances made her debut at the age of seven in her uncle Michael Kelly's opera *Blue-Beard* at Drury Lane on 16 January 1798. After playing children's roles with success, she performed at Drury Lane and the Italian Opera. She attained great popularity over 36 years, and was a superior actress in melodramas. Charles Lamb, who once proposed marriage, made her the heroine of his essay 'Barbara S ——,' *London Magazine*, May 1825. She was associated with all the great performers of her time, especially Edmund Kean. Upon her retirement she founded in Dean Street, Soho, an academy for the training of young actresses, but the enterprise was unsuccessful despite the backing of the Duke of Devonshire. Subsequently she devoted herself to giving readings of Shakespeare and private lessons. She died at Ross Cottage, Feltham, Middlesex, on 6 December 1882 and was buried in Brompton Cemetery. (*DNB, OCT*)

KELLY, Lydia Eliza **362, 363**

b. 1795

Lydia Eliza Kelly was born on 2 June 1795, the daughter of the actor Mark Kelly (1767-1833) and his wife Mary Jackson (d. 1827). Lydia was the younger sister of the more prominent performer Frances Maria Kelly (1790-1882, *q.v.*). After acting at Glasgow and Worthing, she made her debut in London at the age of 15 with the Drury Lane company (performing at the Lyceum) in the title role in *Rosina* on 11 October 1810 (**362**). After three years, she acted again in the provinces, mainly at Edinburgh, until she returned to London as Juliet on 21 January 1815. But she never proved as popular as her sister Frances and spent the remainder of her career at the Bath Theatre, where she settled in 1821. In addition to the portraits of her in the Garrick Club, there are pictures of Lydia Kelly as Beatrice in *Much Ado about Nothing*, Juliet and Desdemona.

KELLY, Michael **364, 365**

1762-1826

The popular Irish tenor Michael Kelly was born in Dublin on 12 August 1762, the eldest of the fourteen children of Thomas Kelly, a prosperous wine merchant. His mother was a Miss McCabe, from a respectable Westmeath family. After showing an early talent for music, nurtured by prominent teachers, Kelly made his stage debut on 17 May 1776 as the Count in *La buona figliuolo* at the Fishamble Street Theatre, Dublin. Upon the advice of Rauzzini, who had given him some singing lessons, Kelly went in 1779 to Italy, where he spent four years studying and travelling. In Vienna he met Haydn, Gluck and Mozart and performed in the Emperor Joseph's Court Theatre.

In February 1787 he departed Vienna to take up an engagement at Drury Lane, where he made his first appearance on 20 April as Lionel in *A School for Fathers*. Kelly remained a featured singer and composer at Drury Lane for some 33 years, including the period 1792-1794, during which that theatre's company played at the King's Theatre while the new Drury Lane was being built. Among his major successes were Sir George Orbit in *The Honey Moon*, Colonel Blandford in *The Cherokee*, Armstrong in *The Iron Chest* and Selim in the extraordinarily popular *Blue-Beard*. After his last stage appearance at Drury Lane, as Frederick in *No Song No Supper* on 17 June 1808, he continued to stage manage and provide music for productions there. He also served as acting manager of the Haymarket Theatre from 1801 to 1811. From 1787 he published and sold his music from his house at No 9, Lisle Street; his prosperity from that business allowed him in 1802 to lease another house at No 9, Pall Mall, which he called the Music Saloon, from which he also sold wines. But his preoccupation at the theatres gave him little time to attend other enterprises, and he was obliged in September 1811 to file for bankruptcy.

Kelly passed the last years of his life ravaged by gout so severe he 'was unable to put a foot to the ground.' His pain perhaps was made more tolerant during the time he spent at Brighton in good company, including that of George IV. Kelly died at Margate on 9 October 1826 and was buried at St Paul, Covent Garden, on 17 October.

When Kelly was at Drury Lane in the early years of his career he had met Anna Maria Crouch (née Phillips), a beautiful young actress with whom he performed for many years, and who became his mistress. Her death in October 1805 ended the long liaison. Kelly died without issue and intestate. Several of his brothers went on the stage (see the *BDA*, 8).

Although Kelly was not a good actor and had an unremarkable voice, he gained great popularity because of his stage presence and craft. He was, as one reviewer put it, 'a pretty good playhouse singer, nothing more.' He was relatively unschooled in composition, but he managed to write some elegant airs. In 1826 Kelly published his *Reminiscences* in two volumes. He was a member of the 'School of Garrick,' a congenial club of stage veterans, and of the Academy of Ancient Music and the New Musical Fund. (*BDA*)

KEMBLE, Charles Robert

1775-1854 **224, 366-370, 750, S25, B165**

Charles Kemble was born at Brecon, South Wales, on 25 November 1775. He was the eleventh child of the country managers Roger Kemble and his wife Sarah (née Ward). Many of his elder siblings appeared on the stage before Charles was ten, including John, Sarah, Stephen and Elizabeth. Charles, like his brother John, was sent for classical studies to the English College at Douai and then obtained a position in the Post Office in London. But before long, he too adopted the family profession, making an appearance at Sheffield in 1792-93 as Orlando in *As You Like It.* After his apprenticeship in country towns, he was brought to London by his brother John to appear as Malcolm in the inaugural production of *Macbeth* at the new Drury Lane Theatre on 21 April 1794 and was reported to have been 'very respectable.' That was an apt description of the rest of his career. He proved to be an accomplished actor and earned commendation in such parts as Mercutio, Macbeth (**369**), Benedick, Romeo and Charles Surface, but he was never an inspired talent and did not challenge the great eminence of his brother John and his sister Sarah. Nevertheless, Charles played an enormous number of roles and was an important presence in the London theatre during the first third of the nineteenth century. He had an eloquent manner of speech and played in the 'Kemble manner.' William Macready called him 'a first-rate actor in second-rate parts.' Yet he found Kemble's Mirabel in *The Inconstant* 'a most finished piece of acting' and his Cassio 'incomparable.'

In 1822 Kemble assumed the management of Covent Garden and appeared on 11 March as Charles Surface in *The School for Scandal.* He offered a number of highly regarded productions, including a revival of *King John* on 24 November 1823 with historically accurate costumes by Planché (*q.v.*). But the finances were shaky and Kemble was sinking into bankruptcy until in 1829 he brought out his daughter Frances Kemble (*q.v.*) as Juliet in a production in which he acted Mercutio – considered his greatest comic role – and his wife Maria came out of retirement to act Lady Capulet. His daughter proved a sensation, and her popularity over the season managed to return the theatre to solvency. Kemble accompanied Frances on a successful two-year tour of America. When Kemble returned to London he made some appearances at the Haymarket and Covent Garden. He was in weak health and growing deaf, so he made a last round of farewell performances at Covent Garden in 1836 and assumed a post as Examiner of Plays for the Lord Chamberlain, a sinecure he held until 1840. He was succeeded in that position in 1840 by his son John Mitchell Kemble, a distinguished philologist. On 10 January 1837 Charles Kemble was honoured by the Garrick Club – of which he was an original member in 1831 – with a dinner at the Albion Hotel. He acted a few more times at Covent Garden in 1840, when Queen Victoria expressed her wish to have her consort see Kemble perform. Kemble made his last stage appearance on 10 April 1840, as Hamlet, when he showed himself as 'the master yet.'

He spent his last years as a 'venerated relic' at the Garrick Club. He died on 12 November 1854 and was buried in Kensal Green Cemetery. His wife Maria Theresa had died in 1838. For information on his children and a long list of portraits of him, see the *BDA* (8: 315-321). For his biographies see the *BDA* and Jane Williamson, *Charles Kemble, Man of the Theatre* (1970).

KEMBLE, Mrs Charles Kemble, Maria Theresa née De Camp 391, 392
1775-1838
Born in Vienna on 17 January 1775, she was the daughter of the musician George Louis De Camp and his wife Jeanne Adrienne Dufour. Her father brought his large family to London by 1777, the year in which he joined the band at Covent Garden Theatre. His wife did not perform in London but two of Maria Theresa's sisters, Adelaide and Sophia, and a brother Vincent, as well as other members of the family, were on the London stage. At the age of eight Maria Theresa danced the part of Cupid in the ballet *Les Ruses de l'Amour* at the King's Theatre on 1 May 1783. She continued to appear in children's roles at the King's, then at the Royal Circus, the Haymarket and Drury Lane. At the Haymarket on 15 August 1792 she played Macheath in a bizarre production of *The Beggar's Opera*, in which Charles Bannister and J. H. Johnstone appeared as Polly and Lucy. At the new Drury Lane Theatre on 14 May 1794 Maria performed Lady Helen in *The Children of the Wind.* She remained at Drury Lane through the first six seasons of the nineteenth century, appearing in the roles of young women. Among her numerous parts were Charlotte in *My Grandmother*, Lucy Lockit in the *Beggar's Opera*, Statira in *Alexander the Great*, Olivia in *Twelfth Night* and Patie in *The Gentle Shepherd* (the role in which she was painted by De Wilde, **392**). She also was engaged regularly during summers at the Haymarket through 1800.

By 1800 Maria was betrothed to Charles Kemble (*q.v.*), who was also at Drury Lane under his brother John's management. The Kemble family opposed the alliance, but after a long wait, Charles and Maria finally married at St George, Bloomsbury, on 2 July. When the family moved over to Covent Garden that autumn the new Mrs Kemble went with them, appearing that season as Maria in *The Citizen*, Ophelia in *Hamlet* and Dorinda in *The Tempest.* The following season she acted Mrs Ford in *The Merry Wives of Windsor* (**391**). Mrs Kemble remained at Covent Garden through the 1812-13 season and then went off to the provinces, playing at Brighton, Dublin, Edinburgh and Glasgow. After a few more performances at Covent Garden in 1815 and 1819, she retired from the stage, though she did return ten years later for one performance at Covent Garden on the occasion of her daughter Fanny's debut as Juliet on 5 October 1829.

Preferring the country, Mrs Kemble lived for a while at Craven Hill while Charles lived in lodgings in town to be close to his work. She did not accompany him on his tour to America from 1832 to 1834. Her last two years were passed at a cottage in Addlestone, near Chertsey, where she died on 3 September 1838, at the age of 63. She was buried in the Addlestone churchyard. The *BDA* lists 28 portraits of her, most of which date before her marriage. (*BDA*)

KEMBLE, Elizabeth
See Elizabeth WHITLOCK

KEMBLE, Frances
See Elizabeth WHITLOCK

KEMBLE, Frances Anne, later Mrs Pierce Butler 372, 373, B44, B166
1809-1893
Fanny Kemble was born in London on 27 November 1809, the eldest daughter of the actors Charles Kemble and his wife Maria Theresa (née De Camp). She was the niece of the great actors John Philip Kemble and his sister Sarah Siddons. All are noticed on these pages. It is said that Frances had no liking for the stage but went upon it to help save her father from bankruptcy. Heavily in debt, Charles Kemble was managing the company at Covent Garden when Fanny made her debut there as Juliet (**372**) on 5 October 1829, with her father acting Mercutio and her mother acting Lady Capulet. Fanny was a great success and followed Juliet with Lady Teazle, Portia (**373**), Isabella, Euphrasia, Calista and Belvidera. In 1830 she was the original Julia in Knowles's *The Hunchback.* She was so popular that her father was soon out of debt.

In September 1832 she and her father went to America, where they toured for two years, winning acclaim. In June 1834 in New York she married Pierce Butler, a Philadelphian who was also a Georgia plantation owner, retired from the stage and lived on Butler Island and in

Philadelphia. Butler's infidelity and his ownership of slaves led to a divorce in 1849, and Fanny returned to England and the stage, acting sometimes with Macready and giving readings from Shakespeare with her sister Adelaide Kemble Sartoris. The last of these readings was given in New York in October 1868. Fanny retired to a cottage in Lenox, Massachusetts, where she wrote poems and reminiscences. There she became one of the first to take up the fashion of wearing what came to be known as 'bloomers.' Subsequently, in 1877, she returned to London, where she died on 15 January 1893 and was buried in Kensal Green Cemetery.

Fanny Kemble was a strong and intelligent woman, independent, with a forceful personality. And she possessed her full share of the famed Kemble beauty. Audiences were enthralled by her acting, and had she been more determined to follow a stage career perhaps she could have risen to the level of esteem accorded to her aunt Sarah Siddons.

She was a passionate abolitionist, who fought a private war with her husband over slavery. Pierce Butler lost much in the American Civil War, including his Philadelphia mansion and his slave property; he was arrested for treason. After the war he returned to Butler Island to manage the plantation with the help of his former slaves, now sharecroppers. He died of malaria in August 1867.

Fanny Kemble's books include *Journal of a Residence on a Georgia Plantation in 1838-39* (1863, edited with an introduction by John A. Scott, 1961). *Fanny Kemble's Journals* were edited with an introduction by Catherine Clinton (2000). Biographies of her were written by Margaret Armstrong, *Fanny Kemble, a Passionate Victorian* (1938), Henry Gibbs, *Affectionately Yours, Fanny* (1947) and *Fanny Kemble* (1967), and J. C. Furnas, *Fanny Kemble* (1982). (*OCT, EB)*

KEMBLE, Henry **375, 376**

1848-1907

Henry Kemble was born in 1848, the illegitimate son of Henry James Vincent Kemble (1812-1857) and the grandson of the estimable actor Charles Kemble (*q.v.*). Henry's father failed as an actor, went to Cambridge, had his army commission bought for him by his sister Fanny Kemble (*q.v.*) and drifted through his life; his affair with Mary Ann Thackeray furnished Henry James with material for *Washington Square.* The elder Henry died insane in August 1857. Young Henry's education was provided for by his aunt Fanny. In 1867 he made his debut on the Dublin stage. He appeared at Drury Lane in 1874, was with John Hare at the Court Theatre and was associated with the Bancrofts. He created the role of the Earl of Loam (**376**) in Barrie's *The Admirable Crichton* at the Duke of York's on 4 November 1902.

Henry Kemble became a member of the Garrick Club in 1878. He died in April 1907. He was an amusing man and an excellent comedian. His short and stout stature, captured in Allen's portrait (**375**), contributed to his being nicknamed 'Harry the Beetle.'(*OCT*)

KEMBLE, John Philip **377-390, 750, G1007, G1022, S063, B45-B48**

1757-1823

John Philip Kemble, the leading actor on the London stage between Garrick and Kean, was born at Prescott, Lancashire, on 1 February 1757, the first son of the provincial managers Roger Kemble and his wife Sarah (née Ward). His elder sister was the famous Sarah Siddons (*q.v.*); many of his siblings were also actors and some are noted on these pages. He received early schooling at Worcester and in a Catholic seminary at Sedgley Park, near Wolverhampton, before being sent to the English College at Douai, intended for the priesthood. When a child he had made some appearances in his father's company, and after Douai he returned to England in 1775 to take up the family calling. He acted at Wolverhampton, Cheltenham and Liverpool, and when he applied for a position with Tate Wilkinson at York, Kemble listed a catalogue of 86 roles he had in his repertoire. He made his debut at York on 20 January 1779 – the day that David Garrick died – as Orestes in *The Distrest Mother* and was next seen as Ranger in *The Suspicious Husband.* By 1781 Kemble's reputation was firmly established at York, where he had also written a few plays, and he next acted at Edinburgh and at the Smock Alley Theatre in Dublin, appearing at the latter theatre as Hamlet on 2 November 1781. Now ready for London, he made his debut at Drury Lane as Hamlet (**386**) on 30 September 1783 and was praised for electrifying transitions, an interesting observation, because such a comment was not often made later about his acting style, which has been characterized as formal and declamatory. Among his other roles that season was Richard III (**380**). On 6 December 1783 he appeared with his sister Sarah as Mr and Mrs Beverley in *The Gamester*. On 10 December he acted King John to her Constance. His biog rapher James Boaden described Kemble's portrayal of King John as 'The most cold-blooded, hesitating, cowardly and creeping villainy,' though other critics found him slow, monotonous and cold. Soon established as the leading actor in London, he went from triumph to triumph, acting such roles as Coriolanus (**381**) – for which he seemed born to play – Cato (**385**) and Rolla in Sheridan's potboiler *Pizarro*. (His performances as Coriolanus, Hamlet, Rolla and Cato are memorialized in Lawrence's larger-than-life-size portraits.)

In December 1787 Kemble married the actress Priscilla Brereton, widow of the actor William Brereton and daughter of the Drury Lane prompter William Hopkins. The following year he took over the management of Drury Lane Theatre, which he retained until that theatre was razed in 1791 to make way for a new theatrical facility. The new Drury Lane Theatre opened on 12 March 1794 with a concert of Handel's music. The first theatrical production was *Macbeth* on 21 April 1794, with Kemble in the title role and his sister Sarah in her great role of Lady Macbeth (**390**). At the end of the 1801-2 season Kemble, no longer able to tolerate Richard Sheridan's financial shenanigans at Drury Lane, left there to embark on a Grand Tour. In April 1803 he concluded his negotiations for the management of Covent Garden Theatre, which he assumed in 1803-4, bolstered by a company that included his sister Sarah, his brother Charles, W. T. Lewis and the difficult but brilliant George Frederick Cooke. Kemble retained that management until 1812, and then acted in the provinces until he returned to act at Covent Garden as Coriolanus on 15 January 1814, when the audience rose to welcome him back.

Kemble became ill in May 1816, and when he played Macbeth at Edinburgh in June he was described as 'the ruin of a magnificent temple, in which the divinity still resides.' His farewell performance came at Covent Garden on 23 June 1817; when he came on as Coriolanus – probably his greatest role – the house rose for a five-minute ovation. After occupying himself with travel, Kemble died at Lausanne on 26 February 1823 and was buried in a cemetery outside that city. His wife Priscilla survived him by 22 years, dying at Leamington in 1845. They had no children.

As the *BDA* notes, the handsome, elegant and intelligent Kemble was in private often aloof and intimidating. He was nicknamed 'Black Jack' by friends and enemies alike. Though his drinking did not approach the severity of Cooke and Kean's, Black Jack often heard the chimes at midnight. He enjoyed the highest esteem in his profession and clearly was a fine manager and a great actor, and he wore well the mantle inherited from Garrick as the high-priest of Shakespeare. He wrote or adapted some 58 plays. His superb library of old plays was bought by the sixth Duke of Devonshire and with a large amount of Kemble documents went in 1914 from Chatsworth House to the Huntington Library in California. The *BDA* lists some 197 portraits and engravings of Kemble. Thirteen are in the Garrick Cub, along with some figurines.

KEMBLE, Sarah
See Sarah SIDDONS

KEMBLE, Stephen George 393, 394, 750
1758-1822
Born at Kington, Herefordshire, on 3 April 1758, Stephen Kemble was the third child of the strollers Roger Kemble and his wife Sarah (née Ward), the progenitors of a large clan of actors and managers. He was the brother of Charles and John Philip Kemble and Sarah Siddons (*q.v. all*). After receiving some schooling at Douai, Stephen was apprenticed to a surgeon at Coventry but soon joined the family calling. He passed his early professional years at York, Leeds and Dublin. In 1783-84 he was engaged at Covent Garden while John Philip and Sarah were

at the rival house, Drury Lane. Stephen made his Covent Garden debut as Othello on 24 September 1783. Playing Desdemona was the young actress Elizabeth Satchell, whom he would soon marry. Though he performed a few more roles (Richard III, Sealand in *The Conscious Lover* and Bajazet in *Tamerlane* (**393**) among others, he was not reengaged at Covent Garden, and he migrated back to the provinces. After a busy season at Edinburgh in 1786-87, Kemble and his new wife played a summer season at the Haymarket in London. Stephen made his debut there on 16 May 1787 as Dominick in *The Spanish Fryar*, followed two nights later as Claudius in *Hamlet*; his wife played Ophelia.

Kemble returned each summer to the Haymarket through 1791. In February 1790 he led a company that played at Coventry through June; he acted Hamlet, Lear and Othello. In March 1791 he assumed management of the new Theatre Royal in Newcastle. His theatrical empire expanded in November 1791 when he acquired the leases of the theatres in Glasgow and Edinburgh. The former lessee, John Jackson, went to law over the terms of the lease of the Edinburgh house, but after long arbitration Kemble prevailed. He opened the Edinburgh theatre on 18 January 1794 with *Hamlet*, in which he acted Hamlet and his wife Ophelia. His subsequent six-year management was very successful until the quality of the company deteriorated to a deplorable state. In 1800 Kemble gave up the enterprise to his old nemesis Jackson. In 1806 he relinquished the management of the Newcastle circuit to Macready.

During the 1790s Kemble gained a considerable amount of weight, to some 18 stone. So when he acted Falstaff at Drury Lane in the autumn of 1802 he required no padding. After brief engagements in and out of London and some stage management for Elliston at Drury Lane in 1818-19, Kemble died at the Grove, near Durham, on 5 June 1822 and was buried in the Durham Cathedral. Stephen Kemble wrote a few plays, including, with his son Henry Stephen Kemble, *Flodden Field*, based on Scott's *Marmion* and produced at Drury Lane on 3 December 1818. (For Kemble's children see the *BDA*, 8: 401-402.)

As an actor Kemble did not possess sufficient talent to be ranked with his brother John or sister Sarah. But he was competent. His greater skill was in managing and producing. Falstaff was his best role. There are some eight portraits of him in that role, including De Wilde's watercolour in the Garrick Club. (**394**)

KEMBLE, Mrs Stephen George, Elizabeth née Satchell 371

1762?-1841

Born about 1762 in London, Elizabeth Satchell was the daughter of John Satchell, a musical instrument maker of Great Pulteney Street, Golden Square. She had at least three sisters who went on the stage (see the *BDA*, 8: 403). Elizabeth made her debut at Covent Garden as Polly in *The Beggar's Opera* on 21 September 1780, when it was reported that her person was 'exquisitely pleasing.' Other roles followed: Ophelia, Patty in *The Maid of the Mill*, Cecilia in *The Son-in-Law* and Constantia in the premier of Macklin's comedy *The Man of Mode*, on 10 May 1781. Reviewers claimed that she showed promise. Over the next several seasons she made steady progress, and, noted as a 'rising actress,' in 1783-84 she appeared as Juliet, Perdita, Desdemona and Cordelia.

On 29 November 1783 Elizabeth married the Covent Garden actor Stephen Kemble (*q.v.*), the son of Roger and Sarah Kemble and the brother of John Philip Kemble and Sarah Siddons. When her husband was discharged from Covent Garden at the end of 1783-84, Mrs Kemble went with him to play in the north. She made her debut at Edinburgh in January 1786 as Desdemona. She was back in London at the Haymarket in the summer of 1787, when she was the original Yarico in Colman's *Inkle and Yarico* on 4 August. She played at the Haymarket regularly in the summers through 1796. Though she appeared over the following years in various provincial theatres, her career was mainly at Edinburgh, helping her husband manage, between 1792 and 1800. There she acted about 150 roles that ran the spectrum of the eighteenth-century female repertory.

When the Edinburgh enterprise bankrupted them, Mrs Kemble returned to London to make her first and only appearance at Drury Lane, as

Ophelia, on 29 October 1800, when her brothers-in-law John and Charles Kemble acted Hamlet and Laertes, respectively .

Elizabeth Kemble died on 20 January 1841 at the Grove, near Durham, and was buried at Durham Cathedral by the side of her husband (who had died some nineteen years earlier). James Boaden, the biographer of J. P. Kemble and Sarah Siddons, praised Elizabeth warmly, writing that 'The stage never in my time exhibited so pure, so interesting a character as Miss Satchell.' Other critics said that she possessed an elegant figure and a 'natural and impressive style.' Her Juliet was 'delicious' and her Yarico was 'incomparable.' Her children Frances Crawford Kemble (1787-1849) and Henry Stephen Kemble (1789-1836) had stage careers and are noticed in the *BDA*.

KENDAL, Dame Madge Margaret Rafto née Robertson 395, 820

1849-1935

She was born on 15 March 1849 at No 58, Cleethorpes Road in Grimsby, Lincolnshire, the daughter of Margaretta and William Robertson, both of the theatrical profession. She was the 22nd child of her parents; her brother Thomas William Robertson (see 719) became a successful dramatist; another brother, E. Shafto Robertson, and a sister, Fanny Robertson, became actors. Margaret first appeared on the stage as the child Marie in *The Struggle for Gold* at the Marylebone Theatre on 20 February 1854. She continued to act children's parts for some 11 years, appearing at Bristol and London in such roles as Eva in *Uncle Tom's Cabin*, Cinderella, a fairy in *A Midsummer Night's Dream* (with Ellen Terry as Titania) and Alice in *Marriage at Any Price*. She made her London debut as an adult in Ophelia at the Haymarket Theatre on 29 July 1865, billed as Madge Robertson. Over the next several years at the Haymarket she acted Blanche in *King John*, Desdemona, Georgina in *Our American Cousin* and Jessica in *The Merchant of Venice*. Also in the company, which also toured, was William Hunter Grimston, whom she married in 1869. He acted under the name of Kendal, and their careers then were intertwined for a number of years. William Kendal was not as fine an actor as his wife, but he was an excellent theatre administrator; with Sir John Hare, Kendal and his wife managed the St James's Theatre with great skill and prosperity from 1879 to 1888. On 7 October 1889 Madge Kendal made her first appearance in New York, as Susan Hartley in *A Scrap of Paper*, at the Fifth Avenue Theatre. During the remainder of her career in London and on tours with her husband, she acted numerous leading and featured roles, and also appeared in a number of films. She retired in 1908, though she returned to the stage for a Gala evening, on 27 June 1911, at His Majesty's Theatre, to play Mistress Ford in the letter scene from *The Merry Wives of Windsor*. In 1926 she was made DBE, and in 1927 she received the Grand Cross of the British Empire. Mrs Kendal died at Chorleywood, Hertfordshire, on 14 September 1935. Her husband had died some years earlier, in 1917. In 1933 she published her autobiography *Dame Madge Kendal*. *See* also Thomas Pemberton, *The Kendals* (London 1900).

KENDAL, William Hunter real name Grimston 396

1843-1917

The actor and manager William Hunter Kendal (whose real name was Grimston) was born in London on 16 December 1843. He made his London debut as Louis XIV in *Life's Revenge* at the Soho Theatre on 6 April 1861. Kendal played the following year at that theatre – renamed the Royalty – appearing with Charles Wyndham and Ellen Terry. He then was a member of the companies at Birmingham and Glasgow, at the latter place performing with Helen Faucit, Charles Kean and Dion Boucicault. In 1866 he was engaged by Buckstone at the Haymarket, where he remained until 1874, appearing mainly in young romantic leads such as Orlando in *As You Like It*, Romeo, Capt Absolute in *The Rivals*, Dazzle in *London Assurance* and Young Marlow in *She Stoops to Conquer*. In 1869 he married the actress Madge Robertson (*q.v.*), who was also a member of the Haymarket company, and thereafter they often appeared together. Kendal entered into partnership with John Hare, first at the Court and then at the St James's, during which time he acted numerous roles. He also appeared at the Prince of Wales's Theatre under the Bancrofts in 1876-78. Kendal was somewhat overshadowed in acting by his wife (who was made DBE in 1926, after his death), but he was by all accounts a fine actor and good businessman. He retired from the stage in 1908. Kendal died on 6 November 1917.

KENNEY, James **397**
1780-1849
The popular dramatist James Kenney was born in Ireland in 1780. His father James Kenney managed for many years Boodle's Club in James's Street, London. Kenney's first play, *Raising the Wind*, originally performed as an amateur theatrical, was produced at Covent Garden on 5 November 1803. The farce ran 38 nights that season and remained in the repertory for some years. Many of his subsequent pieces enjoyed similar popularity, including *The World* (1808), *Love, Law, and Physic* (1812, **477**), *Spring and Autumn* (1827) and *Sweethearts and Wives* (1823). In all he wrote over 50 plays. His last was a serious drama, *Infatuation*, written for Charlotte Cushman at the Princess's Theatre, 1845. Kenney died in Brompton on 25 July 1849. His wife Louisa (d. 1853) was the daughter of the French critic Louis Sebastian Mercier and the widow of the playwright Thomas Holcroft. (*DNB*)

KERR, Frederick real name Frederick Grinham Keen **G0994**
1858-1933
Christened Frederick Grinham Keen, he was the son of Grinham Keen, a solicitor of Esher. He was educated at the Charterhouse and Caius College, Cambridge, and was intended for his father's profession, but he opted for the stage instead and went to America in 1881. His first appearance was at Wallack's Theatre in New York on 4 January 1882 as Sir Toby in *The School for Scandal*. After acting several more roles in New York, he returned to London, where he made his debut at the Gaiety Theatre on 6 December 1882 as Sir Henry Harkaway in *My Life*. From then, over almost 50 years on the stage, Kerr acted numerous roles in London and New York. Among his last were James Blake in *The Gold Diggers* at the Lyric in December 1926, Lord Trench in *The High Road* at the Shaftesbury in September 1927, and at the Fulton in New York, Octave de Corquefou in *A Kiss of No Importance* in December 1930. He also appeared in films, including *Born to Love*, *Waterloo Bridge* and *The Man from Toronto*. Kerr directed productions at various theatres. In 1931 he published his memoirs, *Recollections of a Defective Memory*. Kerr became a member of the Garrick Club in March 1920. He died on 2 May 1933 at the age of 74. Kerr was married to Lucy Houghton (née Dowson); his son Geoffrey Kerr (b. 1895) and his daughter Molly Kerr (b. 1904) had stage careers in London and elsewhere. His grandson is the film actor John Kerr, son of Geoffrey Kerr.(*WWWT*)

KEYS, Louisa
See Louisa Henrietta Hannah MILLS

KING, Henry **793**
d. 1889
Henry King, who is shown as No. 18 in O'Neil's large canvas of the game in the Billiards Room, was elected to the Garrick Club in December 1847 (and then again in March 1853) and died in January 1889.

KING, Thomas **3, 23, 398-402**
1730-1805
The son of a successful tradesman, Thomas King was born on 20 August 1730 in the parish of St George, Hanover Square. His education was at Westminster School, after which he was apprenticed to a solicitor but was drawn to the stage. He became a strolling player, and, in October 1748, he was seen at Windsor by David Garrick and on the nineteenth appeared at Drury Lane as Allworth in *A New Way to Pay Old Debts*. More supporting roles followed, and in the summer of 1749 he acted leading characters at Bristol: Ranger in *The Suspicious Husband*, Benedick in *Much Ado about Nothing*, Romeo, and George Barnwell. Playing opposite him and encouraging his career was Hannah Pritchard, a powerful ally. After another season at Drury Lane acting secondary roles King returned to Bristol in the summer of 1750 and then joined Thomas Sheridan's company at Smock Alley in Dublin. For four years he gained invaluable experience from the enlightened manager and developed a

talent for delivering prologues and epilogues and playing a line of fops, clever servants, elegant gentlemen and eccentrics. In October 1759 King returned to Drury Lane as a major member of the company, and by the mid-1760s he was earning £8 weekly, near the top of the pay scale. He became Garrick's close friend and indispensable cohort.

At Drury Lane over the years that followed Tom King was the initial and usually inimitable interpreter of dozens of characters in new plays, among them Lord Ogleby in *The Clandestine Marriage* (**23**, **398**) Sir Peter Teazle in *The School for Scandal* (**3**, **402**?), Belcour in *The West Indian* and Puff in *The Critic*. Among his parts in old plays were Pistol in *2 Henry IV*, Scrub and Archer in *The Beaux' Stratagem*, Tattle, Jeremy and Ben in *All for Love*, Osric in *Hamlet*, Kastril in *The Alchemist*, Rodrigo in *Othello*, Tom in *The Conscious Lovers*, Sparkish in *The Country Wife*, Touchstone in *As You Like It* (**401**, another of his particularly successful parts), Shylock in *The Tempest* (one of his failures), Malvolio in *Twelfth Night*, Bayes in *The Rehearsal* and Sir John Brute in *The Provok'd Wife*.

King was one of the most dependable, hardest working actors of his time and one of the most amiable. His home life was equally admirable: in the summer of 1766 he married the actress-dancer Mary Baker and lived happily ever after. His career regularly involved him in provincial appearances and he had, as well, skill in management (tested to the limit when he struggled to run Drury Lane with the capricious Richard Brinsley Sheridan as proprietor). Further, he was instrumental over the years in developing the Drury Lane Theatrical Fund for the assistance of retired and disabled players. His amiability and *joie de vivre* drew him to gambling, and despite his handsome income, his finances were touch and go over the years.

After 55 years on the stage, Thomas King retired in 1802 following a final benefit at which he acted Sir Peter Teazle one last time and said his farewell to his loyal Drury Lane patrons. Plagued for years by gout, King died on 11 December 1805. He was buried, appropriately, at the 'actors' church,' St Paul, Covent Garden. Mary King joined him there in December 1813. In 1820 the critic William Hazlitt remembered seeing Tom King in performance in his late years: 'there was King, whose acting left a taste on the palate, sharp and sweet like a quince; with an old, hard, withered face, like a John-apple, puckered up into a thousand wrinkles; with shrewd hints and tart replies.' (*BDA*) [EAL]

KING, William Augustus Henry **403**
1894-1958
William King, born on 23 February 1894, served as a distinguished scholar at the British Museum, having joined the staff in July 1926; he was Deputy Keeper of British and Medieval Antiquities from 1952 until his retirement in February 1954. He wrote five books on porcelain and pottery, including *Chelsea Porcelain* (1922) and *English Porcelain Figures of the Eighteenth Century* (1925). King was elected to the Garrick Club in 1937; he resigned in 1957, shortly before he died on 21 February 1958.

KIRKWOOD, Pat **892**
b. 1921
The actress Pat Kirkwood, who is shown as No.19 in Gilroy's scene of the Garrick Club Outing, was accompanied to the event by her husband Hubert Gregg (No. 18). She was born at Pendleton on 24 February 1921, the daughter of William Kirkwood and his wife Norah (née Carr). She made her stage debut at the Selford Royal Hippodrome in 1936 in a variety show. After similar appearances in variety and pantos in the provinces, she made her London debut on 24 December 1937 at the Prince's Theatre as Dandini in *Cinderella*. During more than 40 years on the stage she performed in numerous pantomimes, variety shows, revues, cabarets, and light comedies. Her stage roles include Ruth in *Wonderful Town*, Mrs Squeezum in *Lock Up Your Daughters*, Constance in *The Constant Wife* and Mrs Markham in *Move Over Mrs Markham*. She has also appeared on television and starred in radio series. (*WWT*)

KNIGHT, Edward **404-406, 630**
1774-1826
Born in Birmingham in 1774, Edward Knight played with touring provincial companies in

Wales and the north of England until he joined Tate Wilkinson's company at York about 1803. He joined the Drury Lane company at the Lyceum in 1809, making his first London appearance there on 14 October as Timothy Quaint in *The Soldier's Daughter* and Robin Roughhead (**404**) in *Fortune's Frolic*. He also made favourable impressions as Label in *The Prize*, Jerry Blossom (**406**) in *Hit or Miss*, Scrub in *The Beaux' Stratagem*, Varland in *The West Indian* and Sam in *Raising the Wind*, among other roles. When the company moved into its new Drury Lane Theatre his first role there was Simple in *The Merry Wives of Windsor* on 23 October 1812. Knight remained at Drury Lane the remainder of his career, playing scores of characters and specializing in domestics, rustics and farmers. A short man, some five feet two, with a shrill voice, he was said to be unequalled in various lines of pert servants, like Arnulf (**405**) in *Plots! Or the North Tower*. In his *Dramatic Biography*, Oxberry wrote that Knight's country boys are never unsophisticated; 'they are shrewd, designing, knowing.'

Illness caused Knight to retire from the stage in 1825-26. He died at his house in Great Queen Street on 21 February 1826 and was buried in a vault at St Pancras New Church. After the death of his first wife, whom he had wed at Leeds, in 1807 Knight married Susan Smith, the sister of the actress Sarah Bartley (*q.v.* as Sarah Smith). (*DNB*)

KNIGHT, Mrs Edward, Susan née Smith 355

1788-1859

Susan Smith, born in 1788, was said to be the sister of the more prominent actress Sarah Smith (*q.v.*), who became Mrs George Bartley. In 1807 she married the actor Edward Knight (*q.v.*), probably at York, where they were both members of Tate Wilkinson's company. She came with Knight to London in 1809 and went with him to the new Drury Lane Theatre in 1812. Though not as fine an actress as her sister Sarah, Mrs Knight became somewhat of a favourite. She is shown as Lady Allworth in Clint's large canvas of a scene from *A New Way to Pay Old Debts* (**355**), which features Edmund Kean as Sir Giles Overreach.

KNIGHT, Joseph FSA 407

1829-1907

The distinguished editor and critic Joseph Knight was born on 24 May 1829, the son of Joseph Knight and his wife Marianne (née Wheelwright). In 1863 he became a barrister at Lincoln's Inn. From 1883 he was editor of *Notes and Queries*, and also served as drama critic for the *Globe* and *Athenaeum*. Among his most important contributions were many of the lives of actors for the *Dictionary of National Biography*. Among his other works was a *Life of David Garrick* (1894). He became a member of the Garrick Club in March 1883, and he died on 23 June 1907.

KNIGHT, Thomas 409, 410, 411

d.1820

Thomas Knight was born into a well-regarded Dorsetshire family, was intended for the law, and was placed under the actor Charles Macklin for tuition in elocution. He was attracted to the stage and made his first appearances at Richmond. After acting at Lancaster and Edinburgh, he joined Tate Wilkinson's company at York, first appearing there as Lothario in *The Fair Penitent* in August 1782. While under Wilkinson he developed into a good actor. Engagements followed at Sheffield and Bath, and after an apprenticeship of some 25 years in the provinces, Knight made his first appearance in London at Covent Garden on 25 September 1795 as Jacob Gawkey in *The Chapter of Accidents*. De Wilde painted the picture of him in that role (**409**) soon after. Knight's rustic simplicity charmed audiences and he was kept busy in a number of similar parts, including Farmer Harrow (Roger) in *The Ghost*, the role in which he was painted by Zoffany (**411**). Though he toured in the summers with his actress wife Margaret (the sister of the more famous Elizabeth Farren), whom he had married in London in March 1788, Knight was a mainstay at Covent Garden through the season of 1803-4. He took his farewell of London on 15 May 1804, playing Farmer Ashfield in *Speed the Plough* and Lenitive in *The Prize*. Knight then assumed the management of the theatre at Liverpool, which he ran successfully for 16 years. He enjoyed the comfortable life of a country gentleman at homes in Lichfield and Woore. He died suddenly at his country home in Woore on 4 February 1820. His wife Margaret had died earlier, at Bath, on 28 June 1804. Knight made generous bequests to a number of his family. He had been a fine comedian and was characterised as 'an admirable actor, and a worthy man.' In addition to the portraits of him in the Garrick Club by De Wilde, Zoffany and Wageman (**410**), pictures of Knight were painted by Woolley, Bond and an anonymous artist. (*BDA*)

KNYVETT, Charles **750**
1752-1822
Charles Knyvett, who is pictured as No. 14 in Harlow's large canvas of the Trial Scene in *Henry VIII* (**750**), was born on 22 February 1752, probably in London. He studied under Benjamin Cooke, and by May 1775 he was playing in the Drury Lane band. During his long career in London music, he directed the Handel Memorial Concerts at Westminster Abbey, served as a Governor of the Royal Society of Musicians and played and sang at various concert venues. He died in January 1822. His sons Charles (1773-1859?) and William (1779-1856) were also active in London musical circles. (*BDA)*

KNYVETT, William **750**
1779-1856
William Knyvett, who is pictured as No. 4 in Harlowe's large canvas, was born on 21 April 1779, the son of the musician Charles Knyvett (1752-1822, *q.v.*) and his wife Rose, of the parish of St George, Hanover Square. He participated in numerous festivals and concerts in London with his father and brother, the younger Charles Knyvett. By 1775 he was a principal alto in the Concerts of Ancient Music. He was elected to the Royal Society of Musicians in 1800 and played in many of that society's benefit concerts. Knyvett was also a popular composer and singer. He died on the Isle of Wight on 17 November 1856. (*BDA*)

L

LACY, Harriette Deborah
See Harriette Deborah TAYLOR

LAMBERT, Mary Anne
See Mary Anne Elizabeth 'Fanny' STIRLING

LAMBTON, Lieutenant General Arthur **793**
1836-1908
Born on 19 October 1836 at Biddick Hall, Durham, Lambton was the fourth son of William Henry Lambton (brother of the 1st Earl of Durham) and his wife Henrietta, a daughter of Cuthbert Ellison of Hebburn, MP. After Eton, he entered the army in 1854 and served for many years, in the Crimea, Egypt, and the Sudan. After rising to the rank of Major General in 1890 he retired in 1892. Lambton was married to Alice, the daughter of Robert Lister. He was elected to the Garrick Club in February 1868 and died on 2 March 1908.

LANGE, Josef **412**
1751-1829
Lange was an actor of some reputation in Germany and in Vienna. At the age of 21 he acted Hamlet in Franz Heufield's adaptation of the play at the Habsburg Court Theatre in Vienna in January 1773. He was a 'monotonous Hamlet.' Some years later, in April 1816, the aging Lange played King Lear at the Theater an der Wien. (Simon Williams, *Shakespeare on the German Stage 1586-1914.*

LANGFORD, Joseph Munt **793**
d. 1889
Joseph Munt Langford, who is shown as No. 40 in O'Neil's large canvas of members in the Billiards Room (**793**), was elected to the Garrick Club in 1850 and died in 1889.

LAWRENCE, Gerald **413**
1873-1957
Gerald Lawrence, who had a long career as a romantic actor, was born at Eastwood,

Nottingham, on 23 March 1873. He appeared with the Benson Company at Stratford-upon-Avon in 1895, subsequently made two tours to South Africa, and on 17 September 1898 appeared at the Lyceum in London as Young Siward in *Macbeth*. He acted with Tree's Company at Her Majesty's in 1899, playing the Dauphin in *King John* and Orsino in *Twelfth Night* (**413**). In 1903 he joined Irving at the Lyceum, staying until 1905, was at Drury Lane and toured the United States as a leading man. Lawrence produced Shakespearean plays at the Court Theatre and in Berlin in 1909, when he appeared as Hamlet, Orlando and Romeo. In October 1912 he acted Captain Brassbound in *Captain's Brassbound's Conversion* at the Little Theatre. Lawrence served in the Royal Navy, 1914-1918. After the war he continued to produce and act in London and elsewhere until 1938; among his notable parts were the title roles in his revival of *Monsieur Beaucaire* (1923), *Beau Brummel* (1928) and *David Garrick* (1925, and throughout the rest of his career). His first wife was the actress Lilian Braithwaite (1873-1948); their daughter was the well known actress Joyce Carey (1898-1993). His second wife was the American actress Fay Davis (1872-1945), who appeared with him in many productions. Later he married the actress Madge Compton (d. 1970). Lawrence became a member of the Garrick Club in 1944. He died on 16 May 1957. (*OCT, WWT*)

LAWSON, Nigel, Baron of Blaby **965**

b. 1932

Nigel Lawson was born on 11 March 1932, the son of Ralph Lawson and his wife Joan Elizabeth (née Davis). He was educated at Westminster School and Christ Church, Oxford, and after service with the Royal Navy joined the editorial staff of *The Times* and then became City Editor of the *Daily Telegraph*. Subsequent to his serving as special assistant to Prime Minister Sir Alec Douglas Home, he represented Blaby in Parliament from 1974 until 1992. He has been a key figure in shaping Britain's fiscal and economic policies. Among his many important posts have been Financial Secretary to the Treasury (1979-1981), Secretary of State for Energy (1981-1983) and Chancellor of the Exchequer (1983-1989). He is Chairman of the Central Europe Trust and is on the boards of a number of banks and financial organizations. In 1992 he was created a life peer and Baron of Blaby. Lord Lawson became a member of the Garrick Club in 1967. His books include *The Power Games* (1976, with Jock Bruce-Gardyne), *The View from No. 11 – Memoirs of a Tory Radical* (1992) and *The Nigel Lawson Diet Book* (1996, with his wife Thérèse Lawson).

LAWTON, Frank **892**

1904-1969

Frank Lawton was born in London on 30 September 1904, the son of Frank Molkeley Lawton and his wife Daisey (née Collier). He made his first appearance on the London stage at the Vaudeville Theatre in *Yes!* on 29 September 1923. After other parts at the Vaudeville, Shaftesbury and St James's theatres, he enjoyed success as Littler in *Sadie Dupont* in December 1927 at the Strand. As Woodley in *Young Woodley* he scored a greater success, first at the New Theatre in February 1928 and then at the Savoy the following month. He toured in the role and also appeared in the film in 1930. Over the next two decades he was seen in a number of roles in London and on 1 February 1934 made his first appearance in New York at the Ritz as Charles Tritton in *The Wind and the Rain*. In New York for several seasons he acted Thierry Keller in *Promise* at the Little Theatre (December 1936), Alan Howard in *French without Tears* at the Henry Miller (September 1937) and Percy Bysshe Shelley in *I Am My Youth* at the Playhouse (March 1938). He returned to London in 1938, served in the Second World War and was awarded the U. S. Legion of Merit. He re-appeared on the stage in September 1945, touring as Richard in *Three Waltzes*. Among his later roles were Tom Collier in *The Animal Kingdom*, Leonard Ferris in *Mid Channel* and Nigel Wainwright in *Summer in December*. In 1950 he toured as Evan Davies in *September Tide*. Lawton also appeared in a number of films. He was married to the actress Evelyn Laye (1900-1996), who is shown with him in Gilroy's group (**892**). He became a member of the Garrick Club in 1942. His death occurred on 10 June 1969.

LAYE, Elsie Evelyn CBE **892**
1900-1996
Evelyn Laye was born in London on 10 July 1900, the daughter of Gilbert Laye and his wife Evelyn (née Froud). She first appeared on the stage as Nag-Ping in *Mr Wu* at Brighton in August 1915. She made her London debut in the revue *Honi Soit* at the East Ham Palace on 24 Aril 1916. Her career extended some 61 years, during which she acted numerous roles in London, New York and on tour. She received the CBE in 1973, and she died in February 1996. In the picture of the Garrick Club Outing (**892**) she is seen with her husband Frank Lawton.

LEE, Henry? or R.? **600**
1765-1836
The actor identified as 'R. Lee' in the Nixon drawing of a scene on stage at the Bowmen's Lodge in 1799 was most likely Henry Lee (1765-1836), who was acting in the provinces by 1787. He managed for a while at Salisbury in 1791, and was at Covent Garden by September 1796. His afterpiece *Throw Physic to the Dogs* was acted at the Haymarket Theatre on 6 July 1798. Lee spent most of career as a journeyman actor in the provinces. His wife Sarah Jane Lee (d. 1797) was also mainly a provincial actor. After she died in 1797, Lee married a Miss Lloyd. Henry Lee died in London on 30 March 1836. *(BDA)*

LEE, Jenny, later Mrs J. P. Burnett **414**
1846-1930
Jenny Lee was born in London in 1846, the daughter of the artist Edwin George Lee. She made her first appearance on the London stage as Henry in *Chilperic* at the Lyceum on 22 January 1870. After playing some other parts at the Lyceum and elsewhere in London, in 1872 she accompanied E. A. Sothern to America to play Mary Meredith in *Our American Cousin*. She then acted for two years in San Francisco, where in 1875 she first played her famous role of Jo in *Bleak House* (**414**). She first acted Jo in London at the Globe Theatre on 21 February 1876, and for the next 20 years was associated almost solely with this role, which she played throughout the world. In 1880 she went to Australia, returning to London in 1885 to play Jo at the Strand. Some of her later roles included Mrs James Blackwood in *The Chetwynd Affair* (August 1904), Mrs Bedwin in *Oliver Twist* (July 1905) and Mistress Quickly in *The Merry Wives of Windsor* (April 1906), all at His Majesty's. She appeared as Jo in a scene from *Bleak House* at a matinée at the Lyric Theatre on 7 February 1921 for the benefit of the Dickens Memorial House. She was married to the actor and dramatist J. P. Burnett. Jenny Lee died on 3 May 1930.

LEE, Nathaniel **415**
c. 1646?-1692
The playwright Nathaniel Lee (also an actor) was born about 1646, the son of the clergyman Richard Lee. Young Nat went to Cambridge and then came down to London to search for theatrical employment. His first recorded part was the Captain of the Watch in *The Fatal Jealousy* at Dorset Garden Theatre on 3 August 1672; he is also known to have played Duncan in *Macbeth*. According to the prompter Downes, writing in 1708, Lee was a failure as an actor, though Colley Cibber said Lee was remarkably good at reading his own plays to actors. In any case, Lee gave up acting almost as soon as he attempted it and turned to playwriting, his first effort being *Nero*, which was given, unsuccessfully, at Drury Lane Theatre by the King's Company in May 1674. His next play was *The Rival Queens* (often called *Alexander the Great*), first performed on 17 March 1677 at Drury Lane to great applause. It became a stock play and attracted audiences and top performers into the nineteenth century. Lee went on, sometimes writing alone, sometimes in collaboration with John Dryden, through 1683, when his last play, *Constantine* was produced.

Then Lee lost his mind. He seems to have had a breakdown, caused or partly caused by excessive drinking, and was confined to Bedlam until April 1688. He had little income, though Drury Lane gave him a small pension, and he was able to earn a little through the publication of some of his plays. But Lee threw his life away in May 1692; he was found on the street, literally dead drunk. (*BDA*) [EAL]

LEECH, John
See Index of Artists

LEIGH, Anthony **417**
d. 1692
The player Charles II called 'his actor,' Anthony Leigh (sometimes Lee), was from a good Lancashire family, but his birth date is not known. He was first mentioned in the Lord Chamberlain's accounts on 27 December 1671, when he and several other actors were arrested for performing in and about London without a license. Though he joined the Duke's players sometime during the 1671-72 season at their new theatre in Dorset Garden, Leigh was not mentioned in the bills until 10 January 1676, when he acted Rash in *The Country Wit.* He was then named regularly in Duke's Company productions through 1682, when the patent troupes united. Among his roles were a few still remembered today: Old Bellair in *The Man of Mode*, Aelius in *Timon of Athens*, the title role in *Sir Patient Fancy*, Fryar Dominic in Dryden's *The Spanish Fryar* (**417**) and Antonio in *Venice Preserv'd.* His specialty was fops, and he seems from comments of the time to have been one of the best in the business. He was also a popular speaker of prologues and epilogues.

Tony Leigh during the 1680s at Drury Lane Theatre or, occasionally, the larger Dorset Garden, was seen in such roles as Oldfox in *The Plain Dealer*, Harlequin in Mountfort's *Doctor Faustus*, Scaramouch in *The Emperor of the Moon* and Falstaff in *The Merry Wives of Windsor* – the characters' names indicate his comic preferences. Colley Cibber in 1740 remembered Leigh's 'mercurial' talent and how skillful the actor was in controlling it. He died on 21 December 1692. The Index of Sitters in *Pictures in the Garrick Club* gives flourishing dates for Leigh that suggest that he may have lived beyond 1692; he did not. A later portrait of John Dunstall as Dominic engraved by Walker, after Dodd, is strikingly similar to Kneller's portrait of Leigh (**417**). (*BDA*) [EAL]

LEIGHTON, Frederick Lord, Baron of Stretton **793**
1830-1896
The academic painter Frederick Leighton was born at Scarborough in 1830. He was schooled in art in Rome and elsewhere in Europe. The most famous of his paintings, purchased by Queen Victoria, was 'Cimabue's Madonna Carried in Procession through the Streets of Florence.' He also painted a number of scenes from the plays of Shakespeare. He became a popular President of the Royal Academy in 1878. His opulent home in Kensington is now a museum. Leighton was elected to the Garrick Club on 8 June 1864. He died on 25 January 1896.

LEKAIN, real name Henri-Louis Cain **418**
1729-1778
The French actor known as Lekain and called by his benefactor Voltaire the greatest tragedian of his time, was born Henri-Louis Cain on 31 March 1729 in Paris. He spurned his father's trade of goldsmith and engaged in amateur theatricals. Voltaire was so impressed by his performances in them that he brought him into his house and provided coaching and money, and a small theatre. His work there brought Lekain a debut at the Comédie Française as Titus in Voltaire's *Brutus* in 1750. Despite his liabilities of small stature, harsh voice, and ugliness, Lekain became very popular with the public, and he was frequently compared favourably with Garrick, with whom he was friend and correspondent. Garrick, who practised a more natural style of acting, respected Lekain, though he disagreed with his more feverish and heroic style.

Along with the actress Clairon, Lekain introduced reforms in costuming and more realistic scenery, and, like Garrick, abolished the custom of spectators sitting on the stage. Among his notable triumphs were his performances as Oreste in Racine's *Andromache* and Genghis Kahn in Voltaire's *L'Orphelin de la Chine.* After playing Vendome in Voltaire's *Adélaïde du Guesclin,* he went out into the Paris winter night, caught a chill, and died on 8 February 1778. His son published the *Mémoires de H. L. Lekain* in Paris in 1801. *See* also *Réflexions sur Lekain et sur l'art théâtrale,* by Françoise Talma (1825). (*OCT*)

LESLIE, Fanny **419**
1856-1935
The actress Fanny Leslie Gough, whose anony-

mous portrait is missing from the Garrick Club, was born in 1856 and died in 1935.

LEVERIDGE, Richard **420**
c. 1670-1758
The popular bass singer Richard Leveridge was born about 1670 and apparently began his professional career in 1694-95. That season he sang in the St Cecilia's Day celebration (John Blow's *Te Deum and Jubilate*, according to the 5th edition of Grove) at Stationers' Hall, presumably on 22 November 1694, and he was Ismeron in *The Indian Queen* at the Dorset Garden playhouse in the autumn of 1695. From then to 1751, when he was past 80, he busied himself singing songs between the acts and within plays, playing musical roles in plays and 'operas' (called semi-operas because actors acted and singers sang in many of them) and entertaining at concert venues in and around London. Dick, as he called himself, also composed songs, sometimes the music, sometimes the lyrics, and sometimes both, and from as early as 1714 to 1736 or later he kept a convivial coffee house in Tavistock Street.

Leveridge was a popular singer, but the musical antiquarian Hawkins felt that the singer 'had no notion of elegance;' – 'it was all strength and compass.' Dr Burney put it more gracefully: Leveridge's appeal was to the lovers of Comus and Bacchus, not Minerva and Apollo. But he was applauded for a large number of singing roles and dozens of songs, one of the most popular being Henry Purcell's mad song from D'Urfey's *Don Quixote*, 'Let the Dreadful Engines,' originally composed for John Boman. Leveridge died on 22 March 1758 at the age of 88. (*BDA*) [EAL]

LEWES, Charles Lee **421, 422**
1740-1803
Born in Bond Street on 19 November 1740, Charles Lee Lewes was the son of a hosier who later became a letter carrier. Charles engaged in some amateur theatricals, according to his *Memoirs*, but his early career is difficult to trace because of the possibility of confusing Lewes with Philip Lewis, another minor London actor of the 1760s. Lewes tried provincial companies – in Doncaster, Sheffield and other towns – and then appeared as Prince Henry in *King John* on 23 September 1767 at Covent Garden. There through 1782-83 he was seen in many minor roles, among them Burgundy in *King Lear*, Montano in *Othello* and Cloten in *Cymbeline*; he made more progress in pantomimes, taking leading characters in such popular works as *Harlequin Doctor Faustus* and *The Rape of Proserpine.* His most successful part was Young Marlow in the 15 March 1773 premiere of *She Stoops to Conquer.* Lewes appeared in country theatres in the summers, and in the 1780s he gained some attention with lectures of his own devising patterned after George Alexander Stevens's *Lecture upon Heads* – satirical monologues on various types of people (a Frenchman, a Sailor, a Libeller and the like).

In the autumn of 1783 Lewes moved to Drury Lane, playing for his first appearance Marplot in *The Busy Body* on 16 September. Though he acted some important characters there – Falstaff in *The Merry Wives of Windsor,* Touchstone in *As You Like It*, Witwoud in *The Way of the World* – he was in competition with John Palmer and not making the progress he hoped for. He tried Ireland, acting in comedies and giving his *Lecture*, and then he packed up his family and went to India, where he fared no better. His problem, it would seem, was a comic talent of no great distinction and a conviction that he should be better paid for it. Back in London he tried Covent Garden again, peddled his *Lecture* and other sketches, took benefits for himself at the Haymarket, and, again, went off to perform in provincial theatres. On 24 June 1803 Covent Garden granted him a farewell benefit, though he was not a member of the company; two days later – some sources say a month later – Charles Lee Lewes died. (*BDA*)[EAL]

LEWIS, Sir George James Ernest **423**
1910-1945
Sir George Lewis was born on 25 February 1910, the son of the second Baron George Lewis and his wife Marie. The younger Lewis was a member of the firm of Lewis, Lewis, and Gisborne & Co, solicitors in Ely Place, Holborn. He succeeded his father as baron in 1927. Lewis became a member of the Garrick Club on 6 July 1933. He died on 2 January 1945.

LEWIS, William Thomas **424-429**
c. 1746-1811
Born in Ormskirk, Lancashire, about 1746, William Thomas Lewis was the son of William Lewis, a linen draper turned actor. After the elder Lewis's death Mrs Lewis became Mrs William Dawson, and she and her family were strolling players in Ireland. Young William Thomas Lewis played juvenile parts – Peter in *Romeo and Juliet* and Fleance in *Macbeth* to name two – in 1756, and about 1759 he was sent off to Armagh for schooling. He acted in Dublin in the 1760s, and in February 1771 his Belcour in *The West Indian* caught the attention of the play's author, Richard Cumberland. Cumberland liked Lewis's comic talent, found him 'young, handsome, and volatile,' and recommended him to David Garrick at Drury Lane in London. Garrick was not interested, but Lewis received a contract from Covent Garden and made his first London appearance, as Belcour again, on 15 October 1773. Critics liked his fire and spirit but felt Lewis went too far and needed to reign in his energy. He went on that season to appear as Aimwell in *The Stratagem*, Mercutio in *Romeo and Juliet* (**425**), Prince Hal in *1 Henry IV* and Valentine in *Love for Love*, among other characters. The management found him promising, and Lewis spent the following 35 seasons there, acting at least 194 parts in comedies, tragedies, and farces, among them Claudio in *Much Ado*, Edgar in *King Lear*, Archer in *The Stratagem*, Mirabel in *The Way of the World*, Cassio in *Othello*, Plume in *The Recruiting Officer* and Charles Surface in *The School for Scandal* – an impressive repertoire to which he added, year after year, many characters in new plays. Lewis, like his step-father, was also involved in theatre management – as deputy manager at Covent Garden by 1782, a position he held for 21 years and in which he was greatly admired by his colleagues. He also managed in Liverpool with Knight. For his labours he received good pay: £20 weekly by 1793-94.

Some critics found Lewis too much the same in too many parts, but most seem to have agreed with George Frederick Cooke that Lewis was 'humorous, whimsical, and at the same time elegant' – a rather neat balancing act for a comedian. Lewis died on 13 January 1811, leaving a wife (Henrietta Amelia, née Leeson, an Irish actress) and at least six children. (*BDA*) [EAL]

LISTON, John **430, 438, 477, 949, B50-B55, G1006**
1776-1846
John Liston was born in 1776, perhaps in Norris Street, in the parish of St James's; supposedly his father was a cook's shopkeeper. He was educated under Dr Barrow at the Soho Academy. Liston served for a while as master of the grammar school of St Martin's in Leicester Square and participated in amateur theatricals. He soon turned professional and made appearances at Weymouth, York, Dublin and with Stephen Kemble's company on the northern circuit. His first appearance in London was at the Haymarket Theatre as Sheepface in *The Village Lawyer* on 10 June 1805, followed that season by Zekiel in *The Heir-at-Law*, Farmer Ashcroft in *Speed the Plough*, Jacob Gawky in *The Chapter of Accidents* and similar comic roles. The next season he made his debut at Covent Garden as Jacob Gawky on 15 October 1806. Over the next 30 years Liston, one of the most comic of actors, excelled in farce and low comedy and was a leading player on the London stage. His popularity is testified to by the numerous portraits and figures of him at the Garrick Club. Among his greatest triumphs was Paul Pry at the Haymarket on 13 September 1825, a performance described by Genest as a perfect piece of acting. Liston remained a member of the summer company at the Haymarket until 1830 and was at Covent Garden until 1822. His first appearance at Drury Lane came on 28 January 1823 as Tony Lumpkin in *She Stoops to Conquer*.

He spent the last years of his career engaged by Madame Vestris at the Olympic Theatre, until his retirement in 1837. Subsequently he moved to a house facing Hyde Park Corner. He died there of 'a softening of the brain' on 22 March 1846 and was buried at Kensal Green. Liston, a favourite of George IV, had the highest salary of any comedian and left an estate of £40,000. Though he had a reputation as a practical joker, he also had a melancholy side that made him often appear grave. But of his acting Hazlitt wrote: 'his jaws seem to ache with laughter, his eyes look out of his head with wonder, his face is unctuous all over, and bathed with jests.' Leigh Hunt wrote that in Liston's 'best performances he may be called natural in every sense of the word … [He] passes from the simplest rustic to the most conceited pretender with undiminished easiness of attainment.'

In addition to the pictures in the Garrick Club, many other portraits and engravings of Liston were made. Liston's wife Sarah (née Tyrer), whom he had married in 1807, also acted in London. For Liston's biography, see Jim Davis, *John Liston Comedian* (1985). (*DNB, OCT*)

LISTON, Mrs John, Sarah, née Tyrer 439
1780-1854
Sarah Tyrer, a pupil of Kelly and Mrs Crouch, performed in the concerts at the Rotunda in Dublin and appeared on the London stage in the early years of the nineteenth century. She made her debut at Drury Lane on 21 May 1801 as Fidelia in *The Pirates* and then sang as Madge in *Love in a Village*. Her most famous character was Queen Dollalolla in *Tom Thumb,* in which De Wilde depicts her (**439**). When Liston (whom she had married in 1807) took his leave of Covent Garden on 31 May 1822, Mrs Liston, who was acting infrequently by then, retired. (*DNB*)

LITCHFIELD, Mrs John, Harriet, née Sylvester Hay 440, 441
1777-1854
Harriet Sylvester Hay was the daughter of John Sylvester Hay, a surgeon on an East Indiaman and later at the Royal Hospital in Calcutta. She was born on 4 March 1777, but where we cannot be certain. By 1792 she was in England, and on 15 September she played Julia in *The Surrender of Calais* at Richmond. Applauding her in the audience was the popular actress Dorothy Jordan. Harriet found a position in Edinburgh in early 1793. As Miss Sylvester she gained experience there and in Glasgow and Dumfries – attracting the attention of Robert Burns – and in Liverpool. On 27 May 1796 at Covent Garden she made her London debut, playing Edward in *Everyone One Has His Fault* to great applause. The male costume, said the *Monthly Mirror,* 'became her much; her voice possesses uncommon sweetness and flexibility; her action … was unembarassed, her manner playful and interesting, and her conception of the character just …' The following 14 September she married John Litchfield, an actor, and two weeks later she gave birth to a son.

Harriet made some stage appearances at the Haymarket in February 1797, advertised as Mrs Litchfield, then she returned to Covent Garden on 20 September 1797 as Marianne in *The Dramatist.* She worked on at Covent Garden, slowly increasing her salary from £4 weekly in 1798-99 to £12 in 1805-6 and adding to her repertoire a respectable string of such secondary roles as Julia in *The Rivals*, Lady Anne in *Richard III*, Regan in *King Lear*, Lucy in *The Recruiting Officer* and, most importantly, Emilia in *Othello*, one of her best characters. After her years at Covent Garden she acted occasionally at the Haymarket, where she made her final appearance, as Emilia, on 8 October 1812. She and her husband went into retirement, she dying on 11 January 1854. Their marriage, which had got off to a hasty start, had lasted 58 years. (*BDA*)[EAL]

LLOYD, Frederick OBE 442, G1029
d. 1995
Frederick Lloyd served as General Manager of the D'Oyly Carte Opera Company at the Savoy Theatre. He was co-author, with Robin Wilson, of *Gilbert & Sullivan. The D'Oyly Carte Years* (1984). Lloyd became a member of the Garrick Club in November 1953. He died in July 1995 (not in 1962 as stated in *Pictures in the Garrick Club*).

LOCKE, William John 443
1863-1930
Born on 20 March 1863, the eldest son of John Locke of Barbados, William John Locke was educated at Queen's Royal College, Trinidad, and St John's College, Cambridge. From 1897 to 1907 he was Secretary of the Royal Institute of British Architects; he was also an Honorary Corresponding Member of architectural societies in Holland, Spain, Portugal and the United States. He was mainly an author, however, writing 35 novels and six dramas, including *The White Dove* (novel, 1900), *The Beloved Vagabond* (novel, 1906, made into play 1908)), *The Joyous*

Adventures of Aristide Pujol (novel, 1911, made into play 1912), *The Red Planet* (novel, 1917), *Joshua's Vision* (novel, 1928), *Butterflies* (1908, play) and *The Man from the Sea* (1910, play). Locke became a member of the Garrick Club in 1907. He was a recipient of the Chevalier de l'Ordre de la Couronne of Belgium. His wife Aimée was the daughter of Theodore Heath. Locke died on 15 May 1930.

LOGAN, Mary
See Mary GIBBS

LONSDALE, Frederick. Leonard 444
1881-1954
Originally named Lionel Frederick Leonard, he was born on 5 February 1881 in St Helier, Jersey, Channel Islands. He became best known for his popular comedies of contemporary manners, adroitly handled and replete with epigrammatic wit. Among these were *Spring Cleaning* (1923), *Aren't We All Well* (1923), *The Last of Mrs Cheney* (1925) and *On Approval* (1927). Earlier he had been a librettist of musicals, including *The Balkan Princess* (1910), *The Maid of the Mountains* (1916) and a version of *Monsieur Beaucaire* (1919). Lonsdale died 14 April 1954 in London. He had become a member of the Garrick Club in 1918. (*OCT*)

LOVEGROVE, William 445-447
1778-1816
William Lovegrove was born on 13 January 1778 in Shoreham, Sussex, the son of a plumber-engineer. Young Lovegrove did some amateur acting in London, playing Hamlet at some point in a private theatre in Tottenham Court Road. He gained more experience in Richmond in 1799 and then Dublin, Manchester, Plymouth, York, Margate, Worthing, Bath and Bristol before engaging at the Lyceum in London with the Drury Lane company. As a strolling player he had appeared in such roles as Jaques in *As You Like It*, Edgar in *King Lear* and Sir Anthony Absolute in *The Rivals*. His first appearance with the Drury Lane troupe was on 3 October 1810 as Lord Ogleby in *The Clandestine Marriage* (**445**). He acted at the Lyceum in 1811-12 and at the new Drury Lane in 1812-13, playing many supporting roles from his sizeable repertoire. He died of a cerebral hemorrhage in June 1816. (*BDA*) [EAL]

LUPTON, Thomas Goff 355
1791 1873
Thomas Lupton, one of the persons tentatively identified in Clint's picture of a scene from *A New Way to Pay Old Debts*, was born in Clerkenwell, London, on 3 September 1791, the son of the goldsmith William Lupton and his wife Mary. He received tuition from George Clint and Samuel W. Reynolds. Between 1811 and 1820 he exhibited some crayon portraits at the Royal Academy. Lupton developed the method of using steel for mezzotint engravings. He published a number of such engravings in collections. He was sometime President of the Artists' Annuity Fund. He died at No 4, Keppel Street, Russell Square, on 18 May 1873.

M

MACKLIN, Charles **448, 449**

1699-1797

Charles Macklin (or sometimes Melaghlin, McLaughlin, Mecklin, Maclean, etc.) was born in County Donegal, Ireland, in 1699. He was sent to a boarding school, exhibited some theatrical ability, trained as a performer at Bristol and other provincial theatres and may have gained some experience as a harlequin in London as early as 1720. The first certain evidence of his performing dates 24 September 1730, when a playbill has him at Bartholomew Fair playing Sir Charles Freeman in *The Beaux' Stratagem.* He seems to have been willing to play almost anything anywhere throughout much of his career, for his is a history of hopping from one theatre to another (and usually squabbling with his managers if not his fellow performers) – not what one might expect from an actor who helped reform his profession. He was a stocky, bluff, blunt, stubborn, testy Irishman with a will of his own, mostly self-educated, thirsty for public approval and willing to work hard and fight hard to succeed. He had two 'wives' and a son and daughter, to all of whom he was almost too devoted. His daughter Maria had a modest stage career, partly engineered by Macklin; his dissolute son was a terrible disappointment. Only to his stage career was Macklin really married.

He acted roles large and small in good plays and bad, and managers would normally have found his varied talents very 'useful' indeed. He could sing (Peachum in *The Beggar's Opera* was one of his favourite roles), dance in pantomimes, write comedies and farces (but he had to fight to be paid for his efforts), teach (he was one of the best acting coaches of the century and ran an academy of oratory for a while) and manage (though he wasn't cut out for that kind of work). But what he is remembered and honored for are a handful of roles, especially Shylock in *The Merchant of Venice* and Macbeth but also Sir Archy MacSarcasm in his own *Love à la Mode*, Touchstone in *As You Like It* and Sir Pertinax Macsychophant in his *Man of the World* (**448**). His interests as an actor are evident in such varied characters as Brazen and Appletree in *The Recruiting Officer*, Teague and Abel in *The Committee*, Foppington in *The Careless Husband*, Poins and Prince Hal in *1 Henry IV*, Osric and the Gravedigger in *Hamlet*, Face in *The Alchemist*, Sir Jasper in *The Country Wife*, Malvolio in *Twelfth Night*, Marplot in *The Busy Body*, Iago in *Othello* (another of his rare ventures into tragedy) and Sir Wilful in *The Way of the World.*

But his repertoire, while it confirms his usefulness, hardly suggests an actor who was willing to face public disapproval and the alienation of his cohorts by playing 'the Jew that Shakespeare drew' – as Pope called his Shylock. Macklin clearly had, in addition to all his other good and bad qualities, a willingness to take risks. Today, we are so accustomed to Shylock being played as a serious, almost tragic character that we can hardly imagine how audiences on 14 February 1741 at Drury Lane (eight months before Garrick's Richard III sensation at Goodman's Fields Theatre) must have taken Macklin's innovation. They had been accustomed to Granville's *The Jew of Venice* – a Restoration watering down of the Shakespeare play with Shylock played as a comic character. Macklin was thorough in his study of the play, but the effect was not stodgy or antiquarian but electric in its theatricality and realism.

Of the many descriptions of Macklin's Shylock (which he continued playing with great success for decades) one of the best was by the German visitor Lichtenberg: 'Imagine a rather stout man with a coarse yellow face and a nose generously fashioned in all three dimnensions, and a long double chin, and a mouth so carved by nature that the knife appears to have slit him right up to the ears, on one side at least, I thought. He wears a long black gown, long wide trousers, and a red tricorne … The first word he utters, when he comes to the stage, are slowly and impressively spoken: 'Three thousand ducats.' The double 'th' and the two sibilants, especially the second after the 't,' which Macklin lisps as lickerishly as if he were savoring the ducats and all that they would buy, make so deep an impression in the man's favour that nothing can destroy it. Three such words uttered thus at the outset gave the keynote of the whole character.'

Macklin continued acting into the 1780s, despite age, infirmities, and faltering memory, but his stage career ended on 7 May 1789 at Covent Garden Theatre, where he was to play Shylock. His memory failed him utterly. The poor old man was replaced by Thomas Ryder and never took the stage again. He died on 11 July 1797, aged 98, bowed but not broken. (*BDA*) [EAL]

MACREADY, William Charles
1793-1873 **450, 451, B56-B61**
William Charles Macready, a leading figure in the development of production techniques in the middle of the nineteenth century, was born in London on 3 March 1793. His father was the Irish actor-manager William Macready (1755-1829), who is noticed in the *BDA* (10: 39-44), and his mother was Christina Ann (née Birch), a provincial actress. The elder Macready acted at Covent Garden for ten years beginning in 1786 and also managed for a brief period the Royalty Theatre in Wellclose Square. After receiving some schooling in Kensington, Birmingham and Rugby, young Macready, though intended for the bar, turned to acting. He made his stage debut on 7 June 1810 in his father's company at Birmingham as Romeo and for some four years played young leading characters like George Barnwell and Young Norval in *Douglas*. In 1811 at Newcastle he first acted Hamlet. There he also played Beverley to Mrs Siddons' Mrs Beverley in *The Gamester* and Young Norval to her Lady Randolph. He developed a repertoire of over 70 roles during those years in the provinces.

Macready made his debut at Covent Garden on 16 September 1816 as Orestes in *The Distrest Mother*. A number of leading roles followed, including Rob Roy (**B58**) in the stage adaptation of Scott's novel, and by the 1820s he was recognized as one of the leading English actors. He was famed for playing Shakespearean roles, especially Hamlet, Othello, Iago, Lear and Richard II. His Benedick, Coriolanus, Shylock (**B59**) and Antony were also well regarded. After seven years at Covent Garden, Macready's unpleasant relationships with the management of that theatre caused him to engage at Drury Lane, where he made his first appearance on 13 October 1823 in the title role in *Virginius*. He remained at Drury Lane for thirteen years. His best and probably most successful new part there was the leading role in Knowles's *William Tell* (**B60**, **B61**), a portrayal that drew extravagant praise.

In June 1824 Macready married Catherine Frances Atkins, a provincial actress. In September 1826 he and his wife, and her sister, set off to America, where on 2 October he was well received as Virginius at the Park Theatre in New York. He left New York in 1827, acted some roles successfully in Paris, and he was back at Drury Lane in October 1830. That December he played one of his most powerful roles, Werner in Byron's tragedy. In November 1832 he acted Iago to the Othello of Kean, whom he much disliked, though he did appear as a pallbearer at Kean's funeral.

Though he was an actor of great talent, probably Macready made his greatest mark in the history of the British stage as a manager and producer at Covent Garden from 1837 to 1839 and Drury Lane from 1841 to 1843. A meticulous and cultured man, Macready did his best to maintain a high quality of texts and production. He imposed strong discipline upon his actors, supervised thorough rehearsals, insisted on accurate costumes and scenery and rejected corrupted texts of Shakespeare's plays in his notable revivals.

His achievements were marred by his second visit to America, in 1849, when his feud with the American tragedian Edwin Forrest erupted in the calamitous riot at the Astor Place Opera House in New York, when partisans clashed and 22 persons were killed. Macready barely managed to escape with his life, made his way back to England, and after some appearances in county towns, began a round of farewells. His last performance was at Drury Lane on 26 February 1851, as Macbeth (**B57**). He retired to his country home at Sherborne, Dorset, and after his wife died in 1852 and he married Cecile Louise Frederica Spencer in 1860, he moved to Wellington Square, Cheltenham. He died at Cheltenham on 27 April 1873 and was buried in Kensal Green cemetery.

Macready had been passionate about his work, and often displayed quarrelsome propensities. But he was an actor in his time second only to Kean and a producer who influenced his theatre as

Garrick had done in the previous century. Among the books published about him are William Archer, *William Charles Macready* (1890); Alan S. Downer, *Eminent Tragedian William Charles Macready* (1966); William Toynbee, ed, *The Diaries of William Charles Macready, 1833-1851* (1969); J. C. Trewin, *Mr Macready: a Nineteenth-Century Tragedian and his Theatre* (1955); and Richard Moody, *Astor Place Riot* (1958). (*DNB, EB*)

MADDOCKS, Walter? Joe? 600
d. 1823?
According to a notation on John Nixon's drawing of the green room of the theatre of the Royal Kentish Bowman at Dartford Heath in 1799, one of the persons pictured is 'Joe Maddocks.' Perhaps the figure is actually Walter Maddocks (d. 1823), an actor who was in the provinces for a number of years before he settled at Drury Lane for three decades, playing a line of beggars, bailiffs, shepherds and soldiers. Walter Maddocks in his early years at Norwich was called 'Jas' [James] Maddocks. Otherwise, no actor called Joe Maddocks is known to us, nor is one in the *BDA*.

MAEDER, Clara
See Clara FISHER

MAGAN, James
See James MIDDLETON

MALIBRAN, Maria Felicidad née Garcia 452
1808-1836
This exceptional mezzo-soprano was born Maria de la Felicidad Garcia, the daughter of the tenor Manuel Garcia. A precocious child, she sang in Naples at the age of five and was brought by her father to London in 1817. Several years later she was a sensation singing at a musical club in Paris, and on 7 June 1825 she appeared as Rosina in *The Barber of Seville* at the King's Theatre, London, and displayed evident talents. On 23 June she sang Felicia in the first performance of Meyerbeer's *Crociato*. Her father took her to New York to perform for several seasons in his company at the Park Theatre, where she appeared in operas by Mozart and Rossini. On 25 March 1826, against her wishes, her father married her to a wealthy French merchant named Malibran, but she left him in about a year. After leaving New York in October 1827, Mrs Malibran divided her time between Paris and London and was soon acknowledged as a great singer. She made triumphant tours through Italy. Her marriage to Malibran having been annulled, on 26 March 1836 she married the violinist Charles-Auguste de Bériot (1802-1870), who had accompanied her on her tours. That April back in London she fell from her horse and was seriously injured. In September 1836 she was at the Manchester Festival, but, not fully recovered, she died on 23 September at the Mosely Arms Hotel. She was buried in the collegiate church at Manchester, but her remains were later removed and taken to Brussels, where she was re-interred in the cemetery of Laeken in a mausoleum erected by Bériot. Malibran's charm, according to *Grove's Dictionary*, 'seems to have lain chiefly in the peculiar colour and unusual extent of her voice, in her excitable temperament, which prompted her to improvise passages of strange audacity on the stage, and in her strong musical feeling …' The pencil and watercolour drawing by Fletcher (**452**), after Chalon, is a version of the portrait engraved by R. J. Lane, and is purported to show her as Fidalma in *Il matrimonio segreto*. A number of biographies of her have been published, including April Fitzlyon, *Maria Malibran, Diva of the Romantic Age* (1987) and Howard Bushnell, *Maria Malibran: a biography of the Singer* (1979).

MANSEL, Robert 453
d. 1824
Robert Mansel, from Wales, made his stage debut on 3 January 1798 with the Jones company at the Fishamble Street Theatre in Dublin. He used that as a stepping stone to Covent Garden in London, where he played Young Marlow in *She Stoops to Conquer* on 19 September of that year to luke-warm reviews. For £3 weekly he also, in 1798-99 and 1799-1800, acted such parts as Tressel in *Richard III*, Malcolm in *Macbeth* and Ratcliffe in *Jane Shore*. Mansel then left London to spend the remainder of his career touring provincial towns – Belfast,

Edinburgh, York, Hull, Doncaster – and it was while on the road that he had a stroke. He died on 22 October 1824 in Wansford. (*BDA*) [EAL]

MARDYN, Charlotte **454**
b. 1789
One of the facts that seems certain in William Oxberry's overblown memoir of Charlotte Mardyn in his *Dramatic Biography* (1825) is that she was born in poor circumstances in Ireland in 1789. She served as a housemaid in Plymouth in the early 1800s and married a Mr Mardyn. She was acting in London about 1811 and at Bath in 1814. In September 1815 she made her first appearance at Drury Lane as Amelia Widenhaim in *Lovers' Vows* and then acted Albina Mandevill in *The Will.* Other roles in London included Sylvia in *The Recruiting Officer*, Peggy in *The Country Girl* and Jacintha in *The Suspicious Husband.* In Oxberry's opinion she was unfit to play leading comedy roles at metropolitan theatres. Her first husband seems to have disappeared, and she took up with a 'gentleman of rank and fortune' – a 'Baron R——,' whom she may have married. Oxberry claims that despite the rumours about her many 'errors,' she was 'more sinned against than sinning.'

MARRABLE, Frederick
See Index of Artists

MARSHALL-HALL, Sir Edward QC **456**
1858-1927
Born in Brighton on 16 September 1858, the youngest son of Dr Alfred Hall and his wife Julia Elizabeth (née Sebright), he was educated at Rugby and at St John's College, Cambridge (BA 1882). He became a barrister, Inner Temple, 1883, and a Bencher, 1910. A distinguished barrister, Marshall-Hall practised in London and in the South-Eastern and Sussex Sessions. He was knighted in 1917. He became a member of the Garrick Club in 1891 and died on 24 February 1927.

MARTIN-HARVEY
See Sir John Martin HARVEY

MARTIN-TURNER, Grahame **892**
d. 1999
Grahame Martin-Turner, who is shown as No. 24 in Gilroy's picture of the Garrick Club Outing in 1967, was a Director of De la Rue when he was elected to the Garrick Club in March 1951. He also was a Director of the Bowaters Group. He became a Life Member of the Garrick Club, where he was often seen, and served on the House Committee. He died in December 1999.

MARTYR, Margaret, née Thornton
d. 1807 **458-460**
Margaret Thornton Martyr's birthdate and parentage are not known for certain, but she may have been the daughter of a London tailor. Her declared stage debut, advertised as 'A Young Lady,' was at Covent Garden Theatre, as Rosetta in the musical *Love in a Village* on 13 February 1779, though she had already sung at the Vauxhall pleasure garden and did again in the summers that followed. Miss Thornton seems to have been a singing member of the Covent Garden troupe for the 1779-80 season but appeared at Drury Lane once, for Mrs Wrighten's benefit. By 13 November 1780 she had married a Captain Martyr, whose name she kept throughout her career and by whom she had a daughter. From 1780 to 1804 Margaret was a regular in the winters at Covent Garden and spent her summers at Vauxhall or provincial theatres. She was a popular singer, actress and dancer with a salary that reached £10 weekly in 1786-87. Her husband had died in prison, and later, in 1784, she formed a liaison with the oboist William Thomas Parke that brought her at least two more children. Margaret was a pert, attractive woman, well-suited to breeches parts – 'Sportive, playful, arch, and free' she was called in Bellamy's *London Theatres* in 1795. Her assignments over the years included Polly and Lucy (and also Macheath) in *The Beggar's Opera*, Louisa in *The Duenna*, Rose in *The Recruiting Officer* (**458, 459**) and roles in pantomimes. Margaret Martyr died on 7 June 1807. (*BDA*)[EAL]

MARY, QUEEN OF SCOTS **937**
1542-1587
Mary Stuart was born at Linlithgow Palace,

Lothian, Scotland, on 8 December 1542, the only child of King James V of Scotland and his French wife, Mary of Guise. The death of her father only six days after her birth left her Queen of Scotland, with her mother as regent. She grew up tall and beautiful. In April 1558 she married Francis, eldest son of Henry and Catherine of France; Francis was still a boy. Upon the death of Henry in 1559 and the ascension of Francis, Mary became queen consort of France. When Elizabeth Tudor came to the throne of England in 1558 Mary became next in line for the English throne. Francis died in 1560 and Mary returned to Scotland. But her rule was factious and turbulent because she was a Roman Catholic, and Elizabeth refused to acknowledge her as a rightful heir. Mary's disastrous love affairs and marriage to Henry Stewart, Earl of Darnley, in July 1565, and, after Darnley's murder, to James Hepburn, 4th Earl of Bothwell only served to exacerbate her unwise political actions and provoked the rebellion of the Scottish nobles. She fled to England, where Elizabeth had her incarcerated for 18 years, until she was beheaded at Fotheringhay Castle, Northamptonshire, on 8 February 1587. (*EB*)

MASSEY, Mrs E. **461**
fl 1776-1783
After some years acting in the provinces, Mrs Massey and her husband joined Colman's company at the Haymarket, where on 7 August 1777 she appeared as Queen Elizabeth in *Richard III*. The next season she was at York but returned to the Haymarket the summer of 1778, when her roles included Cordelia, Lady Macbeth and Queen Catherine in *Henry VIII*. She continued to appear summers at the Haymarket until 1781 and then went to act in Dublin. For a performer of so little status, she must have made some impact in London to become the sitter for the three portraits noted in her entry in *Pictures in the Garrick Club* (**461**). (*BDA*)

MATHEWS, Charles **462-477, B169**
1776-1835
Biographical information on Charles Mathews, whose great gallery of theatrical portraits, formed the nucleus of the Garrick Club collection, is given in the companion volume, *Pictures in the Garrick Club*, pp. xxxix and pp. 256-265. The reader is also referred to the *DNB; Mr Mathews at Home* by Richard L. Klepac (1979); and *The Life and Correspondence of Charles Mathews, the Elder, Comedian. By Mrs [Ann] Mathews,* edited by Edmund Yates (1860).

MATHEWS, Charles James
1803-1878 **478-595, 950, B105**
Biographical information on Charles James Mathews, the son of Charles Mathews and the husband of Lucia Elizabeth Vestris (*q.v.*) is given in the companion volume, *Pictures in the Garrick Club*, pp. 266-267 and pp. 268-312, *passim.*

MATHEWS, Lucia Elizabeth
See Lucia Elizabeth VESTRIS

MATTOCKS, Mrs George, Isabella, née Hallam **596, 597**
1746-1826
Isabella, born in 1746, was the daughter of the elder Lewis Hallam and a member of a large family of performers who were responsible for the development of the American theatre. When many of the clan left for the new world in 1752, Isabella was left in the custody of her aunt, Ann Barrington, who carefully guided the youngster's early stage career. Isabella began, as did many child actors, playing the Duke of York in *Richard III*, in this instance at Covent Garden Theatre on 22 September 1752; that night her aunt was seen as Lady Anne. Isabella made her first 'adult' appearance on 10 April 1761 as Juliet to Ross's Romeo, with Ann Barrington playing Lady Capulet. The youngster also danced that evening and in later appearances showed her talent as a singer and guitarist. Over the years at Covent Garden (and in the summer of 1773 at Liverpool), she acted a formidable repertoire of important roles in comedy and tragedy, among them Cordelia in *King Lear*, Jessica and Portia in *The Merchant of Venice*, Ophelia in *Hamlet*, Hermione in *The Winter's Tale*, Lady Macbeth, Mrs Ford in *The Merry Wives of Windsor* – to name only some of her Shakespearean characters. From 7 April 1765 she was advertised as Mrs Mattocks, having married, against the wishes of her

relatives, the mediocre actor and fairground singer George Mattocks. Though the marriage lasted for years, both were unfaithful.

Isabella Mattocks appeared in so many roles at so many theatres in and out of London that she attracted much critical attention over the years, but most of the comments were guarded. In 1773, for instance, the *Macaroni and Savoir Vivre Magazine* said, 'She has an exceeding good natural voice that stamps her a very good second singer; which, on the whole, from a pleasing person, together with a good share of judgement, renders her one of the most useful performers in the theatre she is engaged in.' Francis Gentleman in *The Theatres* in 1772 called her 'figure happily dispos'd, tho' small,/ Striking in nought, agreeable in all ...' And so they went, damning with faint praise a performer who was well liked, but not very well liked.

Mrs Mattocks made her final stage appearance on 7 June 1808. Her husband had died in 1804, leaving her little; she had managed her career successfully, however, and left a comfortable estate to her daughter Isabella Anne, whose husband squandered it. But Isabella Mattocks left many friends in the theatre; they gave her a benefit at the King's Theatre in 1813 that brought in £1092. She died at her house in High Street, Kensington, on 25 June 1826. (*BDA* [EAL]

MAUDE, Cyril Frances **S26**
1862-1951

The actor-manager Cyril Maude was born in London on 24 April 1862, the son of Capt Charles Maude and the Hon Mrs Maude. Though intended for the military, he determined for the stage, and after some early training his poor health forced him to leave England for Canada, and then the United States, where he began his stage career in Denver and then New York. In 1885 he returned to England, making his first appearance in London at the Criterion on 18 February 1886 as Mr Pilkie in *The Great Divorce Case.* After numerous appearances in various London theatres he became in 1896 co-manager with Frederick Harrison of the Haymarket Theatre and until 1905 he was responsible for presenting many fine productions in which he often acted with his wife Winifred Emery, whom he had married in 1888. Subsequently, after acting in Charles Frohman's company at the Duke of York's in 1906, he took over the management of the Playhouse (formerly the Avenue Theatre at Charing Cross), which he conducted until 1915. Tours took him to North America, and he continued to perform a number of parts in London until he retired in 1927. He excelled in the roles of old men like Sir Peter Teazle, Lord Ogleby and Andrew Bullivant in *Grumpy* (1914). He also appeared in films, notably *Peer Gynt, Heat Wave* and *Girls Will Be Boys.*

After the death of Winifred Emery in 1924, he married in 1927 Beatrice Mary Ellis, the daughter of John Ellis, a Vicar at Leicester, and the widow of P. H. Trew. Maude enjoyed his later years in Torquay. He was twice President of the Royal Academy of Dramatic Art. He joined the Garrick Club in 1927. His book *Behind the Scenes with Cyril Maude* was published in 1927. Maude died on 20 February 1951, aged 88. (*OCT, WWWT*)

MAYHEW OF TWYSDEN, Rt Hon Lord, Patrick Barnabas Burke Mayhew
b. 1929 **G0984-G0986**

Patrick Mayhew, who is seen in three caricatures drawn by Charles Yorke for the menu of the Garrick Club Dinner in 1998, was born on 11 September 1929, the son of S.G. H. Mayhew, MC. He was educated at Balliol College, Oxford (MA), and was President of the Oxford Union Society (1952). He served in the Royal Dragoon Guards and was called to the Bar, Middle Temple, in 1955 and became a Bencher in 1980 (QC 1972). His service in politics and Conservative governments includes MP for Tunbridge Wells, 1974-1997; Under Secretary of State, Department of Employment, 1979-1983; Minister of State, Home Office, 1981-1983; Solicitor General, 1983-1987; and Attorney General, 1987-1992. In 1997 he was created Baron of Kilndown, Kent (a Life Peer). Lord Mayhew became a member of the Garrick Club in 1988. He is married to Jean Elizabeth Gurney (OBE 1997), the daughter of John Gurney, and has four sons. (*WW*)

MCDONALD, Ean G0997
fl. 1903
Little is known to us about the actor Ean McDonald who played Morton Mackenzie in the production of *The Light that Failed* at the Lyric Theatre on 7 February 1903 and is pictured in Beaumont's set of caricatures of the cast. (**G0997**).

MEADOWS, Drinkwater 598, G1037
1799-1869
Born in 1799 and said to be a native of Yorkshire (or Wales), Drinkwater Meadows spent a number of years acting in provincial companies in the north of England. In 1817 he was engaged at the Bath Theatre, and finally on 28 September 1821 he made his first appearance in London, at Covent Garden Theatre as Scrub in *The Stratagem*. Meadows remained at Covent Garden, playing numerous supporting roles, until 1844. Some of his characters were Crabtree in *School for Scandal*, Filch in *The Beggar's Opera*, Medium in *Inkle and Yarico,* Simon Pure in *A Bold Stroke for a Wife* and the original Raubvogel in *Return Killed* (the role in which Meyer depicted him, **598**). He later acted at the Lyceum and under Charles Kean's direction at the Princess's, where he remained until he retired in 1862. Meadows served as Secretary of the Covent Garden Theatrical Fund. He died at Prairie Cottage, the Green, Barnes, on 12 June 1869. Joseph Knight described him as a conscientious and reliable actor and a 'careful, retiring man, shunning publicity … much respected and little noticed.' Meadows joined the Garrick Club in 1832 but resigned in 1867, two years before his death. Five volumes of 'Correspondence with Drinkwater Meadows of Covent Garden Theatre Illustrated with portraits', by Charles Britiffe Smith are in the Club Library. (*DNB*)

MELLON, Harriot, later Mrs Thomas Coutts, then Duchess of St Albans 599-600
1778?-1837
Harriot Mellon (or possibly Malone) may have been born in 1778, the daughter, perhaps, of Lieutenant Matthew Mellon and Sarah (last name unknown). The earliest certain theatrical information we have of her is a playbill dated 16 October 1787: she acted, with great success, Little Pickle in *The Spoiled Child* with Thomas Bibby's troupe at Ulverstone. With her in the company was her mother Sarah, now Mrs Entwisle (her first husband had died), who worked backstage and seems to have spent much of her time running Harriot's life. The youngster sang, danced and acted children's roles and then more mature parts as she grew up, and the Entwisles joined Stanton's company at Stafford and neighbouring towns. Her repertoire in the early 1790s included Cowslip in *The Agreeable Surprise*, Celia and Audrey in *As You Like It*, Lydia Languish in *The Rivals* and Beatrice in *Much Ado about Nothing.* She was seen by the Drury Lane manager Richard Brinsley Sheridan in October 1794, and within a year Miss Mellon was in London.

Her debut at Drury Lane was probably as Lydia Languish, on 30 October 1795, though she had been an extra in *Lodoiska* earlier that month. A critic wrote that she was 'strikingly handsome, her voice musical, her action powerful when not checked by fear, and there were some tones of archness …' In the Drury Lane company was Dorothy Jordan, whose line was almost exactly that which Harriot was developing; Mrs Jordan was a splendid model but at the same time a roadblock in the younger player's path. Some of Harriot's roles her first season in London were Lady Godiva in *Peeping Tom*, Lucy in *The Recruiting Officer* and Lady Blanche in *King John* – as well as Amanthis in *The Child of Nature*, which she played for Mrs Jordan when Dorothy was ill, and Penelope in *The Romp*, for Maria Theresa de Camp, when she needed a replacement. The singer-actor Michael Kelly noted how valuable Harriot was at Drury Lane and how esteemed she was by her colleagues.

She spent the summer of 1796 acting at Liverpool, was treated kindly by Sarah Siddons, who had a brief engagement there, and Harriot played a number of important characters, including Ophelia in *Hamlet*, Hero in *Much Ado*, Estifania in *Rule a Wife and Have a Wife*, Rosalind in *As You Like It*, the title role in *Polly Honeycomb* and Miranda in *The Tempest.* When she returned to London in September one critic said she 'improves amazingly.' Miss Mellon returned to Liverpool for summer engagements and kept developing her own style of playing flirts, mischievous wenches, charming soubrettes, and hoydenish country girls. How much her mother had to do with the development of her daughter's career we cannot tell, but her influence was evidently considerable, and by 1804 Harriot was beginning to declare her independence. Her stepfather, who had been serving in the Drury Lane band, was dismissed and, with Mrs Entwisle, moved to Cheltenham, leaving Harriot in London.

It was during a visit Harriot made to Cheltenham that she met, perhaps through her mother, a number of aristocrats as well as the aging, married banker Thomas Coutts, one of the richest men in England. Though she continued her stage career and benefited greatly from Dorothy Jordan's gradual withdrawal from the public eye, Harriot's schedule was reduced and her relationship with Coutts developed into what was apparently a true love – though for the rest of her life there were those who saw her as avaricious. When Mrs Coutts died in 1815 Harriot left the stage, married Coutts, and began a new career as a London hostess, giving extravagant parties for her aristocratic friends and donating large sums of money to charities. Coutts died in 1822, and five years later Harriot added a title to her wealth by marrying the young Lord Burford, Duke of St Albans, who wanted her money as much as she wanted his rank. 'I am a Duchess at last,' she wrote her friend Sir Walter Scott. 'All this is very flattering to an old lady … What a strange, eventful life has mine been, from a poor little player child, with just food and clothes to cover me, dependent on a very precarious profession, without talent or a friend in the world … [Y]our affectionate friend. HARRIOT ST. ALBANS.' She resumed her entertainments, attended court regularly, and enjoyed growing old wealthily. The Duchess died on 6 August 1837. (*BDA*) [EAL]

MENAGE, Arabella, later Mrs Michael William Sharp **601**
d. 1817
The birth date of Arabella Menage is not known. She was the daughter of the French Drury Lane dancer Mons Menage and his wife Arabella. Our subject danced as a child in *Harlequin's Invasion* on 27 December 1792 and may have appeared earlier. By 1798-99 the younger Arabella was performing regularly at Drury Lane, usually in the chorus but occasionally in named roles: Nelly in *No Song, No Supper* and Irene in *Blue-Beard* were two. At the Haymarket in 1801 she was Patty in *Inkle and Yarico* and Rosina in *The Castle of Sorrento.* Her highest salary at Drury Lane seems to have been £5 weekly. In 1804 she married the painter Michael William Sharp (d. 1840), to the chagrin of Sarah Siddons, who called her 'a naughty little dancing Girl.' Mrs Sharp died on 9 January 1817. Her husband, a member of a large family of musicians and actors, died in 1840. (*BDA*) [EAL]

MENUHIN, Sir Yehudi KBE, Baron of Stoke d'Aberon **S49**
1916-1999
The great violinist and conductor Yehudi Menuhin was born in New York on 22 April 1916, the son of Moshe and Martha Menuhin. He studied under private tutors in America and Europe, and at the age of seven made his debut playing Mendelssohn's *Violin Concerto* with the San Francisco Symphony, and at the age of ten he played in Paris, at 11 in New York and at 13 in Berlin. During his long career he was seen on most of the world's concert stages, playing with the leading orchestras and conductors, and was recognized as one of the great violin virtuosos of the twentieth century. During the Second World War he devoted his time to giving concerts for American and Allied troops, and in 1945 he played at Bergen-Belsen for recently liberated inmates. Menuhin settled in London in 1959 and in 1963 opened the Yehudi Menuhin School of Music at Stoke d'Aberon, Surrey. He made many recordings and served as conductor and soloist for the Menuhin Festival Orchestra, which toured the USA, Australia and New Zealand, and he appeared regularly on British and American television. Throughout his public life he was devoted to humanitarian causes and social justice and was the recipient of many honours from governments and societies. He was knighted in 1965, but did not assume the title until he became a British citizen in 1985. In 1993

he was made a life peer. Sir Yehudi became a member of the Garrick Club in March 1956. He was also a member of the Athenaeum. In addition to essays, among his many publications are *Violin: Six Lessons* (1972), *Violin and Viola* (1976), *The Music of Man* (1979, with Curtis Davis), his autobiography *Unfinished Journey* (1977, with four additional chapters in 1997 as *Unfinished Journey: Twenty Years Later*).

Sir Yehudi died in Berlin on 12 March 1999. (*WW, EB*)

MEREWETHER, Charles George QC 793
d. 1880
Charles Merewether, who is shown as No. 29 in O'Neil's scene of Members in the Billiards Room, was elected to the Garrick Club in 1851 and died in 1880. No doubt he was related to Henry Allworth Merewether, below, perhaps as brother, son or nephew. (*DNB*)

MEREWETHER, Henry Allworth QC 793
1812-1877?
Henry Allworth Merewether QC is shown as No. 27 in O'Neil's scene of Members in the Billiards Room. He was the son of Henry Allworth Merewether (1780-1864), serjeant-at-law, who is noticed in the *DNB*. The younger Merewether was a recorder of devizes and a bencher of the Inner Temple. He became a member of the Garrick Club in 1864. A notation in the Roll of Members states he died in 1878, but the *DNB* gives 1877.

MERRIVALE, Gladys
See Dame Gladys COOPER

MERRY, Anne
See Anne BRUNTON

MIDDLETON, James, stage name of James Magan 602, 603
c. 1769-1799
James Magan was born in Dublin, probably in 1769, and was trained, like his father, in surgery. James became attracted to the stage and applied to Covent Garden Theatre in London, probably late in 1787; he was advised to get some experience at Bath, where he made his official debut as Othello on 31 January 1788, advertised as 'A Gentleman.' He then appeared as Romeo and acted both roles in Bristol before returning to London in September. At some point he began using James Middleton as a stage name. At Covent Garden he acted Romeo again, followed by Chamont in *The Orphan*, O'Donovan in *The Toy*, Harry Neville in *The Dramatist* and Florizel in *The Winter's Tale*. It was a promising beginning, but Middleton was a spendthrift and an inebriate, and the Covent Garden management dropped him after 1788-89. His mental instability was increased by the death of his wife Sophia in August 1789. He tried Dublin, Cork, a new wife, Edinburgh and Belfast in that order, expanding his repertoire to include Hamlet, and he was engaged again at Covent Garden for 1793-94 at £6 weekly.

Middleton's acting was noted by some critics, and though they likened his voice to that of Spranger Barry, which was a nice compliment, they accused him of ranting and crying too much and generally being too extravagant both in his acting and in his private life. His worst offence occurred on 19 December 1796, when he was acting Nerestan in *Zara*: after the first scene he walked out of the theatre, and Davenport had to read the rest of his part. Middleton went to a tavern and sent a message to the playhouse saying he would act no more that evening. He was dropped from the roster, returned to Dublin again, misbehaved, and lost his position once more. Middleton came back to London in 1798, desperate, and Drury Lane hired him at £6 per week. He worked for most of the season, his last appearance being on 17 April 1799. Steeped in debt, borrowing constantly from members of the company, and 'filthy in person, depraved in principle,' he was finally sent to Newgate, was rescued by Charles Kemble, gave recitations in a small theatre in Pimlico and died, drunk, on 18 October 1799. The willingness of the two patent theatres to engage Middleton at a good salary, and the interest of artists in painting him, suggest that the actor had much talent but little sense. (*BDA*)[EAL]

MIKARDO, Ian G1020
1908-1993
The politician and writer Ian Mikardo was born

on 9 July 1908 and was educated at Portsmouth. He began his political career as MP for Reading, 1945-1950, and advanced to the National Executive Committee of the Labour Party 1950-1959, 1960-1978 (chairman 1970-1971). He served as chairman of the Select Committee on Nationalised Industries,1966-1970, President ASTMS, 1968-1973, and Vice-President Socialist International, 1978-1983 (Hon President from 1983). Among his books are *Centralised Control of Industry* (1944), *The Second Five years* (1948), *The Problems of Nationalisation* (1948), *Socialism or Slump* (1959) and *Back-Bencher* (autobiography, 1988). He died on 6 May 1993. (*WWW*)

MILLAIS, Sir John Everett
See Index of Artists

MILLS, John **606**
d. 1736
This actor and manager appeared on the stages of Drury Lane and Dorset Garden by 1695 and soon became an important player. In 1709 he contracted to perform at the Queen's Theatre, but he returned to Drury Lane in 1710. There he remained the rest of his life acting major roles in an extensive repertoire, among which were Othello, Julius Caesar, Chamont in *The Orphan*, the Ghost and Hamlet in *Hamlet*, Osmyn in *The Mourning Bride*, Horatio in *The Fair Penitent* and Gloucester in *King Lear*. He also assisted in the management of Drury Lane. Though some critics complained of his ranting, Mills was described as 'the most useful actor that ever served a theatre.' He excelled as Pierre in *Venice Preserv'd* (**606**). Mills died in November 1736. (*BDA*)

MILLS, Louisa Henrietta Hannah née Keys **607**
d. 1804
Louisa Mills was the daughter of the country actors Mr and Mrs Simon Keys. Louisa Keys was on provincial stages as a child before she made her London debut at Sadler's Wells on 9 April 1792 singing in *Queen Dido*. After a few more performances at the Wells she acted in Ireland and in 1797 joined Tate Wilkinson's York circuit. In April 1797 at York she married the provincial actor Henry Mills. As Mrs Mills she returned to London, this time to Covent Garden, on 3 October 1798, as Sophia in *The Road to Ruin* and Little Pickle in *The Spoiled Child* (**607**). One reviewer wrote that as the farcical Little Pickle she exhibited 'astonishing point and spirit' and in some instances was more entertaining than Mrs Jordan, who created the original. Mrs Mills continued at Covent Garden through the 1803-4 season in similar roles, including Priscilla Tomboy in *The Romp* and Alambra in the musical farce *Paul and Virginia*. She also appeared at the Haymarket Theatre, in the summer of 1801. Consumption forced her to leave the stage in May 1804, to be supported by the generosity of Thomas Harris, the Covent Garden manager, and other friends. She died while being cared for at her brother's residence in Canterbury on 7 July 1804. Louisa Mills' sister, Sarah Jane Keys, was also on the London stage and married the actor-manager Henry Lee. Louisa's brother (first name unknown) was a theatrical musician. (*BDA*)

MILNE, Alan Alexander **G1013**
1882-1956
The English humourist and author A. A. Milne was born in London on 18 January 1882, the son of John Vince and Sarah Marie Milne. His father owned a private school called Henley House, in Mortimer Road, where Alan and his brothers David Barrett Milne and Kenneth John Milne were first educated. Among the teachers for a while was H. G. Wells. Milne took a BA in mathematics (1903) at Trinity College, Cambridge, and then, assisted by a gift of £1000 from his father, he set off for London to become a free-lance writer. In 1905 his first book, *Lovers in London*, appeared. In the First World War Milne served in France as a signal officer in the Royal Warwickshire Regiment. Upon his return he wrote the plays *The Dover Road* and *Mr Pim Passes By* and the detective story *The Red House Mystery*. But it was as a writer of verses and stories for children that he achieved his lasting fame, with *When We Were Very Young* (1924), *Winnie-the-Pooh* (1926), *Now We Are Six* (1927), and *The House at Pooh Corner* (1928), the latter two with illustrations by Ernest Shepard and dealing with the adventures of Christopher Robin. The stories

were inspired by the real Christopher Robin Milne, the son that was born to A. A. Milne and his wife Dorothy de Selincourt on 21 August 1920. Unhappily, the son remained estranged from his father and mother during his adult life. In 1929 Milne wrote *Toad Hall,* based on Kenneth Grahame's *The Wind in the Willows*. His last book was *Year In, Year Out* (1952). He published his autobiography, *It's Too Late Now,* in 1938. In October 1952, Milne suffered a stroke that incapacitated him until his death on 31 January 1956 at Hartfield, Sussex. He had joined the Garrick Club in May 1919. Christopher Robin Milne wrote of his father, 'He knew about me, he knew about himself, he knew about the Garrick Club – he was ignorant about anything else. except, perhaps, about life.' For years the Garrick Club received royalties bequeathed by A. A. Milne from his writings. Recently the Club received a substantial settlement when Disney Corporation bought the rights to the Pooh stories and characters. A number of books have been written about Milne, among them *A. A. Milne, a Critical Biography* by Tori Haring-Smith (1982) and *A. A. Milne: the Man Behind Winnie-the-Pooh* by A. Thwaite (1990).

MILNE, Christopher Robin **608**
1920-1996
Christopher Robin Milne was born on 21 August 1920, the son of Alan Alexander Milne, who wrote the popular series of Winnie the Pooh stories in which Christopher Robin was often featured. His mother was Dorothy Daphne Milne (née Selincourt). He served in the Royal Engineers in the Second World War.

The drawing by Shepard (**608**) depicts him as a young child. Christopher Robin Milne was blessed and cursed by being so closely associated with the Pooh stories. He was a bookseller and author of a number of books and stories, including *The Enchanted Places* (1976, the story of his childhood and relations with his parents), *The Path Through the Trees* (1979, the story of his adult life), *The Hollow on the Hill* (1982) and *The Open Garden* (1988). *Beyond the World of Pooh*, a collection of his essays, was published in 2000. Milne joined the Garrick Club in March 1976, but resigned in November 1984. He died on 20 April 1996, leaving his wife Leisley de Selincourt, a cousin whom he had married against his parents' wishes, and a daughter Clare.

MIRREN, Dame Helen **970**
b. 1945
Helen Mirren was born Ilynea Lydia Mironoff on 26 July 1946 in London. She is the daughter of a Russian-born émigré, said to have been an aristocrat who escaped from the Revolution. In England he became a musician and driving instructor. His wife was Scottish. Helen did some training at the National Youth Theatre and a teacher's college, and made her professional debut at the Old Vic in 1965 as Cleopatra, receiving enthusiastic reviews. After appearances at Manchester, in 1967 she joined the Royal Shakespeare Company, where she remained for some 15 years. With the RSC she gave impressive performances at Stratford and London in a number of roles, including Cressida (1968), Hero (1968), Lady Anne in *Richard III* (1970), Ophelia (1970), Miss Julie (1971) and Lady Macbeth (1974, **970**). She also played Nina in *The Seagull* at the Lyric in 1975 and Isabella in *Measure for Measure* at the Riverside Studio in 1974. In 1972 she was with Peter Brook's experimental company touring Africa and North America.

She began her film career in 1967 with *Herostratus,* followed by Peter Hall's film of *A Midsummer Night's Dream* in 1968. Among her other numerous films are *The Age of Consent* (1969), *Caligula* (1979), *Excalibur* (1981), *Cal* (1984, Best Actress Award Cannes Film Festival), *White Nights* (1985), *The Comfort of Strangers* (1990), *The Madness of King George* (1994, Oscar nomination for Best Actress) and the star-filled *Gosford Park* (2001, Oscar nomination). She returned to the London stage in 1994 with a brilliant portrayal of Natalya Petrovna in *A Month in the Country* (and in New York, Tony Award for Best Actress, 1995). In 1998 she again acted Cleopatra, to Alan Rickman's Antony, in a disappointing production at the National Theatre. But in the summer of 2000 she made retribution with a riveting performance of Lady Torrance in *Orpheus Descending* at the Donmar Warehouse. In 2001 she appeared in New York with Ian McKellan in an acclaimed production of *The Dance of Death.*

It is as a television star that Mirren has become best known to a wider audience, especially as DCI Jane Tennison in the several series of *Prime Suspect*, for which she received numerous awards. She was honoured with a DBE in 2003. Dame Helen currently lives in America.

MITCHENSON, William **676, 823**
1821-1870
William Mitchenson, who is depicted as Tibbytight in *Puss in Boots* in the missing picture by Meyer (**676**), made his debut in that character at Covent Garden in December 1832, at the age of eleven. He continued to perform in pantomimes in London for a number of years. He is also pictured with Kate Vaughan (*q.v.*) in **823**. Mitchenson died on 20 October 1870.

MOLIÈRE Jean Baptiste Poquelin
1622-1673 **609, B62, B63**
Molière was baptised Jean-Baptiste Poquelin in Paris on 15 January 1622. As the son of an upholsterer in the royal household, he received a good education at the prestigious Collège de Clermont. Renouncing his father's trade, and adopting the name of Molière, he joined with nine others to form a theatrical troupe called somewhat pretentiously the Illustre-Théâtre. From those humble beginnings he eventually became France's greatest writer of comedy and head of a theatrical enterprise at the Palais Royal that after his death evolved into the Comédie Française. Molière was supported by Louis XIV but was often plagued and conspired against by the sacred and secular authorities who found heresy and sedition in his great plays *Tartuffe, L'École des femmes* and *Don Juan*. Other masterpieces include *Les Précieuses ridicule, Le Misanthrope, L'Avare, Le Bourgeois gentilhomme* and *Le Médicin malgré lui*. While performing Argan in the fourth performance of his own *Le Malade imaginaire* at the Palais Royal on 17 February 1673, Molière collapsed on stage, was taken to his house on the Rue de Richelieu, and died. Last rites were denied to him, and he was buried without ceremony, after sunset, on 21 February.

Molière's genius derives in part from the vigour of his language, his use of creative theatrical devices, and his penetrating observation of human behaviour. 'Molière seems [in *Tartuffe*] to put his finger on what was new in his notion of what is comic: a comedy, only incidentally funny, that is based on a constant double vision of wise and foolish, right and wrong seen together, side by side. That is his invention and his glory' (W. G. Moore, *Moliere: a New Criticism* (1968). *See* also Burnim and Wilton, *The Richard Bebb Collection in the Garrick Club*, B162 and B163.

MOODY, John, stage name of John Cochran **610-613**
1727-1812
John Cochran was born in 1727 in Cork, the son of a hairdresser. Because the lad took it into his head to pass himself off as an Englishman, he changed his name to Moody (presumably from the character in Cibber's *The Provok'd Husband*, which he later acted) and declared that he was born in Stanhope Street, Clare Market, in London. He was a hairdresser for a few years and then sailed to the West Indies, joining a troupe of players in Kingston, Jamaica, with whom he is said to have acted Hamlet, Romeo, King Lear and other leading roles. Moody worked his way back to England and in 1758 was acting in Norwich. David Garrick saw him playing Lockit in *The Beggar's Opera* and hired him to act at Drury Lane in London. There on 12 January 1759 Moody substituted for Holland as Thyreus in *Anthony and Cleopatra* and on 22 May was advertised as the 'gentleman' playing Henry VIII.

In his first full season, 1759-60, Moody showed Londoners, among other characters, Seyward in *Macbeth*, Henry VIII again, Catesby in *Jane Shore* and, most importantly, Sir Callaghan O'Brallagan in *Love à la Mode*. The last role was one of several Irish characters he made a speciality in the seasons that followed: Major O'Flaherty in *The West Indian*, Sir Patrick O'Neale in *The Irish Widow* and Connolly in *The School for Wives* were all written for him. Over the years Drury Lane also used him in such roles as Teague in *The Committee* (**613**), Ben and Sir Sampson in *Love for Love*, Lord Burleigh in *The Critic*, Sir Lucius O'Trigger in *The Rivals* and Oldfox in *The Plain Dealer*. He made excursions elsewhere: Covent Garden, the Haymarket, several summers in Bristol and some appearances in Leeds, York, Liverpool and Plymouth. He worked his way up to £8 weekly at Drury Lane by 1789 but showed little ambition and was regularly called lazy by his critics. His last appearance was on 26 June 1804, when he came out of retirement after 10 years to play Jobson in *The Devil to Pay* (**611**) for a hospital benefit. John Moody died on 26 December 1812, aged 85. He had been married twice: to Anne (family name unknown), who died in 1805, and to Kitty Ann Worlock, a dancer, who survived him and died in 1846. (*BDA*) [EAL]

MORE, Kenneth Gilbert 892, G1003
1914-1982
Kenneth More was born at Gerrards Cross, Buckinghamshire, on 29 September 1914, the son of Charles Gilbert More and Edith Winfred (née Watkins). After attending Victoria College, Jersey, he first appeared on the stage in 1936 at the Windmill Theatre in a revue sketch. He served in the Royal Navy in the Second World War, and returned to the stage to play the role of the Reverend Arthur Platt in *And No Birds Sing* at the Aldwych in November 1946. More was to become one of the leading actors of his day, appearing in numerous plays and films until 1978. On stage he acted, among other roles, Sir Robert Morton in *The Winslow Boy* (New Theatre 1970), Andrew Perry in *Signs of the Times* (Vaudeville, 1973) and the Duke in *On Approval* (Vaudeville, 1977). But it was in 35 films that he made his greater reputation: among them were *Scott of the Antartic* (1948); *Doctor in the House* (1954, British Film Academy Award as best actor); *The Deep Blue Sea* (1955, Venice Volpi Cup as best actor); *The Admirable Crichton* (1957); *The Longest Day* (1962); *A Night to Remember* (1958); *The Thirty-Nine Steps* (1959); *Sink the Bismark!* (1960); *Oh! What a Lovely War* (1968); *The Battle of Britain* (1969) and *Journey to the Centre of the Earth* (1976). He also appeared on television; his best remembered role was as Young Jolyon in *The Forsyte Saga* (1966-1967). More wrote three autobiographical books: *Happy Go Lucky* (1959), *Kindly Leave the Stage* (1965) and *More or Less* (1978). He became a member of the Garrick Club in 1954. He died on 12 July 1982. The theatre in Redbridge bears his name.

MORGAN, Roger Hugh Vaughan Charles CBE G0982
b. 1926
Roger Morgan was born on 8 July 1926, the son of the novelists and playwrights Charles Langbridge Morgan and Hilda Vaughan. He was educated at Phillips Academy, Andover (USA), Eton and Brasenose, Oxford (MA). Morgan served in the Grenadier Guards, 1944-1947 (Capt 1946), as Librarian of the House of Commons, 1951-1963, and of the House of Lords 1963-1991. He was honoured with a CBE in 1991. In 1955 Morgan joined the Garrick Club; he is a Senior Trustee and Life Member.

MORISON, Stanley Arthur 614
1889-1967
The typographer and scholar Stanley Morison was born on 6 May 1889 at Wanstead, Essex. He became the foremost historian of printing and typography in Britain and wrote many articles and books on the subject (including *Four Centuries of Fine Printing*, 1924) and on literary and humanistic history. For many years he was on the staff of *The Times* and designed Times New Roman, perhaps the most successful typeface of the twentieth century. He was engaged with several periodicals and was editor of *The Fleuron*, 1926-1930, an influential journal on typography, editor of *The History of the Times* and editor of the *Times Literary Supplement* (1945-1947). He was also on the Editorial Board of the *Encyclopaedia Britannica* and wrote many articles for it. Morison became a member of the Garrick Club in 1931. He died in London on 11 October 1967.

MORTON, Charlotte Jane
See Charlotte Jane CHAPMAN

MORTON, Thomas 615
1764?-1838
The playwright Thomas Morton was born in Durham about 1764, the youngest son of John Morton of Wickham. After some education at a school in Soho Square, London, he entered Lincoln's Inn in 1784 but was not called to the Bar. His appetite for the theatre was whetted by amateur acting, and his first play, *Columbus; or, A World Discovered*, was successfully acted at Covent

Garden on 1 December 1792. Thereafter he wrote numerous plays, mostly comedies and melodramas. *Speed the Plough* (Covent Garden, 8 February 1798) had a long run and was frequently revived. Other notable pieces were *The School of Reform* (Covent Garden, 15 January 1805) and *Town and Country, Which is Best?* (Covent Garden, 10 March 1807). Morton died on 28 March 1838. One of his sons, John Maddison Morton became a writer of farces. In addition to De Wilde's portrait of him (**615**), there is a portrait of Morton by Sir Martin Archer Shee. 'He was a man of reputable life and regular habits, who enjoyed, two years before his death, the rarely accorded honour of being elected (8 May 1837) an honorary member of the Garrick Club.' (*DNB*)

MOSSOP, Henry 616

1729?-1774

Henry Mossop was probably born in Dublin in 1729, the son of Reverend John Mossop of Trinity College. Henry was given a proper education and entered Trinity College with the intention of becoming a clergyman, but he came to London and turned to the stage, despite being refused by both Garrick at Drury Lane and Rich at Covent Garden. With almost everything against him, he returned to Dublin and found work with Thomas Sheridan at Smock Alley Theatre, where he appeared as Zanga in *The Revenge* on 30 November 1749. Benjamin Victor served him a death blow: 'a wild awkward youth, that had never taken the business and propriety of acting in consideration.' Mossop modelled himself after James Quin but copied Quin's 'faults instead of the beauties.' That did not stop Mossop, for he went on to act Cassius in *Julius Caesar*, Gloster in *Jane Shore*, Othello, King John, Macbeth and other important characters, determined (and apparently encouraged by Sheridan) to overcome his shortcomings and find success in the theatre.

Critical comments remained mixed for years: 'no carriage; his action wild, ranting irregular' (Lord Orrery), 'the most melodious clear voice I ever heard' (Tate Wilkinson), 'playing which appears natural, because it is divested of all pomp and ceremony' (John Hill), 'a sameness in most of the characters he acts' (*Theatrical Review*, 1757) and 'as wretched a performer as ever graced the stage' (Edward Purdom). But he doggedly worked his way up, at Drury Lane, then at Dublin again, Drury Lane again, and Dublin once more (as manager). After all that experience he was classed by Thomas Davies as (after Garrick and Spranger Barry) 'the most valuable actor on the stage.' He was hard-working, careful in his attention to the minute details of his profession, and, indeed, very good when playing the fiery characters most suited to him. But he had too much going against him from the start, and all his effort did not take him to the top of his profession. He gambled too much, and his health deteriorated by 1771. In 1772 he was bankrupt, and the patent theatres in London had no place for him. He died on 27 December 1774, almost penniless. (*BDA*) [EAL]

MOUNTAIN, Mrs John, Rosemond, née Wilkinson 617, 618

c. 1768-1841

Rosemond Wilkinson was born about 1768, the daughter of Wilkinson the slackwire and tightrope walker who also made theatrical wigs and dressed hair. (She was not related to the York Theatre manager Tate Wilkinson, though she was for a time employed by him.) Rosemond's first stage appearance may have been in the summer of 1782, but her first recorded role was Madame Hazard in *Mount Parnassus,* a burletta given at the Royal Circus on 4 November of that year. She was both an actress and a singer and quickly gained not only an audience but the handsome sum (for a youngster) of two guineas weekly. With her family she went north in 1784 and attracted the attention of Tate Wilkinson when she acted Patty in *The Maid of the Mill* and Rosetta in *Love in a Village.* Tate took her into his company, gave her some of Dorothy Jordan's roles when Mrs Jordan left York, and by 1786 Miss Wilkinson received offers from Liverpool and London. She had a successful summer in Liverpool, met and was smitten by the musician John Mountain, signed a three-year contract with Covent Garden Theatre, and against her relatives' better judgment, got married. On 4 October 1786 she made her debut as Fidelia in *The Foundling* and Leonora in *The Padlock.* Covent Garden became her home for most of the ensuing decade, though she appeared also in Dublin, Liverpool, York, Bath, Bristol and Birmingham. In 1800, after some voice training with Rauzzini in Bath, she changed her affiliation to Drury Lane and was with that troupe until her retirement in May 1815. Her salary had reached a peak in 1805-6, when she was earning £15 weekly.

In addition to the roles just mentioned, Mrs Mountain was seen as Lucinda in *The Conscious Lovers*, Dorinda in *The Beaux' Stratagem*, Jessica in *The Merchant of Venice*, Sylvia in *The Old Bachelor*, Caelia in *As You Like It*, Perdita in *The Winter's Tale*, Ophelia in *Hamlet* and many others. Critics praised her 'amiable simplicity' (Oxberry), 'correct ear and good taste' (*Monthly Mirror*) and 'engaging regularity of features' (Waldron). Her marriage seems to have been a happy one, and her husband's musical support enhanced her career over the years. They had one child. Rosemond Mountain died on 3 July 1841. (*BDA*) [EAL]

MUNDEN, Joseph Shepherd
1758-1832 **355, 429, 619-630**

Born in 1758 in Brook's Market, Leather Lane, Holborn, London, Joseph Shepherd Munden was the son of a poulterer. He was placed with an apothecary, then a law stationer and then a lawyer, after which he spent two years in Liverpool, earning his living as a scrivener while gaining experience as an actor. On 11 January 1779 he performed in *The Gentle Shepherd* with a group of northern players at the Haymarket Theatre in London, but for ten years Munden worked chiefly in the provinces, spending some time as a manager with Whitlock. His niche was in comedy, and after the death of the comedian John Edwin in 1790 Munden was able to get an engagement at Covent Garden Theatre in London at £6 weekly. His debut was as Sir Francis Gripe in *The Busy Body* and Jemmy Jumps in *The Farmer* on 2 December 1790; the critic 'Anthony Pasquin' compared Munden unfavourably with both the deceased Edwin and the reigning comedian John Quick: Munden equalled 'Neither the Quick nor the dead.' The *World* was more favourable: Munden was 'rather under the middle size, his figure good, his voice powerful and melodious, and his articulation the clearest and most rapid we ever witnessed.' The *Gazetteer* claimed that he acted 'Without the aid of grimace or buffoonery.' But grimace and buffoonery captured audiences, and within a few years critics reported that Munden went too far: 'he is too fond of grimace,' commented Waldron in 1795, and the *Morning Herald* in 1798 complained about his ad libs. Leigh Hunt in 1807 said with irony that Munden had an 'innumerable variety of as fanciful contortions of countenance as ever threw women into hysterics.' Charles Lamb still found him irresistible: 'When you think he has exhausted his battery of looks ... suddenly he sprouts out and entirely new set of features, like Hydra. He is not one, but legion; not so much a comedian as a company. If his name could be multiplied like his countenance, it might fill a playbill. He, and he alone, literally *makes faces*.'

Lamb's praises helped make Munden one of the most popular low comedians of his day, and it is worth noting that in the Garrick Club collection of theatrical portraits there are almost as many depictions of Joseph Munden as of David Garrick and J. P. Kemble: as Marrall in *A New Way to Pay Old Debts* (**355**), Project in *Speculation* (**429**), Autolycus in *The Winter's Tale* (**619**, **620**, reported as lost but now found), Crack in *The Turnpike Gate* (**621**), Peregrine Forester in *Hartford Bridge* (**622**) and Old Brummagem in *Lock and Key* (**630**) – in addition to portraits out of character by Drummond, Knight, Opie, Shee and Turmeau. Munden's many roles also included Peachum in *The Beggar's Opera*, Sir Francis Wronghead in *The Provok'd Husband*, Sir Peter Teazle in *The School for Scandal*, Scrub in *The Beaux' Stratagem*, Dogberry in *Much Ado about Nothing*, Sir Anthony Absolute in *The Rivals* and one of his lesser-known favourites, Dornton in *The Road to Ruin*.

Munden lived with Mary Jones, an actress who performed as Mrs Munden in the 1780s and bore him four daughters; in 1789 she ran off with the actor John Hodgkinson, and that year Munden married the player Frances Butler. After about 50 years on the stage Joseph Munden retired, on 31 May 1824; for his farewell at Drury Lane he acted two of his most popular parts, Sir Robert Bramble in *The Poor Gentleman* and Old Dozey in

Past Ten O'Clock. He died on 6 February 1832. (*BDA*) [EAL]

MUNNINGS, Sir Alfred James
See Index of Artists

MURRAY, Charles **632, 633**
1754-1821
Born in Cheshunt, Hertfordshire in 1754, Charles Murray was the son of Sir John Murray (1718-1777), baronet of Broughton, who is noticed in the *DNB*, and his second wife, née Webb. He enjoyed a classical education, studied pharmacy and surgery, and served as a surgeon's mate in the Mediterranean. In 1773 he began to perform in private theatres, using the name Raymur to spare family embarrassment. He joined Wilkinson on the York circuit, and in 1777 he went to Norwich, where he assumed his real name and where his reputation grew over the next eight years. At Norwich he married his first wife, who died at age 21 in January 1780. Two years later he was living with Anne Payne (née Acres), an actress who was estranged from her husband, the actor Jonathan Payne. It is not clear whether or not Murray married her after Payne died in 1784.

Murray made his first appearance at Bath on 8 October 1785 as Sir Giles Overreach in *A New Way to Pay Old Debts*, and he was the original Albert in *Werter* on 3 December 1785. At Bath and Bristol he played a number of leading roles, including Macbeth, Shylock, Iago, Iachimo, Evander in *The Grecian Daughter* and Pierre in *Venice Preserv'd*. His successes in the provinces brought him an engagement at Covent Garden Theatre, where he made his debut on 30 September 1796 as Shylock, for which he received mixed reviews. There were complaints of 'a drawl in his recitation' and deficiencies in majesty and grace, but in the judgment of the *Monthly Mirror* he was better suited to roles of older tragic figures (Shylock aside) like Lear, Evander, or Old Norval than 'any actor we remember to have seen.' Such roles, including Tobias in *The Stranger* (in which he is pictured by De Wilde, **632**), became his line at Covent Garden, where he remained through 1816-17. By then his ill health and infirmities were evident, and he made his farewell on 17 July 1817 as Brabantio in *Othello*. He eventually settled in Edinburgh, where his son William Henry Murray (q.v.) was manager of the theatre. Charles Murray died in Edinburgh on 8 November 1821. His private character was highly commended. In addition to the Edinburgh manager William Henry Murray, his children by Anne Payne Murray were Maria Murray, an actress who married the actor and author Joseph Leatherley Cowell and became the matriarch of a large theatrical family, and another daughter, Harriet Murray, who became an actress and married the actor Henry Siddons, the son of the famous Sarah Siddons. (*BDA*)

MURRAY, Henry **634**
d. 1884
A Henry Murray was elected to the Garrick Club in March 1867 and died in January 1884. The sitter in this elusive picture (**634**) probably was the son of the actor-manager Henry Leigh Murray (q.v.). Or possibly the picture is really of Henry Leigh Murray himself.

MURRAY, Henry Leigh
real name Wilson **635**
1820-1870
This actor, whose real surname was Wilson, was born in London on 19 October 1820 and acted with amateur players in a theatre in Catherine Street, the Strand, about 1838, playing such roles as Buckingham in *Richard III*, Cassio, Macduff and Iago. In December 1839 he made his professional debut at Hull as Ludovico in *Othello*, and then under the name of Leigh in September 1840 he appeared at the Adelphi Theatre in Edinburgh. He left Edinburgh in 1845, to make his London debut at the Princess's Theatre on 19 April 1845 as Sir Clifford in *The Hunchback*. Over the next 20 years he acted a wide range of characters at various London theatres: the Lyceum, Strand, Olympic, Adelphi, Drury Lane and St James's. Because of his ill health, he was given a benefit at Drury Lane on 27 June 1865. He died on 17 January 1870 and was buried in Brompton Cemetery. His wife Elizabeth (d. 1892), an actress, was the daughter of the provincial manager and playwright Henry Lee

(1765-1836). His brother Gaston Murray (1826-1869) also acted in London. (*DNB*)

MURRAY, William Henry 636, 637
1790-1852
Born in 1790 at Bath where his father Charles Murray (*q.v.*) was acting, William Henry appeared on that stage as an infant and juvenile. His sister Maria married the actor Joseph Leatherly Cowell. Another sister, Harriet, married Henry Siddons, the son of Sarah Siddons. Beginning in 1803-4 William was at Covent Garden playing various small parts. In November 1809 he appeared at Edinburgh, where he was associated with the theatre there for 42 years. When Henry Siddons died, William took over the management of the theatre in Shakespeare Square on behalf of his widowed sister. He continued to act supporting roles. In addition to managing that theatre successfully, for a while he ran the Adelphi (formerly the Caledonian) and the playhouse in Leith Walk. In 1848 he gave up stage managing but appeared on stage, making his farewell at the Adelphi on 22 October 1851 as Sir Anthony Absolute in *The Rivals*. Murray was described by Joseph Knight as 'An excellent actor in juvenile parts where no deep emotion or pathos had to be displayed.' He was also good in comedy and in character parts. In manner he was 'staid, formal, and a trifle pedantic.' Murray wrote a number of plays of little consequence. He became a member of the Garrick Club in 1843 but spent most of his life in Edinburgh. Murray died in 1852. In addition to his portraits in the Garrick Club (**636**, **637**), a portrait by Sir William Allan is in the Scottish Portrait Gallery.

N

NARES, Owen Ramsey 638
1888-1943
The matinee idol Owen Nares was born in 1888, at Maiden Erleigh, the son of W. O. Nares and his wife Margaret (née Beverley). He trained for the stage under Rosina Filippi and appeared at the Haymarket Theatre in 1909 and in *Old Heidelberg* at the St James's Theatre in 1910. He toured the provinces, had his career interrupted by illness for two years, and then returned to London where he appeared continuously for eleven years. Among his popular roles were Lord Monkhurst in *Milestones* (1912), Julian Beauclerc in *Diplomacy* (1913), the dual role of the Bishop and Armstrong in *Romance* (1915) and Mark Sabre in *If Winter Comes* (1923, at the St James's where he was manager for a while). He toured the provinces with his own companies for a number of years. In London again he played Roger Hilton in *Call it a Day* (1935), Robert Carson in *Robert's Wife* (1937) and Max de Winter in *Rebecca* (1940). He died suddenly on 31 July 1943, at the age of 55. Nares was a fine actor and a handsome man with great appeal as a romantic figure. He became a member of the Garrick Club in 1929. (*OCT*)

NAPIER, Major-General George Thomas Conolly 793
d. 1874
Identified as No. 16 in O'Neil's large canvas of a game in the Billiards Room, Major General Napier was a member of a large family of military men and politicians. He became a member of the Garrick Club in 1868.

NEWLAN, Fanny
See Fanny PEARCE

NICKALLS, Guy Oliver 892
1899-1974
Born on 4 April 1899, the son of Guy Nickalls and Ellen Gilbey (née Gold), Guy Oliver Nickalls was educated at Eton and at Magdalen College, Oxford, where he rowed with many winning

crews. He was the eight oar in the crew that represented the UK in the 1920 and 1928 Olympics, winning two silver medals. He served in the First World War, was with the Foreign Office, 1919-20, and was a member of the advertising firm of Alfred Pemberton, Ltd, from 1926. Nickalls's interest in rowing was pervasive; he published books and gave broadcasts on the sport. He became a member of the Garrick Club in March 1929. Nickalls died on 26 April 1974.

O

O'CONNELL, John Morgan **793**
d. 1876
The barrister John Morgan O'Connell, who is shown as No. 6 in O'Neil's scene of members in the Billiards Room, was elected to the Garrick Club in February 1864. He died in January 1876.

O'DOWD, Sir James Cornelius **793**
1829-1903
James Cornelius O'Dowd was born on 1 January 1829, the eldest son of the barrister J. K. O'Dowd. After being educated at Trinity College, Dublin, he became a barrister, Middle Temple 1859, and was Deputy Judge Advocate-General of the Army 1869-1899. He held various other military judicial positions, and was Professor of Law at the Staff College from 1896. He also was part-proprietor and co-editor with Sir William Howard Russell of the *Army and Navy Gazette*, and wrote a number works on military legal issues. O' Dowd was knighted in 1900. Sir James became a member of the Garrick Club in 1854 and died on 15 December 1903.

OLDFIELD, Anne **639-641**
1683?-1730
Anne Oldfield was probably born about 1683 and introduced to the stage by the playwright George Farquhar. She evidently joined Drury Lane Theatre under the management of Christopher Rich in 1699-1700, her first known role being Candiope in *Secret Love*. She was called Mrs Oldfield when *The Grove* was published in 1700, an indication that Anne was probably then near her majority. Colley Cibber, a promising actor himself, later said that Anne was not at first given much responsibility at Drury Lane, though the records show her acting and speaking prologues and epilogues during the early years of the new century. By 1703 she was in the middle of the pay roster, though well below the leading ladies Elizabeth Barry and Anne Bracegirdle. Her opportunity came on 7 December 1704, when the would-be playwright Cibber tailored Lady Betty Modish in *The*

Careless Husband to Anne's talents – 'an agreeably gay Woman of Quality a little too conscious of her natural Attractions,' wrote Cibber, and he purposely made the description as applicable to Lady Betty as to Mrs Oldfield.

That kind of character became Anne's line in the years that followed at Drury Lane and the Queen's Theatre: Sylvia in *The Recruiting Officer*, Mrs Sullen in *The Stratagem*, Lady Lurewell in *The Constant Couple*, Mrs Loveit in *The Man of Mode*, Letitia in *The Old Bachelor*, Millamant in *The Way of the World*, Lady Brute in *The Provok'd Wife* and Lady Townly in *The Provok'd Husband*. She also appeared in serious characters – Jane Shore, Cleopatra in *All for Love*, Calista in *The Fair Penitent* are typical – but she said, according to the prompter Chetwood, 'I hate to have a Page dragging my Tail about. Why do they not give [Mary] Porter these parts? She can put on a better Tragedy Face than I can.' And she was probably right: her own vanity made her ideal for sophisticated, graceful ladies of quality. In his preface to *The Provok'd Husband* Cibber said, 'The spectator was always as much informed by her Eyes, as her Elocution … The qualities she *acquired* were the *Genteel* and the *Elegant*. The one in her Air, and the other in her Dress …' These were characteristics that Anne Bracegirdle had before her, and Mrs Oldfield's 1731 *Life* reported that in a contest held (probably in 1706-7 if at all) the two played the title role in *The Amorous Widow* in competition and Oldfield acted Bracegirdle off the stage.

Anne also commanded the most favourable of terms from managers. According to the Drury Lane treasurer Zachary Baggs, in 1708-9 Anne was earning over £250 for acting only 39 times. After about 1715 she seems not to have taken more than two or three new parts per season, and at her benefit in March 1729 (the first of the season, a prize in itself) she cleared an estimated £500. She may not have needed the money. Since about 1703 Anne had lived with Arthur Mainwaring, the Commissioner of Customs, by whom she had a son and from whom she inherited a generous estate; after Mainwaring died in 1712 she had a similar affair with Brigadier General Charles Churchill. In both relationships she won the acceptance of families in high society.

Anne Oldfield's last stage appearance was on 28 April 1730 as Lady Brute in *The Provok'd Wife*. She died on 23 October and was buried in Westminster Abbey. It was the end of an era for Drury Lane, where she had been a leading lady for so many years. (*BDA*; Joanne Lafler, *The Celebrated Mrs. Oldfield*, 1989) [EAL]

OLIVIER, Sir Laurence Kerr, Baron of Brighton **642, 643, S50, S51,**
1907-1989 **G1003, B65, B66, B147, B148**

Laurence Olivier, regarded as the greatest English actor of the twentieth century, was born on 22 May 1907 at Dorking, Surrey, the son of the Reverend G. K. Olivier and his wife Agnes Louise (née Crookenden). At the All Saints Choir School, at the age of nine, he made his theatrical debut as Brutus in an abridged *Julius Caesar*, and five years later, in 1922, he appeared as Katherine in a special boys' performance of *The Taming of the Shrew* presented by Oxford's St Edwards School at the Stratford Festival, Stratford-upon-Avon. After attending the Central School of Dramatic Art in London in 1924, Olivier joined the Birmingham Repertory Theatre Company, under the management of Sybil Thorndike; in 1929 with the English Stage Society he appeared in the West End in the title role of *Beau Geste* and as Stanhope in *Journey's End*. He also went to America in 1929, making his Broadway debut in *Murder on the Second Floor*. Back in London he appeared in a number of contemporary and classical roles. In 1935 he and John Gielgud alternated performances as Romeo and Mercutio at the New Theatre.

In 1937 Olivier joined the Old Vic Company, where he triumphed in an unabridged *Hamlet*, which he later took to Elsinore. Over the years at the Old Vic, the Chichester Festival (of which he was the first director), the National Theatre (which he was instrumental in founding and served as the first director), Stratford and elsewhere, Olivier displayed an astonishing energy and versatility as an actor. He played Oedipus and Puff in a double bill at the New Theatre in 1945 (**B147**, **B148**). On alternating nights he acted Antony to Vivien Leigh's Cleopatra in Shakespeare's play and Caesar to her Cleopatra in Shaw's play. He was spectacular as Coriolanus and engaging as Brazen in *The Recruiting Officer*. In 1957 he acted the title role in a superb revival of *Titus Andronicus* and was masterful as the broken-down comedian Archie Rice in *The Entertainer*. He gave memorable performances as Shylock, Othello, Richard III (**643**, **B66**), Tyrone in *Long Day's Journey into Night* and Edgar in *The Dance of Death*.

Among the first of his many film roles, and the one that made him a star and matinee idol in America, was the tormented Heathcliff in *Wuthering Heights* in 1939. During the Second World War he served in the Royal Navy Fleet Air Arm, but was demobilized in 1944 to make his brilliant and patriotic film version of *Henry V* (**B66**, special Academy Award). Notable among his more than 50 films are *Hamlet* (1948, Academy Award), *Carrie* (1950), *Richard III* (1956), *The Prince and the Showgirl* (1957), *The Entertainer* and *Othello* (1961), *Sleuth* (1972) and *Marathon Man* (1976). Olivier also appeared in television productions, notably in *A Voyage Round My Father* (1982) and *King Lear* (1983). He also narrated *The World at War* (1963).

He was knighted in 1947 and created Baron (life peer) of Brighton in 1970. He became a member of the Garrick Club in 1936. Honorary degrees were awarded to him by Tufts University (1946), Oxford (1957), Manchester (1968), Sussex (1978), Edinburgh (1964) and London (1968). He married three times, to actresses: those with Jill Desmond and Vivien Leigh ended in divorces, and in 1961 he married Joan Plowright. He wrote *Confessions of an Actor* (1982) and *On Acting* (1986).

Lord Olivier died on 11 July 1989 and was buried in Poet's Corner, Westminster Abbey. He lies with Garrick and Kean. Olivier has been the subject of some 25 books, including those written by Melvyn Bragg, John Cottrell. Robert Daniels, W. A. Darlington and Anthony Holden. (*WWW, EB, OCT*)

O'NEIL, Henry Nelson ARA
See Index of Artists

O'NEILL, Eliza later Lady Wrixon-Becher
1791-1872 **644, 645**
The very talented actress Eliza O'Neill was born in 1791 in Drogheda, the daughter of the manager of the theatre there and his wife (née Featherstone). She made her first stage appearance as a child at her father's theatre and subsequently acted in Belfast and Dublin. At Dublin she earned acclaim as Jane Shore and Juliet. In 1814 she was engaged at Covent Garden, where she made her debut as Juliet on 6 October. She was a great success and was extravagantly hailed as the new Mrs Siddons. She remained a favourite at Covent Garden for five years, excelling as Lady Teazle, Mrs Oakly and Lady Townly in comedy and acclaimed in tragic roles like Juliet and Belvidera. In 1819 she was betrothed to William Wrixon Becher, a wealthy member of the Irish Parliament. She made her farewell from the stage at Covent Garden on 13 July 1819 as Mrs Haller in *The Stranger* and on 18 December of that year married Becher, who subsequently inherited a baronetcy from an uncle. Lady Becher died on 29 October 1872. She possessed beauty, grace and simplicity and was highly praised by Hazlitt. Though a great tragic actress, she fell short of transcendent genius. (*DNB*)

O'REILLY, William
See William BAILEY

ORGER, Mary Ann Ivers **355, 630**
1788-1849
This actress was born on in London 25 February 1788. Her father was a country musician named William Ivers and her mother was a sometime actress. Mary Ann appeared as an infant in *Henry VIII*, played the young girl in *Children of the Wood* at Newbury in 1793, and for some years acted with Henry Thornton's company in the nearby towns east and south of London. She married a Quaker, George Orger, of High Wycombe, in July 1804, and though she retired from the stage for a while, she resumed in 1805 with performances at Glasgow and Edinburgh. Announced as Mrs Orger from Edinburgh, she made her London debut at Drury Lane on 4 October 1808 as Lydia Languish in *The Rivals*. She played with the Drury Lane company until about 1845, and made appearances at the Haymarket, the Olympic (with Madame Vestris),

and at Covent Garden, mainly in a line of supporting characters like Susan in *The School for Authors* and Jane in *Wild Oats*. Oxberry called her as a very useful actress and 'a voluptuous beauty in her general appearance,' qualities not readily apparent in the Garrick Club pictures. She died on 1 October 1849. Three of her sisters also acted: one married Mr Hughes of Drury Lane; another, Mrs Fawcett, was a country performer; and the third, Mrs Lazenby, acted at the Olympic. Mary Orger's daughter Caroline (1818-1892) married the musician Albert Robert Reinagle (*BDA* 12: 306, *DNB*)

O'TOOLE, Peter Seamus G1002
b. 1932
Peter O'Toole was born on 2 August 1932 in Connemara, County Galway, Ireland, the son of Patrick Joseph and Constance Jane (née Ferguson) O'Toole. He grew up in Leeds and trained at RADA. He made his stage debut at the Leeds Civic Theatre in 1949, served in the Royal Navy, and from 1955 to 1958 was with the Old Vic Company in Bristol; he made his London debut with that company at the Old Vic in London in 1956 as Peter Shirley in *Major Barbara*. As one of Britain's leading actors, whose range extends from classical drama to contemporary farce, O'Toole's principal stage roles have included Jimmy Porter in *Look Back in Anger*, Alfred Doolittle in *Pygmalion*, Lysander in *A Midsummer Night's Dream*, Shylock, Petruchio and Hamlet. He made his Broadway debut as Henry Higgins in *Pygmalion* at the Plymouth Theatre in 1987. His first film was *Kidnapped* in 1960, and later he became an international star with stunning performances in *Lawrence of Arabia* (1962), *Becket* (1963), *Lord Jim* (1965), *The Lion in Winter* (1968), *Man of La Mancha* (1972) and *The Ruling Class* (1972). His television appearances include *Svengali* (1982), *Kim* (1984) and the miniseries *Masada* (1981), acclaimed as one of the finest performances of his career. O'Toole has been nominated seven times for an Academy Award; In 2003 the Academy gave him a special award for his achievements. He received an Emmy Award for his performance of Bishop Cauchon in the minseries *Joan of Arc* (1999). He has published two volumes of memoirs: *Loitering with Intent: the Child* (1992), and *Loitering with Intent: the Apprentice* (1996). O'Toole became a member of the Garrick Club in 1963.

OXBERRY, William 355, 646
1784-1824
William Oxberry was born on 18 December 1784 in Moorfields, facing Bedlam. After apprenticeships with a painter, a bookseller and a printer, he made appearances in local amateur theatres. He then played in the provinces until he made his professional London debut at Covent Garden as Robin Roughhead in *Fortune's Frolic* on 7 November 1807. He made no great impression and soon went to act at Glasgow where he fared better, making some reputation as Sir David Daw in *The Wheel of Fortune*. He returned to London to play with the Drury Lane company at the Lyceum, where he acted Leo Luminati in *Oh! This Love* (**646**), and at the new Drury Lane Theatre in 1812. He remained at Drury Lane through the season 1819-20, appearing in supporting and featured roles like Master Stephen in *Every Man in His Humour*, Slender in *The Merry Wives of Windsor*, Moses in *The School for Scandal* and Job Thornberry in *John Bull*. In many of his other roles, it is said, he 'failed to rise above mediocrity.' After also failing as manager of the Olympic, in 1821 Oxberry took over Craven's chophouse in Drury Lane, a place where literary and theatrical people congregated. For a while he had been editor of *The Monthly Mirror*, and he was the author of a number of books, including *The Theatrical Banquet, or the Actors' Budget* (1809) and *Oxberry's Anecdotes of the Stage* (1824). He also edited the *New English Drama*, 113 plays in 22 volumes, 1818-1824. He died of a stroke on 9 June 1824. After Oxberry's death, his widow published his *Dramatic Biography*. His son William Henry Oxberry (1808-1852) was also an actor and author (*q.v.*)

OXBERRY, William Henry G1034
1808-1852
This actor was born on 21 April 1808, the son of William Oxberry (*q.v.*), actor and author. After some time in his father's printing office and an apprenticeship with a surgeon, young

Oxberry appeared in some amateur theatricals and then made his professional debut at the Olympic Theatre on 17 March 1825 as Sam Swipes in *Exchange No Robbery*. Over the next 27 years he made a career as a comic dancer and as an actor in burlesques. He appeared at most London theatres, and he also managed a few, including the Lyceum (English Opera House) in the 1830s and the theatre at Windsor. In 1841 at Covent Garden he acted Flute in *A Midsummer Night's Dream,* and in June 1843 he was at the Princess's playing the ridiculous schoolmaster in *The Swedish Ferryman*. Oxberry wrote a number of forgotten plays, most of which have remained unpublished. He died from lung disease on 29 February 1852, leaving behind a widow and three children whom he wished would be supported by the income from his 30 plays yet unacted. In his will he also requested that his heart be preserved in some medical museum as a specimen of a broken heart. Those requests, and others in his will concerning his funeral, were not observed. He was the editor of *Oxberry's Weekly Budget of Plays* (1843-1844) and *Oxberry's Dramatic Chronology* (1850).

P

PACKER, John Hayman **647**

1730-1806

John Hayman Packer was born in the Strand on 21 March 1730, the son of a saddler in Glass House Street. When Ann Packer, his widowed mother, died in October 1763 she left John and his sister a considerable estate. Packer gave up his father's trade for the theatre, appearing in 1754 at Newcastle under the name of Hayman. He made his debut in London at Covent Garden on 24 January 1758 as Johnson in *The Rehearsal.* Garrick then engaged him for Drury Lane, where Packer appeared on 19 September 1758, now advertised as Mr Packer, as Selim in *The Mourning Bride.* His subsequent roles that season were Rosencrantz, Benvolio, Catesby in *Richard III* and Albany in *King Lear*, among many others. Packer remained throughout his London career at Drury Lane, with Garrick until 1776 and then for 28 more seasons until 1804-5, when he retired. He acted dozens of roles during the five decades he was a utility actor. In summers he played at Bristol and Richmond.

A fall down a flight of stairs in January 1806 hastened his death, which occurred on the following 16 September. He was buried at St Paul, Covent Garden. A useful actor, Packer lacked the 'animation and fire' for leading roles. One critic unkindly called him 'a very reputable saddler; though a miserable actor.' (*BDA*)

PAGET, William George

See 3rd Marquis of ANGLESEY

PALMER, Jane

See Jane POWELL

PALMER, John **3, 648-652, B67**

1744?-1798

Born in 1744, or perhaps 1742, in the parish of St Luke, Old Street, John 'Plausible Jack' Palmer was the son of the Drury Lane house servant Robert Palmer (1699-1787). Our subject is not to be confused with a second actor named John Palmer (1728-1768), not related, who was nicknamed 'Gentleman Palmer.' Our Palmer made his stage debut at the Haymarket Theatre on 28 April 1762 as the Oxford scholar in Samuel Foote's farce *The Orators*. Then Palmer acted, for his father's shared benefit at Drury Lane, Buck in *The Englishman in Paris* on 20 May at the very same time he was scheduled to perform in *The Orators* at the Haymarket. That was not the way to begin an acting career, but it was an indication of Palmer's eagerness to play any role, large or small, anywhere, without seriously considering what he was doing. In this case, Foote sacked Palmer from the Haymarket, and the boy went off to Portsmouth. When he returned in the autumn of 1762 he was hired by Garrick at Drury Lane and spent the season acting mostly bit parts, but at his father's benefit in May 1763 Palmer played George Barnwell in *The London Merchant*. When he was not given a raise in salary for 1764-65 Palmer quit and joined the company at Norwich. There he married Frances Berroughs but quickly deserted her for a Yarmouth mistress, incurring the ire of his wife's family and friends and forcing him back to his bride, with whom he returned to London expecting but not finding employment. The rest of his life was not exactly patterned after those early years of witless behaviour, but John Palmer managed in time to get himself into a variety of awkward and sometimes even dangerous situations.

He supported himself and his wife by delivering Stevens's *Lecture on Heads* at a variety of London and provincial venues, and during the rest of the 1760s, still trying to find himself but not looking very hard, Palmer busied himself at a variety of theatres acting such roles as Harcourt in *The Country Girl*, Faulconbridge in *King John*, Edmund in *King Lear*, Young Wilding in *The Lyar*, Kastril in *The Alchemist*, Cassio in *Othello*, Launcelot in *The Merchant of Venice*, Iachimo in *Cymbeline* (**651**), Chamont in *The Orphan* and the character that gave Palmer his nickname, the coxcomb Lord Plausible in *The Plain Dealer*. Most of those roles he played at Drury Lane, where Garrick hired him for 1766-67. But in addition to acting at Drury Lane and gaining popularity with audiences, restless Palmer worked in the summers at Liverpool, Birmingham, Dublin, and, beginning in 1776, the Haymarket in London. Among his most popular roles was one for which he was particularly well-suited: the smooth, hypocritical Joseph Surface in *The School for Scandal* (**3**). But Palmer, restive this time because he wanted a company of his own, thought he saw a chance to get around the Licensing Act of 1737, which restricted straight plays to Drury Lane, Covent Garden, and, in the summers, the Haymarket.

Courageous but foolhardy, he joined with his friend the Reverend William Jackson and laid plans to build a new playhouse in the vicinity of the Tower. Jack supposed that, with the reverend's help in getting the support of the magistrates in the Tower Hamlets district and the Lieutenant of the Tower, he should be able to erect a theatre and produce plays there without running foul of the Licensing Act. He sold shares under false pretences to prospective renters, put up his own money and negotiated bank loans. By 20 June 1787 the Royalty Theatre in Wellclose Square was ready to open, offering *As You Like It* (with Palmer playing Jaques) and *Miss in Her Teens*. The opening went off well enough and the theatre actually remained open until April 1788, but the entertainments had to be mostly variety shows, not plays, and the company members were officially branded vagabonds, as in olden times. The venture ultimately failed, Palmer lost his shirt, and the managers of the three patent houses, who had opposed the project from the beginning, kept their monopoly.

By 1790 Palmer was back at Drury Lane for £17 weekly (for he was still a popular actor), and there he worked during the winter seasons until his death. His final appearance was in Liverpool on 2 August 1798; he acted the title role in *The Stranger*, a strenuous part which he struggled to complete. He died onstage and the audience supposed that his collapse was part of the show. He had been plausible to the end. (*BDA*) [EAL]

PALMER, Robert L. **653-655**
1757-1817
Robert L. Palmer was born in Banbury Court, Long Acre, in September 1757. He was the son of the Drury Lane Theatre house servant Robert

Palmer (1699-1787) and the brother of the actors John Palmer (1744-1798) and William Palmer (d. 1797), all of whom are noticed in the *BDA*.

Robert made his debut at Drury Lane, at the age of six, as Mustardseed in *A Midsummer Night's Dream* on 23 November 1763, a night that was to begin his association of some 54 years with that theatre. He outgrew juvenile roles and by 1775 was acting in the summer with his brothers at Birmingham. In the summer of 1776 he was engaged by Foote at the Haymarket Theatre. He also acted at Dublin and Edinburgh. But it was at Drury Lane that Palmer developed an extensive repertoire of over 300 roles: comic eccentrics, gallants, braggarts and foreigners. He was reported to have been excellent in comic French characters and he occasionally played Harlequin. He was a member of 'the School of Garrick' (**655**). Palmer died in Pimlico on 25 December 1817 and was buried at St Martin-in-the-Fields. In addition to the three portraits of him in the Garrick Club the *BDA* lists another nine. (*BDA*)

PARKE, John 750

1745-1829

The oboist John Parke, who is pictured in Harlow's large scene of the Trial in *Henry VIII* (**750**), was born in 1745, the son of John and Frances Parke, probably of the parish of St Margaret, Westminster. His younger brother was the celebrated oboist William Thomas Parke (1761-1847). In 1768 John Parke was engaged as principal oboist for the opera at the King's Theatre. Later engagements included principal oboist at Vauxhall Gardens and Drury Lane Theatre, where he began an enduring friendship with Garrick. The Duke of Cumberland also became a friend and patron. Parke played at the major music festivals and was a member of the Royal Society of Musicians for almost 50 years. He died in London on 2 August 1829. He had ten children by his wife Hannah. The eldest, Maria Hester Parke, later Mrs John Beardmore (1775-1822), became a professional singer and pianist who performed in London. His son Henry Parke (1893-1835) became a distinguished architect who is noted in the *DNB*. The other children pre-deceased their father. For more information and other pictures of John Parke see the *BDA* 11: 199-200.

PARSHALL, Horace Field 892

1903-1986

Horace Field Parshall was born on 16 June 1903, the son of Horace Field Parshall, DSC, and Annie Matilda Rogers. Educated at Eton and at New College, Oxford, he was called to the bar as barrister, Inner Temple. He served with distinction in the Second World War and eventually became Director-General of the St John's Ambulance Association, 1950-1960. He was a Director of Pyrene Co, Ltd, 1947-1968 (Deputy Chairman 1962-1968). Parshall became a member of the Garrick Club in December 1954. He died on 18 February 1986. He is shown in Gilroy's picture of the Garrick Club outing (**892**) with his third wife, Lady Phyllis Gabrielle Gore, the daughter of M. von den Portem, New York.

PARRY, Henry Sefton S55

1822-1887

In *PGC* S55 was called the bust of an unknown man, but it has since been identified as that of Henry Sefton Parry, the theatrical manager and builder of theatres. He was born in 1822 into a theatrical family and grew to learn many skills: painting scenery, cutting costumes and stage-carpentry, among them. In 1859 he went to Cape Town with his wife and established professional entertainments there. Then he travelled with a small company to many parts of the world. On returning to England he built a number of theatres, which he planned and managed. In October 1866 he opened the Holborn Theatre, of which he remained lessee until 1972. He opened the Globe Theatre, on the grounds of the old Lyon's Inn on Newcastle Street, the Strand, in November 1868 and managed it until 1881. The Avenue Theatre, at the corner of Craven Street, facing the Thames, was built by him and was inaugurated in March 1882, under Burke's management. Parry also was involved in building theatres in Greenwich, Hull and Southampton.

Parry suffered a paralytic stroke, from which he died at Cricklewood Lodge, Middlesex, on 18 December 1887, and was buried in Old Willesden churchyard. (*DNB*)

PARSONS, Ian Macnaghten CBE 892
1906-1980
The publisher and editor Ian Parsons was born on 21 May 1906, the son of Edward Percival Parsons and his wife Mabel Margaret. He was educated at Winchester and at Trinity College, Cambridge. In 1928 he joined Chatto and Windus, where he became a partner in 1930, and Director in 1953 (Chairman 1954-1974). He was also a Director of Scottish Academic Press and Sussex University Press. Among his publications were several anthologies of poetry, including the *Poems of C. Day Lewis* (1977). He was married to Marjorie Tulip Richie in 1934. He became a member of the Garrick Club in July 1936. Parsons was honoured with an OBE in 1944 and a CBE in 1971. He died on 29 October 1980.

PARSONS, William
1736 1795 **39, 40, 613, 656-663**
William Parsons was born in London on 29 February 1736, the son of William Parsons, a carpenter in Bow Lane, Cheapside. After attending St Paul's School and apprenticing to a surveyor and perhaps an apothecary, Parsons developed his interest in amateur theatricals into a professional endeavour. He began his stage career at York in the mid-1750s, and about 1757 he joined the company at Edinburgh. After five years there he began an engagement with Garrick at Drury Lane on 21 September 1763, when he played Filch in *The Beggar's Opera*. He was soon seen that season as Douglas in *1 Henry IV*, Rosencrantz in *Hamlet*, Charino in *Love Makes a Man*, Robert in *All in the Wrong* and Polonius (his most substantial role). At Drury Lane over 32 years he appeared in some 200 roles, few of them of capital importance, but in many supporting roles he was excellent. His forte became old men like Colonel Oldboy in *Lionel and Clarissa* (**657**) and country clowns like Scrub in *The Stratagem*. His best role was thought to be Corbaccio in *Volpone*. At the Haymarket, where he appeared regularly in summers, he introduced numerous characters in new comedies. Parsons's last appearance was as Sir Fretful Plagiary in *The Critic* on 19 January 1795. After much suffering from asthma he died at Frog Hall, his home at Stangate, St George's Fields, Lambeth, on 3 February 1795, and was buried in St Margaret's Churchyard at Lee, near Blackheath.

Parsons was an actor of great merit and a person of modesty and sociability. He was on the committee that formulated the Drury Lane Theatrical Fund and was one of 'the School of Garrick' (**661**). He retained his interest in the arts as an amateur painter and draughtsman. A watercolour drawing by him called 'A Composition of Fancy' was reported in *PGC* (**931**) as location unknown,' but it has now been located; it was engraved by Angus in 1790. Some 38 portraits of Parsons are recorded in the *BDA*.

PATON, Mary Anne later Mrs Wood 664
1802-1864
The vocalist Mary Ann Paton was born in October 1802 in Edinburgh, the eldest daughter of George Paton, writing master, and his wife (née Crawford). By the age of eight she was appearing at public concerts as a singer and performer on the harp and pianoforte. When the family moved to London in 1811, she was heard in some private concerts, but illness interrupted her career for six years. She re-appeared, at Bath in 1820 and at Huntingdon in 1821 and in 1822 made her London debut at the Haymarket as Susanna in *The Marriage of Figaro*, in which role she is pictured by Stewart (**664**). She afterwards performed the Countess in the same opera, Rosina in *The Barber of Seville*, Lydia in *Morning, Noon and Night* and Polly in *The Beggar's Opera*. At Covent Garden she acted Mandane in *Artaxerxes*, Rosetta in *Love in a Village*, Adriana in *The Comedy of Errors* and Clara in *The Duenna*. A critic in 1823 described her as 'gifted with extraordinary powers … Not yet twenty-one, yet her technical attainments, we are disposed to think, are nearly as great as those of any other vocalist in this country … She is beautiful in her person and features.' In 1824 she played Agatha in *Der Freischutz* and in 1826 triumphed as Rezia in *Oberon*, a role 'she was created for,' according to the composer Weber, who also conducted the piece.

On 7 May 1824 she married Lord William Pitt Lennox, but she divorced him in Scotland in 1831. That year she became the wife of the tenor Joseph Wood. After an engagement at the King's Theatre in 1831 and at Drury Lane in 1832, she resided with her husband at Woolley Moor, Yorkshire. They visited America in 1840, and when they returned she went into a convent for a year. She emerged to give a few concerts at the Princess's Theatre, and then settled at Bulcliffe Hall, near Chapelthorpe, where she died on 21 July 1864. Her sisters Isabella and Eliza were also professional singers. (*DNB*)

PATRICK, Nigel Dennis Wemyss 892
1913-1981
The actor Nigel Patrick, shown as No. 9 in Gilroy's picture of the Garrick Club Outing (**892**), was born on 2 May 1913, the son of the actors Charles Wemyss and Dororthy Turner. He started his career in 1932, first appeared in the West End in 1934 and played many roles before serving in the Second World War. After the war he continued his stage career, acting and directing many plays, including *The Pleasure of His Company* (Haymarket 1959), *Present Laughter* (Queen's 1965), *Best of Friends* (Strand 1970) and *Dear Daddy* (Ambassadors 1976). His films include *The Browning Version, Breaking the Sound Barrier, The Informers, The Battle of Britain* and *The Great Waltz.* He became a member of the Garrick Club on 5 November 1952; he died on 21 September 1981.

PAYNE, William Henry Schofield G1033
1804-1878
Born in London in 1804, Payne was apprenticed to a stockbroker, but at the age of eighteen he ran away with a travelling theatrical company in Warwickshire. After some engagements in Birmingham and London, playing with Grimaldi and Bologna at Sadler's Wells, in 1825 Payne joined the Pavilion Theatre, where he remained many years. In December 1831 he made his first appearance at Covent Garden in the pantomime *Hop o' my Thumb and his Brothers.* During his long career he performed numerous parts, from pantomime to tragedy. Often he appeared with Grimaldi at the Wells and sometimes with Charles Kemble and Edmund Kean. He also figured in some ballets. In the 1840s and 1850s he was at Vauxhall Gardens, the Theatre Royal Manchester, the Crystal Palace and Covent Garden. Payne died in Dover on 18 December 1878. By his first wife (née Rountree) he had four children, all of whom had careers on the stage. The watercolour by C. M. Donald in the Garrick Club (**G1033**) shows Payne as Tasnar in *Puss in Boots*, a pantomime that opened at Covent Garden Theatre on 24 February 1833 and ran for 42 nights. (*DNB*)

PEARCE, Fanny née Newlan G1035
1767-1843
Fanny Newlan was born in Dublin in 1767 and by 1790 was performing with Astley's company in Ireland. About the turn of the century she came with Astley to London, where she soon married an actor named Pearce. After his death she acted at Covent Garden about 1820 Widow Casey in *Fontainbleau*, and she was the original Irish Girl in *Family Jars* at the Haymarket. Her last role was in *The Frolics of the Fairies* at the Strand. She died in London in 1843, her demise accelerated by having been 'tossed by an infuriated bull.' (*BDA*)

PEILE, Mr 297
fl 1777-1781
The 'Young Gentleman' who was announced as making his first appearance on the stage as Dorilas in *Merope* at Covent Garden Theatre on 17 January 1777 was later identified as a Mr Peile. He remained at Covent Garden for another four seasons, through 1780-81, playing mainly supporting roles but occasionally important parts like Hotspur in *I Henry IV*, the Duke in *The Chances*, Don Pedro in *Much ado About Nothing* and Banquo in *Macbeth* (the role in which Romney pictured him with Henderson, **297**). At the end of the 1780-81 season he left Covent Garden and seems to have dropped out of theatrical records. (*BDA*)

PENLEY, Sampson 355
d. 1838
Sampson Penley, who is pictured as Allworth in Clint's large canvas of a scene from *A New Way to Pay Old Debts*, was on the stage from a very young age and after spending time in the provinces appeared at Drury Lane on 28 February 1815 as Young Norval in *Douglas*. An anonymous engraving of him in that role was published. Penley also appears as Kenmure with H. E.. Johnston as Donald in an engraving by J. Findlay (after W. M. Craig) of a scene in *The*

Falls of Clyde (1820). In the *Harvard Theatre Collection Catalogue of Dramatic Portraits* (2: 313) Penley is called Perley. Oxberry wrote of him in *Dramatic Biography* (1825), 'He personates *fops* and *pert servants* with some ability, and can boast of a fine figure, and finer teeth, which are seen to great advantage from the Dress Boxes and second *Tier*.'

PHELPS, Samuel **665, 666, B171**
1804-1878
This British actor-manager was born on 13 February 1804 in St Aubyn Street, Plymouth Dock, in Devon, the seventh child of Robert M. Phelps and his wife Ann (née Turner). His younger brother Robert Phelps (1808-1890) was educated at Trinity College, Cambridge, and became master of Sidney Sussex College. Samuel worked several years as a journalist in Plymouth and London and engaged in amateur theatricals before he turned professional on the York circuit. After touring in Ireland and Scotland and to Exeter and Plymouth, he appeared at the Haymarket Theatre under Webster for a short summer season, making his debut on 28 August 1837 as Shylock. That summer he also acted Hamlet, Othello and Richard III. That autumn Phelps began an engagement with Macready at Covent Garden, appearing on 27 October 1837 as Jaffeir in *Venice Preserv'd*; he next played Othello to Macready's Iago. Over the next eight years Phelps was seen in a number of leading roles. He was an estimable and powerful actor, but his major contribution to the English stage was to be made in managing and producing.

Phelps's took over the lease of Sadler's Wells Theatre in 1844, opening his management on 27 May with *Macbeth*; he acted the leading role and Mrs Warner played Lady Macbeth. Until 1861 Phelps acted in and directed almost the entire Shakespeare canon, including the first production of *Antony and Cleopatra* since Garrick's production in the middle of the eighteenth century and the first production of *Pericles* since the Restoration. He did away with the singing witches in *Macbeth* and abandoned Cibber's text of *Richard III* for the Bard's.

His productions were admired for their imagination, integrity and scenic beauty. With these productions Phelps raised the Wells to a position of importance. He played leading roles in many of them. Among his best parts was Bottom, which he first played in October 1853. He also appeared in a number of non-Shakespearean roles, including Lord Ogleby in *The Clandestine Marriage*, Penruddock in *The Wheel of Fortune* and John Thornberry in *John Bull*.

Phelps's distinguished tenure at Sadler's Wells came to an end in 1862, a year after his indispensable business manager, Thomas Greenwood, retired. He then played on for another 15 years, under various managements; his last performance was as Cardinal Wolsey in *Henry VIII* at the Imperial Theatre in 1878.

Phelps had long resided in his house at No 420, Camden Road. He died on 6 November 1878 at Anson's Farm, Coopersdale, near Epping; he was buried in Highgate Cemetery. Phelps became a member of the Garrick Club in 1874. The portrait by Forbes-Robertson of him as Cardinal Wolsey (**665**) is one of the best of him. Biographies include Shirley S. Allen, *Samuel Phelps and Sadler's Wells Theater* (1971) and W. M. Phelps and John Forbes-Robertson, *The Life and Life-Work of Samuel Phelps* (1886). *See* also Dennis Arundell, *The Story of Sadler's Wells 1863-1977* (1978). (*DNB, EB, OCT*)

PHILIPPS. Thomas **667**
1774-1841
The singing actor and composer Thomas Philipps was born in London in 1774. He made his first appearance as an actor at Covent Garden on 10 May 1796 as Philippo in *The Castle of Andalusia*. He was engaged at the Crow Street Theatre, Dublin, in 1801, and returned to London in 1809, when on 26 June at the English Opera House he played Hartwell in *Up All Night* (**667**). After two more years in London, Philipps reportedly earned some £7000 from a tour of America. He retired from the stage early to become a teacher of singing and a composer of ballads. In 1828 he was a member of the Catch Club. Philipps died on 27 October 1841, having been injured in a railway accident. Though his stage career seems to have been a modest one, he was called by the singer Michael Kelly in 1826 'the best acting singer on the English stage.' His publications include *Elementary*

Principles and Practice of Singing (1826), a *Collection of Moral Ballads* and many songs and ballads. (*DNB*)

PHILLIP, John RA 668

1817-1867

The painter John Phillip was born in Aberdeen on 19 April 1817 and early on exhibited a talent for art. But he was first an errand-boy to a tinsmith in Aberdeen and then at 15 was apprenticed to a painter and glazier in Wallace Nook. He then studied under James Forbes, a local portrait painter, and in 1835 he produced a genre picture, ' The Pedlar or Newsvendor,' which was purchased by Lord Panmure, who later gave it with several other subjects by Phillip to the Mechanics' Institution in Brechin. Phillip also painted scenery for the theatre in Aberdeen.

In 1836 Phillip went to London under the patronage of Lord Panmure, where he studied under Thomas Mugrave Joy, and in 1837 he was admitted to the Schools of the Royal Academy. Next year he began to contribute portraits and historical subjects to the RA shows, and continued until 1850, among his exhibits being 'Presbyterian Catechising', 'The Spae-wife' and 'A Scottish Washing.'

His delicate health forced him in the winter of 1851-52 to Seville, where, influenced by the works of Velasquez, he changed his style to the potent colouring and chromatic splendour which characterized his best paintings. In subsequent years he returned to Spain several times; during the six months he spent there in 1860 he produced a prodigious number of canvases, watercolours, and pencil sketches. He became an associate member of the RA in 1857 and a full member in 1859.

Phillip died, apparently from a stroke, in Campden Hill, Kensington, on 27 February 1867. In 1873 over 200 of his works were shown in the London international exhibition, the catalogue for which was compiled by his longtime friend T. Oldham Barlow, who had engraved many of the pictures. Phillip also painted a number of portraits of distinguished persons, including Sir J. E. Millais, Richard Ansell and Princess Beatrice. He made several self-portraits, but the best likeness of him is the one in the Garrick Club by C. E. Cundell (**668**) in 1867. (*DNB*)

PHILLIPS, Anna Maria

See Anna Maria CROUCH

PINERO, Sir Arthur Wing 669-671, S27

1855-1934

One of the leading playwrights of the last quarter of the nineteenth century, Arthur Pinero was born in Islington, London, on 24 May 1855, and was descended from Portuguese Jews. He was the son of the solicitor John Daniel Pinero and his wife Lucy (née Daines). He abandoned his study of law at the age of 19 to become an actor, making his first appearances at the Theatre Royal, Edinburgh, in June 1874. Though he acted for some ten years, his main direction was for playwriting. His first play, *Two Hundred a Year*, was produced at the Globe in London on 6 October 1877. After several minor pieces, he achieved popularity with *The Magistrate*, a farce that was performed at the Court Theatre in 1885. Other farces, *The Schoolmistress* (1886) and *Dandy Dick*, were also written for the Court Theatre. With *The Profligate* in 1889 Pinero turned more serious and fused sentimentality with serious social ideas. Then with *The Second Mrs Tanquery* at the St James in 1893, with Mrs Patrick Campbell in the title role, he established himself as a playwright of importance, writing the first of several plays that depicted women in battle with society. He wrote numerous other plays, including *The Notorious Mrs Ebbsmith* (1895), *Trelawny of the Wells* (1898), *Iris* (1901) and *Mid-Channel* (1909). In 1909, at the height of his career, Pinero was knighted. His subsequent dramatic efforts were less successful. In thought Pinero was in the school of Ibsen and in structure in that of Scribe and Sardou. His plays did stir public controversy, and he was a very good storyteller. His social dramas drew fashionable audiences, but it is his farces – 'literate, superbly constructed, with a precise, clockwork inevitability of plot and brilliant use of coincidence' (*EB*) – that have stood the test of time. Pinero became a member of the Garrick Club in 1884. He was also a member of the Athenaeum and the

Dramatists. He died in London on 23 November 1934. (*OCT*)

PITT, Ann 297, 672
1720?-1799
Ann Pitt's parentage is unknown, but her brother Cecil Pitt was a wealthy dry goods merchant in London. She was acting on the London stage by 12 January 1745, when she played Angelica in *The Anatomist* at Drury Lane. Except for some appearances in the provinces and at the Haymarket in summers, Ann Pitt spent some 47 years engaged at Drury Lane, playing a line of serving maids, nurses, old women and eccentrics. Among her regular roles were Lappet in *The Miser*, the Nurse in *Romeo and Juliet* and Lady Bountiful in *The Beaux' Stratagem*. The last role she seems to have played on any stage was the Spanish Lady in *Barataria* in June 1792, and that appearance was at Covent Garden, not Drury Lane. She died in London on 18 December 1799 and was buried in the family plot of Charles Dibdin the Younger in the cemetery at St James's Chapel, Pentonville. Ann Pitt's daughter Harriett Pitt (1748?-1814) had been the mistress of the actor-manager Charles Dibdin (1745-1814) and the mother of Charles Isaac Mungo Dibdin (1768-1833). Our subject Ann Pitt's other child, Mary Ann Richards, was sired by the scene painter John Inigo Richards (d. 1810). In addition to the portrait now in the Garrick Club (**672**), Ann Pitt is shown as Lady Wishfort in *The Way of the World* in an engraving by Walker, after Dodd, 1776. She also is seen as one of the Witches in the painting by Romney (?) of a scene in *Macbeth*, in the Garrick Club, **297** (*BDA*)

PLANCHÉ, James Robinson 673
1796-1880
The antiquary, costume designer, and dramatist James Robinson Planché was born in Old Burlington Street, Piccadilly, on 27 February 1796, the son of Jacques Planché, a watchmaker. After some early education in geometry and perspective he was articled to a bookseller. He soon developed his interest in the stage, acting as an amateur in private theatres in Berwick Street, St Pancras, Catherine Street and Wilton Street. His burlesque *Amoroso, King of Little Britain*, was produced at Drury Lane on 21 April 1818. He wrote some ten pieces for the Adelphi Theatre in 1820-21, but it was his historical costume designs for Charles Kemble's revival of *King John* at Drury Lane in 1823 that firmly established his reputation and led to his becoming one of the most prominent theatrical practitioners in London. The production was among the first historical dramas to be brought out with authentic dress of the period. His designs appeared in *Costumes of Shakespeare's King John*, by J. K. Meadows and G. Sharp, 1823-1825.

After viewing the coronation of Charles X at Paris, Planché made drawings of the costumes and spectacle for a production at Covent Garden Theatre on 10 July 1825. On 12 April 1826 he provided the libretto for Carl Maria von Weber's last composition, *Oberon, or the Elf King's Oath*, especially prepared for Covent Garden. Planché was manager of the music at Vauxhall Gardens in 1826-27 and in 1830 took over the management of the Adelphi Theatre. In 1831 he joined Mme Vestris at the Olympic Theatre, writing with Charles Dance the burlesque *Olympic Revels*, for her opening night on 3 January 1831. In 1839, when Mme Vestris went over to Covent Garden Theatre, Planché followed as director of costume, supervisor of the paint room and reader of plays submitted for production. He later worked for the Haymarket and Lyceum theatres. His last dramatic piece was *King Christmas*, a one-act masque at the Gallery of Illustrations on 26 December 1872.

Planché also developed a reputation as an antiquarian scholar, and became a member of the Society of Antiquaries on 24 December 1849. Later he helped form the British Archaeological Association in December 1848. He became Somerset Herald on 1 June 1866 and reported on and re-arranged the armoury at the Tower of London. In 1834 he published his *History of British Costumes*. Among his numerous other writings were *Regal Records, or a Chronicle of the Queens Regnant of England* (1838), *The Conqueror and his Companions* (1874) and *Suggestions for Establishing an English Art Theatre* (1879). He wrote some 72 pieces for the stage, many of them Christmas and Easter tales. His wife Elizabeth St George (1796-1846), whom he married on 26 April 1821, wrote some dramas and farces. Planché was one of the original members of the Garrick Club in 1831; he resigned in 1853, rejoined in 1865 and resigned again in 1869. He died at No. 10, St Leonard's Terrace, Chelsea, on 30 May 1880.

PLATT, Bartholomew 'Batt' **674**
d. 1758
'Batt' Platt was singing speciality songs at various London venues as early as 1715. His name appears over the years in advertisements for taverns and the Southwark and Bartholomew fairs. He seems to have been a regular attraction at Sadler's Wells. He also sang at Goodman's Fields Theatre, 1731-32. He was described as 'a favourite singer with the vulgar.' Platt dressed and sang in the character of a madman when he sang 'Mad Tom.' Platt died at Winslow, Buckinghamshire, on 24 July 1758. (*BDA*)

POOLE, Elizabeth **675, 676**
1820-1906
Elizabeth Poole appeared on the London stage for first time at the age of seven and was seen for several years in children's roles. In the 1830s she made appearances at the English Opera House, playing the Heir of Ormond in *The Feudal Lady* and the title role in *Tom Thumb*. The catalogue of portraits in the Harvard Theatre Collection lists 15 portraits of her, but we know little more about her career. She married a Dr Bacon. She died on 15 January 1906.

POOLE, Martha
See Mrs Peter DICKONS

POPE, Alexander **677-682**
1762-1835
Born on 24 March 1762, according to 'The Manager's Notebook,' Alexander Pope was probably from Cork and was certainly the son of Thomas Pope, a miniaturist. Trained as an artist, Alexander was also attracted to the stage and made his first professional appearance as Oroonoko on 10 October 1781 in Cork. There he also acted Charles Surface in *The School for Scandal* and continued his two careers in the years immediately following. On 8 January 1785 Pope made his London debut, again as Oroonoko, at Covent Garden. The *European Magazine* branded his type of acting as 'the art of recital,' and critics during the ensuing years found Pope at fault in almost every category of the player's art. He had an expressionless, mawkish countenance, said the German visitor Brandes in 1785; his face was 'as hard, as immovable, and as void of meaning as an oak wainscoat,' wrote Leigh Hunt in *Dramatic Essays*; he had an awkward strut, stiff speech, and was seldom in character, claimed Henry James Leigh in 1786; he rants and writhes, declared John Williams in 1788; he has too much sameness, complained Waldron in 1795; 'Mr Pope has attained to that point, which he will never surpass – mediocrity,' carped Thomas Dutton in 1800 – and so on. Pope had some advocates, but few players of his day received such harsh criticism and still survived in the London theatre world.

He survived in the theatre chiefly by making himself useful, as so many secondary actors did, and settling for a modest salary (£12 weekly at Covent Garden in 1796-97, £14 by 1806-7), spending many of his summers labouring in provincial theatres, and marrying well or well enough, thrice. His first wife, almost twice his age, was Elizabeth Younge, who also had twice his acting talent and twice his salary; they married in 1785; she died in 1797. His second wife was Maria Ann Campion, an actress of promise, like Alexander; she brought him £200 annually when they married in 1798; she died in 1803. His third wife, Clara, whom he married in 1807, was an accomplished painter, who exhibited 41 paintings between 1808 and 1833; she outlived him. Pope, who had studied for a while with Hugh Douglas Hamilton in London, practiced miniature painting and exhibited 59 pictures at the Royal Academy between 1787 and 1821.

Despite the critics, Alexander's acting career encompassed dozens of important roles, such as Shore and Hastings in *Jane Shore*, Alexander the Great, Othello, Richard III, Romeo, Hotspur in *1 Henry IV*, King Lear, Hamlet (**677**), Cato, Aimwell in *The Beaux' Stratagem*, and Macbeth – but seldom was he distinguished. In 1820 at Drury Lane, according to Winston's *Drury Lane Journal*, Pope proudly told the audience he had acted for them for 35 years, 'never neglected his duty, could not retire the stage, and performed such parts as were allotted him …' The theatre had little use for Pope toward the end of his career; he became a pensioner of Covent Garden Theatre, where he had kept up his Fund payments for 44 years. Alexander Pope died at 73 on 12 March 1835. (*BDA*) [EAL]

POPE, Mrs Alexander the first, Elizabeth, née Younge **682, 683**
c. 1740-1797
Elizabeth Younge was born about 1740 in Southwark, and when near the age of 28 she came to the attention of David Garrick, who trained her in acting and brought her out as Imogen in *Cymbeline* at Drury Lane on 22 October 1768, advertised as 'A Young Gentlewoman' making her stage debut. The straightforward prompter William Hopkins took note of her: 'Mrs Younge – an elegant figure in both dresses, a very good voice, but wants management, – a great deal of acting about her, and would make a great figure if she had a better face. Upon the whole she played the part amazingly well, and had deserved applause.' Garrick liked her so much he raised her salary from £2 to £3 weekly on the basis of her first few appearances. Then she tried Jane Shore ('so, so – spoke much too low,' wrote Hopkins), Ovisa in *Zingis* ('played very bad, and much disliked') and, for her benefit, Perdita in *Florizel and Perdita* (no comment). Her career seemed, from these remarks, to be sinking, but she signed on at Richmond for the summer of 1769 and came back to the Garrick fold in 1769-70 to play such important roles as Juliet, Maria in *The London Merchant*, Lady Anne in *Richard III*, Angelica in *Love for Love* and Calista in *The Fair Penitent*. Garrick had high hopes for her but could come to no agreement on a contract, so Elizabeth spent the summer in Bristol and most of the 1770-71 season acting in Dublin.

On 26 September 1771 she returned to Drury Lane to play Imogen, followed by more leading chacacters, among them Fidelia in *The Plain Dealer*, Indiana in *The Concious Lovers*, Lady Brute in *The Provok'd Wife*, Viola in *Twelfth Night* and Monimia in *The Orphan*. Through 1778-79 she added such characters as Queen Elizabeth in *The Earl of Essex* (**683**), Zara in *The Mourning Bride*, Rosalind in *As You Like It*, Desdemona in *Othello*, Cordelia in *King Lear*, Lydia Languish in *The Rivals*, and Belvidera in *Venice Preserv'd* – a splendid line of heroines, often of the tender variety. Offstage she could be tough as nails negotiating with Garrick. By the late 1770s she was earning £12 weekly. When she left Drury Lane to act at Covent Garden in 1779-80 her departure was apparently because of money: she wanted £20 weekly plus a benefit free of house charges and an extra stipend for clothes, which Sheridan at Drury Lane would not give her. Meanwhile, during the summer months, she augmented her income by touring some country towns – Bristol, Edinburgh, Liverpool, Manchester and Cork.

Elizabeth Younge began her engagement at Covent Garden on 10 November 1779 as Marcelia in *The Duke of Milan* and then acted some of her old Drury Lane characters, as well as such important new roles as Estifania in *Rule a Wife and Have a Wife*, Statira in *Alexander the Great* and Andromache in *The Distrest Mother*, as well as youthful characters like Juliet that she was now too old to play credibly. In the summer of 1784 when she was acting in Ireland (at about 44) she also tried to recapture her youth by marrying the young artist-actor, Alexander Pope, then 24. She had a much more successful career than he; in 1786, for example, she was earning £20 per week and he £9. In the years that followed their careers were usually pursued together, but they seldom acted as a team. They evidently had a comfortable marriage, Alexander being content with a famous wife but one whose influence was helpful to him.

Elizabeth excelled in both comedy and tragedy, though she never matched Elizabeth Farren in the one or Sarah Siddons in the other. But for characters requiring softness she was first rate, and she had a remarkably wide range of characters she could play well, making her the kind of high level 'useful' player who was both reliable and invaluable. Mrs Pope acted at Covent Garden for the rest of her life, now playing more mature roles: ladies of fashion or title. But her health was poor in the mid-1790s, and she died on 15 March 1797. She had worked out an arrangement with Pope that allowed her to control her own property, but, strangely, Elizabeth died intestate, and her property, worth some £7000, passed to him. (*BDA*) [EAL]

POPE, Mrs Alexander the second, Maria Ann née Campion, stage name Mrs Spencer 686
1775-1803
Born in Waterford in 1775, Maria Ann Campion was the daughter of a merchant. She made her theatrical debut at the Crow Street playhouse in Dublin on 13 February 1790 as Monimia in *The Orphan*, but her effort was marred by an attack of stage fright. In March and April she was seen as Juliet (**686**), Rutland in *The Earl of Essex*, Desdemona in *Othello* and Cordelia in *King Lear*. Miss Campion (who, beginning in 1795 called herself Mrs Spencer, a stage name probably), spent the next five years gaining experience in Galway, Cork, Derry, Waterford and Belfast as well as Dublin; she also worked at York and Hull, with Tate Wilkinson's company. Finally, on 13 October 1797 she made her London debut at Covent Garden, playing Monimia with great success. The critics liked Mrs Spencer's 'unaffected simplicity' and 'artless innocence' and compared her favourably with Mrs Cibber. Maria Ann was an actress who appeared unconscious of her pretty face and elegant form. The *Monthly Mirror* thought her worth a long article that praised her judgment, attractiveness and taste but hoped she would develop a voice with more consistency and smoothness and bring her gestures under better control.

On 24 January 1798 she married the actor Alexander Pope, who had been widowed in March 1797. His own career as an actor was modest, but his first wife had been near the top of the acting profession; his new wife was closer to him in age and was, like him, still developing her career. The couple toured the provinces in the summers and acted at Covent Garden in the winters, she earning £8 weekly and he £12, though her roles were usually significant: Indiana in *The Conscious Lovers*, Lady Macbeth, Portia in *The Merchant of Venice*, Desdemona in *Othello*, Statira in *Alexander the Great* and the like, along with smaller parts. But at the turn of the century she was settling into attitudes and postures. Like her husband, Mrs Pope showed promise but never achieved stardom. She acted Desdemona on 10 June 1803 but became ill in the third act and could not finish her role. On the eighteenth she suffered a stroke and died. (*BDA*) [EAL]

POPE, Jane 684, 685
1744?-1818
The daughter of William Pope, peruke-maker and Drury Lane Theatre barber, Jane Pope was born about 1744. (The *BDA* contains a typographical error and shows her born about 1774.) Jane's first certain mention in the bills was on 3 December 1756, when she was Lalcon in a production of *Lilliput* at Drury Lane in which most of the roles were taken by children. Her adult debut was on 23 October 1759 as Corinna in *The Confederacy*. Also in that cast was Kitty Clive, the consummate comedienne, who advised young Jane and became a life-long friend. Jane followed Lalcon with Dolly Snip in *Harlequin's Invasion*, Biddy in *Miss in her Teens*, Prue in *Love for Love* and Miss Notable in *The Lady's Last Stake*. She was engaged at Drury Lane until 1808 and developed a fine repertoire of comic roles that included Cherry in *The Stratagem*, Beatrice in *Much Ado about Nothing*, Flora and Violante in *The Wonder*, Miss Sterling in the premiere of *The Clandestine Marriage*, Olivia in *The Plain Dealer*, Polly and Lucy in *The Beggar's Opera* (though critics said she was a dreadful singer), Lady Minikin in *Bon Ton*, Audrey in *As You Like It*, Letitia in *The Old Bachelor*, Mrs Malaprop in *The Rivals*, Mrs Page in *The Merry Wives of Windsor* (**685**), Mrs Candour in *The School for Scandal* and a host of other choice characters, many of them calling for the kind of pertness that was second nature to 'Popsie,' as she was called. Remarkably, in her maturity she specialized in maturity; Hazlitt said she was 'the very picture of a duenna, a maiden lady, or antiquated dowger.' She took some of Kitty Clive's old roles and made many of them her own; William Hawkins especially liked her Nell in *The Devil to Pay*, Beatrice in *Much Ado* and Phyllis in *The Conscious Lovers*, all of which he called matchless. By 1775

she was earning £8 weekly, a good salary for a specialist in low comedy, and she augmented that with engagements in Dublin and Liverpool during some summers, though she did not tour as much as many of her colleagues.

Jane Pope by 1807 was having trouble with her memory, so she sensibly announced her retirement, making her last appearance on 26 May 1808. At the end of the evening, in the character of Audrey in *As You Like It*, she bid her audience farewell. Jane died on 30 July 1818. (*BDA*) [EAL]

POQUELIN, Jean Baptiste
See MOLIÈRE

POTT, Emily G1025
d. 1781
Reynolds's model for his painting of Thais (**G1025**) was reputed to have been the notorious courtesan Emily Pott, also sometimes known as Emily Warren, Emily Bertie and Emily Coventry. Supposedly Reynolds had used her many times as a model. Reynolds seemed to have enjoyed the gossip and speculation surrounding his picture of Thais. Emily Warren had been a lover of the Hon Charles Greville, who may have commissioned the portrait and who bought it. In 1778 Emily left him for Robert Pott. Emily never saw the finished picture, which was exhibited at the RA in 1781. In the spring of that year she died at sea on her way to India. The Garrick Club picture is a copy by an unknown artist of the original Reynolds now at Waddesdon Manor.

POVEY, Mary Ann 687
1804-1861
Born in Birmingham in 1804, she became a member of the Oratorio Choral Fund Society when seven. In the rare instance of a new performer appearing on another actor's benefit night, Miss Povey was introduced to Drury Lane audiences on 3 June 1817, for the benefit of the singer Thomas Cooke, her mentor. Subsequently she was seen at that theatre, at the English Opera and in the summer seasons at the Lyceum. Among her best roles were Polly Peachum in *The Beggar's Opera*, Jessica in *The Merchant of Venice* and Julia Mannering in *Guy Mannering* – all roles in which she was pictured in engravings. She married Edward Knight, son of the Drury Lane actor of that name.

POWELL, Ann later Mrs Thomas Warren and then Mrs John Martindale 695
c. 1761-1821
Ann Powell, who is shown standing next to her mother in Mortimer's picture of her family (**695**), was born in late 1760 or early 1761, probably in London. She was the elder daughter of the estimable William Powell (*q.v.*) and his wife Elizabeth (née Branson, later Mrs John Abraham Fisher (*q.v.*). She was probably the Miss Powell who acted at China Hall, Rotherhithe, in the summers of 1777 and 1778, when her roles included Desdemona in *Othello* and Miss Neville in *She Stoops to Conquer*. She was still a minor when she married Thomas Warren of the Inner Temple in October 1780. She re-appeared on the London stage, at Covent Garden, on 10 December 1788 as Elvira in *Percy*. During the remainder of that season there, now called Mrs Warren, she acted a number of leading roles, including Mrs Sullen in *The Stratagem*, Indiana in *The Conscious Lovers* and Olivia in *A Bold Stroke for a Husband*. But she never again acted in London. Warren having died, she married John Martindale on 8 August 1795. Martindale became a proprietor of Covent Garden Theatre through the one-eighth share Ann had inherited from her father William Powell. Ann Martindale died at her house in King Street, London, in September 1821.

She was also pictured in a portrait by George Romney, which was engraved by Hodges; as Rosetta in *The Foundling*, engraved by Scott, after Stothard; and by M. Brown as Helena in *All's Well that Ends Well*. The Brown drawing was sold at Christie's in 1793 and was engraved by Thornthwaite for *Bell's Shakespeare*, 1786. Ann seems not to have acted either Helena or Rosetta in London. The portrait by Romney was with Agnew's in 1969. (*BDA*)

POWELL, Elizabeth, Mrs William Powell née Branson, later Mrs John Abraham Fisher 695
d. 1780
Elizabeth Branson was the daughter of Covent Garden house servants, a Mr and Mrs Branson.

She seems not to have tried the stage until after she married the actor William Powell (*q.v.*). While Powell was co-managing the new Theatre Royal in Bristol, in 1766, she appeared there as Ophelia, Cordelia and Beatrice. When he acted and managed at Covent Garden from 1767 to 1769, she served in that theatre's wardrobe, her acting talents evidently insufficient to warrant her a position on the stage. After Powell's premature death in 1769, she inherited his share in Covent Garden and Bristol. On 27 February 1772 at St Paul, Covent Garden, she married the composer, musician and philanderer John Abraham Fisher. She also proved unfaithful and had an affair with the actor George Maddocks. As Mrs Fisher, she died at Brompton on 7 May 1780. Her two daughters, Elizabeth Mary and Ann Powell, also shown in **695**, are noticed on these pages. (*BDA*)

POWELL, Elizabeth Mary later Mrs George White 695

fl. 1760s-1820s?

Elizabeth Mary Powell, who is standing on the table in Mortimer's picture of the Powell family (**695**), was the younger daughter of the actor William Powell and his wife Elizabeth Powell (née Branson, later Mrs John Abraham Fisher). Both parents are noticed on these pages. Though her sister Ann Powell (*q.v.*) acted for a few seasons in London, Elizabeth Mary seems not to have gone on the stage. She married George White, a clerk in the House of Commons. He became a one-eighth shareholder in Covent Garden Theatre through his wife's inheritance from her father William Powell. (*BDA*)

POWELL, Jane Mrs William née Palmer?, earlier Mrs Farmer, later Mrs John James Renaud 688-692

c. 1761-1831

Jane Powell, whose maiden name may have been Palmer, was born in Cranbrook, Kent, about 1761. On 29 August 1787, advertised as a lady making her first stage appearance, she acted Alicia in *Jane Shore* at the Haymarket Theatre in London. One newspaper identified her as Miss Palmer, another as Mrs Farmer. She apparently had a good reception, but, whoever she really was, she did not appear again for a year: on 9 September 1788 she acted Alicia again, identified as Mrs Farmer. She was praised this time for her beauty but criticized for her awkwardness. John Philip Kemble must have found her promising, for he engaged her at Drury Lane for a 17 November 1788 debut as Juliet to his Romeo; Kemble noted on his playbill that she was a beautiful creature and, 'She will be a good actress.' So he gave her that season, among other characters, Anne Bullen in *Henry VIII*, Sigismunda in *Tancred and Sigismunda*, Virgilia in *Coriolanus* and Lady Grace in *The Provok'd Husband* and paid her £3 weekly.

In the summer of 1789 Mrs Farmer acted at Liverpool, met and conquered William Powell (not the promiment actor but the Drury Lane house servant and, later, prompter) and returned to Drury Lane in the autumn as Mrs Powell, playing Lady Anne in *Richard III* on 12 September. She spent some summers acting in the provinces, but her winter home for most of her career was with the Drury Lane company, where she added to her repertoire such important roles as Desdemona, Olivia in *Twelfth Night*, Lady Percy in *1 Henry IV*, Lavinia in *The Fair Penitent*, Mrs Sullen in *The Beaux' Stratagem*, Sylvia in *The Recruiting Officer*, Statira in *Alexander the Great*, Hamlet, and Portia in *The Merchant of Venice*. She reached a salary of £15 weekly in 1808-9. With the Kemble clan Jane performed at Covent Garden in 1811 and within a few years she was spending more and more time at such secondary venues as the Surrey Theatre and with Mrs Butler's troupe in Edinburgh (for 11 years). She had left Powell before 1808, married John James Renaud in 1813, and made her last stage appearance on 30 September 1829, playing one of her best roles, Gertrude in *Hamlet* with Edmund Kean in the title role. Mrs Renaud died in London on 31 December 1831.

Jane Powell at her peak was much praised for her acting, being favourably compared by some to Sarah Siddons, with whom she often performed. Her Hamlet was not just a stunt; Thomas Gilliland in 1804 had high praise for her 'uncommon powers' as the Danish prince. (*BDA*) [EAL]

POWELL, Sidney 956
fl. 1956
Although the figures in Julian Barrow's painting of 'Members in the Coffee Room' are said to be fictitious, the wine waiter in the white coat has been identified as Sidney Powell, who began working at the Garrick Club in 1956 and is now retired. Hough in the *Ace of Clubs*, calls him 'a glorious institution.'

POWELL, Thomas Harcourt 793
d. 1892
When Thomas Powell, who is shown as No. 11 in O'Neil's scene of members in the Billiards Room, was elected to the Garrick Club in March 1862 he was described as of the 'Guards' and living at Bury St Edmunds. He died on 2 September 1892.

POWELL, William 59, 693-695
c. 1735-1769
William Powell – the actor and manager, not the Drury Lane house servant and prompter – was born at Hereford in 1735 or 1736. He seemed headed for a business career, spent some ten years in a City countinghouse, and married Elizabeth Branson (or Branston) in 1759. She seems to have had relatives at Covent Garden Theatre, and William had, as friends, the actors Charles Holland and William Parsons. It was through Holland that Powell met David Garrick, who happened at the time (1763) to be casting about for someone to act some of his characters while he was touring the Continent. Powell was given a trial and some training by Garrick, and practically fell into a professional stage career at Drury Lane. On 8 October 1763 Powell appeared as Philaster in George Colman's alteration of Beaumont and Fletcher's play and created, after some initial faltering, a sensation. The prompter Hopkins noted Powell's great promise, and Horace Walpole said Powell had turned the heads of Londoners, including the King's. On 22 November Powell acted Jaffeir in *Venice Preserv'd* and then Lusignan in *Zara*, Lord Townly in *The Provok'd Husband*, Leon in *Rule a Wife and Have a Wife*, Oroonoko, the Ghost in *Hamlet*, Othello, and other characters – almost all to satisfaction. Powell's salary jumped from £3 to £8 weekly, Drury Lane made money, and everyone was happy.

But Garrick must have seen that all was not well with Powell. The manager's letters from the Continent were cautious: to his brother George he said Powell 'must have a Master to watch his English' and to Powell on 12 December 1764 he advised: 'Study hard, my friend, for Seven years & you may play the rest of your life ...' How many different meanings of 'play' Garrick intended cannot be known, but it was advice Powell should have heeded. Perhaps he thought he really was heeding it when he decided to gain experience in the provinces and in management. In the summer of 1764 he began an association with the Jacob's Wells Theatre in Bristol, acting King Lear for his debut. About 1766 he joined John Arthur and Matthew Clarke in the management of the new Bristol Theatre Royal, and in addition to encountering managerial problems and quarrelling with Arthur, Powell began to neglect his acting. The season of 1766-67 at Drury Lane was his last; Garrick felt betrayed, especially when Powell became involved in the Covent Garden patent, which the widow of John Rich made available for purchase. Powell became an assistant to Colman in the management and served the company as leading actor. But despite his years of business training Powell as a co-manager was frequently at odds with his cohorts, spent too much of his time womanizing and let his health deteriorate. His work at Covent Garden and in Bristol came to an end on 3 July 1769 in Bristol: he died of pneumonia brought on by foolishly stripping and lying in the damp grass after playing cricket. He was only about 33. Garrick wrote, 'poor Powell had some requisites of an Actor, but he was carele[ss], & gave to his pleasures ... the time he shd have Employ'd in Study – alas poor Stage!' (*BDA*) [EAL]

POWER, William Grattan Tyrone G1005
1797-1841
Tyrone Power was born on 2 November 1797 near Kilmacthomas, Waterford. His father was of a well-to-do Waterford family, and he died in America before Tyrone was a year old. Tyrone's mother Marie, daughter of a Colonel Maxwell

who was killed in the American Revolution, settled in Cardiff, where young Tyrone joined a troupe of strolling players at the age of 14. After touring in the provinces and in South Africa, Power was engaged at Covent Garden in 1826 and soon became well regarded as a delineator of Irish characters. Power made his last appearance in London on 1 August 1840 at the Haymarket Theatre, when he played Captain O'Cutter in *The Jealous Wife*. Brooke's watercolour portrait of him as Clement Cleveland in Thomas Dibdin's *The Pirate* (**G1005**) was anonymously engraved. (That melodrama was first performed at the Surrey Theatre on 7 January 1822, with Finn in the role of Clement Cleveland the Pirate.) There are 26 items listed for Tyrone Power in the Harvard Theatre Collection catalogue of engraved theatrical portraits.

Power made four visits to America, and during his return voyage from the last, which he made to look after property he had bought in Texas, he was lost with another 122 persons when, on 14 March 1841, the steamship 'President' out of New York bound for Liverpool went down. He left his widow (née Gilbert), whom he had married in 1817, and four sons. One son, Harold Power, became an acclaimed concert pianist and was the father of Tyrone Power (1869-1931), a matinee stage idol in America who appeared in D. W. Griffith's films in the 1920s. (That Tyrone Power was the father of the popular film star Tyrone Power Jr [1914-1958], who acted on the New York stage in the 1930s and appeared in numerous films.) Our subject's son Sir William Power was sometime agent-general for New Zealand and wrote various books on travel; another son, Maurice, became an actor but died suddenly in 1849.

In 1836 Tyrone Power published his two-volume *Impressions of America*. He also wrote some romances and several plays, including a comedy called *Married Lovers*, which he produced. He was an original member of the Garrick Club in 1831.

PRAED, Winthrop Mackworth **793**
d. 1890

The W. M. Praed identified as No. 30 in the key to O'Neil's painting of a game in the Garrick Club Billiards Room (**793**) was William Mackworth Praed, who at the time he became a member of the Club in May 1862 was a banker living at No 4, Bryanston Square. Probably he was the brother of Charles Tyringham Praed of the 25th Regiment, also living at No. 4, Bryanston Square, when he was elected to the Club in March 1864, having been proposed by W. M. Praed. They seem obviously related to the William Mackworth Praed (1802-1839), author, publisher and MP, who is noticed in the *DNB*. But his biography states that he had two daughters and makes no mention of any sons. Other persons with that surname, M. N. Praed Esq and Bulkeley C. Praed, were members of the Garrick Club at the end of the nineteenth century.

PRINSEP, Valentine Cameron
See Index of Artists

PRITCHARD, Mrs William, Hannah née Vaughan **253, 696, 697**
1709-1768

One of David Garrick's most talented leading ladies, Hannah Vaughan was born on 28 October 1709 in Angel Court, about two blocks from Drury Lane Theatre, and was christened, according to the registers of St Martin-in-the-Fields, on 15 November. Most of her relatives were connected in one way or another with the theatre: her father Edward Vaughan was a stay maker, a brother was a fan maker, two others were actors and are noticed in the *BDA*. Her husband (as of 1730) William Pritchard (1707-1763) was an actor and theatre treasurer (also noticed in the *BDA*), and two of their children married into the profession. Yet there is little information about Hannah's theatrical beginnings. Her first certain notice was at Drury Lane on 5 May 1733, when she may have acted the First Phillis in *The Livery Rake*. She then was Loveit in *A Cure for Covetousness* at Bartholomew Fair on 23 August, a part in which her singing drew attention. In September one R. S. (probably Richard Savage) in the *Gentleman's Magazine* found promise in her voice, diction, reason and sense, and he was right: beginning in the autumn of 1733 with Theophilus Cibber's renegade troupe at the Haymarket Theatre she appeared as Nell in *The Devil to Pay*, Ophelia in *Hamlet*, and Belina in

The Mother-in-Law, among other parts large and small. Thomas Davies said of her Belina that Mrs Pritchard had a 'genteel person, for she was then young and slender … [H]er expressive yet simple manner; her unembarassed deportment and proper action … charmed all the spectators …' He even compared her favourably with Anne Oldfield, the elegant leading lady who had recently died. Mrs Pritchard and the rest of Cibber's seceders returned to Drury Lane by mid-March 1734, and that house became her theatrical home base for many years. There and occasionally at the late summer fairs, Lincoln's Inn Fields, the Haymarket, Bristol and Richmond she acted such characters as Sylvia in *The Old Bachelor*, Lady Fidget in *The Country Wife*, Lady Wou'dbe in *Volpone*, Lady Townly in *The Provok'd Husband*, Dol Common in *The Alchemist*, Mrs Sullen in *The Beaux' Stratagem*, Lucy in *The Beggar's Opera*, Mrs Foresight in *Love for Love*, Lady Anne in *Richard III* and Lady Macduff in *Macbeth*. In addition, she played in pantomimes and developed her skills in all sorts of comic and tragic characters. At Drury Lane in 1740-41, a crucial season for her, she added some significant new roles: Desdemona in *Othello*, a much-acclaimed Rosalind in *As You Like It*, Viola in *Twelfth Night* and Nerissa in *The Merchant of Venice* (in the production in which Charles Macklin introduced his serious Shylock).

John Rich stole Hannah from Drury Lane to act at Covent Garden Theatre in 1741. There she came on in some important new roles, including Sylvia in *The Recruiting Officer*, Lady Brute in *The Provok'd Wife*, Margery in *The Country Wife* and Gertrude in *Hamlet* (in which she surpassed the celebrated Mary Porter). But Hannah had a falling out with Rich, broke her articles and returned to Drury Lane in September 1742. Joining that troupe at the same time was young David Garrick. Hannah first acted with him on 5 October 1742, playing Monimia to his Chamont in *The Orphan*. They then appeared as Jane Shore and Hastings in Rowe's tragedy and as Richard III and Queen Elizabeth. Their partnership, though sometimes disrupted by changes in companies and made volatile by artistic temperaments on both sides, continued, mostly at Drury Lane, until her retirement in 1768.

Hannah's career remained to the end a mixture of comic and tragic characters, among them Belvidera in *Venice Preserv'd*, Calista in *The Fair Penitent*, Beatrice in *Much Ado about Nothing*, Clarinda (to Garrick's Ranger) in *The Suspicious Husband*, Emilia in *Othello*, Lady Macbeth (**253**), Meropé in Hill's tragedy, Cleopatra in *All for Love* and Millamant in *The Way of the World*. She was a talented actress in whom the critics rarely found a fault. John Hill in *The Actor* (1755) said that on stage Mrs Cibber was Mrs Cibber, but 'when Mrs Pritchard plays Merope, she is Merope; when she represents the wife of Theseus, she *is* the wife of Theseus; and nothing of herself appears, but all the character.' She was superb as Gertrude in Hamlet, and her portrayal of Lady Macbeth was a masterpiece, judged by Mrs Thrale to be superior to that of Mrs Siddons. Samuel Foote, who could when he wished skewer any notable person with his wit and venom, was so taken with Hannah's 'unblameable Conduct in private Life,' 'her Easiness of Disposition,' her 'good Voice … pleasing Figure, and a correct Judgment' that 'I would, were I a Patentee, rather have her in my service, than any Woman in England.'

But nature was against her. She began to put on weight. In 1750, when Mrs Pritchard was in her prime, Hill, who so lavishly praised her talent, had to note that her starving Jane Shore was simply too 'plump and rosy.' Garrick, in a cranky letter to his brother George in 1767 complaining about having to work up Oakly (to Hannah's Mrs Oakly in *The Jealous Wife*) said, 'I have not play'd Oakly these three Years – Sick – Sick – Sick – & Mrs Pd will Make me Sicker – great Bubbies, Noddling head, and no teeth – O Sick – Sick – Spew – .' Perhaps she could not face retirement or had not saved enough for her old age. Now a widow, she subscribed to the Drury Lane Theatrical Fund (a retirement plan) but not until 1766, and an anticipated share in an inheritance that year did not materialize. She acted a reduced schedule in the mid-1760s, but she performed as long as she could. Lady Macbeth (with Garrick) was her last character, on 25 April 1768. After that, in deference to her, Garrick did not play Macbeth again. Mrs Pritchard died on 20 August, too soon to appreciate Garrick's compliment. She was buried in the churchyard of St Mary, Twickenham, and a memorial tablet was placed in Poet's Corner, Westminster Abbey; later it was removed to the Triforium. (*BDA*, and Anthony Vaughan, *Born to Please: Hannah Pritchard, Actress*, 1971)[EAL]

PURSER, John **41, 698**
1776-1808
The actor John Purser, who was born in 1776 in the vicinity of Covent Garden, the area in which most of his adult life was spent, was probably related to the house servants named Purser at Drury Lane. He appeared on that stage as a child in a *Pasticcio* in May 1784 and then did a long stint in the provinces. Some 16 years later, announced as from Margate, he returned to Drury Lane on 30 October 1800 as Old Philpot in *The Citizen*. Purser remained engaged as an actor and singer at Drury Lane through the season 1807-8. He died on 15 June 1808 at the age of 32, and his ashes were placed in the grounds of St Paul, Covent Garden. In addition to the De Wilde portraits of him in the Garrick Club as Sneer (**41, 698**), Purser probably is depicted as one of the figures in that artist's scene from *All the World's a Stage*. That painting, formerly at the National Theatre and now at the Theatre Museum, is reproduced in the *BDA* 5: 284.

PYE, Harriet
See Mrs James ESTEN

Q

QUARTERMAINE, Leon **G0993**
1876-1967
Leon Quartermaine was born at Richmond, Surrey, on 24 September 1876, the son of Fred Quartermaine and his wife Alice Ann (née Egg). He made his stage debut at the Alexandra Theatre in Sheffield on 19 February 1894 as Fred Ingleford in *£1000 Reward* and was subsequently seen in numerous plays and films for many years. Among his film roles were Jaques in *As You Like It* (1936), Stephen in *The Dark World* (1935) and the Russian in *Settled Out of Court* (1925). Among his stage roles were James Vickery (**G0993**) in Forbes-Robertson's production of *The Light that Failed* that opened at the Lyric on 7 February 1903. Late in his career of over 50 years, in 1944-45 with the Gielgud Repertory Company, he acted Scandal in *Love for Love*, the Ghost in *Hamlet*, Theseus in *A Midsummer Night's Dream* and the Cardinal in *The Duchess of Malfi*.

Quartermaine died on 25 June 1967 at the age of 90. His second wife was the actress Fay Compton (1894-1978), from whom he was divorced, and he was the brother of the actor Charles Quartermaine (1877-1958). Leon was elected to the Garrick Club in February 1915 and resigned in 1940. (*WWWT*)

QUICK, John **429, 699-703**
1748-1831
George III's favourite actor, John Quick, was born in Whitechapel, London, in 1748, the son of a brewer. He began his stage apprenticeship in Kent and Surrey by the age of 12 and played, according to early memoirs, Altamont in *The Fair Penitent* at Croydon when he was 14. In the summer of 1766 Samuel Foote hired Quick for the Haymarket, where he appeared first on 18 June as Folly in *The Minor* and Jasper in *Miss in Her Teens*. There and at the King's Theatre that summer he took such roles as Trippet in *The Lying Valet*, Sir Charles in *The Beaux' Stratagem*, Burgundy in *King Lear* and Silvius in *As You Like It*. Quick was probably in the provinces in 1766-67 and then at the

Haymarket in the summer of 1767; on 14 September 1767 he made his Covent Garden debut as James in *The Mock Doctor*. He acted there during the winter seasons for more than three decades, building a huge repertoire of chiefly comic roles suitable for the 'little fellow' image nature gave him. Among his characters were Peter in *Romeo and Juliet*, Dr Caius and Slender in *The Merry Wives of Windsor*, Mungo in *The Padlock*, Tony Lumpkin – an excellent part for his whimsy and vitality – in the premiere of *She Stoops to Conquer*, Isaac Mendoza in *The Duenna* (**700**, **702**, **703**) Foresight in *Love for Love* and Touchstone in *As You Like It*. Remarkably, he tried Richard III and, said the *Public Advertiser* on 8 April 1790, 'he was *earnest* in the attempt, and succeeded tolerably,' but the audience, expecting buffoonery, were not satisfied. They wanted their amiable Quick.

For they loved him, especially in older characters, and he was popular for years, onstage and off, in London and provincial towns. Seldom was he criticized for overdoing facial expressions, though like almost all low comedians his grimaces were part of his stock in trade, and caricaturists delighted in making his Richard III look ridiculous. But an indication of his standing at Covent Garden was his salary: £14 weekly by 1793-94, the second highest in the troupe. Since he spent most of life being well-behaved – a churchgoer, healthy, not a heavy drinker, comfortably married with a family, pleasing almost everybody from the King on down – he received relatively little bad publicity. *The Children of Thespis* (1792) called him 'smart tiny QUICK, giving grace to a joke.' He reduced his workload around the turn of the century, cutting back on his touring to the provinces and ending his full-time engagement at Covent Garden. On 24 May 1813 he came out of retirement to make what may have been his last appearance: Don Felix in *The Wonder* at the Haymarket, for the benefit of Mrs Mattocks. The 'prince of low comedians,' as Thomas Bellamy called John Quick, died at Islington on 4 April 1831 at 84. (*BDA*) [EAL]

QUIN, James 704-706, B76-78, B179
1693-1766
Of Irish extraction, James Quin was born in King Street, Covent Garden, on 24 February 1693, virtually next door to London's two major theatres, where he spent so much of his career. He was the son of James and Elizabeth Grindzell Quin; the elder Quin had studied at Trinity College, Dublin, and Lincoln's Inn, London, and had pretensions to poetry. Young James was taken by his parents to Dublin in 1700 or 1701 and may also have been a student at Trinity College. He sought employment in the theatre and his first appearance may have been at Smock Alley as Abel in *The Committee* in 1714. By February 1715 he was in London acting, at Drury Lane, Vulture in *The Country Lasses*. He continued playing such small parts as Guildenstern in *Hamlet*, Gloucester in *King Lear*, Voltore in *Volpone* and Aaron in *Titus Andronicus*. In September 1717 he turned up at Southwark Fair acting Vincent in *Twice Married*, and in the middle of the 1717-18 season he joined John Rich's troupe at Lincoln's Inn Fields, where he was seen in more important parts: Hotspur in *1 Henry IV*, Horatio in *The Fair Penitent* and Antony in *Julius Caesar*. From that point on he seems to have gravitated toward heavy parts in both comedy (Sir John Brute in *The Provok'd Wife*) and tragedy (Claudius in *Hamlet*). Over the years he played many important roles under John Rich, among them Pinchwife in *The Country Wife*, Falstaff (his best character) in *The Merry Wives of Windsor* and *1 Henry IV*, King Lear and the Ghost in *Hamlet*. At Drury Lane again (from September 1734) he was seen in many of his standard characters and also Othello, Richard III, Brutus in *Julius Caesar*, Sullen in *The Stratagem* and the title role in *Volpone*. His majestic manner and declamatory style he must have learned from Barton Booth, who had learned it from the best Restoration actor, Thomas Betterton. And that style served him well and gained him fame until the arrival on the theatrical scene of Charles Macklin and David Garrick in 1741.

The playwright Richard Cumberland left us in his *Memoirs* the most vivid description of Quin and Garrick onstage together, playing Horatio and Lothario respectively in *The Fair Penitent*: Quin, 'with very little variation of cadence, and in a deep full tone, accompanied by a sawing kind of action, which had more of the senate than of the stage in it … rolled out his heroics with an air of dignified indifference, that seemed to disdain the plaudits, that were bestowed upon him.' Then, 'when after long and eager expectation I first beheld little Garrick, then young and light and alive in every muscle and in every feature, come bounding on the stage … heavens, what a transition! – it seemed as if a whole century had been swept over in … a single scene.' Cumberland, like many of the discerning playgoers, accepted Garrick's new style almost at once, but many playgoers found Quin perfectly satisfactory, because he was what they were used to, and his style seemed appropriate for the kinds of characters he usually played. One might have expected Quin to either change with the times or retire and give the stage to the new generation. But, as some critics noted, Quin by the 1740s was too set in his ways. And there were many, including Garrick, who appreciated Quin's style and respected his talent. Indeed, Quin and Garrick became good friends.

It is significant, however, that from 1741, Quin began changing the even tenor of his ways. He gave up his engagement at Drury Lane after the 1740-41 season, appeared at Smock Alley in the summer of 1741 and signed on again at Covent Garden for the 1740s. He began spending more time relaxing and indulging himself at Bath and less time treading the boards. His last appearance was on 15 May 1751 at Covent Garden as Horatio in *The Fair Penitent*, after which he undertook only benefits for friends. He lived out a life of pleasure at Bath, dying there on 23 January 1766, not long after a visit with the Garricks at Hampton. (*BDA*) [EAL]

R

RAE, Alexander **707-710**

1782-1820

Alexander Rae was born in London in May 1782. When a young man, he worked for an East India agent, but he declined an offer of employment in India and embarked on a theatrical career. He appeared as Hamlet at Bath on 28 January 1806. That role became one of his favourites (**708**). After gaining more experience at Bath and Bristol, he was engaged at the Haymarket in London, where he made his debut as Octavian in *The Mountaineers* on 9 June 1806. That summer he also acted, among other roles, Hamlet, Sir Edward Mortimer in *The Iron Chest* and Lovewell in *The Clandestine Marriage*. At the end of the summer season at the Haymarket, Rae went to Liverpool, where he played four seasons. Back in London he made his debut at Drury Lane on 14 November 1812, as Hamlet, followed by Norval in *Douglas*, Hastings in *Jane Shore*, Romeo and George Barnwell. He acted Bassanio to Kean's Shylock, Richmond to his Richard III, Othello to his Iago and Macduff to his Macbeth. Rae continued at Drury Lane to 1820, offering a number of important leading and secondary roles, such as Edgar in *King Lear*, Aboan in *Oroonoko*, Plume in *The Recruiting Officer* and Horatio in *The Fair Penitent*. He also served as stage-manager at Drury Lane, a position which, it is said, led him into a life of dissipation. He abandoned his home and family to take up with an actress. Rae left Drury Lane in 1820 for an ill-fated venture into management at the Royalty Theatre. Though he had gathered good actors, Rae found he could not pay salaries, and he fell into ruin. After an operation for gallstones from which he never recovered, he died on 8 September 1820. Rae was reported to have been an actor with judgment and elegance. Hamlet remained his finest portrayal and came second only to that of Kemble in his day. (*BDA*)

RAFTOR, Catherine

See Mrs George CLIVE

RANSOME, Arthur Michell CBE 711

1884-1967

The writer Arthur Ransome was born on 18 January 1884 in Leeds, Yorkshire, the son of Professor Cyril Ransome (d. 1897). After being educated at Rugby he went to work for a publisher and then became a war correspondent in the First World War. He made several trips to Russia before and after the revolution, and as a result he wrote *Old Peter's Russian Tales* (1916), *Six Weeks in Russia* (1919) and *Racundra's First Cruise* (1923), among other books. His earliest work was a *History of Storytelling* (1906), and he later wrote biographies of Edgar Allen Poe (1910) and Oscar Wilde (1912). Ransome was best known for his colourful adventure novels for children, among the most popular of which is the *Swallows and Amazons* series (1931). He was an avid fisherman, as Gilroy depicts him (**711**), and wrote *Rod and Line* (1922) and *Mainly About Fishing* (1959). The *Autobiography of Arthur Ransome* was published in 1976. He was elected to the Garrick Club in 1943 and was made CBE in 1953. Ransome died on 3 June 1967.

RATTO, Frank Louis MC 712

d. 1974

Frank Ratto was a barrister and the President of the Pensions Appeals Tribunal. He was elected to the Garrick Club in February 1929, became a life member, and was a keen card player there until his death on 24 May 1974.

RAYMOND, James Grant 713

1768-1817

Born James Grant, the son of an Army officer who lost his life in South Carolina in the American Revolutionary War, he studied for the Scottish Episcopal Church, but became a midshipman and then an actor. He was at the Crow Street Theatre in Dublin in early 1792, acting major roles like Oroonoko, Jaffeir in *Venice Preserv'd* and Castalio in *The Orphan*. He made his debut in London at Drury Lane Theatre as Osmond in *The Castle Spectre* on 26 September 1799, when he was received favourably. Raymond remained at that theatre the rest of his life, mainly in good supporting roles. In the 1811-12 season he began managing Drury Lane, but the heavy managerial responsibilities and the constant perilous financial circumstances of the theatre wore him down. He died on 24 October 1817 at his house, No 3, Chester Street, Grosvenor Place, and two days later was buried in the churchyard of St Paul, Covent Garden. Raymond had, according to an early memoir, 'assembled many pictures, chiefly dramatic, in which were preserved the best portraits and most highly-wrought scenes.' The disposition of that collection is unknown to us. Raymond acted Frederick in *The Stranger* – the role in which he is pictured by De Wilde (**713**) – at Bath on 22 October 1814. He had first played it at the Lyceum (with the Drury Lane company) on 4 August 1814. (*BDA*)

READE, Charles 793

1814-1884

The admirable storyteller Charles Reade was born near Ipsden, Oxfordshire, on 8 June 1814, the eleventh and final child of John Reade and his wife Anna Maria (née Scott-Waring). He was educated at Oxford, served as Dean of Arts at Magdalen College and became Vice-President of Magdalen, a position he treated as a sinecure. Reade spent most of his career writing 40 plays that were produced in London and 14 novels, many of which treat the social injustices of his time. His best work is said to have been *The Cloister and the Hearth* (1861), an historical romance about the father of Erasmus. He had a long relationship with the actress Laura Seymour, who became his housekeeper in 1856 and died in 1879. Reade died in London on 11 April 1884 and was buried in Willesden churchyard, beside the remains of Laura Seymour. Most of Reade's dramas suffer from an excess of theatrical effects. He became a member of the Garrick Club in 1839. (*DNB*).

REDDISH, Samuel 651

1735-1785

The son of a tradesman, Samuel Reddish was born in Frome, Sussex, in 1735 and at 15 was apprenticed to a surgeon. He gave that up and tried the stage, first in Norwich, then at Richmond, Surrey, and finally in London, where neither patent theatre showed an interest in him. But he was engaged by Henry Woodward for the

Crow Street Theatre in Dublin, where he made his debut as Lord Townly in *The Provok'd Husband* on 12 October 1759. After that he tried Edinburgh, Dublin again, Norwich again, Cork, Dublin again, and so on, attracting creditors wherever he went and fleeing them in the nick of time. By 1770 he was involved in company management at Bristol, and on 18 September 1767 he made his Drury Lane debut as Lord Townly; with him was his wife Polly (née Hart), who acted at Drury Lane for a few seasons until Samuel replaced her with Mary Anne Canning.

Reddish turned out to be a useful enough actor, playing such roles as Iago in *Othello*, Alexander in *The Rival Queens*, Romeo, Lothario in *The Fair Penitent*, Jaffeir in *Venice Preserv'd* and Faulkland in *The Rivals*. His salary at Drury Lane was £12 by 1777-78, and he was usually hard-working, good at prologues and epilogues, and a quick study, but many critics found him unsuitable for the characters he acted. In 1772 *The Theatres* said Reddish had no 'expression, dignity, or ease' and was limited by a weak voice, a lack of spirit, and no grace. By 1774 he was behaving erratically, occasionally not knowing what character he was to act, sometimes hissed off the stage, and often missing engagements. His Bristol connection dissolved, he gave up Drury Lane, tried Covent Garden briefly, returned to Edinburgh and Dublin. Reddish received aid from the Drury Lane Theatrical Fund, but there was little that could be done to save him; he died on 13 December 1785 at the Asylum for Lunatics at York. (*BDA*)[EAL]

REES-MOGG, Lord William, Baron of Hinton **1965**

b. 1928

The publisher and editor William Rees-Mogg was born on 14 July 1928, the son of Edmund Fletcher Rees-Mogg and his wife Beatrice (née Warren). He was educated at Charterhouse School and at Balliol College, Oxford, where he was President of the Oxford Union. He began his journalistic career with the *Financial Times* (1952-1956), where he advanced to Assistant Editor (1957-1960). With the *Sunday Times* he was City Editor (1960-1961), Political and Economic Editor (1961-1963) and Deputy Editor (1964-1967). He served as Editor of *The Times* from 1967 to 1981. Other important posts included Chairman of the Arts Council of Great Britain, 1982-1989, Vice-Chairman of the Board of Governors, BBC, 1981-1986, and Vice-Chairman of the Conservative Party's National Advisory Committee on Political Education, 1961-1963. He is also a director of several financial institutions and author of, among other books, *The Reigning Error: the Crisis of World Inflation* (1974), *Blood in the Streets* (1988), *The Great Reckoning* (1991) and *The Sovereign Individual* (1997).

Rees-Mogg was knighted in 1981 and was created a life peer, Baron of Hinton, in 1988. He has been a member of the Garrick Club since 1965.

REEVE, John **714**

1799-1838

This actor, the son of the hosier Thomas Reeve, was born at his father's shop on Ludgate Hill on 2 February 1799. He was the nephew of the musician and theatrical composer William Reeve (1757-1815), who is noticed in the *BDA*. At Winchmore Hill, near Enfield, he was a schoolmate of Frederick Yates (1795-1842), who became an actor and is noticed below. After working for his father, Reeve was placed with a hosier named Neville in Maiden Lane, and after three years he became a clerk at Gosling's Bank in Fleet Street. With other clerks at the bank he participated in theatricals at Pym's Theatre, Wilson Street, in Grey's Inn Road. On 8 June 1819 he acted Sylvester Daggerwood in *New Hay at the Old Market* at Drury Lane. He acted a few nights at the Haymarket Theatre and then began an engagement at the Lyceum in July 1819, where he specialized in imitations. Reeve's career developed slowly while he played at minor theatres in London and in Macready's company at Bath and Bristol. In 1823 he was back in London at the Adelphi, where he again succeeded as a mimic, and in April 1826 he began an engagement at the Haymarket that lasted until 1830 and during which he came into his own as a favourite comedian in many of Liston's old parts. After appearances at the Adelphi, Covent Garden and the Queen's Theatre, Reeve went to America, where he was not a success. He returned to England and to the

Adelphi Theatre, enjoyed some triumphs and ended his career at the Surrey in 1837 in a new drama called *The Wandering Tribe*, in which he was 'conspicuously imperfect.' Soon after, he died of a stroke at his house, No 46, Brompton Row, on 24 January 1838, at the age of 39, and was buried in Brompton churchyard.

Reeve was a good farceur and an effective droll, but his excessive drinking ruined his potential. He was often imperfect in his lines and sometimes went on without knowing any of the part. He relied on the indulgence of his audiences, and when he broke down in roles he had not even read he would wink at the audience and chuckle, 'You know I am fond of my glass and will excuse it.' In the earlier part of his career among his best roles were Scout in *The Village Lawyer*, Major Sturgeon in *The Mayor of Garratt*, Lissardo in *The Wonder*, Lubin Log in *Love, Law, and Physic*, Tony Lumpkin in *She Stoops to Conquer* and the title role in *Paul Pry*. In addition to Ambrose's portrait of him (**714**) in the Garrick Club, Reeve's portrait was painted by T. C. Wageman. Engraved portraits of him as Sylvester Daggerwood, Jerry Hawthorn and Bill Mattock (in *The Queer Subject*) were also published. (*DNB*)

REINHOLD, Frederick Charles **715**

1737-1815

Born in 1737 in London, Frederick Charles Reinhold was the son of the emigré bass singer from Dresden, Henry Theodore Reinhold (1690?-1751), who is noticed in the *BDA*. Frederick's sister sang on the London stage as Miss Reinhold and later Mrs Willems. Frederick himself was steeped in music from childhood and belonged to the boys choirs of the Chapel Royal and St Paul's Cathedral. As a juvenile he made his first stage appearance at Drury Lane Theatre on 5 February 1752 in an unspecified role in the entertainment *Queen Mab*. In the 1750s he began singing at Marylebone Gardens in summertime and in the choruses of various oratorio performances in London. He was kept busy as a bass singer in the choruses at the Haymarket and Drury Lane in the 1760s. Reinhold made his first appearance at Covent Garden on 30 October 1769 as Giles in *The Maid of the Mill*. On 17 January 1770 he sang Hawthorn in *Love in a Village*, the role in which he is depicted in Zoffany's exceptionally fine-toned picture (**715**). In 1783 he was appointed organist of St George the Martyr, Bloomsbury, and in 1784 he began his long association with the Handelian concerts at Westminster Abbey and the Pantheon and in the spring oratorios at Drury Lane from 1784 through 1792.

Reinhold sang some 80 roles in operas, pantomimes and comic operas; his last appearance was as Polyphemus in *Acis and Galatea* on 2 March 1798 at Covent Garden. He died at Somers Town on 28 September 1815 and was buried on 6 October at St Paul, Covent Garden. He was also pictured as Artabanes in *Artaxerxes* in an anonymous engraving (reproduced in the *BDA* 8: 416) based on a Covent Garden performance on 25 January 1777. (*BDA*)

RENAUD, Jane

See Jane POWELL

REYNOLDS, Frederic **750**

1764-1841

The person identified as T. Reynolds (No.12) in Harlow's painting of the Trial Scene in *Henry VIII* perhaps was Frederic Reynolds, the dramatist who is noticed in the *DNB*. He was born in Lime Street, London, on 1 November 1764, the son of a prominent Whig attorney. He entered the Middle Temple on 12 January 1782 but abandoned the law for playwriting. His first play, *Werter*, based on Goethe's novel, was produced at Bath on 25 November 1785 and then at Covent Garden Theatre on 14 March 1786. Subsequently Reynolds wrote nearly 100 plays, many of which were printed and some produced. From 1814 to 1821 he was engaged at Covent Garden as a 'thinker' – perhaps what is now called a dramaturg. He later performed the same duties for Elliston at Drury Lane. His last play was a pantomime at the Adelphi, Christmas 1840. He died on 16 April 1841. He had married in March 1799 Elizabeth Mansel (d. 1848), who acted at Covent Garden in the 1790s and is noticed in the *BDA* 10: 70-72. In 1826 he published his autobiographical two-volume *The Life and Times of Frederic Reynolds*. Reynolds became a member of the Garrick Club in November 1831, soon after its founding, but he resigned in February 1834. His son Frederic Mansel Reynolds (d. 1850) was also a dramatist and is noticed in the *DNB*.

RICH, John stage name Lun **716, 717**
1692-1761
John Rich, the son of the lawyer-theatre manager Christopher Rich, was baptized at St Andrew, Holborn, on 19 May 1692. Almost nothing is known of John's childhood, and in 1714, when his father died, the lad may or may not have been prepared to take over not only a theatrical troupe but a new playhouse in Lincoln's Inn Fields, then nearing completion. His father's will gave him that responsibility, however, and John began his pre-destined career. First, he appeared, on 18 December 1714, costumed in mourning for his father, to speak an epilogue on the stage of the new theatre. Then, on 10 November 1715 he tried playing the Earl of Essex in *The Unhappy Favourite*, his first and apparently last attempt at serious acting. He seems to have been searching for his place in the theatre world, and he finally found it in dance. He engaged a pair of French children, the Sallés, to dance in the 1716-17 season; their specialty was harlequinades, and John Rich may have danced with them in 'A new Italian Mimic Scene between a Scaramouch, Harlequin, Country Farmer, His Wife, and others' on 26 December 1716; by the following June the piece had been turned into a pantomime, possibly of Rich's devising. From 1716-17 onward Rich concentrated his attention on his own dancing ability and the growing appeal of Italianate pantomimes. He called himself 'Lun' whenever he played Harlequin.

However, Rich and his brother Christopher Moyser Rich, who was a silent partner, almost bankrupted the Lincoln's Inn Fields company, and they had to farm out their theatrical patent to stay in business. Ultimately Rich succeeded, becoming London's favourite harlequin in pantomimes and entr'acte entertainments and winning audience acceptance of variety bills instead of evenings of just one play. To his credit, he understood the changing taste of London audiences and eventually forced his competition at Drury Lane Theatre to begin offering similar bills.

Thomas Davies in his *Life of David Garrick* described a typical Rich pantomime: a serious main plot and a comic subplot, similar to Renaissance Italian intermezzi between acts of straight plays: 'By the help of gay scenes, fine habits, grand dances, appropriate music, and other decorations, he exhibited a story from Ovid's Metamorphosis, or some other fabulous writer. Between [*sic*] the pauses or acts ... he interwove a comic fable consisting chiefly of the courtship of Harlequin and Columbine, with a variety of surprising adventures and tricks which were produced by the magic wand of Harlequin, such as sudden transformation of palaces and temples to huts and cottages; of men and women into wheelbarrows and joint-stools ...' and the like. John Weaver, Rich's chief rival at Drury Lane, kept to the classical story and, apparently, presented mute dance entertainments, but eventually he, too, added comic impurities, to the chagrin of sophisticated but delight of general theatregoers. One of Rich's most popular offerings was *The Necromancer, or, Harlequin Doctor Faustus*, which opened on 20 December 1723 with Rich, of course, as Harlequin. The pantomimes and other commedia dell'arte-type entertainments received so much popular attention that some critics felt Rich was not paying sufficient attention to Shakespeare and legitimate drama, but the records show that he came close to matching Garrick's serious offerings, though with lesser talent. Garrick at Drury Lane scorned the trivial nature of pantomimes, but he eventually produced them, too.

Garrick also recognized Rich's talent: in the prologue to his own *Harlequin's Invasion* in December 1759 (after Rich had given up performing and his patent) Garrick said

> When Lun appeared with matchless art and whim,
> He gave the power of speech to every limb;
> Tho' mask'd and mute convey'd his quick intent,
> And told in frolic gesture what he meant.

An example of one of Rich's turns was Harlequin hatched from an egg, in *Harlequin a Sorcerer*, first performed on 21 January 1725 at Lincoln's Inn

Fields: 'a masterpiece of dumb show from the first chipping of the egg, his receiving of motion, his feeling of the ground, his standing upright, to his quick harlequin trip round the empty shell,' remembered John Jackson in 1793. That was not stage spectacle but mime, and Rich was evidently an expert at both. He also helped popularize ballad operas by presenting John Gay's enormously successful *Beggar's Opera*, which opened on 29 January 1728 and ran for an unheard of 32 uninterrupted nights, making Rich richer. Four years later he opened the fine new Covent Garden Theatre, in which he was able to produce some elaborate popular attractions, such as, in 1755-56, *The Rival Queens*, to which he added a lavish depiction of Alexander's triumphal entry into Babylon.

This was a remarkable career for a person who was accused of lacking taste and being stupid. Rich was eccentric, certainly: he kept dozens of cats, he mangled people's names and, said Davies, he could be vulgar and ungrammatical. But Rich was probably more clever than he seemed, and the stupidity may have been an act; he was, after all, a skilled performer and the son of a crafty lawyer. He grew into an excellent patentee and manager and competed successfully with Garrick at Drury Lane for years. He moved in high social circles and founded the lively Beefsteak Club, a social group that included Dr Johnson and the Prince of Wales.

John Rich died at his house next to Covent Garden Theatre on 26 November 1761. (*BDA*) [EAL]

RICHARDS, Elizabeth Rebecca
See Mrs John EDWIN

RICHARDSON, Sir Ralph David
1902-1983 **S52, B153**

Ralph Richardson, who, with Gielgud, Guinness and Olivier, formed a quartet of some of the greatest actors of the twentieth century, was born on 19 December 1902 at Cheltenham, the son of Arthur Richardson and his wife Lydia (née Russell). He made his first stage appearance at Brighton in 1921 as Lorenzo in *The Merchant of Venice*, toured the provinces, and joined the Birmingham Repertory Company in 1925. His debut in London came in 1926 at the Haymarket as Arthur Varwell in *Yellow Sands*. From 1930 to 1932 he was at the Old Vic, where he played in *Oedipus at Colonus*, and during the 1930s he gained prominence in West End productions of modern plays. After serving in the Fleet Air Arm during the Second World War, he returned to act at the Old Vic and co-direct with Olivier. He received acclaim in such roles as Falstaff (**S52**), Uncle Vanya, Peer Gynt, Cyrano, the Inspector in *The Inspector Calls* and Bluntschli in *Arms and the Man*. In 1956 he played Prospero and Volpone at the Royal Shakespeare Theatre, and during the 1970s he distinguished himself in a number of performances, many at the National Theatre, including in *No Man's Land*, *Home*, *What the Butler Saw*, *The Cherry Orchard*, *The Double Dealer* and *The Wild Duck*. Richardson brought to his roles a unique personality, 'one that was charming and refined, but also mischievous and capable of hinting at sinister or tragic depths in the character he played' (*EB*). Among his 75 films were remarkable portrayals in *The Fallen Idol*, *Anna Karenia*, *The Heiress*, *Our Man in Havana*, *Long Day's Journey into Night* (Cannes Film Festival Award for Best Performance), *Breaking the Sound Barrier* (British Academy Award) and *Dr Zhivago*.

Richardson was knighted in 1947 and was given the Order of St Olaf (Norway) in 1950, an Hon DLitt from Oxford in 1969 and a Special SWET Award in 1981.

He was a member of several London clubs, including the Athenaeum and the Savile. After suffering a severe stroke, Sir Ralph died in London on 10 October 1983, survived by Meriel Richardson (née Forbes Robertson), his wife of 39 years, and a son. The *Oxford Companion to the Theatre* describes him as 'an unselfish and unspectacular actor' who brought to all his parts the same 'integrity of purpose.' Though recognized as one of finest Shakespearean actors of his time, he was also 'a subtle interpreter of modern parts.' *See* John Miller, *Ralph Richardson; the authorized biography* (1995) and Garry O'Connor, *Ralph Richardson: an actor's life* (1985

RIVINGTON, Gerald Chippindale **718**
1893-1977

Born on 13 December 1893, the son of Charles

Robert Rivington of Castle Bank, Appleby, Westmorland, Gerald Rivington attended Harrow (and later became Chairman of the Governors, 1953-1964). After service in the First World War, he became Vice-President of the Publishers' Association, 1921-1931 and a Liveryman of the Stationers' and Newspaper Makers' companies. He was elected to the Garrick Club in 1918 and died on 2 March 1977.

ROBERTSON, Madge
See Dame Madge KENDAL

ROBERTSON, Thomas William **719**
1829-1871

Born on 9 January 1829 at Newark-on-Trent, the playwright Thomas William Robertson, who is shown as a child in the Garrick Club's portrait by an unknown artist (**719**), was the eldest of a large number of children of William Robertson, a comic actor at the Derby and Lincoln theatres, and his wife Margaret Elizabeth Marinus, an actress. His great-grandfather was James Robertson (d. 1795), a principal actor on the York circuit for many years. His grandfather, also named James Robertson, by his marriage to the actress Miss Robinson, had seven children, including William, the father of our subject.

Our subject's sister Margaret was better known as the actress Madge Kendal (*q.v.*). Two brothers also went on the stage: Frank Craven Robertson (1846-1879), who acted in Liverpool and then in London; and Edward Shafto Robertson (1844?-1871), who acted in London in 1870 and was drowned in the shipwreck of the *Avoca* on a voyage from Melbourne to India.

Thomas William began his career as a child actor on the Lincoln circuit. After some schooling at Spalding and Whittlesea, he returned to the Lincoln company (which was managed by his father William), where typically of country companies he was called upon to do many jobs. He prompted, painted scenery and wrote songs. He also acted a number of leading roles, including Hamlet, Charles Surface, Young Marlow and Jeremy Diddler. In 1848 he went to London and became a starving writer who supported himself by acting at minor theatres. His first play, *A Night's Adventure*, was produced in 1851 by William Farren at the Olympic Theatre and ran four nights. Many slight pieces followed while he served as prompter at the Olympic.

Robertson married the actress Elizabeth Burton (real name Taylor) at Christ Church, Marylebone, on 27 August 1856. They toured Irish and English towns and then Robertson gave up acting and turned to writing magazine sketches and translating French plays. He also became a member of a Bohemian literary set. His first stage success, *David Garrick*, adapted from his novel, was slow finding its audience until it was produced by Sothern at the Haymarket in 1864. Roberston established his reputation with *Society*, a sketch of Bohemian manners that was produced first in Liverpool and then under the Bancrofts on 11 November 1865 at the Prince of Wales's Theatre, where it ran 26 weeks. Other successes followed at the Prince of Wales's, including his major achievement, *Caste*, on 6 April 1867, and *M. P.*, on 23 April 1870.

With his numerous plays, Robertson influenced the technique of comedy writing that became known as the 'cup and saucer' school – portions of antiphonal duets, domestic interiors and occupations, and conflicts between the worldly and callow and the tender and sentimental. Many of his plays were published in *Principal Dramatic Works of Thomas William Robertson, with a Memoir by his Son* (2 vols 1889) and in *Lacy's Acting Editions of Plays*.

Robertson's first wife died on 14 August 1865. On 17 October 1867 he married Rosetta Feist, a German, at the English Consulate in Frankfurt. After suffering failing health for several years, he died at his house, No 6, Eton Terrace, Haverstock Hill on 3 February 1871 at the age of 42. He was a brilliant conversationalist, and in his Bohemian days he was widely popular at the Savage and Arundel clubs. There are numerous photographs of him, and a small bust of him was at the Arundel. (*DNB*)

ROBINSON, Mrs Thomas, Mary née Darby **720, 721**
1758-1800

The comprehensive notice of Mary Robinson provided in the *BDA* (13: 30-47) relates the somewhat romantic and importunate early life of this beautiful actress, who, it is said, was born 'in the midst of a tempest' on 27 November 1758 in the remnant of a medieval monastery in Bristol. Her father, a prosperous sea captain from Bristol named Darby – who supposedly had been born in America and whose first name was probably William – lost his fortune in a wild scheme to establish a 'whale fishery' on the coast of Labrador. The family having been deserted by Darby, Mary Darby was shunted from one boarding school to another, but then through a series of introductions she was presented by the dramatist Arthur Murphy to David Garrick during his last season of management at Drury Lane Theatre. Impressed by her voice and beauty, Garrick offered to train her and bring her on as Cordelia to his Lear. That event never occurred.

On 12 April 1774 Mary married Thomas Robinson, a solicitor's clerk, who proved a heavy drinker and gambler. Eventually debt caused them to flee to Tregunter, where Mary gave birth to her child Maria Elizabeth in the dormitory of a flannel factory run by Methodists because she was denied lodging at the manor house. When the Robinsons returned to London, he was imprisoned for £1200 debt, and Mary remained with him. Subsequently released, they took an apartment in Newman Street, and she was visited by Richard B. Sheridan, the new manager of Drury Lane, who like Garrick before him, was charmed by her voice and beauty and offered her an engagement. With Garrick in the audience, on the night of 10 December 1776, she acted Juliet. The prompter noted in his *Diary* 'a genteel Figure – a very tolerable first appearance and may do in time.' One critic called her 'a theatrical genius in the rough.'

At Drury Lane over the next four years, Mrs Robinson appeared in a number of leading roles, including Statira in *Alexander the Great*, Fanny in *The Clandestine Marriage*, Ophelia in *Hamlet*, Octavia in *All for Love*, Cordelia in *King Lear*, Viola in *Twelfth Night* and Rosalind in *As You Like It* (**721**). It was her performance at the age of 22 of Perdita in Garrick's alteration of *The Winter's Tale* on 20 November 1779 that captured the attention and passion of the young Prince of Wales, who signed his love letters to her 'Florizel.' She began an affair with him but the dissolute prince soon deserted her, never having provided her with a promised bond of £20,000. Subsequent 'attachments' occurred, despite the fact that Mary was still living with her libertine husband. Among them was Lt Col Banastre Tarleton, a dashing cavalry commander (whose portrait by Reynolds is in the National Gallery), with whom she consorted and travelled until about 1785.

She made her last appearance at Drury Lane on 31 May 1780 and her first at Covent Garden on 31 December 1782, as Rosamond in *Henry the Second*. After acting that season at Covent Garden such roles as Alicia in *Jane Shore* and Oriana in *The Knight of Malta*, she made her final appearance on the stage as Victoria in *A Bold Stroke for a Husband* on 15 May 1783.

From about the age of 25 Mary Robinson suffered a rheumatic fever that drove her from spa to spa on the Continent in a quest for a cure. Mrs Thrale gossiped that Mary's troubles were the result of 'Venereal Indulgences.' She died from complications caused by gall-stones at the age of 42 on 26 December 1800 at Englefield Cottage, Surrey, and was buried in Old Windsor churchyard.

In the 1790s she had turned to writing novels and essays. Her novels included *Vancenza* (1792), *Angelina* (3 vols 1797) and *Elinda, or the Abbey of St Aubert* (1799). She also published several volumes of poems. Her daughter Maria Elizabeth published Mary Robinson's *Memoirs* in 1801. Though she never rose to the first rank as an actress, as a personality and fashion plate she became a person of notoriety. She was attacked and satirized in such pieces as the anonymous *Letters to Perdita*. But her beauty was substantial and attracted a number of portraitists. In addition to the copy of the Reynolds portrait of her at the Garrick Club, **720** (after the original at Waddesdon Manor), another five of her by that artist (with many copies) exist, including the one from 1783-84 now in the Wallace Collection. In all, the *BDA* lists 81 pictures of her and numerous engravings. (*BDA*)

ROCK, Edward Anthony **722, 723**

d.1815

This specialist in portraying Irishmen, whose real name may have been O'Rourke, turned from hairdressing to acting by 1784, when he was a member of the company at Brighton. He first appeared at Covent Garden Theatre on 15 November 1786 as the Irish Haymaker in *Rosina.* He continued at that theatre in a repertoire of modest roles through the season of 1794-95 and also appeared at the Haymarket. In February 1796 he began an engagement with Stephen Kemble at Edinburgh which continued through 1808-9, acting numerous roles, mostly in his line, but some of more importance, such as Sterling in *The Clandestine Marriage,* Sir Peter Teazle in *The School for Scandal* and Sir Anthony Absolute in *The Rivals.* After a brief return to Covent Garden, Rock became deputy manager at the Crow Street Theatre in Dublin in 1809, in which position he served until his death in that city on 5 November 1815. His reputation was established as a stage Irishman (as depicted by De Wilde in **722** and **723**), and he was described as second only to Johnstone in the Irish character. His wife also acted in London (*q.v.*).

ROCK, Mrs Edward Anthony née Essex **724**

fl. 1776-1793

When still Miss Essex, this actress made her first appearance at the Haymarket Theatre on 12 June 1776 as Maria in *The Contract.* She played several other roles there that summer, when a Miss J. Essex, probably her sister, was also in the company. Though on the Drury Lane pay list for the 1776-77 season, she made only one known appearance at that theatre, as Silvia in *The Old Bachelor* on 19 November 1776. That night the prompter wrote in his *Diary,* 'a small mean Figure and a shocking Actress, so bad she is to do the Part no more.' She did manage to obtain an engagement at the China Hall, Rotherhithe, in the summer of 1777. Perhaps some seasoning in the provinces made her eligible for an engagement at Covent Garden Theatre beginning in 1787-88. By then she had married the actor Edward Anthony Rock (*q.v.*). She remained at Covent Garden through 1792-93, acting a line of secondary roles, including chambermaids and vocal parts in pantomimes and musical pieces. After a summer at the Edinburgh Theatre Royal in 1793, Mrs Rock seems to have retired or died. Her husband continued to act and co-manage at Edinburgh and Dublin until his death in 1815. Though she was an actress of inconsequential importance, De Wilde depicted her as Viletta (**724**, a role she did not act in London) for *Bell's British Theatre.* (*BDA*)

ROMANZINI

See Maria BLAND

ROSS, David **725, 726**

1728-1790

David Ross was born in London on 1 May 1728, the son of Alexander Ross (d. 1753), who had moved from Edinburgh to London in 1772 to take up a position as a solicitor of appeals. David's grandfather was Alexander Ross, vicar of Easterfarn. When David Ross was a student at Westminster School, an indiscretion earned him the hostility of his father, who was sufficiently angered to leave his son only one shilling on the first day of every May (his birthday), 'thereby to put him in mind of his misfortune he had to be born.' Eventually David successfully contested the will.

Ross began his professional acting career at the Smock Alley Theatre, Dublin, in May 1749, playing Clerimont in Fielding's *The Miser.* That season at Dublin he also appeared as Orlando in *As You Like It,* Macheath in *The Beggar's Opera* and Edmund in *King Lear,* among other roles. Garrick engaged him for the season of 1751-52 at Drury Lane, where he made his debut on 3 October 1751 as Young Bevil in *The Conscious Lovers.* He was well received, and, according to one critic, he demonstrated that he was capable of 'restoring to the stage the long-lost character of the real fine gentleman.' Capital roles followed: Castalio in *The Orphan,* Lord Townly in *The Provok'd Husband,* Barnwell in *The London Merchant* and Essex in *The Earl of Essex.* Ross remained at Drury Lane through 1756-57 and then went over to Covent Garden in the autumn of 1757. At the latter house he acted numerous major roles, including Prince Hal in *1 Henry IV,* the title roles in *Douglas* and *King John,* Jaffeir in *Venice Preserv'd,* Oakly in *The Jealous Wife* and Antonio in *The Merchant of Venice.* On 8 October 1757 he played Hamlet, the role in which Zoffany depicted him (**726**). He grew fat and lazy and lost his engagement at Covent Garden at the end of the 1772-73 season.

He also suffered from gout, which prevented him from playing for long periods of time. After five years, Ross returned to Covent Garden, but acted infrequently, though he appeared as Lear and Othello. His last performance in a London patent house came on 17 February 1778, as Sir Charles in *The Careless Husband.*

In the 1760s Ross had ventured into theatrical management in the provinces. He ran the theatres at Manchester and Edinburgh. At the latter city he opened the Canongate Theatre in 1767 and then the new Theatre in Shakespeare Square in 1769. He gave up his enterprises in the north in 1781 and afterwards did little acting, and only in the provinces. He was appointed titular Master of the Revels for Scotland in October 1772, a position he held the rest of his life. He died in London on 14 September 1790 at the age of 62 and was buried at St James, Piccadilly.

Ross had been a good and promising actor, possessed of charm, ease, elegance and a fine voice. But he squandered his talents by lack of will and application. Tate Wilkinson called him 'the Prince of negligence.' He did enjoy the company of influential acquaintances, including that of Boswell, who was chief mourner at his funeral. Ross's wife Frances Murray, a somewhat 'celebrated' woman of the town whom he had married in the 1750s, may have done some acting in Edinburgh, but not in London. (*BDA*)

RUSSELL, Charles Ritchie, Baron of Killowen **728**

1908-1986

Charles Ritchie Russell was born on 12 January 1908, the son of Francis Xavier, Baron Russell of Killowen (1867-1946, *q.v.* **729**) and his wife Mary Emily Ritchie, daughter of the 1st Baron Ritchie of Dundee. Like his father he was educated at Oriel College, Oxford, and was called to the Bar at Lincoln's Inn, 1932. He became a QC in 1948 and a Bencher in 1952. After serving in the Army from 1939 to 1945, he became Attorney-General to the Duchy of Cornwall (1951-1960), Judge of Chancery Division, High Court of Justice (1960-1962), President of the Restrictive Practices Court (1961-1962) and a Lord Justice of Appeal (1962-1975). Charles Russell was created a life peer in 1975. He became a member of the Garrick Club in 1939 and died on 23 June 1986.

RUSSELL, Lord Francis Xavier, Baron Russell of Killowen **729**

1867-1946

Francis Xavier Russell was born on 2 July 1867, the 4th son of Lord Russell of Killowen (1832-1900). He was educated at Oriel College, Oxford, and was called to the Bar, Lincoln's Inn, 1893. Russell became a QC in 1908, a Judge of the High Court, 1919-1928, a Lord Justice of Appeal, 1928-1929, and a Lord of Appeal in Ordinary, 1929-1946. He was created a Life Peer in 1929. Lord Russell married the Hon Mary Emily, 5th daughter of the 1st Baron Ritchie of Dundee in 1900. He became a member of the Garrick Club in 1893 and remained so for 53 years, until his death on 20 December 1946. He also served as a Trustee and was entered in the Roll of Members as 'Frank' Russell. *See* also his son, Charles Ritchie Russell, above (**728**).

RUSSELL, Samuel Thomas **171, 730**

c. 1770-1845

The son of Samuel Russell and his wife, both performers, Samuel Thomas Russell was born about 1770. In 1773 he was advertised as 'Master Russell, age 3' in the Norwich Theatre Royal playbill, and with his parents the child performed in some capacity at other provincial playhouses. On 18 September 1776 at the Haymarket Theatre in London young Samuel appeared at Ned Shuter's benefit doing imitations and reciting 'Bucks Have at ye all.' That was a pattern for a few years, augmented by juvenile parts: Tom Thumb, the Quaker Boy in *A Bold Stroke for a Wife* and the Duke of York in *Richard III* at the Haymarket, the China Hall in Rotherhithe, Marylebone Gardens, and similar venues. Then the boy and his parents toured country theatres, attracted the attention of the Prince of Wales and thus arrived at Drury Lane. Samuel the younger on 22 January 1795 acted Charles in *The School for Scandal* (which displeased His Royal Highness) and Fribble in *Miss in Her Teens* (which didn't). Critics told the lad he just wasn't cut out for well-bred characters, and Fribble was more his type. That, of course, did not keep Russell from trying fashionable comic characters like Sparkish in *The Country Girl*, but he was indeed better suited to rogues, countrymen and eccentric servants. By the end of the century he had added to his Drury Lane repertoire such characters as Roderigo in *Othello*, Fag in *The Rivals*, Osric in *Hamlet*, Tattle in *Love for Love*, Feste in *Twelfth Night* and, especially, Jerry Sneak in *The Mayor of Garratt* (**171**, **730**).

Russell was especially popular at Margate (partly because he married the proprietor's daughter), and as the years wore on he delved more and more into management, becoming stage manager at the Surrey Theatre and, from 1819, Drury Lane. He was a dependable comedian, sometimes tipsy, and a favourite at 'giving out' the next day's bill, for he remained adept at reciting and joking. Russell gave his farewell to the audience on 1 July 1831 at the Haymarket, playing Jerry Sneak. He died on 25 February 1845. (*BDA*) [EAL]

RUSSELL, Sir William Howard **731**
1820-1907
William Russell was born in Ireland on 28 March 1820, the son of John Russell, of Lilyvale, and his wife Mary, the daughter of Captain John Kelly, Castle Kelly, Dublin. He was educated at Trinity College, Dublin, and then, as a special correspondent to *The Times*, covered many of the major events that occurred in the middle of the nineteenth century. He reported on the Crimea (1854-1856), the American Civil War (1861-1862), the Franco-German War (1870) and South Africa (1879-1880). He was charged by Nubar Pasha to select the guests at the opening of the Suez Canal, and accompanied the Prince of Wales as Honorary Private Secretary to India (1875-1876). Russell also published a number of letters and diaries from his expeditions. In writing of the battle of Balaclava in 1854 he applied to the English infantry the phrase 'the thin red line,' which has passed into the language. His letters describing the suffering of the British Army in that winter of 1854-1855 brought home to the public the dreadful conditions under which the troops lived, and inspired in part the work of Florence Nightingale. He was knighted in 1895. His first wife, whom he married on 16 September 1846, was Mary Burrowes (d. 1867), and his second was Countess Antoinetta Malvezz, whom he married on 18 February 1884. Russell became a member of the Garrick Club in 1853. He died on 10 February 1907 and was buried in Brompton Cemetery. (*DNB*)

RUTHERSTON, Mrs **892**
fl. 1967
Mrs Rutherston, who is shown as figure No. 30 dancing with the Garrick Club staff member Frederick Barker in Gilroy's scene of the Garrick Club Outing, is said by Richard Hough (*The Ace of Clubs*) to be the wife of a member. But we find no Rutherston in the Roll of Members. Possibly she was a member of staff.

RYAN, Lacy **49**
c. 1694-1760
Born about 1694, Lacy Ryan was named as a member of the Queen's Theatre troupe as early as December 1709 and is known to have acted Rosencrantz in *Hamlet* on 1 July 1710 at Greenwich. He then moved to Drury Lane, where he was kept busy with small roles and then major characters until 1718, when he joined the manager John Rich at Lincoln's Inn Fields. There (and at Covent Garden from 1732 on) he remained until his death in 1760, playing such important Shakespearean roles as Hamlet (as early as 26 February 1719, his best role), Hotspur, Prince Hal, Iago, Wolsey, Benedick and the Ghost in *Hamlet* (as late as 18 March 1760, his last appearance) (**49**). Some of his non-Shakespearean parts were Pinchwife and also Horner in *The Country Wife*, the title role in *Oroonoko*, Tom in *The Conscious Lovers*, Mosca in *Volpone*, Mirabell in *The Way of the World* and Lothario in *The Fair Penitent.* Despite the importance of his roles and the energy he showed during a long career, Ryan was seldom described as anything more than an 'able' actor.

He was better-known because of at least three scuffles in real life: in 1713 he had a fight with some Thames watermen and received such a blow on his nose that his voice was altered; in 1718 Ryan killed a drunken Irishman named Kelley when Kelley drew his sword on the actor in a tavern; and in the worst, on 16 March 1735, Ryan was set upon by one or two footpads who left him with part of his face shot away. Remarkably, he recovered sufficiently to act again, though his voice was never the same, and for an actor brought up in the period of Thomas Betterton and Barton Booth, that must have been devastating. The public, as one would expect, was most sympathetic, and Ryan continued acting many of his old parts, even though critics wished he would abandon youthful characters for which he now lacked the necessary fire. Ryan died in August 1760. (*BDA*)[EAL]

RYDER, Thomas **732**
1735-1791
Thomas Ryder was born in 1735, the son of Preswick and Sarah Ryder, both provincial performers. Our subject acted in Edinburgh in 1757 in a variety of roles, among them Aimwell in *The Stratagem*, Alexas in *All for Love*, Ben in *Love for Love*, Chamont in *The Orphan*, Filch in *The Beggar's Opera*, Prince Hal in *2 Henry IV* and Sir Andrew Aguecheek in *Twelfth Night*. He could sing, dance and act a variety of character types – a utility actor in the best sense, and always valuable to a company. On 7 December 1757 he made his first appearance at Smock Alley Theatre in Dublin, as Plume in *The Recruiting Officer*, and the next night he acted Romeo to the Juliet of Elizabeth Hopkins. Ryder performed there and at Crow Street through 1764-65, after which he toured the Irish towns, built a new theatre in Belfast, spent too much on town and country homes for himself and his wife (the actress Rosetta Comerford), managed Smock Alley and Crow Street, and developed a sizeable and faithful following in Ireland. Then Ryder pulled up stakes in 1786 and headed for London.

At Covent Garden on 25 October 1786 he acted Sir John Brute in *The Provok'd Wife* and unsettled many spectators by playing Brute as a brute. Ryder acted at Covent Garden until November 1790 in his usual variety of roles, after which he managed the Edinburgh theatre, acted in Belfast and then retired to Dublin, where he died on 26 November 1791.

The portrait of Ryder (**732**) attributed to Roberts in *PGC* is now credited to C. R. Ryley and is a study of Ryder as Lovegold in *The Miser*; an engraving by Angus, after Ryley, of Ryder in that role was published by Lowndes in his *New English Theatre* (1788). (*BDA*) [EAL]

S

SACHEVERELL, Charlotte
See Charlotte CHARKE

ST ALBAN, Duchess of
See Harriot MELLON

SALLIS, Peter **G1003**
b. 1921
Peter Sallis was born in Twickenham on I February 1921, the son of Harry Sallis and his wife Dorothy Ann Frances (née Barnard). He trained for the stage at RADA. After making his professional debut as a Soldier and a Servant in *The Scheming Lieutenant* at the Arts in September 1946, he worked in various repertory theatres, and in May 1951 he returned to London to act Fedotik in *The Three Sisters* at the Aldwych. Subsequently he was seen at numerous London theatres in a variety of roles, including Waitwell in *The Way of the World*, Retrosi in *Venice Preserv'd*, Joe Scanlon in *The Matchmaker*, the Stage Manager in Orson Welles's production of *Moby Dick* at the Duke of York's in June 1955, Simon and Barère in *Danton's Death* at the Lyric, Hammersmith, January-April 1959, and Roat in *Wait Until Dark* at the Strand, July 1966. His films include *Anatasia, The Doctor's Dilemma, The Scapegoat* and *Saturday Night and Sunday Morning*. He also has appeared on a number of television shows, including *The Mary Tyler Moore Show, The Carol Burnett Show* and *Last of the Summer Wine*. Sallis became a member of the Garrick Club in December 1978. (*WWT17*)

SALOMON, Johann Peter **773**
1745-1815
The violinist and impresario Johann Peter Salomon was born in January 1745 at Bonn, in the house at No 515, Bongasse, the same house in which Beethoven would be born 25 years later. His father Philipp Salomon was an oboist in the Elector of Cologne's band and in the Bonn theatre. Johann joined the court band at the age of 11. In 1780 he played in Paris and then embarked for England, making his first public appearance in

London playing a concerto on the violin and leading the band at Covent Garden Theatre on 23 March 1781. That year he played in Edinburgh and in the Professional Concerts in London; in 1783 he became a member of the Royal Society of Musicians.

By 1785 Salomon was one of London's foremost artists. In 1786 he organized a series of concerts at the Hanover Square Rooms, where some of the most important musical events in London's musical history would take place. He also led the concerts of the New Musical Fund and of the Academy of Ancient Music. While on the Continent in 1790 he met Haydn and persuaded him to come to London, and it was during Haydn's two visits, 1790-91 and 1794-5, that the 'Salomon' – or 'London' – symphonies were composed and played. Haydn lived with Salomon for a year in 1790 at his residence, No 12, Great Pulteney Street. Salomon also was influential in stimulating Haydn to undertake his great oratorio *The Creation.*

Throughout his career in London Salomon was constantly associated with opera, concerts and the theatre. His distinguished pupils and protégés included Pinto, Clement, Braham, Hague and Cudmore; and his friends were Hazlitt, Shield, Arnold, Ayrton and Clementi, among many others. He died at his house, No 70, Newman Street, London on 28 November 1815 and was buried in the South Cloister of Westminster Abbey, having been one of the most influential and beneficial musicians of his time. In addition to the portrait of him in the Garrick Club (**733**), given to the circle of George Harlow, portraits of Salomon were done by William Beechey (Faculty of Music, Oxford), George Dance (Royal College of Music), Thomas Hardy, William Lane (Royal Collection) and William Owen. (*BDA*)

SAMUEL, Adrian Christopher Ian CMG, CVO 892

b. 1915

Ian Samuel, who is shown as No. 22 in Gilroy's scene of the Garrick Club Outing in 1967, was born on 20 August 1915, the son of George Christopher Samuel and Alma Richards. After being educated at Rugby School and St John's College, Oxford, he entered HM Consular Service in 1938 and served in various posts in North Africa. In the Second World War he was in the Royal Air Force. Subsequently his career in the Foreign Office took him to Embassies in Ankara, Cairo and Damascus. From October 1959 to 1963 he was Principal Private Secretary to the Secretary of State for Foreign Affairs and then Minister at HM Embassy in Madrid, 1963-1965. After resigning from the Foreign Service in 1965 he became Director of British Energy Chemical Contractors Association and British Agrochemicals Association. His publications include *An Astonishing Fellow; a Life of Sir Robert Wilson* (1986). Samuel was elected to the Garrick Club in May 1967.

SARGENT, Sir Harold Malcolm Watts 734

1895-1967

The conductor Malcolm Sargent was born on 29 April 1895, the son of Henry Edward Sargent of Stamford, Lincolnshire. He attended Stamford School, was articled as a pupil at Peterborough Cathedral and received a MusB at Durham. He earned a diploma at the Royal College of Organists at 16 and became in his early 20s England's youngest Doctor of Music. His conducting debut was in 1921 with the Queen's Hall Orchestra. He joined the staff of the Royal College of Music in 1923, and then established a number of concerts with various orchestras. Sargent helped Sir Thomas Beecham form the London Philharmonic in 1932. Subsequently, throughout the world, he became Britain's best-known conductor. He led the BBC Symphony Orchestra from 1949 to 1957 and, unsurpassed as a choral director, he conducted the Royal Choral Society and the Huddersfield Choral Society for many years. In addition to conducting orchestras in many of the major cities throughout Europe and North America, at home he led the Gilbert and Sullivan Operas, the Promenade Concerts (as shown in **734**) from 1947 to his death, the Covent Garden operas and the Edinburgh Festivals, among numerous other venues. He was knighted in 1947. Other of his numerous honours include DMus Oxon (Hon 1942); LLD Liverpool (Hon 1947); St Olaf Medal (1947); and Chevalier of the Legion of Honour (1967). Sir Malcolm became a member of the Garrick Club in 1927. He died in London on 3 October 1967. His biography by Charles Reid was published in 1968. (*WWW*)

SATCHELL, Elizabeth
See Mrs Stephen George KEMBLE

SATTERTHWAITE, Commander Edward Sidney **735, 892**
1900-1992
E. S. Satterthwaite was born at Bromley, Kent, on 11 February 1900, the son of Sidney Clement Satterthwaite and his wife Constance Stephenson Clarke. He was educated at Newton College Preparatory School and Christ's Hospital, Horsham, Sussex. He joined the Royal Navy on 15 July 1917, serving on his first ship, *HMS Vincent*, from 1917 to 1920. After many sea appointments and adventures (including qualifying as a free balloon pilot), in 1940 he was posted to Ottawa as Secretary to his mentor Vice-Admiral A. E. Evans, head of British Admiralty Technical Division. Satterthwaite served Evans a total of 18 years in various appointments until the Admiral's death in a flying accident in December 1944. Satterthwaite's final naval appointment, in the rank of Acting Captain RN, was as supply officer of *HMS Ganges*. He was a keen sportsman, playing rugby for the Navy and Kent, hockey for the Navy and Suffolk and cricket for the United Services. He was also an expert yachtsman, with many prizes and cups to his credit.

After retiring from the Royal Navy, Satterthwaite worked for three years with the estate agents Lofts and Warner. On 1 January 1953 he was appointed Secretary of the Garrick Club. Satterthwaite introduced an immensely popular Derby Day outing for members (**892**) and for the staff an annual outing to the seaside.

Sadly, London clubland reached a crisis in the 1960s. Social habits were changing, hotels and restaurants were providing stiff competition both for customers and staff, costs were rocketing with inflation and revenues falling. By the time 'Satters' or 'The Commander,' as he was known to many, retired as Secretary on 31 December 1972, having been elected a Life Member, the worst of the storm was over. He had made the Club his life and retained the loyalty of the long-serving members of the staff. For the next twenty years Satterthwaite was a frequent user of the Club.

He had married Jane Quick (**892**) on 29 August 1936; they had two daughters, Sarah, born 24 January 1941, and Nona, born 3 November 1942. From 1974 he and his wife lived in Broughton, Hampshire. Commander Satterthwaite died on 22 February 1992.

SCOFIELD, David Paul CBE, CH **S53, B154**
b. 1922
This brilliant and powerful actor was born at Hurstpierpoint, Sussex, on 21 January 1922, the son of Edward H. and M. Scofield. He attended the Vardean School in Brighton and trained for the stage at the Croydon Repertory School in 1939 and at the London Mask Theatre School in 1940. He toured with companies entertaining troops in 1941, was with the Birmingham Repertory Theatre 1942-1945 and then with the Royal Shakespeare Theatre at Stratford-upon-Avon 1946-1948. At the last he enjoyed great success as Henry V, Cloten in *Cymbeline*, Don Adriano in *Love's Labour's Lost*, Lucio in *Measure for Measure* and Hamlet. In London at the Arts Theatre he acted Tegeus Chromis in *A Phoenix Too Frequent*. Scofield has continued to play major roles at most of London's major theatres. Among his most memorable performances were Pierre in *Venice Preserv'd* (Lyric Hammersmith 1953), the drunken priest in *The Power and the Glory* (1957), Thomas More in *A Man For All Seasons* (Globe 1960), Coriolanus (Stratford, Canada, 1963), Uncle Vanya (London 1970), Volpone (London 1977) and Salieri in *Amadeus* (National Theatre 1979). Among his films are *A Man For All Seasons* (Academy Award 1966), Tobias in *A Delicate Balance* (1974) and the French King in Branagh's version of *Henry V* (1989).

Scofield was awarded a CBE in 1956 and was named Companion of Honour in January 2001. He holds honorary doctorates from Glasgow, Kent and Sussex universities. Possessed with an extraordinary voice and 'a strongly moulded face', he has been a masterful and compelling performer in the British theatre for over 60 years. (*WW, OCT*) *See* also Burnim and Wilton, *The Richard Bebb Collection in the Garrick Club*, B154.

SCOTT-WARING, Harriet Pye
See Mrs James ESTEN

SEYLER, Athene CBE 736, 951
1889-1990
Athene Seyler, whose busy career spanned almost six decades, was born in London on 31 May 1889, the daughter of Clarence H. Seyler and his wife Clara (née Thies). She trained for the stage at the Royal Academy of Dramatic Art and made her first stage appearance on 11 February 1909 at the Kingsway Theatre as Pamela Grey in *The Truants*. Subsequently she graced the stage of almost every major London theatre, specializing in comedy. She was successful in a variety of roles, including Madame Ranevska in *The Cherry Orchard* (**736**), Fanny Farrelli in *Watch on the Rhine*, Vita Louise in *Harvey*, Mrs Malaprop in *The Rivals*, the Nurse in *Romeo and Juliet*, Miss Moffat in *The Corn is Green* and Lady Fidget in *The Country Wife*. Among her last roles was Martha Brewster in *Arsenic and Old Lace*, at the Vaudeville in February 1966. She appeared in a number of films from 1932, and she directed several stage productions. She served on the Arts Council of Great Britain, as Hon Treasurer of British Actors Equity Association and as President of the Royal Academy of Dramatic Art and the Theatrical Ladies Guild. In 1959 she was honoured with a CBE. Her book *The Craft of Comedy* was published in 1944. In her later years Seyler lived in the Coach House, No 26, Upper Mall, in Hammersmith; she died on 12 September 1990 at the age of 101. (*WWW, WWT*)

SHAKESPEARE, William 737, S28, S30, S44, B84-B87, SP0001
1564-1616
William Shakespeare was baptised in Holy Trinity Church at Stratford-upon-Avon on 26 April 1564, but his birthday is traditionally said to have occurred on 23 April. He was the son of John Shakespeare, a burgess of Stratford, and his wife Mary Arden, of Wilmcote, Warwickshire. Shakespeare became the greatest dramatist and poet in the English language. Most of his plays were first acted at the Globe Theatre on the Bankside, London, where Shakespeare was also an actor and partner in the management. After retiring to live at 'New Place' in Stratford, he died on 23 April 1616 and was buried in Holy Trinity Church. The first folio of his collected plays was published by some fellow actors in 1623 and is now one of the most valuable books in the language. His 36 (or 37) plays have been translated and produced throughout the world, and today he remains the most widely known and produced dramatist. By his wife Anne Hathaway (d. 1623) he had three children: Susanna, baptised on 26 May 1583, and twins Hamnet and Judith, baptised on 2 February 1585.

SHARP, Mrs Michael William
See Arabella MENAGE

SHEREK, Hon Major Henry G0976
1900-1967
Born on 23 April 1900 and educated abroad, Henry Sherek was with the Rifle Brigade in 1919 and was re-activated in 1940. He retired from the Army as an Honorary Major in 1944. He married in 1937 the Hon Kathleen Mary Pamela Corona Boscawen, daughter of the 7th Viscount Falmouth. Since the Second World War he produced some 110 plays in the London and New York, notable among them being *Idiot's Delight, Edward My Son, The Cocktail Party, The Confidential Clerk, The Queen and the Rebels, Under Milkwood, Fanny's First Play, The Petrified Forest, Private Lives, The Philadelphia Story* and *The Playboy of the Western World*. Sherek became a member of the Garrick Club in February 1961. He died on 23 September 1967.

SHERIDAN, Richard Brinsley 738
1751-1816
Born in Dorset Street, Dublin, on 30 October 1751, Richard Brinsley Sheridan was the son of the theatre manager, actor and teacher of oratory Thomas Sheridan (*q.v.*) and his wife Frances, a playwright. Though Richard went to grammar school in Dublin and had strong feelings for his Irish heritage, most of his life was spent in England, to which he became equally devoted. His life was fraught with incident, from two duels at Bath for his beloved (singer Elizabeth Linley, with whom he eloped to France), to the success of four sparkling comedies in five years, to the

managership and near-financial ruin of Drury Lane Theatre, to dazzling oratory (and protection from creditors) as a Member of Parliament, to regular drunken bouts featuring claret and brandy, to death in debt but burial in Poet's Corner at Westminster Abbey. He belonged to the world of the theatre, where he brought people more merriment than they had enjoyed since the days of Congreve, as well as to the theatre of the world, where he championed the revolutionary Irish, American and French. He was sometimes irresponsible and disorganized but just as often light-hearted and witty, as when he was accosted by a highwayman and offered the thief an IOU. Though he is not known to have been an actor, much of his life was an act, full of intrigues, wordplay and pretense. Sheridan was asked whether he was a rogue or a fool; he replied that he was somewhere between the two. His life in politics was merely the other side of the theatrical coin. It is difficult to castigate Sheridan for his financial ineptitude after he has entertained you with *The Rivals*, *The School for Scandal*, *The Duenna* and *The Critic*.

Yet that part of his life spent in the theatre did serious damage to England's greatest playhouse and the hundreds of people who worked there. Employees went without pay while Sheridan enjoyed the good life; the patentee sat in the Piazza Coffee House watching 'by his own fireside' as Drury Lane burned to the ground in 1809. He had little interest in tragedy and seemed at times to be a man who could not take life seriously, even when seriousness was thrust upon him.

Sheridan's career as an author began in the 1770s with satirical and political epistles. His first play was *The Rivals* (1775), which was not immediately successful but attracted audiences after Sheridan doctored it and improved the casting. Then, in a striking flurry of creativity between 1775 and 1779, while at the same time taking over the managership of Drury Lane, Sheridan turned out his four major comedies and three lesser pieces. After that the playwright in him was content with play doctoring and staging. He wrote some new scenes in 1780 for Woodward's *Harlequin Fortunatus* and staged in it a spectacular, audience-catching battle; he cooked up a pantomime called *Robinson Crusoe* in 1781 that had 40 performances; in 1798 he tinkered with Thompson's *The Stranger*, from Kotzebue, and in 1799 he turned out his last major theatrical work, *Pizarro,* again from Kotzebue. By that time Drury Lane's finances were in a shambles and Sheridan was turning over stage management to others. He seemed to have enjoyed the power and notoriety of heading England's premiere theatre but only wanted it to further his political ambitions.

His appearances as a political orator dazzled the House of Commons; one speech, in 1787, was over five and a half hours long and brought cheers; another, in 1798 was delivered over three days, and seats for it fetched £50. But his political career began to wane in the early years of the new century, and by 1812 he had lost his positions both in Parliament and at Drury Lane. He was debt-ridden, unprotected by membership in Parliament, and dependent on the kindness of friends. His body was giving way on him, too, and Sheridan died on 7 July 1816. (*BDA*; Fintan O'Toole, *A Traitor's Kiss: The Life of Richard Brinsley Sheridan*, 1997)[EAL]

SHERIDAN, Thomas 739, B173

1719-1788

Born in 1719 in Quilca, near Dublin, the son of the schoolmaster Dr Thomas Sheridan and his wife Elizabeth. Thomas Sheridan the younger was the godson of Jonathan Swift and grew up among people interested in drama and education. By the age of 13 young Tom was engaged in theatrical activity, playing Antony in *Julius Caesar* at Mme Violante's booth in George's Lane. The boy was sent to Westminster School in London and received BA and MA degrees from Trinity College, Dublin. He kept his interest in education throughout his life, but the attraction to theatre was strong, so Tom made a career that encompassed both. At Smock Alley Theatre he arranged to have Guarini's *Pastor Fido* produced on 31 January 1740 for his family's benefit, and on 29 January 1743 Tom acted the title role in *Richard III* at that playhouse. Then his play *Captain O'Blunder* was presented in February and his *Brave Irishman* in the summer. He also acted Hamlet on 28 February 1743, followed by Brutus in *Julius Caesar*, Othello, Cato and other major roles, establishing himself in his own mind as Dublin's leading actor and the man who could save the theatre.

That streak of arrogance got Tom Sheridan into trouble again and again in the years that followed: he fought with Theophilus Cibber in 1743 over a robe for Cato to wear, with David Garrick in 1745 over salary arrangements, with a drunken member of the audience in 1747, with a fund-raiser for a hospital over the use of musicians for a benefit in 1750, and so on. He apparently felt his enemies resented his rules and practices, which he laid on like a teacher in a classroom instead of a theatre manager with a business to run.

In 1743 Dublin had two rival troupes – one in Smock Alley and another in Aungier Street – competing in a town that could not really support both. The rival proprietors united, planning to form a joint company at Aungier Street, and they offered Thomas Sheridan a good salary (apparently £6 weekly) to run the united company. Sheridan wanted to take over the management and pay the propietors £500 annually. They refused, so Sheridan leased Smock Alley, recruited the actors who had been squeezed out of the merger and published his plan to save theatre in Dublin. But then he received an attractive offer from London and gave up his Smock Alley plan, which then collapsed.

Sheridan made his London debut at Covent Garden on 31 March 1744 as Hamlet, followed by Macbeth, Lord Townly in *The Provok'd Husband* and Brutus in *Julius Caesar*. In 1744-45 he joined Garrick at Drury Lane, appearing first on 20 October 1744 as Horatio in *The Fair Penitent* and then Pierre in *Venice Preserv'd*, Tamerlane, and others. But he couldn't sit still: in the middle of the season he went back to Dublin, conferred with the proprietors, had a benefit at Smock Alley and returned to London to finish the season. Then he did roughly the same thing all over again: Dublin to confer, London to recruit, and Dublin again to get ready to manage Smock Alley, with Garrick and George Anne Bellamy as visiting actors.

The 1745-46 season was successful, and in the autumn of 1746 Sheridan began instituting some of his reforms: offering subscription plans to theatregoers, developing the theatre's wardrobe, instituting better rehearsal discipline and charging extra for on-stage seating. All went well for a while, but in 1754 Sheridan announced that he was quitting the stage following a riot at Smock Alley that left his theatre a wreck. That was not the end of his theatre career, for he was to quit the stage again and again before his death.

Sheridan acted at Covent Garden again in 1754-55, then wrote a book on British education, went back to Dublin to serve as Master of the Revels, became manager of Smock Alley once more, returned to London in 1759 after deciding again to quit Ireland – and so it went. In the meantime, in 1747, Thomas Sheridan had married Frances Chamberlaine. The most notable of their children was, of course, Richard Brinsley Sheridan (*q.v.*), the playwright-theatre manager-politician who inherited some of his father's restless, erratic ways but added to them a gift for comedy that his father lacked.

Though Thomas Sheridan acted many roles during his theatrical career, most of the characters he played were of a serious nature, and rarely did critics praise his acting; he was, it would seem, more orator than actor and more manager than performer. A letter written by the actor William 'Gentleman' Smith dated 24 March 1814 was blunt: Thomas Sheridan 'certainly might be a Master of the Theory of the drama, but nothing further. In eccentric & extravagant characters He had weight & Hyperbolical Fustian Dignity [suitable for] Cato, Brutus, Coriolanus – He had no natural Talents …' His sound judgment was sometimes noted, but it seems to have been the judgment of a stern schoolmaster rather than a creative artist.

Thomas Sheridan's late years were spent mostly writing and being cared for by his daughter Elizabeth. He died on 14 August 1788. (*BDA*) [EAL]

SIDDONS, Henry **741, 749**

1774-1815

Born at Wolverhampton on 4 October 1774, Henry Siddons was the eldest child of the actress Sarah Siddons and her husband William Siddons. Henry's birth occurred while his parents were touring the provinces, before his mother became famous. After some schooling in Croyden and at Dr Barrow's Academy in Soho, Henry was sent to the seminary at Charterhouse, intended for the priesthood. But while at school, he acted some children's roles in his parents' productions, and he played the Child to his mother's Isabella at her re-appearance at Drury Lane on 10 October 1782; he is pictured in that role in Hamilton's painting in the Garrick Club (**749**).

In the 1790s he strolled the northern provincial towns, acted with his uncle Stephen Kemble's company in Edinburgh for a while, and finally, on October 1801, returned to London to play Herman in *Integrity* at Covent Garden. In the cast was his future wife, Harriet Murray. He acted Hamlet on 12 October 1801 and Othello on 28 October; he was favourably received and the reviews were encouraging. At the end of the season, for his benefit on 21 May 1802, his mother joined him to act Lady Randolph to his Douglas.

After remaining at Covent Garden through 1804-5, Siddons left Covent Garden and went over to Drury Lane, where he acted until the end of 1808-9; he then left the London stage for good. In 1809 he became patentee of the Edinburgh Theatre; that theatre opened under his management on 14 November with *The Honeymoon*, in which he acted the Duke and his wife was Juliana. He enjoyed a six-year stint as manager at Edinburgh and appeared in some 80 roles, including Captain Absolute in *The Rivals*, Charles Surface in *The School for Scandal*, Don Felix in *The Wonder*, Posthumus in *Cymbeline*, Puff in *The Critic* and Shylock. Three comedies written by him were produced during that time, and several of his entertainments had been performed earlier in London.

Henry Siddons died of tuberculosis in Edinburgh on 12 April 1815, the third of Mrs Siddons's children to be so afflicted. He was buried in Greyfriars Churchyard. Information on his widow and four children is given in his notice in the *BDA* 13: 390-391.

SIDDONS, Sarah **390, 742-745, 747-750,**
1755-1831 **644, G1018, B88, B89**

The supreme 'Tragic Muse,' Sarah Siddons, was born at the Shoulder of Mutton Inn in Brecon, Wales, on 5 July 1755. She was the first of the twelve children of the provincial actor-managers Roger Kemble and his wife Sarah (née Ward), many of whom enjoyed estimable stage careers, including her brothers John Philip, Charles and Stephen and her sisters Frances and Elizabeth. Like her siblings, Sarah went on in children's parts, and her first recorded performance was as Princess Elizabeth in a family production of *Charles the First* at the King's Head, Worcester, on 12 February 1767. When a young woman she made a reputation playing at Cheltenham and Gloucester, and was engaged by Garrick, who brought her on at Drury Lane as Portia in *The Merchant of Venice* on 29 December 1775. Her debut was a failure. She had little more success in her other roles that season, and when she appeared as the original Julia in Bates's opera *The Blackamoor Wash'd White* the play was hissed. Singing and comedy were not to be her forte. When she acted Lady Anne to Garrick's Richard III on 27 May 1776, during his last round of farewell performance, she was intimidated and 'lamentable.' So back to the provinces she went, for more seasoning. After playing at Liverpool and Manchester, she showed the promise of her great powers during several seasons at Bath and Bristol. Richard B. Sheridan, the new manager at Drury Lane, brought her back to London, where on 10 October 1782 she acted the lead in *Isabella, or, The Fatal Marriage* (**749**). All had changed. The house was drenched in tears – a phenomenon that was to occur often during the rest of her career. Sarah achieved a triumph and her portrayal of the pathetic Isabella was called 'infinite.' Other acclaimed performances followed: Euphrasia in *The Grecian Daughter*, Calista in *The Fair Penitent*, Zara in *The Mourning Bride*, Lady Randolph in *Douglas* – all roles in which she would be unequalled. She remained in the Drury Lane company through 1801-2, except for some summers away in the provinces.

Her first performance in London of Lady Macbeth occurred on 2 February 1785 (**742**, **743**, **748**). She set such a magnificent standard in that role that some say it has never been approached. Lamb wrote some years later, 'We speak of Lady Macbeth, while in reality we are thinking of Mrs S.' Her performance of Lady

Macbeth was followed a month later with a portrayal of Desdemona to her brother John's Othello. On 7 February 1792 she was Queen Elizabeth to his Richard III. Among her other great roles were Queen Katharine in *Henry VIII* (**750**), Mrs Beverley in *The Gamester,* Constance in *King John* and Mrs Haller in *The Stranger.*

When John Philip Kemble assumed the management at Covent Garden Theatre in 1803 Mrs Siddons went with him, remaining there through 1811-12. She made her farewell with a round of her famous characters, culminating with Lady Macbeth on 29 June 1812, before a house packed with emotional spectators. After the sleepwalking scene – according to one newspaper reporter, 'the greatest act that in our memory adorned the stage' – the audience applauded for five minutes, and the curtain was then dropped, causing the performance to be concluded at that point. Then she spoke an eight-minute farewell speech. The audience wept and so did brother John. Subsequently, Sarah gave some private readings at Windsor Castle, appeared at Drury Lane on 25 May 1813 to act Mrs Beverley for the benefit of the Theatrical Fund, and she returned to Covent Garden for one night, on 11 June 1813, to act Lady Macbeth for the benefit of her brother Charles Kemble. In November 1815 she acted at Edinburgh for the benefit of the children of her deceased son Henry Siddons, playing Lady Macbeth, Lady Randolph, Constance and other favourite characters.

Though she gave a few more performances over the next several years for various charities, essentially she retired to her residence, Westbourne Farm, in Paddington, receiving friends, writing letters, sculpturing, travelling and generally enjoying her unaccustomed leisure. She left Westbourne Farm in 1817 to reside at No 27, Upper Baker Street, where she died on 8 June 1831, at the age of 76. She was buried in the churchyard of St Mary's, Paddington. Hazlitt lamented, 'She raised tragedy to the skies … Who shall make tragedy once more stand with its feet upon the earth, and with its head raised above the skies, weeping tears and blood?' In 1849 a monument to her was raised in Westminster Abbey, and a small sculpture, modeled after Reynolds's painting of her as the Tragic Muse, was unveiled by Henry Irving on Paddington Green in June 1897.

Mrs Siddons was never the social lioness. In fact, she was somewhat shy and domestic and was not an intellectual. She was a faithful wife to a somewhat uninspiring husband, the pedestrian actor William Siddons, whom she married at Coventry in November 1773. He died at Bath in March 1808. Some dalliances with the artist Thomas Lawrence and an uncharacteristic episode with the fencing master P. Galindo were reported. Harnessed to the world of the theatre, she worked hard most of her life to maintain her family (see the information on them in the *BDA*, vol 14).

As the *BDA* has noted, 'She was a genius in her art, as beautiful as she was talented.' In later years her increased girth sometimes caused her to be stuck in chairs, from which she had to be assisted. But her great beauty is seen in many of the more than 300 portraits and engravings listed in the *BDA*. Most of the leading artists of her day painted her portrait: Thomas Beech, William Beechey, George Clint, Richard Cosway, Samuel De Wilde, Thomas Gainsborough (a fine example of her beauty, at the Tate), William Hamilton, George Henry Harlow, John Hoppner, Thomas Lawrence (who did numerous portraits of the Kemble and Siddons family) and Joshua Reynolds (especially 'The Tragic Muse,' now at the Huntington Art Gallery, with a copy at Dulwich College). A lengthy notice of her is provided in the *BDA*. Other biographies include: James Boaden, *Memoirs of Mrs Siddons* (1827); Yvonne Ffrench, *Mrs Siddons, Tragic Actress* (1953); and, especially, Roger Manvell, *Sarah Siddons, Portrait of an Actress* (1971). Her interesting and revealing correspondence with Hester Lynch Piozzi was edited by Kalman A. Burnim and published in *The Bulletin of the John Rylands Library* 52 (Autumn 1969). Large collections of Sarah's letters are in the Harvard Theatre Collection and in private hands in London.

SHUTER, Edward **740**

1728?-1776

The low comedian Edward Shuter may have been born in 1728 or a few years later. In response to a notice in *Theatrical Biography* in 1772 the wag himself claimed: 'my Mother sold Oysters in the Winter, and Cucumbers in the Summer, yet I do solemnly aver, that I was not born in a Cellar [as the biographer had said], but in a front room up two pairs of stairs, at one Mr. Merit's, an eminent Chimney-Sweeper, in Vere-street, St. Gile's.' He may or may not have been a potboy at age 12, a footboy for the acting Lampes in Preston, a tapster and who knows what and what not, but he certainly was an apprentice to the theatre manager Thomas Chapman at Richmond. He acted the Cook in *Chrononhotonthologos* there on 8 September 1744, and at Covent Garden on 15 April 1745, for Chapman's benefit, Master Shuter played Johnny in *The Schoolboy*. Then he repeated that character at Drury Lane for Morgan's benefit, and on 13 June 1746 Ned, as he was usually called, appeared as Osric in *Hamlet*, with Garrick in the title role. Next came a Witch in *Macbeth* on 27 June. That was a strong beginning for a youngster, even if the roles were small.

Shuter went back to Richmond and Twickenham to act for Chapman and in 1746-47 was in the Hallam troupe (operating illegally at the Gooman's Fields Theatre), playing such secondary roles as Trapland in *Love for Love*, Perriwinkle in *A Bold Stroke for a Wife*, Filch in *The Beggar's Opera*, Syringe in *The Relapse* and Polonius in *Hamlet*. In the summer of 1747 Shuter acted with Samuel Foote at the Haymarket and then Garrick hired him for Drury Lane in the autumn; Ned finally settled in at Covent Garden beginning with the 1753-54 season. Garrick thus lost a promising actor and graciously admitted it. On 21 May 1753 while playing Bayes in *The Rehearsal*, he said to Shuter, who was in some unspecified role, 'you are a good Actor and I am sorry you have left me' – which got 'a Clap' from the audience, according to the prompter Cross. Though Shuter acted occasionally at other venues in and out of London over the years between then and 1775-76, Londoners found him regularly in the winters at Covent Garden under the management of John Rich. That manager's taste ran to pantomimes and comedy and was probably Shuter's main reason for changing companies. Who knows how he would have fared had he stayed under Garrick's tutelage; he clearly needed discipline at Covent Garden, and Rich seems not to have given it.

Among Shuter's popular roles with Rich's troupe were Falstaff in *The Merry Wives of Windsor*, Touchstone in *As You Like It*, Scapin in *The Cheats of Scapin*, Justice Woodcock in *Love in a Village*, Mercutio in *Romeo and Juliet*, Kate Matchlock in *The Funeral*, Statira in *The Rival Queens*, Sir Callaghan O'Brallaghan in *Love à la Mode*, and three of his most notable characters: Scrub in *The Beaux' Stratagem*, the original Hardcastle in *She Stoops to Conquer* and the original Sir Anthony Absolute in *The Rivals*. He had a repertoire of over 200 roles and several related lines: farcical servants, country boobies, aged beaux and squires, eccentrics, highwaymen (and also comical magistrates), burlesque female roles, and comic Irishmen – many of which he augmented with ad libs and buffoonery and some of which he spoiled with drunkenness. His loyal spectators usually forgave his behaviour, unless he was too inebriated to perform, but onstage and off as the years wore on Ned Shuter became his own worst enemy, gross and insensitive, too eager for the approval of the gallery, indiscreet – 'a deplorable object!,' the comedian John Moody called him, referring to some of Shuter's actions in 1775 that were apparently too dreadful for his friends to describe. 'He is very profligate and wicked,' Moody said; 'he has been but once on the stage these six weeks.' More's the pity, for Shuter was truly talented, a natural comedian who played not just farcical characters in plays of little consequence but roles of substance that were a challenge for him and drew from critics of the time extended analyses. But again and again contemporaries registered their disappointment: 'Mr. Shuter has it in his power to be a good comedian,' wrote the critic in *The Theatrical Review* for 1757, 'but he often drops the comedian, to be laughed at as a comical man.' Shuter seems to have been a loose cannon, on and off the stage, too funny for his own good. Shuter died at age 48 or possibly younger, on 1 November 1776.

The portrait of Shuter as Scapin was inadvertently reproduced twice in *Pictures in the Garrick Club*. The picture intended to be Bartley as Hamlet shown with 51 is a repetition of 740. (The portrait reproduced in the *BDA* 13:337 was intended to be that of Shuter as Scapin, but is actually the Garrick Club portrait by Isaac Pocock of George Bartley as Hamlet.) (*BDA*) [EAL]

SHUTER, George **750**
fl. 1817
The Mr Shuter who appears as No. 9 in Harlow's scene of the trial in *Henry VIII* was probably George Shuter, the son of the famous eighteenth-century comedian Edward Shuter. George Shuter was said to be a great favourite at Wolverhampton; his wife and children were also on provincial stages.

SIM, Alastair CBE **751**
1900-1976
Alastair Sim, who made a career of playing eccentrics, was born in Edinburgh on 9 October 1900, the son of Alexander Sim and his wife Isabella (née McIntyre). He left the family tailoring business for the stage, appearing as a messenger in *Othello* at the Savoy in 1930. After playing the Cardinal in *The Venetian* in London and the Old Vic season in New York in 1932-33, Sim appeared in and produced a number of plays by James Birdie. Though his stage appearances were many, including Dandy Dick in Chichester and London in 1973 and Captain Hook in *Peter Pan* in several revivals, it was in films that he became best known. He created a number of memorable characters: the Headmistress (in drag) in *The Belle's of St Trinian's* (1954), Cockerill in *Green for Danger* (1946), Scrooge (1951) and the title role in *An Inspector Calls* (1954), among the most notable in more than 50 films. He also appeared in a television series *Misleading Cases* with Roy Dotrice from 1967 to 1971. In 1951 he received a Hon LLD from Edinburgh University and was Rector of that institution from 1948 to 1951. In 1953 he was honoured with a CBE. Sim became a member of the Garrick Club in 1943. He died on 19 August 1976.

SIMEON, Louisa
See Mrs William CHATTERLEY

SIMMONS, Samuel **752-759**
c.1773 or c.1777-1819
Samuel Simmons seems to have been born about 1773 (though the *DNB* suggests 1777), the son of a house servant at Covent Garden Theatre, and he was first recorded in the playbills on 4 November 1783 as the Boy in *The Poor Soldier*. He was then seen there and at the Haymarket in such childrens' roles as the Duke of York in *Richard III*; by 1793-94 he was no longer called Master Simmons in the bills and had probably just turned 21. Some modern sources confuse him with his father, and his name was occasionally given as Simmonds. In any case, he acted regularly at Covent Garden in minor roles and served as a dancer and singer. By 1814-15 'little' Simmons, as the critic Hazlitt called him, was earning £9 weekly and in demand also at Liverpool. According to the *Authentic Memoirs of the Green Room* Simmons carved a nice niche for himself in three types of comic roles: simpletons, 'forward coxcombry still accompanied with silliness' and 'ridiculous fretfulness.' The little comic with a large talent was pictured most frequently as Beau Mordecai in *Love a la Mode* (**752**, **753**) and Master Matthew in *Every Man in His Humour* (**755**, **756**). His last appearance was as Moses in Sheridan's *The School for Scandal* on 8 September 1819. Three days later he died. (*BDA*)[EAL]

SIMPSON, Elizabeth
See Mrs Joseph INCHBALD

SINCLAIR, John **760, 761**
1791-1857
This singer was born the son of a cotton-spinner in Edinburgh on 9 December 1791. After service in a military band, he made his London debut at the Haymarket Theatre on 7 September 1810 as Cheerly in *Lock and Key*. He later was engaged at Covent Garden, where he sang tenor roles, acquiring great popularity as Apollo on *Midas* (**760**, **761**). He went to Italy for further training in 1819 and received instruction at Naples from Rossini, who wrote the role of Idreno in *Semiramide* for him. Sinclair returned to London and appeared at Covent Garden on 19 November 1823 as Prince Orlando in *The Cabinet*. After engagements at the Adelphi and Drury Lane and a brief visit to America, Sinclair retired to Margate, where for some years he was the director of the Tivoli Gardens. He died at Margate on 23 September 1857. He had married

in 1816 the daughter of Captain Norton. One of Sinclair's daughters was married to the American tragic actor Edwin Forrest.

Sinclair had a fine tenor voice, with a somewhat effeminate style. He composed a number of Scottish songs – 'Come sit ye doon,' 'The Mountain Maid' and 'Johnny Sands' among them – which remain popular today. (*DNB*)

SINDEN, Lady Diana née Mahony 892
b. 1927
Lady Diana Sinden, who is identified as No. 32 in the key to Gilroy's painting of the Garrick Club Outing in 1967, was born Diana Mahoney on 18 July 1927. She married the actor Donald Sinden on 3 May 1948. She is an actress and Vice President of the Theatrical Ladies Guild.

SINDEN, Sir Donald (Alfred) CBE
b. 1923 **762, 965, B90, G0981, G1002**
Donald Sinden was born on 9 October 1923, the son of Alfred Edward Sinden and his wife Mabel Agnes (née Fuller). He made his first stage appearance in 1942 and was with the Leicester Repertory Theatre in 1945, the Shakespeare Memorial Theatre Company at Stratford, 1946-47, the Old Vic and Bristol Old Vic, 1948, and the Haymarket 1949-50. Under contract with the Rank Organisation from 1952 to 1960, he appeared in 23 films, among which were *The Cruel Sea* and *Doctor in the House*. He returned to the theatre, playing in *Odd Man In* at the St Martin's in 1957. Subsequently he has appeared in most major theatres and with companies throughout Britain in a variety of roles ranging from light comedies and farces to classics. His numerous parts have included Lord Foppington in *The Relapse* with the RSC (Aldwych 1967), Malvolio and Henry VIII (Stratford and the Aldwych 1969-70), Sir Harcourt Courtly (**762**) in *London Assurance* (Aldwych 1970, New Theatre 1972, and a tour of America) for which he won a Drama Desk Award, Stockman in An *Enemy of the People* (Chichester 1975), Benedick in *Much Ado about Nothing* (Stratford and Aldwych 1976-77), King Lear (Stratford and Aldwych 1976-77), for which he received the *Evening Standard* and the Variety Club Award for Best Actor, 1977, and Othello (Stratford and Aldwych 1979-80). He continues to grace the London stage at this writing.

He received the CBE in 1979 and was knighted in 1997. Sir Donald's services to his profession include: Trustee, British Actors Equity Association (1982-), Arts Council Drama Panel (1973-1977), London Academy of Music and Dramatic Art Council (1976-), Arts Council of Great Britain (1982-1986), Chairman British Theatre Museum Association (1971-1977) and Theatre Museum Advisory Council (1973-1980). He is currently (since 1983) President of the Royal Theatrical Fund. His books include *A Touch of the Memoirs* (autobiography, 1982), *Laughter in the Second Act* (autobiography, 1985), *The Everyman Book of Theatrical Anecdotes* (ed. 1987), *The English Country Church* (1988) and *The Last Word* (ed. 1994). He joined the Garrick Club in 1960 and was a Trustee 1980-2000. (WW; see also Burnim and Wilton, *The Richard Bebb Collection in the Garrick Club*, B90)

SKEFFINGTON, Sir Lumley St George, Bart 763
1771-1850
The fop and playwright Skeffington was the son of Sir William Charles Skeffington and was born in St Pancras on 23 March 1771. He socialized and dined in select circles and earned a reputation as a fancy and eccentric dresser; in *English Bards and Scotch* Reviewers, Byron treated him with irony for his habits. In the early 1800s Skeffington had several of his plays produced in London without much success: among them were *Word of Honour* (Covent Garden, May 1802), *The High Road to Marriage* (Drury Lane, May 1803) and *Maids and Bachelors* (Covent Garden, June 1806). He succeeded to his baronetcy in 1815. His reckless extravagance soon dissipated the family fortune, and after some years of incarceration in the King's Bench he lived quietly in south London, adorned by false hair and rouged cheeks. He died in Southwark on 10 November 1850, without issue, and his title became extinct. (*DNB*)

SMITH, Sir Charles Aubrey CBE
1863-1948 **764, G0995**
C. Aubrey Smith was born on 21 July 1863, the son of the physician Charles John Smith and his

wife Sarah Ann (née Clode). He was educated at Charterhouse and Cambridge. At the latter place he was a talented cricketer. Later he became captain of the Sussex team and also led English teams in Australia and South Africa. Smith is better remembered for his long and distinguished film career, but his stage career was also estimable. He first acted in Hastings in 1892, did some touring and made his London debut on 13 March 1895 at the Garrick Theatre as the Rev Amos Winterfield in *The Notorious Mrs Ebbsmith*. From then until 1943 he was seen on the stages of England and America in numerous roles, often as a distinguished and wise older man, in which manner he is captured in Gilroy's picture (**764**). Some of his parts were Gilbert Torpenhow in *The Light that Failed* (**G0995**), Sir Arthur Little in *Caesar's Wife*, Henry Higgins in *Pygmalion*, George Marden in *Mr Pim Passes By*, Sir John Dorle in *Mixed Doubles*, John Middleton in *The Constant Wife* and Sir Travers Ryecroft in *The Way to Treat a Woman*. He began his cinema career in silent films in 1915 and was seen in many films into the 1940s. He eventually settled in Beverly Hills, California, where he died on 20 December 1948 at the age of 85. Smith received the CBE in 1938 and was knighted in 1944. He had become a member of the Garrick Club in 1906. He was also a member of the Green Room, the Players (NY), and the Masquers (Hollywood). (*WWWT*)

SMITH, Clara Ann
See Clara Ann DIXON

SMITH, George **765**
1777-1836?
George Smith was born in London in 1777, the son of a successful tradesman. He had a good singing voice as a boy and was in St Paul's choir until his voice broke. After an apprenticeship with a stationer he returned to performing and was perhaps the G. Smith who was an archer in *William Tell* at Sadler's Wells on 12 May 1794. Regular singing engagements followed at Vauxhall Gardens and the Wells and at the Royal Circus, the Amphitheatre in Peter Street (Dublin), Manchester, and finally Drury Lane, on 10 October 1806, when he sang Hodge in *Love in a Village*. Other favourite parts were Peter in *Up All Night* (**765**), Father Luke in *The Poor Soldier* and, in Edinburgh in 1819, Macheath in *The Beggar's Opera* and Young Meadows in *Love in a Village*. Wheeler, the stage doorkeeper at Sadler's Wells, reported that Smith did not get along in his profession because of his idleness and sottishness and gradually declined into chorus parts. George Smith may have died in 1836. (*BDA*) [EAL]

SMITH, Hannah Waldo
See Hannah ASTLEY

SMITH, Mrs Theodore, Maria née Harris
fl. 1772-1796 **768**
Born Maria Harris, this actress was already the wife of the composer Theodore Smith by the time she made her debut at Drury Lane on 20 October 1772 as Sylvia in *Cymon*, the role in which she is depicted by De Wilde (**768**). She received enthusiastic applause and played with similar success Clarissa in *The School for Fathers*, Laura in *The Chaplet*, Helen in *Cymbeline* and Leonora in *The Padlock*, among other roles. She remained at Drury Lane through 1784-85 in a similar line, adding such roles as Perdita in *Florizal and Perdita* and Rosetta in *Love in a Village*. William Hawkins described her in his *Miscellanies* (1775) as having 'a smart little figure, with an admirable sweet musical voice.' Her interpretation of Ophelia and her singing in that role were admired by the German visitor Lichtenberg. According to one memoir Mrs Smith ran off with a Mr Bishop after retiring from the stage in 1774. But in January 1776 she was still with her husband when their son was christened. She was still alive in January 1796. (*BDA*)

SMITH, Richard **59**
fl. 1741?-1781?
The Richard Smith who is identified by Ashton as the Messenger in Mortimer's painting of a scene from *King John* (**59**) was probably the actor of that name who is noticed in the *BDA* (14: 155-57). He appeared regularly as a utility actor (often 'a walking gentleman') at the Haymarket and Covent Garden in the 1760s and 1770s. The *BDA* reproduces the picture and states that the figure on the right is Robert Bensley as Hubert,

and the figure left with right arm extended is William Smith as the Bastard. Ashton calls that latter figure Robert Bensley as Hubert. Valentine's engraving does not solve the matter, as it identifies only two of the three figures: Bensley as Hubert (presumably on the left) and Powell as King John (center). The figure on the right is not captioned.

SMITH, Richard John **766**
1786-1855
Richard Smith, known as O. Smith, was baptized at St Michael le Belfry, York, on 26 February 1786. He was the sixth child of the actor Walter Smith (1732-1809) and his actress wife Henrietta (1752-1822), the daughter of Richard and Martha Scarse. Both of Richard Smith's parents acted on the London stage in the eighteenth century and are noticed in the *BDA*. Richard Smith is said to have started his theatrical career playing juvenile roles at Bath. After touring with provincial companies and acting at Edinburgh and Glasgow, he was engaged at the Surrey Theatre in 1810 for the pantomimes. His performance of Obi in the melodrama *Three-fingered Jack* earned him the sobriquet of 'O' – otherwise Obi – Smith. Playing mostly demons, monsters, assassins, and the like, Smith appeared throughout his career at the Lyceum, Drury Lane, Covent Garden and the Adelphi. He was the first Zamiel in Soane's adaptation of *Der Freischütz* at Drury Lane on 10 November 1824, and he acted the title role in *Don Quixote* (**766**) at the Adelphi in January 1833. Smith accumulated a large amount of theatrical prints, cuttings, magazine articles, playbills and memoirs that now form under his name a twenty-five- volume 'Collection of Materials Towards a History of the Stage' at the British Library. He died on 1 February 1855 and was buried in Norwood cemetery.

SMITH, Sarah, later Mrs George Bartley, née Williamson **767**
1783?-1850
There is conflicting information about the parentage and early years of this actress, but she seems to have been born in 1783, the daughter of a country actor named Williamson and his wife, who was supposedly the daughter of General Dillon of Galway. Some testimony suggests that Sarah's surname was actually O'Shaugnessy. In any event, she adopted the stage name of Miss Smith, apparently after her mother's second marriage, when she appeared in Salisbury as Edward in *Every One Has His Fault.* She was 16 when she played Joanna in *The Deserted Daughter* at Liverpool. After some years at Edinburgh, York, Birmingham and Bath, she made her debut at Covent Garden on 2 October 1805 as Lady Townley in *The Provok'd Husband.* Later her reputation was enhanced when she recited Collins's 'Ode to the Passions,' memorialized by De Wilde's drawing (**767**). Though she continued in London as a successful tragic actress, Miss Smith was overshadowed first by Mrs Siddons and then by Eliza O'Neill. She joined Drury Lane in January 1813, and on 23 August 1814 she married the actor George Bartley. She went with him to America in 1818 and returned to England in 1820 to act in the country and then again in London. After suffering some years with paralysis, she died in London on 14 January 1850. Sarah Smith's finest characters were Belvidera in *Venice Preserv'd* and Estifania in *Rule a Wife and Have a Wife.* Leigh Hunt highly praised her genius for high tragedy and low comedy. (*DNB*)

SMITH, Susan
See Mrs Edward KNIGHT

SMITH, William **3, 769**
1730-1819
William Smith was born in London on 22 February 1730, the son of the wholesale grocer William Smith (1700-1782). He received some education at Eton, but left there because of improprieties while drunk and went to St John's College, Cambridge. With his tall figure and good looks, Smith opted for the stage, appearing for the first time, at Covent Garden, in the title role of *Theodosius* on 8 January 1753, when he was announced as 'a Gentleman.' He was supported by Mrs Cibber as Athenais and Spranger Barry as Varanes. Thus Smith began a career at Covent Garden, where he was to remain for twenty years before he moved over to work under Garrick at

Drury Lane beginning on 22 September 1774. During those years he played numerous roles, mainly in comedies, in which he excelled as the fashionable gentleman and earned the sobriquet 'Gentleman Smith.' He became a solid favourite of audiences in such roles as Loveless in *The Relapse*, Heartfree in *The Provok'd Wife* and Oakly in *The Jealous Wife*. In the earlier part of his career he had success in playing roles in tragedy: Edgar in *King Lear*, Macbeth, Osman in *Zara*, Richard III and Valasquez in *Braganza*, among others. His greatest role, and one probably written by Sheridan with Smith in mind, was the original Charles Surface in *The School for Scandal* at Drury Lane on 8 May 1777 (**3**).

After Garrick's retirement in 1776, Smith remained at Drury Lane until his retirement in June 1788. He spent the following 30 years in relative good health, enjoying the races, hunting and the company of friends of gentility and nobility. He died on 13 September 1819, at age 89, leaving an estate valued at some £18,000. Smith's skills were summarized by one critic, who praised his ease, elegance and vivacity: 'being the unaffected gentleman in private life, he is necessarily so on the stage.' (*BDA*)

SNOW, Sophia
See Mrs Robert BADDELEY

SOTHERN, Edward Askew
1826-1881 **770, 771, B91, B92, G1017**
This popular actor, the son of a merchant and ship owner, was born in Liverpool on 1 April 1826. Using the stage name Douglas Stuart, he made his professional debut in 1849 at St Helier, Jersey, as Claude Melnotte in *The Lady of Lyons*. In engagements at St Helier, Weymouth and Birmingham, he acted a large number of roles, including Hamlet. In the early 1850s he went to America, playing in Boston, Washington, Baltimore and other cities. He then settled in Lester Wallack's company in New York. During his four years with Wallack he changed his name from Stuart to Sothern. Subsequently he joined Laura Keene's company, in which he acted many roles, mainly in light comedy, including Charles Surface, Bob Acres, Benedick, and Charles Courtley in *London Assurance*. At Laura Keene's Theatre on 12 May 1858 he played the small part of Lord Dundreary (**770**, **771**, **G1017**, **B91**) in Tom Taylor's *Our American Cousin*, a role that eventually became his signature part. In that role he made his London debut on 11 November 1861 at the Haymarket Theatre. Although the production was not well received at first, it eventually caught on and ran 496 nights. Sothern developed his role into a series of monologues. The Dundreary whiskers became a fashion, as did the character's attire. After a few more parts, in April 1864 Sothern acted the title role in *David Garrick*, which became another very popular character. Sothern continued to act in England, mainly in the provinces, until he returned to America in 1874. He reappeared at the Haymarket in London in May 1878. By 1880 his health and popularity had waned. He died in his house in Vere Street, Cavendish Square, on 21 January 1881. Sothern was a confirmed wag and prankster and good company. He had many aristocratic friends with whom he often shared his fine stable of horses. He became a member of the Garrick Club in 1864. He wrote *Stranger than Fiction* and *The Light that Lies in Woman's Eyes*, plays that were seen in New York. His sons Lytton Edward Sothern (1856-1887) and Edward H. Sothern (1859-1933) were both actors in London for a while, and the latter became especially popular in romantic comedies in America. (*DNB*; see also Burnim and Wilton, *The Richard Bebb Collection in the Garrick Club*, Nos B91, B92)

SPENCER, Mrs
See Mrs Alexander POPE

SPENCER, Lord Charles **600**
1740-1820
The person identified as 'C. Spencer/Manager' in Nixon's drawing of the Green Room in the theatre of the Royal Kentish Bowmen (**600**) is probably Lord Charles Spencer, who appeared in private theatricals at Blenheim organized by his brother George, fourth Duke of Marlborough. (*See* Sybil Rosenfeld, *Temples of Thespis*, 1978.) Charles Spencer, the second son of Charles Spencer, third Duke of Marlborough (1706-1758), was MP for Oxfordshire from 1761 to 1784 and from 1796 to 1801. He held many important posts during his

career in government, including treasurer of the king's chamber, lord of the admiralty and postmaster general. He died at Petersham on 16 June 1820.

SPENCER, William Robert **600**
1769-1834
The poet and wit William Robert Spencer, who is identified as one of the figures in Nixon's drawing of the green room of the theatre of the Royal Kentish Bowmen, was born in 1769 the younger son of Lord Charles Spencer (1740-1820), who is noticed above. He appeared in private theatricals organized at Blenhein by his uncle George, the fourth Duke of Marlborough. Educated at Harrow and at Christ Church, Oxford (no degree), he served as commissioner of stamps from 1797 to 1826. He was very popular in London society and followed no career in public life but published a variety of verses, translations and prologues. His burlesque *Urania* was performed at Drury Lane in 1802. In his later years he lived in poverty and poor health in Paris, where he died on 24 October 1834. (*DNB*)

STANTON, Charlotte
See Mrs Thomas GOODALL

STEPHENS, Catherine, Countess of Essex
1794-1882 **750, 773-776**
Born in London on 18 September 1794, Catherine Stephens was the daughter of Edward Stephens, a wood carver and gilder in Park Street, Grosvenor Square. She was placed under the singing tutor Gesualdo Lanza in 1807, and during her five years with him she sang in concerts in Bath, Bristol, Margate, Southampton and other places. In 1812 Thomas Welsh became her teacher, and on 23 September 1813 Catherine made her debut at Covent Garden as Mandane in *Artaxerxes* (**773**). She met with immediate success and was compared favourably to the divas Catalani and Billington. She next sang Polly in *The Beggar's Opera* on 22 October and Clara in *The Duenna* on 12 November. In 1814 she appeared at the Concert of Antient Music and at the festivals in Norwich and Birmingham. As a principal performer at Covent Garden until 1822, Miss Stephens was seen and heard in a number of important roles with conspicuous success: among them were Mrs Cornflower in *The Farmer's Wife*, Ophelia to the Hamlets of J. P. Kemble and C. M. Young, Sylvia in *Cymon* and Hermia in *A Midsummer Night's Dream*. On 12 March 1818 she was the original Diana Vernon in *Rob Roy Macgregor* (**774**, **775**) and on 16 March 1819 she played Susanna in the first production of *The Marriage of Figaro* at Covent Garden. In 1822-23 she joined Elliston's company at Drury Lane, appearing on 20 February 1824 as Mrs Ford in Reynolds's operatic version of *The Merry Wives of Windsor* (**776**). She returned to Covent Garden in 1827-28. She also earned a great reputation as a concert singer, featured in various concerts and festivals throughout the kingdom. She retired in 1835 and on 19 April 1838 she married George Capell Coningsby, fifth Earl of Essex. He was an octogenarian widower who died soon after, on 23 April 1839, and as the Countess of Essex she was able to live in comfort for another 43 years. She died at No 9, Belgrave Square on 22 February 1882 and was buried in Kensal Green. She was said to have 'the sweetest soprano voice of her time' and was reportedly unequalled as a ballad singer. Of her Polly and Mandane Leigh Hunt wrote, they 'are like nothing else on the stage, and leave all competition far behind.' In addition to her pictures in the Garrick Club, her portraits were painted by John Linnell and Sir William Newton; a portrait of her by John Jackson is in the National Portrait Gallery. One of her sisters made a debut as Polly in *The Beggar's Opera* at Drury Lane on 29 November 1798 and appeared in other roles through 1801; she was judged an extremely fine singer, with a voice unequalled except by Mrs Bland. In 1806 she married the singer George Smith. Mrs Smith seems to have died in 1828, without achieving any of the lasting reputation enjoyed by her sister Catherine. *See* the *BDA* 14: 260-61. (*DNB*)

STERLING, Clara Ann
See Clara Ann DIXON

STEEVENS, George **772**
1736-1800
This editor and scholar of Shakespeare was

widely read in Elizabethan literature. He was a friend of Garrick, who provided him with quartos of Shakespeare's plays from his fine library. In 1766 Steevens published an edition of twenty of Shakespeare's plays and in 1773 a complete and annotated edition in ten volumes 'with the corrections and illustrations of various commentators; to which are added, notes by Samuel Johnson and George Steevens.' He often quarreled with his literary associates. *See* Arthur Sherbo, *The Achievement of George Steevens* (1990). In *PGC* Ashton states that Steevens is noticed in the *BDA*. But he is not; Ashton confused him with the entertainer and manager George Alexander Stevens (1710-1784).

STIRLING, Mary Anne later Lady Gregory, née Kehl **777, 778, 804**
1815-1895
This actress whose career spanned much of the middle part of the nineteenth century was born Mary Anne (but called Fanny) Kehl in Queen Street, Mayfair, in July 1815. Her father was Capt Kehl of the Horse Guards and military secretary with the War Office. Using the name Fanny Clifton, she made appearances in the early 1830s at the Coburg, Surrey, East London and Pavilion theatres. At the Pavilion she met the country actor Edward Stirling (or Lambert), a player of 'walking gentlemen,' whom she married and accompanied to theatres in Liverpool, Manchester and Birmingham. As Mrs Stirling she returned to London to appear in the West End at the Adelphi. Subsequently she was seen in many soubrette and low comedy roles at various London theatres, including the St James's, Strand, Haymarket and Drury Lane. Among her more important later roles were Cordelia, Katharine in *The Taming of the Shrew*, Lady Teazle, Lady Bountiful in *The Beaux' Stratagem*, Mrs Hardcastle in *She Stoops to Conquer* and the Nurse in *Romeo and Juliet* (with Ellen Terry as Juliet, **804**). Perhaps her greatest success was as Peg Woffington in *Masks and Faces* (1852), the role in which she is pictured by Phillips (**778**). Another excellent portrayal was as Maritana in *Don Cesar de Bazan* (1841).

Mrs Stirling retired from the stage in 1885. Her husband, from whom she had separated, died in August 1894. He had written some 200 pieces, mainly burlesques, farces and melodramas that were seen at various London theatres. Later in 1894 she married Sir Charles Hutton Gregory, consulting engineer to the crown agents for the colonies, with whom she had been living for some time. Lady Gregory died on 31 December 1895, leaving an estate of £11,556 to her second husband. By all accounts she was an excellent actress, somewhat extravagant in style, especially in comedy. (*DNB*)

STORACE, Ann Selina, later Mrs John Abraham Fisher the second
1765-1817 **779,780**
Ann (or Anna) Storace, known as Nancy, was born on 27 October 1765 in London, the daughter of Stefano (or Stephen) Storace, an Italian musician who had come from Naples to England as early as 1747. Her mother was Elizabeth Trusler, the daughter of the proprietor of Marylebone Gardens, one of London's musical pleasure gardens; she married Storace in 1761, when Stephen was director of the band there. In this musical family also was Nancy's brother Stephen, who became a composer and conductor. Nancy received her initial musical training from her father and then from Sacchini and Rauzzini, two of the best Italian musicians in England. Nancy may have made her first public appearance as a singer in Southampton in August 1773, and the two youthful Storaces were at the Salisbury music festival in October, Nancy singing and Stephen playing the violin to responsive audiences and critics. The next year she sang at the Haymarket Theatre in London, and in 1777 she is known to have participated in the oratorios at Covent Garden and taken the role of Cupido in Rauzzini's *L'ali d'amore* at the King's Theatre. She made appearances in Brighton and at the Hereford Three Choirs Festival and, in 1778, was in London again before heading off to Naples with her parents.

Her stay on the Continent lasted nine years and saw her in Naples, Florence, Leghorn, Parma, Milan, and, in 1783, Vienna, where the family stayed for four years. Nancy was not yet twenty, but her singing in Italy and Austria was attracting audiences and gaining her a good press: one Vienna critic was quite taken with her: 'She united in her person, like none other alive, and only a few singers of the past, all the gifts of nature, education, and technique which one may desire for performance in Italian comic opera.' And under the noses of her parents in 1783 the eighteen-year-old found herself an English husband in Vienna, the musician John Abraham Fisher. Her choice was a disaster, and the marriage quickly fell apart. When the Emperor Joseph II heard how badly Fisher treated his wife, he threw Fisher out of Austria. Meanwhile, close to hand was Mozart, with whom she had what was apparently a platonic relationship. He dashed off some vocal works for her and cast her as Susanna in *Le Nozze di Figaro* in 1786. She was just 21.

Nancy and her brother were engaged at the King's Theatre back in London in the spring of 1787. On 24 April she made her reappearance in London, singing Gelinda in *Gli schiavi per amore*, produced by her brother. Considering her considerable reputation in Vienna and the fact that composers of stature there had been, as Mozart was, much taken with her voice, Nancy's reception back in London was not warm. Dr Burney, for example, thought her voice had 'a certain crack and toughness' that made it less than ideal for a serious singer. According to Stephen Storace, the Italians in London, including the composer Cherubini, believed that anyone not born in Italy could not be a singer.

On 24 November 1789 at Drury Lane she was Adela in the première of Cobb's *The Haunted Tower* (**779**), which received 56 performances that season; Nancy was paid £10 per night and established herself as one of London's favourite singers. Though she did not abandon Italian opera, the rest of her career was devoted chiefly to popular musical theatre pieces like *No Song No Supper, The Cherokee*, *The Duenna*, *The Spanish Barber*, *Mahmoud* and *The Iron Chest*. What she had, in addition to a charming voice, was an 'enchanting vivacity' – friskiness, the *Public Advertiser* called it – that more than made up for her plain features and awkward stage movement. She was sometimes arrogant in her behaviour, however; in 1794 she refused to perform for their majesties at Buckingham Palace, saying she was 'better engaged.'

Nancy did not marry again after the disintegration of her relationship with Fisher, but in the 1790s she fell in love with the singer John Braham, 12 years her junior, and had some happy years singing (often with him) in musical theatre works. They toured the Continent, and returned to perform at London's major patent houses. She made her farewell appearance at Drury Lane on 30 May 1808 as Floretta in *The Cabinet* and retired to Dulwich. Braham left her in 1816 to marry a Mrs Wright, leaving Nancy quite shattered. She died on 24 August 1817. (*BDA*) [EAL]

STUART, Douglas
See Edward SOTHERN

SUETT, Richard **42, 781-783**
c. 1758?-1805
Born about 1758 in Chelsea, Richard Suett was the son of John Suett, a butcher. Young Suett seems to have been given training in church choirs and performance experience at pleasure gardens and at the Haymarket Theatre, but the earliest certain note of him as a professional was on 22 June 1771, as Master Suett, at the Grotto Gardens in a musical piece called *The Gamester*. Then he joined Tate Wilkinson's troupe at York as a singer, and in 1773-74 his name appeared on the bills as Mr Suett. Word reached London of Suett's talent as singer and actor, and Drury Lane hired him to appear on 7 October 1780 as Ralph in *The Maid of the Mill* and then Squire Richard in *The Provok'd Husband*, Mungo in *The Padlock*, Moll Flagon in *The Lord of the Manor* and other parts.

Drury Lane became Suett's home base for the rest of his career, and he amassed dozens of roles there, including Filch in *The Beggar's Opera*, Dick in *The Lying Valet*, Waitwell in *The Way of the World*, Lord Plausible in *The Plain Dealer*, Feste in *Twelfth Night*, Touchstone in *As You Like It*, Hardcastle in *She Stoops to Conquer* and many more. He was also a popular comedian at the Haymarket in the summers. By his last season with the Drury Lane troupe, 1804-5, he was earning £12 weekly.

Dicky Suett, as he was called in his day, was a sociable, heavy-drinking man with a 'tall, thin, ungainly figure' that was ideal for the kind of low comedy he liked to play, but he seems to have lacked the skill – or understanding – to give his comic creations much depth, as William Parsons of the previous generation had been able to do on occasion. But audiences loved Dicky for his mugging (another Parson trait), his ad-libbing and his interpolated 'O La!' that could trap a clap. Charles Lamb told the story that on his deathbed (on 6 July 1805) Dicky's last words, to his actor-friend Robert Palmer, who was at his bedside, were just that: 'O La! O La! Bobby!' (*BDA*) [EAL]

SUMBEL, Mary
See Mary WELLS

SUSSEX, Augustus Frederick, Duke of 784
1773-1843
Augustus Frederick, the sixth son of King George III and Queen Charlotte, was born at Buckingham Palace on 27 January 1773. He spent much of his youth abroad, studying at Göttingen University and developing intellectual tastes. While in Rome in 1793 he married Lady Augusta Murray, daughter of the fourth Earl of Dunmore, in a ceremony conducted by a clergyman of the Church of England. The marriage ceremony was repeated that December at St George, Hanover Square, under the names of Augustus Frederick and Augusta Murray, but was annulled by the King. Prince Augustus generally ignored the ban and had two children by Augusta Murray. In 1801 he was made Baron Arklow, Earl of Inverness and Duke of Sussex. He incurred the displeasure of his father again by his liberal views supporting abolition of the slave trade, removal of restrictions on Jews, Catholic emancipation and reform of Parliament, among other causes. He was elected President of the Society of Arts in 1816 and served as President of the Royal Society 1830-1839. He was highly sought after as chairman of anniversary dinners. The Duke, who had remarried, to Lady Cecilia, daughter of the Earl of Erran, died from erysipelas on 21 April 1843 and was buried at his request at Kensal Green Cemetery. As one of the founding members of the Garrick Club in 1831, he was a moving force in its formation and was its first Patron. (*DNB*)

SUTRO, Alfred OBE G1010
1863-1933
The dramatist Alfred Sutro was born in London on 7 August 1863, the son of the physician Sigismund Sutro. He was educated at the City of London School and in Brussels. He wrote a number of plays, many of which were highly successful, including *The Cave of Illusion* (1900), *Freedom* (1916), *A Marriage has been Arranged* (1904), *The Perfect Lover* (1905), *The Laughing Lady* (1922) and *A Man with a Heart* (1925). Sutro became a member of the Garrick Club in March 1906; he was also a member of the Beefsteak Club. In 1918 he was honoured with an OBE. His wife, Esther Stella Sutro (author of *Nicolas Poussin*, 1923), was the daughter of J. M. Isaacs, of South Knoll, Upper Norwood. Sutro died on 11 September 1933. (*WWWT*)

SWETE, E. Lyall 785
1865-1930
The writer, director and performer E. Lyall Swete was born in Wrington, Somerset, on 25 July 1865, the son of the physician Edward Horace Walker Swete and his wife Sara Ann (née Bailey). He was educated at Trinity College, Stratford-upon-Avon, and Worcester Cathedral School. He made his first appearance on the stage at Margate on 26 September 1787 in *The Road to Ruin*, and after some years of touring he joined Benson's company at the Lyceum, where he made his London debut as Michael Williams in *Henry V* on 15 February 1900. Subsequently, until 1928, he appeared in dozens of plays in the West End and on Broadway, and he also wrote and directed. Among his numerous roles were Polonius in Oscar Ashe's production of *Hamlet* at the Adelphi in 1905 (with Irving as Hamlet), Enobarbus in Benson's production of *Antony and Cleopatra* at the Lyceum in 1900, Frank Thompson in *Outward Bound* at the Garrick in 1923 and Cardinal Wolsey in *Henry VIII* at the Empire in 1925. He wrote among other pieces *Clare de Lune*, Empire, New York 1921 (for Ethel and John Barrymore, and also acted Ursus), *Aphrodite* (New York 1919, also directed), *A Burgomeister of Belgium* (New York 1919, also acted the title role) and *Miss Elizabeth's Prisoner* (Imperial 1903, also acted Mr Valentine). The

last play he directed was *Payment* at the Arts in 1928. He joined the Garrick Club in 1904. Swete was married to Ethel Mary Brough, daughter of the author William Brough.

Swete died in London on 19 February 1930.

SYLVESTER HAY, Harriet
See Mrs John LITCHFIELD

SYNGE, Captain C. E. **793**
d. 1871
Captain C. E. Synge, who is shown as No. 2 in O'Neil's picture of members in the Billiards Room, was elected to the Garrick Club on 6 January 1855, when he gave his address as the Army & Navy Club. He died in February 1871.

T

TALFOURD, Sir Thomas Noon **786**
1795-1854
Thomas Talfourd, who was an original member of the Garrick Club when it was formed in 1831, was born on 26 May 1795 at Reading, the son of Edward Talfourd, a brewer, and his wife, who was the daughter of the minister Thomas Noon. Talfourd combined careers in law and literature, publishing *Poems on Various Subjects* and a number of essays. Talfourd also wrote theatrical criticisms for the press. He was in the same circle as Hazlitt, Godwin and Wordsworth. In 1817 he was called to the Bar from the Middle Temple and became recognized as an excellent lawyer and orator. In July 1849 he was elevated to the bench in the Court of Common Pleas, an office he filled with great efficiency until his death on 13 March 1854. He had also been elected MP for Reading in 1835, 1837 and 1847. As a man of letters he was best known for his tragedy *Ion*, which was produced by Macready on 26 May 1836. In addition to the portrait by Lucas (**786**), a portrait of him by Pickersill is in the National Portrait Gallery and a bust of him by Lough was placed in the Crown Court at Stratford. (*DNB*)

TANNER, Stella
See Mrs Patrick CAMPBELL

TAYLEURE, John **787**
1782-1861
John Tayleure, who appears as Tag in Clint's scene from the *Spoiled Child* (**787**), acted in London and probably in Scotland during the early decades of the nineteenth century. By 1834, Tayleure kept a shop near St Martin-in-the Fields Church, where he sold theatrical pictures and autographs. He also published prints and lithographs, including an engraving (by T. Landseer, after E. Prentis) of his wife Jane Tayleure as Mrs Grimley and a lithograph (by G. E. Madeley) of her as Madame la Marquise de Viellecour in *Promotion*. Tayleure seems to have stocked his shop with prints from Charles

Mathews' collection. One of his regular customers was John Dillon, a playwright, who was a partner in the firm of Morrison, Dillon and Company. John Dillon was the complier of the print collection that came to the Garrick Club through Sir Charles Ibbetson. John Tayleure, who was not a member of the Garrick Club, died on 28 March 1861. A portrait of Tayleure was engraved by R. Grave, after T. Hargreaves. Tayleure is also shown on an anonymous lithograph of a song sheet of 'That Says Nothing,' published at Glasgow, 1822; he holds a copy of 'The New Marriage Act.'

TAYLOR, Charles **788-791**
1781-1847
A native of Bath, where his mother kept a tavern, Charles Taylor performed in provincial theatres until he made his first appearance in London as William in *Guilty or Not Guilty?* at the Haymarket in 1804. Later that year he engaged at Covent Garden, first appearing as Lubin in *The Quaker* (**789**). He became a noted mimic and imitator of country performers. Other favourite roles included Canton in *The Clandestine Marriage* and Major Galbraith in *Rob Roy Macgregor*. Taylor became a member of the Garrick Club in December 1831, the year the Club was formed. He resigned in 1845.

TAYLOR, Sir Charles **792, 793**
1817-1876
When he was proposed for membership in the Garrick Club on 16 March 1847, Charles Taylor gave his address as the Athenaeum Club. He was admitted on 30 April. In his letters Thackeray wrote of him as a friend. Taylor served on the Committee in the 1850s, during the period of the controversy between Thackeray and Dickens over the admission of Edmund Yates. At the Committee meeting on 20 March 1888 it was proposed that members be allowed to invite guests for luncheon in the Visitor's Room and that 'sixpence be charged for each person at the Table.' The motioned carried 8 to 4. But the amendment to the motion that luncheon be limited to mutton chops, cold meat or sandwiches was defeated, 6 for, 7 against. Taylor died in 1876.

TAYLOR, Harriette Deborah, later Mrs Walter Lacy **952**
1807-1874
Born in London in 1807, the daughter of a tradesman, Harriette Taylor first appeared at the Bath Theatre in November 1827 and quickly became popular, playing such roles as Julia in *The Rivals*, Portia in *The Merchant of Venice* and Lady Macbeth. On October 30 1830 she made her London debut at Covent Garden as Nina in *Carnival of Naples*. She was successful as Rosalind in *As You Like It* and in other roles. After acting under Ben Webster's management at the Haymarket in 1837, she went back to Covent Garden in August 1838 to act under Macready's management. She played Lady Teazle in *The School for Scandal*, a production in which Charles Surface was acted by Walter Lacy, whom she soon married, and now acting as Mrs Lacy she played a series of capital roles in comedy and tragedy. She excelled as Juliet in *Romeo and Juliet* and in the title role of Jerrold's *Nell Gwynne*. She made her farewell from the stage at the Olympic in 1848 and died in Brighton on 28 July 1874. (*DNB*)

TEARLE, Sir Godfrey Seymour **202**
1884-1953
Godfrey Tearle was born in New York on 12 October 1884, the son of the Shakespearean actor Osmond Tearle (1852-1901) and his second wife Marianne Conway, the daughter of the American actor F. B. Conway. He began his stage career in 1893 by acting in his father's company. Tearle had a long and distinguished career on stage and in films. Some of his roles were Maddoc Thomas in *The Light of Heart* (1940), Antony in *Antony and Cleopatra* (**202**, London 1947 and New York 1948), Othello and Macbeth (Stratford 1948-49) and Sloper in *The Heiress* (1950). He also produced some plays as actor-manager. In 1951 he received a knighthood for his services to the stage. He had a four-year relationship with the actress Jill Bennett (*q.v.*), whom he had met when they were performing at the Royal Shakespeare Theatre in Stratford in 1949. In 1983 Jill Bennett published *Godfrey: A Special Time Remembered*. Tearle became a member of the Garrick Club in 1923. He died on 8 June 1953. (*WWW, OCT*)

TEMPEST, Dame Marie Susan 794, 795
1866-1942
Marie Tempest was born in London on 15 July 1866, the daughter of Edwin and Sarah Etherington. After making her first appearances in musical comedy beginning in 1885, she took on regular comedy roles in 1899 and was seen as Nell Gwyn in *English Nell* in 1900 and Becky Sharp in 1901. She played numerous roles for more than 50 years on the stage in London, New York and on extensive tours throughout the world. Among her many charming portrayals were Judith Bliss in *Hay Fever*, Olivia in *Mr Pim Passes By* and Mrs Nolan in *Midsummer Madness* (the role in which Sherington depicted her, **795**). In 1935 she celebrated her stage jubilee with a command performance at Drury Lane before George V and Queen Mary with scenes from *The Marriage of Kitty* and *Little Catherine*. She was made DBE in 1937 and died on 14 October 1942. (*OCT*)

TENDUCCI, Giusto Ferdinando 796
c. 1735-1790
Born about 1735 in Siena (and thus sometimes called Senesino), Giusto Tenducci became at age nine a *castrato* to preserve his singing voice. He performed at Venice in *Ginevra* in 1753 and at Naples in *Farnace* in 1756 – and presumably elsewhere in other operas in between, for he gained enough fame to be engaged in 1758 at the King's Theatre in London. There, on 11 November, Tenducci sang Idaspe, the second man, in Galuppi's *Attalo*. The following January he participated in *Il Ciro riconoscuito* and *Il trionfo della gloria* to critical acclaim. He toured to the Theatre Royal, Norwich, and returned to London for engagements at the King's Theatre, the Haymarket and various concert halls. Then things went wrong. Tenducci was arrested for debt in 1761 and received compassionate benefits arranged by his cohorts. He then apparently went to Scotland but returned to London, to Covent Garden Theatre in late 1761 to sing in Arne's *Artaxerxes*, and during the rest of the 1760s he appeared at Ranelagh Gardens, Covent Garden, the Lock Hospital, the King's Theatre, Smock Alley Theatre in Dublin, Edinburgh, Covent Garden again, the King's again, and York. He seems to have toured much more extensively than most opera singers, and he may have been fleeing creditors.

During these wanderings the singer baffled everyone by marrying Dorothea Maunsell. Her father, Thomas Maunsell, a Dublin counselor, had engaged Tenducci to give Dorothea singing lessons and ended up doing everything he could to separate the newlyweds. He interrupted Tenducci's performances, imprisoned him and threatened his daughter with confinement in a madhouse – if we can believe the accusations in a 1767 pamphlet. Tenducci continued singing in recitals, however, and public sentiment began to swing in the couple's favour. They went to Edinburgh, where Dorothea began a singing career herself, and in 1769 they were in London, where she sang at the Haymarket. By 1770 Tenducci, despite all his offstage adventures, was keeping up his rather erratic singing career, sometimes as a first man in opera and sometimes as a member of a chorus.

In 1771 the couple went to the Continent with Tenducci's mother and sister, with whom he sometimes left his wife while he toured Italy making concert appearances. That was a mistake. Tenducci had not been recognizing Dorothea as his wife – because of Italian attitudes toward *castrati* marrying – and Dorothea, feeling doubly neglected, had a change of heart and sought refuge with William Long Kingsman in Naples. The Tenducci marriage was anulled in July 1775, by which time Dorothea was married to Kingsman, with her father's blessing.

Tenducci was engaged by Sheridan at Drury Lane in 1776-77 and 1777-78 to sing solo and in choruses, and he appeared at various concert halls. He returned to Dublin to perform and then came back to the King's Theatre in London, singing the title role in Gluck's *Orfeo* in May and June 1785. But Lord Mount Edgcumbe called it 'a performance of an old man, who had never been very capital.' According to the *Scots Magazine* of March 1790, Tenducci died at Genoa, apparently in debt. (*BDA*) [EAL]

TERRISS, Ellaline, later Mrs Seymour Hicks S32
1871-1971
Born in Stanley, the Falkland Islands, on 13 April

1871, Ellaline Terriss was the daughter of the actor-manager William Terriss (*q.v.*) and his wife Amy (née Fellowes). She made her debut as Mary Herbert in *Cupid's Messenger* on 14 February 1888 at the Haymarket Theatre, under the management of Beerbohm Tree. A three-year engagement with Charles Wyndham at the Criterion followed, and she was subsequently seen in modest roles at various London theatres. She played Cinderella with great success at the Lyceum in 1893, and crossed the sea to appear in the same role at the Abbey Theatre in New York in April 1894. After marrying the actor and playwright Seymour Hicks, she was a leading lady in his plays and acted numerous other roles in London, becoming a star player in music halls and in straight and musical plays. In 1914 with her husband she entertained British troops in France, and she also accompanied him in 1927 to Canada, where they remained five months. Among her last roles was Mrs Thornton in *The Miracle Man* at the Victoria Palace in May 1935. Between 1939 and 1946 she was in South Africa. Upon her husband receiving his knighthood in 1935 she became Lady Hicks. In 1928 she had published her reminiscences, *Ellaline Terris; by Herself and with Others*. She died on 16 June 1971, at the age of 100. (*WWWT, EB*)

TERRISS, William Charles James, original surname Lewin 797. S33
1847-1897

William Terriss, one of the leading actors of the last quarter of the nineteenth century, was born in St John's Wood, London, on 20 February 1847, the son of George Herbert Lewin, a barrister. After some schooling at Christ's Hospital, a fortnight's stint in the merchant service and some study of medicine, he became a partner in a large sheep farm in the Falkland Islands. He gained some stage experience in Birmingham and made his first London appearance, as Lord Cloudwrays in *Society*, on 21 September 1868 at the Prince of Wales's Theatre, under the Bancroft management. At the Lane and other London venues he was then seen in a number of roles and scored his first real success as Doricourt in *The Belle's Stratagem* at the Strand at the end of 1873. Terriss acted Romeo (**797**) to Adelaide Nielson's Juliet at the Haymarket and Comte de la Roque in the premiere of *Monsieur le Duc* at the St James's in 1879. When he joined Ellen Terry and Henry Irving at the Lyceum in 1881 Terriss became an established star, acting Cassio, Mercutio, Don Pedro and Romeo and touring with Irving in America in 1884-85.

Terriss left Irving at the end of 1885 and began his association with the Adelphi Theatre, becoming the leading man in a series of melodramas. Among his roles were Lt Hawkesworth in the London premiere of Belasco's *The Girl I Left Behind Me* and Lewis Dumont in the first London performance of Gillette's *Secret Service* in August 1897. Terrriss last played that role on 15 December 1897. The following day, as he was approaching the Adelphi private entrance, he was stabbed to death by a disgruntled and insane actor named Richard Archer Prince, who was convicted and committed to the Broadmoor Criminal Lunatic Asylum

The portrait of Terriss as Romeo (**797**) described in *PCG* as a watercolour is actually a hand-coloured print, after a photograph.

Because of his gallant bearing and debonair style, Terriss was nicknamed 'Breezy Bill.' In 1888 he had married Isabel Lewis, who acted as Miss Amy Fellowes. They had two sons (one an actor) and a daughter, Ellaline (1871-1971), a popular actress (*q.v.*) who married the actor and playwright Seymour Hicks. (*DNB*; see also George Rowell, *William Terriss and Richard Prince*, 1987)

TERRY, Daniel 798, 799
c. 1780-1829

Born in Bath about 1780, Terry spent five years as a pupil of the architect Samuel Wyatt, but turned to acting, first playing at Bath as Heartwell in *The Prize* about 1803. He joined the company at Sheffield in 1803, and he then spent some years at Edinburgh and Liverpool, where he was seen in such supporting roles as Cromwell in *Henry VIII* and Edmund in *King Lear*. At Edinburgh, where Sir Walter Scott became his champion, he was elevated to Falstaff in *Henry IV* and *The Merry Wives of Windsor* and created the role of Roderick Dhu in Eyre's adaptation of *The Lady of the Lake* on 15 January 1811. On 18 November 1811 he acted Lord Ogleby in *The*

Clandestine Marriage, the role in which he made his London debut at the Haymarket on 20 May 1812. During that season at the Haymarket he acted numerous roles, including Shylock, Iago, Major Sturgeon in *The Mayor of Garratt* and Barford in *Who Wants a Guinea?* (the role in which De Wilde depicts him in **798**). On 8 September 1813 he made his first appearance at Covent Garden, as Leon in *Rule a Wife and Have a Wife.* He remained at that theatre through 1822, when on 16 October he appeared as Sir Peter Teazle in *The School for Scandal.* In 1825 he became manager of the Adelphi with Frederick Henry Yates. But financial setbacks put him under the strain of collapse, and, after leaving the Adelphi and an engagement at Drury Lane, he suffered a paralyzing stroke and died in June 1829. Scott had thought highly of his acting in all forms of drama and gave him financial support and friendship at Edinburgh, where Terry was well known. Terry wrote five theatre pieces, including the music dramas *Guy Mannering* (Covent Garden, 12 March 1816) and *The Heart of Mid-Lothian* (Covent Garden, 17 April 1819). He was responsible for an important publication, *British Theatrical Gallery* (1825), a collection of theatrical portraits and brief biographies. Daniel Terry was not related to the famous Terry theatrical family.

TERRY, Edward O'Connor G1004
1844-1912
Edward Terry was born in London on 10 March 1844. He made his first stage appearance at Christchurch as Wormwood in *The Lottery Ticket,* and after several provincial tours appeared at the Surrey Theatre, London, on 14 September 1867 as Finnikin Fussleton in *A Cure for the Fidgets.* His debut in the West End came as the First Gravedigger in *Hamlet* at the Lyceum on 29 August 1869. Then he was engaged at the Strand Theatre for seven years and at the Gaiety beginning August 1876 and lasting until May 1885. In 1886 Terry became manager of the Olympic, and on 17 October 1887 he opened Terry's Theatre. His great success there was as Dick Phenyl (**G1004**) in Pinero's *Sweet Lavender,* which opened on 21 March 1888 and ran 700 nights. In the early 1900s he toured Australia, South Africa, Canada and America with his company. Terry served as a Justice of the Peace in Surrey, as Grand Treasurer of English Freemasons and trustee of the Actors' Benevolent Fund. He became a member of the Garrick Club in February 1884. Terry died on 2 April 1912.

TERRY, Dame Ellen Alice, later Mrs G. F. Watts and then Mrs James Carew 800-804, 820, 953, 954, B93, B175
1847-1928
Ellen Terry, who became one of the most popular actresses on the British stage, was born in Coventry on 27 February 1847, the fourth daughter in the large family of the provincial actors Benjamin Terry and his wife Sarah (née Ballard). Ellen was the sister of Kate, Marion, Florence, George, Charles and Fred Terry, and the grand-aunt of Sir John Gielgud. She made her debut on the London stage in the child's role of Mamillius in Charles Kean's production of *The Winter's Tale* at the Princess's Theatre on 28 April 1856. Subsequently, with Kean's company she was seen in other juvenile parts, including Prince Arthur in *King John* in October 1858 and Puck in *A Midsummer Night's Dream* in October 1856. She left the Princess's when Kean's management ended in 1859, toured with her sister Kate, was a member of the Royalty Theatre for a while and acted at Bristol and Bath. In 1863 she returned to act in London for a brief period until she retired upon her marriage in 1864 to the painter G. F. Watts, whose model she had been. But she reappeared in 1866, at the Olympic, as Helen in *The Hunchback.* On 26 December 1867 she acted with Henry Irving for the first time, playing Kate to his Petruchio. Soon after, she again withdrew from the stage, this time to live with the architect and stage designer Edward Godwin (1833-1886). With him she had two children, Edith, and Edward Gordon Craig (1872-1966), the visionary whose concepts about stage design revolutionized methods of presentation in the theatre of the twentieth century.

Terry was persuaded to return to the stage by the producer Charles Reade. After an absence of six years, she was seen as Phillipa Chester in *The Wandering Heir* at the Queen's Theatre on 28 February 1874. With the Bancrofts in 1875 she was a great success as Portia in *The Merchant of*

Venice. After some other appearances in London, including as Lady Teazle in *The School for Scandal* at the Gaiety in 1877, she joined Henry Irving at the Lyceum in December 1878.

Terry's artistic partnership with Irving began on 30 December 1878 when she played Ophelia to his Hamlet. Her tender and pathetic portrayal of Ophelia was accounted one of her finest. (The Garrick Club painting of her in that role, **801**, is now credited to G. F. Watts [see Index of Artists] and not to Violet Lindsay.) In Irving's striking and realistic mise-en-scènes she acted Portia (**800, 803**), Beatrice, Lady Macbeth (**802**), Imogen, Volumnia, Desdemona and Cordelia, and established herself as one of the most popular and intelligent actresses of her time.

She acted Portia in Irving's final performance at the Lyceum on 19 July 1902. By then her close 24-year personal relationship with Irving was also coming to an end, and a month earlier she had appeared as Mistress Page in Beerbohm Tree's revival of *The Merry Wives of Windsor* at Her Majesty's on 10 June. She had begun in the 1890s a brilliant correspondence with George Bernard Shaw. (The letters from that so-called 'paper courtship' were edited by Christopher St John and published, with a preface by Shaw, in 1931.) On 20 March 1906 at the Court Theatre she played Lady Cecily Waynflete in Shaw's *Captain Brassbound's Conversion*, a role he had written with her in mind.

Her jubilee of 50 years on the stage was celebrated in 1906 with her performances of Mistress Page, Hermione in *The Winter's Tale* and Francisca in *Measure for Measure,* among other roles, and she was honoured by the profession at Drury Lane on 12 June. In 1907 she married the American actor James Carew, who was 30 years her junior, but they soon parted. Subsequently, she appeared in the United States, gave lectures on Shakespeare's heroines, and made occasional appearances in plays at various London venues. Among her later roles were the Nurse in *Romeo and Juliet* (**804**) at the Hampstead Everyman in 1919 and Mrs Long in *Pride and Prejudice* at the Palace Theatre in 1922. She also appeared in several films. In May 1922 she received an honorary LL. D. from St Andrew's University, and in 1925 she was created Dame Grand Cross of the British Empire. Dame Ellen served as Vice-President of the Actors' Orphanage Fund. In 1908 she published her autobiography, *The Story of my Life.*

Ellen Terry died on 21 July 1928 at her cottage, Small Hythe, in Kent. That cottage is now the Ellen Terry Memorial Museum, having been given to the National Trust in 1939 by her daughter, Edith Craig. Biographies of Ellen Terry include Nina Auerbach, *Ellen Terry, Player in her Time* (1987), Joy Melville, *Ellen and Edy: a Biography of Ellen Terry and her Daughter, Edith Craig* (1987) and Tom Prideaux, *Love or Nothing; the Life and Times of Ellen Terry* (1975). A sound recording of the voices of Terry and Irving was issued by Richard Bebb in 1974. (*WWWT, EB*)

TERSI, Maria Theresa
See Maria BLAND

THACKERAY, William Makepeace
1811-1863 **805-807, S34, S35, S0060**
This English novelist, regarded in his day as second only to Dickens, was born in Calcutta on 18 July 1811, the son of Richmond Thackeray, an administrator in the East India Company. In 1816 he was sent home to England, had an unpleasant period at Charterhouse School, attended Trinity College, Cambridge, 1828-1830, left without taking a degree and studied law at the Middle Temple, 1831-1833. In 1832 he came into a patrimony of £20,000 that he squandered through gambling and imprudent investments. While in Paris studying art he married, in 1836, a poor Irish girl, returned to London, gave up some of his dilettante habits and turned seriously to journalism. He wrote under several pen names in various magazines. The serial publication in 1847-48 of his novel *Vanity Fair*, appearing under his own name, brought him success and fame.

Thackeray travelled and lectured in the United States from 1852 to 1856 and then returned to London, where he became a fixture at the Garrick Club, which he had joined in 1833. In 1858 his literary quarrel with Dickens and Edmund Yates found its way to the Garrick Club's Committee, who eventually denied Yates admission despite Dickens's support. Only in the last months of his life did Thackeray patch up the quarrel with Dickens.

Thackeray died in London on 23 December 1863 at the age of 52 and was buried in Kensal Green Cemetery. A commemorative bust was placed in Westminster Abbey. His wife went insane, but long survived him. His attachment to Jane Brookfield, the wife of a Cambridge friend, had ended at the insistence of her husband.

Vanity Fair showed his gift for depicting the London scene and the contrast between rich and poor and good and evil. It is regarded as one of the great historical novels. Thackeray's other important works were *The Luck of Barry Lyndon* (1844, later revised as *The Memoirs of Barry Lyndon*, 1856), *The History of Henry Esmond* (3 vols, 1952), *The Newcomers* (1853-1855) and *The Virginians* (1857-1869). *See* Gordon N. Ray, *Thackeray* (2 vols, 1955-1958, and 1972), Geoffrey Tillotson, *Thackeray the Novelist* (1954 and 1974), and F. G. Kitton, 'The Portraits of Thackeray,' *Magazine of Art* (July 1891). For Thackeray and the Garrick Club, see Richard Hough, *The Ace of Clubs* (1986). (*EB*)

THOMSON, George Malcolm 892, G1028
1899-1966
The prolific author and journalist George Malcolm Thomson was born on 2 August 1899 in Leith, Scotland, the eldest son of the journalist Charles Thomson and his wife Mary (née Eason). After attending Edinburgh University he became a journalist, writing for the *Evening Standard* and *Daily Express*. During the Second World War he was Principal Private Secretary to the first Baron Beaverbrook. Thomson wrote some 34 books; among them are *The Crime of Mary Stuart* (1967), *A Kind of Justice* (1970), *Sir Francis Drake* (1972), *The Warrior Prince: Prince Rupert of the Rhine* (1976), *The First Churchill: the Life of John, 1st Duke of Marlborough* (1979), *The Prime Ministers* (1980) and *Kronstadt '21* (1985). He became a Life Member of the Garrick Club, to which he was elected in 1947. Thomson died on 20 May 1996.

THORNDIKE, Dame Agnes Sybil CH, later Mrs Lewis Casson 808, S36
1882-1976
The versatile actress Sybil Thorndike was born at Gainsborough, Lincolnshire, on 24 October 1882, the daughter of Arthur John Webster Thorndike, a canon of Rochester Cathedral, and his wife Agnes Macdonald (née Bowers). Sybil trained at the Guildhall School of Music, London, and for some time worked as a pianist. In 1904 she studied at Ben Greet's Academy, and her early stage career was closely interwined with Greet's theatrical activities. Her first professional appearance was with his company at Downing College, Cambridge, on 14 June 1904, when she acted Palmis in *The Palace of Truth* and walked on in *The Merry Wives of Windsor*. Her first London appearance was as Janet Moriee in *The Marquis* at the Scala Theatre on 9 February 1908. She performed in Annie Horniman's company at Manchester (1908-9 and 1911-13) and in 1914 rejoined Greet at the Old Vic, under Lilian Bayliss, playing Adriana in *The Comedy of Errors* on 30 November. Over the next four years at the Old Vic, in a variety of roles, modern and classical, tragic and comic, she was instrumental in establishing that theatre's name, especially as the home of Shakespeare. Lady Macbeth, Portia, Rosalind, Viola, Constance, Imogen and Mistress Ford were among her major parts. She also acted Lady Teazle, Kate Hardcastle and Lydia Languish, as well as the male roles of Lear's Fool and Prince Hal.

Her long career spanned some 65 years, during which she appeared in most of the major roles in the theatrical repertory, playing in theatres in London, all over Europe, Australia and America. In March 1924 at the New Theatre, London, she created the title role in Shaw's *St Joan*. Other significant roles included Hecuba in *The Trojan Women*, Miss Moffat in *The Corn is Green*, Medea, Candida, Isabel Linden in *The Linden Tree*, Mrs St Maugham in *The Chalk Garden*, Mrs Callifer in *The Potting Shed* and Abby Brewster in a revival of *Arsenic and Old Lace*. She opened the Chichester Festival in July 1962, acting Marina in *Uncle* Vanya. With her husband Sir Lewis Casson, she toured Australia and New Zealand, South Africa, Kenya, Turkey and Israel, giving recitals.

In June 1931 she was appointed Dame Commander of the British Empire and in 1970 was created a Companion of Honour. She received honorary degrees from the universities of Manchester, Edinburgh, Southampton, Surrey and Oxford. She has been the subject of biographies by Sheridan Morley, Elizabeth Sprigge and John C. Trewin. Her writings include *Religion and the Stage* (1928) and, with her brother Russell Thorndike, a biography of Lilian Bayliss (1938). Dame Sybil died in London on 9 June 1976. (*WWWT, OCT, EB*)

THORNTON, Margaret
See Margaret MARTYR

THURLOW, Lady Mary Catherine
See Mary Catherine BOLTON

TOKELY, James **809**
1790-1819
Born in 1790, Tokely made his debut at Drury Lane in 1813. He was at the Haymarket Theatre in 1817. He died in 1819 at the age of 29. Cruikshank drew and engraved Tokely as Peter Pastoral in *Teasing Made Easy*, the same character in which he is pictured by De Wilde (**809**)

TOOLE, John Lawrence
1830-1906 **810-812, S37, B163**
The comedian and manager John L. Toole was born in London on 12 March 1830, the youngest son of James and Elizabeth Toole. His father was the celebrated Toastmaster of the East India Company. Originally a clerk in a wine merchant's office, young Toole turned to the stage, joining Dillon's company in Dublin. He appeared in London at the Lyceum in 1856, as Fanfaronade in *Belphegor*. In 1858 he joined Ben Webster's company at the New Adelphi, remaining for nine years. One of his successes there was Bob Cratchit in his friend Dickens's *A Christmas Carol*. Toole eventually played in almost every theatre in the United Kingdom, and he toured the United States, Australia and New Zealand. In 1879 he took over the lease of the Charing Cross Theatre in William Street, gave it his name in 1882, and managed it until 1895, when gout forced his retirement. The theatre was pulled down to make way for an extension of old Charing Cross Hospital.

Toole had become a member of the Garrick Club in 1864. He died on 30 July 1906 in Brighton, where he had retired. Toole and Henry Irving were great friends, and they appeared together in a revival of *Robert Macaire* at the Lyceum on 14 June 1883 (see Burnim and Wilton, *The Richard Bebb Collection in the Garrick Club*, B163). (*OCT, WWW*)

TORR, Miss **750**
fl. 1817
We know nothing more about the Miss Torr who is identified as No. 18 in Harlowe's large canvas of the trial scene in *Henry VIII* in 1817.

TRAVERS, Ben CBE **813**
1886-1980
The prolific playwright and novelist Ben Travers was born in Hendon on 12 November 1886, the son of Walter Francis and Margaret Burgess Travers. After some schooling at the Charterhouse School in Surrey he went into the wholesale grocery business and was posted to the business office in Singapore, where he sent much of his time studying the plays of Pinero. In 1911 he returned to London and secured a position at the Bodley Head publishers. In 1914 he joined the Royal Naval Air Service and rose to the rank of major. In 1916 he married Violet Mouncey. After the war Travers settled at Burnham and devoted himself to writing. His first play, *The Dippers*, was produced by Charles Hawtry at the Criterion on 22 August 1922 and ran 173 performances. His second farce, *A Cuckoo in the Nest*, adapted from his own novel, opened at the Aldwych on 22 July 1925 and was an enormous success, running 376 performances. He wrote another eight plays for the Aldwych company between 1926 and 1933, including perhaps his best, *Rookery Nook* (1926), establishing him as the leading writer of English farces and an institution in the theatre.

Another notable farce was *Banana Ridge* (1938), in which Travers himself acted the small role of the Malaysian-speaking servant Wun. Starring were Robertson Hare and Alfred Drayton, who also appeared in his *Spotted Dick* (1939). After serving in the Second World War in the Royal Air Force, Travers returned to write more farces. In all he wrote some 22 plays, the last being *The Bed before Yesterday* (Lyric, December 1975), written at the age of 89 and highly praised as among his best achievements. He also wrote five novels, a number of short stories, and 18 screenplays (some from his own plays). Despite their great popularity in Britain, his plays were not very successful in America, apparently because they are so deeply grounded in the English farce tradition. Travers became a member of the Garrick Club in 1929. In 1976 he was honored with a CBE. He died in London on 18 December 1980 at the age of 94.

TREDCROFT, Edward **793**
d. 1888
Edward Tredcroft, who is shown as No. 12 in O'Neil's scene of members in the Billiards Room, was described as of the Fourth Dragoons when he was elected to the Garrick Club in March 1849. He died in May 1888.

TREE, Anna Maria,
later Mrs James Bradshaw **814-816**
1801 1862
Anna Maria Tree was born in London in August 1801. Her father, who lived in Lancaster Buildings, St Martin's Lane, was with the East India House. As a youngster Anna appeared in some choruses at Drury Lane, and in 1818 at Covent Garden she played Rosina in *The Barber of Seville*. Other roles in musical pieces followed, including Susanna in *The Marriage of Figaro* (**814**), until 1819, when she began to act a series of Shakespearean parts – including Ariel, Viola (**816**), Imogen, Ophelia and Rosalind – for which she won much praise. She remained at Covent Garden until her retirement in June 1825. Soon after, she married the property owner James Bradshaw. Mrs Bradshaw died on 18 February 1862. She was the sister of Ellen Tree (*q.v.*), who became the wife of the actor-manager Charles Kean. (*DNB*)

TREE, Ellen, later Mrs Charles Kean
1805-1880 **817**
Ellen Tree was born in the south of Ireland in December 1805. Her father moved to London soon after and settled with his family at Lancaster Buildings, St Martin's Lane. Possibly he was involved in the theatre. Ellen had three sisters who also found their way into the theatrical profession. An elder sister danced at Drury Lane as Miss Tree and then Mrs Quin. Another, Anna Maria Tree (1801-1862, *q.v.*), acted at Covent Garden and became Mrs James Bradshaw (q.v.). And a third also acted at Drury Lane in the 1820s and became the wife of John Philip Chapman, a proprietor of the *Sunday Times*.

Ellen Tree made her professional debut in London at Covent Garden near the end of the season 1822-23 playing Olivia in an operatic version of *Twelfth* Night, in which her sister Anna Maria played Viola. Her subsequent engagements at Bath and Birmingham were not auspicious, but she re-appeared in London, at Drury Lane, on 23 September 1826 as Violante in *The Wonder*. She remained at Drury Lane for three seasons, offering mainly a line of young women in comedies, including Lady Teazle, Miranda in *The Busybody*, Charlotte in *The Hypocrite*, Miss Hardcastle in *She Stoops to Conquer* and Angelica in *Love for Love*. In 1829-30 she went over to Covent Garden Theatre, where she acted until 1833, appearing in such new roles as Lady Elizabeth in *The First of May* and Mariana in *The Wife* (with her future husband Charles Kean). She was not well received in the male title role in Talfourd's *Ion* at the Haymarket Theatre on 10 August 1836. She also acted the title role in *Black-Eyed Susan* and assumed the male role of Romeo to Fanny Kemble's Juliet. She was in America from 1836 to 1839, then returned to Covent Garden, where her original roles were the Countess in *Love* in 1839 and Isoline in *John of Procida*, both by Sheridan Knowles.

While performing in Dublin, on 29 January 1842 she married Charles Kean, and that night acted with him as Juliana in *The Honeymoon*. That year she also appeared in many Shakespearean parts at the Haymarket Theatre in London. She then travelled with Kean to America. Her professional career from that point was interwoven with that of her husband. When Kean took over the Princess's Theatre in London in 1850 and embarked on his very successful revivals of Shakespeare with lavish and meticulously detailed costumes and settings, Mrs Kean appeared in many of them, playing Viola, Desdemona, Hermione, Lady Macbeth, Constance, the Queen in *Richard II* and Queen Katharine in *Henry VIII*. She also acted in other pieces, including the heroines in *Pauline* (1851) and *Trial for Love* (1852). When Charles Kean died in 1868, she retired from the stage and lived quietly until her death on 20 August 1880. Mrs Kean received high praise for her portrayals of Viola, Constance and, especially, Gertrude in *Hamlet.* The actress Helen Faucit described her: 'She had in youth much beauty and fascination, and in riper age was handsome and intellectual.' (*DNB*)

TREE, Sir Herbert Beerbohm 818-820
1853-1917
This outstanding romantic actor and one of the most successful managers of his time was born in London on 17 December 1853, the son of Julius and Constantia (née Draper) Beerbohm. He was half brother to Max Beerbohm (1872-1956), the sophisticated writer and caricaturist. Educated in England and Germany, Herbert engaged in amateur theatricals for several years before turning professional in 1878. Adopting the surname of Tree, he made numerous appearances in and around London and the provinces (espcially at the Crystal Palace and at Brighton). He was firmly established by 1883, when he scored a great success as Prince Borowski in *The Glass of Fashion* at the Globe in London on 8 September. Over the next 30 years he was seen in dozens of major leads in London and throughout England, including Petruchio, King John, Bottom, Macbeth, Falstaff (**820**), Cardinal Wolsey, Othello, Antony, Hamlet (**819**), Fagin in *Oliver Twist,* Sir Peter in *The School for Scandal,* Henry Higgins in *Pygmalion* and Zakkuri in *The Darling of the Gods.* His portrayal of Svengali in *Trilby,* which he had produced in Manchester in September 1895 and for the first time in London at the Haymarket on 30 October 1895, was accounted his greatest. The demonic spell that he cast in that role is memorialized in Morrow's caricature (**818**).

In 1887 Tree became the lessee and manager of the Haymarket Theatre, which he ran for ten years, through 1896. The following year he took over the proprietorship of and rebuilt Her Majesty's Theatre (later renamed His Majesty's after King Edward VII). As producer at both theatres he presented numerous fine productions in the Irving tradition, ranging from poetic drama to children's plays, among the most remarkable being some of the plays of Shakespeare, particularly *Richard III, King John, Henry VIII* and *A Midsummer Night's Dream.*

In 1904 he founded the Academy of Dramatic Art (later called the Royal Academy of Dramatic Art), which has trained so many important actors and actresses for the profession. He was decorated by the crowned heads of Germany and Italy and in 1909 was knighted by King Edward. He served as President of the Theatrical Managers Association, President of the Actors' Association, and a Trustee of the Actors' Benevolent Fund. In 1884 Tree became a member of the Garrick Club. He published his *Thoughts, and Afterthoughts* in 1913. He died in London on 2 July 1917. *See* Max Beerbohm, *Herbert Beerbohm Tree: Some Memories of Him and His Art* (1920), and Madeleine Bingham, *The Great Lover: The Life and Art of Herbert Beerbohm Tree* (1978). (*WWWT, EB*)

TROLLOPE, Anthony 821
1815-1882
This novelist with a realistic view of Victorian life was born at No.16, Keppel Street, Russell Square, on 24 April 1815, the son of Thomas Anthony Trollope and his wife Frances (also a novelist). His unhappy time at Harrow School entailed bullying from peers and masters and left him with an unsatisfactory education. His early years as a junior clerk in the General Post Office made him equally dissatisfied until he obtained a position as a postal surveyor in Ireland. On 11 June 1844 in Dublin he married Rose Heseltine, the daughter of Edward Heseltine, a bank manager. While in Ireland he wrote *The Macdermots of Ballyeloran* (published 1847), and upon his return to England as a postal inspector in the southwest, he wrote his first novel of distinction, *The Warden* (1855). Subsequently he produced his best-known novels: *Barchester Towers* (1857), *Doctor Thorne* (1858), *Framley Parsonage* (1861), *The Small House at Allington* (1864) and *The Last Chronicle of Barset* (1867). These novels are distinguished for their depiction of ecclesiastical circles and the landed aristocracy. Eventually he returned to London, retired from the post office, was unsuccessful as a candidate for Parliament,

and wrote a number of other novels, especially *Orley Farm*, *Sir Harry Hotspur of Humblethwaite*, and (published posthumously) *Mr Scarborough's Family*. Trollope has been called a master of pathos and humour and a keen and realistic observer of the manners and habits of the social classes.

He spent his last years in the small Sussex village of Harting. On a visit to London in November 1882 he suffered a stroke and died on 6 December. Trollope became a member of the Garrick Club in 1862. Trollope himself wrote that the first time he really felt popular was when he joined the Club. In addition to the picture of him by O'Neil (**821**), his portrait by Samuel Lawrence is in the National Portrait Gallery; it was engraved by Lowenstam and prefixed to Trollope's *Autobiography* (1883). *See* C. P. Snow, *Trollope: His Life and Art* (1975) and Christopher Herbert, *Trollope and Comic Pleasure* (1987). (*DNB*, *EB*)

TWISS, Frances
See Frances KEMBLE

TYRER, Sarah
See Mrs John LISTON

U

UNDERHILL, Cave **822**
1634-1713
Cave Underhill (which was his real name) was born on 17 March 1634 in the parish of St Andrew, Holborn, the son of a clothworker. What drew him to the stage we know not, but his first recorded part seems to have been Sir Morgly Thwack in *The Wits* at the Lincoln's Inn Fields playhouse on 15 August 1661. He followed that with what became one of his most notable characters, the Gravedigger in *Hamlet*, and a singing part, Feste in *Twelfth Night*. Another Shakespearean role that gained him a following was Trincalo in *The Tempest*, and Cave was frequently nicknamed Trincalo. He was regularly employed in the Duke's Company under Sir William Davenant, then in the United Company (from 1682) at Dorset Garden Theatre and Drury Lane, then in Thomas Betterton's troupe of veterans at Lincoln's Inn Fields and from 1705 at the new Queen's Theatre. Cave acted Sir Sampson Legend in the premiere of *Love for Love* on 30 April 1695; later he was Kent in *King Lear* and Obadiah in *The Committee* (**822**).

He was a busy, popular actor, best at droll, dead-pan comic roles but clearly adept in blunt, earthy supporting parts. His face, said Colley Cibber in his *Apology* years later, was 'full and long; from his Crown to the end of his Nose was the shorter half of it, so that the Disproportion of his lower Features, when soberly compos'd, with an unwandering Eye hanging over them, threw him into the most lumpish, moping Mortal that ever made Beholders merry.' Cave Underhill died in 1713. (*BDA*) [EAL]

USTINOV, Sir Peter Alexander CBE
b. 1921 **G1021**
Peter Ustinov was born in London on 6 April; his father was a journalist and his mother was a painter. His grandfather had been a Russian officer in the Czar's army. Peter was educated at Westminster School and trained at the London Theatre School. He made his professional stage debut at the age of seventeen, as an old man in

The Wood Demon. Many stage roles followed, but it as a film actor that he has made his career of some 60 years, appearing in more than 70 films. In 1951 he received an Academy Award nomination as Nero in *Quo Vadis?*. He received Oscars for the best supporting actor in *Spartacus* (1960) and *Topkapi* (1964). He played Hercule Poirot in six films in the 1970s and 1980s.

The multi-talented Ustinov wrote a number of notable plays that were acted in London and New York: *The Love of Four Colonels* (1951), *Romanoff and Juliet* (1956) and *Halfway Up the Tree* (1967), to name a few. In his comedy *Beethoven's 10th* (1983), he also starred as the composer. He acted and directed his film version of *Billy Budd.* In 1969 he received an Oscar nomination for his screenplay *Hot Millions.* Ustinov is a master story teller, and he has published collections of short stories. His autobiographical works include *Dear Me* (1977), *Ustinov at Large* (1993) and *Ustinov Still at Large* (1994).

For his humanitarian efforts as Ambassador at large for UNICEF since 1969, he was awarded that organisation's Medal for Distinguished Service in 1993. He received the CBE in 1975 and was knighted in 1990. Sir Peter was elected into the Garrick Club in 1948 and is a Life Member. (*EB*)

V

VAUGHAN, Hannah

See Mrs William PRITCHARD

VAUGHAN, Kate **823**

1852?-1903

Kate Vaughan, whose real name was Catherine Candelon, a child of a theatre musician, was trained as a dancer and inaugurated a new school of 'skirt-dancing.' She also performed in burlesques at the Gaiety from 1876 to 1883 and then turned to standard comedy, appearing in such roles as Lydia Languish, Miss Hardcastle and Lady Teazle during her management of the Vaughan-Conway company, 1886-1887. Touring took her to Australia and South Africa. She died in 1903. The pencil drawing portrait of her, reported as unlocated in the GCP, has been found; in it she is shown with the actor William Mitchenson (q.v.) Possibly it is a costume design by C. Wilhelm (1859-1925) for an unknown production. (*OCT*)

VALENTINE, Sydney **G0996**

1865-1919

Born on 14 February 1885, Sydney Valentine made his stage debut at Dover on 26 December 1882 with the Charles Dickens Repertory Company, and after some touring he appeared for the first time in London at the Prince's Theatre on 21 April 1884 as Sam Gaythorne in *Cut Off with a Shilling.* Over the next 30 years he acted numerous roles in London and New York, some of them with Irving's company at the Lyceum in 1895-1896 and at the Haymarket under Frederick Harrison and Cyril Maude from 1897 to 1900. At the Lyric in February 1903 he appeared as J. G. Fordham in *The Light that Failed* (**G0996**). Later in his career he played, among other roles, Roebuck Ramsden in *Man and Superman* at the Coronet, Notting Hill, in September 1912 and at the Hudson Theatre, New York, the same month. At His Majesty's on 5 July 1915 he acted Cranmer in an all-star revival of *Henry VIII* given in aid of the King George Actors' Fund; he was sometime chairman of that fund. Valentine became a member of the Garrick Club in January 1918. He died on 23 December 1919 at the age of 54. (WWT3rd ed)

VERNON, Joseph **824**
c. 1731-1782
Joseph Vernon was born in Coventry about 1731 (or perhaps as late as 1739), an illegitimate child. His singing voice as a boy was so splendid that the actor Richard Yates and then the Drury Lane manager David Garrick took Vernon on as an apprentice. The boy's first professional advertisement was the playbill for 26 December 1750, when he sang in the masque *Alfred*; the prompter Richard Cross noted that Vernon sang very well. By 1751-52 the Drury Lane bills cited the singer now as Master and now as Mr, so he was probably near his majority. By 1752-53 and later Vernon appeared in plays: Loveless in *The Double Disappointment*, Donalbain and Malcolm in *Macbeth*, Squire Richard in *The Provok'd Husband*, Fabian and Feste in *Twelfth Night*, Verges and Balthasar in *Much Ado about Nothing*, Launcelot and Lorenzo in *The Merchant of Venice*, Ferdinand in *The Tempest*, Macheath in *The Beggar's Opera*, Hawthorn in *Love in a Village* and many others. He also sang and acted at the Haymarket, the Chapel of the Lock Hospital, the King's Theatre and Covent Garden as well as in Dublin.

He ruffled some feathers when, in 1755, he wed, illegally and without her friends' consent, the young performer Jane Poitier, and some members of his audience hissed him. He married a second time, in 1773, to Margaret Richardson. Since he was known as a womanizer, Vernon was also supposed to have married two other women. He died on 19 March 1782, remembered as a good popular singer and an adequate actor. (*BDA*) [EAL]

VESTRIS, Lucia Elizabeth née Bartolozzi, later Mrs Charles James Mathews
1797-1856 **825-827, B94-B100**
Born in London on 3 January 1797, this singer and manager was the daughter of the engraver Gaetano Stephano Bartolozzi (1757-1821) and the granddaughter of Francesco Bartolozzi (1727-1815), a Florentine stipple engraver in the service of George III. Lucia was married briefly to Auguste-Armand Vestris (1788-1825), a member of the Vestris dynasty of dancers in Paris and London (see the *BDA* 15: 146-154). She appeared in Italian operas in London in 1815 and scored a success in the title role of Moncrieff's *Giovanni in London* in 1817. After several years in Paris she returned to London to perform at Covent Garden and Drury Lane and became a favourite in breeches parts. In 1830 she took over the lease of the Olympic Theatre, which she opened with Planché's burlesque *Olympic Revels*. With a strong company that included John Liston and Maria Foote, she presented a number of burlesques and extravaganzas. Also in the company was Charles James Mathews (*q.v.*), whom she married in 1838, and subsequently they managed the Lyceum and Covent Garden until 1854.

Madame Vestris was an excellent manager; she insisted on realistic props and accurate costumes and is credited with introducing the box set, with a ceilinged room, in November 1832. She died in London on 8 August 1856. Biographies of her have been written by Leo Waitzkin, *The Witch of Wych Street* (1933); Charles Pearce, *Madame Vestris and her Times* (1969); Clifford Williams, *Madame Vestris* (1973); and William Appleton, *Madame Vestris and the London Stage* (1974).

VIOLETTE, Eva Maria
See Mrs David GARRICK

W

WAKER, Mr **828**
fl. 1790
An actor of this name performed in Dublin about 1790. Other than the portrait by Herbert in the Garrick Club and the engraving by Fisher, after F. West, as Roger in *The Ghost*, we know little more about Waker.

WALDRON, Mrs
See Sarah HARLOWE

WALLACE, Ian Bryce OBE **G0987, G1011**
b. 1919
Ian Wallace, who is caricatured in a drawing by Charles Yorke on the menu of the Garrick Club dinner in 1997, was born in London on 10 July 1919, the son of Sir John Wallace, Kirkcaldy, Fife, and Mary Bryce Wallace (née Temple). He was educated at the Charterhouse and Trinity Hall, Cambridge (MA). After service in the Second World War, he made his stage debut at Sadler's Wells in *The Foreign Reel* in 1945 and has since sung principal roles with the New London Opera Company, at Glyndebourne, Edinburgh, Berlin, Parma and with the Welsh National Opera. He has appeared regularly on television and radio as singer, actor, compere and panelist. His recordings include Gilbert and Sullivan operas with Sir Malcolm Sargent and humorous songs by Flanders and Swan. Wallace devised, wrote and presented three series of adult education programmes on opera entitled *Singing for your Supper*, for Scottish Television, 1967-1970. St Andrews University awarded him an Hon DMus in 1991. His publications include the autobiographical volumes *Promise Me You'll Sing 'Mud'* (1975) and *Nothing Quite Like It* (1982) and *Reflections on Scotland* (1988). He received the OBE in 1983. Wallace joined the Garrick Club in 1954 and is a Life Member.

WALLACK, James William **829**
1791?-1864
Born in Hercules Buildings, Lambeth, probably in 1791 (but maybe on 24 August 1795), James William Wallack was the son of the performers William Wallack (c. 1760-1850) and his wife Elizabeth Field Granger (c. 1760-1850), who are noticed in the *BDA*. James's elder brother Henry John Wallack (1790-1870) became a leading actor and theatrical manager in England and America; his three children Fanny, Julia and James William Wallack II also became prominent actors.

Our subject, James William Wallack, performed with other members of his family at the Royal Circus by the age of four. In 1807 he appeared as the Negro Boy in the pantomime *Furibond; or, Harlequin Negro* at Drury Lane. After playing three years in Dublin he returned in 1812 to the new Drury Lane Theatre, where he acted until 1818 in such roles as Malcolm in *Macbeth*, Laertes, Axalla in *Tamerlane*, Joseph in *The School for Scandal*, Alcibiades in *Timon of Athens* and Iago. Wallack made his debut in New York at the Park Street Theatre on 7 September 1818 as Macbeth. After appearing in a number of major parts, he returned to London. Subsequently he shuttled between London and New York frequently and became an important manager in the latter city when, with his brother Henry John Wallack, he took over the National Theatre in 1837. He assumed management of the Lyceum Theatre in New York in 1852 and renamed it Wallack's Lyceum. There he presented for nine seasons successful productions of Shakespeare and some contemporary drama. His son Lester was stage manager and his son Charles treasurer. Wallack, who was from the older Kemble school of acting, gave up performing in 1859 and devoted himself entirely to managing. In 1861 he built a new theatre at Broadway and 13th Street, called Wallack's Theatre. Wallack died in New York, from complications of gout, on 25 December 1864. He had been one of the original members of the Garrick Club in 1831.

Wallack's son Lester (real name John Johnstone Wallack, 1810-1888) enjoyed a career as a popular actor in America and also managed Wallack's Theatre; he wrote his *Memories of Fifty Years* (published posthumously in 1889). Lester Wallack married Emily Millais, sister of the artist Sir John Everett Millais. That artist made some sketches of James William Wallack. (*DNB*, *OCT*, *EB*)

WARD, Dame Geneviève **830**
1837-1922
Born in New York on 27 March 1837, she was the daughter of Samuel Ward. Her maternal grandfather had been a mayor of the city. She married in 1855 Count Constantine de Guerbel. Originally an opera singer, she studied in Italy and made her debut in 1857 at La Scala under the name of Mme Ginevra Guerrabella. She enjoyed success singing in Paris, London and New York; she made her first appearance in New York at the Academy of Music on 10 November 1862, as Violetta in *La Traviata*. During a tour of Cuba she caught diphtheria, and consequently her singing voice was ruined.

After teaching singing for some years in New York, she decided to turn actress, went to England, and made an appearance at the Theatre Royal, Manchester, on 1 October 1873 as Lady Macbeth. She was immediately hailed and after offering Constance in *King John*, Adrienne Lecouvreur, Medea and Lucrezia Borgia at Manchester, she ventured to London, where on 20 March 1874 at the Adelphi Theatre she appeared as Alexina in *Elizabeth, or the Exiles of Siberia*. From then on Ward became a major actress on the London stage, appearing in capital roles at many theatres and playing in America and South Africa. At the Lyceum on 21 August 1879 she appeared as Stephanie de Mohrivart in *Forget-Me-Not*, a role she acted over 2000 times throughout the world. Among her portrayals were Lona Hessel in *The Pillars of Society*, Katherine in *Henry VIII* (with Irving), the Queen in *Cymbeline*, Emilia in *Othello*, Mrs Borkman in *John Gabriel Borkman* and Queen Anne of Austria in *The Man in the Iron Mask*. Ward managed the Olympic Theatre in 1883, which she opened on 6 January with a production of *Forget-Me-Not*. She joined Irving at the Lyceum in 1891. In 1909 she toured with Benson's company as Queen Margaret in *Richard III*. Ward enjoyed great success as Volumnia in *Coriolanus*, a role she first acted at His Majesty's on 19 April 1910 and often acted during the 1910s. She played it at the Old Vic in April 1920 and toured in that part with Benson in the autumn of 1920. She was made a DBE in March 1921. Dame Geneviève died on 18 August 1922 at the age of 85. (*WWWT*)

WARD, John **831, 832**
1704-1773
John Ward was born in 1704, perhaps at Leominster, but little is known about his origins or youth. His first appearance on the stage occurred at Lincoln's Inn Fields Theatre on 17 November 1722, when he acted Ascanio in *The Spanish Curate*. He remained at that theatre under John Rich's management for another three seasons. There he met his future wife, the actress Sarah Butcher (1711-1786), the daughter of provincial actors. After leaving London, the Wards probably toured for several years before settling in at Smock Alley Theatre, Dublin, where John Ward made his debut on 27 April 1730 as Friendly in *Flora*. They also played at the Aungier Street Theatre in Dublin and toured the Irish and English towns. It was at Clonmel on 2 September 1735 that Mrs Ward gave birth to Sarah Ward, who would marry Roger Kemble and become the matriarch of the great Kemble clan. In 1741-42 the Wards took up an engagement at Drury Lane, where John made his first appearance on 19 September 1741 as Laertes in *Hamlet*. His roles that season included Douglas in *Henry IV*, Duke Frederick in *As You Like It* and Trebonius in *Julius Caesar*. But the following season they were gone from Drury Lane and on the road again. In May 1746 Ward took a company to Stratford-upon-Avon, where they performed with much success. On 9 September 1746 the Wards acted Othello and Emilia in what may have been the first production of a Shakespearean play in Stratford, for the benefit of restoring Shakespeare's bust in the Holy Trinity Church. Over the next two decades Ward led his company throughout England and Wales, giving high quality performances. He died at Leominster on 30 October 1773 and was buried in Leominster churchyard. His wife Sarah died in 1786. They had numerous children but only three survived. The sons William and Stephen were not talented. The daughter Sarah acted in the provinces but her main distinction came as the mother of Charles Kemble, John Philip Kemble and Sarah Kemble Siddons. (*BDA*)

WARD, Mrs Thomas Achurch, Sarah, née Hoare **833**
1756?-1838?
Sarah Hoare, who probably was the daughter of provincial actors, was born about 1756. She had two sisters who went into the profession: Katharine Hoare, later Mrs Sparks Powell (1762-1807), and Letitia Hoare, who became the common-law wife of a Cheapside haberdasher named Sage. They may have been related to the banker Henry Hoare (d. 1828) and the dramatist Prince Hoare (1755-1834). By the summer of 1775 Sarah Hoare was acting in Younger's company on the Birmingham circuit. Sometime that summer she married Thomas Achurch Ward (1747-1835), who was also an actor in the Birmingham company. The Wards obtained an engagement at Covent Garden for the 1776-77 season, when Mrs Ward made her debut on 14 November 1776 as Rodogune in *Ethelinda*. Other roles followed: Zara in *The Mouring Bride*, Queen Eleanor in *King Henry the Second*, Roxana in *Alexander the Great* and Euphrasia in *The Grecian Daughter*. Mrs Ward was employed in and out of London for several seasons, and in 1782 she joined Drury Lane, where she remained until June 1793. She then went to the Manchester Theatre, where she was greeted favourably, and acted such capital roles as Lady Randolph in *Douglas*, Calista in *The Fair Penitent*, Mrs Beverley in *The Gamester* and Belvidera in *Venice Preserv'd*. She died at Manchester, probably in 1838. This Mrs Ward is not to be confused with the Sarah Ward who became the wife of Roger Kemble and the matriarch of the Kemble dynasty. (*BDA*)

WARRE, Arthur **783**
d. 1902
Arthur Warre, who is shown as No. 24 in O'Neil's picture of members in the Billiards Room, was a Lieutenant in the Royal Navy when he was elected to the Garrick Club in July 1856. He was re-elected in February 1874, at which time his 'profession' was given as 'None Late Member.' Warre died on 4 May 1902.

WARREN, Emily
See POTT

WARREN, Mrs Thomas, Ann
See Ann POWELL.

WARREN, Mrs William
See Anne BRUNTON

WATERHOUSE, Keith Spencer CBE, FRSL **965**
b. 1929
The prolific writer and journalist Keith Waterhouse was born in Hunslet (Leeds), Yorkshire, on 6 February 1929, the fourth son of Ernest and Elsie Waterhouse. He left school at the age of 15, worked at odd jobs and became a newspaperman in Leeds. Then he came to London as a journalist, eventually obtaining positions as a columnist with the *Daily Mirror* (1970-1986) and the *Daily Mail* (beginning in 1986). He is a regular contributor to *Punch* and other periodicals. He is also a playwright, screenwriter and novelist with great skill at creating comedy and satire 'out of depressing conditions.' His first novel, in 1957, *There is a Happy Land*, was followed by the very successful *Billy Liar* in 1959 (made into a play in 1960, a film in 1963 and a musical in 1974). Together with Willis Hall, his collaborator on the production of *Billy Liar*, Waterhouse wrote several other plays and revues, including *All Things Bright and Beautiful* (1962), *They Called the Bastard Stephen* (1964) and *Whoops-a-Daisey* (1968). His play *Jeffrey Bernard is Unwell* was produced in 1991, and had a successful revival in 2000 with Peter O'Toole in the title role. Waterhouse is a recipient of a number of prizes and awards for his writings, including television series. He was honoured with a CBE in 1991. He became a member of the Garrick Club in 1977.

WATSON, Miss
See Mrs BROOKS

WEBB, Richard **297**
d. 1784
The actor Webb who is identified as one of Witches in Romney's scene from *Macbeth* (**297**) was probably Richard Webb. He made his debut on the stage as Young Aboan in *The Royal Slave* at Drury Lane on 27 April 1770. Subsequently

he played in the provinces, mainly in Edinburgh, where from 1771 to 1779 he developed a repertoire of some 80 roles. He specialized in bluff squires, judges, landlords, wise men and eccentrics. Webb joined Colman's company at the Haymarket in the summer of 1777 and remained with that summer playhouse through 1782. In 1780-81 he also became a member of the Covent Garden company, in which his roles included Don Lopez in *The Wonder*, Jemmy Twitcher in *The Beggar's Opera* and Charles in *As You Like It*. In 1784 he was imprisoned for debt at the King's Bench, where he died in July of the same year. Both Webb and his wife were obese, each weighing about 16 stone. Mrs Webb (*q.v.*) was acting with her husband in Edinburgh and London. (*BDA*)

WEBB, Mrs Richard, née Child, formerly Mrs Day **834**
d. 1793
This actress played under her maiden name, Miss Child, at Norwich in March 1764 and by 1765 was married to an actor named Day. Together they toured numerous provincial towns. They may have acted at Dublin in 1770-71. As Mrs Day she was at the Theatre Royal, Edinburgh, in 1772-73. What happened to Mr Day is not known, but by May of 1774 she assumed the name of Mrs Webb, though it is not clear whether or not she ever married the actor Richard Webb. She appeared regularly in major roles in Edinburgh through 1779, and she and Webb joined Colman at the Haymarket Theatre in London in the summer of 1778. When she made her debut there on 12 June 1778 as Mrs Cross in *Man and Wife,* one critic alluded to her obesity, finding her '*first rate* in point of bodily size, and *second rate* as to theatrical merit.' But she did have some talent for tragedy – in the parts of Queens in Shakespeare – and possessed a 'most powerful and harmonious voice.' With Richard Webb she joined the Covent Garden company in the autumn of 1779. Among her numerous roles in London – which were of greater significance than those of her partner, but not as major as those she had enjoyed in Edinburgh – were Lady Oldcastle in *Separate Maintenance*, Mrs Cheshire in *The Agreeable Surprise* and the Landlady in *William and Susan*. Most of her assignments were in light comedies, musical comedies and interludes. She first appeared as Lady Dove in *The Brothers* (the role in which she was depicted by De Wilde, **834**) at Covent Garden on 25 April 1787. Mrs Webb's large girth can be seen in De Wilde's picture and in other pictures of her, including a caricature of her as Cowslip. Her husband died in debtor's prison in July 1784. Mrs Webb, who resided in the Covent Garden area (Bedford Street from 1779 to 1782, Broad Court, Bow Street, in 1787, and No 19, Catherine Street, the Strand, in 1791), died of a stroke on 24 November 1793 and was buried at St Paul, Covent Garden. (*BDA*)

WEBSTER, Benjamin Nottingham
1797-1882 **835, 836**
The actor-manager and prolific dramatist Ben Webster was born at Bath on 3 September 1797, the son of a musical composer, pantomimist, and dancing-fencing master in that city and his wife Elizabeth Moon, of Leeds. Ben had numerous brothers and half-brothers, including Frederick Webster (1802-1878), an actor and stage manager at the Haymarket. Ben made his first appearance on the stage at Warwick performing Harlequin, acting some small speaking roles and playing second violin in the theatre orchestra. That inauspicious beginning was followed by some years in the provinces, including Manchester and Liverpool. He made his London debut as a smuggler in the opening entertainment of the Coburg Theatre (later the Old Vic) on 11 May 1819. After some inconsequential engagements at Richmond, Croyden and Birmingham, Webster engaged at Drury Lane, appearing there on 28 November 1820 as Almagro in *Pizarro*. He was associated with that theatre until 1829, when he went over to the Haymarket, at which theatre he remained for many years, becoming lessee and manager in 1837. In 1844 he also took over the Adelphi and in 1859 replaced the latter with the New Adelphi. At these theatres he produced many notable plays, with some of the best actors in London; he also appeared in many of the productions. The *DNB* lists dozens of roles which he acted until he retired in February 1874. Prominent among them were Triplet in *Masks*

and Faces (1852), Lorin in Boucicault's *Geneviève* and Luke Fielding in *Willow Copse*. He was an excellent actor of characters that displayed 'serious purpose, puritanical fervour, and grim resolution.'

Webster wrote about 100 plays, many now not traceable; several were adapted from the French. A number were published in Webster's *Acting National Drama*. Webster died at his residence, Churchside, Kensington, on 2 November 1882.

The Websters' children were involved in the theatre. Their son John Webster acted at several London theatres in 1837 and 1838. Ben's namesake son, Ben Webster, wrote some plays for the Adelphi from about 1865 to 1873. Our subject's grandson, Benjamin Webster (1864-1947) was a prominent actor in London and New York; he married the actress Dame May Whitty (1865-1948); their daughter Margaret Webster (b. 1905) made an outstanding reputation as a director of Shakespearean plays.

In addition to the portraits of Benjamin Nottingham Webster in the Garrick Club (**835**, **836**) and several engravings of him in character, many photographs of him exist. Webster had become a member of the Garrick Club in February 1838. (*DNB, OCT*)

WEICHSEL, Elizabeth
See Elizabeth BILLINGTON

WELLINGTON, Arthur Wellesley, First Duke of **918**
1769-1852
The 'Iron Duke' was born in Dublin on 1 May 1769, the son of Garret Wellesley, 1st Earl of Mornington. He was educated at Eton and the military academy at Angers, France, and entered the Army in 1787. He rose rapidly and obtained a peerage. His victories in India brought him a knighthood (1804); those in Spain and Portugal (1808-1814) made him Viscount Wellington; and that over Napoleon at Waterloo (1815) the Duke of Wellington. He was richly rewarded by Parliament and foreign sovereigns and became one of the most influential and popular men in Europe. Wellington served as Prime Minister 1828-1830, in which capacity, because of his reactionary views, he was less successful and popular. He retired from public life in 1846, died on 14 September 1852 and was buried under the dome of St Paul's, next to Lord Nelson.

WELLS, Julia Elizabeth
See Julie ANDREWS

WELLS, Mary, Mrs Ezra, née Davies, later Mrs Joseph Sumbel **837**
1762-1829
Mary Wells was characterized by one of her contemporaries as 'a noted and infamous woman.' Her three-volume autobiography, *The Memoirs of the Life of Mrs Sumbl, late Wells* (1811), is cavalier about facts and is imaginative with anecdotes; it was written, according to one early reviewer, by a person whose mind was not 'always perfectly collected.' She was born Mary Davies in December 1762, one of the daughters of Thomas Davies, a woodcarver and gilder in Birmingham, who – according to Mary's *Memoirs* – was employed by Garrick to dig up the root of the celebrated mulberry tree at Stratford and fashion a box from it. After some early experience in Birmingham, York and elsewhere in the provinces, in November 1778 at Shrewsbury – at the age of sixteen – Mary married the actor Ezra Wells, to whose Romeo she had acted Juliet at Gloucester. Shortly after, he deserted her.

Eventually Mary Wells made her way to the London stage, where on 4 September 1781 at the Haymarket Theatre she was the original Cowslip in O'Keeffe and Arnold's *The Agreeable Surprise*. The nickname Cowslip stuck with her many years, and sometimes she was called by the nickname Becky. In the 1780s she acted a spectrum of roles, musical, comic and tragic, at the Haymarket, Drury Lane and Covent Garden. Among her many roles were Ann Lovely (**837**) in *A Bold Stroke for a Wife*, Imogene in *Cymbeline*, Mrs Page in *The Merry Wives of Windsor*, the title role in *Jane Shore*, Audrey in *As You Like it*, Lady Easy in *The Careless Husband* and Lady Randolph in *Douglas*.

On 11 May 1786 she appeared for her benefit at Covent Garden in Edward Topham's farce *Small Talk or, The Westminster Boy*. Because it was an old and established rule among the youth of Westminster School not to permit any exhibition on the stage reflecting their body, a large group of Westminster boys mustered and dispersed throughout the boxes. When in the second act Mrs Wells appeared in the dress of a Westminster scholar, they made such an uproar that the piece was prevented from being heard.

By the late 1780s, Mrs Wells had developed a reputation for unconventional and sometimes eccentric behaviour, some of it caused by an incipient insanity exacerbated by drink. She caused a sensation at Weymouth in 1789, when she failed in her attempts to attract the attention of their Majesties on the esplanade, and, in order to follow the King and Queen to Plymouth, she paid ten guineas a week for hire of a yacht, 'a gun mounted on the deck, on which she sat astride, singing God save the King.' After affairs with some of London's leading figures, including Frederic Reynolds, Horne Took, the elder Colman and Sheridan, she lived with the sometime-playwright Edward Topham, by whom she had four children. After five years he left her destitute and miserable. Much of her distress was caused by her indiscretion in backing the considerable debt of her brother-in-law, Emanuel Samuel, husband of her sister Anna Davies, an actress who had made her debut at the Haymarket in July 1786. Mrs Wells bailed Samuel out of the Fleet Prison, arranged an appointment for him in the West Indies and financed his voyage. Plagued by her creditors, Mrs Wells passed several years in prison or trying to avoid prison.

It was in 1796 while in the Fleet Prison for debt she met the shady character Joseph Haim Sumbel, a Moorish Jew and former secretary to the Ambassador from Morocco. Sumbel had been confined to the Fleet for contempt of court, having refused to answer interrogatories concerning a large quantity of diamonds found in his possession. In October 1798 in the Fleet, Mary Wells married Sumbel in a wedding of 'Eastern grandeur,' solemnized, as one reporter put it, with all 'Jewish magnificence.' In preparation, she had converted to Judaism, taking the ritual bath in the Mikvah, and adopting the name Leah. The *Morning Post* commented that 'Mrs Wells was always an odd genius, and her becoming a Jewess greatly satisfies her passion for eccentricity.' The new Leah Sumbel wrote a public letter to that newspaper disclaiming any passion for eccentricity and affirming that it was 'studying and examining with great care and attention, the Old Testament, that has influenced my conduct.' After their release from the Fleet, the Sumbels settled at No 79, Pall Mall, next door to the Duke of Gloucester. The new Mrs Leah Sumbel lived there in 'splendid misery,' for Joseph Sumbel proved to be a man of vicious and irrational temperament, who often locked her up without food and apparently kept a harem. One night he fired a pistol at her but missed.

A public exchange of charges and accusations followed, including a debate over whether or not Mary (Leah) was really a Jewess. According to certain stories in the press, the marriage had not been a legal Jewish ceremony and she had broken the Sabbath and the dietary laws, by running away from Sumbel in a carriage on a Saturday and by eating 'forbidden fruit – namely, pork grisken and rabbits.' A long and unresolved litigation ensued, but soon Sumbel died, in 1804, while on visit to Altona, near Hamburg, and was buried in the local Jewish cemetery.

Though Mary continued to call herself Mrs Sumbel, she renounced Judaism, writing: 'I am now once more received into the bosom of Christianity as a repentant sinner, fully confident, as such, that the Almighty will pardon my transgressions.' After some more years of acting on the London stage, she claimed on the Covent Garden Theatrical Fund in 1809, and by then, according to the actor-manager James Winston, was 'unquestionably insane.' After some twenty more years of misery and illnesses she died in 1829, at the age of 67, and was buried in the old churchyard of St Pancras. Mrs Wells had been a good actress when not suffering abberations of mental illness. Frederic Reynolds described her as a beautiful woman on the stage. The *BDA* lists some 28 portraits of her.

WESTON, Thomas **838**

1737-1776

Thomas Weston's father was reputed to be an undercook in the kitchen of George II, and Thomas was originally apprenticed there as a turn-broach. After some time as a midshipman and as an actor with a strolling company, he appeared about 1759 at a Bartholomew Fair booth. He then made his first appearance in a London theatre on 28 September 1759 when he played Sir Francis Gripe in *The Budy Body* at the Haymarket. Some years more were passed in the provinces, particularly at the Smock Alley Theatre in Dublin, until Weston returned to London to play at Drury Lane in the summer of 1761. He continued to be engaged at the Haymarket and Drury Lane, off and on, through 1775-76, appearing mainly in inconsequential comic pieces that made him a favourite with the gallery. Contemporary critics gave him high praise for his comic abilities and inimitable and simple manner. 'It was impossible,' related James Northcote to Hazlitt, 'from looking at him, for anyone to say that he was acting. You would suppose they had gone out and found the actual character they wanted, and brought him upon the stage without him knowing it.' But he was a difficult man, overbearing and insolent by several accounts, and unlettered and possessed of few ideas. He also drank a good deal. Weston died sometime in January 1776. There are 11 pictures of Weston listed in the *BDA*, including four renditions of him as Scrub in *The Beaux' Stratagem*, two with Garrick as Archer. Garrick declared that Weston's portrayal of Scrub was one of the finest jobs of acting he had ever seen. (*BDA*)

WEWITZER, Ralph **839**

1748-1825

Of Norwegian or perhaps Swiss heritage, Ralph Wewitzer was born on 17 December 1748 in Salisbury Street, the Strand. He was apprenticed to a jeweller but, since all his siblings took to the stage, it was almost inevitable that he would too. On 12 May 1773 at Covent Garden he made his debut, at his sister Sarah's benefit, as Ralph in *The Maid of the Mill.* He then found himself in debt and fled to Dublin, where audiences were responsive and he earned enough to settle his financial problems and return to Covent Garden. He spent most of his performance time there through 1789 and then at Drury Lane until 1819. He was also seen at provincial theatres – Liverpool, Bristol, Birmingham, Edinburgh, Richmond – and at the Haymarket some summers. During his 44 or so years onstage he mastered over 400 roles, most of them small but some substantial: Lopez in *The Duenna*, the French Officer in *The Touchstone*, Shadrach in *The Quaker*, the Old Woman and Dr Caterpillar in *Harlequin Teague*, Crazy in *Peeping Tom*, Solomon in *The Stranger*, Dr Caius in *The Merry Wives of Windsor* (**839**) and many others. He specialized in eccentrics and dialect characters of all kinds except Irish and Scots. His salary was modest: £2 weekly in 1776-77, £7 in 1796-97 and the years following, but back down to £3 by 1819. *The Roscius* said Wewitzer 'lived a life of good humour, cheerfulness and ease.' He enjoyed good benefit receipts and augmented his salary with a number of publications from 1785 on: collections of theatre songs and anecdotes, historical gatherings and miscellaneous theatricana. But he was dependent in his latter years on a stipend from the Drury Lane Theatrical Fund, and when Ralph Wewitzer died on 1 January 1825 he was apparently in debt.

Wewitzer's second wife, three sisters and brother had stage careers which are recorded in *BDA*, along with details about his publications. (*BDA*) [EAL]

WHITE, Lt Col the Honourable Charles William **793**

fl. 1864-1869

In O'Neil's painting (1869) of a scene in the Billiards Room, the figure numbered 5 in the key is Charles William White, MP, who was also a member of the Fusilier Guards. When he completed his candidate's application for membership in the Garrick Club White gave his rank as Lieutenant Colonel and his address as Belgrave Square. He was elected to the Garrick Club in March 1864.

WHITE, Elizabeth

See Elizabeth HARTLEY

WHITE, Elizabeth

See Elizabeth Mary POWELL

WHITFIELD, John **840**

1752-1814

This actor, manager and playwright was

probably the son of the Covent Garden tailor and wardrobe keeper Robert Whitfield and his wife, a dresser at that theatre. Both parents are noticed in the *BDA*. Whitfield spent some seasons acting at Norwich and Canterbury before he appeared at Covent Garden on 26 September 1774 as Trueman in *George Barnwell*. His wife Mary made her debut there as Harriet in *The Miser* on 30 September. The Whitfields remained at Covent Garden, off and on, through 1802-3 and were for some seasons engaged at Drury Lane. John developed a repertoire of over 200 roles, usually of the supporting variety but sometimes leading parts like Horatio in *The Fair Penitent* and George Barnwell in *The London Merchant*. His Shakespearean roles included Benvolio, Paris, Laertes, Salanio in *The Merchant of Venice* and Fenton in *The Merry Wives of Windsor*, among others. He was a mature and useful professional actor, and some critics believed he was not being used to advantage by the managers. Whitfield died on 27 January 1814 and was buried at St Paul, Covent Garden, beside his wife Mary, who had died in December 1795. In addition to the portrait by Harding in the Garrick Club (**840**), Whitfield was pictured by James Roberts (engraving by Thornthwaite) as Captain Dormer in *A Word to the Wise* (1795) and by W. Loftis as Sir George Wealthy in the *Minor* (watercolour at the Folger Library). (*BDA*)

WHITLOCK, Elizabeth, Mrs Charles Edward, née Kemble 374. 841
1761-1836
Born at Warrington, Lancashire, on 2 April 1761, She was the daughter of the provincial actors Roger and Sarah Kemble and the sister of Charles and John Philip Kemble and Sarah Siddons. Like her siblings, Elizabeth began her acting career by playing children's roles in her parent's touring company. She was an experienced stroller by nineteen and on 22 February 1783 made her London debut at Drury Lane as Portia in *The Merchant of Venice*. She was accounted by the critics as a 'tolerable' actress but no threat to the merits of her sister Sarah. Tate Wilkinson, for whom she acted at York, wrote that although she had talent she was in the fullness of her youth 'wild as a colt untamed.' During two more seasons at Drury Lane she acted Imogen in *Cymbeline*, Lucia in *Cato*, Lady Touchwood in *The Double Dealer* and Marwood in *The Way of the World*, among other roles.

But the influence of her sister and brothers could not keep her at Drury Lane and in 1785 she joined the circuits at Chester and Newcastle, then under the management of Charles Edward Whitlock. She had married Whitlock in June of that year. For some nine years the Whitlocks acted in various venues in the north, including York and Edinburgh. In the latter city, at the Theatre Royal in Shakespeare Square, in 1793 Mrs Whitlock acted nineteen capital roles, among them Alicia in *Jane Shore*, Juliet, Belvidera in *Venice Preserv'd*, Lady Macbeth and Lady Randolph in *Douglas*. While at Edinburgh they were engaged by Thomas Wignell for his Chestnut Street Theatre in Philadelphia. Mrs Whitlock first acted in America at Annapolis and then made her Philadelphia debut on 19 February 1794 as Isabella in *Isabella; or the Fatal Marriage*, with her husband as Count Baldwin.

Playing at the major eastern cities in America, including New York, Boston and Charleston, Elizabeth became a major star and was called 'the American Siddons.' With her husband she returned to London about 1807, returned to America in 1812, and after several more years went once more back to England, where her husband died at Addlestone, Surrey, on 3 March 1822. Having given up the stage, Elizabeth lived in comfort another 14 years and died at Addlestone on 27 February 1836. Her sister Sarah described her as 'a noble, glorious creature, very wild and eccentric.' Sarah's biographer, Thomas Campbell, wrote that Elizabeth was 'just what Mrs Siddons would have been if she had swallowed a bottle of champagne.' The portrait attributed to Downman (**374**) was inventoried by Mathews as of Frances Kemble, later Mrs Francis Twiss (1759-1822), and is tentatively shown as of her in *Pictures in the Garrick Club*. But we believe it to be of Mrs Whitlock. For Frances Kemble, see the *BDA* 8: 329-332.

WIGNELL, Mrs Thomas
See Anne BRUNTON

WILKINSON, James Pimbury 842
b. 1787
James Wilkinson, who was perhaps the son of the manager of the York circuit, Tate Wilkinson, spent most of his career in the provinces. He made his first London appearance at the English Opera on 15 June 1816 as Simon Spatterdash in *The Boarding House* and then continued there for a while and at the Adelphi for a few years. Though not regarded as a capital performer, Wilkinson was pictured in a number of characters, especially in engravings published in *Terry's Theatrical Gallery* and the *British Stage.*

WILKINSON, Rosemond
See Mrs John MOUNTAIN

WILKINSON, Tate 843
1739-1803
The peripatetic actor-manager Tate Wilkinson was born on 27 October 1739 in London, the son of a clergyman. According to Tate's own *Memoir* of 1790 his education was irregular. His father died while being transported to America for performing illegal marriages, and Tate turned his back on a life in the clergy in favour of a career on the stage. He tried Covent Garden Theatre, but he failed to impress the manager John Rich and antagonized Peg Woffington, the company's leading actress. His problems with people of importance were usually caused by his natural talent for mimicry. Peg was infuriated when she thought Tate mimicked her from a box while she was acting. On the other hand, he impressed David Garrick at Drury Lane when Wilkinson gave his impersonation of the actor-manager Samuel Foote, Garrick's antagonist. Over the years he was in and out of favour with those he aped. Tate's career, which took him all over the three kingdoms again and again, was a series of successes and failures, and his memoir records many of them frankly and with equanimity; he was at heart an honest (though windy) man in a tumultuous profession.

Because Wilkinson acted so regularly at provincial theatres he had the opportunity to build a repertoire of important roles, among them Aimwell in *The Beaux' Stratagem*, Hastings in *Jane Shore*, Horatio, Hamlet, and the Ghost in *Hamlet*, Petruchio in *The Taming of the Shrew*, Lord Chalkstone in *Lethe*, King Lear, Richard III, Cadwallader in *The Author*, Coriolanus, Shylock, Othello, Mrs Amlet in *The Confederacy*, Bayes in *The Rehearsal* and Romeo. But acting was not really his forte, and when he performed from time to time in London he was rarely seen in leading roles. In the first part of his career – from about 1757, when he was taken on at Drury Lane by Garrick, to 1766, when he joined Joseph Baker in the management of the York circuit – he attracted audiences and enemies with his mimicry, which he frequently displayed within characters he played – as in *Puzzle* in Foote's farcical *Tea.*

Then Wilkinson visited York and was enticed into helping Baker salvage the foundering York circuit, which consisted in 1766 of York and Hull plus a changeable assortment of other towns in central England. Wilkinson had seen many good and bad companies during his wanderings, though he was still only 26 years old, and he proved an ideal partner for Baker. Tate, using much of his own savings, established the circuit as York, Hull, Leeds, Wakefield, Doncaster and Pontefract, set up the best wardrobe outside London, refurbished old playhouses and built new ones. He ended the practice of actors going door to door, hat in hand, soliciting benefit patrons, began offering, as in London, spring oratorios, and stopped filling out playbills with 'preludes, interludes, or afterludes.' He gained the respect of local burghers and married a York native, Jane Doughty, with whom he started a family. All this activity did not prevent him from making regular visits to other provincial theatres and to London to recruit actors and keep up his many contacts with fellow stage professionals. Nor did he settle for managing just the York circuit: he leased the Edinburgh Theatre Royal in 1779.

Tate Wilkinson was also a theatre historian; in 1795 he published *The Wandering Patentee* which, along with his *Memoir* details his remarkably active career and gives a vivid picture of provincial theatres in eighteenth-century Britain. Wilkinson nurtured a great number of important players who performed for him: John Philip Kemble, Sarah Siddons, Dorothy Jordan,

Thomas King, Charles Mathews, Elizabeth Farren, the Fawcetts and many less experienced players ('Blooms from my garden,' he called them). He was probably better known by audiences all over the country than any other actor of the period, and he must have known more theatre folk than anyone else of his time. Tate Wilkinson died on 16 November 1803, leaving the management of the York circuit to his son John. (*BDA*) [EAL]

WILLIAMS, Michael Leonard G1002
b. 1935
Michael Williams was born in Manchester on 9 July 1935, the son of Michael Leonard and Elizabeth (née Mulligan) Williams. He attended St Edward's College and trained at RADA. In 1959 he made his stage debut at the Nottingham Playhouse as Auguste in *Take the Fool Away*, and in 1961 he made his London debut at the Duchess Theatre as Bernard Fuller in *Celebration*. Most of his stage work has been with the Royal Shakespeare Company, which he joined in 1963: Puck in *A Midsummer Night's Dream*, Filch in *The Beggar's Opera*, Guildenstern in *Hamlet*, the Fool in *King Lear* and Troilus, among many roles. He made his film debut in 1966 as the Herald in *Marat/Sade*, a role he had played on the stage with the RSC and in New York in 1965. Other principal films include *In Search of Alexander the Great* (1980), *Enigma* (1981), *Educating Rita* (1982) and *Henry V* (1990). On television he has been seen in *My Son, My Son* (1978), *Love in a Cold Climate* (1980), and in the series *Elizabeth R.* (1971), *A Fine Romance* (1980-1981), *September Song* (1992-1994) and *Conjugal Rites* (1993-1994). Leonard married the actress Judi Dench in 1971. He became a member of the Garrick Club in 1977.

WILLIAMSON, Sarah
See Sarah SMITH

WILLIS, Sir John Ramsay 955
1908-1988
John Willis, the Judge of the High Court of Justice, Queen's Bench Division, 1966-1980, was born on 1 January 1908, the son of Dr and Mrs J. K. Willis, of Cranleigh, Surrey. He was educated at Lancing and at Trinity College, Dublin, and called to the Bar, Gray's Inn, in 1932. He served in the Army in France, India and Burma during the Second World War, rising to Lt Colonel. He became a Bencher at Gray's Inn in 1953 and QC in 1956; he served as Recorder of Southampton, 1955-1966, Deputy Chairman of East Suffolk QS 1965-1971, and Member of the Parole Board 1974-1975. He was knighted in 1966. Sir John was married to Peggy Ellen Branch in 1935 and then to Barbara Ringrose in 1959. He became a member of the Garrick Club in 1955 and died on 29 Octber 1988.

WILSON, Richard 296, 844
1744-1796
Richard Wilson's father was a cleric at Durham Cathedral who died young, leaving a widow and large family. Richard, born in 1744, was sent to London to be a jeweller's apprentice with his father's brother, but he was attracted to the stage and spent his early years as a strolling player at Leeds, Carrickfergus, Norwich and Edinburgh – where his first role is known: King Lear, on 23 November 1772 at the Theatre Royal in Shakespeare Square. He also tried Scapin in *The Cheats of Scapin*, Ben in *Love for Love*, Constant in *The Provok'd Wife*, Prince Hal in *1 Henry IV*, Ranger in *The Suspicious Husband* and Polonius in *Hamlet* (**296**) – a mixed bag of characters, but he was best in low comedy and musical pieces. Samuel Foote saw Wilson's work in Edinburgh and engaged him for the summer of 1774 at the Haymarket in London, where he made his debut on 30 May as Mungo in *The Padlock* and an unspecified part in *The Nabob*. After another summer at the Haymarket he was hired for the 1775-76 season at Covent Garden and acted there through the 1782-83 winter season, while appearing regularly at the Haymarket most of his summers. Among his most successful roles were Jerome in *The Duenna* and Sir Tunbelly Clumsy in *The Man of Quality*.

Wilson was regularly plagued by creditors, and critics complained of his lack of diligence. His audiences too often had to settle for someone else reading Wilson's part when the actor failed to appear. In 1786 he fled town to avoid creditors and performed in Ireland and Scotland, but he returned to Covent Garden and the Haymarket for 1790-91. He suffered from gout, tried to keep creditors at a distance, borrowed heavily from the Covent Garden manager, tried his hand at playwriting, shared management duties in Dundee, acted in the provinces, and ended up in debtors' prison, where he died on 14 June 1796. He had five wives over the years, two of whom he may actually have married. The portrait in the Garrick Club (**844**) attributed to Roberts in *PGC* is now credited to Ryley and shows Wilson as Ben in *Love for Love*. (*BDA*) [EAL]

WILSON, Sarah
See Sarah HARLOWE

WOFFINGTON, Margaret **845-849**
1717?-1760
She was carefree, fetching, witty, talented, generous, hard-working, caustic, catty, self-centred, vain, tough, passionate, vulnerable, haughty – everything and more that one could ask in an actress. She was Margaret Woffington of Dublin, born perhaps in 1717. Her early years are so shrouded in mystery that her many biographers over the centuries have spilled much ink second-guessing their subject. Fortunately, most of the unanswered questions about her and the many colourful tabloid-type tales of her private life (laid out in the *BDA* for all to see) did not have much bearing on the stage career that concerns us here. Her earliest theatrical employer may have been the lively Signora Violante, an Italian equilibrist, whose troupe entertained at the Smock Alley Theatre in Dublin in 1729-30, though the earliest mention of Miss Woffington in the bills came in December 1731: she acted Macheath in a Lilliputian version of *The Beggar's Opera* at Violante's 'booth' theatre in Dame Street. Peg and her sister Mary, to whom Peg was devoted throughout her life, were in that show again in London, at the Haymarket Theatre on 4 September 1732. By 1735 Peg was at the Aungier Street theatre in Dublin, singing, dancing and acting such parts as Dorinda in an alteration of *The Tempest*, Ophelia in *Hamlet* and Rose in *The Recruiting Officer* – but the critics, if any saw her work, were silent, so we have no way of knowing if the neophyte showed promise or not. But during those years she had the opportunity to learn from, among others, the Elrington family of actors and the actor-manager John Ward. Then traces of her are lost until the winter of 1739, when she was again at Aungier Street to play Polly in *The Beggar's Opera* and, more importantly, Silvia (a breeches part) in *The Recruiting Officer*. On 25 April 1740 she acted Sir Harry Wildair in *The Constant Couple*, another breeches role and one with which she was identified for the rest of her career. The Dublin audiences loved it.

On 6 November 1740 Peg acted Sir Harry at Covent Garden Theatre in London, an appearance commanded by the Prince of Wales. Her 1740-41 season under John Rich's management also brought her before London audiuences as, among less familiar characters, Cordelia in *King Lear* (with Dennis Delane), Letitia in *The Old Bachelor* and Cherry in *The Stratagem*. Her success was remarkable, and London had found a new idol. Peg, after an argument with Rich over salary, moved to Drury Lane, where she first appeared as Mrs Sullen in *The Stratagem* – with Kitty Clive as Cherry – on 22 September 1741. They would be rivals for years, as would George Ann Bellamy and anyone else who endangered Peg's position in the limelight (but who can say if her rivalries, and some of her love affairs, were not at least partly the creation of the scribblers, including Horace Walpole, who relished such gossip). Also in 1741-42 at Drury Lane Peg acted Rosalind in *As You Like It*, Lady Brute in *The Provok'd Wife*, Nerissa in *The Merchant of Venice* and Belinda *The Man of Mode*.

While Peg Woffington was establishing herself as London's new model of elegance and beauty at Drury Lane, David Garrick was stunning them at the Goodman's Fields Theatre as a volatile Richard III. On 26 May 1742 he came over to Drury Lane to act King Lear, with Peg playing Cordelia. They were struck with one another and almost immediately left London for Dublin, where they played Richard III and Lady Anne, Ophelia and Hamlet, Fondlewife and Letitia in *The Old Bachelor* and Silvia and Plume in *The Recruiting Officer*. Then, when they returned to London, they set up housekeeping, something with which Peg was familiar but which was not Davy's cup of tea.

So they eventually went their separate ways socially but continued, for years, a compatible relationship in the theatre. At Drury Lane Peg acted most of her previous characters plus Isabella in *Measure for Measure*, Viola in *Twelfth Night* and Cleopatra in *All for Love*, among others.

But even after Garrick became manager of Drury Lane, Peg was dissatisfied with the roles she received – she was in competition with Susanna Maria Cibber and Kitty Clive – and signed on at Covent Garden again for 1748-49, where she was clearly the leading lady. Indeed, she was seen as Portia in *Julius Caesar*, Calista in *The Fair Penitent*, Desdemona in *Othello*, Lady Macbeth, Gertrude in *Hamlet* and Lady Fanciful in *The Provok'd Wife*. She was given more serious roles at Covent Garden (though often opposite the lumbering Quin), but in 1750-51 Mrs Cibber came over from Drury Lane, and Peg had to compete again for good parts (she was given Gertrude because Mrs Cibber was Ophelia, for example). It was good experience, and Peg was a willing worker and frequently substituted for ailing actresses. She had the talent in both comedy and tragedy, and the only flaw mentioned by critics was her voice, which Colley Cibber said was 'not that Silver Tone some possess' – and that deficiency may have been most apparent when she had to share the stage with an actress like Mrs Cibber, who was a professional singer. So again Peg felt dissatisfied and left for Dublin in 1751.

At Smock Alley Theatre she joined Thomas Sheridan's company for three seasons before returning in the autumn of 1754 to Covent Garden, where she added to her repertoire, among other characters, Zara in *The Mourning Bride* and Jocasta in *Oedipus*. But time was taking its toll. Margaret Woffington had been on the stage over 20 years and had been living an eventful offstage life with her numerous competitors in the theatre and with her various lovers. Her last stage appearance was at Covent Garden as Rosalind in *As You Like It* on 3 May 1757. She was speaking the epilogue when she had a paralytic seizure. One of the liveliest of actresses spent the rest of her days an invalid. Margaret Woffington died on 28 March 1760. (*BDA*) [EAL]

WOLFIT, Sir Donald
1902-1968 **43, 850, G1003, G1012, G1014**
The distinguished actor-manager Donald Wolfit was born on 20 April 1902, the son of William Pearce Woolfitt [sic] and his wife Emma (née Tomlinson). He began his theatrical career at York in September 1920 as an extra in *The Merchant of Venice* and first appeared in London in November 1924 at the Haymarket as Phirous in *The Wandering Jew*. He was with the Old Vic in 1929-30, toured Canada as Robert Browning in *The Barretts of Wimpole Street* in 1931-32, and played Mowbray in Gielgud's *Richard of Bordeaux* in 1932. Then followed his long association acting in and producing Shakespearean plays at the Stratford Memorial Theatre; he also acted for many seasons at a number of London theatres and various festivals. During the Second World War Wolfit made an important contribution to home front morale with 112 performances of lunch-time Shakespeare at the Strand Theatre. Among his notable roles were the title role in *Tamburlaine* and Lord Ogleby in *The Clandestine Marriage* (Old Vic 1951), Oedipus in *Oedipus Rex* and *Oedipus at Colonus* (King's Theatre, Hammersmith 1953), and many major leads in Shakespeare: Hamlet, Othello, Shylock, Richard III, Malvolio and Macbeth. Wolfit also made numerous film and television appearances. He was made CBE in 1950 and was knighted in 1957. Sir Donald served as President of the Royal General Theatrical Fund. His autobiography *First Interval* was published in 1955. He was married three times: to Chris Frances Castor, Susan Katherine Anthony and Rosalind Den Payne (the daughter of the actor-director B. Iden Payne). Rosalind Payne appeared with Wolfit in many of his productions. Sir Donald became a member of the Garrick Club in 1942. He died on 17 February 1968. An extensive collection of his papers, mainly dealing with his career as actor-manager, are at the Harry Ransom Humanities Research Center, University of Texas, Austin. (*WWW, OCT*)

WONTNER, Arthur **851**
1875-1960
Born in London on 21 January 1875, Arthur Wontner trained for the stage under Sarah

Thorne at the Theatre Royal Margate. He was with Louis Calvert's Shakespeare touring company and over the next several years toured with Lewis Waller, visited Australia and New Zealand in Sir Herbert Beerbohm Tree's company, and reappeared in London in 1906 in *Raffles* under Charles Frohman. For another 42 years Wontner was associated with some of the best managers and finest actors. He played Laertes to Irving's Hamlet, was with Granville Barker's company, and appeared with Lilah McCarthy, Mrs Patrick Campbell, Martin Harvey and John Hare. Under his own management at the Criterion he produced and acted. Between 1926 and 1929 he acted in New York and toured America. Back in London in 1929, he appeared at Drury Lane as Richelieu and was seen there as Fouchée in *Napoleon* (**851**) and Malvolio in 1932. He continued acting on the stage until 1948 and also appeared in many films (portraying Sherlock Holmes in five of them) and television productions. He served on the London Theatre Council and as Treasurer of British Actors' Equity and for more than 25 years was a member of the Committee of the Actors' Orphanage. He became a member of the Garrick Club in 1916. Wontner died on 10 July 1960.

WOOD, Mary Ann
See Mary Anne PATON

WOODWARD, Henry **852-854**
1714-1777
The son of a tallow chandler, Henry Woodward was born on 2 October 1714 in Southwark. He went to Merchant Taylor's School, received some training in dance and acting from the Covent Garden manager and harlequin John Rich and was cast in a juvenile version of *The Beggar's Opera* on 1 January 1729. Young Woodward then joined Goodman's Fields Theatre in the autumn of 1730 and was given such parts as Simple in *The Merry Wives of Windsor*, the Page in *The Orphan*, Dicky in *The Constant Couple*, Filch in *The Beggar's Opera* and the title role in *Tom Thumb*. The lad gained further experience at the Richmond Theatre and at Fielding's Southwark Fair booth. On 21 April 1732 (the *BDA* mistakenly dates this 1752) he played the lead in *Harlequin's Contrivance* at Goodman's Fields and began his career in pantomimes. Throughout his stage life he had multiple lines: low and high comedy characters in plays and athletic leading roles in harlequinades. *The Theatrical Review* (1757) noted the paradox: 'His figure is perfectly genteel, his voice smart, agreeable, and pliant, and both seem to point out the parts of a genteeler cast, as those which he is likeliest to look, and consequently to perform; and yet ... it is not in those he succeeds best; and he never pleases his audience more, than when he is obliged to distort that genteel figure, into the aukward deportment of a Scrub [in *The Beaux' Stratagem*] or the like.'

By 1733-34 Woodward was acting regularly at Goodman's Fields in the winters and the Haymarket in the summers; to these activities he sometimes added work at the fairs in early autumn. He was a busy, hard-working, sober, serious, frugal player who specialized in comic characters: Jacques in *Love Makes the Man*, Clodpole in *The Lover's Opera*, Tom in *The Funeral*, Rodrigo in *Othello*, Osric in *Hamlet* and Tattle in *Love for Love*. He took his lines to Drury Lane after the Licensing Act of 1737 closed down Goodman's Fields, and then Covent Garden from 1741. He was then engaged by the Dublin manager Thomas Sheridan. At Smock Alley Theatre on 28 September 1747 Woodward played Marplot in *The Busy Body*. Presenting satirical entertainments at the rival theatre on Capel Street was Samuel Foote, and Woodward had the audacity to present a monologue titled *Coffee* in opposition to Foote's *Dish of Chocolate*. That led to paper wars not unlike the pompous challenges of swordsmen and boxers – wars which created audience interest and certainly made it look as though the comedians were at one another's throats, which they sometimes were. But the sober side of Woodward seems to have prevented him from getting as deeply involved in antic entertainments and paper wars as Foote regularly was. By the time of his 1747 Dublin visit, Woodward had established himself as one of the best comic actors of his time and a favourite in such characters as Marplot, Bobadil in *Every Man in His Humour*, the Fine Gentleman in *Lethe*, Brass in *The Confederacy* (**854**), Mercutio in *Romeo and Juliet*, Petruchio in *Catherine and Petruchio* (**853**) and, as always, Harlequin.

In the autumn of 1748 Woodward returned to London to act at Drury Lane under David Garrick's management. There he remained until 1758, acting and presenting pantomimes of his own devising, with excursions to Dublin. His trips made him a favourite with the Irish and involved him in 1758 in the management of Smock Alley, shared with the actor Spranger Barry. The venture ended up losing Woodward some £3000. He then headed for a return engagement at Covent Garden, where he remained for eight seasons. In 1770, when his contract ended, he published a notice of his intention to go to Scotland with Samuel Foote and the summer Haymarket troupe. Then Woodward came back to Covent Garden, for over £16 weekly, and there he stayed in the winters until his death. He had given up harlequinades by this time, but in the 1770s he was still adding new characters to his repertoire, among them the first Captain Jack Absolute in *The Rivals*. His final appearance on the stage was as Stephano in *The Tempest* on 13 January 1777. He died the following 17 April. (*BDA*) [EAL]

WORSTHORNE, Sir Peregrine Gerard 965

b. 1923

The editor and writer Peregrine Worsthorne was born on 22 December 1923, the son of Col Koch de Gooreynd, OBE (who assumed the surname of Worsthorne by deed poll, 1921) and Baroness Norman. After attending Stowe School, he took a degree at Cambridge, furthered his education at Oxford and served in the Second World War. After holding a position as sub-editor at the *Glasgow Herald*, 1946, Worsthorne joined the *Times* editorial staff, 1948-1953 and then the *Daily Telegraph*, 1953-1961. He was Deputy Editor of the *Sunday Telegraph*, 1961-1976, Associate Editor, 1976-1986, and Editor, 1986-1989. Among his books are *Perigrinations. Selected Pieces* (1980), *By the Right* (1987) and *Tricks of Memory: An Autobiography* (1993). He was knighted in 1991. In 1950 he married Claude Bertrand de Colasse, who died in 1990, and then in 1991 Lady Lucinda, daughter of Viscount Lambton. Sir Peregrine became a member of the Garrick Club in 1971.

WRENCH, Benjamin 855-857

1778-1843

Wrench spent his early career at York and Edinburgh and was at Bath in 1805. He was engaged at Drury Lane from 1809 to 1815, making his debut as Belcour in *The West Indian* on 7 October 1809; among his roles were Captain Absolute in *The Rivals* and Loveless in *A Trip to Scarborough*. Wrench was at the English Opera House (Lyceum) 1816-1818, and then at Covent Garden. He scored a great success at the Adelphi in 1821 as Tom in *Tom and Jerry*. He died in 1843. His wife Hannah Henrietta Wrench, who died after 1827, acted in London and is noticed in the *BDA* as Mrs William Perkins Taylor. (*DNB*)

WRIGHTEN, James 858

1745-1793

Born in 1745, James Wrighten worked as a copper-plate printer before turning to the stage and performing with a travelling company. About 1769 in Birmingham he met and married the actress Mary Ann Matthews, and the two were hired by Drury Lane in London for the 1769-70 season. Mrs Wrighten was a talented actress and had a substantial career in England and, as Mrs Pownall, in America; James, on the other hand, acted mostly minor roles, like Burgundy in *King Lear*, Snake in *The School for Scandal* and Surly in *The Alchemist*. He found his real theatrical calling in the summer of 1785 at the Haymarket Theatre, where he served as a prompter. He became the Drury Lane prompter in the autumn of 1785, replacing Ralph Harwood. Though he never developed an acting career that amounted to much, he was a useful performer and, as Michael Kelly said in his *Reminiscences* in 1826, 'a man most esteemed and respected' as a prompter. He was not thought of that way by his wife, however, who in 1789 published a pamphlet calling her husband 'gross and filthy.' Wrighten was of great service to Drury Lane, however, and he was a devoted secretary to the Theatrical Fund which aided indigent retired players. Wrighten died on 2 April 1793 at the age of 48. (The Index of Sitters in *Pictures in the Garrick Club* does not supply Wrighten's birth year, though the specific information about his age at his death, from a

Kemble MS at the British Library, seems reliable.) (*BDA*) [EAL]

WRIXON-BECHER, Lady
See Eliza O'NEILL

WROUGHTON, Richard **859**
1748-1822
Richard Wroughton was born at Bath in 1748, the son of a Colonel 'Rotton,' the spelling of whose name was changed (by Richard, one supposes) for stage use by 1768, probably to disarm critical punsters. Richard was originally intended for medicine, but on 24 October 1768 he was acting Zaphna in *Mahomet* at Covent Garden Theatre in London. He then tried Tressel in *Richard III*, Altamont in *The Fair Penitent*, the title role in *George Barnwell*, Malcolm in *Macbeth* and other characters. He settled in for 15 seasons at Covent Garden. Friendly, faithful, and hard-working, Wroughton was earning £12 weekly by 1786, but he felt he was unjustly treated by the management, quarrelled over the favoured treatment the younger Holman (*q.v.*) was receiving, and lost his position. It seems likely that Wroughton misjudged his own acting talent, which seems to have been ordinary, but Holman's career fared not much better with the critics.

Wroughten had become involved in the management of Sadler's Wells from 1784 and handled the business so well that the two patent houses saw his venture as a serious threat to them. Wroughton also toured the provinces, performing in Dublin and perhaps Edinburgh, but returned to London to act and to serve as the acting manager at Drury Lane almost to the end of the century. He announced his retirement in 1798, but within two years he was back at Drury Lane, helping in the management. In 1810 he joined a group of fellow players to petition the King for a third patent, but Covent Garden and Drury Lane prevented the attempt. Remarkably, he continued acting at Drury Lane for another five years, testifying to his ability to get along even with enemies. Wroughton finally retired for good after the 1814-15 season and 37 years in the profession. During that time he amassed over 200 roles, some leading, some secondary. Among them were such Shakespearean characters as Prince Hal in *1 Henry IV*, Laertes and the Ghost in *Hamlet*, Romeo, Jaques in *As You Like It* and Edgar in *King Lear*. The variety in his repertoire was certainly useful, but the critics found him second rate. The *Druriad*, for example, warned him never again to play Plume in *The Recruiting Officer*, and when he and Mrs Jordan acted Romeo and Juliet the *Monthly Mirror* said the play 'has not often been so ill performed.' The unkindest cut was the *Druriad*'s 'there never was a story of more woe/ Than Wroughton croaking love-sick Romeo.' That seems to have been about as close to a rotten pun as the critics dared get.

But Wroughton was well-liked by people in and out of the theatre, proved adept at management and left a 'handsome fortune' to his widow Elizabeth when he died on 7 February 1822. (*BDA*) [EAL]

WYNDHAM, Sir Charles **860, B177**
1837-1919
Born on 25 March 1837 and christened Charles Culverwell, he was the son of the surgeon Robert James Culverwell. Although he qualified as a physician, he was drawn to amateur theatricals in which he used the surname Wyndham, which he legally adopted in 1886. After a short-lived professional engagement at the Royalty Theatre in 1862, he went to America and enlisted with Union forces in the Civil War. During the war he also made appearances on the stage, notably as Osric in John Wilkes Booth's *Hamlet* at Washington in April 1863. He returned to England in 1864, made some reputation as a light comedian, and took a company to tour America from 1871 to 1873 and again in 1883. Wyndham took over the Criterion Theatre and built the Wyndham on the corner of Charing Cross Road and the New Theatre in St Martin's Lane, and he proceeded to turn them into some of the most important venues in London. He also continued to act, especially the title role in *David Garrick* (**860**), the popular play by Robertson that opened at the Criterion on 15 November 1886. Wyndham was knighted in 1902. He became a member of the Garrick Club in 1886.

In 1860 Wyndham married his first wife Emma Silberrad, who died in 1916. That year he married Mary Moore (1862-1931), the widow of the playwright James Albery. She was a fine actress who played leading roles opposite Wyndham, and after his death on 12 January 1919 she continued to conduct his managerial enterprises. After Mary Wyndham died, her son Bronson James (by Albery) and Sir Charles Wyndham's son Howard (1865-1947) by his first wife (who had been the sister of the American dramatist Bronson Howard) took over control.

Y

YATES, Frederick Henry **861, 862**
1797-1842
Frederick Henry Yates was born on 4 February 1797, the son of Thomas Yates, a tobacco importer in Russell Square. He was educated at Charterhouse School, worked later in the commissariat department and was with Wellington in the Peninsula. Urged on by his friend, the comedian Charles Mathews, he turned to the stage. He appeared, it seems, for the first time in Boulogne, France, as Fustian in *Sylvester Daggerwood*. He was at Edinburgh in February 1818, playing Shylock, Iago, Richard III and Bolingbroke (in Kean's Richard II). Announced as from Edinburgh, Yates made his debut at Covent Garden on 7 November 1818, as Iago. He remained at that theatre through 1824-25. Though he acted roles like Macduff, Buckingham, Casca and Glenalvon in *Douglas*, Yates made his reputation mainly as a comic actor, following the line of Mathews. Among his roles were Moses in *The School for Scandal*, Dick in *The Apprentice*, Boniface in *The Stratagem*, Mordecai in *Love à la Mode* and Flexible in *Love, Law and Physic*. He also presented entertainments in which he imitated other well-known actors.

In March 1825 Yates and Daniel Terry purchased the Adelphi Theatre for £25,000. They opened it on 10 October 1825 and enjoyed a successful first season, highlighted by Fitzball's *The Pilot* that played for 200 nights. When Terry soon retired from the partnership, Yates was joined by Mathews, and when the latter died in June 1835 Yates continued on at the Adelphi (also acting there and elsewhere in London) until 1842. Among his late roles were Robert Macaire in *L'Auberge des Adrets*, Fagin in *Oliver Twist*, Mr Gay in *Jack Sheppard* and Pickwick in *The Peregrinations of Pickwick*. He had also managed the Caledonian Theatre (renamed the Adelphi) with William Henry Murray in Edinburgh and, with Braham, the Coliseum in Regent's Park

Yates suffered a stroke in Dublin in 1842 and returned to London, where he died at No 4, Mornington Crescent on 21 June 1842 and was buried in the vaults of St Martin-in-the-Fields. He was an original member of the Garrick Club in 1831, but resigned in 1840. In 1823 he had married the actress Elizabeth Brunton (1799-1860), the sister of the more famous Anne Brunton (later Mrs Merry and noticed in the *BDA* as Mrs Thomas Wignell). Their son, the journalist and novelist Edmund Yates is noticed in the *DNB*.

Yates, short in stature, was a sound and versatile actor and a resourceful manager. (*DNB*)

YATES, Richard **864, 865**
1706?-1796
Richard Yates, who became an important actor at Drury Lane and also was active at the late summer fairs in London, may have been born about 1706. Identifying his activities in the 1730s is sometimes difficult, because Yeates the elder and younger (no relation) were active at the fairs about the same time. Our subject may have been the Yates who acted in *The Rival Milliner* at the Haymarket Theatre on 19 January 1736 and went on to play at Lincoln's Inn Fields Theatre, at Covent Garden in 1737-38, and at Drury Lane in 1739-40. If so, some of his more important roles were Brazen in *The Recruiting Officer*, Mrs Fardingale in *The Funeral*, Roderigo in *Othello*, Jeremy in *Love for Love*, Pantaloon in *Harlequin Shipwrecked* and Dapper in *The Alchemist*. That Yates also turned up at Bartholomew Fair in 1739 and 1740 and at Goodman's Fields Theatre in 1740-41 and 1741-42 playing somewhat larger roles. To confuse matters further, the Richard Yates we have been following paraded under the name of David ap Shinken at Goodman's Fields. Playgoers of the time, of course, knew who was who at the theatres. In any case, Richard Yates built up a sizeable repertoire of secondary roles, making himself one of those 'useful' actor-dancer-singers of the period.

From 1742-43 until 1766-67 Yates acted primarily at Drury Lane (under David Garrick's management from 1747-48), adding to his list of important characters such new ones as Jeremy and Ben in *Love for Love*, Foigard in *The Stratagem*, a Witch in *Macbeth*, Harlequin in *Harlequin Grand Volgi*, Sparkish in *The Country Wife*, Malviolio in *Twelfth Night* (**864**), Pistol and Fluellen in *Henry V*, The Drunken Man in *Lethe*, Dogberry in *Much Ado about Nothing*, and Jerry Blackacre in *The Plain Dealer* (which he learned at the age of about 50). He moved to Covent Garden in 1767 for a few years, then journeyed to Edinburgh and back to Drury Lane. He finally settled at Covent Garden in the autumn of 1782. Throughout his career he made appearances at fairs and sometimes managed booth theatres.

Though Yates usually acted small parts in comedies, he became a favourite, saved his money and augmented his income by marrying twice, both times to actresses. He and his successful second wife had enough money to buy into the King's Theatre (opera house) in London in November 1773. There he became noted for his stinginess, according to W. T. Parke in his *Musical Memoirs*, and was described as a 'dwarf-like manager, who had an eye to every thing ...' Yates sold his share in the opera house in 1778 and returned to acting in Edinburgh and Norwich. He died on 21 April 1796 at the age of 79, 83, 89, 90 or 97, depending on which source one uses; his ending was thus just as obscure as his beginning. Better known and more talented than Dicky Yates was his second wife, Mary Ann, who was one of London's leading actresses (*q.v.*). (*BDA*) [EAL]

YATES, Mrs Richard the second, Mary Ann, née Graham **863**
1728?-1787
Mary Ann Graham was probably born in 1728 in Birmingham, the daughter of the captain's steward on the *Ariel*, William Graham and his wife Mary. Her early years are a blank, but she seems to have made her first stage appearance in Dublin as Anna Bullen in *Henry VIII* on 22 January 1753 under the manager Thomas Sheridan, who presumably used his oratorical expertise to train Mary Ann. She then came to London, where she may have begun her theatrical chores at Drury Lane as a dresser and bit-part player. The first certain evidence we have of her acting there dates from 25 February 1754, when she appeared as Marcia in *Virginia*; the prompter Cross noted her as 'a gentlewoman who never appear'd on the stage before.' Paul

Hiffernan in *The Tuner* in March described Miss Graham as 'a new Actress with a graceful Figure, pleasing Voice, and praiseworthy Deportment.' She acted the title role in *Jane Shore* for her benefit on 29 April. After a few more appearances, Miss Graham disappeared from the stage, and when she returned it was as Alcmena in *Amphitryon* on 15 December 1756, advertised as Mrs (Richard) Yates. Her husband (*q.v.*), a secondary player in the company, seems to have devoted at least some of his time to managing her career, though Mary Ann proved to be quite capable of managing herself, and she worked her way to the top of London's select list of prima donnas.

Mrs Yates seems to have received training from the author Arthur Murphy and from David Garrick, but her acting, which was often described over the years as imperious, haughty or lofty, seems to have been patterned more after the declamatory style of the early eighteenth century. Since her forté was tragedy, that style worked effectively. Though she appeared in comedies – Lady Townly in *The Provok'd Husband*, Violante in *The Wonder*, Sylvia in *The Recruiting Officer* and the like – she was most comfortable in serious drama: Calista in *The Fair Penitent*, the title roles in *Zara* and *Jane Shore*, Lady Randolph in *Douglas*, Monimia in *The Orphan*, Belvidera in *Venice Preserv'd*, Desdemona in *Othello*, Cordelia in *King Lear* and Andromache in *The Distrest Mother* – among many other characters. In the 1760s she established herself as the equal of Mrs Cibber and Mrs Pritchard, Garrick's other queens, but when Cibber and Pritchard died (in 1766 and 1768 respectively) Mrs Yates, then in her prime, lost her Drury Lane engagement because of a disagreement with Garrick over salary. The *Universal Museum* made it clear that she was carrying her husband: 'Dicky could not say a word for himself.'

She moved to Covent Garden, where she first appeared on 16 October 1767 as Jane Shore and then was seen in 1767-68 in some of her old characters as well as Cordelia in *King Lear*, Lady Macbeth, Cleopatra in *All for Love* and Gertrude in *Hamlet*. James Harris attended her benefit on 13 March 1769 and scribbled a note to John Hoadly about it: 'Never a fuller [house] – pit and boxes thrown together: she acted the part of Electra in the *Orestes* of Voltaire, translated on purpose for her [by Dr Thomas Francklin]. For tone, and justness of elocution, for uninterrupted attention, for everything that was nervous, various, elegant, and true, in attitude and action, I never saw her equal but Garrick.' But, again, Mrs Yates demanded more salary than Covent Garden's manager Colman would pay (£600 for the season for herself plus 'the usual salary for her husband,' according to the papers). Colman said he wouldn't have Mrs Yates for any price. So she and her husband bought into the opera house – the King's Theatre – where their interests remained until 1778. Mrs Yates proposed offering a season of both operas and plays but was turned down by the Lord Chamberlain, for the Licensing Act of 1737 restricted straight plays to Drury Lane, Covent Garden, and, during the summers, the Haymarket.

During her absence from the London stage Mary Ann and her husband acted in Edinburgh and with Richard's company at Birmingham. James Dibdin's *Annals of the Edinburgh Stage* noted that Mrs Yates drank heavily, often coming on stage 'more than half seas over.' On 15 October 1774 she returned to Drury Lane, where she quickly began fighting with Garrick over salary. She was such an attraction that Garrick put up with her behaviour; by 1778-79 she was being paid £800 for the season and was evidently worth it. On 17 February 1775, when *Braganza* was premiered, by the end of the play, wrote Walpole to Mason, 'They clapped, shouted, huzzaed, cried bravo, and thundered out applause' for the play and its star.

Her last regular stage appearance was on 11 May 1783 at Covent Garden, as Hermione in *The Winter's Tale*. She came back in 1785 to act the Duchess in *Braganza* at Drury Lane for Mrs Bellamy's benefit and then performed in Birmingham, Edinburgh and York, but critics said her time was past, and it was. She died in May 1787 at 59. (*BDA*) [EAL]

YOUNG, Sir Charles George **S39**

1795-1869

Born on 6 April 1795, the son of a Lambeth physician, Charles Young was educated at

Charterhouse School. He entered the College of Arms in 1813 and in 1820 was made York Herald. In 1842 he was appointed Garter principal King-of-Arms and was knighted. In his capacities as York Herald and Garter King he served as secretary to missions for investing European heads of state. He made numerous contributions to heraldic literature, most of them privately printed, and also to *Notes and Queries*. Sir Charles died at his house in Prince's Terrace, Hyde Park, on 31 August 1869. He was one of the original members of the Garrick Club when it was formed in 1831. (*DNB*)

YOUNG, Charles Mayne 750?, 866-872
1777-1856
Born on 10 January 1777, the son of the London surgeon Thomas Young and his wife Anna, Charles Mayne Young was educated at Eton and Merchant Taylors' School. He worked as a clerk before appearing (as Mr Green) at Liverpool in the title role in *Douglas* 1798. He was also seen at Manchester and Edinburgh, where in 1802 he became friends with Sir Walter Scott. In 1807 at the Haymarket he made his London debut as Hamlet (**867**) on 22 June and was subsequently seen there as Hotspur in *1 Henry IV*, Petruchio in *The Taming of the Shrew*, Rolla in *Pizarro* and other major roles. The following year he acted with John Philip Kemble, his model and mentor, at Covent Garden, where he was seen as Macbeth, Prospero in *The Tempest*, Joseph Surface in *The School for Scandal*, Richard III, Cassius in *Julius Caesar* (**866**), Othello and Iago, King John (**871**) and King Lear, among other chiefly Shakespearean roles. When Kemble reduced the number of his own appearances, Young became to many followers England's leading tragedian.

Leigh Hunt found Young's Cassius most promising. On 5 April 1812 he wrote, 'It is full of fire, and yet marked with the nicest discrimination – a rare combination, in which this actor promises to excel all his contemporaries … [I]f Mr. Young proceed[s] in this manner to study his part *ambitiously*, and to read his part with that searching and patient eye which will alone enable us to catch all the pith and scope of his eloquence … he will soon oust Mr. Kemble from the throne which his grave cant has usurped …' On the other hand, when William Hazlitt saw Young play Prospero at Covent Garden on 23 July 1815 he found it 'indescribably bad. It was grave without solemnity, stately without dignity, pompous without being impressive … Mr. Young did not personate Prospero, but a pedagogue teaching his scholars how to recite the part, and not teaching them well.'

In 1822 Young was with Edmund Kean at Drury Lane, making his debut there as Hamlet on 17 October and during the season sharing leads with him. The following season found Young back at Drury Lane. He retired on 31 January 1832 after playing Hamlet, with Macready as the Ghost. Young died on 28 June 1856 at Brighton. Considering his rivals – Kemble, Kean, and Macready – Charles Mayne Young held his own well enough, but his declamatory style was too like Kemble's for audiences exposed to the excitement Kean generated. (*DNB*; Gamini Salgado, ed. *Eyewitnesses of Shakespeare*, 1975) [EAL]

YOUNG, George 750
fl. 1817
The George Young who is identified as No. 16 in Harlow's 1817 painting of the Trial of Queen Katherine in *Henry VIII* is unknown to us. Ashton suggests the possibility that it could be the English actor Charles Mayne Young (1777-1856). *See* **872**.

YOUNGE, Elizabeth
See Elizabeth POPE

Brief Lives of the Artists

A

ABBEY, Edward Austin RA **281**
1852-1911
Abbey was born in Philadelphia and studied at the Pennsylvania Academy from 1860-1871. He was employed by Harper Brothers, who sent him to England in 1878. He settled here for the rest of his life, making a number of visits to the Continent and to the United States. Abbey first exhibited at the Royal Academy in 1885 and was elected Academician in 1898. He was noted for his illustrations of historical subjects.

ALLAN, Sir William RA, PRSA **332**
1782-1850
Sir William Allan was born in Edinburgh in 1782 into a family of modest background. Educated at the High School, Edinburgh, he showed an early love of art and was apprenticed to a coach-painter. He came to London and entered the Royal Academy Schools, exhibiting his first pictures, 'Paul and Virginia' and 'Inver, near Dunkeld,' there in 1803. He would have been only fifteen when Henry Erskine Johnstone (**332**), a fellow native of Edinburgh and five years older than Allen, appeared in London at Covent Garden as Young Norval in *Douglas* in October 1797. Johnstone played the role again at Drury Lane in September 1803, and it is likely that Allan's youthful work dates from that period, for in 1805 he left for Russia, where he remained until his return to Edinburgh in 1814. During the later part of his career, Allan worked largely as a portrait, genre and history painter of no outstanding merit. A portrait by him of his friend, Sir Walter Scott, is in the National Portrait Gallery. He was elected Royal Academician in 1835 and President of the Royal Scottish Academy in 1838; he received a knighthood in 1842. Allan died in Edinburgh in 1850.

AMBROSE, C. **714**
fl. 1824-1848
The name of this lacklustre painter is identifiable only through the 30 portraits he exhibited at the Royal Academy between the above years. Apart from the Garrick Club's portrait of Reeve, he is known to have painted the dramatist James Sheridan Knowles.

'APE'
See Carlo PELLEGRINI

ARNOLD, Samuel James
See Brief Lives of the Sitters

ARROWSMITH, Thomas **648**
1792–c.1829
The above numbered portrait of John Palmer was attributed to Arrowsmith in Mathews's inventory, No 109. *Pictures in the Garrick Club* notes that it is unlikely to have been by this deaf and dumb portrait painter and miniaturist. Robert Walters points out in his 1909 catalogue of the Club's pictures that James Saxon exhibited a portrait of Palmer as Cohenberg at the Royal Academy in 1796 (**465**).

AUBREY, John **52**
John Aubrey was presumably an amateur and painted **52** from a photograph.

AYRES, Elsa **79**
fl. 1955
Elsa Ayres, née Gronvold, was married to the sculptor Arthur James John Ayres (b. 1902). They lived in London.

B

BALDRY, G.W. (Grace Baldry?) 800
fl. 1897
This little known artist exhibited one picture, entitled 'Judith', at the Royal Academy in 1897.

BANNISTER, Jane 30
fl. 1783–c.1829
Jane Bannister was the actress daughter of Charles Bannister (see Index of Sitters). She first appeared on the London stage as Amelia in *The English Merchant* at the Haymarket Theatre on 27 August 1783. After several more performances in London, at Drury Lane, she acted in amateur productions given by the Earl of Barrymore at the theatre in Brighton. At the latter place she married the actor James Swendall in 1790 and passed the remainder of her career in provincial theatres. She was still alive in 1829. Her portrait of her father was engraved in 1804.

BARBER BEAUMONT, John Thomas
1774-1841 **315, 947, 957, all after**
Barber Beaumont, a miniature painter, entered the Royal Academy Schools in 1791, gaining several medals and exhibiting there from 1794 to 1806. His interests then moved towards insurance, and in 1807 he founded the County Fire and Provident life insurance offices in premises designed by himself in Regent Street. In 1816 he established the Provident Institution and Savings Bank in Covent Garden. During the Napoleonic invasion scare he raised a rifle corps and on one occasion had them fire in Hyde Park at a target, which he was himself holding, at a range of 150 yards.

BARRON, Hugh 301, after?
c. 1747-1791
Hugh Barron was the son of an apothecary. He was a musical prodigy on the violin and became one of the best amateur performers of his day. He was a pupil of Sir Joshua Reynolds. After working for some time as a portrait painter, he visited Italy by way of Lisbon, living in Rome in 1771-1772. He returned to London and settled in Leicester Fields, and he exhibited periodically at the Royal Academy between 1782 and 1786. The Club's portrait of the actor, Charles Holland, (**301**) is thought to be a copy after his work. Redgrave described Barron's paintings as 'feeble imitations of his great master.'

BARROW, Julian 956
b. 1939
Julian Barrow was born in Cumberland. He studied painting and drawing in Florence. He has lived in his Tite Street studio in Chelsea and worked from there for over 30 years. He specializes in landscapes and country house views as well as conversation pieces and interiors. Barrow has travelled extensively in the United States and the Middle East and has exhibited on more than 20 occasions at the Royal Academy. He is President of the Chelsea Arts Society.

BATONI, Pompeo 234, after
1708-1787
The Garrick Club's portrait of David Garrick (**234**) is a copy after the original in the Ashmolean Museum, Oxford. Batoni was a highly renowned portrait painter of his day in Rome. English *milordi* making the Grand Tour frequently engaged him to paint their portraits. Garrick sat for the Ashmolean portrait in Rome at the age of 47 in 1764.

BEACH, Thomas 182, 183, 184 attr. to, 292, 390, 647 attr. to,
1738-1806 **796, 831 attr. to**
Thomas Beach was born in Dorsetshire in 1738. He studied at the St Martin's Lane Academy in London and became a pupil of Sir Joshua Reynolds in 1760 at the age of 22. He settled initially in Bath, whence he travelled in Dorset and in Somerset, specializing in portraiture of the local gentry, both single portraits and groups, which are usually on a small scale. From 1772 to 1783 he exhibited at the Society of Artists, of which he was a member and later Vice-President. By 1785 he also had a London address in St James's Square, where he had a painting room, and from there he exhibited at the Royal Academy from 1785 until 1797. The Garrick Club possesses four single portraits by him together with his 'Macbeth' (**390**),

with John Philip Kemble as Macbeth and Sarah Siddons as Lady Macbeth. Beach exhibited this painting at the Royal Academy in 1786.

BEECHEY, Sir William RA **377**
1753-1839
Beechey was born at Burford in Oxfordshire in 1753. Initially articled to a solicitor, he attended the Royal Academy as a student at the age of 21 in 1774. He started exhibiting at the Royal Academy from 1776 and, over a period of 62 years, he showed 375 paintings, virtually all of them portraits. From 1782 to 1787 he worked in Norwich, returning from there to London, where he established a successful practice. As an artist of the second rank (he was a rival to Hoppner), his reputation became eclipsed towards the end of his career by that of Lawrence. Opie once remarked that 'his pictures…seemed only fit for sea captains and merchants.' He found favour, however, with the royal family, securing the appointment of portrait painter to Queen Charlotte. In 1798 he was knighted and made a member of the Royal Academy. Beechey had no particular connection with the stage, and the Club's picture is a version, from Charles Mathews's collection, of the original at Dulwich Picture Gallery, commissioned by Desenfans about 1798.

BEERBOHM, Sir Max
1872-1956 **269, 317, 423, 669, G1010**
Max Beerbohm was born in London in Palace Gardens Terrace in 1872, son of a corn merchant from the Baltic who had settled in England. After receiving his education at Charterhouse and Merton College, Oxford, he came to know, through Sir William Rothenstein, Aubrey Beardsley and Oscar Wilde. He made a short visit to the United States as secretary to his half-brother, the actor, Sir Herbert Beerbohm Tree. Returning to London he succeeded Bernard Shaw as dramatic critic of the *Saturday Review* in 1898. Beerbohm became friendly with a number of leading literary men of the day including Henry James, Swinburne and G.K. Chesterton. In 1910 he married the actress Florence Kahn and they went to live in Italy. Beerbohm is chiefly remembered for the polished and witty style evident in his novel, *Zuleika Dobson*, in his collection of stories, *Seven Men*, and in his innumerable caricatures.

BELT, Richard C. **S37**
fl. 1873-1885
Belt exhibited 20 works at the Royal Academy between 1873 and 1885. (**S37** was shown there in 1885.) He was involved in a libel action, which he won, and which lasted from 1882 until 1884. It was claimed that all his works executed between 1876 and 1881, including the statue of Lord Byron in Park Lane, London, were in fact by two of his assistants.

BENNETT, Frank Moss **228**
1874-1953
Bennett was born in Liverpool and studied at the St John's Wood Art School, at the Slade School and at the Royal Academy Schools. He exhibited at the Academy from 1898 to 1928.

BING, Robert **822**
fl. 1697-1720
Bing, or Byng, was known to have been active, with his brother, Edward, as a drapery painter in the studio of Sir Godfrey Kneller. He also practiced for a time in Salisbury.

BLANCHE, Jacques-Emile **794**
1861-1942
Born in Paris in 1861, Blanche considered himself an Englishman by adoption. He had his tweed suits made in Savile Row, bought his hats from Lock's and his shoes from Lobb. Harold Nicholson, in Blanche's obituary for *The Times* in 1942, wrote 'he had known Victorian London and possessed a knowledge of our country life; he had observed the transition from nineteenth century to twentieth century England and been intimate with such diverse figures as Wilde, Beardsley, Henry James, George Moore and Sickert, and since he was equally intimate with three generations of French artist and writers, he formed a valuable hyphen between the two cultures.'

Blanche's portraits include those of numerous distinguished contemporaries in the world of literature, art and the theatre, including George

Moore, Aubrey Beardsley, Walter Sickert, Charles Ricketts, Charles Shannon, Marcel Proust, Colette and the Garrick Club's image of Marie Tempest.

BLEECK, Peter Van
See Peter VAN BLEECK

BOEHM, Sir Joseph Edgar (S34)
1834-1890
Boehm's career spanned the Victorian era and he became one of its best-known and most prolific portrait sculptors. He was born in Vienna in 1834 and settled in England in 1862, 'from which time he produced a great outpouring of work, much of it monumental.'

BRADLEY, William 157
1801-1857
From humble beginnings in Manchester, where he received some instruction from Mather Brown, Bradley came to London in his early twenties and obtained an introduction to Sir Thomas Lawrence. He exhibited a number of portraits at the Royal Academy and the British Institution over a period of some 20 years. His sitters numbered, among others, W. C. Macready, one of the original members of the Garrick Club in 1831.

BRIGGS, Henry Perronet RA
1791-1844 **366, 367, 450, 673**
Briggs was born at Walworth and entered the Royal Academy Schools at the age of 20. He is first recorded as having exhibited at the Royal Academy in 1814 where, apart from the following year, he showed regularly up until the year of his death. His earlier exhibits included many history paintings but, from the time of his election as an Academician in 1832, he devoted himself almost exclusively to portraiture.

BROCK, Charles Edmund RI 231
1870-1938
Brock was born in London, but went to school in Cambridge, where he studied under the sculptor Henry Wiles. He remained in Cambridge for many years, working as a portrait painter and illustrator.

BROCKEDON, William 268
1787-1854
Brockendon was born at Totnes, in Devon, and grew up to be something of a polymath. His interest in painting was matched by his travel writings and his inventions. After his father's death in 1802, he spent six months in London, at the age of fifteen, at the home of a watchmaker, learning the trade his father had practiced. By 1809, however, he changed tack and spent six years studying to be a painter and, from 1812 until 1841, he exhibited fairly regularly at the Royal Academy. He also wrote a number of travel books.

BROCKHURST, Gerald Leslie RA
1890-1978 **G0976**
Gerald Brockhurst was a portrait painter who worked up a very fashionable practice between the first and second world wars. He was also an engraver. He exhibited at the Royal Academy between 1915 and 1949 and went to live in the United States in 1939.

BROUGH, Robert 7
1872-1905
Brough exhibited in Scotland during the 1890s, and at the Royal Academy between 1897 and 1904 (including the Club's painting of George Alexander in *The Prisoner of Zenda,* in 1902). The brief career of this talented painter was brought to an abrupt end when he was killed in a railway accident at the age of thirty-two.

BROWN, Mather 682
1761-1831
Brown was an American by birth. He received some instruction from Gilbert Stuart before coming to London in 1781; he entered the Royal Academy Schools the following year. There, he received his education as an artist from Benjamin West. He executed work for Boydell's *Shakespeare Gallery*, exhibited at the British Institution and showed a large number of portraits as well as historical and biblical compositions at the Royal Academy from 1782 until the year of his death. His later work often made up for in size what it lacked in quality.

BUCHEL, Charles A. 115, 172, 328, 376
1872-1950
Buchel was an artist of German origin. He painted and drew primarily theatrical personalities and worked for a number of years for Herbert Beerbohm Tree. He exhibited seven paintings at the Royal Academy between 1898-1902, including one of Beerbohm Tree as 'Herod, King of the Jews.'

BUNBURY, Henry William 885, 886
1750-1811
William Henry Bunbury was the son of the Reverend Sir William Bunbury Bt, of Mildenhall, Suffolk. He started drawing caricatures while still at school at Westminster. Much of his work was engraved and etched, including such humorous works as *Geoffrey Gambado* and *An Academy for Grown Horsemen.* Always an amateur, his caricatures were coarsely drawn and often coarse in subject matter, but his subjects were never lampooned in an unkind manner. As a result of his genial nature, he was popular during his lifetime and became friends with Garrick, Goldsmith and Reynolds. He had his portrait painted both by Lawrence and by Reynolds.

BURNELL, Benjamin 144, 338
fl. 1790-1828
Little is known of this artist beyond the listings of his exhibited work at the British Institution and the Royal Academy, where he showed landscapes, portraits and biblical subjects over a period of 38 years. He initially entered the Royal Academy Schools as an architectural student but later took up painting.

BUSS, Robert William
1804-1875 **10, 167, 168, 478, 825**
Buss studied painting under George Clint, whose work he is known to have copied. During the earlier years of his career he painted portraits of a number of the leading actors and actresses of his day; later he moved into historical and genre subjects.

BUTLER, Timothy S 25 attr. to
b. 1806
Butler won a silver medal at the age of 18 from the Society of Arts and went on the following year to attend the Royal Academy Schools. According to Rupert Gunnis, Butler became a popular portrait-sculptor who achieved excellent likenesses. He exhibited over 100 busts at the Royal Academy between 1828 and 1879, including two busts of Charles Kemble, in 1844 and 1846, sculpted when Kemble would have been about 70.

C

CARRICK, Thomas **212**
1802-1875
Born near Carlisle, the son of a cotton mill owner, Carrick became a self-taught miniature painter. He left home and took employment with a chemist in Carlisle. But his heart was in miniature painting and he acquired a reputation in the north painting, among other portraits, one of Charles Kean, who was then beginning to make a name for himself as a provincial actor. Carrick moved to Newcastle-upon-Tyne and then to London, where he exhibited miniatures virtually every year from 1841 to 1863.

CHALON, Alfred Edward RA **452 after**
1780-1860
The younger brother of John James Chalon, Alfred Edward was born in Geneva. He was intended for a commercial career, but entered the Academy Schools at the age of 17 and first exhibited there in 1810. He went on to become a highly successful and fashionable painter of portrait watercolours with true Victorian colouring and finish.

CHILDE, James Warren **479-594, 826**
1778-1862
Graves notes two artists by the name of J. W. Childe as exhibitors at the Royal Academy, one showing landscapes from 1798 to 1810 and the other listed as a miniature painter, exhibiting portraits from 1815 until 1853. The *DNB*, however, states that both are in fact the same man, who adopted miniature painting in the course of his career. Many of his portrait exhibits were of popular actors and actresses of the day. The Garrick Club possesses a series of the actor, Charles James Matthews, in 74 parts.

CLINT, George ARA **111, 137, 150, 213, 216, 224, 286, 345, 351, 355, 430, 462, 463, 477, 630, 787, 825, 829, G1040**
1770-1854
George Clint was born in Brownlow Street, Drury Lane, in 1770, the son of a hairdresser. Clint had a varied career, starting as apprentice to a fishmonger and progressing through employment in an attorney's office to becoming a house painter. He painted the stones of the arches in the nave of Westminster Abbey. In his forties, his studio in Gower Street drew actors and actresses as a result of his having painted a number of dramatic scenes, among which is the Club's painting of William Farren, Charles Farley and Richard Jones in *The Clandestine Marriage*. He also executed a number of theatrical single portraits. Apart from his paintings, he was known as a mezzotint engraver. His engraving, after Harlow, of the trial scene in Shakespeare's *Henry VIII* attracted a lot of interest when it was shown at the Royal Academy. Clint exhibited 100 pictures, including a number of theatrical scenes, at the Royal Academy between 1802 and 1845. He was elected ARA in 1821.

CODNER, Maurice **18, 93, 299**
1888-1958
Codner was born at Stoke Newington, the son of an iron merchant. He attended Colchester School of Art and became a fashionable portrait painter. The entry for him in the *DNB* describes his portraits, in a somewhat dismissive manner, as 'what are called good likenesses, a superficial representation of features being more in demand than a penetrating analysis of character.' The Garrick Club possesses two of the best examples of his work in the portraits of Sir Seymour Hicks (**93**) and Alan Aynsworth (**18**).

COLLIER, The Hon John
1850-1934 **138, 173, 810, 820**
Collier was the son of a judge, Lord Monkswell. After Eton and study on the Continent, he worked for a time in the City. He attended the Slade School of Art and then specialized in portraiture and subject paintings. Collier was elected to the Garrick Club in 1872 and resigned seven years later in 1879.

COPE, Sir Arthur Stockdale RA
1857-1940 **830, 851**
Arthur Cope, the son of Charles West Cope, was a prolific portrait painter. By 1905, when Graves published his *Dictionary of Royal Academy Exhibitors*,

Cope, starting in 1876, at the age of nineteen, had already shown over 100 paintings. The quality of his work is variable. He was elected Academician in 1910 and knighted in 1919.

CORBETT, J. **128**
d. 1815?
Corbett was born in Cork. He was a pupil of his fellow countryman James Barry and practiced portrait painting for a while in London, before returning to his native land, where he died in poverty.

COSWAY, Richard **19, 70, 206, 223,**
1742-1821 **947, all attr. to**
The Garrick Club presently has no work attributed with any confidence to Richard Cosway.

COWARD, Sir Noel Pierce
See Brief Lives of the Sitters

CUNDELL, Charles Ernest **668**
fl. 1860-1869
Charles Cundell finds no mention in the standard art dictionaries. He exhibited three portraits at the Royal Academy between 1860 and 1869.

D

DANCE, George RA **218**
1741-1825
George Dance the Younger was the fifth son of George Dance the Elder, architect of the Mansion House. The younger George succeeded his father as Surveyor to the Corporation of the City of London by right of purchase in 1768. He was responsible for the rebuilding of Newgate Prison and for the design for the front of Guildhall. In his later years he turned to portrait drawing and caricature. He saw published '*A Collection of Portraits sketched from the Life since the year 1793, by Geo. Dance, esq., and engraved in imitation of the original drawings by Will. Daniell, ARA* (folio 1809 and 1814. Dance was a fellow of the Society of Antiquaries and a Founder Member of the Royal Academy.

DANCE-HOLLAND, Sir Nathaniel RA
1735-1811 **13, 237**
Sir Nathaniel Dance-Holland was the third son of George Dance the Elder. He studied under Francis Hayman. He spent eleven years in Italy, from 1754 to 1765, and on his return to England set himself up as a portrait painter in London. He was a Founder Member of the Royal Academy, where he exhibited sporadically from 1769 until 1790. Dance-Holland appears in the 1770s to have inherited money, and to have given up portrait painting in 1782. That year he resigned his membership at the Academy on his marriage with a Mrs Dunner, an immensely wealthy widow. (He exhibited a further three landscapes as an Honorary Exhibitor.) He took the name of Dance-Holland on his marriage, became a Member of Parliament for East Grinstead, and was created a baronet in 1800. On his death, his estate was valued at over £200,000.

DAVID, Villiers **403**
1906-1985
Villiers David was a wealthy amateur artist who occasionally exhibited. During the Second World War, when the value of his South American

holdings was suffering, he was heard to mutter, as he walked up St James's Street, 'Oh dear! Down to the last six million.' Augustus John painted a lively portrait of him.

DE LOUTHERBOURG, Philippe Jacques (Philip James) RA **236, 865**
1740-1812
De Loutherbourg was born at Basel and educated there with a view to entering the ministry of the Lutheran Church. Having determined to pursue an artistic career he went to Paris and became a pupil of Carle Van Loo and Casenova. His precocious talent resulted in his being elected an Associate of the French Academy at the age of 22 and a full Member five years later. He became known for his large wild and romantic landscapes and his battle scenes. After marriage, he travelled to Switzerland and Italy. Garrick discovered him on a trip to Paris in about 1771 and brought him back to England, were he engaged him at a salary of £500 a year, to oversee the scenery and stage apparatus at Drury Lane. De Loutherbourg brought about a revolution in theatre scenery painting and lighting effects and also assisted Garrick in a fundamental overhaul of theatrical costume. De Loutherbourg first exhibited at the Royal Academy in 1772 and continued with large numbers of works up until the year of his death. He became a full member of the Royal Academy in 1781. He quarreled with Garrick's successor, Sheridan, and left the theatre. He was known for his well-received invention, a machine he called the 'Eidophusikon', which showed moving tableaux accompanied by special lighting effects and music. De Loutherbourg was known to have indulged a taste for mysticism, healing powers and the occult at his house in Hammersmith Terrace.

DEVAS, Anthony ARA **261, 276**
1911-1958
Anthony Devas was born at Bromley, Kent. He attended the Slade School of Fine Art (1927-1930), from where he developed a successful career for himself as a fashionable portrait painter. He was elected ARA in 1953 and died five years later at the age of 47.

DE WILDE, Samuel
1751-1832
5, 12, 20, 34-35, 39, 40-42, 50, 55-56, 64, 71-76, 80, 95-96, 104, 108-109, 113, 123, 124, 127, 129, 130, 140, 145-146, 148, 151, 158-159, 161, 169-171, 179, 180-181, 188-189, 193-96, 201, 203-205, 209, 214, 219, 220-222, 258-260, 267, 272, 285, 302-305, 308-309, 313, 316, 334, 335, 339, 340, 342-343, 346, 371, 378-379, 391-394, 397-398, 404, 409, 421-422, 424-426, 431-435, 438-440, 445-48, 458-459, 464-470, 473, 595- 596, 602, 607, 610, 615, 617, 619-623, 632, 644, 646, 653- 658, 667-689, 690- 692, 698-699, 707-709, 713, 722-724, 730, 752-757, 760-761, 765, 767, 773, 781-783, 788-790, 798, 809, 814, 833-834, 837, 839, 841, 852, 855-856, 859, 866-868, 873, G1006 attr. to

Samuel De Wilde was born in Holland in 1751. When he was an infant, his widowed mother brought him to England, where they settled in Soho. De Wilde entered the Royal Academy Schools in 1769. He first exhibited at the Society of Artists in 1776 and at the Royal Academy two years later. From the 1790s (in his forties) he appears to have devoted himself almost entirely to theatrical portraiture, exhibiting some 80 theatrical subjects at the Royal Academy between 1792 and 1821.

In the early years of the nineteenth century, Charles Mathews (1776-1835), the actor, formed a renowned collection of theatrical paintings and drawings, which included many De Wildes. De Wilde worked for John Bell, a publisher of theatrical prints, and later for George Cawthorn, producing both small paintings and drawings. At least seventeen of De Wilde's pictures, which eventually ended up in Mathews's possession, were among those the artist had exhibited at the Royal Academy.

By far the greater part of the Mathews collection had been acquired after the actor's death by an original member of the Garrick Club, John Rowland Durrant. Durrant subsequently gave it to the Club, in 1835. Mathews was a good friend of De Wilde and bought or commissioned paintings directly from him. Apart from taking advantage of several major picture sales, Mathews also purchased a number of De Wilde's theatrical paintings on the dispersal, in 1819, of the noted collection of Thomas Harris. Harris, who had been manager of Covent Garden, was a major patron of theatrical painting in the late eighteenth century. Harris had also commissioned a number of theatrical portraits from Gainsborough Dupont. Ten of these are now in the Club's collection, some of them having come via Mathews's collection.

In 1819, Mathews's son, Charles James Mathews, recounted how, in the autumn of his life, De Wilde was frequently to be found at the corner of Drury Lane Theatre, a portfolio under his arm. He died in 1832 at the age of eighty-four.

DIGHTON, Robert
c. 1752-1814 **57, 83, 162, 163, 659, 700**

Dighton, who styled himself 'drawing master', was in fact an accomplished man of many talents including those of actor, caricaturist, portrait painter, etcher and humourist. Dighton exhibited at the Free Society of Artists from 1769 until 1773. His etchings were chiefly satirical portrait heads of leading members of the bar.

There was a scandal in 1806 when it was discovered that Dighton had walked off with a number of valuable prints from the British Museum. Samuel Woodburn, a highly regarded art dealer, bought a Rembrandt landscape etching from Dighton in May of that year. On visiting the British Museum to compare it with their impression, he found that the paste marks on the back of the print matched those on a page in the museum's guard book, from which the item was, of course, missing. After an inquiry, no action was taken against Dighton, for want of evidence, although the unfortunate Keeper of the Department, the Reverend William Beloe, was dismissed for not keeping a firmer eye on him. There appears to have been some sort of rough justice lately in the fact that a drawing by Dighton belonging to the Garrick Club (**561** in the Club's 1936 catalogue) was stolen from the lavatory in the Ladies' Room. The remaining pictures are now screwed to the wall. All the Club's Dightons were in Charles Mathews's collection. Dighton also acted and sang in several London theatres and pleasure gardens, and his wife, Mrs Dighton (née Bertles), also performed. For Dighton's career as a professional actor see the *BDA*, 4: 412-415.

DOBSON, William **415**
1610-1646

Dobson was the son of a gentleman who had squandered his estate. Apprenticed to Robert Peake, a portrait painter, he came to the attention of Van Dyck, who introduced him to Charles I. After Van Dyck's death in 1641, Dobson was appointed sergeant-painter to the king. His portraits have a stylistic affinity to Van Dyck and Lely. He died at the age of 36 in 1646. There is a problem in that (**415**) is supposedly a portrait of Nathaniel Lee, the mad poet, but Dobson died at roughly the same time that Lee was born.

D'ORSAY, Alfred Count **78**
1801-1852

D'Orsay was born in Paris, the son of a general in the Grand Army of the Empire. He visited England on the coronation of George IV. On his return to France he made the acquaintance of the Earl and Countess of Blessington. A few years later he moved to Italy, where Byron sat to him for his last portrait. It was at this time that Charles James Mathews, (*q.v.*), living in Italy at the expense of his father, met D'Orsay and Lady Blessington. In 1827 D'Orsay married and almost immediately separated from Lord Blessington's daughter by his first marriage, a girl at that time of little more than fifteen years. Following Lord Blessington's death in 1829, D'Orsay and Lady Blessington made their way to London and there established themselves as platonic companions. For the next 20 years they were a powerful force in the literary and artistic circles centred in Mayfair and Kensington. D'Orsay was a sculptor as well as a painter and his statuettes of Napoleon and Wellington achieved wide popularity. Towards the end of his life he fell into financial difficulties and was obliged to retire to France where, shortly before his death, he was appointed Director of the Fine Arts by Louis Napoleon, at that time President of the French Republic. D'Orsay was a founder member of the Garrick Club in 1831 but was removed four years later for non- payment of dues. *See* also the Index of Sitters for Lady Blessington.

DOWNES, Bernard **740**
fl. 1761-1775
The attribution of the Garrick Club's painting is based on the fact that Downes exhibited a painting relating to this subject at the Society of Artists in 1762. He was noted as having been a member of the Society in 1766 and exhibited at the Royal Academy from 1770 until 1775. Samuel Redgrave describes his work as being 'without merit.'

DOWNMAN, John ARA **374**
1750-1824
Downman was born in Devonshire but came early to London, where he was a pupil of Benjamin West. He studied at the Royal Academy and became a prolific portrait painter. He worked in oils and made tinted drawings. The tentative attribution to him of the Garrick Club's **374** is not convincing.

DRESSLER, Conrad **S55**
1856-1940
Born in London of German descent, Dressler studied at the Royal College of Art and in France. He stayed with Ruskin in 1886 and later became a member of the Art Workers' Guild. He established his own foundry in Chelsea and exhibited sculpture busts and medallions at the Royal Academy from 1883-1899. He then met William de Morgan and together they invented the tunnel kiln. Later in his life, Dressler went to live in Paris, and then in the United States. **S55** has now been identified as the theatrical manager and theatre builder Sefton Henry Parry.

DRUMMOND, Rose Emma **112, 225**
fl. 1815-1857
Rose Emma Drummond exhibited at the Suffolk Street Gallery and, from 1815 to 1835, at the Royal Academy. She painted miniatures, predominantly of well-known actresses. A great number of her portrait drawings in this manner were reproduced in the periodicals *The Ladies' Monthly Museum* and *La Belle Alliance (1817-1823).*

DRUMMOND, Samuel ARA
1770-1844 **441, 611, 624, 943, 952**
Samuel Drummond was born in London. His father had fought for the Pretender in the '45 rebellion. At the age of fourteen he ran away to sea and spent some six or seven years in the Service. He then took up painting and, self-taught, he provided illustrations for the *European Magazine.* He entered the Royal Academy Schools in 1791 and first exhibited there in the same year, showing over 300 works at the Royal Academy over the following 43 years. Drummond was elected ARA in 1808. He received a commission from the Directors of the British Institution for a large canvas of 'Admiral Duncan receiving the Sword of the Dutch Admiral De Winter'; that picture was presented to the Greenwich Hospital. Drummond's later work became somewhat slapdash.

DUGDALE, Thomas Cantrell RA, ROI, RP
1880-1952 **53**
Dugdale was born at Blackburn, Lancashire. He studied at the Manchester School of Art, the Royal College of Art and at the Académie Julien in Paris and served in the Near East during the First World War. He followed a career as portrait painter and textile designer, being elected Royal Academician in 1943. Dugdale was a member of the Garrick Club from 1938 until his death in 1952.

DUMMET, Joan **S6**
b. 1905
Joan Dummet was a sculptor and pastel painter who studied under Jules van Biesbroeck.

DUPONT, Gainsborough **(87 attr. to), (120, 210, 306, 460, 597,**
1754?-1797 **603, 633, 677, 683, 701)**
Gainsborough Dupont was the nephew of Thomas Gainsborough He was apprenticed to Gainsborough for seven years and also entered the Royal Academy Schools in 1775. He learned to paint from his uncle and was his only assistant. After his uncle's death, Dupont completed a number of the Gainsborough's pictures and produced studio replicas. Dupont was also a skilled mezzotint engraver who made a number of prints after his uncle's work.

Joseph Farington (1747-1821), the gossipy member of the Royal Academy, noted in his diary entry for 21 April 1795, 'Gainsborough, did not leave his nephew Dupont anything which was thought "hard". Mr. Harris of Covent Garden Theatre considering Dupont as wanting employ commissioned him to paint portraits of the Actors of that Theatre and only to proceed with the commission which he had no others.' After his uncle's death, he [Dupont] inherited his studio properties and lived for a time in Mrs Gainsborough's house, but he was of too timid and retiring a disposition to inherit his practice, though he was patronized by William Pitt and by the royal family.'

DURHAM, Joseph **S35**
1814-1877
Durham was a prolific sculptor who exhibited no fewer than 128 items at the Royal Academy between 1835 and 1878, the last being shown a year after his death. His best-known work today is undoubtedly the gilded sculpture of the Prince Consort forming the centre-piece of the Albert Memorial. This sculpture originally decorated the gardens of the Royal Horticultural Society before being moved to its present site.

Rupert Gunnis tentatively dates the Garrick Club's bust of Thackeray as 1864, after the novelist's death. Among Durham's other works may be numbered the portraits of Newton, Milton, Bentham and Harvey in front of Burlington House, Jenny Lind 'the Swedish Nightingale' and W. H. Smith.

E

EDRIDGE, Henry ARA **185, 741**
1769-1824
Edridge was a miniature painter and landscape draughtsman. He became a pupil of William Pether, the mezzotint engraver, but later developed a style of small-scale portraiture in which the full-length figure was sketched in pencil or pencil and pen, and then the head was described in detail and finished in watercolour. He also made delightful watercolour landscape drawings somewhat in the style of Thomas Hearne.

ELAND, John Shenton **101**
1872-1933
Eland studied at the Royal Academy Schools from 1893 and then in Paris. He exhibited at the Royal Academy from 1894 and worked as a portrait painter, printmaker and sculptor. He died in New York.

ELLERBY, Thomas **791**
fl. 1821-1857
Ellerby worked in London as a portrait and genre painter. He exhibited at the Royal Academy from 1821 until 1857

ELWES, Simon RA **444**
1902-1975
Elwes was born near Rugby in Staffordshire. He studied at the Slade School of Fine Art from 1918-1921 and then in Paris until 1926. From 1927 he exhibited at the Royal Academy and was elected Academician 40 years later, in 1967. Elwes enjoyed a very successful career as a society portrait painter.

EPSTEIN, Sir Jacob **S8, S36**
1880-1959
Epstein was born in New York City into a family of prosperous orthodox Jewish merchants. He took an early interest in drawing, and shortly after the turn of the century he moved to Paris where he studied in museums as well as at the Beaux Arts School and the Académie Julien. He moved to London in 1905 and took naturalisation in

1911. For most of his career, his work was controversial. He was much influenced by African art. He received a commission to decorate the British Medical Association's building in the Strand, carving eighteen over-life size nudes symbolizing the stages of life. Following complaints, they were inspected by a police officer, who pronounced them to be 'rude.' The Bishop of Stepney then climbed the scaffolding to look at them and declared that they were innocent of any offence. Controversy never entirely left Epstein's work, but the latter part of his career brought him many commissions for works that subsequently were displayed in prominent locations.

ETTY, William RA **887**
1787-1849
Etty was born in his father's bakery shop in York, the son of respectable Methodist parents, and was sent at the age of twelve to an apprenticeship in Hull with a letter-press printer. After seven years of this drudgery, he moved to London and shortly thereafter was accepted by Royal Academy Schools. He decided to devote himself to painting 'God's most glorious work, Woman.' It was only after years of industry and perseverance that he received recognition.

EVES, Reginald Granville RA **60, 309, 329, 729**
1876-1941
Eves was born in London and studied at the Slade School from 1891 until 1895 under Brown, Legros and Tonks. He worked in Yorkshire until 1900 and then settled in London as a successful portrait painter, being elected Academician in 1939, shortly before his death.

F

FAWKES, Wally Walter, originally Ernest
b. 1924 **965**
Wally Fawkes came to England from Vancouver, British Columbia at the age of seven. He was a bandleader as well as a clarinettist and saxophonist, and was co-founder of the Humphrey Lyttleton Band. He commenced his career as a cartoonist after the Second World War, joining the *Daily Mail* in 1945, and worked for a number of newspapers and magazines. Fawkes adopted the name of 'Trog' for his cartoons. He started the 'Flook' strip in 1949 under such story-writers as Sir Compton Mackenzie and later with George Melly, Barry Norman and Barry Took.

FLETCHER, C. J. **452**
fl. c. 1836
C. J. Fletcher exhibited at the Royal Society of British Artists, Suffolk Street.

FLETCHER, Geoffrey Scowcroft
b. 1923 **888, 889, G1042**
Geoffrey Fletcher was born at Bolton in Lancashire. He studied at the Slade School of Art under Schwabe and exhibited at the Royal Academy. He lived at Ashtead in Surrey.

FLETCHER, Hanslip **890**
1874-1955
Hanslip Fletcher was born in London and educated at Merchant Taylors' School. He exhibited at the Royal Academy and specialized as a watercolourist and etcher in architectural subjects. His work was featured in newspapers and magazines, including the *Daily Telegraph* and the *Sunday Times.*

FORBES-ROBERTSON, Sir Johnston **665**
1853-1937
See Brief Lives of the Sitters

FORD, Edward Onslow
See ONSLOW

FOSTER, Richard **G1041**

b.1945

Richard Foster was born and brought up in Norfolk. He studied art at the Studio Simi in Florence and at the City and Guilds, London. He lives presently in London, with a house in Norfolk. He paints portraits and landscapes and travels extensively in connection with both. He is a member and former Vice President of the Royal Society of Portrait Painters, has exhibited frequently at the Royal Academy and has had a number of one-man shows in London.

FOSTER, Thomas **90**

1798-1826

Foster died by his own hand at the early age of 29 at a hotel in Piccadilly, leaving a letter saying that his friends had deserted him and that he was tired of life. During his short career he painted portraits. Foster was a frequent visitor to the studio of Joseph Nollekens and was a friend of Sir Thomas Lawrence.

FOSTER, William **152, 362, 405, 406**

fl. 1771-1812

This artist specialized, during the latter part of his career, in portraits of actresses in pencil and watercolour.

FRANCIS, Clive **G0981, G1002, G1003**

b. 1946

Clive Francis was born at Eastbourne, Sussex, in 1946 and trained at the Royal Academy of Dramatic Art and thereafter at a number of provincial repertory theatres including Worthing, Eastbourne, Derby and Leicester.

His first engagement on the London stage was in 1966 at the Globe Theatre in *There's a Girl in my Soup*. In 1987 he joined Alan Ayckbourn's company at the Royal National Theatre and later he spent a season with the Royal Shakespeare Company. He has performed in a one-man show of *A Christmas Carol*. Francis has also appeared in a number of television performances.

Apart from his acting career, Francis is a caricaturist and book illustrator, having designed the covers for the number of theatrical autobiographies. He has also seen published illustrated books of his drawings celebrating the lighter side of *Hamlet* and *Macbeth*.

FUCHS, Emil **S27**

b. 1866

This is presumably the Austrian sculptor who was born in Vienna in 1866. Emil Fuchs studied under Victor Tigner in Vienna and then under Ernst Herter in Berlin.

FULLWOOD, Charles **155**

fl. 1900-1915

This artist was probably the Charles Fullwood who exhibited at the Royal Society of British Artists, Suffolk Street, and who was also noted as a copyist.

FURNISS, Harry **319**

1854-1925

Harry Furniss was an Irish draughtsman and caricaturist. He exhibited drawings at the Royal Academy between 1884 and 1889 and became a member of the Garrick Club in 1885.

G

GAINSBOROUGH, Thomas RA
1727-1788 **293, 294, 704, all after**
The Club only possesses copies after known Gainsborough portraits. The artist was a leading portrait and landscape painter, draughtsman and etcher of the eighteenth century, who worked around Ipswich, in London and Bath. His work contains great poetry and beauty.

GARDENER **S16**
fl. c. 1774
Gunnis mentions a fine contemporary wax portrait of David Garrick by Gardener as being in the Royal collection. The Club's version is modeled on an engraving by J. K. Sherwin.

GARRATT, Arthur P. **8**
fl. 1899-1908
This little-known artist exhibited four works at the Royal Academy between 1899 and 1901.

GIBSON, John RA **S0063**
1790-1866
Gibson was born in North Wales, the son of a market gardener. The family moved to Liverpool when Gibson was nine, then five years later, aged fourteen, he was apprenticed to a sculptor named Lege, working for a Liverpool firm of statuaries. It was in Liverpool that he came to the attention of William Roscoe, the renowned collector, who commissioned a bas-relief from him. Gibson left for Rome in 1817 and spent the greater part of the remainder of his life there. He received encouragement and instruction from Canova and Thorwaldsen and went on to enjoy a successful and productive career. Gibson was elected a member of the Royal Academy in 1838.

GILBERT, Sir John RA, PRWS **805, 891**
1817-1897
Gilbert was an immensely prolific illustrator (nearly 30,000 illustrations for *The Illustrated London News*). He gave up his career as an estate agent at an early age in order to take up painting. He illustrated about 150 books and was elected President of the Old Watercolour Society in 1871, knighted the following year and elected Academician in 1876. He exhibited at the Royal Academy between 1838 and the year of his death. Gilbert was a better draughtsman than painter, his pictures being for the most part of a turgid, romantic nature. He became a member of the Garrick Club in 1852.

GILROY, John T. Young **43, 77, 119, 149 176-177, 262, 264, 442, 631, 711-712, 718, 728, 734-735,**
1898-1985 **764, 850, 892, G1020, G1029**
'Jack' Gilroy was born in 1898 at Newcastle-upon-Tyne. He studied at the King Edward VII School of Art, Newcastle, and after service in the First World War, won a scholarship to the Royal College of Art. He settled in London, living near Holland Park, and exhibited widely. He joined the staff of the Camberwell School of Art for a brief period from 1921. He was principally a portrait painter, both in oils and watercolour, but he also designed a number of highly successful posters for the Guinness brewery group. Gilroy became a member of the Garrick Club in 1955 and served as Chairman of the Works of Art Sub-Committee from 1970 to 1975.

GLAZEBROOK, Hugh de Twenebrokes **307**
1855-1937
Glazebrook studied under Poynter at South Kensington, and in Paris. He was primarily a portrait painter and exhibited at the Royal Academy from 1885.

GLEICHEN, H.S.H, Count **S1, S2**
1833-1891
Prince Victor Ferdinand Franz Eugene Gustaf Adolf Constantin Friedrich of Hohenlohe-Langenburg married the daughter of an English admiral in 1861. Because of an old German law disqualifying his wife from using his first title, he assumed the name of his second title, Count Gleichen. In fact, Gleichen's mother was half-sister to Queen Victoria. Gleichen had a distinguished career in the Royal Navy, fighting in the Baltic, in the Crimean War and in China, where he was recommended for the Victoria Cross. Illness obliged him to retire at the age of

33, in 1866, and it was then that he took up modelling and sculpture. A material setback following the collapse of a bank caused him to practice sculpture as a serious profession. Queen Victoria granted him a suite of apartments in St James's Palace, where he worked successfully, and later he built himself a house at Ascot on the proceeds. In 1887 he was promoted to the rank of admiral, on the retired list.

GOODMAN, Walter **356, 777**
1838-1895
Walter Goodman was born in London in May 1838. He studied under J. M. Leigh and was admitted as a student at the Royal Academy Schools, at the age of nineteen, in 1857. In 1864 he left for the West Indies, where he remained for five years, writing and painting, mostly in Cuba. While in Cuba he was arrested and imprisoned in More Castle under suspicion of having been implicated in the Cuban revolution of 1869. Expelled from the island, he spent a year in New York before returning to London, where he devoted himself to portrait painting. Goodman exhibited just three paintings at the Royal Academy between 1872 and 1888.

GOTTO, Basil **S 26**
1866-1954
Gotto studied under Bouguereau in Paris and then at the Royal Academy Schools in London. He started exhibiting at the Royal Academy in 1889.

GRAHAM, John **311**
1754-1817
Graham was born in Edinburgh. He was apprenticed to a coach painter and came to London, where he studied at the Royal Academy, exhibiting over 30 paintings there between 1780 and 1797. In 1799 he opened an academy in Edinburgh, where he had David Wilkie and William Allen among his first students. His work seems to have consisted mainly of portraits, genre subjects and historical scenes.

GRANT, Benjamin **S12**
b. 1738
By 1775 Grant was in partnership with James Hoskins. He appears to have suffered financial difficulties toward the end of his life, for Farington, in his diary of 3 August 1808, states that he had been approached by Flaxman 'respecting Grant, a man 70 years old who has for 40 years been employed by the Royal Academy to repair casts etc. He is now old and destitute.'

GREEN, James **131**
1771-1834
Green was the son of a builder from Essex. He was apprenticed to a natural history painter in London, where he worked in watercolour, painting images of shells and insects. On the expiry of his apprenticeship he entered the Schools of the Royal Academy, attracting the attention of Sir Joshua Reynolds. Green painted in oil as well as in watercolour and many of his pictures were engraved. Between the years 1793 and 1834, the year of his death, he exhibited over 160 pictures at the Royal Academy.

GREENHILL, John **290, after**
1644-1676
The Club's only example after Greenhill is an indifferent copy in oils, probably after an engraving from one of two versions in chalks in Magdelene College, Oxford, and the Ashmolean Museum, Oxford. Initially, the subject had been commissioned by Horace Walpole for his gallery of historical portraits at Strawberry Hill. Greenhill was born at Salisbury, son of the Registrar of the Diocese. He went to London about 1662 and became a pupil of Lely, whose style he emulated well. He also made a close study of Van Dyck. Apparently he got into company with bohemian characters living in the area of Covent Garden and on the night of 19 May 1676, returning from the Vine Tavern, he fell drunk into the gutter, was carried to his lodgings in Lincoln's Inn Fields and died later that night, aged 32.

GREY-EDWARDS, Mrs F. M.
b. 1892
Mrs Grey-Edwards, née Lee, was born in Massachusetts in the United States in 1892. She studied at the Boston Museum of Fine Arts and later, in London, at the Slade School of Art (1925-27) under Wilson Steer and Henry Tonks. She exhibited at the Royal Academy.

GRIEVE, William **270**
1800-1844
William Grieve, son of John Henderson Grieve, was one of a family of scenery painters. He worked as a boy at Covent Garden Theatre, but subsequently moved to Drury Lane and to Her Majesty's Opera House. He became the most renowned practitioner in his profession when Clarkson Stanfield and David Roberts, both of whom are represented in the Club by large-scale works (**935, 932**), abandoned scene painting.

GRISONI, Giuseppe **116**
1699-1769
Grisoni, born Pierre Joseph Grison, was a Walloon painter and sculptor, born in Mons, Belgium, in 1699. He studied in Florence and arrived, at age sixteen, with John Talman, the architectural draughtsman, in London. According to an article in *Thieme-Becker* he had little success in England and, after auctioning off his own work in 1728, he returned to Italy within the next year or two and remained there for the rest of his life. The portrait of Colley Cibber, of which there is more than one version, must therefore be an early work.

GUNN, Sir Herbert James RA, PRP
1893-1964 **17**
Gunn was born in Glasgow and studied at the Glasgow School of Art, the Edinburgh College of Art and at the Académie Julien in Paris. He exhibited prolifically, mostly portraits, at the Royal Academy from 1923 and was elected Academician in 1961. Gunn became a member of the Garrick Club in 1935.

H

HAILSTONE, Bernard **642, G1021**
1910-1987
Hailstone studied at Goldsmiths' School of Art and at the Royal Academy Schools. He worked up a successful portrait practice before joining the Auxiliary Fire Service in the Second World War, when he painted scenes of the Blitz. In 1944 he went to South-East Asia to paint Lord Mountbatten. He started exhibiting at the Royal Academy in 1939; his portrait of Sir Laurence Olivier was shown there in 1969.

HALLE, Charles Edward **102**
1846-1914
Charles Edward Halle was the son of the musician Charles Halle. He studied under Baron Marochetti and L. von Mottez. He started to exhibit at the Royal Academy from the age of twenty. Later he joined the 'Secession' artists at the Grosvenor Gallery, where he became an assistant director. Halle was on terms of close friendship with Burne-Jones, Watts, Alma-Tadema and Herkomer.

HALLIDAY, Edward Irvine **813**
1902-1984
Halliday studied at the City School of Art, Liverpool, at the Royal College of Art and in Paris and Rome. He worked up a successful portrait practice, exhibiting regularly at the Royal Academy from 1929, giving addresses in London. He also made a number of portraits of members of the royal family.

HAMILTON, William RA
1750/51-1801 **295 attr. to, 749**
Hamilton was born in London, the son of a Scottish assistant to Robert Adam. His father sent him to Rome in his early youth, where he studied under Zucchi. Returning to England, he entered the Royal Academy Schools in 1769. He made designs for Boydell's *Shakespeare* and Macklin's *Bible*, and was much employed in book illustration. He exhibited extensively at the Royal Academy from 1774 until the year of his death.

Among his painted portraits of actors and actresses he made a number of Mrs Siddons. His work was effete, having Stothard's prettiness without his strength.

HARCOURT, George RA **230**
1868-1948
Harcourt was born in Dunbartonshire, Scotland. He studied for three years with Sir Hubert Herkomer and became a portrait and genre painter. He began exhibiting at the Royal Academy in 1893 and was elected Academician in 1926. For much of his life he lived at Bushey in Hertfordshire.

HARDING, H. J. **380**
fl. 1818-1825
H. J. Harding exhibited nine miniature paintings at the Royal Academy between 1823 and 1825.

HARDING, Sylvester **46, 84, 99, 114, 288 after, 461, 674, 678, 741, 772 possibly by, 840**
1745-1809

Sylvester, or Silvester, Harding was born at Newcastle-under-Lyme in 1745, but placed as a child in the care of an uncle in London. At the age of fourteen he left London and ran away with a group of strolling players. Sixteen years later he returned to the capital and took up miniature painting, exhibiting at the Royal Academy in 1776 and regularly thereafter until 1802. In 1786 he joined his brother Edward in starting a book and print seller's shop in Fleet Street, moving six years later to Pall Mall. He specialized in drawing portraits of famous actors and actresses and employed these in such publications as *Shakespeare illustrated by an assemblage of Portraits and Views appropriate to the whole suite of our Author's Historical Dramas* (1793). He was the father of George Perfect Harding.

HARDY, Thomas **21**
1757-c.1805
Hardy was a portrait painter and mezzotint engraver. He entered the Royal Academy Schools in 1778, and exhibited there from 1778 until 1798.

HARLOW, George Henry **190-191, 314, 363, 381, 471, 733 circle of, 742, 743, 750 after, 774, 775 after, 869, 870**
1787-1819
Harlow was born in London where he was brought up and, according to Redgrave, spoiled by his mother. His father, a merchant residing in Canton, died before George's birth. George received instruction from Henry de Cort, Samuel Drummond and then, for eighteen months, from Sir Thomas Lawrence. Dissatisfied with the treatment he received from Lawrence, he left, or was required to leave, and was from then on obliged to make his own way. He first exhibited at the Royal Academy at the age of 27, in 1805, and continued to show portraits there until 1818 when he left for Italy. Early the following year he was back in England, where he died of the mumps, aged 31. Harlow's group portrait of four different characters, all played by Charles Mathews and with Mathews looking on, was engraved by Meyer.

HAYMAN, Francis RA **49, 696, 697**
c.1708-1776
Hayman was, according to Horace Walpole, a Devonian. Brian Allen notes that a John Hayman, presumably the artist's father, was married at Ottery St Mary in the diocese of Exeter in 1700. As a young man, Francis Hayman was employed to paint scenery by the manager of Drury Lane Theatre, Charles Fleetwood. He used the skills acquired there to paint a series of large canvases between 1741 and about 1761 for Jonathan Tyers, to be used in the supper boxes and pavilions in Vauxhall Gardens. Hayman started painting his theatrical pictures in the early 1740s, at about the same time that he was making illustrations for Sir Thomas Hanmer's edition of Shakespeare. Although his standing as an artist was later eclipsed by Hogarth, Hayman was highly thought of in his own day. He was eager to promote the founding of an institution that would provide academic training for young artists, along the line of academies on the Continent. He was appointed President of the Society of Artists, was a friend of Hogarth and Garrick and subsequently became a Founder Member of the Royal Academy in 1769 and Librarian in 1771.

HAYTER, John **370 after**
1800-1891
John Hayter was a brother of Sir George Hayter. He exhibited at the Royal Academy over a period of 64 years, from 1815 until 1879.

HERKOMER, Sir Hubert von ARA **263**
1849-1914
Herkomer was born in southern Bavaria. His father was a joiner and craftsman and his mother a music teacher. The family emigrated to the United States and then came to England in 1857, when the young Hubert was eight years old. Herkomer received his training at the Southampton School of Art, then at the Munich Academy and lastly at the South Kensington Art Schools. His early years were a bit of a struggle, but he really made his name in 1875 with his painting 'The Last Muster – Sunday at the Royal Hospital, Chelsea.' It went to the Royal Academy and was sold for £1,200. He exhibited regularly at the Academy from 1869 until 1904, mostly portraits and genre subjects.

Herkomer built up a strong practice as a portrait painter and attracted a number of distinguished sitters. He painted, among others, Cecil Rhodes, H. M. Stanley, Lord Derby, Richard Wagner in watercolour and similarly a very telling portrait of John Ruskin (National Portrait Gallery). The Club's robust portrait in oils of Sir William Schwenk Gilbert offers a penetrating analysis of the features of that inspired wordsmith and dramatist.

Herkomer tried his hand at composing operas, acting and lecturing. He built a house at Bushey, 'Lululand', named after his second wife, and a tower, rather unimaginatively called 'Mutterthurm' at Landsberg. He painted large group portraits, somewhat in the manner of the Dutch seventeenth-century artists. Among these were 'The Chapel of the Charterhouse' and 'The Council of the Royal Academy.' Herkomer became a member of the Garrick Club in 1913. The following year, in 1914, he painted 'The Firm of Friedrich Krupp.' It was the year of Herkomer's death.

HEWSON, Stephen **843**
fl. 1775-1805
Hewson was a little known miniature painter who exhibited at the Society of Artists, the Free Society and the Royal Academy, primarily portraits but also genre subjects.

HICKEL, Joseph **412**
1736-1807
Joseph Hickel was from a Bohemian family of painters. At the age of 20 he entered the Academy in Vienna, specializing in portraiture. While there, he came to the attention of the Empress Maria Theresa, who sent him on a funded mission to Milan, Palma and Florence. In these cities, Hickel, noted for his rapid brushwork, painted countless portraits of distinguished personalities in the service of the Empress. On his return to Vienna he was commissioned to paint a portrait of Joseph II and was subsequently appointed to be a member of the Vienna Academy. Hickel was extraordinarily prolific, and over his career he painted some 3000 portraits. Apart from his work in court circles, Hickel painted a series of portraits of actors, to be found in the Actors' Gallery in the Vienna Hofburgtheater. The Garrick Club's portrait of Joseph Lange as *Hamlet* is a version of one of these paintings.

HICKEY, Thomas **1, 255 attr. to**
1741-1824
Hickey was born in Dublin and studied at the Academy there. He was in Italy from about 1760 to 1766 and back in Dublin by 1767, where he exhibited from 1768 to 1770. He came to London and entered the Royal Academy Schools in 1771 at the age of 30. He exhibited at the Royal Academy from 1771 to 1776, giving his London address as Jermyn Street, then in 1779 from Bath and again in London in 1792. He made his first visit to India, via Portugal, about 1784 and remained there until 1791. Then, from 1792 to 1794, he accompanied Lord Macartney when the latter acted as plenipotentiary in an embassy sent to Peking in an attempt to improve the treatment meted out to English subjects by the Chinese. By 1798 he was back in India, where he appears to have remained for the rest of his life, being buried in Madras. The Garrick Club's painting of Mrs Abington was identified by Horace Walpole as having been No 150 in the Royal Academy Exhibition of 1775.

HIGHMORE, Joseph 705 attr. to, 717
1692-1780
Highmore was the son of a coal merchant. Though he was designated by his family to study with a solicitor, he abandoned the law in 1715 and set up as a portrait painter, spending the next ten years in Kneller's Academy in Great Queen Street. He established a highly successful practice, his career running more or less in tandem with that of Hogarth. He retired in 1761, sold his art collection and moved to Canterbury where he indulged in literary pursuits and where he died at the age of 88.

HOGARTH, William 98 attr. to, 706 attr. to
1697-1764
Sadly, the Club owns no paintings by William Hogarth. Hogarth was one of the earliest major artists to take an interest in theatrical painting. His portrait of Richard III, circa 1745, (Walker Art Gallery, Liverpool), commemorates Garrick's performance in the role at Goodman's Fields Theatre in 1741. It was the performance that effectively launched Garrick's career. Hogarth had earlier painted a group of child actors performing Dryden's *Indian Emperor, or the Conquest of Mexico* and made several versions of a scene from John Gay's popular ballad-opera *The Beggar's Opera.*

HOLROYD, Sir Charles RPE
1861-1917 **604, after Millais**
Holroyd was born in Leeds but settled in London. He studied at the Slade School of Art and later taught there. He exhibited at the Royal Academy between 1885 and 1895. Holroyd became the first Keeper of the Tate Gallery and a Director of the National Gallery.

HONE, Horace ARA
1756-1825 **382, 745 attr. to, 881 attr. to**
Hone worked in watercolour and enamel. He spent some time in Dublin and, in 1795, was appointed miniature painter to the Prince of Wales. He later returned to London and had a very active practice until within a few years of his death.

HONE, Nathaniel RA 616
1718-1784
Nathaniel Hone was born into a Presbyterian family in Dublin in 1718, the son of a merchant of Dutch origin. He was entirely self-taught. He came over to England as a young man practicing as a portrait painter. He spent some time in Italy in his early thirties and then returned to England to pursue a successful career, first as a painter of miniatures, then, at some time in the 1760s, of full-scale portraiture. Hone was a Founder Member of the Royal Academy. He seems to have had ambitions to challenge Reynolds's leading role as a portrait painter but was no match for him. Hone was a rather malicious man and there was a famous falling out with the first President of the Royal Academy. Hone submitted to the Academy a painting that he titled 'The Conjurer.' The subject was clearly an attack on his business competitor, Sir Joshua, and it implied that the latter had stolen most of his compositions from famous Renaissance paintings. There was also said to be an alleged portrayal of Angelica Kauffmann, whom Reynolds was known to admire, in the top left corner. Following complaints, Hone re-painted this area.

HOSKINS, James S 12
fl. 1770-1791
James Hoskins and his first partner, Samuel Euclid Oliver, started working for Wedgewood in 1770 modelling 16 low relief busts. By 1775 Hoskins' firm had become known as 'Hoskins and Grant' and from that date they supplied Wedgewood with a number of busts of famous poets, playwrights, authors and scientists including, in 1779, the Club's black basalt bust of Garrick. Hoskins held the post of 'moulder and caster in plaster' to the Royal Academy from the time of its foundation in 1769 until his death in 1791.

HOYOLL, Philip 835
1816-1875
Hoyoll was born in Breslau, Germany, and studied at the Dusseldorf Academy from 1834 to 1839. He moved to London about 1864, when he started exhibiting at the Royal Academy.

HUDSON, Thomas 117
1701-1779
Thomas Hudson was born in Devonshire in 1701. He was a pupil of Jonathan Richardson

the elder. When a young man, he ran off with and married his master's daughter. Hudson subsequently worked up a very successful portrait practice in London in which he frequently painted the faces and hands of his subjects, leaving the drapery to Joseph Van Haeken, that skillful practitioner who, with his brother, Alexander, also worked for Allen Ramsay, among others. On one of his numerous visits to Bideford in Devonshire, Hudson came across the youthful Joshua Reynolds and took him on as a pupil in his studio. Reynolds left after two years and soon outstripped his master with the result that Hudson's fame declined. Remaining on good terms with Reynolds, Hudson made a second marriage to a wealthy widow and retired to a contented old age at Twickenham, near Pope's Villa. Like his master Richardson and his pupil Reynolds, Hudson was an enthusiastic collector of Old Master drawings.

J

JACKSON, John RA **451**

1778-1831

John Jackson was born in North Yorkshire, the son of a tailor. He came to London in 1804, putatively on a bursary from Sir George Beaumont, and was admitted as a student at the Royal Academy. He was elected Academician in 1817. He went to Italy in 1819, where he painted Canova's portrait. He was quite a prolific painter although he was never in a position to charge much for his pictures. The *DNB* notes that 'his religious opinions were earnest but gloomy' [he was a Wesleyan Methodist] 'and are said to have ruined his health and spirits in his last years, while the low state of his finances at his death is partly attributable to his extravagant generosity in support of Wesleyan institutions.'

JACKSON, Raymond 'JAK'

1927-1997 **11, 962, 971, 972**

Raymond Jackson studied at the Willesden School of Art. He started his career making pocket cartoons. By the age of 24 he had become editorial cartoonist for the London *Evening Standard* and for *The Mail on Sunday*. In the 1970s his cartoons gave offence to some in Trade Union circles.

JAGGER, Charles **223 attr. to**

c. 1770-1827

Charles Jagger was a miniaturist who worked in Bath and does not appear to have exhibited in London.

JOHNSON, Thomas **99 after**

1709-1767

Thomas Johnson was a draughtsman and mezzotint engraver. Many of his prints are after subjects of his own composition, although he also made prints after Rubens and Kneller.

JOSEPH, George Francis ARA **645**

1764-1846

Joseph entered the Royal Academy Schools at the age of 20 in 1784 and first appeared as an exhibitor four years later. He gained the gold medal in 1792 for his 'Scene from Coriolanus.' Apart from subject and history paintings, as well as fancy subjects and book illustrations, he is known primarily as a portrait painter. He retired from London to Cambridge in 1836 and died ten years later.

K

KAUFFMAN, Maria Anna Angelica Catherina RA **291**

1741-1807

Angelica Kauffman was born at Coire, in Switzerland, in October 1741. She showed early talent both for music and painting and grew up to be fluent in French, German, Italian and English. Her cosmopolitan, cultivated background and amiable disposition brought her many friends in artistic and literary circles. She went with her family as a young girl to live in Italy, where she stayed for a number of years and where she commenced her career as a painter. In 1766, at the age of 25, she arrived in London from Venice, accompanying Lady Wentworth, the wife of the English ambassador. In her mid-twenties she contracted a clandestine marriage with an imposter claiming to be a Count de Horn, but the family bribed him to leave England and secured a deed of separation from the Pope. Horn subsequently died and Angelica Kauffman, who retained her maiden name, re-married at the age of 40 another painter, Antonio Zucchi, with whom she retired to Italy. She was much admired by Garrick, Goldsmith, Fuseli, and by Reynolds and Nathaniel Dance-Holland, the last being reputedly in love with her. Probably at Reynolds's behest she was one of the original 36 founder members of the Royal Academy. From the date of its foundation in 1769 until 1797 she exhibited no fewer than 82 paintings there. She appears to have been employed by the Adam brothers, and her work features as part of the decoration in a number of their houses both in London and the country. Her work drew acclaim through the prints from her subjects engraved by Bartolozzi and others. She learned engraving and was employed by Alderman Boydell in illustrating his *Shakespeare Gallery*; she also did some illustrations for Bell's *British Theatre*. Kauffman's paintings are rather vapid in colour and her drawing weak, but she displayed an attractive neo-classical charm.

KEELEY, John **811 attr. to**
1849-1930
Keeley was a Birmingham artist who worked mostly in watercolours. He exhibited more than 300 works at the Royal Birmingham Society of Artists from 1872.

KELLY, Sir Gerald Festus RHA, PRA **86**
1879-1972
Kelly was born in London of Irish parents. He studied at Trinity Hall, Cambridge and in Paris where, in 1904, he became a member of the Salon d'Automne. He was elected a member of the Royal Hibernian Academy in 1914, Royal Academician in 1930 and President of the Royal Academy in 1949. He was knighted in 1955. Kelly became a member of the Garrick Club in 1923 and resigned in 1931.

KETTLE, Tilly **725, 863**
1734-1786
Tilly Kettle was born in London, the son of a house painter. He received his early training from his father, studied in the Duke of Richmond's gallery of casts and at the Academy in St Martin's Lane. He exhibited portraits at the Society of Artists, of which he became a Fellow. He was in practice as a portrait painter in London from 1764 until 1769. In 1770 he left for India, where he remained for seven years. There he amassed a considerable fortune painting portraits of nabobs and native princes; he sent home a number of pictures for exhibition.

Kettle returned to England in 1777, married, and built a house for himself in Old Bond Street, opposite Burlington Gardens. He also at that time exhibited pictures at the newly formed Royal Academy. Unfortunately he over-stretched himself, became bankrupt and was obliged to retire to Dublin. In 1786 he set off again, at the age of 52, overland to India, hoping to repair his fortunes, but he fell ill near Aleppo, where he died.

KIRCHOFFER, Henry **874**
1781-1860
Henry Kirchoffer was an Irish portrait, landscape and miniature painter, who was born in Dublin. He became a member of the Dublin Academy in 1826 and from 1830 was its Secretary. In 1835 he resigned his membership at the Academy and went to London, where between 1837 and 1843 he exhibited at the Royal Academy.

KNELLER, Sir Godfrey, Bt **47 after, 65,**
1646-1723 **417 after, 639 attr. to**
Godfrey Kneller was born Gottfried Kniller at Lübeck, North Germany, son of an established family. He studied painting in Amsterdam under Ferdinand Bol and may have had some instruction from Rembrandt towards the end of the latter's life. He spent some time in Italy working in Rome, Naples and Venice before coming, almost by chance, to England, where he stayed. Young and courteous, Kneller was recommended to Charles II and came to be employed in royal circles through his reign and that of James II, William III and Queen Anne. He amassed a large fortune, although it took a dip on account of the 'South Sea Bubble.' His work was very highly rated in his own day, bringing praise from such figures as Pope, Dryden and Pepys. As a result of all this adulation he became somewhat arrogant. He was knighted in 1692 and made a baronet in 1715. He lived at Great Queen Street, Lincoln's Inn Fields, and built a house for himself at Whitton, near Hounslow, that still exists under the name of Kneller Hall. Kneller was an extraordinarily prolific painter but he had a great deal of help from assistants and his reputation took a dive after his death, never to recover.

KNIGHT, John Prescott RA
1803-1881 **97, 226, 625, 687, 799**
Knight was born in Stafford, the son of the actor Edward Knight (see the Index of Sitters). He studied at Sass's Academy and with George Clint. He exhibited over 200 works at the Royal Academy between 1824 and 1878, both portraits and genre subjects. He was elected Academician in 1844.

L

LAMBDA, Peter **S3**
fl. 1953-1974
The sculptor Lambda became a member of the Garrick Club in 1967 and resigned in 1974. He exhibited at the Royal Academy in 1952 and 1955.

LAMBERT, Edward F. **347, 436**
fl. 1823-1846
Edward Lambert was a history painter and engraver who worked in London. Between 1823 and 1846 he exhibited at the Royal Academy and at the Suffolk Street Gallery.

LANCASTER, Sir Osbert CBE **895, 896, G1030**
1908-1986
Osbert Lancaster was born in London in 1908. After Oxford, he studied unsuccessfully for the bar and then attended the Slade School of Art. From 1939 his cartoons appeared regularly in the *Daily Express* featuring the languid figure of Maudie Littlehampton. Lancaster published a number of books over the years, and in 1951 he started designing stage sets and costumes for productions in the West End and at Glyndebourne. He was knighted in 1975 and died in 1986. Sir Osbert Lancaster became a member of the Garrick Club in 1962.

LANDSEER, Sir Edwin Henry RA **871**
1802-1873
Landseer was born in London in 1802. He had no formal education and started drawing animals at a very early age. By the time he was eleven he had secured the silver palette of the Society of Arts. In 1824 he made his first trip to Scotland, visiting Sir Walter Scott at Abbotsford. Scottish scenery and wild life had a profound effect on his work and his sometimes rather sentimental but very accurate depictions of animals touched the hearts of his contemporaries. There is frequently a sadistic streak in the subject matter of his work, and there may have been some mental unbalance, which resulted in his suffering from severe depression later in life. On the surface, however, Landseer had a cheerful disposition and he was much sought after in aristocratic circles. He became a full member of the Royal Academy in 1831, was knighted by Queen Victoria in 1850 and on his death in 1873, was buried in St Paul's Cathedral.

LANE, Anne Louisa **235**
fl. 1770-1789
Anne Louisa Lane was a miniature painter and sister of William Lane. She exhibited between 1769 and 1776 at the Society of Artists and then between 1778 and 1782 at the Royal Academy.

LANE, Richard James **368 attr. to**
1800-1872
Richard Lane was born at Berkeley Castle, Hereford, in 1800. His mother was Thomas Gainsborough's niece. At sixteen he was articled to Charles Heath, the renowned line engraver, becoming himself an able engraver and later, lithographer. He also produced a large number of sensitive pencil and chalk portrait drawings.

LAWRENCE, Sir Thomas PRA **372 after, 383-85, 386 studio, 733 attr. to, 744, 745 after, 746 after, 747 after, G1022**
1769-1830
Lawrence, born in Bristol, the fourteenth of sixteen children, was a child prodigy, drawing from the age of five and producing excellent portrait likenesses at ten. In 1779 Fanny Burney stayed at the Black Bear, an inn in Devizes, of which Lawrence's father was then landlord, and declared his son to be 'a most lovely boy of ten years of age who seems to be not only the wonder of the family, but of the times for his astonishing skill in drawing.' By 1780 the family were living in Bath. Lawrence came to London in 1786 and briefly attended the Royal Academy Schools. In 1790, at the age of 21, as Waterhouse aptly puts it, he 'burst on the world' with his full-length portraits of Queen Charlotte (National Gallery) and Miss Farren (Frick Collection, New York). Two years later he was made Painter in Ordinary to the King in succession to Reynolds. Some of the finest of his portraits were made when the Prince Regent commissioned him to paint the principal leaders who had formed the alliance against Napoleon. This series hangs

together in the 'Waterloo Chamber' at Windsor Castle. Lawrence exhibited at the Royal Academy from 1787 until the year of his death. He was elected RA in 1794 and PRA in 1820. He was knighted by the Prince Regent in 1815. Like Richardson, Hudson and Reynolds, Lawrence formed a very distinguished collection of Old Master Drawings.

LE CLEAR, Thomas **85**
1818-1882
Thomas Le Clear was a portrait and genre painter. He was born in Owego, New York, in 1818. Self-taught, he worked in London, Canada, and from 1839 in New York by way of Buffalo.

LEECH, John **416, 897-922**
1817-1864
John Leech was born in London and, like Thackeray, with whom he established a life-long friendship, was educated at Charterhouse School. Leech was originally destined for the medical profession but, apparently on account of some family financial crisis, he was obliged to start earning his living in his early twenties as a free-lance illustrator. With the help of Thackeray he got a job with *Punch* magazine. He formed close friendships with Charles Dickens and with the Victorian painter W. P. Frith, and knew Millais and Trollope. Leech became a member of the Garrick Club in 1849. He was a rather nervous horseman, but that didn't prevent him from riding to hounds with unbounded enthusiasm. He made delightful illustrations to several of R. S. Surtees's sporting novels and is also known for having illustrated Dickens's *Christmas Carol.*

LENS, Bernard the 3rd **846**
1682-1740
Of the third generation and best known of this family of painters, Lens was born in London in 1682. He studied at the Academy of Painting in Great Queen Street, Lincoln's Inn Fields, and became the best-known miniature painter of his day. He was appointed limner to George I and George II and was drawing master to, among others, the Duke of Cumberland and Horace Walpole. He taught drawing at Christ's Hospital and practiced etching. Lens drew and engraved 62 plates illustrating *A New and Compleat Drawing Book*, which was not published until after his death.

LESLIE, Charles Robert RA **132**
1794-1859
Charles Robert Leslie was born in London, the son of American parents. His father, Robert Leslie, was a successful clockmaker in Philadelphia, and a personal friend of Benjamin Franklin. Robert Leslie had come to London with his family in 1793 with a view to increasing his business. The family returned with Robert Leslie to America in 1799 on the death of his Philadelphia partner; then Robert Leslie, himself, died in 1804, when his son, Charles, was only ten years old. The boy was able to complete his education owing to the kindness of the professors at the University of Pennsylvania. On the strength of a drawing of the actor George Frederick Cooke, made from memory, a subscription was raised to send Charles Leslie to study painting in Europe, and he arrived at Liverpool in 1811 with a letter of introduction to Benjamin West, then President of the Royal Academy. Leslie made his reputation with historical and literary subjects as well as portraits. He exhibited at the Royal Academy from 1813 until the year of his death. He always retained a keen interest in the theatre. Apart from his work as a painter, C. R. Leslie is remembered for his delightful *Memoirs of the Life of John Constable, R. A.*, a study of his intimate friend, published initially in 1843 (the full edition in 1845, eight years after Constable's death).

LETHBRIDGE, Walter Stephens **265**
1771-1831
Lethbridge was born at Charlton, Devon, son of a farmer. He was apprenticed to a house painter and acted as assistant to a journeyman painter before coming to London, where he studied it the Schools of the Royal Academy. He exhibited at the Academy, primarily as a miniature painter, from 1801 until 1829. He retired to Stonehouse, Plymouth, the following year and is reputed to have died the year after that.

LINDO, F. **54**
fl. 1755-1765
Lindo was a portrait painter in oils and crayons.

Waterhouse describes him as having made 'a good many portraits in Lowland Scotland and in Aberdeenshire 1760-62 ... and he usually manages to make his sitters look rather "common".'

LINSELL, C. **197**
fl. 1801-1830
Linsell was a miniature painter who exhibited at the Royal Academy between 1801 and 1830.

LION, Flora **330**
1876-1958
Flora Lion was a portrait, figure and landscape painter who studied at the Royal Academy Schools and at the Académie Julien in Paris.

LITTRET de M de MONTIGNY, C. A.418
c. 1735-1775
Claude Antoine Littret de Montigny was a draughtsman and engraver. He was born in Paris in 1735. He came to London about 1768 and died in Rouen in 1775.

LOCKWOOD, Sir Frank QC, MP **320**
1846-1897
Sir Frank Lockwood became a member of the Garrick Club in 1882.

LODGE, Francis Graham **923**
b. 1908
Francis Lodge was the son of the figure and landscape painter Carron Lodge. He was born at Burton on Trent and, as a self-taught draughtsman, went to work for the *Observer* and for *Everyman.*

LONG, Edwin Longsden RA
1829-1891 **939, 940, 942**
Edwin Long was born at Bath in 1829. He came to London, where he studied at the British Museum and at a private art school. He commenced his career primarily as a portrait painter. He travelled to Spain with John 'Spanish' Phillips and initially was much influenced by Velazquez. Later, his religious and eastern subjects met with great success. His chief patroness was Baroness Burdett-Coutts (1814-1906). He painted portraits of the Baroness and of Henry Irving. There was a marked falling off in the quality of his later work.

LONSDALE, James 14, 365, 472, 626, 861
1777-1839
James Lonsdale, a portrait painter, was born in Lancashire but came early to London, where he worked as a pupil in Romney's house in Hampstead. He bought Opie's house in Berners Street on the latter's death and lived there for the rest of his life. He was appointed Painter in Ordinary to the Duke of Sussex. The Duke, who was the sixth son of George III, was the first Patron of the Garrick Club. Lonsdale was one of the Founder Members of the Society of British Artists. Redgrave has pointed out that 'his portraits made little attempt at flattery.'

LOW, Sir David Alexander Cecil **G1013**
1891-1963
David Low was a political cartoonist, caricaturist and illustrator. He was born in Dunedin, New Zealand, and educated at Boys' High School, Christchurch. Low was self-taught, although he did a short spell at Canterbury School of Art. He arrived in London in 1919 and started working for the *Evening Standard* in 1927. He subsequently worked for other newspapers and periodicals, producing over 14,000 drawings over a period of 50 years. He was knighted in 1962.

LUCAS, John **786**
1807-1874
Lucas was born in London in 1807. He was apprenticed to the engraver S.W. Reynolds, but at the conclusion of his apprenticeship he set himself up as a portrait painter. In this field he achieved enormous success, exhibiting no fewer than 96 paintings at the Royal Academy between 1828 and his death in 1874. He was reputed to get a very good likeness, and for that reason many of the most eminent people of the day sat to him.

LUTYENS, Robert **614**
d. 1972
Robert Lutyens was Sir Edwin Lutyens's only son. He collaborated on several buildings with his father towards the end of the latter's life, but he also practised as a journalist, interior decorator and artist. He became a member of the Garrick Club in 1944 and died in 1972.

M

MACBETH-RAEBURN, Henry RA, RE 414
1860-1947
Henry Macbeth-Raeburn was born in 1860, son of Norman Raeburn, RSA. He studied at the Royal Scottish Academy Schools and at the Académie Julien in Paris. He commenced as a portrait painter at the age of 24 and then, six years later, took up engraving. Macbeth-Raeburn exhibited widely and was elected to membership of the Royal Academy in 1933. He lived at Newbury in Berkshire and later at Dedham in Essex.

MacLEAN, Alex RBA 92
1867-1940
MacLean was a painter of marine, landscape and figurative subjects. He exhibited at the Royal Academy and was a member of the Royal Society of British Artists, Suffolk Street.

MACLISE, Daniel RA 155 after, 806, 807, 924 previously attrib
1806-1870
Maclise was born Daniel McLeish at Cork, Ireland, son of a Scottish Highlander who had been stationed in Ireland in the army. In 1825 he made a sketch of Sir Walter Scott when the latter was visiting a bookshop in Cork. Scott signed the drawing; a lithograph was made from it and over 500 copies were sold. Maclise came to London in 1827, where he sketched Charles Kean as Norval in *Douglas*. The lithograph of that sketch met with similar success. Between 1830 and 1838 he contributed 80 portrait drawings to *Fraser's Magazine*, subsequently known as the *Maclise Portrait Gallery*. The subjects included Sir Walter Scott, Coleridge, Thackeray, Wordsworth, Count d'Orsay, Charles Lamb, Carlyle, Disraeli and Leigh Hunt. He met Charles Dickens in 1830 and a warm friendship sprang up between them.

Maclise really made his name as a history painter. He began exhibiting at the Royal Academy in 1829 and showed work fairly regularly there up until his death. In 1835 he was elected Associate Member of the Royal Academy, at which time he changed his name from McLeish to Maclise. He became a full Academician five years later. His work was highly acclaimed at the time, although there was a faltering interest in the painting of historical subjects towards the end of his life. He declined the offer to be made President of the Royal Academy after Eastlake's death and is said to have refused a knighthood. He died from pneumonia at the age of 64 at his house in Cheyne Walk.

MARRABLE, Frederick 925
1818-1872
Frederick Marrable was born in 1818, the son of Sir Thomas Marrable, Secretary of the Board of Green Cloth to George IV and William IV. He was articled as a young man to the architect William Blore. In 1856 he was appointed Superintending Architect to the newly established Metropolitan Board of Works, a post from which he resigned six years later, in 1862. He had a good deal of private practice and one of his more important commissions was to design and build the Garrick Club (1860-1864). He lived in Avenue Road, Regent's Park. His death occurred suddenly at the age of 54 while he was inspecting buildings of the Bethlehem Hospital for Convalescents at Witley in Surrey.

MASQUERIER, John James 68
1778-1855
Masquerier's family was of French origin. He was taken to Paris at the age of eleven and studied there under Vincent and Carle Vernet, but he returned to London on account of the Revolution and entered the Royal Academy Schools in 1792. He exhibited over 70 pictures at the Academy between 1795 and 1838. Waterhouse states that he was 'a very successful and very indifferent portrait painter' who travelled a good deal within the British Isles. In 1823, at the age of 45, he retired to Brighton, living off investments from the proceeds of his earlier work and occasionally sending work for exhibition.

MATHEWS, Charles James
1803-1878
See Brief Lives of the Sitters

MAY, Philip William RI **670, 927**
1864-1903
'Phil' May, as he was always known, was born near Leeds in 1864, son of an engineer. His mother was the daughter of an Irish actor, Eugene Macarthy. Phil May's father had been a pupil in George Stephenson's locomotive works at Newcastle-on-Tyne, but hadn't succeeded in business on his own account, as a result of which the son was brought up with the six other children of the family in straightened circumstances. Phil May was orphaned at the age of nine and at one time he was even reduced to begging in the street. After a little acting and drawing, he had his first break at the age of nineteen, in 1883, when he drew a caricature of Irving, Bancroft and Toole leaving a Garrick Club supper. It was published as a print, and the Prince of Wales, Sir Arthur Pinero and Sir Squire Bancroft acquired replicas. Phil May subsequently found well-paid work as a humourous draughtsman for magazines. From 1885 he spent seven years in Australia, returning to London, where he worked for various periodicals and for the *Daily Graphic* newspaper. His work provides a telling image of London street life towards the close of the nineteenth century. May was a heavy drinker and his health also suffered from a destitute childhood. He died from a wasting disease in 1903, aged 39.

MENPES, Mortimer L. RI, RBA, RA
1860-1938 **322, 882, 953**
Mortimer Menpes was born in Australia in 1860. Coming to England, he became a pupil and follower of Whistler. He worked in the style of his master as painter, draughtsman and etcher. He exhibited from 1882 until 1913 at the Society of Painter Etchers in London and, in 1904, wrote an admiring memoir of Whistler entitled *Whistler as I knew him.*

MERCIER, Philip **847**
1689?-1760
Mercier, from a family of Huguenot refugee origin, was born in Berlin and studied at the Academy there. He arrived in England in 1716 and married three years later. He became Principal Portrait Painter and Library Keeper to Frederick, Prince of Wales, situations that didn't last, for unstated private reasons. From 1739 until 1751 he lived in York and made brief visits to Ireland in 1747 and Scotland in 1750. He was in Portugal for a year in 1752. Waterhouse points out that, at an early stage in his career, Mercier must have become familiar with the work of Watteau. With Gravelot, he helped to introduce the French style of painting into England, particularly with his popular fancy pictures.

MERRITT, Anna Massey Lea **804**
1844-1930
Anna Massey Lea Merritt, who was born in Philadelphia, became the wife of the painter Henry Merritt (1822-1877). She worked in portraiture and as a genre painter, exhibiting at the Royal Academy between 1878 and 1893. Her best-known picture, 'Love Locked Out,' which is in the Tate Gallery, is regarded as something of a joke.

MEYER, Henry Hoppner **215 attr., 349,**
c. 1782-1847 **350, 598, 675, 676**
Henry Meyer, born in London about 1782, was a nephew of John Hoppner. He became a pupil of Francesco Bartolozzi, practicing later as an oil painter and watercolour draughtsman as well an engraver. His engraved work adopted the stipple manner of his master.

MILLAIS, Sir John Everett, Bt. PRA
1829-1896 **282, 323, 604 after**
Millais was born in Southampton, the youngest son of John William Millais. The family was of Norman origin but had been settled for generations in Jersey and they returned to the island shortly after the child's birth. Millais showed extraordinary precocity as a draughtsman and, having received some tuition from a Jersey drawing master, he came to London in 1838, at the age of nine, with an introduction to Sir Martin Archer Shee, President of the Royal Academy. He attended the School of Henry Sass; then, in 1840, at the age of eleven, he was entered as a student at the Royal Academy where he carried off every prize. He showed for the first time at the Royal Academy in 1846. Two years later he formed the 'Pre-Raphaelite'

movement, first with Holman Hunt and then Dante Gabriel Rossetti. One of the movement's most avid supporters was John Ruskin. Millais subsequently married Ruskin's wife, Euphemia (Effie) Gray, after she had obtained a divorce from Ruskin on the grounds of 'nullity.'

Many of Millais' paintings from his Pre-Raphaelite period and later became icons, but, in truth, the inspired quality in paint of his detailed observation became diluted with time as he acquired ever-greater status as a highly successful Victorian portrait painter. For all that, his finest portraits, such as those of Gladstone and Henry Irving, are very impressive. The *DNB* comments, 'He was the life of his own family, and regarded with affection by a very large and distinguished circle of acquaintance; but he did not care for ordinary social gatherings, and preferred to spend his evenings at the Garrick Club, where he was sure to meet a number of congenial friends.' Millais was unanimously elected President of the Royal Academy in January 1896, on the death of Lord Leighton, but he himself died later the same year. Millais became a member of the Garrick Club in 1855.

MORELAND, Henry Robert **237**
1719?-1797
The Garrick Club's only painting by Henry Moreland is a copy of a large canvas by Nathaniel Dance. Redgrave described Moreland politely as 'a man of unsettled habits.' In fact, he was intermittently picture dealer, restorer, mezzotint engraver, forger and bankrupt. He was the son of George Henry Moreland and the father of George Moreland. Some of his subject pictures proved popular in mezzotint engraving.

MORLEY, William Hook **351**
1815-1860
William Hook Morley was born in 1815. He became an orientalist and lawyer at the Middle Temple, studying art, architecture, and languages. He died at Brompton Square, London, aged forty-five, in 1860.

MORROW, Albert George **818**
1863-1927
Albert George Morrow worked as an illustrator and also painted figurative subjects. He studied at the Royal College of Art and exhibited nine works at the Royal Academy between 1890 and 1904.

MORTIMER, John Hamilton RA **59, 695**
1740-1779
Mortimer was born in Eastbourne, where his father owned a mill, but came as a young man to London, where he studied under Thomas Hudson and Robert Edge Pine as well as at the Duke of Richmond's Gallery and the St Martin's Lane Academy. He won five premiums from the Society of Arts between 1759 and 1762 and was estimated to hold great promise. He was elected President of the Society of Artists in 1774. Redgrave states that he led a rather dissolute life with bohemian friends in the purlieus of Covent Garden, but reformed after his marriage when he left town to live in Aylesbury. As well as conversation pieces and portraits, Mortimer specialized in history painting and romantic subjects portraying banditti in the manner of Salvator Rosa. He perhaps never reached his full potential, dying at the age of 39 after a short fever.

MORTON, Andrew **369**
1802-1845
Andrew Morton was born in Newcastle-on-Tyne, the son of Joseph Morton, a Master Mariner. He studied at the Royal Academy Schools where he gained a silver medal in 1821. Painting in the style of Sir Thomas Lawrence, he established a very successful portrait practice. He exhibited at the Royal Academy between 1821 and 1845.

MULREADY, Augustus E. **944**
d. 1886
Augustus Mulready was a member of the Cranbrook Colony, a group of artists including Thomas Webster, F.D. Hardy and others, who took their name from the village of Cranbrook in Kent. They set out to paint pictures of simple scenes, frequently including unsentimental portrayals of children. Mulready specialized in painting London street urchins, thus providing, with early photography, a telling record of one aspect of Victorian life.

MUNNINGS, Sir Alfred James PRA, RWS
1878-1959 **61, 62, 63, 671, 928, G1019**
Born the son of a miller at Menham Mill on the Waveney, Suffolk, Munnings left school at the age of fourteen and went to work with a firm of lithographers in Norwich. He showed an early enthusiasm and skill in drawing but had the misfortune, at the age of twenty, to lose the sight of his right eye, as the result of an accident. In 1911 he moved to Cornwall and became acquainted with the Newlyn Group around Stanhope Forbes. Despite his disability, he went to France during the Great War, looking after horses. Between the wars he became immensely sought after as a horse painter, mingling with the gypsies on the racecourses and being invited to country houses to paint owners and their horses. He made a great deal of money and was able to buy his own country house, Castle House in Dedham, Essex. Munnings was elected Academician in 1925. He became President of the Royal Academy in 1944 and was knighted in that year.

His querulous disposition may have been inherited from his father, but was also attributed to attacks of the gout. Apart from his great skill and understanding in the painting of horses, he is frequently remembered for an intemperate outburst against modern art delivered at a Royal Academy dinner. His speech was broadcast live, and listeners were entertained, according to newspaper reports, to grunts from Winston Churchill and a hiccup from the Archbishop of Canterbury. Munnings was elected to the Garrick Club in 1922 and resigned in 1950.

N

NAISH, William **427 attr.**
d. 1800
William Naish was born at Axbridge, in Somerset. He came to London, where he practiced with considerable success as a painter of miniatures, exhibiting at the Royal Academy almost continuously from 1783 until his death in 1800.

NEAGLE, John **85, after**
1760? -1822
The engraver John Neagle was born in London about 1760. He provided a number of illustrations for *The Shakespeare Gallery*.

NIXON, John **66, 160, 164, 238, 257, 599, 600, 652, 684, 702, 763, 779, 875, 929**)
c. 1760-1818
John Nixon was an amateur draughtsman as well as a merchant in Basinghall Street, London. For many years he was Secretary to the Beefsteak Club. He made a number of views of country seats which were engraved by William Watts. He also drew a large number of amusing caricatures, some of which he etched himself.

NOST, John Van the Younger
See John VAN NOST, the Younger

O

O'CONNER, John RHA **930**
1830-1889
John O'Conner was born in Ireland. After working briefly in Belfast and Dublin as a theatrical scenery painter, he came to London, aged eighteen, in 1848, where he later became principal scene-painter at Drury Lane and the Haymarket (1863-1878). From about 1855, he began painting topographical views, mainly of London, and exhibited them at the Royal Academy from 1857 until 1888. He travelled widely on the Continent.

O'NEIL, Henry Nelson ARA
1817-1880 **227, 358,792, 793, 821**
O'Neil was born at St Petersburg, Russia. In 1823, his British parents brought him to England, at the age of six. Thirteen years later, aged nineteen, he entered the Royal Academy Schools. He specialized in history and biblical painting. His work was frequently of indifferent quality and it always carried a strong Victorian flavour. In 1844, the Prince Consort bought his 'Boaz and Ruth.' The Garrick Club possesses several portraits by him, including a group portrait, painted in 1869, of 44 Garrick members around the billiard table. O'Neil had several publications to his name, including *Lectures on Painting delivered at the Royal Academy*, and he was also a talented amateur performer on the violin. O'Neil became a member of the Garrick Club in 1860.

ONSLOW FORD, Edward RA **S21**
1852-1901
Edward Onslow Ford was born at Islington. His father, who was a City businessman, died when Ford was twelve. His mother, discerning his artistic sensibilities, sent him to study in Antwerp and Munich. He returned to England with a German wife and settled at Blackheath. He first attracted attention with a bust of his wife, which he exhibited at the Royal Academy in 1875. From there on his career flourished and he attracted commissions for monumental work and portraiture. As a late Victorian sculptor, he produced portraits of many of the leading figures of his day. He was noted, too, for the small replicas he published of his statues. He was elected Academician in 1895, and he died six years later at the age of 49 from pneumonia, brought about by heart disease.

OPIE, John RA **67, 449, 627**
1761-1807
Opie was born in St Agnes, Cornwall, son of the village carpenter. He was befriended by Dr John Wolcot (1738-1819), the 'Peter Pindar' who wrote the satiric *Lyric Odes to the Royal Academicians*. Wolcot brought Opie to London in 1781 declaring him to be 'the Cornish Wonder.' He quickly achieved a name for himself and was never short of portrait commissions. He exhibited regularly at the Royal Academy from 1782 until the year of his death and was elected a full member in 1788 at the age of 27. Waterhouse wrote that 'he lacked the graces, but was one of the ablest English painters of his time.'

OPPENHEIMER, Joseph **143**
1876-1966
Joseph Oppenheimer (not James Oppenheim as stated in the Garrick Club picture catalogue) was born in Wurzburg, Germany, in 1876. He studied at the Munich Academy of Art from 1892 to 1894 and then travelled for several years in Europe and the Middle East before visiting the United States for the first time in 1900. His work came under the influence of the French Impressionists.

P

PARKINSON, Thomas 1744
c.1789 **89, 651, 768, 838**
Parkinson worked for the most part on theatrical subjects. He exhibited periodically at the Royal Academy between 1774 (when he showed a scene from *She Stoops to Conquer*, executed in the manner of Zoffany) and 1789. His figures are described as being 'rather wooden.'

PARSONS, William
1736-1795
See Brief Lives of the Sitters

PARTRIDGE, Sir John Bernard
1861-1945 **174, 324, 325**
John Bernard Partridge is primarily known as a book illustrator and as a cartoonist for *Punch*, which magazine he joined at the age of 30. He started life as an actor and then moved on to become a stained glass and decorative painter.

PASSAGLIA, Augusto **S28**
1838-1918
Augusto Passaglia was born at Lucques in 1838. He was a pupil of P. Martini and was appointed Professor at the Florentine Academy in 1875. He was very highly thought of in his day and, in 1887, he won the competition to decorate the three pairs of doors of Florence Cathedral. Apart from many commissions for religious subjects, he sculpted a likeness of Victor Emanuel II, now at Lucca. He died at Florence in 1918.

PEAKE, Mervyn **643**
1911-1968
Mervyn Peake, son of a medical missionary, was born in 1911 at Kuling, China. He came to England in 1922, aged eleven, and eight years later was admitted to the Royal Academy Schools, where he studied for three years. In 1936 he was offered the post of Professor at the Westminster School of Art. During the Second World War, when he was given the role of driving instructor, he started to write the first volume of the Gothick trilogy that went under the title of 'Gormenghast,' books which he illustrated himself. Sadly, he developed Parkinson's disease and, suffering from depression, virtually ceased drawing and writing. He died in 1968 at the age of 57.

PEAKE, Richard Brinsley **842**
1792-1847
Richard Brinsley Peake was born in Gerrard Street, Soho, son of Richard Peake, who worked for 40 years in the Treasury Office of the Drury Lane Theatre. The son trained initially as an engraver and was articled to James Heath, remaining with him for seven years, from 1809 to 1817. He then turned to the stage to become a dramatist, writing for the most part comedies and farces. He is said to have written a number of Charles Mathews's later 'At Homes,' performed at the Adephi in 1839. Peake was an original member of the Garrick Club in 1831.

PEARCE, Stephen **635**
1819-1904
Stephen Pearce was born in London. He studied at Sass's Academy and at the Royal Academy Schools. In 1841 he became a pupil of Sir Martin Archer Shee. He exhibited 92 paintings at the Royal Academy between 1839 and 1885 and is chiefly known for his portraiture and equestrian painting.

PELLEGRINI, Carlo 'Ape'
1839-1889 **27, 326, 487, 731**
Carlo Pellegrini was born at Capua in Italy in 1839 to a landed family. He had an easy-going temperament and in his youth he enjoyed Neapolitan society, exercising his talent for caricature among his friends. Having run through his father's inheritance he joined Garibaldi's forces during the Italian War of Independence. At the age of 25 he came to England, where he settled permanently and where he soon found himself obliged to make his own living. He turned his drawing skills to account and from 1869 started having his caricatures, which he signed with the sobriquet 'Ape,' published in *Vanity Fair*. The Garrick Club possesses two in this manner, (**27** & **326**). Pellegrini at one time tried his hand at oil painting, but if the Club's example (**731**) is characteristic, he had little

talent for this medium. Pellegrini died in London from lung disease at the age of 50.

PETTIE, John RA **860**
1839-1893
John Pettie was born in Scotland and went to study at the Trustees' Academy, Edinburgh, at the age of sixteen, in 1855. There he met W. MacTaggert, and W.Q. Orchardson. He began to exhibit at the Royal Academy in 1860, moving to London two years later. The subjects for his earlier work are frequently historical, of the 'ripping yarns' school. Later, he turned more to portraiture. Pettie became an Associate of the Royal Academy in 1866 and a full Member seven years later, in 1873.

PHILLIPS, Henry Wyndham **266, 344, 778**
1820-1868
Henry Wyndham Phillips was the younger son and pupil of the portrait painter Thomas Phillips RA (*q.v.*). The son, too, worked chiefly as a portrait painter. Christopher Wood points out that he was also a Captain in the Artists' Volunteer Corps and Secretary to the Artists' General Benevolent Institution.

PHILLIPS, Thomas RA **133**
1770-1845
Thomas Phillips was born at Dudley, Warwickshire, and was apprenticed by his parents to Francis Egington, a glass painter, of Birmingham. He came to London in 1791 and studied briefly under Benjamin West, who employed him working on the painted-glass windows of St George's Chapel at Windsor Castle. The next year he exhibited for the first time at the Royal Academy, showing a view of Windsor Castle. He came to realize, however, that his real talent lay in portraiture. From a relatively modest start, he subsequently found aristocratic patrons as well as such artistic and literary figures as Blake and Byron to sit for him. Over the years up until the time of his death he exhibited 338 paintings, nearly all portraits, at the Royal Academy. He was elected Academician in 1808.

PICKERSGILL, Henry William RA **454**
1782-1875
Henry Pickersgill, a pupil of George Arnald, became a very prolific portrait painter, showing 384 works at the Royal Academy between 1806 and 1872. His work was valued for presentation portraits. He was elected ARA in 1822 and full Academician in 1826. Pickersgill became a member of the Garrick Club in 1832.

PINE, Robert Edge **239,240**
c. 1730-1788
Born in London, Robert Edge Pine was son of an engraver. Waterhouse points out that he was 'one of the first to do portraits of actors in character parts.' His two portraits of Garrick in the Club's collection are weak derivatives of the painting in the National Portrait Gallery. He painted a powerful, rather weird and unflattering portrait of George II as well as a number of subject paintings, some with political undertones; those activities probably excluded him from being numbered among the Founder Members of the Royal Academy. He did, however, exhibit there on three occasions, over the period 1772 to 1784, after he had left the Society of Artists following an insulting remark from its President. In 1773 he left England and settled in Philadelphia, where he died five years later.

POCOCK, Isaac **51**
1782-1835
Isaac Pocock was born at Bristol in 1782, the eldest son of the noted marine painter, Nicholas Pocock. He studied under George Romney, and later, after Romney's death, under Sir William Beechey. He exhibited periodically at the Royal Academy, mostly portraits, from 1803 to 1818. In the latter year he inherited property at Maidenhead. Pocock started writing plays earlier, and his first piece, the farce *Yes or No*, was produced at the Haymarket Theatre in 1808. Charles Mathews acted the role of Dick Cypher, and the Garrick Club has a painting by Samuel de Wilde of him in this part (**466**). After Pocock came into his inheritance he devoted himself almost entirely to the drama.

POLLOCK, Courtney Edward Maxwell
1877-1943 **S 22**
Courtney Pollock was born in Birmingham in 1877. Like Albert Toft, he was a pupil of the

sculptor Edward Lanteri. As well as sculpting portrait busts, he painted and wrote on art. Pollock was a member of the Royal Society of British Artists. He died in 1943.

POND, Arthur **845**
c. 1700-1758
Pond was a painter, pastel draughtsman, etcher and engraver. He acquired a reputation as a collector and connoisseur. As a young man he went to Rome in the company of Roubiliac to study art. The *DNB* remarks that 'the most notable of his numerous original portraits are those of Alexander Pope, William, Duke of Cumberland, and Peg Woffington.' He was a prodigious etcher, and his output included many subjects relating to the Old Masters. He was elected a Fellow of the Royal Society as well as of the Society of Antiquaries. Pine died in Lincoln's Inn Fields in 1758, and his collection of Old Masters, sold the following year, made £400.

POPE, Alexander
1763-1835
See Brief Lives of the Sitters

PRINSEP, Valentine Cameron RA **395**
1838-1904
Always known as 'Val,' Valentine Prinsep was born on St Valentine's Day in Calcutta, the son of an official in the Indian Civil Service. He was sent to school in England and was himself originally destined for the Indian Civil Service. He formed a close relationship, however, with George Frederick Watts and, mixing with his circle, he resolved to take up the profession of painting. He studied under Watts and then under Gleyre in Paris, where he met Whistler, Poynter and du Maurier. He also established a friendship with Dante Gabriel Rossetti and was influenced by the Pre-Raphaelites. Later he came under the spell of Lord Leighton, whose style pervades much of his work. The Royal Academy elected him Academician in 1894, although his work was always of the second rank. He was a man of considerable personal charm and, in 1884, at the age of 46, he married a wealthy lady and enjoyed her ample support. Prinsep became a member of the Garrick Club in 1864.

PROCKTOR, Patrick RA **941, 970,**
b. 1936 **G1015, G0970**
Patrick Procktor was educated at Highgate School and at the Slade School of Art. He has shown in many one-man exhibitions and has illustrated a number of books. He was elected Academician at the Royal Academy in 1996 and has been a member of the Garrick Club since 1988.

PYE, Thomas **31**
b.1756
Pye is a little known Irish portrait and history painter. He studied in Dublin and exhibited there. He entered the Royal Academy Schools in 1775 and exhibited just one picture there the following year. He is later recorded as living in Rome.

PYLE, Robert **693**
fl. 1760-1768
Pyle painted portraits, conversation pieces and fancy subjects. Waterhouse notes that his figures 'are very stiff and wooden.'

R

READ, Catherine **254, after**
1723-1778
Catherine Read was a fashionable portrait painter, chiefly of ladies and children of the aristocracy.

REMFRY, David **969**
b. 1942
David Remfry was born in Sussex in 1942. He studied painting at the Hull College of Art. He has had a number of exhibitions at the Mercury Gallery, London, in New York, Los Angeles and in Florida. He is a member of the Royal Watercolour Society and a Fellow of the Society of Arts.

RENOUARD, Charles Paul **948**
1845-1924
Charles Paul Renouard was born at Cour-Cheverny in 1845. He trained at the Ecole des Beaux-Arts but, on account of straightened circumstances, was obliged initially to work as a house painter. Later, he assisted his master, Pils, executing ceilings at the Paris Opera in 1875. He started exhibiting sketches of actors at the Salon from 1877 and in 1884 provided material for the publications, *L'Illustration, Paris Illustré* and *Graphic.* He was awarded Chévalier de la Légion d'honneur in 1893.

REYNOLDS, Sir Joshua PRA **125 studio, 229 studio, 241 after, 242 after, 720 after, 738 studio, G1025 after, S14 after?**
1723-1792
Unfortunately, the Garrick Club only possesses studio work or copies of paintings from this leading artist and first President of the Royal Academy. Reynolds's pervading influence can, however, be identified in many of the paintings in the Club's collection.

RICHARDSON, Jonathan **640**
c.1665-1745
At the age of twenty Jonathan Richardson senior became a pupil of John Riley, the portrait painter, and married his niece. He succeeded Sir Godfrey Kneller and Michael Dahl in the stolid portrait style of the period. He lacked imagination in his work and his portraits all tend to have a similarity about them. Horace Walpole described him as 'a formal man, with a slow, but loud and sonorous voice, and, in truth, with some affectation in his manner.' Richardson had some pretensions as an author, and his essays, published in 1715 and 1719, are reputed to have encouraged Hogarth to paint his works on the staircase of St Bartholomew's Hospital. Richardson was an enthusiastic collector of Old Master Drawings, and his collector's mark, the letter 'r' or an 'r' within an artist's palette, is frequently to be found on drawings. Many of the drawings from his collection later passed into the hands of Sir Joshua Reynolds and Sir Thomas Lawrence.

RIVIERE, Hugh Goldwin RP
1869 1956 **28, 283, 369, 638**
Hugh Riviere studied at the Royal Academy Schools and exhibited at the Academy. He lived first in London and then at Midhurst in Sussex. He was the son of Briton Riviere.

ROBERTS, David RA **932**
1796-1864
David Roberts was born at Stockbridge, on the outskirts of Edinburgh, the son of a shoemaker. After apprenticing to a house painter, he took up scenery painting, working first in Scotland and the North Country, then at Drury Lane Theatre and Covent Garden. He was elected Academician at the Royal Academy in 1841 and began to travel extensively in Europe and the Levant. He was a sensitive draughtsman as well as a painter, and many of his travel drawings were reproduced as lithographs.

David Roberts became a member of the Garrick Club in 1835, put up by his friend, Clarkson Stanfield, an original member. Stanfield, Roberts and Louis Haghe, all friends and artist-members, painted large pictures to decorate the smoking room at the old premises in King Street. Shortly before his death, Roberts was enlisted onto the Building Committee for Decoration and Furnishings of the New Building. It is very likely that in this role he was responsible for the original hanging of the Mathews Collection in the Garrick Street premises.

ROBERTS, James **3, 58, 84 after, 165, 186, 187, 685, 732, 769, 844, 864**
1753-c. 1809
James Roberts was born at Westminster, the son of an engraver. Between 1775 and 1781 he made preparatory watercolour drawings on vellum for most of the engraved plates in Bell's *British Theatre*. He was appointed portrait painter to the Duke of Clarence and in 1809 published an instructional manual on watercolour painting. The *DNB* refers to his lack of imagination and slender abilities, and Waterhouse points out that feeble examples of his style are in the possession of the Garrick Club. The figures in the Club's *School for Scandal* (**3**), are very wooden and in his *Hamlet* scene (**769**), the canvas appears to have been cut to fit the frame, as the ghost of Hamlet's father is missing on the left.

ROBERTSON, Walford Graham RBA, ROI, RP **105, 106**
1867-1948
Walford Graham Robertson was born in London and studied at South Kensington under Albert Moore. Later he moved to Witley in Surrey. As well as painting portraits and landscape, he wrote several books and plays. He sketched many well-known figures of the Edwardian era. Robertson became a member of the Garrick Club in 1910.

ROMNEY, George
1734-1802 **297 studio, 618 attr. to**
Romney was born in the north of England but was in London by 1762. He established a very successful practice and became, after Reynolds and Gainsborough, the most fashionable portrait painter in the country. He had no liking for Reynolds and, as a result, never exhibited at the Royal Academy. Neither of the Club's paintings, despite Charles Mathews's attributions, can be given to him with any confidence.

ROTHLISBERGER Paul **S19**
b. 1892
Paul Rothlisberger was born at Neuchatel, Switzerland, in 1892. He trained as a sculptor and became a pupil of Bouchard, Landowski and Bourdelle. He exhibited in the Swiss salons, and in Paris at the Salons d'Automne and at the Tuilleries.

ROUBILIAC Louis Francois **S15, S29**
1705(?)-1762
Roubiliac the sculptor was born of Huguenot descent at Lyons and was apprenticed to Permoser, sculptor to the Elector of Saxony, in Dresden. He came to England about 1732 and Rupert Gunnis relates that Roubiliac, returning from Vauxhall one evening shortly after his arrival, came across a pocket book containing valuables that belonged to Sir Edward Walpole. Walpole was so grateful for its return that he introduced Roubiliac to the noted sculptor, Sir Henry Cheere, who engaged him as his assistant. Not long after, he received his first independent commission, for the famous statue of Handel at Vauxhall Gardens. From then on he never looked back. In 1758 he completed the full-length statue of Shakespeare (now in the British Museum) for Garrick's Temple at Hampton and made a bust of Garrick, which can be seen in the Garrick Club's painting by Soldi (**727**). The Club is fortunate in possessing a gilt bronze high-relief bust of Garrick (**S15**), as well as a terracotta bust of Shakespeare (**S29**). Several busts of notable characters were made for the Chelsea pottery factory. Gunnis remarks that Roubiliac 'was probably the greatest sculptor to work in England during the eighteenth century … his busts are unsurpassed.'

RUSSELL, John RA **36, 649**
1745-1806
John Russell was born at Guildford, son of a bookseller. He was a pupil of Francis Cotes, studied at the St Martin's Lane Academy and entered the Royal Academy Schools in 1770. He specialized in pastel portraiture, although he also made a few oils when travelling around the country to fulfill commissions. He was elected Academician in 1788, exhibiting 330 works at the Royal Academy between 1769 and the year of his death. In 1790 he was appointed 'Crayon Painter to the King and to the Prince of Wales.' Russell became a non-conformist and acquired an

interest in astronomy and the study of the moon, perhaps influenced by Joseph Priestley (1733-1804) and by the Lunar Society (a scientific society that met monthly at full moon) of Birmingham. He invented and patented, in 1797, an apparatus for exhibiting the moon's phenomena and was responsible for at least two prints describing the surface of the moon. He died of typhus in 1806 in Hull and is buried there.

RUTLAND, Violet Lindsay, Duchess of Rutland
See George Frederick WATTS

S

SALISBURY, Frank Owen 457
1874-1962
Frank Salisbury studied at Heatherley's School, at the Royal Academy Schools and on the Continent. He practised as a painter of rather wooden portraits in London. He achieved some fame with his portraits of George V and VI and with historical paintings in the Houses of Parliament. Salisbury became a member of the Garrick Club in 1944.

SARGENT, John Singer RA 802, after
1856-1925
John Singer Sargent was born, as an American citizen, in Florence on 12 January 1856. He studied under Carolus Duran in Paris and travelled to Italy and Spain, where he was deeply affected by the work of Velazquez. He lived in Paris and then in London, making frequent visits to the United States, while he worked up a highly successful portrait practice within fashionable society. Between 1890 and 1910 he executed murals at the Boston Museum of Fine Arts. A room full of his pictures in the Tate Gallery used laughingly to be referred to as 'The Sergeants' Mess', but this was most unfair as he was an artist of great distinction. He died on 15 April 1925 in Chelsea, London.

SAXON, James 15, 16, 648 attr. to
fl. 1795-1817
James Saxon was born in Manchester. He practiced painting in London and Edinburgh, and then spent several years in St Petersburg. He returned to live in Glasgow, and then again in London. He exhibited at the Royal Academy sporadically between 1795 and 1817.

SEAGO, Edward Brian 139, 280, 751, 762
1910-1974
Seago was born in Norwich, son of a coal merchant. He was handicapped as a partial invalid in childhood by a heart problem and the possessive attentions of a neurotic mother but employed the idle hours in teaching himself to draw. Encouraged by Alfred Munnings, and given

some instruction by Bernard Priestman, he was befriended by Lord Melchett, a noted patron of the arts, who introduced him to his distinguished friends, a number of whose portraits he painted. After a spell in the circus world, he visited the United States shortly before the Second World War, painting horses and portraits. During the war, when he was a camouflage officer with the Royal Engineers, he became friends with Field Marshals Auchinleck and Alexander, both of them amateur painters. The latter invited him to record the Italian campaign in 1944.

After the war, he largely abandoned portrait and horse painting and devoted himself almost entirely to a very successful career in painting landscapes. He retained a lasting interest in the theatre and ballet making friendships with, among others, Flora Robson, Noel Coward, Alastair Sim, Peter Cushing, Athene Seyler and Nicholas Hannen. Seago became a member of the Garrick Club in 1957.

SEDLECKA, Irena
b. 1928 **S46, S47, S50, S51, S52, S53**
Irena Sedlecka was born in Czechoslovakia in 1928 and trained at the Academy of Fine Arts in Prague. She came to London in 1968 and has sculpted a number of contemporary actors. *See* Burnim and Wilton, *The Richard Bebb Collection in the Garrick Club*, p. 130.

SHARP, Michael William
d. 1840 **679, 780, 857, 370 copy**
Michael William Sharp appears to have been born in London. His mother, Elizabeth Sharp, was a daughter of the Drury Lane prompter William Hopkins. Sharp studied painting under Sir William Beechey. By 1813 he was living in Norwich as a lodger of the artist John Crome. He made quite a name for himself in Norwich. He showed 46 paintings, several of them theatrical subjects, at the Royal Academy between the years 1801 and 1836. Sharp's wife, Arabell (née Menage), was a London actress. He died at Boulogne in 1840.

SHARPE, Louisa **776, 816, 827 attr. to**
1798-1843
Louisa Sharpe was one of four artist sisters, all daughters of William Sharpe, a Birmingham engraver. About 1816 the father brought them to London, where the family apparently lived in Covent Garden. Louisa began her career as a miniature painter, exhibiting at the Royal Academy from 1817 to 1829. In 1834 she married Professor Wolgemut Seyffart and went to live with him in Dresden, but she continued to exhibit at the Old Watercolour Society until 1842.

SHEE, Sir Martin Archer PRA
1769-1850 **336, 428, 628, 680, 686**
Shee was born in Dublin, the son of a merchant. He received a classical education there but, showing an interest in the fine arts, was allowed to enter the drawing academy of the Royal Dublin Society. In 1788 Gilbert Stuart, the American painter, persuaded him to move to London where, after some early struggles, he was accepted as a student at the Royal Academy Schools in 1790. Ten years later he was elected Academician. Shee's progress as a portrait painter was steady, aided by industriousness and an educated background. During the early part of his career he was overshadowed by Lawrence, whose panache he was unable to emulate. His later work, executed after Lawrence's death and less influenced by him, was condemned by Benjamin Robert Haydon as 'the tip-toe school.' On Lawrence's death in 1830, Shee was elected President of the Royal Academy, as much on account of his character as on his abilities as a painter. Throughout his life he maintained a keen interest in the stage.

SHEPARD, Ernest Howard **608**
1879-1976
E. H. Shepard spent his childhood years in London. At the age of ten his family moved from St John's Wood to Hammersmith. Shepard went to St Paul's School, whence he won a scholarship to the Royal Academy Schools. He served in the Great War as a major and was awarded the military cross for bravery in the field. After the war he contributed drawings for the magazine *Punch*, where he met E. V. Lucas, who introduced him to A. A. Milne. He is best remembered as illustrator of four of Milne's children's books as well as of Kenneth Graham's

classic, *Wind in the Willows*. In the later part of his life he lived at Lodsworth, Sussex, and near Godalming. He died in 1976 at the age of 97.

SHERINGHAM, George 795, 933
1884-1937
George Sheringham was born in London in 1884. He was a pupil of Harry Becker and trained as a painter and book illustrator.

SHERWIN, John Keyse S16 after
1751-1790
Sherwin was born in Sussex, the son of a labourer. He spent three years with Bartolozzi and was admitted as a student at the Royal Academy Schools in 1772. He was a skilled engraver although a much less able history painter. According to Redgrave, his 'Installation of the Knights of St Patrick, 50 or 60 feet long ... was an absolute failure.' His initial comparative success went to his head, making him idle and careless. He died 'forlorn and comfortless,' in a poor lodging at a public-house in Oxford Street, on 24 September 1790, aged 39.

SHOUT, Benjamin & Robert S30
fl. 1778-1826
Benjamin Shout and his son, Robert, ran their family business from a yard in Holborn, London. They specialized in monumental masonry, although Robert made a small number of busts and casts. They were responsible for a great deal of sepulchral work, particularly in Sussex. Robert was made Master of the Masons' Company in 1822. Shelley, writing of Leigh Hunt's studio in a letter to Maria Gisbourne, states 'His room no doubt is still adorned with many a cast from Shout'. In 1809, Robert took on his son, Charles Lutwyche Shout, as an apprentice.

SICKERT, Walter Richard 966, G1024
1860-1942
Sickert was born in Munich, the son of a Danish painter who subsequently took British nationality. The family moved to England when Sickert was eight, and he was educated in London. He had a short spell on the stage, working for Sir Henry Irving and Dame Madge Kendal, but soon gave it up for his true vocation as a painter. At 21 he attended the Slade School of Fine Art under Alphonse Legros, leaving to work with James McNeil Whistler in the latter's Tite Street studio. Sickert's paintings were also influenced by the work of Degas and by that of the French Impressionists. Sickert was a member of the New English Art Club and later the Camden Town Group, both of which wanted to break away from High Victorian art and to seek greater influence from Continental ideas. Sickert retained his interest in the theatre throughout his life, as witnessed by his early little Whistlerian panel of William Penley in Brandon Thomas's *Charley's Aunt* and his late image of Nigel Playfair as Tony Lumpkin in Goldsmith's *She Stoops to Conquer*.

SIDDONS, Sarah
1775-1831
See Brief Lives of the Sitters

SIMPSON, W. Graham 200
1823-1899
William Graham Simpson was born in Glasgow in 1823. He practiced as a painter, water-colourist, draughtsman and lithographer, arriving in London in 1851 to make views of the Great Exhibition. His subsequent career was pursued chiefly as a war artist earning him the sobriquet 'War in the East Simpson.' He covered the Crimean War, the Afghan and Abyssinian campaigns and the Indian mutiny; he was also present in Paris during the period of the Commune. In 1866 he became a draughtsman for *The Illustrated London News*. (Apparently he was not a member of the Garrick Club, although a Walter Simpson was elected in 1864 and was removed five years later for non-payment of dues.)

SIMS, Charles H. RA 91, 413
1873-1928
Charles Sims was born in Islington, London. He was the son of a costume manufacturer. He was lame from infancy and, at the age of fourteen he was placed in the office of a commission agent in Paris with a view to learning French and business practice. He thought of training for a musical career but in 1890 he became a pupil at the

National Art Training School, South Kensington (later the Royal College of Art), then at the Académie Julien in Paris. In 1893 he joined the Royal Academy Schools, but he was expelled for a minor breach of discipline. He married the daughter of an artist and endured a period of struggle until his first one-man show at the Leicester Galleries in 1906 brought success and recognition. He was elected Associate of the Royal Academy in 1907, and full Academician in 1915. In 1918, he worked as an official war artist in France. In 1920, he was appointed Keeper of the Royal Academy Schools, a position from which he resigned after six months due to pressure of outside work. His breezy, cheerful outdoor scenes in which children frequently played a role, were evidently at odds with his inner feelings, for he committed suicide by drowning himself in 1928, apparently as the result of depression. Sims was elected to the Garrick Club in 1918 but resigned in 1925.

SINGLETON, Henry 134, 147, 192, 333
1766-1839
Singleton was born in London. While Henry was young his father died. Assisted in his ambitions to be an artist by his uncle, the miniaturist, William Singleton, Henry entered the Royal Academy Schools in 1783. He exhibited prolifically at the Royal Academy from the age of eighteen until his death. He made a number of portrait paintings but he was mainly employed as a book illustrator, working in the manner of Wheatley. Redgrave notes that towards the end of his life, Singleton completed a series of small-sized pictures from Shakespeare.

SMIRKE, Robert RA 934 attr. to
1752-1845
Smirke was born at Wigton, near Carlisle. He was initially apprenticed to a coach painter, but entered the Royal Academy Schools in 1772. He was elected Academician in 1793. His hopes for election as Keeper in 1804 were frustrated by George III's objections to Smirke's known radical and revolutionary views. His painted subjects are mostly connected with the theatre and literature. He worked for Boydell's *Shakespeare Gallery*, and he also did a large number of poetical illustrations.

SMITH, John Raphael 747
1752-1812
John Raphael Smith was born in Derby, the younger brother of Thomas Correggio Smith. He was apprenticed to a linen draper in Derby and came to London as a shop assistant. He engraved his first mezzotint at the age of sixteen and then went on to become one of the finest mezzotint engravers of the age, being appointed engraver to the Prince of Wales. Smith worked up a successful career as a publisher and dealer in prints and also spent a lot of his time living it up with his great friend, George Moreland. He gave up engraving ten years before his death but carried on with his other activity, that of making small pastel portraits and genre subjects.

SMITH, Percy John Delf 803, possibly by
1882-1948
Percy Smith was a draughtsman, engraver and book illustrator. He engraved and etched a number of subjects relating to the First World War, and later, in 1934, made studies and etchings of scenes in Palestine.

SOLDI, Andrea 727
1703-1771
Soldi was born in Florence in 1703. After periods spent in Constantinople and Palestine, he was persuaded to come to England by some English travellers, whose portraits he had painted in Aleppo. He arrived in 1735 and almost immediately found himself with a busy portrait-painting practice. Sometime later, extravagant living appears to have brought about domestic difficulties from which he seems not to have recovered. During the 1760s he exhibited at the Society of Arts and the Free Society. The former, which had made him a Fellow in 1765, provided him at his request with financial help early in 1771. He died shortly thereafter; Sir Joshua Reynolds was party to the fund-raising to defray the costs of his burial.

SPENCER, Gervase 278 attr. to
d. 1763
Spencer painted miniature portraits in watercolour on ivory. He also worked in enamel and as an engraver. He died in London.

SPICER, Henry **6, 22, 32, 37, 100, 166, 211, 612, 650, 655, 661, 694 attr. to, 858**
1741-1804
Henry Spicer was born at Reephem in Norfolk. He first exhibited, at the age of 25, in the 1766 exhibition of the Incorporated Society of Artists, one of the several societies in existence at the time of the founding of the Royal Academy. He became the Society's Secretary in 1773 and continued to exhibit there until 1783. He exhibited fairly regularly at the Royal Academy from 1774 until the year of his death. He lived at addresses around Covent Garden and Soho. Spencer specialized in small chalk and watercolour portraits as well as miniatures on enamel and ivory.

STAIGG, Richard **455 attr.to**
1817-1881
Richard Staigg was born in Leeds in 1817. He emigrated to the United States as an adolescent in 1831. He was self-taught, but showed the influence of W. Alston. He made extended visits to Europe in 1867-1869 and 1872-1874. Staigg settled in Newport, Rhode Island, dying there in 1881.

STANFIELD, Clarkson RA **156, 935**
1793-1867
Clarkson Stanfield was born in Sunderland. Showing an aptitude for drawing, he was apprenticed to a heraldic painter in Edinburgh at the age of twelve, but he ran away two years later and, in 1808, persuaded his father to let him go to sea in a collier. In 1812 he was press-ganged into the Royal Navy, but his artistic talents didn't go to waste; he kept a sketch-book and painted scenery for naval amateur theatricals. He left the sea at the age of 25 and devoted himself full-time to scenery painting. While working in Edinburgh he met David Roberts, then a scenery painter. Both moved to London and, from 1822, Stanfield started working at Drury Lane.

In 1834 he gave up scenery painting and devoted himself more or less entirely to easel canvases, although he later carried out some work for Macready and Charles Dickens's private theatricals. Stanfield exhibited his first picture at the Royal Academy in 1820 and, in 1823, became a Founder Member of the Society of British Artists. He also showed with the British Institution. He exhibited regularly at the Royal Academy for the remainder of his life and was elected Academician, in 1835.

He travelled a great deal abroad and most of his marine and landscape paintings are of European subjects. He had formed a life-long friendship with David Roberts, and his other friends included Thackeray, Dickens, Macready and Landseer. Stanfield became an original member of the Garrick Club in 1831, and David Roberts, with Stanfield's sponsorship, was elected in 1835. Both were involved with the paintings and decoration of the Garrick Club's King Street premises; Stanfield helped to look after the frames of the Mathews Collection. Stanfield resigned his membership in 1865.

STEVENSON, Gordon **113**
1892-1982
Gordon Stevenson was a portrait painter who was born in New York in 1892. He trained under Joaquin Sorolla in Spain and was also a student of John Singer Sargent, and he travelled throughout the British Isles and the Continent. He was best known for his society portraits in oil, mostly of Americans. Stevenson died in Chicago in 1982.

STUART, Gilbert **135, 380 after, 388 attr. to, 681, 739 after**
1755-1828
Gilbert Stuart was born in Narragansett, Rhode Island, in 1755. After receiving some instruction from the Scottish painter Cosmo Alexander, he accompanied the latter to Scotland in 1772. After his master's death, he returned home, but came back to England in 1755, at the age of 20, where he found a friend and master in his fellow American, Benjamin West. By 1785 he had established himself as a successful portrait painter in London but returned to America seven years later to work in New York, Washington and Philadelphia, settling finally in Boston, where he spent the rest of his life. He exhibited thirteen portraits at the Royal Academy between 1777 and 1785. He is, perhaps, best known for his many portraits of George Washington, but he had other noted sitters including John Adams,

Thomas Jefferson, Sir Joshua Reynolds, John Philip Kemble and Alderman Boydell. His best-loved portrait is that of William Grant skating in St James's Park, a painting now in the National Gallery of Art, Washington.

SULLY, Thomas **232**
1783-1872
Thomas Sully was born in Hardcastle, Lincolnshire, in 1783. He went to the United States at the age of nine and later studied under Belzons, in Charleston. He worked in Norfolk and Richmond in Virginia with his brother, Lawrence. Following the latter's death, he married his widow in 1805 and went to New York the following year. Shortly afterwards he left to study under Gilbert Stuart in Boston, and then came to London, where he had further tuition from Benjamin West. His peripatetic career took him to Philadelphia in 1810, and from there he travelled to a number of American cities, visiting England again in 1837-38, when he painted a full-length portrait of the newly crowned Queen Victoria. After a career during which he had painted countless pictures of well-known individuals, he died in Philadelphia at the age of 89, in 1872.

T

TAYLER, Charles Foot **373 after**
fl. 1836-1871?
Tayler was a portrait painter who worked in Bath. He exhibited at the Royal Academy between 1820 and 1853.

TOFT, Albert **S9, S20, S23, S32, S33, S0059**
1862-1949
Toft was born into a Staffordshire family of pottery and silver decorators, and he worked as a modeller in the Wedgewood Porcelain Factory. He studied at the Stoke School of Art and later was a pupil of Lanteri at the Royal College of Art. He pursued a career as sculptor and medallist, and he had many commissions for war memorials.

TOPOLSKI, Feliks **202**
1907-1989
Feliks Topolski was born at Czenslochova in Poland in 1907. He studied at the Warsaw Academy of Art under T. Pruszkowski. He specialized in book illustration and caricature. Topolski came to London in 1935, later producing a great deal of propaganda material during the Second World War. He became a British citizen in 1947 and painted the 'Cavalcade of Commonwealth' for the Festival of Britain in 1951. He died in 1989.

TURMEAU, John **198, 629, 710,**
1777-1846 **758, 759, 872, G0990**
John Turmeau, a miniaturist, was the son of a London jeweller who may also have painted. The family was of Huguenot extraction, but long settled in England. Turmeau exhibited over a period of four years at the Royal Academy between the ages of 16 and 20. By 1810 he appeared to be living in Liverpool, although he continued to exhibit occasionally in London until 1836. By 1827 he was Treasurer of the Liverpool Academy, and showed his work regularly there. In addition to his work as a miniature painter, he was in trade as a picture dealer and print-seller.

TUSON, G. E. **770**
d. 1880
Tuson painted historical, genre and religious subjects as well as portraits. He exhibited six pictures at the Royal Academy between 1854 and 1859. His masterpiece appears to have been 'The Deputation of the Corporation of the City of Manchester at the Reception of the Sultan Abd-ul-Asis at Buckingham Palace,' painted for Manchester Town Hall. On a visit to Turkey he executed a number of portraits. He finished his career in Montevideo, where he died.

V

VAN BLEECK, Peter **121, 271, 606**
1697-1764
Van Bleeck, born in The Hague, was working in England by 1723. He was primarily a portrait painter. His work includes several pictures of actors and actresses in character. Waterhouse says of him, 'his quality is variable but his best work is neat and distinguished.'

VANDERBANK, John **81**
1694-1739
Vanderbank was born in London and, from 1711, studied at the Kneller Academy. As a result of factions, the artist James Thornhill seceded from the Kneller Academy to form an Academy in Covent Garden, while Vanderbank founded another rival one with Cheron, in 1720, in St Martin's Lane. Vanderbank worked as a history and portrait painter as well as a book illustrator. His drawings are bold and lively but the pictures more sober. Vertue considered that only intemperance prevented him from becoming the leading portrait painter of his day. He died of consumption at the age of 45.

VANDERGUCHT, Benjamin **243 after,**
1753-1794 **244 by or after, 613, 853**
Vandergucht's father and grandfather were both engravers. The latter had come to England from Antwerp in the seventeenth century. Benjamin Vandergucht studied at the St Martin's Academy and was one of the earliest students to be admitted to the Royal Academy Schools, gaining a silver medal in 1774. He exhibited regularly at the Royal Academy, mostly portraits and theatrical scenes in the style of Zoffany. He had received work from Garrick since 1772, and in 1779 he showed a head of Garrick, exhibited after the actor's death and said to be the last portrait Garrick sat for. A number of his works were engraved in mezzotint. In 1786 he ceased practicing as a painter and, as his father had done before him, turned to picture cleaning and dealing.

He was drowned in 1794, aged 41, while

crossing the Thames from Chiswick, near Mortlake when his boat was capsized by a barge. His dealer's stock of old master pictures was sold at Christie's in 1796, and the proceeds went towards the support of his widow and their eleven children.

VAN DER MIJN, Frans **420**
c. 1719-1783
Van der Mijn was born in Antwerp, one of several children of the flower, history and portrait painter Herman Van der Mijn. Waterhouse suggests that Frans may have assisted his father until the latter's death in 1741. Herman came to London about 1721, but Frans was running a successful practice in Antwerp from shortly after his father's death until 1749. He then moved to London, where again he was successful save for the fact that his incessant pipe smoking put off a number of potential clients.

VAN DYCK, Sir Anthony **942 after**
1599-1641
The Garrick Club's triple portrait of Charles I is a small copy after the original canvas by Van Dyck in the Royal Collection. Van Dyck painted the picture in 1635 at the request of the king to provide the Italian sculptor, Gianlorenzo Bernini, with an accurate likeness from which to carve a marble bust. Bernini was the official sculptor to Pope Urban VIII, and so the entire transaction had to be conducted through the king's wife, Henrietta Maria, who was a Roman Catholic. The bust came to England, but was destroyed in the Whitehall fire of 1698; the painting remained in Italy with Bernini and his descendants until 1802, when it was sold there into the English trade. It was returned to England two years later, and subsequently was bought by the Prince Regent in 1819. Many copies of the painting are in existence.

VAN NOST, John, the Younger S11 after,
fl. 1751-1780 **S12 after, S13 possibly**
John Nost the younger was the nephew of the far more famous John Nost the elder for whom he worked and, as Vertue remarked, 'drove on the business, but never studied, nor did himself anything tolerable.' He moved to Dublin about 1750 and, finding no competition, made his reputation there. Gunnis notes that Van Nost took a mask of Garrick from which he made a bust. He also states that the mask came into the possession of Charles Mathews while 'endless copies of the bust were afterwards put on the market; indeed, Macklin, the actor, said to Nollekens that one "was in every barber's shop-window, as a block for wigs".'

VARLEY, John **38, 199**
1778-1842
John Varley was born at Hackney, London, in 1778, the eldest of five children, two others of whom grew up to be artists. Shortly before his father died, in 1791, he placed John, at the age of 13, with a silversmith. The family was living in reduced circumstances and Varley, who, after a brief period with a law stationer, had taken up the profession of draughtsman and water-colourist, had quite a hard time making a living. Varley benefited from the encouragement of the renowned Dr Munro, and sometime after 1798 started as a teacher. He enjoyed phenomenal success, attracting pupils who went on to become notable watercolourists in their own right: W. H. Hunt, Francis Oliver Finch, John Linnell, Samuel Palmer, Copley Fielding, David Cox and Peter de Wint being among the most renowned. Indeed, he has been described as forming the very backbone of the English watercolour school. He exhibited a great deal at the Royal Society of Painters in Watercolour from the time of their first exhibition, in 1805, and produced vast amounts of work, painting for up to fourteen hours a day, although the results became somewhat mannered in the latter part of his career. When in his early forties, Linnell introduced Varley to William Blake, who drew the 'visionary heads' for him, and with whom he enjoyed a friendship that lasted until Blake's death in 1827.

Varley was a colourful figure, weighing seventeen stone and excelling as a pugilist. It is said that, when tired of boxing, he would exercise himself by throwing his wife 'to and fro' across a table with a pupil.' He was also deeply interested in astrology, casting his horoscope daily. He predicted that his house would catch fire, apparently expressing some satisfaction when the forecast proved accurate.

VERELST, Simon **277 attr. to**
1644-1721
Simon Verelst was born in Antwerp in 1644 and came to England during the Restoration. He painted portraits but is primarily known as a flower painter; sometimes he combined the two, surrounding his portraits with flowers. Walpole writes, 'his portraits were exceeding laboured, and finished with the same delicacy as his flowers, which he continued to introduce into them.' Verelst's consuming vanity eventually led to him being certified as mad, and confined. He called himself the 'God of Flowers' and once went to Whitehall in expectation of conversing with the king for two or three hours. Being repulsed, he said, 'he is the king of England, I am the king of painting, why should we not converse together familiarly?'

VERELST, Willem **122**
fl.1734-c.1756
Willem Verelst was from a family of painters and he himself practiced in portraiture and conversation pieces. Waterhouse cites him as the best portraitist of the family, 'painting both life-size portraits and Devis-scale conversation pieces.'

VISPRE, Francois Xavier **245**
b. c. 1730
The younger brother of Victor, who painted still-lives of fruit on glass, Francois Xavier, who was probably born at Besançon around 1730, did the same, but was known too for miniatures and portrait crayons. The brothers worked a good deal together, first in Paris, then London and Dublin. Waterhouse notes that they were Huguenots and were friendly with Roubiliac.

W

WAGEMAN, Thomas Charles
c. 1787-1863 **352 attr. to, 360, 410**
Wageman was born about 1787 and established himself initially as an artist in the Strand. He specialized in portrait drawings, watercolours and miniatures, for the most part of actors in character. He exhibited at the Royal Academy regularly from 1816 until 1848.

WALLER, Richard **666**
1811-1882
A Richard Waller was a member of the Leeds Society of Artists.

WALTON, Henry **399 attr. to**
c. 1746-1813
Henry Walton was born in Norfolk and was a pupil of Zoffany (about 1769-1770). Having a private income, he was not dependent upon his painting. Waterhouse points out that Walton's known visits to Paris may well account for the influence of Chardin on his work. He only exhibited over a period of three years at the Royal Academy, showing one theatrical work. It would appear that he painted pictures mostly for friends, but he retired around 1780 to a property in Suffolk where he did a little dealing and acted as an art adviser.

WARD, Edward Matthew RA **766**
1816-1879
Edward Matthew Ward was born in Pimlico. His father was employed at Coutts' Bank. The son was sent to learn painting under John Cawse, an artist living in Henrietta Street, Covent Garden. Ward got to know a number of actors at this time and his portrait of Richard Smith, the comedian, as Don Quixote (**766**), appears to have been his first picture to be exhibited at the Royal Academy, in 1834. From 1839 until shortly before his death, from suicide, in 1879, he was a regular exhibitor of historical subjects at the Academy, to which institution he was elected Academician in 1855.

WARD, James RA **949**
1769-1859
James Ward was born in London and died, at the age of 90, at Cheshunt. His long career was spent in part as a mezzotinter, a craft he learned from his own brother William and from John Raphael Smith, and in part as a painter, influenced initially by his brother-in-law, George Morland, and as a draughtsman. He painted cattle at a time when breeding techniques were being vigorously pursued and made a number of fine portraits of horses. He exhibited for 63 years at the Royal Academy from 1792; he was elected Academician in 1811. Ward spent the later part of his life in poverty.

WARD, Sir Leslie 'Spy' 29, 107, 284, 456,
1851-1922 **605, 812, 960**
Leslie Ward was the son of Edward Matthew Ward *(q.v.)* and Mary Ada Ward, (no relation to her husband, but grand-daughter of the artist, James Ward). Leslie was sent to Eton. He exhibited at the Royal Academy in 1868, while still at school, and periodically thereafter until 1883. From 1873 he formed a close working relationship with the periodical *Vanity Fair,* and for the rest of his life provided illustrations for that magazine in the form of cartoon drawings of contemporary celebrities. These drawings were produced in the form of coloured lithographs under the pseudonym of 'Spy,' frequently to be cut out, framed, and used as decoration in countless restaurants, clubs and common rooms.

WATSON-GORDON, Sir John PRSA, RA
1788?-1864 **636**
John Watson-Gordon was born in Edinburgh in 1788 (according to some, in 1790). He was a pupil of his uncle, George Watson, and then, at the Trustees' Academy in Edinburgh, of J. Graham. He first exhibited in London at the British Institution in 1814 with two history paintings, then three years later at the Royal Academy. Among other honours, he was appointed Court Painter to the Queen of Scotland. Although his portrait work does not encompass the most distinguished figures of the period, he painted many notable sitters.

WATTS, George Frederick RA
formerly attr. to Violet Lindsay,
Duchess of Rutland **801**
1817-1904
George Frederick Watts was born in London, son of a piano maker. He wished to become a sculptor and was apprenticed at the age of ten to William Behnes. Eight years later he entered the Royal Academy Schools, but only remained for a short while and was effectively self-trained as a painter. He spent three years in Florence 'absorbing' Titian and Michelangelo. At the age of 33 Watts visited the home of Val Prinsep's parents in Holland Park for a three-day visit, but remained with them for the next 30 years. Aged 46, he married Ellen Terry, then sixteen years old, but the marriage only lasted for a year. Ellen Terry posed for him constantly during this period. The Garrick Club's (**801**) is a study for Ophelia, drawn from a photograph after Ellen Terry's departure. Watts painted notable landscapes and later in his life executed large-scale sculpture. Watts re-married in 1886 and moved to Limnerlease, near Guildford, where he died.

WELLINGS William
fl. 1782-1801 **153, 289, 337, 402 attr. to**
Wellings was a little known silhouette and miniature painter who exhibited two pictures at the Royal Academy in 1793: one a portrait and the other a depiction of Kemble and Mrs Siddons as Thomas Cromwell and Queen Katharine in Shakespeare's *Henry VIII.*

WEST, Robert **2**
fl. 1735-1770
Robert West was dubbed 'parent of the arts in Dublin,' where he founded the first 'School of Design.' although little is now known of him apart from a supposition that he studied in Paris under Boucher and Van Loo. The Garrick Club's chalk drawing, with its signed inscription, appears to be the only work that can be ascribed to him with any confidence.

WESTALL, Richard RA **748, G1007**
1766-1836
Richard Westall was born at Hertford. From the age of thirteen he was apprenticed for a period of

five years to a silver engraver. On the expiry of his apprenticeship he entered the Royal Academy Schools. He exhibited regularly at the Academy for over 50 years up until the year of his death, and was elected Academician in 1794. His primary professional engagements were making watercolours and illustrating books, but he also painted in oils, working for Macklin and for Alderman Boydell.

WHEELER, Sir Charles PRA S38, G1007
1892-1974
Charles Wheeler was born in 1892 at Codsall near Wolverhampton. He was a South Kensington Royal Exhibitioner and started exhibiting at the Royal Academy in 1914. He executed a large number of public and corporate commissions. In 1942 he became a Trustee of the Tate Gallery. In 1956 he was elected President of the Royal Academy, a post he held for ten years.

WILENSKI, Reginald Howard 9
1887-1975
Reginald Wilenski was born in London. He was an artist, but was known primarily as an art critic and art historian. His *Modern Movement in Art* (1927), which analyzed the aims and achievements of modern painters, had quite an influence in its day.

WILKIE, Sir David RA 784
1785-1841
David Wilkie, a genre, history and portrait painter, was born at Cults, Fife in Scotland, the son of a minister. He showed great precocity as an artist, being able, as he put it, to 'draw before he could read, and paint before he could spell.' He went to Edinburgh to study at the Trustees' Academy of Design at the age of fourteen in 1799 and, in 1805, embarked by ship from Leith for London. Wilkie had his first success at the Royal Academy with his painting 'The Village Politicians.' which drew great public acclaim. He was elected Academician in 1811. In 1814, he visited Paris with Benjamin Robert Haydon. Wilkie received a knighthood from George IV in 1836. Further travels to Europe and the Levant followed. Wilkie died suddenly in 1841 after leaving Gibralter on the ship 'Oriental,' and his death was commemorated by his friend J. M. W. Turner with his famous painting, 'Peace – Burial at Sea.' now in the Tate Gallery. Throughout his career, Wilkie enjoyed a great success with his genre and history paintings, which embodied the sentiment of the period. His earlier work was much influenced by David Teniers and Jan Steen, but he developed an individual style underpinned by an assured draughtsmanship that made him regarded as one of the most important painters in Britain in the early part of the nineteenth century.

WILSON, Benjamin 246 after, 296 attr. to, 400 attr. to, 848 attr. to, 967 after
1721-1788
Benjamin Wilson, who was born at Leeds, became a close friend of Garrick, his senior by three years. Wilson may be said to have initiated the 'mise en scène' style of theatrical painting, framed within a proscenium, as distinct from the earlier paintings by Hogarth of *The Beggars' Opera* and *The Conquest of Mexico*, where the actors and the playgoers all form part of the picture. This style is evident with such pictures as Wilson's Garrick and Mrs. Bellamy in *Romeo and Juliet*, the composition of which is imitated in the Club's little enamel by Zincke (**967**). Wilson employed Johan Zoffany to work in his studio until the latter was discovered there by David Garrick. Garrick, recognizing Zoffany's talent for theatrical painting, used it to his own advantage, both for the publicity surrounding the paintings in which he was featured and for the prints made after them.

Benjamin Wilson's career was centered mainly on his work as a portrait painter. His most successful period ran through the 1750s and early 60s. In 1769 he gave up portraiture entirely and devoted himself to scientific studies.

WILSON, Thomas Harrington
fl. 1842-1886 **357, 359**
Thomas Harrington Wilson was a genre and portrait painter and engraver who lived in London.

WOOD, William 601
c. 1768-1809
William Wood was a miniature painter who exhibited at the Royal Academy from 1788 until

1807. Redgrave notes that he promoted the establishment, in 1808, of the short-lived Society of Associated Artists in Watercolour. He was also credited with improving the stability of watercolours on ivory. He died in London in 1809, aged 41.

WOOLNOTH, Thomas **see 373**
1785-c. 1836
Thomas Woolnoth was a little known engraver, who, according to Redgrave, was still living in 1836.

WORLIDGE, Thomas **118, 238 after,**
1700-1766 **247, 248, 854, G1023**
Thomas Worlidge was born in Peterborough but came to work in London. There, he became a pupil of the Italian painter, A. M. Grimaldi. The Garrick Club's oil portrait of Garrick as *Tancred* is in Worlidge's 'grand manner.' He also worked as an engraver, producing prints in the style of Rembrandt. Worlidge was noted for his small portrait drawings in pencil or sanguine. He worked a good deal in Bath as well as London. He died in Hammersmith in September 1766 and is buried in Hammersmith parish church.

WYNNE David **S18, S49**
b. 1926
David Wynne is a self-taught sculptor who first exhibited at the Leicester Galleries in 1950 and at the Royal Academy in 1952. He has enjoyed a successful career and has received a large number of commissions, both in England and abroad. Wynne was elected to the Garrick Club in 1982.

Y

YORKE, Charles **G0984-G0987**
b. 1951
Charles Yorke was educated at Eton and at the Ruskin School of Drawing and Fine Art, at Oxford. He has been a freelance caricaturist since 1977 and his work has appeared in a number of newspapers including the *Daily Mail, Sunday Times, Daily Telegraph, Evening Standard* and in the *Spectator*. Charles Yorke was elected to the Garrick Club in 1984.

YOUNGMAN-CARTER, Philip **312**
1904-1970
Philip Youngman-Carter was born in Hertfordshire in 1904. He was a writer as well as an artist, and in 1927 he married the crime writer, Margery Allingham, collaborating with her on many of her books. After service in the Second World War, he went into Fleet Street, becoming features editor of the *Daily Express* and later editor of *The Tatler*.

Z

ZINCKE, Christian Frederick 967, 968
1684? -1767
Zincke was born in Dresden, the son of a goldsmith. He arrived in England in 1706 and became a pupil of Charles Boit, the enameller. Zincke's delicate enamel work soon became very fashionable, and he made many portraits of leading figures of the day. Frederick, Prince of Wales, appointed him to be his cabinet-maker. Zincke was employed both by George II and Queen Caroline. Madame de Pompadour commissioned him to execute a portrait of Louis XV. He retired in about 1746, remaining in London for the rest of his life.

ZOFFANY, Johan RA 23, 33 attr. to, 126 after, 249, 250, 252, 253, 256 attr. to, 401, 411, 429, 662, 703, 715, 721 attr. to, 726, 772 after, 852 after
1733-1810
Johan or Johann Zoffany was born Johannes Zauffaley near Frankfurt am Main. His father, Antoni Frantz, who was architect to the Prince of Thurn and Taxis, was Bohemian by birth and his mother was German. At the age of sixteen he left home to travel to Rome, where he remained for seven years. He went back to Germany in 1757 and made what turned out to be an unhappy marriage. In 1760 he arrived in England. After a period of great privation, during which time his wife left him, he passed into the employment of the clockmaker, Stephen Rimbault, who set him to painting clock faces, and then with the painter Benjamin Wilson, who used him as a drapery painter. At this time Zoffany attracted the attention of David Garrick, who encouraged him to develop his latent talent for theatrical conversation pieces, a genre that had been pioneered by William Hogarth and developed by Benjamin Wilson. Garrick, with an inborn flair for publicity, sat to Zoffany in a number of the roles in which he acted, in the knowledge that mezzotint prints made from the pictures were bound to reach a wide audience and enhance his reputation.

At the same time that Garrick took an interest in Zoffany, Lord Bute introduced the artist into royal circles. Zoffany painted domestic interiors for George III and Queen Charlotte. In 1769, instead of being elected to the new Royal Academy, he had the honour of being nominated by the king. Zoffany had been destined to join Captain Cook's second expedition (to ascertain the existence or otherwise of a 'Southern Continent') as an artist under the direction of Joseph Banks. Banks, however, withdrew on account of cramped accommodation, and so Zoffany's engagement was cancelled.

In 1772, Zoffany returned to Italy with introductions to a number of leading persons and with a commission from Queen Charlotte to paint the Tribuna (with permission from the Grand Duke of Tuscany) containing leading pictures from the Grand Duke's collection, at the Uffizi in Florence. Starting the work with great enthusiasm, Zoffany managed to spin it out over a period of five years, while accepting other commissions. He crowded his composition with figures (some of them not considered by contemporaries to be among the 'great and the good'), thus turning the painting into a *conversazione*, which brought with it some criticism. Zoffany returned to England in 1779, but four years later, perhaps finding that the fashion for theatrical and other conversation pieces had passed, and to repair his finances, he left for India. His six years in India certainly made him a richer man and he came back to England once more, at the age of 56, to live in some style with his second wife at a house at Strand-on-the-Green, where he died 21 years later.

List of Subscribers

M.D. Abrahams CBE DL
Sir Timothy Ackroyd Bt
Jonathan J. Acton Davis QC
Robert A. Albert
Stanley F. Amis FRIBA
Prof. Brian F.Allen
Anthony J. Anderson QC
Benjamin P. Aris
David Barr
John P. Baskett
Rodney C. Bennett-England
His Hon. Judge Andrew J. Blackett-Ord CVO
His Hon. Judge J. Graham Boal QC
Geoffrey C. Bond
Robert M. Booth
James Borwick
Sir Jeffery H. Bowman
David W. Brewer
Richard Briers CBE
Richard N. Brueton
James McL. G. Buckley
Dr Christopher B. Bunker
Anthony J. C. Butcher QC
Christopher H.G. Chapman
Rt Hon. Sir Christopher J. Chataway PC
David Chipp
His Hon. Michael W.M. Chism
Francis Chronnell
William Clegg QC
Philip G. Clough
Stephen J. Cockburn
Michael Codron CBE
Sebastian Cody
Giles H.C. Cole
Hon. Sir Michael B. Connell
Prof. Richard Creese TD
Graham Crowden
Laurence Cuckney
Ian B. Curteis
Anthony Curtis
William Cussans
John O.R. Darby
Sir Michael Davies
Eric de Bellaigue
John L.F. Dean
Peter Dimmock CVO OBE
Nicholas Dromgoole
Michael J. Edwards CBE QC
Peter W. Fane
Stephen F.J. Fay
J.J. Fenwick
Christopher Fildes OBE
Alec Fitzgerald O'Connor FRCS
Christopher D. Floyd QC
Norman Foster
Mark Fox-Andrews
Sven H. Gahlin
Paul Gane
Gordon C. Gardiner
David Garfield Davies FRCS
David Gilmore
Kenneth S. Giniger
John F. Goble
Giles A.E. Gordon
John S. Gordon JP
Sir Alexander M. Graham GBE
Roger Greenhalgh
Prof. Jack W.C. Hagstrom MD
Eben W. Hamilton QC
Dr Marcus W.N. Harbord PhD MRCP
Joseph C. Harper QC
Dr David R. Harper
Bruce A. Harris
Colin Harrison
John Hartley PC
His Hon. Judge Richard O. Havery QC
Dr David Hay
Dr John T. Hayes CBE
Ian Herbert
Rupert C.S. Hill
Prof Jocelyn N. Hillgarth FSA
Jonathan Holmes

Stephen Hood
Sir Christopher K. Howes KCVO CB
Roy Hudd
Luke A. Hughes
Robin P. Hyman
Ian A.N. Irvine
Jonathan James-Moore
Robin R Jessel
Allen C. Jones RA
David R. Kilpatrick
Jeremy King
Dr Roman S. Kocen TD FRCP
Simon R. Kverndal QC
Martin R. Landau FCA
Paul Langridge
Richard Leech
Anthony Legge
Nigel Lindsay-Fynn
Oliver A.W. Lodge TD
Jonathan Lloyd
Peter M. Luttman-Johnson
Iain Mackintosh
Dr Christopher N. Mallinson FRCP
Sir Michael Marshall
Brian Masters
Duncan Matthews
Brig Simon V. Mayall
Hon. David M. McAlpine
His Hon. Judge David D. McEvoy QC
Henry McGee
Prof. James G. McMurtry
Cornelius M. Medvei
Peter S. Miall
Sir Derek Mitchell KCB CVO
Geoffrey B. Mitchell OBE
Frank R. Moat
Alec Monteath FSA (Scot)
Roger H.V.C. Morgan CBE
Michael E. Nelson
Robert J.B. Noel
Dr Michael O'Donnell
Sir John Owen
Nicholas P. Padfield QC
Bruce Palmer
Geoffrey D. Palmer
Dr Roy M. Palmer
Andrew G. M. Patrick
David M. Pittaway QC
Simon M. H. Raison
Michael J. Redington
Prof. Peter Richards
Philip Roberts
James H. Roose-Evans
Michael J. Roper-Hall FRCS
Tom G. Rosenthal
Anthony B. Rota
Joshua Rozenberg
John S.Y. Rubenstein
Richard E.G. Sachs
Nicholas Salmon
Alexander Schouvaloff
John B. Shelley OBE
Bernard Shrimsley
Peter Siddons
Robin J.H. Simon
Sir Donald Sinden CBE
Marshall Stewart
Evan D.R. Stone QC
David C. Suchet OBE
David H. Tatham OBE
Louis Taylor
Gerald L. Tedder
Hugh Tempest-Radford
John L. Thorn
Harry Towb
Ion C.G. Trewin
Dr Barry Turner
John P.Tydeman OBE
John V.V. Veeder QC
David N. Vermont
John H. Vernon MBE
Paul S. L. Viney
Hugh P. S. Wace
Rt Hon. Lord Wakeham
Dr Oliver C. Waldron
Richard R. Walton
Geoffrey Wansell
Richard G. Ware
Sir Ronald G. Waterhouse GBE
His Hon. Judge Brian Watling QC
Moray Watson
Antony C. Whitaker OBE
David H. Whitaker OBE
Michael Whitehall
John Whitney
Jeffry Wickham
Frank Wilding
J. P. Williams
Harry Wolton QC
Edward Woodward OBE
Charles E. Yorke
John S. Yorke